6141

# worship:

# rites,
# feasts,
# and reflections

## Maxwell E. johnson

PASTORAL
PRESS
PORTLAND · OREGON

Worship: Rites, Feasts, and Reflections
by Maxwell E. Johnson

ISBN 1-56929-069-5

© 2004 Pastoral Press

Pastoral Press
A division of OCP Publications
5536 NE Hassalo
Portland, OR 97213
Phone: 1-800-LITURGY (548-8749)
E-mail: *liturgy@ocp.org*
All rights reserved.
Printed in the United States of America

Senior Research Editor: Bari Colombari
Editorial Assistance: Glenn CJ Byer, Michael Prendergast

Publisher: John J. Limb
Editorial Director: Vic Cozzoli
Managing Editor: Eric Schumock
Graphic Designer: Le Vu
Art Direction: Jean Germano
Cover Art: *Saint Jerome in his study*, Albrecht Dürer (1471 - 1528)

# CONTENTS

## FEASTS

## REFLECTIONS

# INTRODUCTION

During the 2002 annual meeting of the North American Academy of Liturgy in Reston, VA, Glenn Byer of Oregon Catholic Press approached me with the kind invitation to consider putting together a collection of my essays on various liturgical topics for publication in the *Worship* series of the Pastoral Press. This invitation to have my work published in this series, which includes essay collections by liturgical scholars such as Thomas Talley,[1] John Baldovin,[2] Bryan Spinks,[3] and Kenneth Stevenson,[4] to name only a few whose work has greatly influenced my own, is both humbling and gratifying. I am, therefore, delighted to accept Glenn's invitation and *Worship: Rites, Feasts, and Reflections* is the result of that acceptance.

With the absence of any of my work on the Prayers of Sarapion of Thmuis,[5] which is perhaps too specialized for a collection of this type, the essays in this volume span the last ten to fifteen years of my teaching, thinking, conference speaking and writing on various topics in liturgical history and theology, especially Christian Initiation, the Eucharist, the Liturgical Year, and various questions in ecumenical liturgical-sacramental theology. With some exceptions, most of the essays in this volume have been published in some form previously. Consequently, I would like to express my gratitude here to those publications and editors for whom they first appeared in print for permission to re-issue them now in a new form. Many of the nine essays in the first section of this volume are concerned with the rites of

Christian Initiation as well as with related eucharistic and ecumenical liturgical topics. The first essay, "The Study of the Rites of Christian Initiation Today," has appeared nowhere else in this particular form but is based on a revision of both "The Role of *Worship* in the Contemporary Study of Christian Initiation: A Select Review of the Literature," *Worship* 75, (January 2001), 20–35, and "What's New about the Past? The Study of Christian Initiation" *Liturgy, The Journal of the Liturgical Conference* 16, (Summer 2000), 53–59. The second essay, "Romans 6 and the Identity of the Church: Towards a Baptismal Ecclesiology," appeared originally in *Catechumenate: A Journal of Christian Initiation* 22, 5 (September 2000), 22–36. "Baptism as '*New Birth ex aqua et spiritu:*' An Investigation of Western Liturgical Sources," was originally presented as a short communiqué at an international scholarly congress on the occasion of the fiftieth anniversary of the death of Anton Baumstark, the Pontifical Oriental Institute, Rome, Italy, and was first published in *Acta of the International Scholarly Congress: Comparative Liturgy Fifty Years after Anton Baumstark* (+1948), Orientalia Christiana Analecta (Rome, 2002), 787–807. The next essay, "The Postchrismational Structure of Apostolic Tradition 21, the Witness of Ambrose of Milan, and a Tentative Hypothesis Regarding the Current Reform of Confirmation in the Roman Rite," appeared originally in *Worship* 70, (1996), 16–34. This essay deals in part with current scholarship on the so-called *Apostolic Tradition*, reflected in the recent commentary by Paul Bradshaw, L. Edward Phillips, and me.[6] "Let's Stop Making 'Converts' at Easter" was first published in *Catechumenate: A Journal of Christian Initiation* 21, (September 1999), 10–20. An abridged version of this essay has also appeared in *Rite* (May/June 2004), 4–8. The next essay, "One Body, One Spirit in Christ: The Eucharist as the Culmination of Christian Initiation," had its origins as a keynote address delivered to the annual meeting of the Federation of Diocesan Liturgical Commissions, October 10, 1996. It appears here in print for the first time anywhere. "The 'Real' and Multiple 'Presences' of Christ in Contemporary Lutheran Liturgical and Sacramental Practice" had its origins as a keynote address for the conference "Church and Eucharist: The Many Presences of Christ," Center for Pastoral Liturgy, June, 1998, Notre Dame, IN, and was subsequently first published in T. Fitzgerald and D. Lysik (eds.) *The Many Presences of Christ* (Chicago: Liturgy Training Publications, 1999), 105–120. "Eucharistic Reservation and Lutheranism: An Extension of the Sunday Worship?" had its origins as a public lecture called "Real Presence, Eucharistic Reservation, and Ecumenism," and was presented to the Summer Institute of Christian Spirituality "Soul Food" Lecture Series, Spring Hill College, Mobile, AL, June 6, 2002, and appeared in print in Clare V. Johnson (ed.), *Ars Liturgiae: Worship, Aesthetics, and Practice: Essays in Honor of Nathan D. Mitchell* (Chicago: Liturgy Training Publications, 2003), 27–54. The final essay in the first section of this volume, "Planning and Leading Liturgical Prayer in an Ecumenical Context," was first published in *Pro Ecclesia* VIII, (Spring, 1999), 187–200.

The next five essays all deal with various issues surrounding the feasts and seasons of the liturgical year. "Liturgical and Theological Reflections on the Transfer of Solemnities and Feasts to the Following or Nearest Sunday" first appeared as "Movable Feasts?" *Rite* (August/September, 2000), 4–7, 12. "From Three Weeks to Forty Days: Baptismal Preparation and the Origins of Lent" was originally a presentation given to the Problems in the Early History of the Liturgy seminar of the North American Academy of Liturgy, January 4, 1990, St. Louis, MO. It was first published in *Studia Liturgica* 20, (1990), 185–200.[7] The next essay, "Tertullian's '*Diem baptismo sollemniorem*' Revisited: A Tentative Hypothesis on Baptism at Pentecost," was, similarly, first given as a presentation to the Problems in the Early History of the Liturgy seminar of the North American Academy of Liturgy, Reston, VA, January 4, 2002. It appeared subsequently in the *Festschrift* for Paul F. Bradshaw that L. Edward Phillips and I recently edited, *Studia Liturgica Diversa: Essays in Honor of Paul F. Bradshaw* (Portland: Pastoral Press, 2004), 31–44. "Let's Keep Advent Right Where it Is!" appeared originally in *Lutheran Forum* 28, (November, 1994), 45–47. The last essay in this section, "The Feast of the Virgin of Guadalupe and the Season of Advent," appears here for the first time in print. It is based on the fourth chapter of my recent book, *The Virgin of Guadalupe; Theological Reflections of an Anglo-Lutheran Liturgist*,[8] a topic of interest I have been exploring in recent years.

Although issues of liturgical theology are not lacking by any means in the above-noted essays, the five essays which make up the concluding section of this volume are more directly concerned with liturgical and/or sacramental theology *per se*. The first essay, "Forever Flesh," appearing originally in the Notre Dame Center for Liturgy's *Assembly* 26, (September, 2000), 34–35, 40, is my brief attempt to present Lutheran theologian and martyr Dietrich Bonhoeffer as a "liturgical theologian" worth much greater attention in this context than he has been given. Similarly, in "The Place of Sacrament in the Theology of Paul Tillich," published originally as "The Place of *Sacraments* in the Theology of Paul Tillich," *Worship* 63, (January, 1989), 17–31, I argue that the concept of "Sacrament" (not *sacraments*) is an important key to unlocking Tillich's own theological system and that, at core, his overall theology *is*, in fact, a *sacramental* one with ecumenical implications. The next essay, "The One Mediator, the Saints, and Mary: A Lutheran Reflection," originally published in *Worship* 67, (1993), 226–238, critiques Lutheran-Roman Catholic dialogue on this issue from a liturgical perspective. "Liturgy and Theology," concerned with the proper interpretation of the "*lex orandi, lex credendi*," first appeared in Paul Bradshaw and Bryan Spinks (eds.), *Liturgy In Dialogue: Essays in Memory of Ronald Jasper*, (London: SPCK, 1994, 202–225).[9] And the final essay, "Can We Avoid Relativism in Worship? Liturgical Norms in the Light of Contemporary Liturgical Scholarship," had its origins as "Liturgical Norms in the Light of Contemporary Liturgical Scholarship?" and was presented to the Problems in the Early History of the Liturgy seminar, North American Academy of Liturgy, Tampa, FL, Jan. 3, 2000. It was first published in *Worship* 74, (March, 2000), 135–154.

Although most of the essays included herein have appeared in print before now, they are not merely reprints of already published work. Rather, to varying degrees, all of these essays have been re-edited and/or corrected and expanded at various places to reflect my current thought on the topic or to bring bibliographies more up to date. Sometimes that re-editing has meant only a new introduction or other minor corrections. At other times it has meant larger rewrites of particular sections or the inclusion of additional material that had been omitted from earlier published versions. At the same time, I have not found any major positions I have taken previously from which I would now want to dissociate myself or with which I no longer agree. In fact, on several issues (e.g., the ecumenical centrality of baptism, the rightness of full infant initiation, the limiting of Christian initiation at Easter to the unbaptized, the avoidance of cultural assimilations of feasts, issues of eucharistic reservation, etc.) I have become more convinced of—or more firmly committed to—my position than ever.

No attempt has been made in this collection to employ only those essays, which reflect one type of style or level of academic difficulty. To that end, some essays will appeal more directly to the specialist than to the general reader and vice versa. Others have a more decidedly pastoral focus. Others are much more academic in focus without, however, ignoring the pastoral dimensions. Some are quite long, taking several pages. Others are shorter, comprising only a few pages. There is, nevertheless, a common thread that runs throughout most of them, namely, an understanding of and commitment to critical historical-liturgical and theological scholarship in ultimate service to the pastoral liturgical life of the churches today. As such, I have not limited myself to liturgical description alone but in several places have been bold enough to prescribe what may, could, and even *should* be done liturgically today.

Finally, I wish to acknowledge with gratitude Glenn Byer, Michael Pendergast, and Bari Colombari of Oregon Catholic Press for their encouragement on this project and for guiding it through to publication under the Pastoral Press imprint. And deep thanks are due to my graduate assistant, Frankie White, a Ph.D. student in Liturgical Studies at the University of Notre Dame, whose untiring work in reference checking, electronic scanning, and, not least, proofreading, along with her work in my classes, has been of immense help to me.

Maxwell E. Johnson
University of Notre Dame
August 2004

## Notes

1 *Worship: Reforming Tradition* (Washington, D.C.: Pastoral Press, 1990).

2 *Worship: City, Church and Renewal* (Washington, D.C.: Pastoral Press, 1991).

3 *Worship: Prayers from the East* (Washington, D.C.: Pastoral Press, 1993).

4 *Worship: Wonderful and Sacred Mystery* (Washington, D.C.: Pastoral Press, 1992).

5 See *The Prayers of Sarapion of Thmuis: A Literary, Liturgical, and Theological Analysis*, OCA 249 (Rome; Pontifical Oriental Institute, 1995); "A Fresh Look at the Prayers of Sarapion of Thmuis,"*Studia Liturgica* 22 (1992), 163–83; "The Archaic Nature of the Sanctus, Institution Narrative, and Epiclesis of the Logos in the Anaphora Ascribed to Sarapion of Thmuis," in Robert F. Taft (ed.), *The Christian East, Its Institutions & Its Thought: A Critical Reflection: Papers of the International Scholarly Congress for the 75th Anniversay of the Pontifical Oriental Institute Rome, 30 May–5 June 1993*, OCA 251 (Rome: Pontifical Oriental Institute, 1996), 671–702; "The Baptismal Rite and Anaphora in the Prayers of Sarapion of Thmuis: An Assessment of a Recent 'Judicious Reassessment,'" *Worship* 73 (March 1999), 140–68; and "The Origins of the Anaphoral use of the Sanctus and Epiclesis Revisited: The Contribution of Gabriele Winkler and its Implications," in H-J. Feulner, E. Velkovska, and R. Taft (eds.), *Crossroad of Cultures: Studies in Liturgy and Patristics in Honor of Gabriele Winkler*, OCA 260 (Rome: Pontifical Oriental Institute, 2000), 405–42.

6 See Paul F. Bradshaw, Maxwell E. Johnson, and L. Edward Phillips, *The Apostolic Tradition: A Commentary* (Minneapolis: Fortress Press, 2002).

7 Two other essays by me on Lent may also be helpful here: "Preparation for Pascha? Lent in Christian Antiquity" in P. Bradshaw and L. Hoffman (eds.), *Passover and Easter: Origins and History to Modern Times* (Two Liturgical Traditions, vol. 6) (Notre Dame, IN: University of Notre Dame Press, 1999), 36–54; and with Lawrence Hoffman, "Lent in Perspective: A Summary Dialogue," in idem, *Passover and Easter: Origins and History to Modern Times*, 55–68.

8 (Lanham, MD: Rowman & Littlefield, 2002).

9 American edition (Collegeville: The Liturgical Press /Pueblo Books, 1995), 203–27.

# ABBREVIATIONS

DBL          E.C. Whitaker, *Documents of the Baptismal Liturgy*, Revised and Expanded by Maxwell E. Johnson (London: SPCK; Collegeville: The Liturgical Press, Pueblo, 2003).

LW           *Luther's Works* [American Edition] (Minneapolis: Augsburg Fortress)

LWSS         Maxwell E. Johnson (ed.), *Living Water, Sealing Spirit: Readings on Christian Initiation* (Collegeville: The Liturgical Press, Pueblo, 1995).

OC           *Oriens Christianus*

OCA          *Orientalia Christiana Analecta*, Rome: Pontifical Oriental Institute

# RITES

# THE STUDY OF THE RITES OF CHRISTIAN INITIATION TODAY: A SURVEY OF CONTEMPORARY SCHOLARSHIP AND ITS IMPLICATIONS

In this essay I want to reflect on the current scholarly study of the historical development and theological interpretation of the rites of Christian initiation in response to two questions: (1) what new and radical interpretations of historical data have emerged in recent years? and (2) what bearing or implications, if any, might these have on either the revision of current liturgical orders for the churches today or for further scholarship on Christian initiation? In the first section of this article, a summary of current scholarly views about the shape of Christian initiation in the early churches, together with some of the documents upon which that shape or order has been based, will be provided. Second, since the related question of confirmation continues to be a significant question for the churches today, specific issues related to this liturgical act will be considered next. Third, and finally, I shall provide some kind of preliminary answer to the second question noted above, though this question will certainly be hinted at all the way through this essay.

## I. The Study of Christian Initiation in the Early Churches

In the 1960's and 70's there were several common historical and influential assumptions made about the origins and early practice of Christian initiation, namely:

1. that there was a single, monolinear, and original unitive pattern of baptism, "confirmation," and first
   Communion, celebrated from antiquity at the Easter
   Vigil (interpreted by a Romans 6 death and burial
   imagery) and prepared for by at least a nascent Lent,
   which, in the course of the Middle Ages, was dis-
   rupted and separated into distinct sacraments and
   ultimately divorced from their "original" connection
   to Easter;
2. that an important document, like the *Apostolic
   Tradition*, ascribed to Hippolytus of Rome (ca. 215),
   thanks to the work of Bernard Botte[1] and Gregory
   Dix,[2] was actually composed by the early-third century anti-pope Hippolytus himself and thus reflected
   our earliest and authoritative piece of evidence for
   reconstructing early initiation practice at Rome; and
3. that any variations to this supposed normative pattern (e.g., that of early Syria) were to be viewed precisely as accidental and unimportant "variations" or
   idiosyncratic departures from this norm.

Today, however, all of these assumptions, due to a new scholarly and critical read of the sources, have been, and are increasingly being, revised. Thanks, in large part, to the seminal work of
Gabriele Winkler on the early Syrian and Armenian liturgical traditions,[3] summarized in English in a highly significant 1978 article,[4] modern liturgical scholars have come to emphasize that
what was normative in early Christian initiation practice was
liturgical diversity and multiple patterns from the very beginning.[5] In other words, there appears to have been no single common pattern, ritual contents, or theological interpretation which
suggest themselves as universally normative, apart from some
rather obvious things like catechesis, the water bath, and the profession of trinitarian faith. Hence, some of what has been viewed
as universally normative was but the result of various developments toward liturgical uniformity brought about in the aftermath of Constantine's imperial ascendancy and the various trinitarian and christological ecumenical councils of the fourth and
fifth centuries. While a three-fold pattern of baptism, "confirma-

tion," and first Communion, for example, *does* appear to be a discernable early *Roman* pattern for initiation (see John the Deacon and the letter of Innocent I to Decentius of Gubbio), other patterns are also available. In Syrian documents like the *Didascalia Apostolorum* and the *Apocryphal Acts of the Apostles,* for example, an initiatory pattern appears consisting of anointing, baptism, and first Communion in that order and, in the non-Roman West, a ritual pattern of baptism, anointing, and handlaying, with or without a concluding "consignation," also exists (see Tertullian, Cyprian of Carthage, Augustine of Hippo, and later Spanish and Gallican documents) as do distinct theological interpretations of the overall meaning of these rites.

As Winkler demonstrated clearly, a John 3:5 interpretation of baptism as "new birth" or "adoption," with Jesus' own baptism in the Jordan as paradigm, for example, seems to have been favored over the strangely silent theology of Romans 6 in several places in early Christianity until a synthesis was formed in the late fourth century which resulted in several transitions within the rites of the Christian East. Such transitions are reflected especially in the writings of the great Eastern mystagogues: Cyril of Jerusalem, John Chrysostom, and Theodore of Mopsuestia. Certainly one of those transitions has to do with the establishment of the theoretical "norm" of Easter baptism including the concomitant development of Lent as a pre-paschal season of catechumenal preparation.[6] Similarly, prior to these immediate post-Constantinian developments, the high point of the rite, at least in the early Syrian tradition, was not the water bath or any postbaptismal rite but the *prebaptismal* anointing of the head (later the entire body) as the pneumatic assimilation of the neophyte to the messianic priesthood and kingship of Christ. While eventually all of the rites of the Christian East would locate or shift the ritualization of the initiatory Spirit gift to a postbaptismal location, with prebaptismal rites becoming exorcistic and merely preparatory in nature (see Cyril, Theodore, Pseudo-Dionysius, and the Byzantine Rite), evidence of the other pattern and interpretation is still discernable in the sources (see *The Apostolic Constitutions,* Aphrahat, Ephrem, the Armenian Rite, the Rite of the Assyrian Church of the East, and the Maronite Rite). It is quite possible as well that the baptismal rites in Egypt (i.e., The Prayers or *Sacramentary* of Sarapion of Thmuis, the *Canonical Responses* of Timothy of Alexandria, the *Canons of Hippolytus,* and the Coptic Rite) reflect a similar transformation as do those in Syria and Syro-Palestine.[7] If some of Winkler's specific conclusions have been challenged,[8] no one today would seriously question the fact of liturgical diversity, the variety of baptismal practices within the distinct churches of Christian antiquity, and the transformative influence on Christian initiation in the aftermath of both Constantine's ascendancy to power and the doctrinal and ecclesiastical shifts beginning with Nicea in 325. Similarly, certainly no one would argue any longer that these diverse patterns reflect idiosyncratic departures from clearly established norms.

The assumed authoritative status of some early documents themselves, such as the so-called *Apostolic Tradition,* attributed to Hippolytus of Rome (ca. 215), has been subject to new scholarly critique. The emerging scholarly view developing on the *Apostolic Tradition* itself is that it is neither Hippolytan, Roman, nor early third century, at least not in the various extant Latin and Oriental versions in which it has come down to us. Hence, the "tradition" of the *Apostolic Tradition* may well reflect a synthesis of various and diverse liturgical patterns and practices already, some quite early and others added later.[9] With specific regard to Christian initiation in this document, where following baptism and a presbyteral anointing, the rite continues with an episcopal handlaying prayer and subsequent episcopal anointing before the neophytes' participation in the Eucharist, it has been argued that these episcopal rites themselves may well be the result of a fourth-century or later addition to an earlier liturgical core, a core which may well go back to the time of Justin the Martyr in the mid-second century.[10] In a 1996 article[11] I attempted to summarize the implications of this growing scholarly opinion for our understanding of the development of these episcopal rites within the Roman liturgical tradition. Therein I suggested, based both on Ambrose of Milan's reference in *De Sacramentis* to the sevenfold gifts of the Holy Spirit imparted by what he refers to as the "Spiritual Seal," and on Pope Innocent I's firm resolve to limit these postbaptismal actions to the bishop within the famous *Letter of Innocent I to Decentius of Gubbio* (CE 416), that

Rome itself probably knew the bishop's handlaying prayer during the time of Ambrose but may not yet have known an episcopal postbaptismal anointing until a later period. For Milan itself, in fact, whatever Ambrose may have meant in his day by the "Spiritual Seal," later "Ambrosian" liturgical sources (the *Ambrosian Manual* and the *Ordo of Beroldus* ) exhibit nothing that could qualify as constituting this "seal" liturgically. Such, of course, has implications for the origins and meaning of confirmation itself.

## II. The Study of Confirmation

Over the past several years contemporary liturgical scholarship has raised serious questions about the origins and theology of "confirmation." In treating the bishop's post-baptismal rites in the earliest extant version (the Verona Latin) of the so-called *Apostolic Tradition* (mid-fifth-century Latin, in which the gift of the Holy Spirit is *not* associated explicitly with these rites!), for example, Aidan Kavanagh argued in a short article that eventually became a book-length treatment of his hypothesis,[12] that these reflect only the traditional structure of what may be termed an episcopal *missa*. That is, this episcopal unit has the overall structure of a "dismissal" rite used to dismiss various categories of people from the liturgical assembly (e.g., catechumens and penitents), a practice known to have happened frequently in Christian antiquity at the close of various liturgies. Different groups of people, before leaving the liturgical assembly, would go before the bishop and receive, often by a handlaying rite, his blessing. Consequently, just as these neophytes had often been "dismissed" from both catechetical instruction and from other liturgical gatherings by a rite which included the laying on of hands, so now, after baptism and anointing by the presbyter, they are again dismissed by means of a similar ritual structure, but this time the "dismissal" is *from* the baptismal bath *to* the eucharistic table. This dismissal rite would later develop theologically into a postbaptismal conferral of the Holy Spirit as is documented in both the *Gelasian Sacramentay* and *Ordo Romanus XI*. Although this episcopal rite, thanks in large part to the letter of Innocent I to Decentius of Gubbio, would be ultimately separated from baptism itself, the origins of what will become this later "confirmation" rite are thus *structural* rather than theological.

In response, Paul Turner questioned Kavanagh's interpretation of these episcopal acts as constituting an actual "dismissal," and suggested, alternatively, that they should be viewed as "the first public gesture of ratification for the bishop and the faithful who did not witness the pouring of water," as it is quite clear that both baptism and the presbyteral anointing happened at a place outside of the liturgical assembly itself.[13] In other words, this unit of the bishop's handlaying prayer and anointing constitutes a rite of "welcome" rather than dismissal, a rite by which those newly born of water *and* the Holy Spirit are now welcomed officially into the eucharistic Communion of the Church. And they are welcomed there by the chief pastor of the community, the bishop, who prays for God's grace to guide the *neophytes* that they might be faithful to what their baptism has already made them to be. In its origins, therefore, what became "confirmation" through various historical accidents and developments, was simply the way that the baptismal rite itself was concluded and the Eucharist begun in some communities. To separate it from baptism brings with it a whole host of theological and pastoral problems quite incongruent with its origins and modern scholarship strongly underscores that.

With regard to "confirmation" in other Western sources, several studies have addressed this in various ways. In 1981 Joseph Levesque published a detailed and in-depth study of the post-baptismal rites of the major Gallican liturgical sources (i.e., the *Missale Gallicanum vetus*, the *Missale Gothicum*, and the *Bobbio Missal*) and concluded that, even with the absence of parallel rites to Roman confirmation, these sources reflect a complete and integral pattern of Christian initiation already (baptism, anointing, footwashing, and a concluding prayer without any ritual gesture attached).[14] Three years later Gabriele Winkler also provided a compelling analysis of these eighth-century liturgical documents and earlier (fifth-century) conciliar decisions from the Gallican tradition (namely, the local councils or synods of Riez, Arles, and Orange).[15] Within the conciliar decrees one encounters the terminology of *confirmare* and *perficere* to refer to something apparently "done" by the bishop apart from the baptismal rite that serves to "complete" baptism. But anachronism in interpreting this terminology must be avoided. That is, as Winkler demonstrated, such practices called *confirmare* and *perficere* in these conciliar decrees do not appear to be regular parts of the rites of Christian initiation but episcopal actions done in extraordinary or irregular situations (e.g., after "emergency baptisms," at the reconciliation of heretics, or in those situations where chrism had not been obtained from the bishop by presbyters prior to conferring baptism). In addition, Winkler argued that the reference to *"in confirmatione"* ("at confirmation") in Canon 2 of Orange was not necessarily a reference to an episcopal "rite" at all but to the bishop "confirming" the local ministries of presbyters during his pastoral visits. Winkler's interpretation, notably, has been followed by Gerard Austin[16] and Aidan Kavanagh[17] in their own studies of confirmation.

In the same article, Winkler also raised serious doubt about the date and authorship of the famous Pentecost homily attributed to Faustus of Riez in the late fifth century, where for the first time the ultimately influential distinction is made between baptism as a "washing" and "birth" to new life and confirmation (as a handlaying rite) interpreted as a confirmation for "battle," a "strengthening," and a pneumatic "augment" of grace. Although undoubtedly Gallican in provenance, the existence of such a rite together with such a sophisticated theological interpretation, according to her, appears to reflect a time period later than the late fifth century.

In 1985 Frank Quinn provided his own detailed survey of the sources for confirmation and its interpretation in Western Christianity.[18] In his August 15, 1971 Apostolic Constitution *Divinae consortium naturae*, Pope Paul VI decreed that, in its essence, *"the Sacrament of Confirmation is conferred through the anointing with chrism on the forehead*, which is done by the laying on of the hand, and through the words: be sealed with the gift of the Holy Spirit."[19] What is extremely important to note here is that, while Paul VI refers to the "dignity of the respected formulary used in the Latin Church" for this anointing, that is, the formula first appearing in the twelfth-century Roman Pontifical ("I sign you with the sign of the cross and confirm you with the chrism of salvation. In the name of . . . "), present in the famous

Pontifical of Durandus, and continuing in use until 1971, he makes a deliberate choice for the chrismation formula of the Byzantine Rite.[20] According to him, this Byzantine formula, "expresses the Gift of the Holy Spirit himself and calls to mind the outpouring of the Spirit on the day of Pentecost."[21] But the Roman tradition of the hand-laying prayer with its invocation of the seven-fold gifts of the Holy Spirit upon the newly baptized did the same for centuries in a legitimately distinct, and, arguably, more clearly biblical manner. In spite of the current official Roman Catholic definition, is confirmation, then, the rite of handlaying with prayer or is it the chrismation? Of course, that something other than the episcopal hand-laying prayer would attract theological attention in the history of Western Christianity is really no surprise. As Quinn noted, something quite similar happened in the theological interpretation of ordination in the liturgical synthesis formed between the medieval Roman and Gallican traditions. Thomas Aquinas, who so clearly defined confirmation as consisting of both chrism and formula in the thirteenth century,[22] for example, also defined the "matter" and "form" of ordination to be the *traditio instrumentorum* rather than the laying on of hands and prayer, an interpretation which continued officially until Pius XII's restoration of handlaying and prayer as ordination's matter and form in *Sacramentum Ordinis* of 1947. Did something like this also happen with the theological interpretation of confirmation? That is, in the medieval West did confirmation's ritual focus actually shift away from an original pneumatic episcopal handlaying prayer to an episcopal chrismation, which it has continued to be in the Roman Rite ever since?

The regular omission of the first postbaptismal anointing and formula in favor of confirmation in the initiation of adults in the Roman Rite has also attracted the attention of liturgical scholars. Quinn himself stated in the conclusion of the above-noted essay that: "Since the prayer accompanying the postbaptismal rite speaks so strongly of incorporation into the church, a principal focus of baptism, it is odd indeed that this rite can be omitted. Even odder is the addition of the image of prophet to the kingship and priesthood with which this rite has been associated for centuries. Ironically, such an assertion removes confirmation's right to be . . ."[23] Similarly, in 1986 Anglican liturgist Bryan Spinks surveyed the postbaptismal (and confirmation) rites of ten modern English language liturgies from the perspective of the call for "vivid signs" of the gift of the Holy Spirit in paragraph 19 of the 1982 World Council of Churches' ecumenical convergence statement, *Baptism, Eucharist, Ministry*.[24] According to Spinks, instead of "vivid signs" of the Spirit's gift in these contemporary hand-laying and anointing rites, one encounters a great lack of both ritual and theological clarity with regard to terminology (e.g., "explanatory rites," or confirmation) and to which signs and/or other ritual gestures (e.g., anointing, handlaying, a postbaptismal kiss, or the extending of the "right hand of fellowship") might best signify this gift in a contemporary ecumenical context. At one point in this essay, Spinks provided the following example of a postbaptismal anointing prayer from his own pastoral experience in Cambridge, England, which serves to unite or synthesize into one prayer and rite the emphases of both the current Roman postbaptismal anointing prayer and that for confirmation: "Jesus the Anointed One anoints you with grace and signs you as one of his flock. You are a member of a chosen race, a royal priesthood, a holy nation, God's own people. May the Holy Spirit which is poured out upon you sanctify and preserve you. N., you are signed with the oil of Anointing in the Name of the Father, and of the Son, and of the Holy Spirit. Amen."[25] If, as in the case of adult initiation in the Roman Rite, only *one* postbaptismal anointing is desired in contemporary initiation rites, an integrated prayer and rite such as this might well provide a model worthy of further ecumenical emulation.

Closely related to the above discussion of confirmation's evolution and meaning is the fact that within Roman Catholic circles today there is a growing awareness (at least among liturgical scholars) that sacramental confirmation "is not a reaffirmation of a previous baptism; it is not the ritualization of a key moment in the human life cycle. It is, rather the gift of the Spirit *tied intimately to the water-bath* that prepares one for the reception of the body and blood of Christ as a full member of the church."[26] For Roman Catholics this new awareness has had two implications, either: (1) that confirmation and first Communion simply be restored to baptism in all cases, whether the candidate is an infant, child, or adult; or (2) that, at the very least, the traditional "canonical" age of 7 be the time at which those baptized in infancy are confirmed and receive first Communion, in that order. If the first is clearly emerging as a general preference among liturgists,[27] the second is, in fact, emerging as the practice in several dioceses in the United States and Canada and will certainly become more frequent in the coming years. And, along these lines, it should be noted that within several contemporary Protestant traditions the Communion participation of *all* the baptized, with first Communion celebrated at the time of even infant baptism, has been, at least, theoretically restored.[28]

Few Roman Catholic liturgical scholars today have addressed the liturgical, theological, and pastoral issues surrounding confirmation as directly and decidedly as Paul Turner has done. In his 1997 "Forum: Confusion Over Confirmation,"[29] Turner highlighted the confusion brought about by the various and disconnected ways that confirmation is employed in the Roman Catholic Church today: (1) as a rite of initiation (in the case of adult baptism); (2) as a rite of maturity (for those baptized in infancy or even in emergency situations); and (3) as connected to rites of reception of Christians baptized already in other communions into full Communion with the Catholic Church. Not surprisingly, Turner's solution is for the end of such confusion by restoring "confirmation" to baptism in all cases (which would also eliminate altogether any need for "emergency confirmations"), by the development of other rites of baptismal affirmation or reaffirmation for those having already been fully initiated at baptism, and by Roman Catholic recognition that not only baptism but what Roman Catholics consider to be the *fullness* of Christian initiation already exists liturgically within the baptismal rites of other Christian traditions, especially today where, increasingly, the equivalent to Roman confirmation (hand-laying prayer for the Spirit's sevenfold gift and, often, an anointing related to the Spirit's seal) appear as the regular postbaptismal rites within most contemporary Protestant worship books.[30] As Turner concludes: "we need better ecumenical conversation on baptism, profession of faith, eucharistic Communion, and orders. We yearn for the day when confirmation will not be necessary for those who share our Christian faith and wish to share our table."[31]

## III. Conclusion: Implications for Further Study and Practice

It should be abundantly clear, based on all of the above studies, that, first of all, the historical-textual-theological study of the classic documents of the rites of Christian initiation is by no means concluded in our own day, in spite of those who would denigrate such classic liturgiological study as a characteristic only of past and, hence, surpassed scholarship. Together with the need for our constant re-reading of the earliest extant liturgical sources (including the New Testament) and previous scholarship on those sources with new critical eyes, attention to other non-Roman Western liturgical traditions, such as the Mozarabic,[32] would seem to be highly important as the diverse liturgical riches and implications of the wider Christian tradition are increasingly uncovered. Along with this, increased attention to baptismal images and feasts besides Romans 6 and Easter, such as Epiphany and/or Theophany as baptismal occasions both in the East and the non-Roman West, may well serve to challenge the recently restored ideal of Easter baptism as the be-all and end-all of baptismal thought and practice. Indeed, the overall dominance of the re-birth imagery of John 3:5 in relationship to the baptismal paradigm of Jesus' own baptism in the Jordan, as well as the sheer paucity of references to Romans 6 (even within an Easter baptism context) in Western sources, including those of the Roman tradition, have yet to attract the wide attention of liturgical scholars.[33] Similarly, the question of what constituted "confirmation" and, thereby, what *should* constitute confirmation today, including the implications for rite, age, and significance, is, by no means, yet answered definitively. Certainly, as noted above, the contemporary practice of uniting confirmation with the reception of Christians into full Communion needs redress and has no historical precedent in favor of it, unless, of course, it is really intended that "separated brethren" and sisters really are heretics after all and in need of reconciliation. And that this should be done at the Easter Vigil, to my knowledge, has no foundation in the history of Christian initiation at all. Yet, even recent Protestant adaptations of the adult catechumenal process provide this kind of option, thus making the Easter Vigil itself into a celebration of receiving new "converts" into particular ecclesial traditions.[34] The danger, of course, is that the entire baptismal basis and orientation of the restored Vigil and catechumenate is overshadowed by this practice.

Second, in light of both the frequent contemporary practice of creating make-shift fonts for the public viewing of baptism on occasions such as the Easter Vigil, and the document *Built of Living Stones* by the United States Conference of Catholic Bishops (USCCB), architectural attention to baptismal space in our churches would seem to be a highly critical need today as well. If public "seeing" of all the sacramental rites is a great contemporary value, we should not forget that for centuries in the Roman Rite, at least, baptism was customarily administered in separate baptisteries apart from the assembly itself even if *during* its public liturgies. In fact, one of the liturgical purposes of the Easter Vigil readings themselves was to occupy the attention of the liturgical assembly while baptisms were simultaneously taking place apart from the assembly. It was the entrance of the newly baptized into the assembly during the singing of the Litany of the Saints for the ratification, confirmation, or sealing of baptism which followed that constituted the public participation of the assembly in this rite. Attention to baptismal space and its location in the *domus Dei* or *domus ecclesiae* may well be near the top of the list on the continuing agenda for liturgical renewal in the immediate future and critical dialogue among architects, liturgical designers, artists, and liturgists would seem to be of paramount importance in this context.

The words of Mark Searle (+1992) remain most helpful in this context:

> The consequences of believing that baptism should occur in the face of the whole congregation are . . . unfortunate. For one thing, it creates proscenium-style sanctuaries, where everything is enacted on-stage before a more or less passive audience and leads to a massive line-up of heavy symbols across the front of the church: font, paschal candle, lectern, altar, presider's chair, perhaps a second lectern for the cantor. It is is essential, if we are to bring our ecclesial imaginations into line with the biblical ecclesiology of Vatican II, that we break that monopoly of symbols that reserves them all to an enclosed area 'up

front.' Putting the font alongside or near the altar fosters clericalism, passive congregations, and a voyeuristic experience of the most personal of all the sacraments. The radical personalism of this sacrament finds its supreme expression in the nakedness of the candidates, where they are reduced to the human condition in order to be raised to the divine. In centuries when Christians were more prudish than they are today, it must have taken a much more profound realization of the meaning of baptism than most of us possess to make such nudity even thinkable. But the same profound realization of the meaning of baptism that led to ritual nakedness also prompted the creation of baptistries, shaped as mausoleums or as martyr-shrines, where the mysteries hidden from outsiders and cherished by insiders, could take place with fitting decency. These baptistries would be visited by the baptized and venerated on the anniversary of their baptism, but they were never intended to accommodate more than the necessary few.[35]

Third, and finally, Paul Turner's statement that "we need better ecumenical conversation on baptism, profession of faith, eucharistic Communion, and orders" spells out a complete agenda for where pastoral-theological scholarship on Christian initiation now needs to go, especially in light of recent ecumenical agreements, such as the significant 1999 Roman Catholic-Lutheran *Joint Declaration on the Doctrine of Justification*. In short, although he does not use these terms, Turner calls here for both a foundational-ecumenical baptismal spirituality[36] and a baptismal ecclesiology. If, since Vatican II, a "Communion ecclesiology," which is closely connected to divisive ecumenical issues, such as orders (especially the historic episcopacy) and the Eucharist, has been a dominant theological concern, a baptismal ecclesiology as the absolute foundation and source for all ecclesiology would appear to be much more fruitful ecumenically. As Turner writes elsewhere:

> The ecumenical movement longs for the day when the rites which prepare baptized Christians for full

Communion will be ripped from our books, and the cat-echumenate now so freely adapted for the *baptized* may become again the proper province of the unbaptized . . . When the disciples warned Jesus that some who were not of their company were exorcising demons in his name they expected him to put a stop to it. Jesus tolerated strange exorcists with the simplest of aphorisms: 'If they're not against us, they're for us.' The church toler-ates baptisms. Is it too much to ask that we tolerate con-firmations as well? Our churches are irresponsibly dawdling toward a common table.[37]

Indeed, our ecclesial identity as church, as the corporate body of Christ, as dead, buried, and risen in Christ, as born anew and adopted through water and the Spirit, and as signed and sealed by the Holy Spirit for life, witness, and mission in the world is given to us freely in baptism. From baptism the various orders of ministry flow. And back to baptism, to our freely given baptismal identity, the Eucharist and other sacraments lead and direct us. "Better ecumenical conversation on baptism, profes-sion of faith, eucharistic Communion, and orders" is precisely the call for better ecumenical conversation about what the "sacramental bond of unity" constituted by baptism actually implies. It is baptism itself that will bring Christians closer to a common eucharistic table. For it is baptism itself that must frame the conversation and it is baptism that serves to raise all other ecclesiological questions anew.

## Notes

1  B. Botte, *La Tradition apostolique de saint Hippolyte* (Münster Westfalen: Aschendorffsche, 1963).

2  G. Dix, *The Treatise on the Apostolic Tradition of St. Hippolytus of Rome* (London: The Alban Press, 1937; reissued 1992).

3  See G. Winkler, *Das armenische Initiationsrituale*, OCA 217 (Rome 1982).

4  "The Original Meaning of the Prebaptismal Anointing and Its Implications." *Worship* 52 (1978), 24–45 (LWSS, 58–81).

5  The best guide, of course, to early Christian liturgical diversity is the study of Paul Bradshaw, *The Search for the Origins of Christian Worship: Sources and Methods for the Study of Early Liturgy*, revised ed. (Oxford/New York: Oxford University Press, 2002).

6  See P. Bradshaw, "'*Diem baptismo sollemniorem*': Initiation and Easter in Christian Antiquity," in LWSS, 137–47; M. Johnson, "From Three Weeks to Forty Days; Baptismal Preparation and the Origins of Lent," elsewhere in the volume, 199–218; and idem, "Preparation for Pascha? Lent in Christian Antiquity," in P. Bradshaw and L. Hoffman (eds.), *Two Liturgical Traditions*, vol. 6: *Passover and Easter: The Symbolic Structuring of Sacred Seasons* (Notre Dame, IN: University of Notre Dame Press, 1999), 36–54, M. Johnson (ed.), *Between Memory and Hope: Readings on the Liturgical Year*, (Collegeville: Pueblo, 2000), 207–22.

7  See G. Kretschmar, "Beiträge zur Geschichte de Liturgie, insbesondere der Taufliturgie, in Ägypten," *Jahrbuch für Liturgik und Hymnologie* 8 (1963), 1–54; P. Bradshaw, "Baptismal Practice in the Alexandrian Tradition: Eastern or Western?" in LWSS, 82–100; and M. Johnson, *Liturgy in Early Christian Egypt*, Alcuin/GROW Liturgical Study 33 (Cambridge: Grove Books, 1995), 7–16.

8  See A. Logan, "Post-Baptismal Chrismation in Syria: The Evidence of Ignatius, the 'Didache' and 'Apostolic Constitutions,'" *Journal of Theological Studies* 49 (1998), 92–108; and B. Spinks, "Sarapion of Thmuis and Baptismal Practice in Early Christian Egypt: The Need for a Judicious Reassessment," *Worship* 72 (1998), 255–70. But see also, M. Johnson, "The Baptismal Rite and Anaphora in the Prayers of Sarapion of Thmuis: An Assessment of a Recent 'Judicious Reassessment,'" *Worship* 73 (1999), 140–68.

9  See P. Bradshaw, M. Johnson, and L.E. Phillips, *The Apostolic Tradition: A Commentary*, Hermeneia Commentary Series (Minneapolis: Fortress Press, 2002); and P. Bradshaw "Re-dating the Apostolic Tradition: Some Preliminary Steps," in J. Baldovin and N. Mitchell (eds.), *Rule of Prayer, Rule of Faith: Essays in Honor of Aidan Kavanagh, OSB* (Collegeville: Pueblo, 1996), 3–17. For an opposing view see A. Stewart-Sykes, *Hippolytus–On the Apostolic Tradition* (Crestwood: St. Vladimir's Seminary Press, 2001).

10  See Bradshaw, Johnson, Phillips, op. cit., 124.

11  "The Postchrismational Structure of Apostolic Tradition 21, the Witness of Ambrose of Milan, and a Tentative Hypothesis Regarding the Current Reform of Confirmation in the Roman Rite," elsewhere in this volume, 63–82.

12  A. Kavanagh, "Confirmation: A Suggestion from Structure," *Worship* 58 (1984), 386–395 (LWSS, 148–58). See also A. Kavanagh, *Confirmation: Origins and Reform* (Collegeville: Pueblo, 1988).

13  P. Turner, "The Origins of Confirmation: An Analysis of Aidan Kavanagh's Hypothesis," in *Worship* 65 (1991), 320–338 (LWSS, 255).

14  J. Levesque, "The Theology of the Postbaptismal Rites in the Seventh and Eighth Century Gallican Church." *Ephemerides Liturgicae* 95 (1981), 3–43 (LWSS, 159–201).

[15] G. Winkler, "Confirmation or Chrismation? A Study in Comparative Liturgy," *Worship* 58 (1984), 2–17 (LWSS, 202–18).

[16] G. Austin, *Confirmation: Anointing with the Spirit* (Collegeville: Pueblo, 1985).

[17] A. Kavanagh, *Confirmation: Origins and Reform* (Collegeville: Pueblo, 1988).

[18] Frank Quinn, "Confirmation Reconsidered: Rite and Meaning," *Worship* 59 (1985), 354–370 (LWSS, 219–37).

[19] Paul VI, "Apostolic Constitution on the Sacrament of Confirmation," in *The Rites of the Catholic Church*, vol. 1 (Collegeville: The Liturgical Press, 1990), 477 [emphasis added].

[20] Ibid., 477.

[21] Ibid., 477.

[22] *Summa Theologiae* 3a, Q. 72, Arts. 1–12.

[23] Quinn, LWSS, 237.

[24] B. Spinks, "Vivid Signs of the Gift of the Spirit? The Lima Text on Baptism and Some Recent English Language Baptismal Liturgies," *Worship* 60 (1986), 232–246; LWSS, 310–26.

[25] Ibid., quoted from LWSS, 318.

[26] G. Austin, *Anointing with the Spirit* (Collegeville: Pueblo, 1985), 155.

[27] See the *Federation of Diocesan Commissions Newsletter* 22, (December 1995), 45; and see my "Eucharist as the Culmination of Christian Initiation," below, 95–124.

[28] Cf. Evangelical Lutheran Church in America, *The Use of the Means of Grace: A Statement on the Practice of Word and Sacrament* (Minneapolis: Augsburg Fortress, 1997).

[29] P. Turner, "Forum: Confusion Over Confirmation," *Worship* 71 (1997), 537–45.

[30] Cf. *Lutheran Book of Worship/Minister's Edition* (Minneapolis: Augsburg, 1978), 311.

[31] Ibid., 545.

[32] I am pleased to note here that my doctoral student, Chris McConnell is writing his Notre Dame doctoral dissertation, *Baptism in Visigothic Spain: Origins, Development and Interpretation*.

[33] See my essay, "Baptism as 'New Birth ex aqua et spiritu': An Investigation of Western Liturgical Sources," below in this volume, 37–62.

[34] See my "Let's Stop Making 'Converts' at Easter," below, 83–94.

[35] Mark Searle, "Foreword," in Regina Kuehn, *A Place for Baptism* (Chicago: Liturgy Training Publications, 1992), v.

[36] I tried to sketch out eight implications for such a baptismal spirituality in my 1997 article, "Back Home to the Font: Eight Implications of a Baptismal Spirituality," *Worship* 71 (1997), 482–504.

[37] Paul Turner, *Confirmation: The Baby in Solomon's Court* (Mahwah: Paulist Press, 1993), 129.

# ROMANS 6 AND THE IDENTITY OF THE CHURCH: TOWARDS A BAPTISMAL ECCLESIOLOGY

> Do you not know that all of us who have been baptized in Christ Jesus were baptized into his death? Therefore we have been buried with him by baptism into death, so that, just as Christ was raised from the dead by the glory of the Father, we too might walk in newness of life. For if we have been united with him in a death like his, we will certainly be united with him in a resurrection like his. We know that our old self was crucified with him so that the body of sin might be destroyed, and we might no longer be enslaved to sin. For whoever has died is freed from sin. But if we have died with Christ, we believe that we will also live with him. We know that Christ, being raised from the dead, will never die again; death no longer has dominion over him. The death he died, he died to sin, once for all; but the life he lives, he lives to God. So you also must consider yourselves dead to sin and alive to God in Christ Jesus. (Romans 6:3–11)

Of the several biblical and liturgical images of baptism, certainly the understanding that baptism sacramentally signifies and effects our participation in the death, burial, and resurrection of Christ is the most readily available and dominant one at our disposal today. Thanks especially to the restoration of the paschal triduum and the concomitant restoration of the adult catechumenate and Easter baptism in the RCIA, as well as in the revised liturgical books of several other Christian traditions today, what we have come to call the "Paschal Mystery," the great mystery of Christ's death and resurrection, has emerged as the key image and central metaphor by which all Christian life and liturgy are interpreted and understood. Within almost all of our churches Easter and its triduum have achieved their rightful place as the very center of the liturgical year, the annual center or core, after a Lent of penitential return to our origins in the font, in which we initiate new members of Christ's body and in which we renew and re-affirm our plunge into the mystery of Christ's death and resurrection as both our sacramental passage through him, with him, and in him from death to life and as the cruciform pattern or model of our common postbaptismal life as his body in the world.

Such a baptismal spirituality, such baptismal "death mysticism," I believe, also has profound implications for what we might call a "baptismal ecclesiology," that is, a theology of the church rooted primarily in and flowing from our baptismal plunge into the death and burial of Christ. As Aidan Kavanagh wrote in 1977:

> I shall take confidence that the restored Roman rites of Christian Initiation have begun to come alive when I read a treatise on Christian ethics that begins with baptism into Christ; when I see episcopal meetings deciding on Church discipline from a baptismal perspective; when I partake in ecumenical discussions that begin not with Luther or Cranmer or Calvin or Trent, but with baptism; when I am lectured on ministry in terms not of modern sexual roles but of baptism; when I can worship in a parish that consummates its corporate life through Lent at the paschal vigil, gathered around the font where all new life begins.[1]

What kind of church, then, would we be and what kind of Christians would we form if we took our baptismal death as death in Christ seriously, if we, as church, fully aware that we are a "dead church" living *after* life, chose to focus on what is truly essential in our postbaptismal life? That is, if we mean what we say and so are truly "dead" and "buried" by our baptism into Christ's Paschal Mystery, then we can afford to be a church, a "dead church," which understands itself as already having death in its past and walking now in "newness of life" as the result only of a most gracious, freely given, and divine gift. If we as church are truly crucified, dead, and buried in Christ so much so that, to paraphrase St. Paul, "it is no longer we who live but Christ who lives in us" (see Galatians 2:20), then there is nothing left to hold on to other than this, nothing left to lose of ourselves and identity that cannot be risked in service to the reign of God as we follow the way of the cross, which we know of and embrace as the only and ultimate way to life. For, if we as church are already dead, then how can even death itself possibly any longer pose a threat to us? The recent reflections of Joseph Cardinal Bernardin published shortly before his death remind us strongly that the experience of impending death itself has a way of confronting us with the need to focus only on what is truly essential in life and "how much of what consumes our daily life is trivial and insignificant."[2] Is this not equally true in terms of ecclesiology, that so much of what consumes our ecclesial life is often trivial and insignificant in comparison to what and who baptism has already made us to be?

An ecclesiology flowing from a Romans 6 theology of baptism, I believe, would lead to an understanding of the church much like that already envisioned in *Lumen Gentium* 18, where the church is spoken of in terms of its identity as simultaneously "holy" and in constant need of purification, where, like all the baptized, so also the church itself is called to continual repentance, reform, and renewal as it seeks to put the "old Adam" to death daily in order that Christ, and Christ alone, may come to life within it. *Lumen Gentium* 18 states clearly: "The Church . . . clasping sinners to her bosom, at once holy and always in need of purification (*sancta simul et semper purificanda*), follows constantly the path of penance and renewal."[3] In such an ecclesiology, I believe that questions of ecumenism, the inclusive-catholic nature of the church, and its mission and priestly service in the world would seem to be of paramount importance as the baptismal image of the crucified and risen Christ is continually formed and reformed in the church's members. I wish to address each of these three areas briefly in what follows.

## I. An Ecclesiology in Service to Ecumenism

A theology of the church flowing from a Romans 6 baptismal perspective would seem to imply a church for whom the ecumenical end of the scandal of Christian division would be among its highest priorities for the sake of the very credibility of its mission and service in the world. For, in spite of all the conversation, legislation, and dialogue in our day and age about the need to preserve our "Catholic," "Lutheran," or other ecclesial identities, the fact of the matter is that baptism already gives us our identity: a core, foundational, identity rooted in death, burial, and resurrection. Hence, a church that knows itself as "dead" and "buried" in baptism can afford to risk itself ecumenically in the pursuit of full and visible Christian unity because it knows already that common Christian identity it shares, having been brought to "newness of life" out of a common watery grave. It knows that its identity is nothing other than to die to itself in order to live faithfully to God!

Pope John Paul II, in his important encyclical, *Ut Unum Sint*, for example, underscores the baptismal basis for Christian unity precisely in the language of Romans 6, when he asks:

> How is it possible to remain divided if we have been 'buried' through baptism in the Lord's death, in the very act by which God, through the death of his Son, has broken down the walls of division? Division openly contradicts the will of Christ, provides a stumbling block to the world and inflicts damage on the most holy cause of proclaiming the good news to every creature.[4]

Similarly, the 1982 Faith and Order statement of the World Council of Churches, *Baptism, Eucharist, Ministry*, also highlights this ecumenical foundation of baptism well:

> Administered in obedience to our Lord, baptism is a sign and seal of our common discipleship. Through baptism,

Christians are brought into union with Christ, with each other and with the Church of every time and place. Our common baptism, which unites us to Christ in faith, is thus a basic bond of unity. We are one people and all are called to confess and serve one Lord in each place and in all the world. The union with Christ which we share through baptism has important implications for Christian unity. 'There is . . . one baptism, one God and Father of us all . . .' (Ephesians 4:4–6). When baptismal unity is realized in one, holy, catholic, apostolic Church, a genuine Christian witness can be made to the healing and reconciling love of God. Therefore, our one baptism into Christ constitutes a call to the churches to overcome their divisions and visibly manifest their fellowship.[5]

And the *Catechism of the Catholic Church* draws attention to the ecumenical nature of the church due to baptism, while acknowledging the tragic divisions that continue to exist:

Baptism constitutes the foundation of communion among all Christians, including those who are not yet in full communion with the Catholic Church: 'For men who believe in Christ and have been properly baptized are put in some, though imperfect, communion with the Catholic Church. Justified by faith in Baptism, [they] are incorporated into Christ; they therefore have a right to be called Christians, and with good reason are accepted as brothers by the children of the Catholic Church.' Baptism therefore constitutes *the sacramental bond of unity* existing among all who through it are reborn.[6]

Because the church into which the baptized are incorporated is *already* and inescapably an ecumenical church, inseparably united by baptism as the *one* body of the *one* Christ, who is not divided (see 1 Corinthians 1:13), Christian unity is, above all, not a demand, not a call, but already a gift to be received and further realized gratefully. The language of the New Testament is clear: "There is one body and one Spirit, just as you were called to the one hope of your calling, one Lord, one faith, one baptism, one

God and Father of all, who is above all and through all and in all" (Ephesians 4:4–6). Through baptism *all* are incoporated into the *one* Christ, the *one* church, the *one* body of Christ. Although we are always baptized within particular ecclesial communities and according to the liturgical rites of those communities, and although we live out our baptism in those distinct ecclesial manners of life, we are not really baptized "Catholic," "Lutheran," or anything else and we should strive to remove such an incomplete theology of baptismal identity from our vocabulary. We are baptized into communion with *Christ* and so, into communion with the *one church* of Jesus Christ; i.e., all the baptized, in a very real way, *already* belong to the same church! It is what the documents of Vatican II and the *Catechism of the Catholic Church* call this "sacramental bond of unity" that must be on the forefront of any discussion of visible Christian unity today.

Any catechesis on baptism, therefore, that fails to take into account the ecumenical nature of baptism and the church is not only incomplete and partial baptismal catechesis but incomplete ecclesiology as well. If the ecumenical goal, certainly, is to realize this baptismal "communion among all Christians" more perfectly in a situation of a full and visible communion of the churches, the most important step toward that goal is the realization that this communion already exists sacramentally between us. If *Christ himself* is not divided, then how dare we be? Indeed, the division of the church is nothing other than a shameful and sinful scandal, which casts into doubt not only the credibility of the church's identity and mission in the world ("a house divided against itself cannot stand," see Mark 3:25), but the claims we want to make about the meaning of baptism as well. The document, *Baptism, Eucharist, Ministry* is correct in asserting: "our one baptism into Christ constitutes a call to the churches to overcome their divisions and visibly manifest their fellowship." If the second millennium of our common ecclesial history in both East and West can be characterized as being marked by the scandal of Christian division, then, perhaps, by the will and grace of God, this third Christian millennium can be the time in which Christian unity is finally restored. But it won't happen without attention to what our one baptism has already made us to be, that is, *Christ* existing as church in the world!

There are, fortunately, concrete signs that such an approach is beginning to happen ecumenically. And, certainly, one of the most hopeful signs of this is the recent Lutheran-Roman Catholic *Joint Declaration on the Doctrine of Justification*, where this doctrine is explicitly related to baptism. As paragraph 25 of this *Joint Declaration* states:

> We confess together that sinners are justified by faith in the saving action of God in Christ. *By the action of the Holy Spirit in baptism, they are granted the gift of salvation, which lays the basis for the whole Christian life . . .*Whatever in the justified precedes or follows the *free gift of faith* is neither the basis of justification nor merits it.[7]

If this document, of course, does not yet signify full communion or full doctrinal agreement between Roman Catholics and Lutherans, it does firmly root continued ecumenical conversation between us in baptism and, as such, raises the ecumenical questions to new levels. That is, with this as the foundation, the other so-called church dividing issues noted in paragraph 43 of the *Joint Declaration* (e.g., the relationship between word and doctrine, ecclesial authority, ministry, and sacraments to name only a few) can now be addressed in a different way altogether. Significantly, the bilateral dialogues between Roman Catholics and Lutherans over the past thirty plus years have already produced an abundance of documents on precisely these issues, and, as Frank Senn reminded me in a recent conversation, of all Protestant traditions, Lutheranism itself actually has a possible "escape clause" with regard even to Lutheran recognition of some role for the papacy in a reconciled church.[8] Therefore, together with the common Roman Catholic-Lutheran recognition now that ". . . [justification] is more than just one part of Christian doctrine," but "stands in an essential relation to all truths of faith . . ." and functions as "an indispensable criterion, which constantly serves to orient all the teaching and practice of our churches to Christ,"[9] it should be quite possible, indeed, for Roman Catholics and Lutherans to move more deliberately toward a situation of increased, and ultimately, full communion with each other. Such are the undreamed of possibilities that arise ecumenically when baptismal death and burial is taken seriously in ecclesiology.

## II. An Inclusivist or Catholic Ecclesiology

A church fully aware of its status as "dead and buried" by baptism into Christ would work passionately, I also believe, to break down the social, ethnic/racial, economic, and gender-related walls of division and separation even within itself, as it seeks to express ever more concretely the great baptismal vision of equality articulated by St. Paul in Galatians 3:27–28: "As many of you as were baptized into Christ have clothed yourselves with Christ. There is no longer Jew or Greek, there is no longer slave or free, there is no longer male and female; for all of you are one in Christ Jesus." Like death itself, which is no respecter of person, sex, age, status, or wealth, baptism also is the "Great Equalizer." Are not racism, classism, and sexism, but concrete signs of the presence of the "old Adam" in us, who must continually be put to death, "drowned" with Christ in the waters of baptism? Hence, a church that knows itself as already "dead and buried" by baptism into the *one* Christ, who is neither "Jew or Greek . . . slave or free . . . male and female," can dare to "put on" this Christ and risk itself and its identity in the pursuit of a full and inclusive catholicity.

If the body of Christ into which the baptized are incorporated is already *one* body in the *one* Christ, however, then it is also constituted by baptism itself as an inclusive, or better, "catholic" body, which transcends all categories of race, ethnicity, social-economic status, and gender. Nathan Mitchell underscores this radically inclusive, "catholic" nature of the church constituted by baptism when he writes:

> We need to redefine church not as 'family' but as 'halfway house, moving people from fear of the world around them into a role as co-creators of a world which is both God's and their own.' . . . This can best be done by reaffirming Paul's bold, pluralistic blueprint for *inclusive* churches where 'there is neither Jew nor Greek, slave nor free, male nor female, for all are one in Christ Jesus.'

Genuine pluralism does not need—or try—to homogenize experience, tame traditions, exclude innovation or devalue diversity. It begins, instead, with the recognition that no single tradition (be it biblical, Western, American or whatnot) possesses all the resources needed to deal with the bewildering challenges of modern public life. Rich as these traditions are, notes Robert Bellah, 'if we cling obstinately to them alone we will be guilty of a narrow and...ultimately self-destructive parochialism. We must be able to embrace the experience of the rootedness of the American Indians, the uprootedness of the Blacks, the emptiness of the Asians, not out of some charitable benevolence but because our own traditions are simply not enough. Cultural defensiveness will be fatal. *If we are to survive on this earth, we must embrace the entire human tradition, make all of it...available to our imagination.*'10

Like the gift of Christian unity flowing from baptism, so too this radically inclusive or catholic vision of the body of Christ as a community of equals is not simply a goal but a reality already. But, like the continual challenge of Christian unity, it is, at the same time, a reality to be increasingly realized in the life of the church. We do not yet know what a church that takes seriously its multicultural and gender-neutral baptismal plunge into Christ will look like in the coming years. The contributions and challenges that Hispanics, Asians, African Americans, women, and other groups to the future of the church in America are making, and will continue to make, are already having and will continue to have profound impacts on its identity and mission. What will it mean when the Roman Catholic Church in the United States, for example, is constituted by a membership of over fifty percent Latino-Hispanic? What will such changes mean for liturgical inculturation and adaptation? What will years of pastoral leadership of women, even if not ordained to the ministries of episcopate, presbyterate, and diaconate in the Roman Catholic Church, come to mean ultimately for the ways in which local parishes are organized for ministry, for how pastoral care is provided, for how liturgy is celebrated, for how theology is actually done and taught, and for how God comes to be imaged? We cannot yet say. And yet, what is at stake in all of this appears to be the very question of "catholicity" itself, of what it means to embrace a baptismal vision of catholic wholeness in Christ. And, like ecumenism itself, that vision and reality are already baptismal gifts to be cherished and realized. Hence, any baptismal catechesis or ecclesiology that dares to ignore this baptismal vision and reality is, at best, incomplete and partial catechesis. For, the body of Christ into which one is incorporated is already this kind of community by definition because Christ Himself transcends all divisions. Aidan Kavanagh was correct. In such a church that knows itself in baptism as both "at once holy and always in need of purification" (*Lumen Gentium* 18), questions about ethics, ecumenism, ordained and other ministries, liturgical inculturation, language and translations, the identity of the liturgical assembly and its ministers, etc., will always be addressed first, before all else, from the perspective of having death and burial in Christ already behind us. Only then, in Kavanagh's words, might we "take confidence that the restored . . . rites of Christian Initiation have begun to come alive."

## III. An Ecclesiology in Service to Mission and Priesthood

A church knowing itself to be "living after life" would know that its goal is nothing other than to die, than to embrace the cross in its mission of solidarity and service in the world in continuity with Christ's own mission. As studies of those who have claimed to have "died" and "returned" from various "near death" experiences in our own day note, such people tend to "return to life" with a renewed and strong sense of purpose, of what we might call a "mission" to be completed in life.[11] Such a renewed sense of purpose and mission must also mark a "dead" church and certainly a baptismal ecclesiology is an ecclesiology in which such mission is central. From all of the models and images by which one might understand the nature and identity of the church,[12] the best model for a baptismal ecclesiology flowing from Romans 6 is probably that of the church as servant, a servant-people of God involved in Christ's own mission of service in the world. In a pastoral letter to his archdiocese, written in 1966, Richard Cardinal Cushing wrote:

> Jesus came not only to proclaim the coming of the Kingdom, he came also to give himself for its realization. He came to serve, to heal, to reconcile, to bind up wounds. Jesus, we may say, is in an exceptional way the Good Samaritan. He is the one who comes alongside of us in our need and in our sorrow, he extends himself for our sake. He truly dies that we might live and he ministers to us that we might be healed . . . So it is that the Church announces the coming of the Kingdom of God not only in word, through preaching and proclamation, but more particularly in work, in her ministry of reconciliation, of binding up wounds, of suffering service, of healing . . . As the Lord was the 'man for others,' so must the Church be 'the community for others.'[13]

Similarly, Lutheran theologian and martyr, Dietrich Bonhoeffer wrote in his classic work, *The Cost of Discipleship* that the call of Christ is always a call to death in him:

> When Christ calls a man, he bids him come and die. It may be a death like that of the first disciples who had to leave home and work to follow him . . . But it is the same death every time—death in Jesus Christ, the death of the old man at his call. Jesus' summons to the rich young man was calling him to die, because only the man who is dead to his own will can follow Christ. In fact every command of Jesus is a call to die, with all our affections and lusts. But we do not want to die, and therefore Jesus Christ and his call are necessarily our death as well as our life. The call to discipleship, the baptism in the name of Jesus Christ means both death and life . . . If we refuse to take up our cross and submit to suffering and rejection at the hands of men, we forfeit our fellowship with Christ and have ceased to follow him. But if we lose our lives in his service and carry our cross, we shall find our lives again in the fellowship of the cross with Christ. The

opposite of discipleship is to be ashamed of Christ and his cross and all the offence which the cross brings in its train . . . Discipleship means allegiance to the suffering Christ, and it is therefore not at all surprising that Christians should be called upon to suffer. In fact it is a joy and token of his grace.[14]

And, with regard to the mission of the church itself, Bonhoeffer could write in his famous *Letters and Papers from Prison* that: "The Church is the Church only when it exists for others. To make a start, it should give away all its property to those in need . . . The Church must share in the secular problems of ordinary human life, not dominating but helping and serving."[15]

A church "dead" and "buried" by baptism into Christ is liberated from the fear of death itself and, therefore, can dare to risk itself in a mission of suffering service in the world because it knows and seeks to know only the cross and suffering with the world as the way to resurrection. You see, death has a way of setting one free from all kinds of constraints, laws, plans, priorities, and old ways of doing things. So, if the church is truly dead and buried in Christ then there is nothing left to lose in offering itself in service in union and solidarity with the crucified Christ himself. What can possibly happen any longer to an individual or a church who know themselves to be already dead? Absolutely nothing, of course! And, as such, the church has been set free by its baptismal death and burial to become truly this "community for others" in the world.

One in our own day who came to understand the mission of the church and his own episcopal ministry within the church in precisely this way was, of course, the Salvadoran martyr, Archbishop Oscar Arnulfo Romero (+1980), champion of El Salvador's poor, oppressed, and disappeared. As is well known, Romero boldly faced the numerous death threats he encountered in response to his ministry in a way that can only be characterized as baptismal: "If they kill me I shall rise in the Salvadoran people." Only one who knew himself already dead and buried in Christ could make such a bold assertion about his own future. But Romero is not alone. Those who suggest that, rather than the patristic era, it is actually our own time that should be termed the "age of the martyrs" are undoubtedly correct. And if the third-century theologian Tertullian was right in claiming that "blood of the martyrs is the seed of the church," then it is also true that this "seed" of the church is precisely that which is planted by our baptismal plunge into Christ's death and burial. And from that watery grave emerges a servant community of the cross which expects nothing other than what its Servant-Master himself endured and experienced. Who knows what kind of church might yet arise when such baptismal-paschal mystery imagery is embraced by the baptized themselves?

Such a servant model is, precisely, of course, a priestly model at the same time as this community of priests, constituted by baptism, offers itself in union with Christ *the* priest for the life of the world. Probably nothing in the contemporary rites of baptism better expresses this understanding than the postbaptismal anointing in the current Roman Rite, an anointing which, unfortunately, is customarily omitted in favor of confirmation in the case of adult initiation:

> The God of power and Father of our Lord Jesus Christ has freed you from sin and brought you to new life through water and the Holy Spirit. He now anoints you with the chrism of salvation so that, united with his people, you may remain forever a member of Christ, who is Priest, Prophet, and King.[16]

Because it is the body of *Christ* into which the baptized are incorporated, all are initiated by baptism into a royal and prophetic priesthood. As such, the community of the church is a particular kind of community which knows itself as engaged in active priestly ministry and self-sacrificial service in the world. The body of Christ is not a community bent on its own survival or self-preservation. The body of Christ, who is priest, prophet, and king, exists that it may die in Christ, so that it may extend itself for the life of others as it continues its baptismal pilgrimage through death to resurrection. The 1994 edition of the *Catechism of the Catholic Church* expresses this baptismal-ecclesiological dimension well:

The baptized have become 'living stones' to be 'built into a spiritual house, to be a holy priesthood.' By Baptism they share in the priesthood of Christ, in his prophetic and royal mission. They are 'a chosen race, a royal priesthood, a holy nation, God's own people, that [they] may declare the wonderful deeds of him who called [them] out of darkness into his marvelous light.' *Baptism gives a share in the common priesthood of all believers.*[17]

In other words, baptism itself is an "ordination" to priesthood and the church itself is a nothing other than a royal, prophetic, and communal priesthood itself. In an article devoted in large part to precisely this priestly identity of the baptized, Aidan Kavanagh writes:

A baptismal element needs to be introduced into our contemporary discussion of ministry . . . But while one cannot discuss baptism without ministerial implications arising, it has unfortunately become usual to discuss ministries without ever feeling it necessary to enter into the implications of this discussion for baptism. That holy orders are rooted in baptism never seems to cross our minds. I suggest that it must . . . [T]he Church baptizes to priesthood: it ordains only to executive exercise of that priesthood in the major orders of ministry. Indeed *Ordo Romanus XI* of the ninth century has the baptized and anointed neophytes vested in stole and chasuble as they are presented to the Bishop of Rome for consignation prior to the beginning of the Easter Eucharist. The point being that *sacerdotium* (priesthood) in orthodox Christianity is not plural but single. It is that of Christ, shared among those in solidarity with whom . . . he was himself baptized in the Jordan, and also in solidarity with whom he now stands as both sacrifice and sacrificer in heaven . . . While every presbyter and bishop is therefore a sacerdotal person, not every sacerdotal person in the Church is a presbyter or bishop. Nor does sacerdotality come upon one for the first time, so to speak, at one's ordination. In constant genesis in the font, the Church is born there as a sacerdotal assembly by the Spirit of the Anointed One himself. *Laos* ['laity'] is a priestly name for a priestly person.[18]

He continues:

> . . . [I]n baptism by water and the Holy Spirit . . . one is anointed with as full a sacerdotality as the Church possesses in and by the Anointed One himself. Ordination cannot make one more priestly than the Church, and without baptism ordination cannot make one a priest at all. Becoming a Christian and becoming a sacerdotal being are not merely correlative processes, they are one and the same.[19]

To be baptized, therefore, to be incorporated by baptism into the body of Christ, is to become a priest within a community of priests in Jesus Christ, our great high priest. However the specific ministries of bishop, presbyter, and deacon are to be ordered in the life of the church, all the baptized, children, men, and women alike, share in this common priesthood of service and offering in union with Christ himself, and all theological reflection on the priesthood of Christ and the church must begin at the font. Indeed, all theological consideration of ordination and ministry flows from our theology of baptism. For does not ordained ministry itself exist to serve the baptized?

## Conclusion

There is no question but that since Vatican II a "communion ecclesiology" has been a dominant theological concern and an increasingly popular, even ecumenical way of approaching the theology of the church. Such an ecclesiology, however, is often closely connected to divisive ecumenical issues, such as orders (especially the historic episcopacy) and the Eucharist, and so often has limited value. Hence, a *baptismal* ecclesiology, as the absolute foundation and source for all theological reflection on the church may be much more fruitful as a foundational approach out of which other divisive issues can be addressed anew. Not only would such an approach to understanding the church be ecumenically helpful but it could well serve to underscore boldly the very nature and identity of the church and its mission in the world as that which is given precisely in baptism already. That is, Eucharist is the means by which our *baptismal* identity is continually renewed, reconstituted, and strengthened. Our ecclesial identity as church, as the corporate body of Christ, as dead, buried, and risen in Christ, as born anew and adopted through water and the Spirit, and as signed and sealed by the Holy Spirit for life, witness, and mission in the world is given to us freely in baptism. From baptism the various orders of ministry flow. And back to baptism, to our freely-given baptismal identity, the Eucharist and other sacraments lead and direct us. There is a real sense in which our life in Christ is always about baptism and its implications.

Finally, our Romans 6 theology of baptism is not merely about what happens or is supposed to happen to baptized individuals. Death, burial, and resurrection in Christ through baptism are about the birthing of that community of grace called the church. That is, our Romans 6 baptismal paradigm about life-long death and resurrection in Christ is not merely a paradigm for individuals *in* the church. It is the paradigm for the church itself. It is not just baptized individuals but it is the *church* which is called to die constantly in order to live. Probably nothing better captures this reality than the text of Fred Pratt Green (1903–2003) for the contemporary hymn:

> The Church of Christ, in every age
> Beset by change, but Spirit led
> Must claim and test its heritage
> And keep on rising from the dead.
>
> Across the world, across the street,
> The victims of injustice cry
> For shelter and for bread to eat
> And never live before they die.
>
> Then let the servant church arise
> A caring Church that longs to be
> A partner in Christ's sacrifice
> And clothed in Christ's humanity.

For he alone, whose blood was shed
Can cure the fever in our blood
And teach us how to share our bread
And feed the starving multitude.

We have no mission but to serve
In full obedience to our Lord;
To care for all, without reserve,
And spread his liberating Word.[20]

Such is the kind of church a baptismal ecclesiology flowing from Romans 6 may well yet engender in our own world, an ecumenical church, an inclusive-catholic church, and a church on mission knowing that its true identity and life only comes when it gives itself up in death, only when it realizes that it is already dead and buried so that it may rise always to newness of life and be the church that baptism calls into being.

## Notes

[1] Aidan Kavanagh, " Christian Initiation in Post-Conciliar Roman Catholicism: A Brief Report," LWSS, 10.

[2] Joseph Cardinal Bernardin, *The Gift of Peace* (Chicago: Loyola Press, 1997), 109.

[3] English translation in A. Flannery (ed.), *Vatican Council II: The Conciliar and Post Conciliar Documents*, vol. 1 (Collegeville: The Liturgical Press, 1984), 358.

[4] *Ut Unum Sint*, 6.

[5] World Council of Churches, "Baptism," para. D.6, *Baptism, Eucharist, Ministry* (Geneva: World Council of Churches, 1982).

[6] *Catechism of the Catholic Church* (Collegeville: The Liturgical Press, 1994), #1271, 323 [emphasis is original].

[7] *Joint Declaration on the Doctrine of Justification*, para. 25 [emphasis added].

[8] See "The Smalcald Articles" in T. Tappert (ed.), *The Book of Concord* (Philadelphia: Fortress Press, 1959), 316.

[9] *Joint Declaration on the Doctrine of Justification*, para. 18.

[10] Nathan Mitchell, *Eucharist as Sacrament of Initiation*, Forum Essays, Number 2 (Chicago: Liturgy Training Publications, 1994), 130–131.

11 See Raymond Moody, Jr., *Life After Life: The Investigation of A Phenomenon–Survival of Bodily Death* (New York: Walker and Co., 1975), especially 108–120. See also, idem, *Reflections on Life After Life* (New York: Bantam Books, 1977).

12 On the use of various models in ecclesiology see Avery Dulles, *Models of the Church*, Expanded Version (New York: Doubleday, Image, 1987).

13 Richard Cardinal Cushing, *The Servant Church* (Boston: Daughters of Saint Paul, 1966), 6–8.

14 Dietrich Bonhoeffer, *The Cost of Discipleship*, unabridged edition (New York: The Macmillan Co., 1963), 99, 101.

15 Dietrich Bonhoeffer, *Letters and Papers from Prison*, revised edition (New York: The Macmillan Co., 1967), 203–04.

16 *The Rites of the Catholic Church*, vol. 1 (Collegeville: The Liturgical Press, 1990), #319, 208.

17 *Catechism of the Catholic Church* (Collegeville: The Liturgical Press, 1994), #1268, 323 [emphasis is original].

18 Aidan Kavanagh, "Unfinished and Unbegun Revisited," LWSS, 267–69.

19 Ibid., 270–271.

20 "The Church of Christ, in Every Age," Text © 1971, Hope Publishing Company, Carol Stream, IL.

# BAPTISM AS "NEW BIRTH EX AQUA ET SPIRITU": A PRELIMINARY INVESTIGATION OF WESTERN LITURGICAL SOURCES

Contemporary liturgical scholarship on the evolution and theology of the rites of Christian initiation has tended to accept, often quite uncritically, a fundamental distinction between baptism as a ritual of regeneration or new birth "in water and the Holy Spirit" (John 3:5), rooted in Jesus' own baptism in the Jordan, as a characteristic emphasis and paradigm of the Eastern liturgical traditions, especially that of early Syria and, quite possibly, early Egypt, and baptism as a ritual of death and burial in Christ (Romans 6) as a characteristic emphasis and paradigm of the churches of the West. So common is this assumption that the clear and continued presence of John 3 language throughout eighth-century Gallican liturgical documents, i.e., the *Missale Gallicanum vetus*, the *Missale Gothicum*, and the *Bobbio Missal*, is often attributed, *de facto*, to Eastern influence within the early Gallican tradition itself. Similarly, it is has been the acceptance of this distinction between such so-called characteristic emphases between "East" and "West" that has led several contemporary liturgists to suggest that the theological interpretation of baptism in the West today should attempt to "recover" the early "Eastern" focus on John 3:5 and so come to enrich "Western" baptismal theology as well. Gerard Austin, for example, writes that: ". . . the theology of baptism must be viewed not only under the aspect of dying (Romans 6), but under the aspect of birth event (John 3) as well. In this regard *the richness of the Eastern tradition* should be tapped."[1] With regard to infant baptism, in particular, the late Mark Searle also called for renewed attention to the early Eastern tradition for the recovery of a whole cluster of initiation images having little to do with passing from death to life, or with sharing in the dying and rising of Christ through baptism. Such images, noted Searle, include seeing the font as *womb*, rather than tomb, literally called the "Jordan" itself in some traditions, as well as interpreting baptism under the metaphors of "adoption, divinization, sanctification, gift of the Spirit, indwelling, glory, power, wisdom, rebirth, restoration, [and] mission."[2] And, at the end of his recent and detailed study of the baptism of Jesus and its influence in early Christianity, again based in Eastern sources, primarily, Kilian McDonnell calls for a "retrieval" of the paradigm of Jesus' baptism and its baptismal theology of new birth in order to "balance" the Romans 6 theological emphasis that the West has inherited.[3]

It is certainly not my intention to provide a critique either of the scholars or of the scholarship on early Eastern liturgical texts which have led to the increased awareness of Jesus' own baptism in the Jordan and the new birth theology of John 3:5 as the dominant initiatory paradigms in early Christianity. Rather, my concern here is with Western liturgical sources alone and with the question of whether or not Western liturgical evidence supports this common assumption that baptism as "new birth" is, primarily, *Eastern* and baptism as "death and burial" is, primarily, *Western*.

In what follows, I provide, first, a short catena of liturgical texts from Rome and North Italy from the patristic through the early medieval period, as well as *some* theological statements about baptism from other authors in North Africa and North Italy, where the liturgical texts themselves are not readily available. Because the extant Gallican texts have been thoroughly examined by Gabriele Winkler[4] and Joseph Levesque,[5] who have both noted not only the overwhelming presence of John 3:5 as a dominant paradigm but the relative absence of Romans 6 theology, those texts will not be included here. Second, I provide a few liturgical texts from various sixteenth-century Protestant Reformers. And, finally, I shall draw some very tentative conclusions as preliminary hypotheses for future work.

## Part One:
## Latin Patristic and Early Medieval Liturgical Texts

### I. Rome

A. The so-called Apostolic Tradition, ascribed to Hippolytus of Rome (ca. 215), according to the Verona Latin Manuscript

(1) Postbaptismal, Episcopal Hand-laying Prayer:

> And let the bishop, laying [his] hand on them invoke, saying: Lord God, who have made them worthy to receive the forgiveness of sins *through the laver of regeneration of the Holy Spirit:* send on them your grace, that they may serve you according to your will; for to you is glory, Father and Son in the Holy Spirit in the holy church, both now and to the ages of ages. Amen.[6]

B. The Verona (or, "Leonine") Sacramentary[7]

(1) The Collect for Pentecost

> O ineffable and merciful God, grant that the children of adoption whom your Holy Spirit has called unto itself [*id ipsum*] may harbour nothing earthly in their joy, nothing alien in their faith; through. . .

(2) In the Canon

> We ask you graciously to accept this oblation which we offer to you for these whom you have deemed worthy to regenerate by water and the Holy Spirit, granting them remission of all their sins; and command their names to be written in *the book of the living* [Psalms 69:28]; through.

(3) The Blessing of the Font

> We offer you [this] prayer, O Lord, the eternal begetter of [all] things, Almighty God, whose *Spirit was borne upon the waters* [Genesis 1:3 Vulgate], whose eyes looked down from on high upon Jordan's stream when John was bap-

tizing [*tingeret*] those who in penitence confessed their sins: and therefore we pray your holy glory that your hand may be laid upon this water that you may cleanse and purify the lesser man who shall be baptized in it: and that he, putting aside all that is deathly, may be reborn and brought to life again through the new man reborn in Christ Jesus. . .

C.  The Letter of John the Deacon to Senarius (ca. 500)[8]

**Chapter 4.** And so by the efforts of himself and others the man…is next permitted to receive the words of the Creed [*symbolum*] which was handed down by the Apostles: so that he who a short time before was called simply a catechumen may now be called a competent, or elect. For he was *conceived in the womb of Mother Church and now he begins to live, even though the time of the sacred birth is not yet fulfilled.*

**Chapter 6.** And so they wear white raiment so that though the ragged dress of ancient error has darkened the *infancy of their first birth,* the costume of *their second birth* should display the raiment of glory, so that clad in a wedding garment he may approach the table of the heavenly bridegroom *as a new man.*

**Chapter 12.** As new men therefore, abandoning the bitterness of sin, they drink milk and honey: so that they who in their *first birth* were nourished with the milk of corruption and first shed tears of bitterness, *in their second birth* may taste the sweetness of milk and honey in the bowels of the Church, so that being nourished upon such sacraments they may be dedicated to the mysteries of perpetual incorruption.

D.  Roman Baptismal Inscriptions[9]

(1)  Baptistery of Saint Lawrence in Damaso

From this noble spring a saving water gushes, which cleanses all human defilement.

Do you wish to know the benefits of this sacred water? These streams *give the faith that regenerates.*

Wash away the defilement of your past life in the sacred fountain. Surpassing joy to share in the life the water brings!

Whoever resorts to this spring abandons earthly things and tramples under foot the works of darkness.

(2) Baptistery of the Lateran, ascribed to Sixtus III (432–440)

*Here a people of godly race are born for heaven; the Spirit gives them life in the fertile waters.*

*The Church-Mother, in these waves, bears her children like virginal fruit she has conceived by the Holy Spirit.*

Hope for the kingdom of heaven, you *who are reborn in this spring, for those who are born but once have no share in the life of blessedness.* Here is to be found the source of life, which washes the whole universe, which gushed from the wound of Christ.

Sinner, plunge into the sacred fountain to wash away your sin.

The water receives the old man, and in his place makes the new man to rise.

You wish to become innocent; cleanse yourself in this bath, whatever your burden may be, Adam's sin or your own.

There is no difference between those who are reborn; they are one, in a single baptism, a single Spirit, a single faith.

Let none be afraid of the number of the weight of their sins: those who are born of this stream will be made holy.

(3) Inscription Placed in the [Vatican] Consignatorium

Here the innocent sheep, cleansed by the heavenly water, are marked by the hand of the supreme Shepherd.

*You who have been begotten in this water,* come to the unity to which the Holy Spirit calls you, to receive his gifts.

You have received the cross; learn to escape the storms of the world: this is the great lesson of which this place reminds you.

E.   The Gelasian Sacramentary[10]

(1) XXVIII. Postcommunion Prayer for Lent V

O Lord we ask you, may your people live at peace among themselves; and serving you with a pure heart and being free from all strife, may they both take a ready delight in their own salvation and with good will pray for *those who await their second birth*. Through. . .

(2) XXVIII. Collect ad Populum

O God . . . look favourably on these whom you have chosen, that, being helped by your fatherly protection, they may be *conceived and born again*.

(3) XXX. For Making a Catechumen

God, who created the human race that you might also restore it, look with mercy on your adopted people, *set the offspring of your new race* within your new covenant, that what they could not attain by nature, the children of promise may joyfully receive by grace.

(4) XXXII. The Blessing After the Salt is Given

. . .Lead him to *the laver of second birth* that with thy faithful people he may be worthy to receive the eternal rewards of your promises . . .

(5) XXXIV. The Exposition of the Gospels to the Elect at the Opening of the Ears

. . . And so now the Church *being pregnant by your conception,* glories that amidst her festal worship *she labours to bring forth new lives* subject to the Christian law; so that when the day of the venerable Pascha shall come, *being reborn in the laver of baptism,* you shall be found worthy like all the saints to receive the promised gift of infancy from Christ our Lord...

(6) XXXV. The Introduction of the Creed to the Elect

Dearly beloved, who seek to receive the sacraments of baptism, *and to be born unto a new creature of the Holy Spirit* . . .

. . . A sinner goes into the waters and comes out justified. He is thrown out who draws you to death, and he is received who leads you back to life, through whose grace it is given to you to become *sons of God,* not brought forth *by the will of the flesh* [John 1:13], but *begotten by the power of the Holy Spirit.*

(7) XXXVI. The Introduction of the Lord's Prayer

Powerful is our Lord God, who is able both to lead you who seek after the faith to *the laver of the water of regeneration,* and to bring us, who have delivered to you the mystery of the catholic faith, together with you to the heavenly kingdom . . .

(8) XL. The Chrismal Mass

**Collect**: O Lord God, who in *bringing new birth to your people* uses the ministry of priests, grant . . .

**Preface**: It is indeed meet humbly to ask your clemency to confirm the creature of chrism unto its use in the sacrament of perfect salvation and life for those *who are to be renewed in the baptism of the spiritual laver* . . .

**The Blessing of Oil**: . . . we pray you O Lord that to those who shall come to *the laver of blessed rebirth* you would grant cleansing of mind and body by the working of this creature . . .

. . . may this unction which we prepare avail unto salvation, which through the *birth of a heavenly generation they are to attain in the sacrament of baptism* . . .

. . . greater honour was granted to chrism when your Son our Lord Jesus Christ had been washed at his own command *in the waves of the Jordan, when your Holy Spirit had been sent from above in the likeness of a dove.*

*Then you showed forth and bore witness by the voice which was then heard, to your Only-begotten Son, in whom you were well pleased* [Mark 1:11] . . .

**The Blessing of the Exorcized Oil**: I exorcize you, creature of oil . . . that this unction, being purified by divine sacraments, *may be for the adoption of body and spirit* to all who shall be anointed with it . . .

(9) XLII. [Holy] Saturday

. . . Come out and depart from this servant of God . . . that he may become his temple, *through the water of regeneration unto the remission of sins* . . .

(10) XLIIL. The Prayers at Each Lesson on Holy Saturday

**The Fourth Lesson (Exodus):** O God . . . now *by the water of regeneration* bring the same freedom unto the salvation of the Gentiles . . .

(11) XLIV. Rites of Initiation at the Easter Vigil

**Blessing of the Font:** Almighty everlasting God, be present at the mysteries of your great goodness, be present at your sacraments, and *for the creation of the new people which the fount of baptism brings forth to you* send down the *Spirit of adoption* . . .

**Consecration of the Font:** . . . open the font of baptism for the renewal of all nations of the world, that by the command of your majesty it may receive the grace of your Only-Begotten by the Holy Spirit: let your Holy Spirit by the secret admixture of his light *give fecundity to this water prepared for human regeneration, so that, sanctification being conceived therein, there may come forth from the unspotted womb of the divine font a heavenly offspring, reborn unto a new creature: that grace may be a mother to people of every age and sex, who are brought forth into a common infancy* . . .

. . . May the font be alive, *the water regenerating,* the wave purifying, so that all who shall be washed in this saving laver by the operation of the Holy Spirit within them may be brought to the mercy of perfect cleansing . . .

. . . May the power of the Holy Spirit descend into all the water of this font and *make the whole substance of this water fruitful with regenerating* power . . . that every one who enters this *sacrament of regeneration may be reborn in a new infancy* of true innocence.

**Postbaptismal (Presbyteral) Anointing:** The Almighty God, the Father of our Lord Jesus Christ, who has made you *to be regenerated of water and the Holy Spirit* . . ., and has given to you remission of all your sins, himself anoints you . . .

**Episcopal Handlaying [*ad consignandum*] Prayer:** Almighty God, Father of our Lord Jesus Christ, who hast made your servants *to be regenerated of water and the Holy Spirit* . . ., and has given them remission of all their sins . . . send upon them your Holy Spirit, the Paraclete . . .

(12) XLV. Collects and Prayers at Mass on the [Paschal] Night

> **Collect**: Almighty everlasting God . . . preserve in *the new offspring* of your family *the spirit of adoption* . . .

> **Secret**: Receive . . . the offerings of your people and of *your new born servants* . . .

> **Preface**: . . . Mary has rejoiced in her most holy childbirth. The Church rejoices in *the type of the regeneration of her sons.* Thus the blessed font flowed from the Lord's side carried away the burdens of our sins so that at these sacred altars the perpetual life *of the new born* might gather living food.

> **In the Action**: . . . Lord, receive this oblation of your servants and of all your family, which we offer unto you *for all whom you have deigned to regenerate by water and the Holy Spirit* . . .

## II. *North Africa*
### A.  Cyprian of Carthage

In the Gospel according to John: "Unless someone is born of water and the Spirit, he cannot enter the kingdom of God. For that which is born of flesh is flesh, and that which is born of spirit is spirit." Likewise: "unless you eat the flesh of the Son of Man and drink his blood, you do not have life in you."[11]

### B.  Quodvultdeus of Carthage

I am to explain to you the sacraments of the past night and of the present holy Creed . . . For you are not yet *reborn in holy baptism,* but by the sign of the cross you have been *conceived in the womb of holy mother church* . . .[12]

### C.  Augustine of Hippo

In infants, who are baptized, the *sacrament of regeneration is* given first, and if they maintain a Christian piety, conversion also in the heart will follow, of which the mysterious sign had gone before in the outward body.[13]

Now the *regenerating Spirit* is possessed in common both by the parents who present the child, and by the infant that is presented and *is born again*.[14]

### III. Spain
A. *Liber Ordinum*[15]

**Blessing of the Font**: Grant that those who take from *this laver a new life* and set aside the record of the old and are accorded the gift of the Holy Spirit by the laying on of hands may...

**Postbaptismal Handlaying Prayer:** O God, who in this sacrament wherein men *are reborn* send your Holy Spirit upon water . . .

**Blessing:** May he by whom *you are reborn of water and the Holy Spirit* bring you to the heavenly kingdom.

### IV. North Italy
A. Ambrose of Milan[16]

*De Sac.* **2.24.** So you were immersed, and you came to the priest. What did he say to you? *God the Father Almighty*, he said, *who has brought you to a new birth through water and the Holy Spirit and has forgiven your sins, himself anoints you into eternal life.*

*De Sac.* **3.5.** But there are those who try to excuse themselves by saying that it [the *pedilavium*] should not be performed as a mystery, not as part of the baptismal rite, not for *regeneration*, but that this washing of the feet should be done as a host would do it for his guests.

*De Myst.* **5.** After this, the Holy of holies (Hebrews 9:3) was unbarred to you, you entered the *shrine of regeneration* . . .

B.   The Ambrosian Manual[17]

**Prayers at the Blessing of the Font:** Almighty, everlasting God, be present at the mysteries of your great goodness, be present at your sacraments, and for the creation *of the new people which the fount of baptism brings forth to you,* send down the Spirit of adoption...

**Another Prayer:** Look . . . with favour upon sinners, and loose the captive. Restore the innocence which Adam lost in Paradise . . . May they receive the likeness of God, which once was lost by envy of the serpent; may the iniquities which follow upon their disobedience be carried away in this pure stream. May they rise up unto rest: may they be brought forward unto pardon, that being renewed in the mystic waters they may know themselves to be redeemed *and reborn* . . .

**Postbaptismal Chrismation:** Almighty God, the Father of our Lord Jesus Christ, who has *regenerated you by water and the Holy Spirit,* and who has given you remission of all your sins, himself anoints you . . .

**Exorcism of the Oil:** I exorcize you, creature of oil... that to all who are anointed with it, *it may be unto the adoption of the sons of God* . . .

**Prayer:** . . . Lead him to the *laver of the second birth,* that with your faithful people he may be worthy to receive the eternal rewards of your promises . . .

**Exorcism of Water:** . . . when he has been *born again of water and the Holy Spirit* . . . let him become a temple of the living God . . .

**Prayer After Baptism:** Almighty, everlasting God, who hast *regenerated your servant N. by water and the Holy Spirit* . . ., and who has given him remission of all his sins, grant him an abiding wisdom . . .

## C.  Zeno of Verona

**Sermons, Book II.29.1–3: Paschal Sermon:** (1) Welcome, my brothers in Christ, *born today!* . . . [Y]our old self has been happily condemned so that he may be forgiven, buried in the wave of the sacred waters so that he may be *quickened in the nest of the womb* and taste the privileges of the resurrection . . . (2) Oh what goodness of our God! What pure love of our good *mother.* She has taken people different in race, sex, age, and rank . . . (3) And lest she should seem to love anyone more or less than another, she grants to all *one birth,* one milk, one pay, one honour of the Holy Spirit . . . Indeed blessed is the one who always remembers that he is *reborn;* more blessed is the one who does not remember what he was before he was *reborn;* most blessed is the one who does not spoil his infancy with the advance of years.[18]

**Sermons, Book 1.55:** To the Neophytes: Why do you stand there, different in race, age, sex, and rank, who soon will be one? Hasten to the *fountain of the sweet womb of your ever-virgin mother* and there know in your nobility and faith that, as one believes, so one will possess blessedness. Oh what a marvellous and truly divine, most blessed honour, in which *she who gives birth does not groan, and the one born never cries!* This is renewal, this is resurrection, this is eternal life, *this is the mother of all,* who has united us, brought us together from every race and nation and straightway made us one body.[19]

**Sermons, Book 11.28:** Invitation to the Font: Come on, why do you stand there, brothers? Through your faith *the life-giving water has conceived you, through the mysteries now it gives birth to you.* Hurry as quickly as you can to what you desire. Behold, now the solemn hymn is sung, *behold soon the sweet crying of infants is heard; behold from the single womb of their parent proceeds a dazzling throng. It is a new thing, that each one is born in a spiritual manner. Run freely to your mother who has no labour if she gives birth to more than she can number. Come in, then, come in, all of you happy ones, in a moment to be babes at the breast together.*[20]

**Sermons, Book I.38.1–2:** Sermon on the Zodiac to the Neophytes: (1) Rejoice, heavenly peoples, *new children in Christ,* and guard with perpetual care against staining in any way *the whiteness of your flowering spiritual birth today.* What is given cannot be repeated. Behold, you who were children, teenagers, young adults, and old people of either sex, guilty and filthy by your worldly birth, now are free of all guilt and *pure babes* and, what is most wonderful and pleasing, suddenly you who were of different ages *are in a moment all the same age.* (2) But I am well aware of your curiosity. With the taking away of your old life, which henceforth is forbidden you, perhaps you would like to know from us under which constellation and *which sign your mother bore you together, so varied, so many, and so different, in a single birth.*[21]

**Sermons, Book 1.32:** Invitation to the Font: Rejoice, brothers in Christ, hasten with all desire and receive the heavenly gifts. Now the saving warmth of the everlasting font invites you, *now our mother adopts you so that she may give birth to you,* but not in the manner in which your mothers bore you when they brought you into the world, themselves groaning with birth pains and you, wailing, filthy, done up in filthy swaddling clothes and surrendered to this world, but with joy and gladness . . . and freed you from all your sins, and she feeds you not in a stinking cradle but with delight from the sweet-smelling rails of the holy altar, through our Lord Jesus Christ.[22]

## Part Two:
## Select Reformation Baptismal Texts

### I. Martin Luther

**Flood Prayer (1523):** Almighty eternal God, who according to thy righteous judgment didst condemn the unbelieving world through the flood and in thy great mercy didst preserve believing Noah and his family, and who didst drown hardhearted Pharoah with all his host in the Red Sea and didst lead thy people Israel through the same on dry ground, thereby prefiguring this bath of thy baptism, and *who through the baptism of thy dear Child, our Lord Jesus Christ, hast consecrated and set apart the Jordan and all water* as a salutary flood and a rich and full washing away of sins: We pray through the same thy groundless mercy that thou wilt graciously behold *N.* and bless him with true faith in the spirit so that by means of this saving flood all that has been born in him from Adam and which he himself has added thereto may be drowned in him and engulfed, and that he may be sundered from the number of the unbelieving, preserved dry and secure in the holy ark of Christendom, serve thy name at all times fervent in spirit and joyful in hope, so that with all believers he may be made worthy to attain eternal life according to thy promise; through Jesus Christ our Lord. Amen.[23]

**Postbaptismal Garment Prayer (1526):** The almighty God and Father of our Lord Jesus Christ, who hath regenerated thee through water and the Holy Ghost and hath forgiven thee all thy sin, strengthen thee with his grace to life everlasting. Amen. Peace be with thee. *Answer.* Amen.[24]

### II. A Rite of Baptism, Used at Strassburg, 1525–30[25]

**Prayer Before Our Father and Apostles' Creed:** . . . Let us pray . . . that the Lord will baptize him with water and the Holy

Spirit, so that the outward washing which he will perform through me will inwardly be fulfilled in deed and in truth by the Holy Spirit; for that *second birth* which is signified by baptism takes place in *water and in the Holy Spirit,* as the Lord says in John 3.

**Prayer After the Apostles' Creed:** . . .seal and confirm his heart in the same with the Holy Spirit according to thy Son's promise, so that thy inward renewal and *regeneration* of the Spirit may truly be signified by this our baptism . . .

### III. Hermann von Wied's "Consultation"

**Prayer Before Baptism:** . . . so let it be thy pleasure *to beget our infants again, and to adopt them into sons* unto the fellowship of everlasting life by the sacrament of baptism.

**Postbaptismal Blessing:** The almighty and everlasting God and Father of our Lord Jesus Christ, *who hath begotten thee again with water and the Holy Ghost,* and hath forgiven thee all thy sins, confirm thee with his grace unto everlasting life.

### IV. Thomas Cranmer and the *Books of Common Prayer*

**Introduction:** Dear[ly] beloved, forasmuch as all men be *conceived and born in sin,* and that no man born in sin can enter into the kingdom of God (*except he be regenerate and born anew of water and the Holy Ghost*) I beseech you to call upon God the Father through our Lord Jesus Christ, that of his bounteous mercy he will grant to these children that thing, which by nature they cannot have, that is to say, they may be baptized with the Holy Ghost, and received into Christ's holy church, and be made lively members of the same.[26]

**Postbaptismal Anointing (1549):** Almighty God, the Father of our Lord Jesus Christ, *who hath regenerated thee by water and the Holy Ghost,* and hath given unto thee remission of all thy sins, he vouchsafe to anoint thee with the unction of his Holy Spirit, and bring thee to the inheritance of everlasting life. Amen.[27]

## Part Three: Commentary

What I find most illuminating in the texts cited above is the liturgical evidence from Rome in the patristic and early medieval documents. Contrary to what might be expected on the basis of current assumptions, there is almost no reference whatsoever to a Romans 6 theology in these texts! That is, according to my brief investigation of the documents, Romans 6 simply does *not* appear anywhere in the *Apostolic Tradition,* the *Letter of John the Deacon to Senarius,* the *Sacramentarium Veronense,* or in the Roman baptismal inscriptions. Furthermore, I can find only *one* allusion to Romans 6 throughout all of the initiation materials included within the *Gelasian Sacramentary,* where, in the context of the *redditio symboli,* after referring to the completion of Christ's resurrection in the baptized, states that "in it [baptism] is celebrated a kind of death and resurrection."[28] But it is certainly not the dominant interpretative metaphor for baptism throughout this document. Rather, John 3, together with some allusion to Jesus' baptism in the Jordan in the prayers for the blessing of the font, is the central image!

Similarly, while the North African tradition had certainly known the theology of Romans 6 in relationship to baptism since the time of Tertullian's *De baptismo,* John 3 remains an important and complementary image even within this tradition. So also is this the case with Ambrose of Milan and the later Ambrosian tradition. If anyone had a Romans 6 understanding of the baptismal sub- or immersion it was Ambrose of Milan, who, like Cyril of Jerusalem, related the threefold baptismal dipping to Jesus' three days in the tomb and referred as well to the "tomb-like" shape of the Milanese font. Yet, liturgically, it is Ambrose himself who gives us our first clear reference to the Western postbaptismal anointing prayer which, from that time on, at least, will explicitly quote John 3:5 as part of the anointing formula. For that matter, while Romans 6 imagery does appear more often in the Mozarabic or Spanish liturgical tradition than elsewhere in the West, John 3:5 continues to be invoked there as well. And in North Italy, i.e., at least in the sermons of Zeno of Verona, the imagery of John 3:5 appears to be even more dominant.

The above selection of texts from the sixteenth-century Reformation point in a similar direction as well. While Romans 6 is clearly Luther's own primary interpretative text for baptismal theology,[29] apart from possible allusion to it in his *Flood Prayer,* Romans 6 is not clearly present in either his 1523 or 1526 baptismal reforms. Similarly, versions of the traditional presbyteral postbaptismal, anointing prayer with their quotation of John 3:5, whether with or without anointing, tended to continue in some way throughout the reformed rites of the sixteenth century. Indeed, is it not part of the Reformation rejection of the "sacrament" of confirmation to argue that baptism itself, as "new birth in water and the Holy Spirit," constituted the "fullness" of Christian initiation in the first place? Hence, nothing else was needed to "complete" baptism.

When all of these texts are combined with the extant eighth-century texts of the Gallican liturgical tradition, analyzed in detail by Winkler and Levesque, one is led to ask just how dominant in and characteristic of the Western liturgical traditions, in fact, is this so-called "Western theological focus" on Romans 6 as the dominant metaphor for baptism and when it was that it became such? In liturgical *texts,* at least, it is John 3:5, not Romans 6, which appears to be the preferred baptismal image. While the practice of Christian initiation at the Easter Vigil may have brought to the rites contextually an added theological focus from a Romans 6 perspective, and so functioned as baptism's overall hermeneutical or interpretative context, and while various theologians like Ambrose of Milan may have preferred to use a Romans 6 interpretation of baptism, such an interpretation does not seem to have had much affect on Western liturgical *texts* themselves.

Several tentative theses, or at least, beginning hypotheses for future work, emerge from this brief investigation: (1) the baptismal theology of John 3:5 is as much "Western" as it is "Eastern;" (2) the celebration of baptism at Easter is not incompatible with a baptismal theology based on John 3:5; and (3) the principle of *lex orandi, lex credendi* in the West suggests a theology of baptism as "new birth." I shall comment briefly on each of these in what follows.

1. *The Baptismal Theology of John 3:5 is as much "Western" as it is "Eastern"*

In spite of what many have decried as the lack of pneumatology in Western sacramental (and other) theology, the clear and persistent presence of a John 3:5 theology of baptism, as well as reference to Jesus' baptism in the Jordan, in Western baptismal texts suggests that neither liturgical scholarship nor liturgical renewal need always look to the East to "balance out" the so-called characteristic "Western" theological emphasis on Romans 6. Such "balance," including the several and diverse images that Searle described for some years in his discussion of infant baptism, are a clear and definite component of the Western liturgical tradition of baptism as well.

As the contemporary shape of Christian initiation rites demonstrates, however, an "Easternization" or "Byzantinization" of Western initiation has certainly taken place throughout the various churches today.[30] Perhaps nowhere is this clearer than in the 1971 Roman revision of confirmation, where the Syro-Byzantine formula, "N., be sealed with the gift of the Holy Spirit" has been adopted, an adoption also paralleled in the current baptismal rites of almost every other Western liturgical tradition today.[31] Such has tended to overshadow the traditional— and already *pneumatic*—Western "handlaying" prayer for the sevenfold Spirit gift. At the same time, with the exception of the baptismal rite in the Lutheran Church, Missouri Synod's 1982 publication of *Lutheran Worship*,[32] has been the systematic excision from Western baptismal rites of the traditional postbaptismal "anointing" prayer, *the* prayer which, since the time of Ambrose of Milan, has underscored the unitive and integral John 3:5 theology of being begotten in baptism "through water *and* the Holy Spirit."[33] While looking to the East is ecumenically laudable and the attempt to complement or balance a Romans 6 theology with the "richness" of other metaphors, paradigms, and images is surely desirable, the West need not *always* look to the East for the recovery of a pneumatological baptismal focus. Rather, in my opinion, the West needs to look at and recover the pneumatological richness of its own tradition as that richness is expressed already within its own classic liturgical texts. The Western "lack of pneumatology," then, is perhaps due, in part, to the failure of the West to pay adequate attention to its own rich textual liturgical and theological tradition, where, with regard to the rites of Christian initiation at least, such an emphasis is anything but lacking.

2. *The Celebration of Baptism at Easter is not incompatible
   with a Baptismal Theology based on John 3:5*

The real or ideal, or real but shortlived[34] practice of Easter
baptism in the West, while hermeneutically significant in context, does not mean, *necessarily,* the replacement of, or preference
for, the baptismal metaphor of Romans 6 for, or over, John 3:5 in
the Western liturgical tradition. In his recent study of baptism
and Easter in Zeno of Verona, for example, Gordon Jeanes notes
the uneasy juxtaposition of John 3:5 and Romans 6 in Zeno's baptismal sermons, saying:

> Death to the old self and to the world and condemnation
> of sin are presented in the liturgical formulae of renunci-
> ations. Their meaning and emphasis are amplified by the
> sermons. But Zeno does not integrate Romans 6 with this
> imagery, nor does he manage to integrate fully the two
> ideas of the font as the life-giving womb of Mother
> Church and as the place of dying and rising. For him the
> font is still essentially the life-giver and the death dealing
> is normally restricted to the preparatory rites... In the
> Church of the second and third centuries baptism was
> about being born of water and the Spirit, about cleansing
> and enlightenment. Dying with Christ was not to the
> fore, *even in the West where the custom of baptism at Easter
> might easily have suggested it.* That motif was taken up by
> the martyr literature, and only when martyrs belonged to
> the past was it freed for the liturgy and became part of
> the Church's new definition of itself over against the
> world... Zeno lived just at the time when this change of
> understanding was happening, and we see in his ser-
> mons the two theologies sitting, slightly uncomfortable,
> side by side.[35]

At the same time, however, all of the references to baptism in
the later *Gelasian Sacramentary* itself appear within the overall
context of the *Lenten* catechumenate and *Easter* baptism. And still
at that date, as we have seen, the dominant image for what is to
take place, or what is taking place at baptism itself, remains John 3:5

and not Romans 6. Such would seem to suggest that the actual *occasion* for the celebration of Christian initiation, i.e., Easter, either had very little overall influence on the developing shape and theology of Christian initiation in the West or that the theology of John 3:5, as well as Jordan imagery, was too well ingrained in the *Western* tradition to be displaced by this emphasis. That is, it is not simply that John 3:5 complements or balances Romans 6 in the Western sources but, at least in the extant Roman liturgical texts, it is the relative *absence* of a Romans 6 theology altogether even at *Easter* that must be noted!

With regard to this, one must wonder just what it is exactly that has led contemporary liturgical scholars and reformers to opt for a Romans 6 theology of baptism as a "normative" and characteristically "Western" theological focus so much so that contemporary Western liturgical revision of Christian initiation has given Romans 6 a normative status for celebrating and interpreting those rites. So strong is this assumption, in fact, that there is even some evidence to suggest that in contemporary liturgical reform there has been a deliberate attempt to downplay or delete entirely the new birth imagery of John 3:5 in favor of the paschal imagery of Romans 6. For example, after a detailed analysis of the "Roman core" of and Gallican additions to the prayer for the blessing of the baptismal water in the *Gelasian Sacramentary* and its use as a source for the blessing of the baptismal water at the Easter Vigil in the current Roman rite, Dominic Serra notes that it is *precisely* the *Gelasian* references to John 3:5 that have been omitted. With specific reference to the texts surrounding the immersion of the Paschal candle into the font during that blessing, Serra writes:

> [T]he new blessing utilizes only those sections of the Roman epiclesis that do not mention the metaphor of rebirth, and... the phrases borrowed from *Ge(lasianum)* 448 [Gallican additions] have been rewritten so that rebirth images are transformed into paschal references . . . This sort of substitution is very apparent in the phrases that surround the optional immersion of the paschal candle . . . The Gelasian text includes a request that the Spirit render the water fecund for regenerating, while the new

blessing asks that "all who are buried with Christ in the death of baptism rise also with him to newness of life" . . . Once again, we have an obvious substitution of a paschal referent for a regeneration image . . . These substitutions and omissions have the effect of transforming the Gelasian prayer, which was based almost entirely on the metaphor of rebirth, into a prayer based almost exclusively on the paschal dimension of baptism. A clue to understanding this suppression of the rebirth metaphor and its replacement with paschal symbolism can be found in the explanatory note about the candle immersion in the *relatio* on the blessing of the baptismal water in *Schema 112.* The note indicates that the reformers were intent upon emphasizing the paschal and Christic symbolism of the candle, thus avoiding any possible phallic interpretation in the rite of candle immersion. In fact, they decided to change the meaning of the texts surrounding this ritual gesture in order to give the candle immersion the meaning of burial and resurrection with Christ.[36]

Accepting the normativity of Romans 6 as *the* baptismal paradigm for the West, then, appears to be a conclusion based on other than explicit and traditional Western *liturgical* grounds. Such grounds include, I would suggest:

1.  the recovery of John 3:5 and Jesus' baptism in the Jordan as the dominant metaphors for baptism in the early Syrian East and the assumption of a different overall focus in the early West;
2.  the overwhelming focus on Romans 6 in the *interpretative* catecheses of Cyril of Jerusalem, John Chrysostom, and Theodore of Mopsuestia (and the resultant shift in baptismal theology in the East) and the *De Sacramentis* and *De Mysteriis* of Ambrose of Milan for the West;
3.  the modern "recovery" of this "Paschal Mystery," as expressed precisely in the writings of these fourth-century mystagogues, as the primary and normative paradigm for Christian life in general;

4.   the concomitant modern restoration of the Easter
     Vigil as the prime time for baptism in the West, in
     accord with the early Western liturgical—if not theo-
     logical—tradition; and
5.   the resultant re-reading of Western liturgical sources
     based on this "recovery" and "restoration."

But in no case, let me underscore, does this "Western" focus
or "recovery" appear to be based on the dominant imagery within the texts of the traditional baptismal rites themselves! And
with this, it seems that "Paschal Mystery" language and
metaphor says much more about *modern* theological approaches
to baptism and sacramental theology in general, and *modern*
attempts to read the early Western liturgical tradition through
paschal eyes than it does about the classic tradition at all, especially as that tradition is expressed within its liturgical texts.

3.   *The Principle of* **Lex orandi, Lex credendi** *in the West*
     *suggests a Theology of Baptism as 'New Birth'*

Whatever Prosper of Acquitaine's famous formula *ut legem
credendi statuat lex supplicandi* may or may not mean in relationship to liturgy as a locus *theologicus*, if a church's theology of baptism *(lex credendi) is* to be read on the basis of the liturgical texts
used in its celebration *(lex orandi)*, then it seems quite clear that,
at the very least, traditional *Western* theologies of baptism are
clearly as expressive of baptism as "adoption, divinization, sanctification, gift of the Spirit, indwelling, glory, power, wisdom,
rebirth, restoration, [and] mission" as are those of the Christian
East. While I am fully aware that a given church's *lex orandi* cannot be read solely on the basis of texts, it should be noted that
within the East Syrian tradition itself, paschal baptism also
became the (theoretical) norm but never in the sense that its primary theological interpretation of baptism departed too far from
either John 3:5 or Jesus' baptism as the dominant paradigms (cf.
Aphrahat, Ephrem, and Narsai), with the prebaptismal anointing itself, even today, retaining much of its classic pneumatological and "Holy Spirit as Mother" emphasis.[37] Similarly, if
the architectural shape of baptismal fonts has anything to say

theologically, then it may also be contextually significant that even in the West evidence of circular "womb-like" fonts and fonts clearly designed to resemble female genitalia (at least in North Africa,[38] the very place of the first reference to *paschal* baptism) have been uncovered.

## Conclusion

All of the above, I repeat, is most tentative and simply sets the stage for further research and investigation. Along with further detailed analysis of the Western liturgical textual tradition, further research in the baptismal commentaries of Augustine, Ambrose, and other early Western theologians would be necessary as would greater attention to the architectural and archaeological evidence. Nevertheless, for some time I have been rather uncomfortable with the too easy assumption that one of these theological emphases on baptism is "Eastern" and the other "Western," that the presence of one of these in the other tradition is due simply to the influence of one on the other or to a process of liturgical cross fertilization, or that in order to balance one tradition's emphasis there is need to explore the "riches" of the other tradition. This brief investigation of a few representative baptismal-liturgical texts of the West confirms for me why I have been rather uncomfortable with this and, along with this, I have come to wonder if an explicit Romans 6 interpretation of baptism was as new to the West as it was to the East in the late fourth century, in spite of *some* early preference for paschal baptism in North Africa and Rome. As I think is the case, the occasion of and preference for paschal baptism itself has no *necessary* correlation to the particular theology of the rite, at least as that rite is expressed in its liturgical texts. How others interpret that rite in such a context is what gave and continues to give it its overall paschal focus.

Finally, contemporary liturgical scholarship, with good reason, has cautioned against an uncritical acceptance of the methodological principle of Anton Baumstark that what is most common from the comparative study of liturgical texts is most ancient.[39] Nevertheless, the common use of John 3:5 in the liturgical expression and theological interpretation of baptism in the classic liturgical texts of several traditions appears to be one of those issues where Baumstark's principle is absolutely correct. Therefore, baptism as "new birth *ex aqua et spiritu*" is part of the ancient, common, and ecumenical liturgical heritage of the church, both East and West, and, in my opinion, we would do well today to recover, pay renewed attention to, and underscore that common heritage strongly.

---

NB: The original presentation of this essay as a short communication at the International Scholarly Congress, "Comparative Liturgy Fifty Years after Anton Baumstark" (+1948), held at the Pontifical Oriental Institute, Rome, Italy, September 25–29, 1998, was made possible through a travel grant from the Institute for Scholarship in the Liberal Arts (ISLA) at the University of Notre Dame. The author wishes here to acknowledge and thank ISLA for this most generous assistance.

## Notes

[1] G. Austin, *The Rite of Confirmation: Anointing with the Spirit* (Collegeville: The Liturgical Press/Pueblo, 1985), 141.

[2] M. Searle, "Infant Baptism Reconsidered," in LWSS, 385.

[3] K. McDonnell, *The Baptism of Jesus in the Jordan: The Trinitarian and Cosmic Order of Salvation* (Collegeville: Michael Glazier Books, 1996), 246–47.

[4] G. Winkler, "Confirmation or Chrismation? A Study in Comparative Liturgy," in LWSS, 202–18.

[5] J. Levesque, "The Theology of the Postbaptismal Rites in the Seventh and Eighth Century Gallican Church," in LWSS, 159–201.

[6] Text from P. Bradshaw, M. Johnson, E. Phillips, *The Apstolic Tradition: A Commentary,* Hermeneia Commentary Series (Minneapolis: Fortress Press, 2002), 118.

[7] DBL, 207.

[8] Ibid., 208–212 [all emphases are added].

[9] L. Deiss, *Springtime of the Liturgy* (Collegeville: The Liturgical Press, 1979), 264–5 [all emphases are added].

[10] DBL, 213–243 [all emphases are added].

[11] Cyprian, *Ad Quirinium* 3.25.

[12] DBL, 150 [emphasis added].

[13] Augustine, *De bapt.* 4.24.32 [emphasis added].

[14] Augustine, *Ep. 98.2* [emphasis added].

[15] DBL, 169–172 [emphasis added].

[16] Ibid., 178–83 [emphasis added].

[17] Ibid., 183–98 [emphasis added].

[18] Texts are cited from G. Jeanes, *The Day Has Come! Easter and Baptism in Zeno of Verona,* Alcuin Club Collections 73 (Collegeville: The Liturgical Press, 1995), 97–8 [emphasis added].

[19] Ibid., 79–80 [emphasis added].

[20] Ibid., 97 [emphasis added].

[21] Ibid., 69–70 [emphasis added].

[22] Ibid., 68 [emphasis added].

[23] Luther, *The Order of Baptism,* 1523, in LW, vol. 51, 97 [emphasis added].

[24] M. Luther, *The Order of Baptism Newly Revised,* 1526, in LW, vol. 51, 109 [emphasis added].

[25] J.D.C. Fisher, *Christian Initiation: The Reformation Period* (London: Alcuin Club/SPCK, 1970), 36–7 [emphasis added].

[26] Ibid., 89 [emphasis added].

[27] Ibid., 94 [emphasis added].

[28] DBL, 176.

[29] Cf. his Small Catechism in T. Tappert (ed.), *The Book of Concord* (Philadelphia: Augsburg Fortress Publishers, 1959), 348–9. Romans 6 imagery is especially present in Luther's 1519 teaching sermon, *The Holy and Blessed Sacrament of Baptism*, in LW, vol. 35, 23–44.

[30] See A. Kavanagh, *Confirmation: Origins and Reform* (Collegeville: Pueblo, 1988), 93.

[31] Cf. the postbaptismal rites in the *Book of Common Prayer* of the Episcopal Church, USA (New York: Oxford University Press, 1979), 308, and the *Lutheran Book of Worship* (Minneapolis/Philadelphia: Augsburg, 1978), 124, where it appears that the handlaying prayer for the sevenfold gift of the Holy Spirit and the chrismation formula of the 1971 *Roman* rite of confirmation have been adapted.

[32] *Lutheran Worship* (St. Louis: Concordia Publishing House, 1982), 203.

[33] Although this prayer, in revised form, does remain in the current Roman rite, *it is* regularly omitted from the celebration of the *Rite of Christian Initiation of Adults*, where confirmation *is* to follow baptism immediately.

[34] See P. Bradshaw, "'*Diem baptismo sollemniorem*': Baptism and Easter in Christian Antiquity," reprinted in LWSS, 137–147.

[35] G. Jeanes, *The Day Has Come! Easter and Baptism in Zeno of Verona*, 256–7 [emphasis added].

[36] D. Serra, "The Blessing of Baptismal Water at the Paschal Vigil: Ancient Texts and Modern Revisions," *Worship* 64 (1990), 153–5. See also idem., "The Blessing of Baptismal Water at the Paschal Vigil in the *Gelasianum Vetus*: A Study of the Euchological Texts, Ge 444–448," *Ecclesia Orans* 6 (1989), 323–344.

[37] Cf. J. Challassery, *The Holy Spirit and Christian Initiation in the East Syrian Tradition* (Rome: Mar Thoma Yogam, 1995).

[38] I am basing this comment on a slide presentation of early baptismal fonts in North Africa presented at the annual meeting of the North American Patristics Society, Loyola University, Chicago, IL, USA, in June, 1994.

[39] See P. Bradshaw, *The Search for the Origins of Christian Worship* (New York/ London: Oxford University Press, 1992), 59–60, 63–5.

# THE POSTCHRISMATIONAL STRUCTURE OF APOSTOLIC TRADITION 21, THE WITNESS OF AMBROSE OF MILAN, AND A TENTATIVE HYPOTHESIS REGARDING THE CURRENT REFORM OF CONFIRMATION IN THE ROMAN RITE

Recent studies on the rites of Christian initiation in the early church have focused renewed attention on the structure of the episcopal postchrismation rites of *Apostolic Tradition* 21 (hereafter, *ApTrad*)—imposition of hands with prayer and (second) anointing—in relationship to what became known as the sacrament of confirmation in the Roman rite. The hypothesis of Aidan Kavanagh[1] that these episcopal rites in *ApTrad* 21 reflect the traditional structure of an episcopal *missa*, in this case, the 'dismissal' of neophytes *from* the baptismal bath *to* the eucharistic table, which later was both pneumaticized into a conferral of the Holy Spirit to the neophytes and ultimately separated from baptism itself is an intriguing possibility.

Kavanagh's view, however, has not been received without criticism. Paul Turner, for example, has challenged his understanding of those postchrismational episcopal acts as constituting

a 'dismissal' in the very *center* of the initiation rite and has suggested, alternatively, that these acts should be viewed instead as
"the first public gesture of ratification for the bishop and the
faithful who did not witness the pouring of water."[2] But whether
in origin *ApTrad* 21's episcopal postchrismational structure was
either a *missa* or a public "ratification," an issue with which neither Kavanagh nor Turner explicitly deal is the provenance and
date of this particular structure in *ApTrad* 21. Kavanagh writes
that such questions are not "of direct concern" since "subsequent
Roman tradition undeniably betrays [*ApTrad*'s] influence in that
church's baptismal usage."[3]

*ApTrad* 21's so-called "influence" on the shape of the Roman
initiatory rites, particularly on the postchrismational episcopal
structure, however, would seem to make these questions of
extreme concern. That is, if the traditional view that *ApTrad*
reflects early third-century *Roman* practice is not accepted, then
it would seem crucial, indeed, to determine exactly when it was
that "subsequent Roman tradition" came to be influenced by the
structure of the postchrismational rite present in this document.

This essay attempts to look critically at the evidence for the
origins of this unique structure and to make some tentative conclusions concerning its adoption into the early Roman rites of
initiation and its relationship to the Roman rite of confirmation
today. In doing so, I shall present first what "early" evidence
there is for *Roman* initiation rites other than *ApTrad* 21. Second, I
shall discuss briefly some contemporary approaches to the question of the origins of the initiation rites in *ApTrad* itself. Third, the
witness of Ambrose of Milan will be investigated in order to
determine what the shape of the Roman rite of initiation known
to him in the late fourth century actually was. And, finally, the
current reformed Roman rite of confirmation will be analyzed on
the basis of this short comparative liturgical study.

## I. Early Evidence for Roman Rites
of Christian Initiation

In addition to the brief mid-second century outline provided
by Justin Martyr in his First Apology (with no post-baptismal
rites whatsoever indicated),[4] two documents, both from the late

fourth century, have sometimes been cited as evidence for the Roman rites of initiation. In his *Altercation of a Luciferian with an Orthodox* Jerome witnesses to a practice of bishops imposing hands on and praying for the Holy Spirit for those neophytes, in rural areas, who had been baptized by presbyters and/or deacons in the absence of bishops.[5] And the *Mai Fragment*, reflecting an Arian argument against Orthodoxy by citing orthodox liturgical texts, refers to the formula of *a* postbaptismal anointing, saying: "The God and Father of our Lord Jesus Christ, who granted you regeneration by water, himself anoints you with the Holy Spirit and the rest."[6] But it is by no means clear if either of these documents actually reflect specifically *Roman* liturgical practice. If they do, it is significant to note that neither refers clearly to the postchrismational structure of *both* episcopal handlaying and (second) episcopal anointing known from *ApTrad* 21. Indeed, our *first* clear witness to *that* precise structure in *Roman* practice is the fifth-century letter of Pope Innocent I to Decentius of Gubbio (AD 416), in which Innocent boldly asserts the following:

> "About the signing of the newly baptized: it is quite clear that no one may perform it except the bishop. For although presbyters are priests (*sacerdotes*), they do not have the highest degree of the priesthood (*pontificatus*). It is not only the custom of the Church which demonstrated that the signing and the gift of the Holy Spirit is restricted to bishops (*pontifices*), but the passage in the Acts of the Apostles which declares that Peter and John were sent to give the Holy Spirit to those already baptized. For when presbyters baptize, whether in the absence of a bishop or in his presence, they may anoint the baptized with chrism (provided that it is consecrated by the bishop) but they do not sign the forehead with this same oil. That is reserved to the bishops when they give the Spirit, the Paraclete."[7]

Although this Roman episcopal postchrismational structure which Innocent commends to Decentius in North Italy is called by him a "custom of the Church," it is important to underscore the fact that prior to Innocent we have no clear evidence for this structure in undisputed Roman initiatory practice at all. Even if it is accepted that *ApTrad* 21 represents *Roman* liturgical practice it must be remembered that the earliest manuscript we possess, i.e., the Verona Latin, is a *fifth-century* document which most scholars agree reflects a mid-fourth century translation (ca. 350). Whatever the original Greek of *ApTrad* may have been we simply do not know. And even if the original Greek text reflected early third-century *Roman* practice we cannot be certain that this Latin translation does not reflect subsequent development and expansion beyond what the Greek would have been. Similarly, a *translation*, especially of church order materials, a genre of "living literature" notorious for prescribing as well as describing practice,[8] does not necessarily equal immediate adoption and liturgical use.

But there is another problem in this context as well. No one reading the *Latin* text of *ApTrad* 21's postchrismational structure would automatically conclude that either the handlaying prayer or the episcopal anointing is about what Innocent calls the giving "of the Spirit, the Paraclete." Rather, the Latin version of the episcopal prayer for the imposition of hands on the neophyte is a prayer not for the gift of the Holy Spirit but for *grace*. And the operating assumption in this prayer is that the gift of the Spirit is not subsequent to baptism but already given in and connected to the water rite itself:

> Lord God, you have made them worthy to receive the forgiveness of sins through the laver of regeneration of the Holy Spirit; send on them your grace, that they may serve you according to your will; for to you is glory, Father and Son with the Holy Spirit in the holy Church, both now and to the ages of ages. Amen.[9]

Similarly, the episcopal consignation or anointing on the forehead of the neophyte which follows this prayer is also not specifically pneumatic (e.g., the *seal* of the Holy Spirit) but refers to all three persons of the Trinity: "I anoint you with holy oil in God the Father almighty and Christ Jesus and the Holy Spirit."[10]

All that this need mean, if scholars are correct in their dating, is that in the mid-fourth century there was available in the West a Latin version of the postchrismational *structure* of *ApTrad* 21 consisting of an episcopal prayer and subsequent anointing. Approximately sixty-six years later this structure is known and advocated by Innocent I as a "custom of the Church." But the *contents* of this structure in Innocent are noticeably different from those of the Latin text of *ApTrad* 21. According to Innocent, as in the later Oriental versions of *ApTrad* 21, the rite is now clearly associated with an episcopal conferral of the Holy Spirit to the neophytes. Kavanagh, therefore, is certainly correct here in stating that Innocent presumably knows a prayer much like that of the later Gelasian Sacramentary,[11] which reads:

> God almighty, Father of our Lord Jesus Christ, who granted regeneration to your servants by water and the Holy Spirit, and who have given them forgiveness of all their sins, send on them, Lord, your Holy Spirit the Paraclete, and give them the Spirit of wisdom and understanding, the Spirit of counsel and might, the Spirit of knowledge and godliness, fill them with the Spirit of the fear of God, in the name of our Lord Jesus Christ, with whom you live and reign, God forever with the Holy Spirit for ever and ever. Amen.[12]

But only this much is clear. Sometime between the middle of the fourth century and March 19, 416, the post-chrismational episcopal prayer of *ApTrad* 21, or a prayer very much like it, became pneumatic in orientation and remained so in the continual evolution of the Roman rites of initiation.[13] Prior to this, however, we simply do not know what the Roman rites of initiation looked like. And the difficult question, therefore, is whether or not this *structure* of prayer with imposition and the anointing itself reflects traditional *Roman* practice or represents a new development in the Roman initiation rites based on or adapted from something like the Latin version of *ApTrad* 21 itself.

## II. Recent Approaches to the Development of Initiation Rites in *ApTrad* 21

Although traditional scholarship, represented especially by Gregory Dix[14] and Bernard Botte,[15] claimed that *ApTrad*, as reconstructed from the various manuscripts and editions, was an early-third century document "written" by Hippolytus of Rome himself (ca. 215), contemporary work has challenged strongly these earlier and widely held conclusions.[16] With regard to the initiation rites of *ApTrad* 21 in particular, the recent Hermeneia commentary on this document by Paul Bradshaw, L. Edward Phillips, and me[17] surveyed the work of several scholars who argued that the initiation materials actually reflect at least two different sources, a possibly older Roman core (focusing on the role of the bishop) and a later North African source (with more detailed instructions regarding the roles of presbyters and deacons) which were conflated to produce the final form of the text.[18] We have suggested beyond this that in addition to specific "sources," which may have been used or conflated in the development of the text, there were possibly three distinct stages in its evolution.

First of all, the earliest text of *ApTrad's* initiation rites, would probably have been something like the following:[19]

And at the hour when the cock crows, let the water be prayed over first. Let the water be drawn into the pool or flow down into it. And let is be thus if there is no exigency. But if there is an exigency that persists and is urgent, use the water that you will find. And let them strip naked. And first baptize the small children. And each one who is able to speak for themselves, let them speak. But those not able to speak for themselves, let their parents or another one belonging to their family speak for them. Afterward baptize the grown men, and, finally, the women, loosing all their hair and laying aside the jewelry of gold and silver that they are wearing. Let no one take any foreign thing down into the water with them.

As he who is to be baptized is descending into the water, let him who baptizes him say thus [as he lays his hand upon him], 'Do you believe in God the Father omnipotent?' And let the one being baptized say, 'I believe.'[20] And the giver . . . shall baptize him once. And then he shall say: 'Do you believe in Christ Jesus, the Son of God . . .?' And when he has said, 'I believe,' he shall be baptized again. And he shall say again: 'Do you believe in the holy Spirit . . .?' Then he who is being baptized shall say, 'I believe,' and thus he shall be baptized a third time.

And so individually wiping themselves, let them now dress and afterward enter the church . . . And afterward let them pray together with all the people, not praying with the faithful until they have carried out all these things. And when they have prayed, let them offer the peace with the mouth.

If our suggested reconstruction here of an earlier stratum is correct, there is no reason why this part of *ApTrad* 21 could not have been in existence already in the mid to late second century. Such a rite, in fact, would have some parallel both to the baptismal instructions in *Didache* 7 and to the description of the baptismal rites and creedal formulae noted by Justin Martyr in his first Apology.

Second, the next stage in the evolution of *ApTrad* 21 would have been the addition of those ceremonies assigned to the bishop alone, namely: the postbaptismal prayer for grace with the imposition of hands, the episcopal anointing, the kiss, and the greeting ('The Lord be with you') of the neophyte. Third, and finally, the more detailed instructions pertaining to presbyters and deacons (e.g., the prebaptismal rites of blessing of oils, renunciation, and anointing with "exorcised oil," and the presbyteral postbaptismal anointing) would have been the last elements added to produce the final form of the text. Not only does the more detailed character of these instructions suggest that they belong to a later date, but we have no other evidence for the use of oil for pre-baptismal exorcism prior to the middle of the fourth century.[21] Consequently, we have concluded in our commentary that the resultant composition of *ApTrad* 21 is not a single coherent rite as practiced by a particular local church but a conflation of different traditions from different periods, and very probably different places.

If our suggestion that *ApTrad* 21 is composed of diverse strata from different places which were conflated and redacted at

some point in the fourth century is correct, it is extremely helpful in attempting to locate the origins and date of what was to
become the uniquely Roman episcopal postchrismational structure. But there is one major problem with this. If the episcopal
ceremonies were the first to be added to the earlier core of the
rite, this would mean that the initially added postbaptismal rites
had the sequence of a hand-laying prayer followed by a *single*
postbaptismal anointing. While this *might* have been the case, the
fact of the matter is that we *do* have evidence of early postbaptismal rites in the West (e.g., Tertullian in *De baptismo*) which consist of an anointing followed by a hand-laying with prayer but
we have *no* evidence anywhere to corroborate the structure he
suggests. Of course this might only mean that there were other
possible ritual structures in Christian antiquity in addition to
those that have survived. But *the* issue seems to be, as is reflected in Innocent I's letter to Decentius later on, the episcopal
*anointing*, and the question, ultimately, therefore, is whether or
not *this* anointing might represent yet another stratum of development, something added to the text even later.

The possibility that the episcopal anointing might be a later
addition to the postbaptismal rites of *ApTrad* 21, in fact, may be
suggested by Canon 19 in the *Canons of Hippolytus*, a source now
recognized as the earliest derivation of *ApTrad* (ca. 336 in Greek
but not available). One good manuscript of the *Canons of
Hippolytus*, clearly dependent here on some version of *ApTrad* 21,
has the bishop merely sign the forehead of the neophyte with
"the sign of love" and makes no reference at all to either anointing or oil in this context. Significantly, J.M. Hanssens argued that
this manuscript was to be preferred as providing the best and,
thus, the original reading.[22] If Hanssens was correct in this
assessment, it would mean that the shape of *ApTrad* 21, prior to
the Verona Latin version, may have had the postchrismational
structure of prayer with imposition of hands and some kind of
"signing" by the bishop, but this episcopal "signing" was not yet
a second postbaptismal *anointing*. But even if Hanssens was correct, it would not necessarily tell us anything about initiation at
Rome. In any case, we are back both at the middle of the fourth
century with the Latin version of *ApTrad* 21 as the first and only
witness to what will become the uniquely Roman postchrismational episcopal anointing, and sixty-six years later in the second

decade of the fifth with Innocent I as the earliest witness that this pattern is or has, in fact, become Roman.

But can we go further than this? Is it possible to suggest a more specific time somewhere between the mid-fourth century and 416 in which the postchrismational structure of *ApTrad* 21 became the postchrismational structure of the Roman rites of initiation? It is here where the witness of Ambrose of Milan might assist us in developing a workable hypothesis.

### III. The Witness of Ambrose of Milan and the Postchrismational Structure of ApTrad 21

It is well known that in the explanations of initiation given within his two mystagogical catecheses, *De Sacramentis* and *De Mysteriis* (both of which are dated ca. 380–390), Ambrose of Milan claims to follow the customs of the church of Rome in everything except for the unique Milanese rite of the *pedilavium*. Does this mean, then, that the postbaptismal rites known and described by him for Milan parallel those known and used at Rome in the same time period? The implication would seem to be that they are, since Ambrose nowhere attempts to defend an alternate practice.

The problem, however, is that Ambrose's postbaptismal rites themselves are not all that clear. In *De Sacramentis* II. 24, Ambrose refers to an anointing immediately after baptism and cites a formula closely resembling the formula for the presbyteral anointing in the later Gelasian Sacramentary: "God the Father Almighty, . . . who has brought you to a new birth through water and the Holy Spirit and has forgiven your sins, himself anoints you into eternal life."[23] And in *De Sacramentis* III. 8–9, after his description of the *pedilavium* in III. 4–7, Ambrose describes the "spiritual seal," saying:

> The spiritual sealing follows. You have heard about this in the reading today. For after the ceremonies of the font, it still remains to bring the whole to perfect fulfillment. This happens when the Holy Spirit is infused at the priest's invocation: 'the Spirit of wisdom and understanding, the Spirit of counsel and strength, the Spirit of knowledge and piety, the Spirit of holy fear.' These might be called the seven 'virtues' of the Spirit.[24]

The structure reflected by Ambrose certainly *appears* to be the same as *ApTrad* 21. Even his description of the "spiritual seal" in relationship to Isaiah 11:2–3 seems to parallel both the postchrismational episcopal prayer of the Gelasian Sacramentary and that presumably already known by Innocent I.

Here, however, one must proceed with the utmost caution. As Pamela Jackson has demonstrated, Ambrose's "spiritual seal" is "elusive," and we simply do not know "what ritual action—*if any*—accompanied the bishop's prayer."[25] Kavanagh suggests that it may have been simply a general prayer for the neophytes or a concluding prayer for the entire rite.[26] And, to muddy the waters even further, whatever this "spiritual seal" may have been for Ambrose, later sources for the Milanese or "Ambrosian" liturgical tradition (e.g., the tenth-century *Ambrosian Manual*[27] and the twelfth-century *Ordo of Beroldus*[28]) have no corresponding rites beyond the one postbaptismal anointing and *pedilavium*.

The facts, therefore, are these:
1. Ambrose claims to be describing a rite which, other than the *pedilavium*, does not depart from that used in the church at Rome;
2. Ambrose witnesses to an immediate postbaptismal anointing which parallels, structurally, the presbyteral anointing in *ApTrad* 21 and cites an anointing formula which parallels that of later Roman practice; and
3. Ambrose refers to something he calls the "spiritual seal," which, again, appears to correspond structurally to the postchrismational episcopal hand-laying prayer of *ApTrad* 21 and which parallels the language of this prayer in the later Roman rite; *but*
4. We don't have a clue about any gesture or ritual act associated with this "spiritual seal" in Ambrose; and
5. The later Milanese liturgical tradition preserves nothing of this "spiritual seal" in its initiation rites.

How, then, are we to interpret Ambrose's claim that the rite he describes is no different from that used in Rome? At least three possibilities suggest themselves.

1. Ambrose knows that the Roman postchrismational rite is actually different from that of Milan so he is attempting to make the Milanese rite *sound* as "Roman" as possible by using his episcopal freedom to cite a Roman prayer for the sevenfold Spirit as a concluding prayer for the rite; or

2. The postchrismational rite in Ambrose's Milan was identical to that in Rome, which already had both an episcopal hand-laying prayer and second chrismation, and Ambrose's "spiritual seal" should thus be interpreted similarly as a hand-laying prayer with second chrismation, a unit which, for whatever reason, disappeared from Milanese usage later on; or

3. The Roman rite itself had already moved in a pneumatic direction with the hand-laying prayer but either it had not yet adopted a second episcopal anointing or it had done so only recently. And Ambrose either knew it as a recent innovation or did not know it at all. Consequently, his "spiritual seal" corresponds structurally only to the postchrismational hand-laying prayer of the Roman rite and Ambrose is, thus, a witness that at Rome it was a prayer for the gift of the sevenfold *Spirit*. But whether Ambrose's similar prayer included any accompanying ritual gesture cannot be known.

Of these three possibilites, the first is similar to that suggested above by Kavanagh, a possibility finding some support in Gallican liturgical sources, where a final collect for the neophytes, following either the single post-baptismal chrismation or the *pedalavium*, often concludes the whole initiation rite.[29] Ambrose, of course, *may* have been doing something similar in Milan, but we have no hard evidence that he was. The second possibility is actually a fairly traditional argument,[30] but like the first, it too is little more than conjecture without any supporting evidence. If Milan once had a postchrismational structure equivalent to what would become "confirmation" in the Roman rite, what would cause it to disappear later, especially in the medieval period when everyone else is adopting the Roman structure? What then of the third possibility?

While the third possibility is also highly speculative in nature, and based more on an argument *ex silencio* than upon hard data, the following fact remains. Ambrose, who is so careful to describe other aspects of the initiation rites in detail, becomes so ambiguous here. And, when this is coupled with the paucity of sources corresponding to the Roman rites of initiation prior to the middle of the fourth century, both Ambrose's claim that Milan does not depart from Rome in this context and his ambiguity regarding what appears to be a significant portion of those rites in ca. 380–390 becomes quite suggestive. Could it be, indeed, that the Roman rite in this time period is itself ambiguous because the very elements by which that rite will come to be distinguished from all other non-Roman Western rites—i.e., the episcopal hand-laying and subsequent episcopal anointing—have not yet fully developed beyond a postchrismational hand-laying prayer for gift of the Holy Spirit, a rite to which Jerome possibly also refers in his *Altercation* in the 380's?[31] Is, then, Innocent I's reference to the episcopal chrismation as a "custom of the Church" actually a reference to a practice relatively unknown at Rome before the mid to late fourth century, a practice which is becoming both pneumaticized theologically and integrated ritually into the Roman rite only in the last quarter of that century?

We know that the fourth century in general was an era in which postbaptismal rites throughout the Christian world were added to rites that did not have them and that the rites which were added—most often, at least in the East, a single postbaptismal chrismation—were those associated with the conferral of the gift or seal of the Holy Spirit.[32] Something similar, then, must have happened in Rome as well but there the pneumatic focus became attached not specifically to an anointing but to an episcopal hand-laying prayer. Since the years between the Councils of Nicea (325) and Constantinople (381) were years of intense pneumatological debate and doctrinal dispute and consensus regarding the Holy Spirit, such ritual development is perfectly logical. Almost everyone in the fourth century is receiving a postbaptismal anointing into their initiation rites, except the churches of North Africa and Rome where a single postbaptismal anointing was already in existence. But what is unique about Rome in this context is that Rome *alone* comes to adopt a *second* postbaptismal anointing, one reserved exclusively to the bishop as the concluding act of his pneumatic hand-laying prayer.

Ambrose, therefore, may indeed be a credible witness to the Roman rite of his day. He knows the Roman rite and reflects that rite as far as he is able. But what he knows and reflects is a developmental stage in what will ultimately become the final form of that rite. In other words, Ambrose's "spiritual seal" and citation of a prayer which is equivalent to the episcopal hand-laying prayer of the later Gelasian Sacramentary, are not references to an anointing but, more likely, to the pneumatically-oriented hand-laying prayer of the Roman rite. If Ambrose had any ritual gesture for his "spiritual seal," then the most likely one would be an imposition of hands. But *whatever* he may have been doing in Milan between the *pedalavium* and the Eucharist, it is quite clear that this "spiritual seal" as a particular ceremony does not remain an integral part of the Milanese or "Ambrosian" initiation rites.

## Conclusion: A Tentative Hypothesis Concerning the Current Reform of Confirmation in the Roman Rite

On March 19, 416 A.D. Pope Innocent I witnesses to the same postchrismational structure present in *ApTrad* 21 and commends this structure to Decentius in Gubbio. But the contents of this structure in 416 are different than they are in the Verona Latin text of *ApTrad* 21. For Innocent this structure is so pneumatic in focus that he can refer to it as the episcopal conferral of the Spirit. If the Verona Latin text actually reflects *Roman* practice then we know nothing about this structure in the Roman rite before the middle of the fourth century. If it does *not* reflect Roman practice specifically but is, rather, "a conflation of different traditions from different periods, and very probably different places," as Bradshaw suggests, then the *most* we know is that this structure was or had become specifically *Roman* by the time of Innocent I. And, if the contemporary scholarly challenges to the traditional early-third century date and Roman provenance of *ApTrad* prove to be convincing, we will be left, therefore, with Innocent I as the earliest witness to both the episcopal hand-laying prayer and anointing in the Roman rite, a "custom of the Church" at Rome probably reflecting late fourth-century pneumatological and ritual developments.

Even here, however, it is important to note that Innocent's language is rather ambiguous. Although the focus of his response to Decentius is on *who* may perform *which* chrismation and *how* this is to be done—whether on the crown of the head or *in frontem*—Innocent does not clearly say that it is the episcopal *anointing* that actually confers the Holy Spirit. He writes about this episcopal anointing specifically because that's what Decentius, presumably, had asked him about, a sure sign, in my opinion, that there must have been some confusion about the postbaptismal anointing(s) in general—at least in Italy—during this period of history. In his response to Decentius, Innocent only says that *when* the bishop gives the Spirit, the Paraclete, an anointing on the forehead of the neophyte is reserved to him exclusively. But *when* the bishop gives "the signing *and* the gift of Spirit" need only refer to the *occasion* of the imposition of hands and its concluding anointing, whether in conjunction with baptism or at some point separated from baptism, without specifying that the anointing *is* the giving of the Spirit. And, since Innocent uses the Acts 8 story of Peter and John conferring the Holy Spirit in Samaria by the laying on hands in a postbaptismal context as his supportive proof text, it is quite plausible that it is the episcopal pneumatic hand-laying prayer he has in mind.[33] In any event, whether Innocent knew either the formula for the episcopal anointing from *ApTrad* 21 or one more akin to that of the later *Gelasian Sacramentary* ("the sign of Christ to eternal life"[34]), this episcopal anointing is clearly not pneumatic, but, respectively, trinitarian or christic in orientation. Indeed, while this anointing formula was to change more than once in the history of the Roman Rite, it was *never* clearly pneumatic but, rather, trinitarian in focus until 1971.[35]

So where then does all this leave us regarding the 1971 Roman reform of the rite of Confirmation? It is well known that in his Apostolic Constitution *Divinae consortium naturae* of August 15, 1971, Pope Paul VI decreed that, in its essence, "*the Sacrament of Confirmation is conferred through the anointing with chrism on the forehead*, which is done by the laying on of the hand, and through the words: be sealed with the gift of the Holy Spirit."[36] What is extremely important to note here is that while Paul VI refers to the "dignity of the respected formulary used in the Latin Church" for this anointing, that is, the formula first appearing in the twelfth-century Roman Pontifical ("I sign you with the sign of the cross and confirm you with the chrism of salvation. In the name of . . .") and continuing in use until 1971, he makes a deliberate choice for the (*single*) chrismation formula of the Byzantine Rite.[37]

Why, however, was this done? According to him, this Byzantine formula, "expresses the Gift of the Holy Spirit himself and calls to mind the outpouring of the Spirit on the day of Pentecost."[38] But did not the Roman tradition of the hand-laying prayer with its invocation of the seven-fold gifts of the Holy Spirit upon the newly baptized do the same for centuries in a legitimately distinct, and, at least, more clearly biblical manner? The further justification for this in that "the most important place [in confirmation] was occupied by the anointing, *which in a certain way represents the apostolic laying on of hands*,"[39] simply defies logic and is based, ultimately, upon the words of Pope Innocent III (+1216), who similarly claimed that "the anointing...with chrism *signifies* the laying on of hand."[40] But why and how does the episcopal chrismation as opposed to an actual laying on of hands do this? If something "signifying" or "representing the apostolic laying on of hands" was desired, would not an actual imposition of hands themselves have been a fuller and clearer sign of this reality?

That something other than the episcopal hand-laying prayer would attract theological attention in the history of Western Christianity is really no surprise. It is well known that something quite similar happened in the theological interpretation of the rites of ordination. Thomas Aquinas, who so clearly defined confirmation as consisting of both chrism and formula,[41] also defined the matter and form of ordination to be the *traditio instrumentorum* rather than the laying on of hands and prayer.[42] But, as Pope Paul VI's 1968 Apostolic Constitution *Pontificalis Romani recognitio* makes clear, the laying on of hands and prayer of consecration, in fact, have been restored as constituting the matter and form of ordination.[43]

My tentative hypothesis regarding the 1971 reform of the Roman rite of confirmation, therefore, is this. While the current rites of ordination constitute a true reform seeking to recover and restore what is of primary rather than secondary significance, the current reform of confirmation reflects, instead, a mere continuation of what has been an unfortunate medieval theological trajectory in the West, a theological interpretation focussed on what was a secondary (the episcopal anointing) rather than primary and more traditional element (the pneumatic hand-laying prayer). The origins and development of the episcopal chrismation in the Roman rite, as we have seen above, are by no means clear. There is really no hard evidence for it as an integral part of the Roman postchrismational rites before Innocent I in the early fifth century. And, in spite of the scholastic theological interpretation emphasizing the episcopal chrismation as the true matter and form of confirmation, the fact is that the formula for its administration was never pneumatic.

By focussing so exclusively on the chrismation, however, by defining that as the essence of confirmation, and especially by adopting the Byzantine formula for its administration, the Roman rite of confirmation is subject to losing the richness and evocative power of the biblical gesture of hand-laying in Christian initiation. Furthermore, by focussing on this chrismation as the *only* postbaptismal anointing in the case of adult initiation and by calling the presbyteral anointing, received now only by those not to be immediately confirmed, an "explanatory rite," and, hence, quite theologically dispensable, the comparatively richer christic, ecclesiological, and thus implicitly pneumatic, imagery proclaimed and evoked by this anointing become silenced.

Therefore, instead of "reforming" the *rite* of confirmation by turning the chrismation formula itself into the *seal* of the Spirit and, thus, bringing to an unfortunate conclusion the medieval theological focus on episcopal chrismation as bestowing the gift of the Spirit, it would have been preferable to do two things. First, as in the case of ordination, the imposition of hands and the prayer for the sevenfold gift of the Spirit should have been restored theologically as constituting confirmation's matter and form.[44] Such a reform or restoration of the essential nature of the

hand-laying prayer would have allowed the traditional presbyteral anointing in baptism to remain an integral component of
*all* baptisms and not just those of infants or others unfortunate
enough not to be confirmed in the same celebration. Second, a
true "reform" of confirmation would have simply restored it to
its ancient Western location immediately following baptism in *all*
cases, as, indeed, the final pneumatic blessing and ecclesial ratification of Christian initiation and public welcome to the
eucharistic Communion of the church. Here I can only underscore the comment made by Frank Quinn some years ago that:
"today . . . an emphasis upon the classic rite of handlaying with
prayer for the Spirit would be quite healthy. Not only does the
prayer offer much food for thought to the preacher; it is absolutely necessary for understanding the rite."[45]

Any Christian ecclesial tradition or Rite, of course, has the
legitmate right to ritualize the gift of the Holy Spirit in Christian
initiation in any way that it sees fit. It is surely not my intent,
especially as a member of a Christian tradition other than Roman
Catholic, to question the legitimacy of current Roman theology
and sacramental practice or to continue Reformation polemics
about the use of chrism in confirmation. But had the 1971 Roman
reform of confirmation restored the laying on of hands and
prayer as the essential matter and form of this sacrament, the
ecumenical implications of this for the West would have been
dramatic. Then, even though discussion about the sacramental
character of confirmation would have continued, especially
when it is celebrated apart from baptism itself, Catholics,
Lutherans, Episcopalians and Reformed, would be talking,
essentially, about the same basic rite: a laying on hands and
prayer for the sevenfold gift of the Holy Spirit. As it is now, not
only does confirmation remain an ambiguous rite still searching
for an adequate theology, but there is no ecumenical clarity about
*which* rite actually constitutes "confirmation" in the first place.

## Notes

1 A. Kavanagh, *Confirmation: Origins and Reform* (Collegeville: Pueblo, 1988).

2 P. Turner, "The Origins of Confirmation: An Analysis of Aidan Kavanagh's Hypothesis," *Worship* 65 (1991), 336, LWSS, 255.

3 Kavanagh, *Confirmation*, 52.

4 *Apology I*, 65.

5 For an English translation see G. Jeanes, *The Origins of the Roman Rite* (Bramcote/Nottingham: Alucin/GROW Liturgical Study 20, 1991), 19–20.

6 Ibid., 41. Whatever the phrase "and the rest" may have included, Jeanes is certainly correct here in interpreting this address to the neophyte as following the pattern of the first postbaptismal anointing and not the subsequent episcopal anointing of the Roman rite. See note 4, 41.

7 Ibid., 44–45.

8 On this see Paul Bradshaw, *The Search for the Origins of Christian Worship* (London/New York: Oxford University Press, 1992), 80–110.

9 English translation from P. Bradshaw, M. Johnson, and L.E. Phillips, *The Apostolic Tradition: A Commentary*, Hermeneia Series (Minneapolis: Fortress Press, 2002), 118.

10 Ibid., 118.

11 Kavanagh, *Confirmation*, 58–59.

12 English translation from Jeanes, *Origins* 17.

13 Cf. Kavanagh, *Confirmation*, 59ff.

14 G. Dix, *The Treatise on the Apostolic Tradition of St Hippolytus of Rome* (London/Ridgefield, CT: Curzon Press, 1992).

15 B. Botte, *La Tradition apostolique de saint Hippolyte* (Münster 1963).

16 Cf. M. Metzger, "Nouvelles perspectives pour la prétendue *Tradition apostolique*," *Ecclesia Orans* 5 (1988), 241–59; idem., "Enquêtes autour de la prétendue *Tradition apos-tolique*," *Ecclesia Orans* 9 (1992), 7–36; and idem., "A propos des règlements écclesiastiques et de la prétendue *Tradition apostolique*," *Revue des sciences religieuses* 66 (1992), 249–61.

17 P. Bradshaw, M. Johnson, and L.E. Phillips, *The Apostolic Tradition: A Commentary*, Hermeneia Series (Minneapolis: Fortress Press, 2002), especially 104–35, of which the fol-lowing is a summary.

18 See J.-P. Bouhot, *La confirmation, sacrement de la communion ecclésiale* (Lyon 1968), 38–45, R. Cabié, "L'ordo de l'Initiation chrétienne dans la 'Tradition apostolique' d'Hippolyte de Rome," in *Mens concordet voci, pour Mgr. A. G. Martimort* (Paris 1983), 543–58, and V. Saxer, *Les rites de l'initiation chrétienne du IIe au VIe siécle* (Spoletto 1988), 118–19.

19 Unless otherwise indicated the text is taken from the edition of Bradshaw, Johnson, and Phillips.

20 This part of the text is taken from the version preserved in the *Testamentum Domini* according to the translation of Grant Sperry-White, *The Testamentum Domini: A Text for Students* (Bramcote/Nottingham: Alcuin/GROW Liturgical Study 19, 1991), 28.

[21] See Bradshaw, Johnson, Phillips, 131.

[22] J.M. Hanssens, "L'édition critique des Canons d'Hippolyte," *Orientalia Christiana Periodica* 32 (1966), 542–43. See also Paul Bradshaw, *The Canons of Hippolytus* (Bramcote/Nottingham: Alcuin/GROW Liturgical Study 2, 1987), 24.

[23] English translation from E. Yarnold, *The Awe-Inspiring Rites of Initiation* (Middlegreen, Slough: St. Paul Publications, 1971), 119.

[24] Ibid., 124–25.

[25] Pamela Jackson, "The Meaning of 'Spiritale Signaculum' in the Mystagogy of Ambrose of Milan," *Ecclesia Orans* VII (Rome, 1990), 94. Jackson suggests (93) that Ambrose "understood the rite not so much as a discrete effective sign, but more as a 'symbolic overflow' of what had just occurred in the font. Associating various dimensions of salvation with specific ritual actions still vivid in the neophytes' sense-memory would not only enable Ambrose's hearers to have a clearer understanding of the manifold aspects of God's grace in their lives, but also serve as a kind of mnemonic device enabling the neophytes to remember them years after their sacramental experience."

[26] Kavanagh, *Confirmation*, 55.

[27] DBL, 183–98.

[28] Ibid., 198–203.

[29] Cf. the *Missale Gothicum*, 264–265, in DBL, 261–2, and the *Bobbio Missal*, 253–254, in DBL, 273–4. On Gallican initiation rites see J. L. Levesque, "The Theology of the Postbaptismal Rites in the Seventh and Eighth Century Gallican Church," *Ephemerides Liturgicae* 95 (1981), 3–43; G. Winkler, "Confirmation or Chrismation? A Study in Comparative Liturgy," *Worship* 58 (1984), 2–17; and F.C. Quinn, "Confirmation Reconsidered: Rite and Meaning," *Worship* 59 (1985), 354–70 (all in LWSS, 159–237).

[30] Cf. L.L. Mitchell, *Baptismal Anointing* (London: Alcuin Club Collections 48, 1966), 85–91.

[31] See above, note 5.

[32] On this development see G. Winkler, "The Original Meaning of the Prebaptismal Anointing and its Implications," *Worship* 52 (1978), pp. 24–45 (LWSS, 58–81).

[33] I am not convinced by Kavanagh's argument (*Confirmation*, 62) that "despite [Innocent's] appeal to Acts 8 and the apostolic hand laying reported there he does not even mention hand laying in this letter. What he derives from Acts 8 is episcopal hegemony in giving the Holy Spirit . . ., but not the mode by which the apostles did this, namely, by hand laying." But is it not equally possible that Innocent does not refer to hand laying because: (1) this is implied already by his references to *when* the Spirit is given and to Acts 8; and (2) episcopal hand laying was not the issue for Decentius, and, therefore, not part of his question? Decentius was concerned only about the ministers and manner of the postbaptismal anointing(s).

[34] Jeanes, *The Origin of the Roman Rite*, 17.

[35] For a succinct overview of the development of confirmation in the West, its formulas, and the importance of the hand laying prayer, see Quinn, "Confirmation Reconsidered," in LWSS, 219–37.

[36] Paul VI, "Apostolic Constitution on the Sacrament of Confirmation," in *The Rites of the Catholic Church*, vol. 1 (Collegeville: Pueblo, 1990), 477 [emphasis added].

37 Ibid., 477. The operating assumption here appears to be that Byzantine chrismation *is* Roman confirmation, but this is questionable, to say the least. Byzantine chrismation is an integral part of the initiation rite and is located at the very place of the presbyteral postbaptismal anointing of the Roman Rite. If the parallel between the two is intended the Roman reform could have simply replaced the traditional first postbaptismal anointing with this one and not included a second one for "confirmation." It is interesting to note also the ecumenical implications of this change for other Western churches, which have attempted to restore some form of postbaptismal anointing to their initiation rites. The *Lutheran Book of Worship*, for example, rather than restoring the traditional (presbyteral) anointing retained by Luther in his 1523 *Taufbüchlein*, inserted in its place the traditional Roman confirmation hand-laying prayer and a signing (with oil as an option) connected to the words, "*N.*, child of God, you are sealed by the Holy Spirit and marked with the cross of Christ forever," *Lutheran Book of Worship* (Minneapolis: Augsburg, 1978), 124. The baptismal rite of the 1979 American Episcopal *Book of Common Prayer* (New York: Oxford University Press, 1979), 308, did something quite similar. Further examples of this are legion in contemporary Protestant initiation rites. Western liturgical revision of initiation rites in general has thus been quite taken with Byzantine-type formularies regarding the Holy Spirit.

38 Ibid., 477.

39 Ibid., 477 [emphasis added].

40 Ibid., 475 [emphasis added].

41 *Summa Theologiae* 3a., Q. 72, Arts. 1–12.

42 Ibid., Suppl., Q. 37. On this see Quinn, "Confirmation Reconsidered," cited here from Johnson, op. cit., 230ff.

43 See *Documents on the Liturgy, 1963-1979: Conciliar, Papal, and Curial Texts* (Collegeville: The Liturgical Press, 1982), 816–19. The recovery of hand-laying and prayer as the essential matter and form of ordination had already been done by Pius XII in his 1947 *Sacramentum Ordinis*.

44 Whether this would have included an additional anointing or not is immaterial, but if it did there is absolutely no reason why it would have to be the Byzantine formula as opposed to a more Western formula, for example, that used in the Gelasian Sacramentary ("the sign of Christ to eternal life"). The recovery of a richer pneumatological focus in the sacramental rites of the West does not automatically necessitate the Western adoption of Eastern formularies. East and West need not ritualize the gift of the Holy Spirit in exactly the same way especially when, as in the case of the confirmation prayer, the Roman West already had a long standing pneumatologically-oriented tradition of its own. On this, see my essay, "Baptism as '*New Birth ex aqua et spiritu*': An Investigation of Western Liturgical Sources," elsewhere in this volume, 37-62.

45 Quinn, "Confirmation Reconsidered," cited here from LWSS, 235–36.

# LET'S STOP RECEIVING
# 'CONVERTS' AT EASTER

Picture the following scenario. During last year's Easter Vigil at St. Mary's Roman Catholic Church, Anywhere, USA, several (already baptized) candidates who had been members of other · Christian traditions were received into full communion with the Roman Catholic Church and confirmed, after having participated in the RCIA process for at least a year of catechesis and a Lent of "purification and enlightenment." Among those received into full communion were former Lutherans and Episcopalians. A few blocks from St. Mary's at Our Savior's Lutheran Church (of the Evangelical Lutheran Church in America, or ELCA) a similar celebration was taking place at the same time, where several now former Roman Catholics and Episcopalians, after participating in the "Lutheran" catechumenal process, called *Welcome to Christ*,[1] were making their "Affirmation of Baptism." And, at St. Alban's Episcopal Church, again just a few blocks away from both St. Mary's and Our Savior's, and also again during the Easter Vigil celebration, several former Lutherans and Roman Catholics were being received into the Episcopal Church, USA, after having been formed by the *Episcopal* version of the cate- chumenate and "renewing" their baptismal vows (in preparation for a handlaying rite by the bishop at another point during the Easter season).[2] In all three of these churches on that night, the new Easter fire had been blessed, the Paschal Candle had been lighted and carried in solemn procession into a darkened church with the "Light of Christ/Thanks be to God" sung three times, the powerful *Exsultet* had been intoned in the glow both of the

Paschal Candle and those lighted candles held by the assembly, the great watery stories of salvation from the Hebrew Bible had been read, Romans 6 and the Easter Gospel had been proclaimed, the Eucharist had been celebrated, all had affirmed or renewed their baptism, and all had been sent forth from the assembly conscious that, in the words of St. Augustine, they were "an Easter people and alleluia was [their] song." But, in the process, in addition to those who might actually have been baptized during the celebration, some that night had become "Catholics," "Lutherans," and/or "Episcopalians" through a similar ritual process called either "confirmation" (Roman Catholic) "affirmation of baptism" (Lutheran), or "reaffirmation of baptism" (Episcopalian). What is wrong with this picture?

Within a variety of parish settings and different Christian traditions throughout the United States the above scenario is played out every year as the Easter Vigil has become increasingly "New Members Night" and/or "Ecclesial Musical Chairs Night" wherein already baptized members of Christ's *one* body pass from one particular way of ecclesial living into another. As such, Easter is rapidly becoming, I fear, the great festival of our Christian *disunity*. For, how ironic it is that at the very moment where our *common* and *ecumenical* Christian life and paschal identity in the dying and rising of Jesus in the power of the Holy Spirit *should* be celebrated, where the celebration of the paschal sacrament of our *one* baptism into Christ and the church is most highly appropriate, we frequently have chosen instead to *use* (abuse?) the Easter Vigil as the prime time for "making converts" to our particular ecclesial tradition (as though being received into full communion is the sacramental equivalent of baptism). Such use of the catechumenal process for "making converts," while obviously wide-spread, common, and even "permitted," certainly represents a radical departure both from the so-called "Golden Age" of the catechumenate, known to us in the writings of those great mystagogues Cyril of Jerusalem, John Chrysostom, Theodore of Mopsuestia, and Ambrose of Milan,[3] as well as the intent of those who sought to restore the catechumenate to the life of the church today.

In addition to various adaptations of the ritual process leading to adult baptism, confirmation, and first Communion—i.e.,

"Rites for Particular Circumstances"[4]—the Roman Catholic RCIA also provides a rite of "Reception of Baptized Christians into the Full Communion of the Catholic Church." This rite, to take place either during or outside of Mass, includes the conferral and reception of confirmation and, at least within Mass, the preferred occasion, the reception of first Communion. In the rite itself, following the profession of the Nicene Creed in the context of the eucharistic liturgy, those being received into full Roman Catholic communion are invited to state simply, "I believe and profess all that the holy Catholic Church believes, teaches, and proclaims to be revealed by God,"[5] and are then confirmed and receive their first Communion.

When compared with previous rites for the "reception of converts," this new rite of reception represents a most welcome change. Prior to 1962, for example, those "converting" from a variety of other religious traditions to Roman Catholicism were required to make an abjuration either of "Hebrew superstition," the Islamic "sect of the infidel," or, in the case of the already baptized, the "heretical errors" of the particular "evil" Protestant "sect" they were leaving.[6] Even as recent as 1964, the following "Profession of Faith" was sought:

I, *N.N.*, ... years of age, born outside the Catholic Church, have held and believed errors contrary to her teaching. Now, enlightened by divine grace, I kneel before you, Reverend Father *N.N.*, having before my eyes and touching with my hands the holy Gospels; and with a firm faith I believe and profess each and all the articles that are contained in the Apostles' Creed, that is: I believe in God..., and life everlasting. Amen. I admit and embrace most firmly the apostolic and ecclesiastical traditions and all the other constitutions and prescriptions of the Church. I admit the sacred Scriptures according to the sense which has been held and is still held by Holy Mother Church, whose duty it is to judge the true sense and interpretation of the sacred Scriptures, and I shall never accept or interpret them except according to the unanimous consent of the Fathers. I profess that the sacraments of the New Law are, truly and precisely, seven in number, instituted for the salvation of mankind, though all are not necessary for each individual: baptism, confirmation, Eucharist, penance, extreme unction, holy orders, and matrimony. I profess that all confer grace and that of these baptism, confirmation, and holy orders cannot be repeated without sacrilege. I also accept and admit the ritual of the Catholic Church in the solemn administration of all the above mentioned sacraments. I accept and hold, in each and every part, all that has been defined and declared by the Sacred Council of Trent concerning original sin and justification. I profess that in the Mass is offered to God a true, real, and propitiatory sacrifice for the living and the dead; that in the holy sacrament of the Eucharist is really, truly, and substantially the Body and Blood together with the Soul and Divinity of our Lord Jesus Christ, and that there takes place what the Church calls transubstantiation, that is, the change of all the substance of the bread into the Body and of all the substance of the wine into the Blood. I confess also that in receiving under either of these species one receives Jesus Christ, whole and entire. I firmly hold that purgatory exists and that the souls detained there can be helped by the prayers of the faithful. Likewise I hold that the saints, who reign with Jesus Christ, should be venerated and invoked, that they offer prayers to God for us, and that their relics are to be venerated. I profess firmly that the images of Jesus Christ and of the Mother of God, ever Virgin, as well as of all the saints, should be given due honor and veneration. I also affirm that Jesus Christ left to the Church the faculty to grant indulgences and that their use is most salutary to the Christian people. I recognize the holy, Roman, Catholic, and Apostolic Church as the mother and teacher of all the Churches and I promise and swear true obedience to the Roman Pontiff, successor of Saint Peter, Prince of the Apostles, and Vicar of Jesus Christ. Besides I accept, without hesitation, and profess all that has been handed down, defined, and declared by the sacred canons and by the general councils, especially by the Sacred Council of Trent and by the Vatican General

Council, and in a special manner concerning the primacy and infallibility of the Roman Pontiff. At the same time I condemn and reprove all that the Church has condemned and reproved. This same Catholic faith, outside of which nobody can be saved, which I now freely profess and to which I truly adhere, the same I promise and swear to maintain and profess, with the help of God, entire, inviolate, and with firm constancy until the last breath of life; and I shall strive, as far as possible, that this same faith shall be held, taught, and publicly professed by all those who depend on me and by those of whom I shall have charge. So help me God and these holy Gospels.[7]

Furthermore, although the revised rite of Reception, mandated by the *Constitution on the Sacred Liturgy* (*Sacrosanctum concilium*) at Vatican II, appears within the RCIA materials, it is *nowhere* indicated that it is to be seen as part of the RCIA process leading to *Easter* initiation! Indeed, it is only within an appendix to the edition of the RCIA approved for the dioceses of the United States, although often imitated elsewhere around the world, that a series of rites called "Additional (Combined) Rites" regularly places *real* catechumens (unbaptized adults), candidates for confirmation and first Communion (uncatechized but baptized adults), and candidates for reception into full communion together into the same overall ritual process of catechumenal formation with the respective initiation rites then celebrated at the Easter Vigil.[8] While the attempt to be so inclusive of people at differing stages in their spiritual journeys *may* be laudable, and while no one would question the need for tradition-specific catechesis and formation, these combined rites, especially with regard to the rite of reception into full communion, present particular problems still needing to be resolved, including those expressed in the scenario suggested above.

It ought never be forgotten, but often is, I fear, that the origins of the restoration of the adult catechumenate are to be located within the various attempts of missionaries in the late-nineteenth and early-twentieth centuries to prepare adult converts for the full rites of Christian initiation in the Roman Catholic Church.[9] Similarly, with regard to the RCIA itself, the intent of this restored catechumenate is also for the conversion of the *unbaptized*. In other words, the adult catechumenate as envisioned by the RCIA is *prebaptismal* in nature and orientation and *not* designed with the reception or transfer of Christians from one ecclesial tradition to another in mind.

Nevertheless, in the "Additional (Combined) Rites" of the RCIA, both real catechumens and other "candidates," including those for reception into membership—and occasionally those seeking restoration to membership—are often joined together within the same catechumenal process. Hence, while adult catechumens receive baptism, confirmation, and first Communion at the Easter Vigil, other candidates are often received into communion with confirmation and receive their first Communion at the same time.

To be fair, attempts are certainly made in all of these combined situations to make clear distinctions between catechumens and candidates so that the dignity of baptism itself is not compromised. In the RCIA, for example, candidates for full communion are not *supposed* to sign the book of the elect, are not *supposed* to be exorcized with the elect, and are not *supposed* to receive other rites designated for catechumens alone. But, by placing various groups together in the same catechumenal process, and by celebrating both Christian initiation and reception/confirmation together at the Easter Vigil, it is not always clear if the distinctions between these groups is all that clear either to the liturgical assembly or to the elect and candidates themselves. Such confusion, in fact, becomes even more problematic when the number of *candidates* is greater than the number of *catechumens* or *elect* in a given parish, a regular phenomenon in several places today. Indeed, this confusion extends even to those who have the responsibility of leading or directing the process. I have heard parish RCIA directors actually describe the RCIA *not* as the ritual process leading from an initial conversion to full Christian initiation through baptism, confirmation, and Eucharist but as a "program people go through who want to become *Catholics*." And I am well aware of situations where some RCIA directors—and even some pastors (!)—simply do *not* know the rites themselves and who not only treat candidates for full communion *as* catechumens but insist on using the terminology *of* "catechumen" to refer to them.

Paul Turner has written clearly about this confusion saying:

> We can only hope that the need for a rite of transferring membership will become minimized. Progress in the ecumenical movement should help us move toward a single eucharistic table for all Christian families. This would reduce the need for a separate rite of 'Reception of Baptized Christians into the Full Communion of the Catholic Church' and purify the purpose of confirmation. . . . Current pastoral practice sadly initiates such candidates in much the same way as catechumens. The two groups are catechized together, and pass through either the same rituals or ponderous adaptations which struggle to challenge the non-baptized without offending non-Catholic Christians. Frequently, candidates are disappointed that they cannot be baptized like catechumens, that they should not sign the book of the elect like catechumens, that they are not called to scrutinies like catechumens, that they are not anointed with the oil of catechumens like catechumens... By making candidates imitate the path of catechumens we have too often made it too difficult for Christians who share one baptism to share one eucharistic table. The ecumenical movement longs for the day when the rites which prepare baptized Christians for full communion will be ripped from our books, and the catechumenate now so freely adapted for the *baptized* may become again the proper province of the unbaptized.[10]

What is often neglected in Roman Catholic dioceses and parishes in this regard are the norms for the rite of "Reception of Baptized Christians into the Full Communion of the Catholic Church" in the *National Statutes on the Catechumenate*, accepted by the Roman Catholic Bishops of the United States in 1986. According to these *National Statutes*, not only are those received into full communion from other Christian traditions *never* to be designated as "converts," a term strictly reserved for those who convert "from unbelief to Christian belief,"[11] but it is also clearly stated that:

It is preferable that reception into full communion *not* take place at the Easter Vigil lest there be any confusion of such baptized Christians with the candidates for baptism, possible misunderstanding of or even reflection upon the sacrament of baptism celebrated in another Church or ecclesial community, or any perceived triumphalism in the liturgical welcome into the Catholic eucharistic community.[12]

The widespread neglect of the *National Statutes'* clearly articulated preference for the rite of reception taking place outside the context of the Easter Vigil has the potential of turning the restored catechumenate in today's churches into little more than a new way to make "converts" out of already baptized Christians, who seek to be received or transferred into another church.[13] It is quite unfortunate that such a powerful and ecumenical statement about the theology of baptism and the common identity and dignity of all the baptized has not been taken more seriously in the pastoral adaptations made of the RCIA today.

What is equally unfortunate is the fact that in restoring the adult catechumenate in other churches today the same dynamic of combining rites and people has also been at work. Both Lutheran and Episcopal adaptations of the catechumenate, for example, have followed the unfortunate precedent set by the "Additional (Combined) Rites" in the USA version of the RCIA. But the prize for turning the catechumenal process into a denominational or parochial event might certainly go to us Lutherans, where, according to the rites themselves, some form of *Luther's* catechism *may* be presented to all (baptismal candidates and affirmers) on the first Sunday in Lent at the "Enrollment of Candidates for Baptism,"[14] and a Lutheran worship book *is* presented on the fifth Sunday in Lent.[15]

What, then, shall we do? The solution to all this is really quite simple. Let's stop receiving "converts" at the Easter Vigil so that the Easter Vigil *and* the Lenten catechumenate itself can function properly in relationship to baptismal preparation and renewal in a way consistent with its origins and with the primary intent of its modern restoration. In so doing, let's all take seriously the preference of the *National Statutes* in order that any and all ecumenical confusion about baptism be avoided. Quite simply, there is neither historical precedent for the reception/confirmation of baptized Christians from other traditions at *Easter*, nor any sound *theological* reason why such *should* take place. If anything, the theology of *baptism* itself mitigates against such a practice and it is *baptismal* theology—not convenience and not some vague notion of inclusivity—that must shape pastoral practice at this point.

So, then, when *should* people be received into full communion, or be received into another Christian tradition through affirmation or renewal of baptism? Please don't misunderstand me. While I agree fully with Paul Turner that "the ecumenical movement longs for the day when the rites which prepare baptized Christians for full communion will be ripped from our books," I also think that the decisions of people who seek to embrace a new manner of living out their baptismal faith *within* a particular ecclesial manner of life should be celebrated fully. However, although tradition-specific catechesis will be necessary for all in this context and basic Christian catechesis a necessity for some, such "candidates" are *not* catechumens and have no place in the prebaptismal catechumenate of Lent. So, then, *when* should rites of reception take place? Well, certainly not on Holy Thursday, unless one considers such "converts" to be the equivalent of those in the "order of penitents," who in the early medieval Roman tradition were reconciled on Holy Thursday. In short, let's separate this process from Lent, the Triduum, and the fifty days of Easter entirely and find other moments in the life of the Christian community where such reception would be appropriate[16] and where it might be easier to avoid confusion or "possible misunderstanding of or even reflection upon the sacrament of baptism celebrated in another church or ecclesial community, or any perceived triumphalism in the liturgical welcome into the Catholic eucharistic community." Now, whether confirmation (or its equivalent) should be part of such rites of reception is another question for another time.

By way of conclusion, try to picture yet another possible scenario. During this year's Easter Vigil, St. Mary's Roman Catholic Church, Our Savior's Lutheran Church, and St. Alban's

Episcopal Church, all located in Anywhere, USA, celebrated most of the Easter Vigil together in one common place. Since St. Mary's was the host parish for this event, Fr. McCarthy presided over the blessing of the new fire and lighting of the Paschal Candle and offering the concluding prayers after each of the vigil readings. An Episcopal deacon from St. Alban's carried the Paschal Candle in procession and intoned the *Exsultet*. Lectors came from all three parishes and a combined choir assisted with the appropriate responsorial psalms and other chants. Pastor Swanson from Our Savior's gave the Easter homily. At the time appointed for baptism and its renewal, an ecumenical "litany of the saints" was sung,[17] the water was blessed by Father Smith from St. Alban's, who also led in the renunciation of Satan and the triple profession of faith. By turns, the "elect" from each parish (including infants) were baptized (including confirmation and/or the appropriate postbaptismal rites) by the respective ministers from those parishes in the presence of this common liturgical assembly. Following a common renewal of baptismal vows, a sprinkling rite, and an exchange of peace, all three parish groups (unfortunately) moved to two separate locations in the building for, unfortunately, two separate celebrations of the Eucharist.[18] Yet, following those celebrations, all three assembled together again for a common concluding rite, the singing of a final hymn ("Jesus Christ is Ris'n Today!" was chosen), and an Easter party in St. Mary's parish hall in honor of all those newly baptized that night in the *same* font. It is to such common and ecumenical origins in the baptismal waters that the forty days of Lent, the Paschal Triduum, and the fifty days of Easter call us each year. Can we not commit ourselves anew to rid ourselves of any and everything that keeps us from this realization? Indeed, as Gordon Lathrop asks:

> If baptism constitutes the assembly that is the church, ought not the Christians in a given locality enact that truth? Can we not do much of the process of baptism together? Could a renewed catechumenate be undertaken by many or even all of the Christian assemblies in a given local place? Could we be present at each other's baptisms? Could we do baptisms on the great feasts and

do them side by side? Could we even consider constructing a single font for the local churches in our towns and
cities?[19]

## Notes

[1] *Welcome to Christ: Lutheran Rites for the Catechumenate* (Minneapolis: Augsburg
Fortress Press, 1997). See also the accompanying volumes: *Welcome to Christ: A Lutheran
Catechetical Guide* (Minneapolis: Augsburg Fortress Press, 1997); and *Welcome to Christ: A
Lutheran Introduction to the Catechumenate* (Minneapolis: Augsburg Fortress Press, 1997).

[2] See *The Book of Common Prayer* (New York: The Church Hymnal Corporation, 1979),
284ff. See also Office of Evangelism Ministries, The Episcopal Church, *The Catechumenal
Process: Adult Initiation & Formation for Christian Life and Ministry* (New York: The Church
Hymnal Corporation, 1990).

[3] E. Yarnold, *The Awe-Inspiring Rites of Initiation: The Origins of the R.C.I.A.*, 2nd ed.,
(Collegeville: The Liturgical Press, 1994).

[4] *The Rites of the Catholic Church*, vol. 1 (Collegeville: Pueblo, 1990), 170–286.

[5] Ibid., para. 491, 280.

[6] Cf. *Rituale Parvum* (Turin: Desclee, 1949), 35–36.

[7] *The 1964 English Ritual: Collectio Rituum* (Collegeville: The Liturgical Press, 1964),
193–195. For "the uneducated and for those who do not have the religious development to
understand the longer formula," the following "Alternative Form" was also provided: "I,
N.N., touching with my hands God's holy Gospels, enlightened by divine grace, profess the
faith which the Catholic, Apostolic, Roman Church teaches. I believe that Church to be the
one true Church which Jesus Christ founded on earth, to which I submit with all my heart.
I believe in God . . ., and life everlasting. Amen. I profess that seven sacraments were instituted by Jesus Christ for the salvation of mankind, namely, baptism, confirmation,
Eucharist, penance, extreme unction, holy orders, and matrimony."

[8] See Ibid., 287–356. According to Dalve J. Sieverding, in fact, Rome was very reluctant
to approve the use of this rite in the United States for use at the Easter Vigil precisely
because ecumenical relations might be harmed as a result! See his recent study, *The
Reception of Baptized Christians: A History and Evaluation*, Forum Essays (Chicago: Liturgy
Training Publications, 2001), 188–189.

[9] Cf. D. Gelpi, *Committed Worship: A Sacramental Theology for Converting Christians*, vol. 1:
*Adult Conversion and Initiation* (Collegeville: The Liturgical Press, 1993), 188–189.

[10] P. Turner, *Confirmation: The Baby in Solomon's Court* (Mahwah/New York: Paulist
Press, 1993), 129. Turner, of course, is being too nice. Too often, in fact, candidates for full
communion *do* sign the book of the elect, are *scrutinized*, etc.

[11] *The Rites*, vol. 1, 341.

[12] Ibid., 347. While the following paragraph makes a concession "for pastoral reasons," it asserts, nevertheless, that "a clear distinction should be maintained during the celebration between candidates for sacramental initiation and candidates for reception into full communion, and ecumenical sensitivities should be carefully respected."

[13] This seems to be particularly the case in university and college campus ministry settings, where candidates for full communion almost always outnumber catechumens. For that matter, in such settings when actual catechumens who become elected to baptism are present other problems appear. The entire catechumenal process, for example, rather than the expected one *year* of the catechumenate and one *year* of postbaptismal mystagogy, is often streamlined or reduced to a single academic year with enrollment into the catechumenate in Advent, Election on the first Sunday in Lent, the Rites of Initiation either at the Easter Vigil, or (assuming that students are on Easter break during the vigil) the second Sunday of Easter, with mystagogy concluding sometime near Spring commencement.

[14] *Welcome to Christ*, 24.

[15] Ibid., 26, 32, and 34.

[16] In addition to Sieverding's study referred to above, note 8, the only detailed study of the Roman Catholic rite of reception into full communion I am aware of is the very helpful book edited by Ronald A. Oakham (ed.), *One at the Table: The Reception of Baptized Christians* (Chicago: Liturgy Training Publications, 1995). This volume should be looked at carefully by all who struggle with this question.

[17] For an example of such an ecumenical litany see *Welcome to Christ*, 70–1.

[18] I say only two separate celebrations because the Episcopalians and ELCA Lutherans have been participating in an "Interim Eucharistic Sharing" agreement on the way toward full communion.

[19] Gordon Lathrop, *Holy People: A Liturgical Ecclesiology* (Minneapolis: Fortress, 1999), 146–7.

# ONE BODY, ONE SPIRIT IN CHRIST: EUCHARIST AS THE CULMINATION OF CHRISTIAN INITIATION

At the 1992 national meeting of the Federation of Diocesan Liturgical Commissions (FDLC), held in Miami, Florida, the following position statement was adopted:

> It is the position of the delegates...that the Board of Directors of the [FDLC] and the Bishops' Committee on the Liturgy urge the National Conference of Catholic Bishops to take the initiative to propose to the Apostolic See a discussion on the restoration of the ancient practice of celebrating confirmation and Communion at the time of baptism, including the baptism of children who have not yet reached catechetical age, so that through connection of these three sacraments, the unity of the Paschal Mystery would be better signified and the Eucharist would again assume its proper significance as the culmination of Christian initiation.[1]

To restore the Eucharist to its proper place and significance as the culmination of Christian initiation in all cases, a place and significance it clearly has already in the Roman *Rite of Christian Initiation of Adults* (RCIA), where baptism, confirmation, and first Communion function as distinct sacramental moments within an integral and unitive celebration, requires that attention be given to a number of different elements. Four such elements come to mind immediately as calling for further exploration:

(1) that the church itself into which one is initiated by baptism and confirmation be understood primarily as a eucharistic community, the continuation of Jesus own "table companionship" with "tax collectors and sinners," the central symbol of which is the Lord's table around which the community gathers and which, with the table of the word, graciously dominates our worship spaces; (2) that in relationship to baptism and Eucharist "confirmation" itself be reconsidered both liturgically and theologically, in spite of its ambiguous history, as forming none other than the Spirit "bridge" between water bath and table, and not independently as some kind of passage rite related to age and/or catechetical preparation; (3) that the Communion of all the initiated be considered not only in relationship to its one thousand-year history in the West but also ecumenically, and in relationship to its potential formative role in the overall faith development of children; and (4) that this call for the actual restoration of confirmation and Communion to baptism in all cases be issued only with an informed awareness of the vast implications for change throughout the life and practice of the church as a whole that such a call entails. It is upon these four elements that I wish to focus today.

## I. The Church as "Eucharistic Community" or "Table-Companionship"

Contemporary biblical scholarship on the life and ministry of Jesus, especially that of the late Norman Perrin, teaches us that Jesus' own table companionship with "tax collectors and sinners" was "the aspect of Jesus' ministry which must have been most meaningful to his followers and most offensive to his critics."[2] But why was this so? As Nathan Mitchell has written recently:

[Jesus] sat at table not as the charming, congenial, ringleted centerpiece of a Rembrandt painting, but as a vulnerable vagrant willing to share potluck with a household of strangers. Normally, a table's prime function is to establish social ranking and hierarchy (by what one eats, how one eats, with whom one eats). Normally, a meal is about social identification, status, and power . . . But the very

*randomness* of Jesus' table habits challenged this system of
social relations modeled on meals and manners . . . It was
not simply that Jesus ate with objectionable persons—
outcasts and sinners—but that he ate with anyone, indis-
criminately. Hence his reputation: He has no honor! He
has no shame! . . . [Such] commensality was 'a strategy
for building or rebuilding peasant community on radically different principles from those of honor and shame,
patronage and clientage.' For Jesus, *healing* (the gift he
brings to a home) calls forth *hospitality* (those healed offer
refreshment, food and drink, a place at table). The table
companionship practiced by Jesus thus recreated the
world, redrew all of society's maps and flow charts.
Instead of symbolizing social rank and order, it blurred
the distinctions between hosts and guests, need and plenty. Instead of reinforcing rules of etiquette, it subverted
them, making the last first and the first last.[3]

No wonder Jesus was such a threat to religion, culture, and
society alike. Such "table habits," if not watched closely and
even curtailed by those in authority, had the potential to transform the world, to subvert the status quo. For this egalitarian,
inclusive, challenging, status and role-reversing "table companionship" was nothing other the concrete sign, prophetic enact-
ment, and very embodiment of the reign of God that Jesus himself proclaimed. It was this for which he was ultimately crucified, the messianic banquet of the end times (see Isaiah 25), here
anticipated, but already joyfully present, in table sharing with
the One whose critics were to label both "drunkard and glutton"
(Matthew 11:19).

What Perrin calls further this "central feature of the ministry
of Jesus"[4] remained a primary characteristic of the earliest
Christian communities as well, a characteristic witnessed to in
the post-resurrection accounts of the Gospels, which closely
associate meals with Jesus' post-resurrection appearances (cf.
Luke 24), in Acts (cf. 2:42, 46), in the New Testament letters (cf.
especially 1 Corinthians 10—11), and in the *Didache* (9, 10, and
14). Indeed, according to Willy Rordorf, it is the continuation of
this joyful table companionship with the crucified, yet risen,

Jesus on the first day of the week, called now by the term "Lord's Supper," that eventually led to the re-naming of this day itself as the "Lord's Day."[5] Perrin writes:

> In all probability, it was the vividness of the memory of that pre-Easter fellowship between the disciples and the earthly Jesus that provided the pattern for the development of that remarkable sense of fellowship between the early Christians and the risen Lord which is such a feature of primitive Christianity—and which has had such an effect on the Jesus tradition. At all events, we are justified in seeing this table-fellowship as the central feature of the ministry of Jesus; an anticipatory sitting at table in the kingdom of God and very real celebration of present joy and challenge. Here a great deal of the private teaching of Jesus to his disciples must have had its *Sitz im Leben*—especially the Lord's Prayer must belong here—and here the disciples must have come to know the special way that Jesus had of 'breaking bread' which gave rise to the legend of the Emmaus road (Luke 24:35).[6]

In reference to the continued meal practices of these earliest Christian communities, Nathan Mitchell also notes that:

> Many of the practices and beliefs we modern Christians take for granted were not so obvious to the earliest generations of believers. Among these was the ticklish question of whether Jewish and Gentile Christians could sit down together at the same table. (For many Jews, eating with Gentiles would have meant breaking God's law and becoming unclean.) Was eucharistic dining destined to be a *barrier* separating persons along racial and ethnic lines, or would it become a *bridge* bringing them together? Underlying this question were even more basic questions: Should the Christian community be a closed one, or one that is multicultural, multi-ethnic and racially diverse? Are the disciples of Jesus radically exclusive or inclusive? . . . Christians such as the evangelist Mark came down strongly on the side of *inclusivity*, and they

structured their reports of Jesus' meals to support this point of view. In so doing, Mark redefined discipleship and holiness in terms of food. Becoming a disciple, participating in the new kind of holiness envisioned by Jesus, meant taking part in an inclusive table fellowship. It entailed a revolutionary (and highly controversial) understanding of social status and hierarchy. It meant associating with—and offering the reign (presence) of God to—persons who, by the normal standards of Judaism, were wicked. The primary personal and social virtue sought among the members of this newly emergent, culturally/racially/ethnically diversified community was to be *diakonia*, service at table, the work of a slave.[7]

Regarding "initiation" into such a diverse and inclusive "table companionship" in the historical ministry of Jesus, it is important to underscore the fact that nowhere do the Gospels record anything specific about rites of entrance or preparation for this meal sharing with Jesus. Rather, to use our own now traditional sacramental language, the meal itself was not the *culmination* of initiation but appears rather as the *inception*, the very *beginnings* of initiation, the "sacrament" *of* initiation, if you will, *the* rite of incorporation into Christ. Nothing, not even baptism, and certainly nothing like confirmation, were required as preparatory steps.[8] Entrance to the meal of God's reign, anticipated and incarnated in the very life, ministry, and meals of Jesus of Nazareth was granted by Jesus himself and granted especially to those who were *not* prepared and *not* (yet) converted, to the godless and undeserving, to the impure, and the unworthy. Conversion itself, it appears, was not a pre-requisite for but a consequence of this encounter with Jesus at table. Indeed, one does not earn the labels of "drunkard and glutton," or "friend of tax collectors and sinners" when following prescribed social, religious, or ritual behavior. One earns such labels only by scandalizing the expectations and suppositions of others.

I am well aware that much of this flies in the face of our own religious and, especially, our educated *liturgical* sensibilities. And it is not surprising that from early on, the church became concerned with the need to shield, guard, restrict, or fence the meal with the result that, depending upon the historical period and tradition, only the baptized, or only the confirmed, or only those who have been to confession, or only the truly converted, or only those who have been prepared properly, or only those who have reached the age of reason, or only those in communion with this particular bishop, or only those who are card-carrying members of this particular ecclesial tradition are welcomed to Jesus' egalitarian, inclusive, challenging, status and role-reversing "table companionship" as it is celebrated here and now at this table. Such exclusion from the church's meal for a variety of reasons is very much a part of the meal tradition we have inherited in our own day.

The overcoming of centuries of such exclusionary development in eucharistic practice, even *within* and between the churches, is not likely to happen in the foreseeable future. There are, however, those who call us prophetically to examine those practices and attitudes seriously and critically. Reformed theologian Jürgen Moltmann wrote over twenty years ago that:

> . . . the Eucharist, like the meals held by Jesus with 'sinners and publicans,' must also be celebrated with the unrighteous, those who have no rights and the godless from the 'highways and hedges' of society, in all their profanity, and should no longer be limited, as a religious sacrifice, to the inner circle of the devout, to those who are members of the same denomination. The Christian church can re-introduce the divisions between the religious and the profane and between those who are within and those who are without, only at the price of losing its own identity as the church of the crucified Christ.[9]

Along similar lines, Nathan Mitchell writes that one aspect of our liturgical obedience to the command of Jesus, to "Do this is memory of [him]," is that:

> "[Our] *table must be as inclusive as God's mercy*. It must embrace the sinner, the 'morally irregular,' the 'ritually unclean.' *It must welcome precisely those for whom there is no room at any other table.*"[10]

While, thanks to a recent study by Andrew McGowan, one must be very cautious about basing current sacramental and liturgical practice on a reconstruction of what the historical Jesus may or may not have done,[11] one thing, at least, should be quite clear: Eucharist and church, table companionship and community, meals and discipleship, Mass, mission, and ministry go together. Indeed, the church into which we are initiated, by whatever means, is, essentially, composed of the table companions of Jesus, the community of Jesus' disciples and servants, whose identity is celebrated and continually constituted at the church's banquet table.

Similarly, the Christian tradition throughout the ages has rightly continued to emphasize the central importance of this meal both by placing a table, the altar, as the very symbolic and functional center of the community's public worship space (with the baptismal font, traditionally, in a separate building—the "baptistery"—altogether) and by asserting theologically that the Eucharist itself, in the words of Thomas Aquinas, is "the summit of the spiritual life, and the goal of all the sacraments,"[12] or, as in the words of Canon 897 in the current Code of Canon Law:

> The eucharistic sacrifice . . . is the summit and source of all Christian worship and life; it signifies and effects the unity of the people of God and achieves the building up of the body of Christ. The other sacraments and all the ecclesiastical works of the apostolate are closely related to the Holy Eucharist and are directed to it.[13]

Given the centrality of table companionship in Jesus' own ministry and the life of the earliest Christian communities, there is something downright biblical about this architectural and theological continuation in the life of the church. And one implication of this for the practice of Christian initiation should be quite clear, namely, initiation into Christ and the church—at whatever age and at whatever level of preparation and understanding—is nothing other than initiation into Jesus' table companionship. Such is certainly the theological understanding behind the introductory statement in the RCIA that in the Eucharist "the newly baptized reach the culminating point in their Christian initiation."[14] And such is certainly behind the statement of Aidan Kavanagh that: "in baptism the Eucharist begins, and in the Eucharist baptism is sustained. From this premier sacramental union flows all the church's life."[15]

## II. A Reconsideration of "Confirmation" within the Whole Initiation Process

If the church is, essentially, a banquet society, a eucharistic community, the historic communal extension of Jesus' own table companionship, then the call to restore "the Eucharist [to] its proper significance as the culmination of Christian initiation" suggests that whatever gets in the way of clearly expressing this reality in the life of the church needs to be seriously re-evaluated. At the very least, especially in relationship to the initiation of young children, it means that a close look must be given to that initiatory rite known as "confirmation," especially in its inseparable relationship to baptism. In the current Roman RCIA the connection between these two sacramental moments is explicit and clear. Paragraph 215 states:

> The conjunction of the two celebrations [baptism and confirmation] signifies the unity of the paschal mystery, the close link between the mission of the Son and the outpouring of the Holy Spirit, and the connection between the two sacraments through which the Son and the Holy Spirit come with the Father to those who are baptized.[16]

But in spite of this, confusion reigns with regard to confirmation in the churches of today. For if the joining of baptism and confirmation surely does "signify the unity of the paschal mystery," the very unity of our Trinitarian God in the saving economy of grace, then what mystery can possibly be signified in the situation of those only *baptized* in infancy, with confirmation separated from baptism by an interval of time that, according to the American Catholic bishops, can range from as few as seven (the traditional canonical age) to as many as *eighteen* years? Is *this*, I ask, the unity of the paschal mystery?

It is the separation of these two ritual moments from the inclusive pattern of initiation—the water bath with its subsequent anointing with chrism and the episcopal unit of pneumatic hand-laying with prayer and concluding consignation with chrism—within the Roman Rite and in those churches following the practice of Rome,[17] which has caused the confusion both historically and theologically. Within that rite a presbyter or deacon may baptize and perform the first post-baptismal anointing, but, until the current RCIA (1972), and then only in the case of adults or children of catechetical age, a bishop as the "ordinary" rather than "original" minister must himself administer that ritual which has come to be called "confirmation." While within Rome the sheer number of available bishops allowed the unitive celebration of initiation to continue there for quite some time,[18] it was primarily in dioceses outside of Rome where the separation of these moments was most clearly evidenced. Such a separation was theologically justified both by the famous letter of Pope Innocent I to Decentius of Gubbio (461), in which Innocent explicitly reserved the second post-baptismal anointing to the bishop (*pontifex*) and referred to this episcopal ritual act of hand-laying and anointing as "delivering the Holy Spirit, the Paraclete,"[19] and, ultimately, by a fifth-century homily of Faustus of Riez, which referred to the gift of the now separated rite of "confirmation" as being that of the Holy Spirit increasing grace and strengthening the candidate for battle, an understanding that, through Thomas Aquinas, was to become classic in Roman sacramental theology.[20] This, combined with the growing privatization of infant baptism, a high infant mortality rate, and the increasing influence of the Augustinian doctrine of original sin, led even further to seeing the split between these two initiatory ritual moments as justified, natural, and logical.

Catholic liturgist, Fr. Paul Turner, in his recent study of confirmation, under the delightful title of *Confirmation: The Baby in Solomon's Court*, notes that what is called confirmation has functioned and continues to function in three distinct ways in the life of the church. Turner writes:

> Our liturgies tell us we have three separate needs: the need to emphasize the gift of the Spirit in the rites of initiation, the need to mark a transfer of membership from

another Christian church . . ., and the need for children baptized in infancy to affirm their baptism and strengthen their faith and commitment . . .

. . . A rite of initiation is not the same as a rite of transfer or of commitment. Rites of transfer only heighten the intolerable situation of Christian disunity. And the need to recommit and celebrate the strengthening of faith is a need best ritualized by a repeatable celebration . . .

. . . If we could start all over and imagine a day when our ancestors devised these rituals, if we could say, 'We need a rite of initiation, a rite of transfer, and a rite of maturity,' would we choose the *same* rite and the *same* name for all three events? Of course not, yet this is the burden we have laid on the sacrament of confirmation.[21]

Similarly, Dominican liturgical scholar Gerard Austin writes:

Confirmation is not a reaffirmation of a previous baptism; it is not the ritualization of a key moment in the human life cycle. It is, rather the gift of the Spirit *tied intimately to the water-bath* that prepares one for the reception of the body and blood of Christ as a full member of the church.[22]

Indeed, as the 1992 FDLC position statement makes clear, along with restoring "the Eucharist [to] its proper significance as the culmination of Christian initiation," confirmation itself also must be restored to baptism in all cases, not just in those rites designed for *adult* initiation. For baptism is the only context in which "confirmation" makes any liturgical, ecclesiological, trinitarian, and sacramental sense as the ritualization of the Spirit gift in Christian initiation. Without that baptismal context, confirmation remains, as many have said, a "rite in search of a meaning or theology."

Let's simply place confirmation back where it belongs—as the inseparable concluding seal of the baptismal rite itself whenever baptism takes place, and, as a consequence, let us be done with all the debates about knowledge, preparation and age. Perhaps then we can get busy on life-long *mystagogy*, and the life-long return to the font as we seek to live out in the Spirit the implications of our new birth! Perhaps only then may we become clear on the Eucharist itself as the "culmination" of initi-ation rather than do the theological gymnastics of trying to fig-ure out why one who has received first Communion already, the very sign of the fullness of initiation according to Catholic theol-ogy, still needs to be confirmed in order to "complete" that initi-ation into Christ.

## III. The Communion of all the Initiated

Closely related to the issue of the intimate connection between baptism and confirmation is the question of Communion reception. If it is nothing other than the inseparable unity of water and the Holy Spirit that makes Christians, that ini-tiates people into the body of Christ, the church, then it should be clear that the very means by which the church sacramentality and liturgically expresses its self-identity *as* church, that is, the Eucharist, must be for *all* who are initiated into the Christian community, which, at heart, is nothing other than the continua-tion of the table companionship of Jesus himself. The recovery of such a foundational understanding of initiation as entry to the eucharistic companionship of the church then calls us rightly to an advocacy for and practice of the Communion participation of all the baptized, along the lines of the pristine tradition of the Orthodox East from as far back as we can go and along the lines of the tradition of Rome and the West for at least the first Christian millennium. As Aidan Kavanagh says: "although no person has a right to baptism, the baptized *do* possess rights to confirmation and the Eucharist."[23] Or, in the words of the *Lutheran Book of Worship*, "Holy Communion is the birthright of the baptized."[24] Or, still, to say that in yet another way:

> If the Eucharist is the weekly constitutive act of the church, and if participation in that Eucharist signifies both our membership in the body and as such our alle-giance to Christ himself, what are we doing when we

baptize infants and young children and then refuse to admit them to the very act that both signifies and effects that membership?[25]

Why among us is the first post-baptismal act for infants often that of an excommunication from the very table companionship into which they were just initiated? Nothing could be more contrary to the spirit of the church's classic tradition. For, as Robert Taft has noted:

> modern historical research and theological reflection have shown that the universal primitive tradition of both East and West viewed the liturgical completion of Christian Initiation as one integral rite comprising three moments of baptism, chrismation, and Eucharist, and without all three the process is incomplete.[26]

The 1992 FDLC position statement clearly indicates this kind of recovery of the intimate connection between the full initiation of young children and eucharistic participation, and, so rightly advocates for the Communion of baptized and confirmed infants. In so doing, the members of the FDLC have joined a large ecumenical company of contemporary Christians, not only those from the Eastern traditions but Episcopalians and Lutherans throughout the world. In 1991, for example, the Evangelical Lutheran Church in Canada (ELCIC) adopted its own *Statement on Sacramental Practices*, which reads in part:

> In baptism we are incorporated into the body of Christ, the Church. In Holy Communion the Church is nourished and strengthened. Therefore we speak of and practise Communion of the baptized . . . The Lord's supper is God's meal for the baptized. Admission to the supper is by Christ's invitation, offered through the church to the baptized.[27]

Similarly, following the lead of its Lutheran neighbors to the north, a task force appointed by the Evangelical Lutheran

Church in America (ELCA) produced and accepted in 1997 *The Use of the Means of Grace: A Statement on the Practice of Word and Sacrament*. In this document the following statement appears:

> Infants and children may be communed for the *first time* during the service in which they are baptized . . . When infants and young children are communed, the parents and sponsors receive instruction and the children are taught throughout their development.[28]

And, it is important to note that in the Episcopal Church in the USA, at least within a number of its dioceses, the practice of communing *all* the baptized from the moment of their baptism on is reaching the status of a norm.[29]

To understand these recent ecumenical developments, it is so important for us to be grounded solidly in the historical development of the relationship between Christian initiation and Communion practices in the tradition of the Western churches. For this the classic study of J.D.C. Fisher, *Christian Initiation: Baptism in the Medieval West*,[30] remains a most helpful and indispensable guide. According to Fisher, the story of Christian initiation in the medieval West is the story of sacramental and liturgical dissolution, disintegration, and separation. While scholars today would want to nuance a number of his positions, Fisher speaks of four unfortunate developments: (1) the separation of confirmation from baptism;[31] (2) the separation of Communion reception from Christian initiation; (3) the separation of initiation from Easter/Pentecost;[32] and (4) the fragmentation of the unitive rite of initiation into three distinct sacraments separated by increasingly larger intervals of time. On the separation of confirmation and Communion specifically, Fisher summarizes, saying:

> For over a thousand years the Church in the West gave confirmation to children at any age at their initiation . . . But when because of practical difficulties and other causes, . . . it came about that the majority of candidates for confirmation were not infants but adolescents, the Church in the West began to say, 'Infants are not now presented for

confirmation: therefore infants do not need confirmation; the Church normally gives confirmation to adolescents: therefore the grace conveyed by confirmation must be the spiritual strength particularly needed by those entering adolescence.' Similarly for a thousand years the Western Church saw nothing objectionable in giving Communion to newly baptized infants. But when in the 12th and 13th centuries the doctrine of transubstantiation was established, making the Church unwilling to tolerate any longer those accidents which were bound to occur sometimes in the communicating of infants, the Communion of infants came to an end, though not at the same time in all Churches. Then after infants had in fact ceased to receive Communion, the Church began to say, 'Infants are not allowed to receive Communion; the Church cannot be supposed to have excluded them from Communion without good cause; therefore infants have no need of sacramental Communion, and the grace which they receive in baptism must be supposed to suffice until they are of an age to commit actual sin.'[33]

It must be noted, however, that it is not the *doctrine* of transubstantiation that led to the decline of infant Communion. More important factors were the changes occurring in Communion practices themselves prior to the promulgation of this thirteenth-century doctrine, namely, the lack of frequent Communion participation on the part of the laity in general, the growing clericalization of the Eucharist due to developments in the theology of priestly ordination, a growing and increasing scrupulosity about the eucharistic elements (e.g., "may lay persons receive Communion in the hand or only in the mouth from the consecrated hands of a priest?", and "are infants able to swallow the host?"), and, especially, the withdrawal of the cup from the laity and the concomitant development of a eucharistic piety centered almost exclusively on the host. When the cup was withdrawn from the laity, previous practices of communing infants by means of a finger dipped in the cup or reception from the cup by means of a kind of "leaf" or "spoon" naturally disappeared as well.[34]

In spite of these historical developments, which certainly underscore that Christian initiation has undergone some serious disintegration and fragmentation, it must be emphasized here that the recent ecumenical calls for restoring both Communion and "confirmation" to baptism at whatever age are not coming about because of a sacramental romanticism, or from any attempt at a liturgical repristination of a supposed, normative "Golden Age" of the church of the first few centuries. Far from it. Rather, such a move is coming about, primarily, because of a new recovery of the fullness of the theology of initiation itself, because of the rootedness of all Christian initiation and life in the very graciousness of God, the God who through both Word and Sacrament always acts first, always acts in love prior to our action, leading us by the Holy Spirit to the response of faith, hope, and love within the community of grace. Again, as Austin states:

> Such a practice [i.e., the uniting of all three sacraments whenever baptism takes place] would underscore the reality that God takes the initiative, that baptism-confirmation-Eucharist form an essential unity, and that admission to Eucharist is built on incorporation into Christ and not upon something extrinsic such as knowledge or age . . . Such an approach would not destroy programs of religious catechesis; rather it would base such programs on personal development and needs and would be ongoing, rather than coming to a halt after the reception of confirmation.[35]

Closely parallel to this central theological orientation of the inseparable unity of the three initiation rites are the insights of a number of contemporary educators and social scientists, who assert that it is precisely within what some have called the "first stage of faith," that is, ages 2–6, where children possess the greatest and longlasting responsiveness to images, rituals, and symbols.[36] Given this, it should become increasingly clear as well that the denial of the Eucharist to the youngest of baptized children is nothing other than the denial of the *primary* way in which they actually *can* participate in the symbolic, ritual, and image-laden liturgical self-expression of the faith community. If we wait until age 7 or later to introduce them to eucharistic participation, that is, until a time in which they can be catechized, prepared, and begin to "understand" the implications of the Eucharist cognitively and rationally, we have waited too long, I fear. Eucharistic faith is not equal to cognitive understanding. Faith is not only rational but pre-cognitive, pre-rational as well. In the Pauline New Testament sense, faith is not intellectual acceptance of or assent to propositional revelation, but trust. And such trust develops, it seems, only in relationship, only in an environment, in a community of trust such as the family or the church. James Fowler writes that:

> We are endowed at birth with nascent capacities for faith. How these capacities are activitated and grow depends to a large extent on how we are welcomed into the world and what kinds of environments we grow in. Faith is interactive and social; it requires community, language, ritual, and nurture. Faith is also shaped by initiatives from beyond us and other people, initiatives of spirit and grace. How these latter initiatives are recognized and imaged, or unperceived and ignored, powerfully affects the shape of faith in our lives.[37]

If I may be anecdotal here, my own experiences of children and Eucharist have convinced me completely not only of the desirability but of the sheer rightness of communing all the initiated. My own daughter, age 2 at the time, who had been a regular communicant—although secretly—from the time of her infant baptism, surprised me greatly during dinner one Sunday noon. After worshipping at a nearby parish that used a style of bread for Eucharist closely resembling mid-eastern pita bread, our dinner that day, although unintentionally, included pita bread as well. I remember my daughter holding a piece of bread in her hand, and pointing both to a Byzantine icon of Christ above our table and to that piece of bread, she said something like, "Christ Jesus there, Christ Jesus right here." In her own way, she had made some rather interesting and proper theological-liturgical-sacramental connections. Similarly, in a parish I once served, where we had moved from once-a-month to every

Sunday Eucharist, I remember a young mother telling me of the influence this had begun to have on her own pre-school daughter, who, without any prompting, had all of a sudden begun to recite the words of institution aloud as she rode along in the car. Alternatively, I was recently told by one of my graduate students of her experience, where a young child she knew had flatly refused to go forward any longer for a blessing at the time of Communion distribution. When asked why, the child responded that the last time he had gone he had been "Xed" out by the Communion minister, who instead of giving him bread had traced an "X" over him, telling him that he didn't belong. Children are formed by symbol, by image, by ritual. Even when we adults think that we are being inclusive in our Communion practices by, at least, giving them a blessing, or, as in one case I have heard of, giving a *grape* (!) to non-communing children, we may, in fact, be only re-enforcing their *exclusion* from Jesus' table. When children stayed in the pews and did not come forward during Communion distribution at all, we were, at least, being consistent in our exclusionary practices.

If children who have not yet reached catechetical age can be baptized, and if confirmation is properly restored as nothing other than the concluding ritualization and sacramentalizing Spirit-gift and seal of baptism, then there is absolutely no reason, theological or otherwise, why these children should not be communed as well. As a Greek Orthodox woman once explained to a youth group I brought to her parish to experience Byzantine Liturgy: "We feed our small children regular food without expecting them to know yet about vitamins and nutrition. So also we Orthodox feed them the spiritual food of the Eucharist without expecting them to know yet the meaning of this Gift. Both foods are necessary for life." But perhaps it was Mark Searle, who best summed up the rationale for restoring both confirmation and Communion to the baptism of young children, saying:

> At a time when the Church is so intent on rescuing the humane values of Christianity and is concerned to do greater justice to the role of the family . . . and a time when the role of the nonrational and pre-rational dimensions of

the life of faith is being recovered, perhaps infant initiation ought to be seen less as a problem to be grappled with than as an opportunity to be grasped. Far from barring children from the font, the chrism, and the altar, the Church should welcome their participation in these sacraments as a reminder both of the catholicity of the Church and of the fact that, no matter how informed or committed we might be as adults, when we take part in the sacramental liturgies of the Church we are taking part in more than we know.[38]

## IV. Some Implications of the FDLC Position Statement

The call for a discussion of the restoration of confirmation and Communion to baptism in all cases has vast implications for some far reaching but concrete changes in the life and practice of the church as a whole, but especially within the United States. Here I can only list and briefly comment on what I see as six of these major implications.

First of all, along with a strong focus on the church as a table companionship, on the public celebration of the Eucharist, as the characteristic mark of the church, comes, I believe, the need to recover in practice the *corporate* and *public* character of baptism and confirmation in all cases as taking place within and leading to eucharistic participation. As the General Introduction to *Christian Initiation* makes clear in the case of infants: "As far as possible, all recently born babies should be baptized at a common celebration on the same day."[39] And, as the Introduction to the *Rite of Baptism for Children* states:

> To bring out the paschal character of baptism, it is recommended that the sacrament be celebrated during the Easter Vigil or on Sunday, when the Church commemorates the Lord's resurrection. On Sunday, baptism may be celebrated even during Mass, so that the entire community may be present and the relationship between baptism and Eucharist may be clearly seen; *but this should not be done too often.*[40]

One way to ensure both "a common celebration on the same day" for "all recently born babies" at a "not too often" Sunday eucharistic celebration, simply, would be to schedule periodic Sunday or festival baptismal Masses at which recently born babies would be baptized, confirmed, and communed together.[41] Such could be easily done, it appears to me, in close connection with a rediscovery of the numerous initiation-oriented feasts present throughout the liturgical year. For good theological reasons we have centered our attention on the connection between Easter, especially the Easter Vigil, and Christian initiation. But even if centered here the baptismal tradition of the church is much richer than this. Over the past twenty years or so, contemporary liturgical scholarship[42] has helped us understand that, while there was an early *preference* for initiation at Easter in the churches of North Africa and Rome, other churches—e.g., those of Syria, Egypt, and the non-Roman Western churches in Gaul and Spain—tended to focus on other occasions like Epiphany, understood, of course, as the great theophany of Christ in the Jordan, and that a Romans 6 (death-resurrection) theology of baptism came to the forefront of sacramental theology universally only within a fourth-century post-Nicene context. Prior to that, the dominant interpretation and paradigm of initiation appears to have been that of Jesus' own baptism in the Jordan and the re-birth imagery of John 3.[43] And from such a focus in this equally ancient and biblical tradition comes a whole cluster of initiation images which have little to do with passing from death to life, or with sharing in the dying and rising of Christ through baptism. Such images, extremely suggestive in the case of infants, include seeing the font as *womb*, rather than tomb, literally called the "Jordan" itself in some traditions, images like "adoption, divinization, sanctification, gift of the Spirit, indwelling, glory, power, wisdom, rebirth, restoration, [and] mission."[44] Other feasts, then, such as Epiphany, the Baptism of our Lord, or Pentecost, or All Saints, or the annual feast of the parish patron saint, all of which could be preceded by some adaptation of the catechumenal process for the parents and sponsors of infants and all of which could receive their own baptismal vigil, would be ideal occasions for such common celebrations. We have clearly recovered the baptismal focus of Lent and

Easter. Why not, for example, Advent as well? Initiation into Christ is more than participation in his death and resurrection. And we would do well in our catechesis and celebration throughout the year to recover and re-emphasize this diversity of images.

The key in all this, however, is the *public* and *corporate* celebration of these three initiation sacraments. I do not believe that the current normal practice in the Christian East should be followed. That is, while in the churches of the East all three sacraments—baptism, chrismation, and first Communion—are administered within the same celebration, these celebrations tend to be rather privatized and limited in terms of the participation of the local Christian community. If all three are to be restored to the time of baptism in the Roman Rite, it is imperative, in the light of official documents, that they be done publicly and corporately at Mass "so that the entire community may be present and the relationship between baptism and Eucharist may be clearly seen."

Second, it seems obvious that the restoration of first Communion to the time of baptism carries with it the implication that Communion from the cup never be merely *permitted* on occasion but likewise *restored* as the normal and regular practice within Roman Catholic eucharistic celebrations. As history teaches us, it was the withdrawal of the cup from the laity that contributed strongly to the cessation of infant Communion in the first place. Consequently, the restoration of the communing of all the initiated, not only at the time of baptism but ever there after, calls for the restoration of such a practice throughout Roman Catholic parish life and practice. After all, it is *only* from the cup that the youngest of initiated children will be able to commune for the first time and on a regular basis until older.

But how is this to be done? In a day and age when, for a variety of reasons, the sharing of the cup itself has come under close scrutiny, the dipping of a eucharistic minister's or parent's finger *in* the cup and then in the mouths of infants will surely not commend itself as a workable solution. Rather, an alternative must be found and it may be that one unending, seemingly unrelated, gift-giving tradition provides us with the beginnings of such an alternative. I find it extremely fascinating and of potential assistance here that in some places the giving of a silver spoon as a normal baby or baptismal gift has continued. What other significance can this silver spoon possibly have other than as a remnant of a once common practice of it being used to administer first Communion? Such, at least, is the opinion of Balthasar Fischer,[45] and it would not be out of the question to restore this practice more broadly. Not only would Hallmark and religious supply stores love the sales boost and be able to market a whole new line of baptism/first Communion-oriented gifts, but as "guardians and keepers of the eucharistic spoon," parents could continue signifying their sacramental responsibilities in the liturgy by presenting this spoon along with their child to the eucharistic ministers each Sunday. Similarly, together with the baptismal candle and garment, this spoon itself could serve as a fitting reminder of the fullness of initiation at a time in which more formal catechesis and ongoing mystagogy begins to take place. Such eucharistic use of the common baby spoon seems to me much better than reserving it for formal dinner occasions or for oatmeal or squash.

Third, the restoration of confirmation and Communion to the time of baptism implies that the provision granted for the *presbyteral* confirmation of adults and children of catechetical age in the RCIA be extended to include younger children as well. What this means is that the FDLC position statement affirms, in principle, that preserving the unity of the paschal mystery signified by these three sacraments is more important than even the presence of the bishop at confirmation. As this proposed conversation goes forward, the following insight of Gerard Austin is well worth serious consideration:

> The East has preserved the presence of the bishop at confirmation by the insistence that he bless the chrism and thus be vicariously present in the chrism used. The West, on the other hand, has sacrificed the unity of the paschal mystery to hang on to the presence of the bishop. It is physically impossible for the bishop to be present at all baptisms. It must be asked—has not a higher value been sacrificed to maintain a lesser one?[46]

Closely related to this canonical issue, of course, is another, more difficult one, I fear. While, according to Canon 891, local conferences of Catholic Bishops can "determine another age" for confirmation than that of the age of discretion,[47] presumably even that of infancy if they so desire, Canons 913 and 914 on eucharistic participation seem to be quite clear that before receiving Communion children are "required [to] have sufficient knowledge and careful preparation," and be "able to distinguish the body of Christ from ordinary food and receive Communion reverently."[48] In fact, Canon 914 explicitly instructs pastors to be "vigilant lest any children come to the Holy Banquet who have not reached the use of reason or whom he judges are not sufficiently disposed."[49] Since Canon Law, then, seems to be directly opposed to restoring Communion to the time of baptism in the case of infants, a fourth implication of this FDLC position statement is nothing less than a call for a fundamental revision of Canon Law itself. Especially here do I see the need to question seriously the whole relationship of "knowledge," "preparation," and "age of discretion" or "reason" and eucharistic participation. This relationship, it must be underscored, is a legacy from the Middle Ages, from the Fourth Lateran Council (1215) to be exact, and stands in direct contradiction to the practice of the universal church of the early centuries and the Eastern Orthodox Churches of today. In this context appeal is often made to 1 Corinthians 11:29: "all who eat and drink without discerning the body, eat and drink judgement against themselves." But, as modern New Testament exegetes tell us, the body to be discerned here is not the body of Christ as eucharistic host but the community as the body of Christ himself, a portion of which was apparently and regularly excluded from the "Lord's Supper" in Corinth.[50] Indeed, in our own day it may well be that by excluding some of the baptized, namely infants, from the table, we, like those in Corinth, are the ones guilty of not truly discerning the "Body."

A fifth implication of the restoration of these three sacraments to the time of baptism in all cases is that the customary link between religious education, age of the candidates, and the reception of the two post-baptismal initiation sacraments of confirmation and Communion would be broken once and for all. If not handled well, a radical break in long standing practices and associations such as these could have devastating consequences for the ongoing life and ministry of parishes. On the one hand, the restoration envisioned might finally make it clear that infants, children, and adults are, indeed, equals in Christ, who all begin the life of faith together in the same way and in the some place by means of water and the Spirit. As such, all are in need of constant and life-long mystagogy, life-long formation in the mystery of faith granted them as sheer gift in the font, the chrism, and the table. Religious education, then, would focus less on "sacramental preparation," as it is called, less on preparatory catechesis, and more on mystagogical catechesis, more on what the gifts received in these sacraments mean for ongoing life in Christ and his body, the church.

On the other hand, however, the anthropological need for passage rites, or the need for rites of faith commitment and baptismal affirmation, needs currently met by first Communion and confirmation, is a need that must be acknowledged and met in some way. With a restored unitive initiation practice for all ages, would it not be possible for Roman Catholics to develop new, and repeatable, rites of faith commitment and baptismal affirmation, rites which mark significant transition moments in life? Lutherans, for example, have a rite called "Affirmation of Baptism," which was intended, originally, to function not only as the culmination of a program of catechetical instruction for adolescents but in numerous other cases:

> . . . by connecting these significant transitions with the baptismal understanding of our dying and rising with Christ. These rites mark moments when the faith given in baptism finds new expression, and the spiritual gifts given in baptism are stirred up to meet new challenges.[51]

Since first reconciliation, for example, sometimes understood as even a fourth sacrament of initiation, would no longer occur in the immediate context of first Communion, this sacrament could now be given renewed attention, finally, as the sacrament of reconciliation with the church into which one, in fact, *has* been fully initiated. And, further, American Catholics are not really strangers to additional rites related to the initiation sacraments at all. There was a time, not that long ago, where, in a number of places in the United States, as in France and Germany, a distinction was made between "first Communion" at about age 7, of course, and "first *solemn* Communion" at a later age. Is there any reason why some kind of special eucharistic celebration marking the culmination of specific catechesis on the Eucharist could not be reclaimed today as well?

Finally, since a change like this would take some time to come about, the last implication I see coming from this proposal is the need for diocesan liturgists and pastors to provide strong, educated, ongoing, and patient leadership. What this proposal asks for is nothing less than a new conversion, a radical conversion which cuts to the very roots of so much that is, and has been, taken for granted in Roman Catholic parish life. This means, then, that just as much, if not more, attention needs to be given to this as has been given to the many dimensions of the RCIA. That is, just as much attention, if not more, must be given to mystagogy as has been given to catechesis; to the role of children *as* children as has been given to so-called mature, adult faith; just as much, if not more, to God's surprising graciousness mediated as sheer gift in the font, the chrism, and the table, as has been given to adult response and commitment.

I sometimes fear that the enormous success of the RCIA in the United States, in part, is due to the fact, rightly or wrongly, that it can so easily be adapted to and interpreted as compatible with our own cultural stress on individualism, personal independence, and, at least, implicit Pelagianism. No one questions the appropriateness of celebrating all three initiation sacraments for adults or children of catechetical age. After all, they have been prepared through the stages of catechumen and elect and have made some kind of faith commitment and decision. But to confirm and commune those infants and children who have not reached catechetical age challenges this attitude radically and calls us as church back to a spirituality which so clearly focusses on community rather than the individual, on dependency rather than independence, on mystery rather than knowledge, and on grace rather than on response. What the late Eugene Maly said a number of years ago in relationship to infant baptism certainly applies also to the full initiation of infants. Maly wrote:

Through infant baptism we *initiate* a person into a faith-community long before he or she can choose whether to belong. And through infant baptism we also *celebrate* a person's salvation long before he or she consciously experiences the need to be saved or can take any responsibility for turning self toward God. Something about this flies in the face of very basic notions in our culture about individual freedom and the importance of personal choice—in short, our insistence on individualism. We want to believe that we choose God (rather than that God chooses us). We want to believe that we can and should save ourselves (rather than that we are saved) . . . [B]iblical faith challenges our basic human temptation to individualism. Infant baptism is . . . one way we have institutionalized our conviction that community is central to Christian life, to God's plan of salvation.[52]

What this FDLC position statement implies, then, at heart, is a radical, counter-cultural, and anti-Pelagian vision of the church. Because this is so, diocesan liturgists and pastors intent on realizing this vision in the church should expect great struggle and conflict as they seek to bring this to new birth.

## V. Conclusion

The Eucharist constitutes the culmination and goal of the initiatory process and continues to serve as the repeatable sacrament of Christian initiation for all who are washed in baptism and sealed by the Spirit gift. Although underscored clearly in the sequence of the RCIA, both the sequence and separation of rites regularly employed in the initiation of infants often robs the Eucharist of its culminating role by setting confirmation in its place. Furthermore, the separation of the initiation sacraments by intervals of seven to eighteen years in the case of those baptized in infancy seriously distorts the unity of the paschal mystery, since it is precisely the integral and necessary connection of these sacraments that signifies the unity of that Mystery in the saving economy of the trinitarian God.

The mere fact that today we note a disjunction and apparent contradiction and tension between the unitive sequence of the RCIA and the initiatory process employed for those baptised in infancy is due, in no small part, to the contemporary recovery of the centrality of eucharistic participation itself. From Pius X's *Quam Singulari* in 1910 through Vatican II's *Constitution on the Sacred Liturgy* (1963) and the Missal of Paul VI (1969) to the present, Roman Catholics in the twentieth century have experienced the eucharistic liturgy and participation in the Eucharist once again, as in the early church, as being at the very center and source of all Christian life and activity. In such a context, together with the development of the RCIA itself and the celebration of Christian initiation at the restored Easter Vigil, it was only inevitable that the question of who may fully participate in the Eucharist and when would be raised anew. As David Holeton says:

> Any church that begins to encourage frequent Communion among the laity in the context of a piety that sees the Eucharist as a communal action rather than as an action done on the behalf of a collection of individuals cannot help but pose new questions as to who is to be included in the eucharistic community. Once the community becomes one in which all are accepted in its corporate life despite age, or intelligence, or social status, the question of universal participation in the Eucharist becomes a real one. Once the community shares in the Eucharist the experience becomes a conversion. You can never be as you were before.[53]

What is happening today, I believe, is an awareness that the sacraments of Christian initiation have been only partially reformed, at least in the case of those baptized in infancy. The next step that needs to happen, and I would place this high on the agenda of the ongoing liturgical renewal, is to bring that reform to its inevitable completion and conclusion in a common process and unitive sacramental sequence so that all who are initiated as one body and one spirit in Christ may truly share in the table companionship of Jesus as the very culmination of their water bath and Spirit seal within that community of disciples called church. This is the catechetical, liturgical, and sacramental challenge that the FDLC position statement makes and, hence, the ongoing agenda which the FDLC has adopted. Such a challenge and agenda, it must be underscored, are ecumenical issues and should be carried out in an ecumenical context—at least with Lutherans and Episcopalians—as well as internally within the Roman Catholic Church.

I would be remiss, however, if I did not express my doubts as to the ultimate success of this position. There is probably too much that would have to change in theological positions, in Canon Law, and, not least, in popular perception for this to become a reality. Nevertheless, there are reasons to be cautiously hopeful. The increasing number of American Roman Catholic dioceses, for example, that have decided to celebrate both confirmation and first Communion together at age 7, in that order, is a positive, first step in the right direction. And, as a temporary measure highly consistent with current Roman Catholic Canon Law, this is to be applauded highly. But it may well be that such a "temporary measure" or first step in this direction is all that, realistically, can be hoped for in the coming years.

## Notes

[1] *FDLC Newsletter* 22 (Washington, D.C. December 1995), 45.

[2] N. Perrin, *Rediscovering the Teaching of Jesus* (San Francisco: Harper & Row, 1976), 102.

[3] N. Mitchell, *Eucharist as Sacrament of Initiation*, Forum Essays, 2 (Chicago: Liturgy Training Publications, 1994), 89–90.

[4] Perrin, op. cit., 107. This is not to say, of course, that the Last Supper of Jesus and the twelve is somehow less definitive of the Eucharist than Jesus' other meal practices. It must not be overlooked, however, that the Last Supper accounts themselves reflect the way in which the early Christians came to understand the significance of the continuation of Jesus' meal companionship among them in a post-Easter context. In other words, rather than giving us a reliable picture of the meal held on the "night he was betrayed," these accounts reflect the liturgical and catechetical traditions of the various Christian communities. On the theological and liturgical nature of these accounts cf. Nathan Mitchell, *Cult and Controversy* (New York: Pueblo, 1982), 10–43.

[5] See W. Rordorf, *Sunday* (Philadelphia: S.C.M. Press, 1968).

6 Perrin, *Rediscovering*, 107–8.

7 Mitchell, *Eucharist*, 99–100.

8 Whether Jesus himself actually baptized others, as is asserted in John 3:22, need not detain us here. Even if he did, there is no evidence to interpret this baptism as a pre-requisite for meal sharing.

9 J. Moltmann, *The Crucified God: The Cross of Christ as the Foundation and Criticism of Christian Theology* (San Francisco: Harper & Row, 1974), 44.

10 Mitchell, *Eucharist*, 100.

11 See Andrew McGowan, "The Meals of Jesus and the Meals of the Church: Eucharistic Origins and Admission to Communion," Maxwell E. Johnson and L. Edward Phillips (eds.), *Studia Liturgica Diversa: Essays in Honor of Paul F. Bradshaw* (Portland: Pastoral Press, 2004), 101–15.

12 *Summa Theologiae* III, q. 73, a. 3.

13 *Code of Canon Law: Latin-English Edition* (Washington, D.C.: Canon Law Society of America, 1983), 336–37.

14 *The Rites of the Catholic Church as Revised by the Second Vatican Ecumenical Council*, vol. 1 (Collegeville: The Liturgical Press, Pueblo, 1990), 147.

15 A. Kavanagh, *The Shape of Baptism* (New York: Pueblo, 1978), 122.

16 *The Rites*, op. cit., 146–47.

17 Outside of Rome itself, in those rites called "Gallican," "Mozarabic," or "Ambrosian," for example, no ritual ceremony comparable to episcopal "confirmation" appears to have existed until the Roman Rite is adopted.

18 Cf. the various medieval pontificals, including that of Clement VIII (1596), i.e., *after* the Council of Trent. Clement's pontifical even directs that infants be held by their sponsors for confirmation. Underscoring that infants are the expected candidates, adult candidates are to stand before the bishop with one foot on the foot of their sponsors.

19 For the text of this letter see G. Jeanes, *The Origins of the Roman* Rite, Alucin/GROW Liturgical Study 20, (Bramcote/Nottingham: Grove Books, Ltd., 1991), 19–20. On the relationship between this letter and the development of confirmation in the Roman Rite see my essay, "The Postchrismational Structure of *Apostolic Tradition* 21, the Witness of Ambrose of Milan, and a Tentative Hypothesis Regarding the Current Reform of Confirmation in the Roman Rite," *Worship* 70 (1996), 16–34, elsewhere in this volume, 63–82.

20 For the text of Faustus' homily see Paul Turner, *Sources of Confirmation: From the Fathers through the Reformers* (Collegeville: The Liturgical Press, 1993), 35–36.

21 Paul Turner, *Confirmation: The Baby in Solomon's Court* (New York: Paulist Press, 1993), 128.

22 Gerard Austin, *The Rite of Confirmation: Anointing with the Spirit* (Collegeville: The Liturgical Press, Pueblo, 1985), 146 [emphasis added].

23 A. Kavanagh, "Initiation: Baptism and Confirmation," in M. Taylor (ed.), *The Sacraments: Readings in Contemporary Sacramental Theology* (New York: Alba House, 1981), 93.

24 *Lutheran Book of Worship*, Minister's Edition (Minneapolis: Augsburg, 1978), 31.

[25] D. Holeton, *Infant Communion—Then and Now,* Grove Liturgical Study, 27 (Bramcote/Nottingham: Grove Books, Ltd., 1981), 23.

[26] Robert Taft, "On the Question of Infant Communion in the Byzantine Catholic Churches of the U.S.A.," in *Diakonia* 17 (1982), as cited by Ruth A. Meyers, "Infant Communion: Reflections on the Case from Tradition," in idem. (ed.), *Children at the Table: The Communion of All the Baptized in Anglicanism Today* (New York: The Church Hymnal Corporation, 1995), 149.

[27] Evangelical Lutheran Church in Canada, *Statement on Sacramental Practices* (1991), 5.8, 6.9.

[28] *The Use of the Means of Grace: A Statement on the Practice of Word and Sacrament* (Chicago: Evangelical Lutheran Church in America, 1997), 42. For a brief survey of changes in contemporary Lutheran practice elsewhere see my article, "The Shape of Christian Initiation in the Lutheran Churches: Liturgical Texts and Future Directions," *Studia Liturgica* 27, 1 (1997), 33–60.

[29] On this see the collection of essays edited by Ruth Meyers (ed.), op. cit.

[30] J.D.C. Fisher, *Christian Initiation: Baptism in the Medieval West* (London: SPCK, 1965). Reprinted by Chicago: Liturgy Training Publications, Hillenbrand Series, 2004.

[31] Scholars today would note that the so-called "separation" of "confirmation" from baptism was a distinct Roman phenomenon which affected the other churches of the West only when they adopted the Roman Rite. In other words, it would be difficult to speak of the "separation" of confirmation from baptism in those churches (Gallican, Mozarabic, etc.) which prior to this had no rites corresponding to Roman episcopal confirmation. Cf. G. Winkler, "Confirmation or Chrismation?" in M. Johnson (ed.), *Living Water, Sealing Spirit: Readings on Christian Initiation* [LWSS] (Collegeville: The Liturgical Press, Pueblo, 1995), 202–218; and P. Turner, "The Challenge of the Confirmation Praxis," *FDLC Newsletter* 22 (Washington, D.C.: 1995), 45–48.

[32] Here again, recent scholarship has questioned the assumed normativity of both Easter as *the* occasion for baptism and a Romans 6 paschal theology for interpreting Christian initiation in the early Church. See below, note 41.

[33] Fisher, op. cit., 139.

[34] For further discussion of changes in Communion practices, in addition to ibid., see N. Mitchell, *Cult and Controversy* (New York: Pueblo, 1982), Ruth A. Meyers, "Infant Communion," in idem. (ed.), op. cit., 146–164, and Eugene Brand, "Baptism and Communion of Infants: A Lutheran View," in Johnson (ed.), LWSS, 350–64.

[35] Austin, op. cit., 145.

[36] Cf. the work of J. Fowler, *Stages of Faith* (San Francisco: Addison-Wesley, 1981), and J. H. Westerhoff, III, *Building God's People in a Materialistic Society* (New York: HarperCollins, 1983), especially 59–78.

[37] J. Fowler, op. cit., xiii, as cited by Meyers, op. cit., 160.

[38] M. Searle, "Infant Baptism Reconsidered," in LWSS, 408–9. See also the recent Notre Dame doctoral dissertation of Clare Veronica Johnson, *Ex Ore Infantium: The Pre-Rational Child as Subject of Sacramental Action—Theological, Liturgical and Canonical Implications* (Notre Dame 2004). Herein Johnson develops a "theology of childhood," based on a Rahnerian theological anthropology in support of full Christian initiation of infants. Johnson's compelling study needs to be published and to enjoy a wide readership.

[39] *Rites*, vol. 1, 10.

[40] Ibid., 369 [emphasis added].

[41] A "Sunday" eucharistic celebration of Christian initiation need not only be interpreted as one of the "regular" Sunday Eucharists. Rather, just as special celebrations of "first Communion" and "confirmation" tend to be scheduled at other times on Sundays (e.g., afternoons and/or evenings) and infant baptisms themselves tend to be celebrated in some places in a similar fashion, there is probably no reason why periodic "Initiation Eucharists" could not be similarly planned.

[42] See Gabriele Winkler, "*Das armenische Initiationsrituale* (Orientalia Christiana Analecta 217, Rome: 1982), and Die Light-Erscheinung bei der Taufe Jesu und der Ursprung des Epiphaniefestes," *Oriens Christianus* 78 (1994), 177–229. Thomas Talley, *The Origins of the Liturgical Year*, 2nd. edition (Collegeville: The Liturgical Press, 1986); Paul Bradshaw, "'*Diem baptismo sollemniorem* ': Initiation and Easter in Christian Antiquity," in LWSS, 137–47; Maxwell Johnson, "From Three Weeks to Forty Days: Baptismal Preparation and the Origins of Lent," in LWSS, 118–36; and idem., "Preparation for Pascha? The Origins of Lent in Christian Antiquity," in Paul Bradshaw and Lawrence Hoffman (eds.), *Two Liturgical Traditions*, vol. 5: *Passover and Easter* (Notre Dame: University of Notre Press: 1999).

[43] On this see especially G. Winkler, "The Original Meaning of the Prebaptismal Anointing and its Implications," in LWSS, 58–81.

[44] Mark Searle, "Infant Baptism Reconsidered," in LWSS, 385.

[45] Cited in Holeton, op. cit., 8, note 3.

[46] Austin, op. cit., 143.

[47] *Code of Canon Law*, 334–35.

[48] Ibid., 340–41.

[49] Ibid., 342–43.

[50] See Brand, op. cit., 362ff.

[51] Evangelical Lutheran Church in America, *The Confirmation Ministry Task Force Report* (September 1993), 9. See also, Turner, *Confirmation*, op. cit., 128ff. Lutherans, however, continue to call this rite "confirmation" when used at the end of the program of catechetical instruction for adolescents. The rite itself appears in the *Lutheran Book of Worship* (Minneapolis: Augsburg, 1978), 198–201.

[52] Eugene Maly, "Still a Case for Infant Baptism?" in M. Taylor (ed.), *The Sacraments: Readings in Contemporary Sacramental Theology* (New York: Alba House, 1981), 95.

[53] Holeton, op. cit., 15.

# THE "REAL" AND MULTIPLE "PRESENCES" OF CHRIST IN CONTEMPORARY LUTHERAN LITURGICAL AND SACRAMENTAL PRACTICE

What would a contemporary Lutheran, or, more specifically, an Evangelical Lutheran Church in America (ELCA), liturgical-sacramental practice and theology look like that took seriously the multiple presences of Christ underscored by paragraph 7 of Vatican II's *Constitution on the Sacred Liturgy* (hereafter, CSL 7)? In attempting to answer such a question, I simply must state up front that there is a certain artificial quality about this exercise from the very beginning. To take what is a *Roman Catholic* "recovery" of the multiple presences of Christ in the church and then apply that "recovery" to a Lutheran—or even Anglican or Protestant—liturgical-sacramental context seems to me, at first sight anyway, to move in a backwards direction. That is, the emphases of CSL 7 on the multiple "real" presences of Christ in the church within its liturgical celebrations—the ministers, the eucharistic species, the sacraments in general, his word, and the community itself at prayer[1]—sound to Lutheran ears, at least, like a Roman Catholic vindication of what the Lutheran Reformers themselves argued within the overall context of the sixteenth century. The Lutheran Confessions, for example, couldn't be clearer in their assertion that what has been called, traditionally, the "means of grace" include, rather broadly, the spoken word, baptism, Eucharist, the power of the keys (confession and absolution), and the "mutual conversation and consolation of brethren,"[2] while being unconcerned with the precise enumeration of what may or may not be called specific "sacraments."[3] Similarly, at least Lutherans would want to point out that with regard to the presence of Christ in the "ministers," the Confessions again not only equate the "Office" of Ministry *with* word and sacrament as the very means by which the church is called into being by the Holy Spirit in the first place,[4] but have no qualms in asserting that the ordained "do not represent their own persons but the person of Christ" (*repraesentat Christi personam*) and that "when they offer the word of Christ or the sacraments, they do so in Christ's place and stead" (*Christi vice et loco porrigunt*).[5] As such, ordination itself can appropriately be called a "sacrament" by Lutherans,[6] if for no other reason, it appears, than that the ordained, "representing" the person of Christ in and to the church through the actual *doing* of the ministry of word and sacrament, become themselves concrete, embodied, or "sacramental' signs of Christ's continued presence. At the same time, a *Lutheran* reading of CSL 7, especially with regard to the presence of Christ in the community itself, would want to underscore that the ecclesiology of the Lutheran Confessions is, precisely, an ecclesiology of the liturgical assembly, which asserts that "the church is the assembly of saints [or believers] in which the Gospel is taught purely and the sacraments are administered rightly."[7] And—might I be so bold as to point out?—it was Luther himself, who, while limiting the number of sacraments to three, based on the defining criteria he *inherited* from the Western medieval tradition, nevertheless, stated, in words that sound downright prophetic *vis-à-vis* modern Roman Catholic sacramental theology, that "if I were to speak according to the usage of the Scriptures, I should have only one *single* sacrament [Christ, 1 Timothy 3:16], but with three sacramental signs."[8]

Hence, when Lutherans read CSL 7, or read in the 1993 *Directory for Ecumenism* that "baptism constitutes the *sacramental* bond of unity existing among all who through it are reborn,"[9] or hear Pope John Paul II say in his 1995 encyclical *Ut Unum Sint* that that "in the fellowship of prayer *Christ is truly present*; he prays 'in us,' 'with us,' and 'for us,'"[10] they recognize a common theological bond, heritage, and participation in the "real" presence of Christ himself. And, they would underscore strongly the following statement about the very *sacramentality* of the word itself offered by Karl Rahner and Heinrich Fries some years ago that:

> *Pulpit fellowship* is already being practiced in many cases; and it no longer presents a disquieting exception, even to Catholic Christians. But one really should think about this more than ever, *since it is precisely a pulpit fellowship which presupposes a community of faith.* Consider the reality of salvation of the word of God; consider Christ's presence in its various forms, including the form of proclamation; finally consider the theological conformity of word *and* sacrament—sacrament as visible word (*verbum visibile*), the word as audible sacrament (*sacramentum audible*).[11]

Because there is so much in common between CSL 7 and the classic Lutheran confessional, liturgical, and theological tradition, *the* question is *not* really how the *Roman Catholic* recovery of the multiple presences of Christ might shape *Lutheran* liturgical-sacramental practice and theology (even if Lutherans would be most grateful for this recovery in Roman Catholic thought and practice). Rather, the question is, what does a Lutheran liturgical-sacramental practice and theology look like when, in an ecumenical context, it takes its own classic tradition seriously? With regard to this I will divide my comments into two major sections: (1) what, in fact, has been and is happening toward a richer liturgical-sacramental life among, especially ELCA, Lutherans; and (2) what factors still need serious attention?

## I. Developments Toward a Richer Liturgical-Sacramental Life Among Lutherans

The general answer to the question of what a *Lutheran* liturgical-sacramental life looks like that takes the multiple presences of Christ seriously is rather simple. Given the commonality in texts, rites, and rubrics in the worship books of Lutherans and Roman Catholics today, it looks very much like post-Vatican II Roman Catholic worship is also supposed to look: i.e., where the word of God is proclaimed clearly, audibly, intelligibly, and with dignity by carefully prepared readers; where ministers, presiding and otherwise, know their particular roles in the assembly and carry them out in a manner befitting the worship of the trinitarian God; where bread that looks, smells, feels, and tastes like (and, of course, *is*) real bread is broken and shared and where wine, rich and good wine, is shared in common; where the other sacraments or "sacramental rites" are seen as corporate and communal events with the rich and abundant use of the sacramental signs of water and oil and the healing and benedictory gestures of handlaying and touch; where the Liturgy of the Hours is the church being itself in its constant, prayerful, eschatological, intercessory, and expectant vigil; where the paschal Triduum, especially the Great Vigil of Easter, prepared for by a renewing, baptismal in orientation, forty-day Lent and an ensuing fifty-day period of paschal joy, are seen as the pulsating center and heart beat not only of the liturgical year but of life in Christ; and where the community itself, both in assembling to do *leitourgia* and in scattering for its missions of *martyria* and *diakonia* knows itself— "fully, actively, and consciously"—as that body of Christ it receives and celebrates so that it may itself be broken for the life of the world. Indeed, within these general themes, there are several positive developments to note and to celebrate among contemporary Lutherans.

First, as the overall intent of the *Lutheran Book of Worship* itself makes clear, the place, dignity, and full celebration of baptism, including infant baptism, within the public liturgical assembly of the church is emphasized, as is the use of full immersion as the preferred mode of baptism, as well as the use of postbaptismal handlaying and anointing to signify the baptismal gift of the "seal" of the Holy Spirit. Here as well, architectural shifts geared toward providing baptismal pools and fonts enabling immersion are to be noted. Similarly, the renewing and formative power of the RCIA within Roman Catholic circles has led to new and recent adaptations of the catechumenal process in Lutheran circles—including Missouri-Synod and Evangelical Lutheran Church in Canada (ELCIC) cooperation—with the development of several catechumenal and liturgical resources under the general title of *Welcome to Christ*.[12] And, along with this, of course, comes the continual need and opportunity for the development and training of parish catechists and sponsors, and the reorganization and renewal of parish life in general centered around sacramental-liturgical formation and catechesis. While still in its infancy among Lutherans, such holds great promise for the future in the changing cultural context of a "post-Christendom" world.

With further regard to issues concerning Christian initiation, it should also be noted here that, like the unbroken initiatory tradition of the Eastern Orthodox Churches, and like the Episcopal Church, USA, the express wishes of the American Roman Catholic Federation of Diocesan Liturgical Commissions in one of its 1992 resolutions,[13] and its Canadian Lutheran (ELCIC) neighbors to the north,[14] the ELCA has also moved decisively toward instituting the communion of *all* the baptized, including the first Communion of newly baptized infants within the baptismal Eucharist. The ELCA's recently approved 1997 statement on sacramental practices, *The Use of the Means of Grace: A Statement on the Practice of Word and Sacrament*, says clearly that "infants and children may be communed for the first time during the service in which they are baptized."[15] Although this "Statement" was not officially adopted until August of 1997, sixty ELCA congregations reported in 1995 that Communion was, in fact, already being given "in infancy" within their parishes. Such is surely a harbinger of things to come within the ELCA.

Second, in spite of still some resistance related to ungrounded Lutheran fears of "becoming *too* Roman Catholic" in liturgical-sacramental practice, there is no question but that the recovery of the Lutheran confessional norm of the centrality of Sunday and feast day Eucharist is gradually happening within the ELCA. Thanks, at least, in part, to the influence of Gordon Lathrop's recent book, *Holy Things: A Liturgical Theology*,[16] Lutherans are increasingly coming to understand that the very *ordo* of Christian liturgy is constituted by the *Sunday* assembly of the *baptized*, who *gather*, hear the *word*, share the *meal*, and are *sent* on mission in the world. Indeed, what some have begun to refer to as "Gordo's Ordo," based on the resurrection appearances of Jesus in the New Testament (cf. especially the Emmaus account in Luke 24), the mid-second century description of Justin Martyr in his *First*

*Apology*, and the liturgical ecclesiology of the Lutheran Confessions, is clearly the conceptual framework behind not only the recent Lutheran liturgical resource *With One Voice*, but the recent ELCA statement *The Use of the Means of Grace*. Whereas in 1989 only 1,690 of the 10,196 reporting ELCA congregations listed every Sunday Eucharist as their normal practice, that number in 1995 almost doubled to 2,305. If, in relationship to Roman Catholic practice, that still sounds rather low, one should remember that within the not so distant past the norm for those churches now comprising the ELCA[17] was usually a first Sunday of the month celebration, and, within the first half of this century, the norm in those churches was the continuation of the late medieval practice of Communion reception only four times a year. To have moved, then, from this to a situation where over 20% of ELCA congregations now celebrate Eucharist *at least* every Sunday is highly significant.

Hand in hand with this recovery of eucharistic frequency it is also important to note that the style of eucharistic liturgy, due in no small part to the ecumenical nature and influence of the liturgical movement, has also changed dramatically, so dramatically, in fact, that contemporary eucharistic celebrations among Lutherans, Roman Catholics, Episcopalians, and others often look, sound, and are, essentially, the same. It is for this reason that I often challenge my Notre Dame Roman Catholic undergraduate students to experience liturgy at some of the local Lutheran and Episcopalian parishes in the South Bend-Mishawaka area and tell me what they perceive that the real differences are in relationship to the experience of their own parishes (with the general exception of the fact that people might regularly sing better in these other places). And, Professor James White likes to say of his own United Methodist parish, Broadway United Methodist Church in South Bend, that the primary difference, compared with Roman Catholic practice, is that Broadway uses real bread while Roman Catholics use real wine.[18] (Another major difference, of course, is that one might actually encounter an ordained *woman* presider, vested in alb, stole, and chasuble, in some of these churches). Lectors, Communion ministers, and lay assistant ministers, who often fulfill liturgical roles traditionally assigned to deacons in some traditions, are frequently employed in contemporary Lutheran practice. Between the minister's, or altar, editions of the *Lutheran Book of Worship* and the supplement, *With One Voice*, ELCA Lutherans now have at least *fourteen* full eucharistic prayers available for their use, a highly significant development when one considers that the use of *any* eucharistic prayer—beyond Preface, Sanctus, and Institution Narrative—has been an issue of some argument and debate within Lutheran circles in the past thirty years or so.

At the same time, the recovery of the centrality of the Eucharist has led to a concern for the inclusion of those unable to attend the Sunday assembly, due to illness, hospitalization, and other factors. Here is to be noted the increasingly frequent Lutheran practice of lay ministers, who are dismissed from the Sunday assembly in order to bring Communion to the sick and homebound from the Sunday liturgy itself, again along the lines of Justin Martyr's own mid-second-century description of this practice and some sixteenth-century Lutheran *Church Order* practices.[19] Using a new-for-Lutherans rite of "Celebration of Holy Communion with Those in Special Circumstances,"[20] in which the already "consecrated" eucharistic gifts are shared in the context of the reading of the word and prayer, has not only fostered some kind of recovery of the propriety of eucharistic reservation for the Communion of the sick but has actually led in some places to the practice of ongoing eucharistic reservation itself. In South Bend-Mishawaka, for example, at least *three* of the seven ELCA parishes regularly reserve the Eucharist—both bread and wine—in a visible ambry somewhere within their liturgical spaces. One of these parishes does so even on the former high altar in the very center of its worship space, and another of them, for good or ill, not only regularly uses this reserved Eucharist for distribution to the assembly on Sundays in addition to the newly consecrated bread and wine, but, in clear imitation of current Roman Catholic practice, actually distributes Communion to the assembly on Good Friday from what has been solemnly reserved in a special place at the conclusion of the Holy Thursday Liturgy the evening before.[21]

Third, an ELCA Lutheran focus on the multiple presences of Christ in the liturgy would not limit the signification of that "presence" either to the particular gender of ministers, presiding and otherwise, nor to being in a situation of "full communion" with a specific ecclesial tradition. With regard to the reading and proclamation of the word of God itself, ELCA Lutherans have not only recently adopted and adapted the *Revised Common Lectionary* but now use regularly the *New Revised Standard Version* of the Bible as that translation has come to be offered, finally, in an actual, large, and dignified lectionary book designed for Lutheran liturgical use. Given the fact that both male and female together reflect the very "image of God," according to Genesis 1:26–27, and given St. Paul's radical *baptismal* reversal of ethnicity, social status, and gender in terms of the identity of the church itself in Christ, according to Galatians 3:28 (i.e., in Christ Jesus "there is no longer Jew nor Greek . . . slave nor free . . . *male nor female*" [emphasis added]), ELCA Lutherans—as several other ecclesial traditions today—have been able to receive gratefully the gift of women's ordination to the office of ministry in the church and have, albeit with some resistance and difficulty, accepted women pastors among those who "do not represent their own persons but the person of Christ" and who, "when they offer the word of Christ or the sacraments, they do so in Christ's place and stead."

Ecumenically speaking, ELCA Lutherans also hold that since "admission to the [Eucharist] is by invitation of the Lord presented through the church to those who are baptized,"[22] eucharistic hospitality toward members of other Christian traditions is practiced. To that end, "all baptized persons are welcomed to Communion when they are visiting in the congregations of [the ELCA],"[23] and "when a wedding or a funeral occurs during [the Eucharist], Communion is offered to all baptized persons."[24] Eucharistic hospitality to individuals, however, should *not* be taken as a substitute for the pursuit of "full" communion between different churches, a goal toward which the ELCA is also oriented and firmly committed.

At the same time, the practice of eucharistic hospitality and the goal of full communion between currently separated churches *are* related. Viewed as constituting a *source* for and means *toward* full communion, rather than simply the *expression* or *summit* of Christian unity, the ELCA and the Episcopal Church, USA, recognizing substantial agreement between themselves on various issues of doctrine and practice, were involved together since the early 1980's in an officially recognized "interim eucharistic" sharing, which led toward the eventual establishment of full communion in *Called to Common Mission* in 2001. But with regard to Lutheran-Roman Catholic eucharistic sharing, echoing the above-quoted statement of Roman Catholic theologians Karl Rahner and Heinrich Fries that "a pulpit fellowship . . . presupposes a community of faith," that Christ is "present" in "the form of proclamation," and that there is a "theological conformity of word *and* sacrament—sacrament as visible word (*verbum visibile*), the word as audible sacrament (*sacramentum audible*)," and pointing to CSL 7, as well as to other recent Vatican statements on the sharing of the "real" presence of Christ in word, baptism, assembly, and prayer in common, ELCA Lutherans might wonder how seriously such "modes" of Christ's *real* presence are actually taken in and by the Roman Catholic Church. Indeed, if Christ is *present* in such multiple ways, then he is "really" present. And if his "real" presence in word is acknowledged to exist in other communions to such an extent that the ELCA and the American Roman Catholic Bishops could actually produce a (now already out of print) "Lutheran-Catholic Service of the Word" for common use, then what *does* the "theological conformity of word *and* sacrament" actually imply? If divided Christians can already share *some* "modes" of that "*real*" presence *officially*, why not the *eucharistic* mode as well? Similarly, with the radical Lutheran World Federation and Vatican "Joint Declaration on the Doctrine of Justification," signed officially October 31, 1999, signifying, finally, a rather explicit and substantial *unity in faith* between Lutherans and Roman Catholics, one can only wonder what kinds of implications for eucharistic hospitality or "interim eucharistic sharing" might eventually result. But in the meantime, because ELCA Lutherans see a theological consistency flowing from the conformity of audible word and visible word (sacrament) welcoming all the baptized to Christ's inclusive, egalitarian, and community building table companionship naturally follows. Both word and sacrament, in Lutheran thought at least, function together under the category of the "proclamation" of the Gospel, one audible, the other visible. Indeed, a *refusal* to commune President Clinton in one of its assemblies—not the *giv-ing* of Communion to him—is what may have constituted an ecclesial-sacramental scandal among ELCA Lutherans.

Fourth, and finally for this section, other liturgical sacramental practices recovered among contemporary ELCA Lutherans in the years since Vatican II should at least be briefly noted as they relate to this question of "multiple presences." Within the *Lutheran Book of Worship* and *With One Voice*, ELCA Lutherans have for their use a style of the Liturgy of the Hours clearly rooted in the "cathedral' rather than "monastic" tradition, at least with regard to Evening Prayer and its *Lucernarium* and Psalm 141. Regular provisions for private confession and absolution as well as corporate confession and absolution have been made in the current worship books. There has even been a recovery of the practice of the laying on of hands and "anointing of the sick," with forms provided for individual use in ministering to the sick and for public celebrations within the context of the eucharistic liturgy or Liturgy of the Word,[25] a practice that several congregations employ on a fairly regular basis. And, of course, at least in principle, the importance of preaching the word of God has remained a constant and abiding emphasis. All in all, with regard then to the multiple presences of Christ in word, meal, assembly, ministers, sacraments, and prayer, the liturgical practice and theology of the ELCA, at least according to its liturgical books and statements, has been one of recovering its classic liturgical-sacramental heritage within a contemporary ecumenical context. As such, an ELCA liturgical-sacramental practice that takes the multiple presences of Christ seriously looks a lot like the vision of Vatican II and the worship books of its own tradition.

## II. Issues Still Needing Serious Attention

All things liturgical and sacramental within the ELCA, however, are not rosy and I certainly do not want to give the deceptive impression that they are. In fact, there are several issues that still need serious attention in the ELCA if liturgical renewal is to go forward from this point. Let me simply list here—without too much additional comment—what I see some of those to be:[26]

1.  in spite of frequent attempts and some notable examples to the contrary, the Eucharist itself remains in too many places but an "occasional service," either monthly, bi-monthly, or "after" others have been dismissed from the principal Sunday assembly. Out of a total of 10,196 parishes, 2,305 celebrating Eucharist every Sunday is still *only* about 20%, and, for that matter, these statistics do not indicate whether the Eucharist is celebrated in these parishes at *every* Sunday service or not;

2.  in spite of a clear preference for the use of full sacramental signs in the celebration of liturgy,[27] minimalistic use of water in baptism (administered in some places even by only a finger dipped in the font and touched to the head of the candidate), mass produced communion wafers instead of real bread, and what I refer to as (often even pre-filled), individualized, "shot glasses" for the reception of the eucharistic wine, has continued in far too many places. Never mind that the concern of the Lutheran Reformers for Communion under both elements was the sacramental significance of sharing the *cup*, not merely the reception of wine;

3.  in spite of the fourteen eucharistic prayers currently available for use, a bare-bones *Verba* (Institution Narrative) alone often constitutes the normative pattern of eucharistic "consecration"—occasionally without even Preface and Sanctus—in still far too many places on "Communion" Sundays;

4.  the recent ELCA acceptance of "full communion" with various Reformed Churches in the United States calls into question—theoretically at least—the overall credibility of the Lutheran confessional position on the real presence of Christ in the Eucharist;

5. the Paschal Triduum has yet to be even *experienced* by the majority of Lutheran *clergy* much less instituted as the annual center of parish life gathered around the light of Christ risen from death, the watery stories of salvation history, the font, and the table of the Lord, after a Lent oriented toward baptismal renewal and affirmation rather than a forty-day "Passion Sunday" or "Good Friday;"

6. occasional proposals to move or do away with the Advent season altogether in the name of an ambiguous "inculturation" in the modern world find some sympathetic response and reveal a church rather unsure of the theological meaning and overall purpose of the liturgical year itself;[28]

7. even the theological and normative priority of Sunday itself as *the* day of resurrection, day of encounter with the crucified and risen Lord, and the day for the Christian assembly around word and table, as expressed in *The Use of the Means of Grace*,[29] is met with some incredulity and resistance;

8. often with synodical and national support, "contemporary" and non-sacramental forms of "worship," in the name of an ambiguous "hospitality" for "seekers," based on what some have called "entertainment evangelism," is permitted to substitute for or provide an alternative to "traditional" Sunday worship (i.e., the classic Sunday worship of the one, holy, catholic, and apostolic church centered in word *and* table);

9. contemporary or locally created "Statements of Faith" are permitted to modify or even replace the classic Nicene and Apostles' Creeds themselves and so call into serious question the precise relationship of some local Lutheran congregations to the historic faith of the church altogether;

10. the medieval and Thomistic emphasis on the *one* office of ordained ministry (that of presbyter or priest) is maintained with a tenacity approaching a *status confessionis* (i.e., a "state of confession" for which there is no compromise permitted), in spite of the fact that the contemporary Roman Catholic and Anglican emphasis on the "three-fold" office and "ordination" of bishops, presbyters, and deacons has moved beyond this context and owes more to a recovery of a Patristic understanding of "orders" *within* the church, including the laity as an "order" itself(!), than it does to the priestly ordination theology of Western Scholasticism[30];

11. in spite of the traditional Lutheran emphasis on the importance of the oral proclamation of the word in the assembly, far too often, in my experience, the overall performance and quality of proclaiming the Sunday readings, on the part of lectors and presiders alike, pales in comparison with the dignity, care, and attention to oral proclamation that I often experience within post-Vatican II Roman Catholic practice; and, related to this, finally;

12. in spite of the classic Lutheran emphasis on preaching the Word, it is downright frightening, but significant, to note that, according to a list of the ten top preachers in the United States appearing in an issue of *Newsweek* a few years ago,[31] Jesuit Father Walter J. Burghardt was included but not one single Lutheran preacher appeared.

No, all is not yet rosy within ELCA liturgical-sacramental practice, even if it is moving, generally, in what I consider to be the right direction. Issues of ecclesiology and ministry, and the recovery of a rich and full liturgical-sacramental practice that corresponds to and expresses its theological understanding still loom large for the future, as the ELCA, now only fourteen years old itself, seeks to find its ecclesial and ecumenical place at the end of the twentieth and beginning of the twenty-first century.

## III. Conclusion

By way of conclusion, lest my reflections have seemed overly critical or negative, let me underscore the fact that it has only been forty years since the CSL was adopted at Vatican II, only thirty-four years since the appearance of the approved ICEL version of the Missal of Paul VI, only twenty-six years since the publication of the *Lutheran Book of Worship*, and only ten years since the final approved version of the RCIA was adopted in the United States. When one considers what *has*, in fact, taken place with regard to liturgical renewal in that relatively short period of time the only response can be one of grateful awe and humble *"eucharistia."*

In spite of the several issues that remain in all of the major liturgical traditions today, what has been accomplished already from these few years of hard work, should also give us both a sense of hope and a renewed call toward the continued implementation of that common ecumenical liturgical-sacramental vision centered in the multiple and "real" presences of Christ among us. Never can we allow the occasional calls for the "undoing" of contemporary liturgical reform, the "reform of the reform," or for a "restorationist-revisionistic" reinterpretation of that reform, based on an incomplete late medieval ecclesiology and sacramental theology, or for Lutherans, a sixteenth-century fundamentalist repristination, to deter or detract us from that continued implementation. For, at stake in all this is not really the liturgy itself but the very identity and life of the people of God whom the liturgy exists to serve in the first place. And it serves them in forming them to be what they celebrate, to become what they receive, in lives of *diakonia* and *martyria*, lives broken and shared for the sake of the world that others too may come to the fullness of life in the "real" presence of the crucified, yet living, Christ, who is known not only in the apostolic teaching and *koinonia*, in the breaking of bread and the prayers (see Acts 2:42), but is known and revealed especially there.

## Notes

[1] A. Flannery (ed.), *Vatican Council II*, vol. 1 (Collegeville: The Liturgical Press, 1975), 4–5.

[2] See "The Smalcald Articles" IV–VIII in T. Tappert (ed.), *The Book of Concord* (Philadelphia: Augsburg Fortress, 1958), 310–13.

[3] See *The Apology of the Augsburg Confession*, Article XIII. 17, in Tappert, 213.

[4] See *The Augsburg Confession*, Article V, in Tappert, 31.

[5] *The Apology of the Augsburg Confession*, Articles VII and VIII. 28, in Tappert, op. cit., 173.

[6] Ibid., Article XIII. 11-12, 212.

[7] *The Augsburg Confession*, Article VII, in Tappert, 32.

[8] M. Luther, *The Babylonian Captivity of the Church*, LW vol. 36, 18 [emphasis added].

[9] *Directory for Ecumenism*, para. 129, in *Origins* 23, 9 (July 29, 1993).

[10] *Ut Unum Sint* 22 in *Origins* 25 (June 8, 1995).

[11] *Unity of the Churches: An Actual Possibility* (New York/Philadelphia: Paulist Press and Fortress Press, 1985), 125 [emphasis added].

[12] Evangelical Lutheran Church in America, *Welcome to Christ: A Lutheran Catechetical Guide* (Minneapolis: Augsburg Fortress, 1997); *Welcome to Christ: A Lutheran Introduction to the Catechumenate* (Minneapolis: Augsburg Fortress, 1997); and *Welcome to Christ: Lutheran Rites for the Catechumenate* (Minneapolis: Augsburg Fortress, 1997).

[13] See *FDLC Newsletter* 22 (Washington, D.C.: Federation of Diocesan Liturgical Commissions, December 1995), 45.

[14] Evangelical Lutheran Church in Canada, *Statement on Sacramental Practices* (Winnipeg: ELCIC, 1991), 5.8, 6.9.

[15] Evangelical Lutheran Church in America, *The Use of the Means of Grace: A Statement on the Practice of Word and Sacrament* (Minneapolis: Augsburg Fortress Press, 1997), 3.37D, 42.

[16] (Minneapolis: Augsburg Fortress, 1993).

[17] The major Lutheran bodies forming the ELCA in 1987 were the former Lutheran Church in America (LCA), The American Lutheran Church (ALC), and the Association of Evangelical Lutheran Churches (AELC). With the exception of the AELC, formed by several former Lutheran Church - Missouri Synod congregations, the LCA and ALC were themselves the result of various Lutheran "mergers" of several Lutheran churches in the United States and Canada in the early 1960's.

[18] J.F. White, "Roman Catholic and Protestant Worship in Relationship," in Idem., *Christian Worship in North America: A Retrospective: 1955-1995* (Collegeville: The Liturgical Press, 1997), 3.

[19] On this see F. Senn, *Christian Liturgy: Catholic and Evangelical* (Minneapolis: Fortress Press, 1997), 353.

[20] *The Occasional Service Book* (Minneapolis/Philadelphia: Augsburg Fortress, 1982), 83–88.

21 On this see the following essay, ""Eucharistic Reservation and Lutheranism: An Extension of the Sunday Worship?" elsewhere in this volume, 141–164.

22 *The Use of the Means of Grace* (statement of the Evangelical Lutheran Church in America), 49.A., 52.

23 Ibid., 49, 52.

24 Ibid., 49B, 52.

25 See *The Occasional Service Book*, 89–98; 99–102.

26 Several of these issues are also cited in my essay, "The 'Joint Declaration on the Doctrine of Justification' and Lutheran-Roman Catholic Unity: Some Unresolved Questions," *Lutheran Forum* 33, 1 (1998), 22–28.

27 See *The Use of the Means of Grace*, 25 and 26, 31–32; and 44A, 48.

28 See S. K. Wendorf, "Let's Move Advent," in *Lutheran Partners* (November/December 1991) and the numerous favorable letters her plea engendered in *Lutheran Partners* (March/April 1992). For my response to this see my "Let's Keep Advent Right Where It Is," elsewhere in this volume, 237–242.

29 *The Use of the Means of Grace*, 6, 13.

30 Until this becomes clear I fear that Lutherans, Roman Catholics, and Anglicans will continue to talk right past each other on questions of ministry and ordination. Interestingly enough, even Thomas Aquinas held that bishops weren't "ordained," since ordination was to priesthood itself. Because the permanent diaconate no longer existed in Thomas' time deacons were "ordained" only as a transitional step toward presbyteral ordination. Bishops—as priests already—could only be "consecrated." It is within *contemporary* Roman Catholic and Anglican practice, due in large part to that Patristic recovery noted above, that bishops and permanent deacons now are also "ordained" to particular "offices" of ministry within the one "priesthood" of Christ and the Church. It appears here that Lutherans remain more in debt to *medieval* theology and practice with an emphasis on "one ordained office" than do modern Roman Catholics and Anglicans. At the same time, I've often wondered what Lutherans think they are doing at the "installation" of newly elected bishops when the presiding minister "may" lay "a" hand on them during the "blessing." If this isn't liturgically an "ordination" to an office—*ut legem credendi statuat lex supplicandi*—I do not know what it is. It looks like an ordination, functions like an ordination, and sounds like an ordination. Therefore, it is an "installation?" Such logic makes about as much sense to me as does the great syllogism of Woody Allen in the movie *Love and Death*: "Socrates was a man. I am a man. Therefore, I am Socrates?" Of *course*, there is only *one* priesthood, *one* "office" of word and sacrament, *one* ministry, *one* church, and, for that matter, even and only one *sacrament*, namely, Christ himself in the power of the Holy Spirit. But how that "oneness" is "ordered" in the life of the church does not imply only "one" *presbyteral* way as the once-for-all, dominically mandated, ecclesial norm for this ordering. If anything, that "oneness" was signified traditionally by the *episkope* of one *bishop* and not by the presbyteral office.

31 K. Woodward, "Heard Any Good Sermons Lately?" *Newsweek* (March 4, 1998), 50–52.

# EUCHARISTIC RESERVATION AND LUTHERANISM: AN EXTENSION OF THE SUNDAY WORSHIP?

In ecumenical conversations Roman Catholics frequently ask Lutherans something like: "If you Lutherans really believe in the real presence of Christ in the Eucharist as you say you do, then how come you do not normally reserve the Eucharist in your churches?" This is, of course, a most legitimate question for Lutherans to be asked by Roman Catholics. But there is a rather interesting assumption behind this question, namely, that the practice of eucharistic reservation in one Christian tradition can be some kind of litmus test for determining whether another Christian tradition "really" holds to a theology of Real Presence. Is this necessarily the case? What *is* the precise relationship between eucharistic reservation and Real Presence? This particular essay will deal with these questions from a Lutheran theological perspective in light of the early history of the practice of reservation and Communion, related doctrinal and/or dogmatic issues, and current Lutheran liturgical-pastoral practice. In spite of their long history of not doing so might there be ways today in which Lutheranism could embrace some form of eucharistic reservation without compromising its confessional position? I believe that such could, indeed, be possible.

## A Variety of "Lutheran" Practices

Let us imagine four Evangelical Lutheran Church in America (ELCA) congregations existing in various places within the same large city, all of which celebrate the Eucharist at every Sunday liturgy and on major festival days.[1] The first congregation, Transfiguration Lutheran Church, has three Sunday Eucharists, one on Saturday evening and two on Sunday morning. Real bread is used for the celebrations. All of the bread and wine needed for all three celebrations is placed on the credence table before the Saturday evening liturgy and hence, whatever remains of those elements after the first or second liturgies is simply used again ("re-consecrated") at the next liturgy. At the end of all three liturgies any remaining bread and wine is scattered and poured on the ground outside. The theological rationale for both practices (using what remains at the next liturgy and eventually disposing of them on the ground) is that "Lutherans" believe that after the liturgy the bread and wine, which *were* the body and blood of Christ, are no longer that body and blood but revert back to common food and drink.

A similar practice and theological rationale is present at the second imaginary congregation, Faith Lutheran Church. At Faith, however, any "hosts" remaining after its two Sunday celebrations are simply stored with "unconsecrated" ones and any wine remaining in the flagon is poured back into the bottle in preparation for the next Sunday's celebrations. At both Transfiguration and Faith distribution of Communion to the sick and homebound requires the presence of the pastor who will use an occasional service called "Celebration of Holy Communion with Those in Special Circumstances," a service which includes two short eucharistic prayers containing the words of institution.[2]

The third congregation, Saint Paul's Lutheran Church, practices a different custom from either that of Transfiguration or Faith. At Saint Paul's any of the elements remaining after each of its two Sunday Eucharists are reverently consumed by the pastor and assisting ministers, a portion is sent with lay Communion ministers to the sick and homebound who will use a service called "Distribution of Communion to Those in Special Circumstances,"[3] and another portion is reserved for the future

Communion of the sick in what is essentially a "tabernacle" on the back wall (former) altar in the very center of the church. Until only recently this "tabernacle" was kept in the sacristy. At Saint Paul's the obvious theological rationale is that there is a permanence to the Real Presence of Christ "in, with, and under" the bread and wine, a presence that does not somehow cease after the celebration of the eucharistic liturgy itself.

The practice of the fourth imaginary congregation, Christus Rex, is similar to that of Saint Paul's but actually goes one or two steps further. That is, Christus Rex regularly sends lay Communion ministers out to the sick and homebound from its single Sunday celebration and reserves both elements in an "ambry" within a side wall of the sanctuary. But, in obvious imitation of Roman Catholic practice, Christus Rex celebrates a "Mass of the pre-sanctified" on Good Friday wherein elements "consecrated" at the Maundy Thursday Eucharist are distributed to the congregation. And further, in equally obvious imitation of an unfortunately common Roman Catholic practice—a practice, in fact, that Roman Catholic liturgists consider to be liturgically scandalous![4]—Christus Rex *regularly* distributes holy Communion at the time of distribution not only from what has just been consecrated at the Sunday liturgy but from the *reserved* sacrament as well! Indeed, there is no question but that approximately half of the relatively small congregation at Christus Rex receives holy Communion from the *reserved* sacrament each week.

While it is certainly true that no liturgical or extra-liturgical "cult" of the Blessed Sacrament exists at Saint Paul's or at Christus Rex, the mere fact that the Eucharist is reserved in these congregations under both elements indicates that within the ELCA—even within the same city—there is no consistency whatsoever in eucharistic practice, especially with regard to the question of what to do with elements remaining after the liturgy itself. Nevertheless, if I were to speculate on which of these four congregations best reflects the most common practice in the ELCA I would have to say that is probably that of both Transfiguration and Faith, where what has been "consecrated" is either re-used or used to the feed the birds. The question, therefore, naturally arises: which of these imaginary congregations is most "Lutheran" in its eucharistic practice and theological interpretation?

That is not an easy question to answer for the simple reason that, while strongly affirming the real presence of Christ in the Eucharist, at times even in language that approximates the Roman Catholic doctrine of "transubstantiation",[5] the *Lutheran Confessions* do not deal *in detail* with the *duration* of Christ's eucharistic presence. What they do say on this issue, however, if limited, is rather significant. In relationship to Corpus Christi processions, for example, Article XXII of the *Augsburg Confession* states: "Because the division of the sacrament [the withdrawl of the cup] is contrary to the institution of Christ, the customary carrying about of the sacrament in processions is also omitted by us."[6] If this article might be interpreted as but critiquing a "misuse" or "abuse" of the sacrament, the *Formula of Concord, Solid Declaration* (1580) is much stronger in its approach. In its rejection of the specific doctrine of transubstantiation, Article VII states:

> [T]hey assert that under the species of the bread, which they allege has lost its natural substance and is no longer bread, the body of Christ is present even apart from the action of the sacrament (when, for instance, the bread is locked up in the tabernacle or is carried about as a spectacle and for adoration). For nothing can be a sacrament apart from God's command and the ordained use for which it is instituted in the word of God.[7]

Such statements would seem to support the practice of either Transfiguration or Faith. Without the sacramental "action," the "ordained use" of the Eucharist, frequently interpreted as the reception or *"sumptio"* of the body and blood of Christ in Communion (often times called "receptionism"), the Eucharist is not the Eucharist and the body and blood of Christ are not present.

But is it really that simple? Herman Sasse, in his now classic study of Luther's eucharistic theology, *This Is My Body*, wrote that:

Luther and the early Lutheran Church avoided forming any theory about the 'moment' when the Real Presence begins and the 'moment' when it ceases. Some later orthodox theologians advanced the theory that Christ's body and blood are present only at the 'moment' when they are being received. This is frequently regarded, within and without the Lutheran Church, as the genuinely Lutheran doctrine . . . [But] as far as Luther himself is concerned, there cannot be the slightest doubt that he never did limit the Real Presence to the instant of distribution and reception. He never abandoned the view that by the words of consecration bread and wine 'become' the body and blood of Christ. Otherwise neither the elevation, which was in use at Wittenberg up to 1542, nor the adoration of Christ, who is present in the elements, could have been justified. He always regarded it as Zwinglianism to neglect the difference between a consecrated and an unconsecrated host, and it has always been the custom of the Lutheran Church to consecrate the new supply of bread or wine or both if more is needed than originally was provided for. The rule that Luther, like Melanchthon and the Lutheran Confessions, followed was that that there is no sacrament, and consequently no presence of the body and blood of Christ, 'apart from the use instituted by Christ' or 'apart from the action divinely instituted.' Since the word 'usus' is explained by 'actio' it cannot mean the same as 'sumptio.' If it has sometimes been understood in this way, it must be said that neither Luther nor the Formula of Concord . . . identified the 'sumptio' (eating and drinking) with the use or action of the sacrament.[8]

In a related footnote Sasse adds:

Luther demanded the dismissal of a pastor who had given to a communicant an unconsecrated host instead of a consecrated one, which had been dropped. This unfortunate man was imprisoned. Luther does not approve of such punishment, but he thinks him unfit for the

Lutheran ministry: 'He should go to his Zwinglians' (Letter of January 11, 1546; WA Br 11, No. 4186). In 1543 Luther and Bugenhagen gave their opinion in a controversy about the question whether consecrated hosts could be preserved together with unconsecrated ones for another consecration. Luther criticizes this. Nothing of the consecrated elements should be saved, but must be consumed. In this connection he gives a clear definition of the sacramental 'time' or 'action': '*sic ergo definiemus tempus vel actionem sacramentalem, ut incipiat ab initio orationis dominicae et duret, donec omnes communicaverint, calicem ebiberunt, particulas comederint, populus dimissus et ab altari descessum sit.*' (WA Br 10, No. 3894, lines 27ff.). In a Table Talk of 1540 Luther goes so far as to allow the blessed sacrament to be carried to another altar (in the same church) or even, as was still customary in some churches, to be brought to the sick in their home (WA TR 5, No. 5314), provided this could be regarded as part of the 'action.' This was tolerated as an exception. However, a reservation of the sacrament was not allowed. The remnants of the elements should be either consumed or burned.[9]

On the basis of the above two quotations from Sasse, it would seem, then, that all four of our ELCA congregations are, in various ways, at odds with the Lutheran sacramental tradition. Both Transfiguration and Faith are at odds in their practice of mixing unconsecrated bread and wine with consecrated bread and wine, either from one service to the next or in preparation for the following week's liturgies. Certainly Transfiguration is at odds by scattering the remaining bread and pouring out the remaining wine on the ground rather than consuming both reverently. But Saint Paul's and Christus Rex are also at odds with that tradition in their own ways. Consistent with Luther's permitted exception of allowing the Eucharist to be taken to the sick as an "extension of the action," both Saint Paul's and Christus Rex do send lay Communion ministers out from the liturgy to the sick and homebound. It would seem, however, that they both depart from the Lutheran tradition in their practices of eucharistic reservation. Here, especially, it would appear that is the practice of Christus Rex which represents the most radical departure in regularly distributing Communion from the reserved sacrament during Sunday liturgies and in adopting the "Mass of the pre-sanctified" for Good Friday.

If this is true, however, that all of these congregations seem to depart in some way from the Lutheran tradition, the reason for that must certainly be that the tradition itself is not all that clear. As we noted in Sasse above, "Luther and the early Lutheran Church avoided forming any theory about the 'moment' when the Real Presence begins and the 'moment' when it ceases." Consequently, even today the avoidance of forming any such theory gets expressed in various ways. On the one hand, *The Use of the Means of Grace* can direct that "any food that remains is best consumed by the presiding and assisting minister and by others present following the service."[10] On the other hand, regarding the Communion of the sick and homebound the same document says: "*Occasional Services* provides an order for the Distribution of Communion to Those in Special Circumstances. As an extension of the Sunday worship, the servers of Communion take the elements to those unable to attend."[11] But, when one reads the rubrics of this particular service it becomes clear that "extension of the Sunday worship" is interpreted as an *immediate* extension of the distribution of Communion from the Sunday worship:

> To underscore the significance of bringing the congregational Eucharist to those unable to participate in the assembly, the Communion should be carried to the absent *without delay* following the congregational celebration. Sufficient ministers should be appointed so that all the absent may receive Communion *within a few hours* of the congregation's service that day.[12]

In other words, one does not get the impression that distribution on Tuesday or Wednesday of the following week, for example, is quite viewed as a similar "extension of the Sunday worship." And, consequently, one starts asking theologically, just how long *does* the presence of Christ remain in the bread and wine as this extension of the Sunday worship? A few hours? A few days? And if the body and blood of Christ do remain in the elements for the purposes of communing the sick and home-bound on *Sundays* does that presence disappear if the Communion minister does not arrive at the place of the sick or homebound until Monday or Tuesday? Is the Real Presence of the body and blood of Christ in the bread and wine a permanent presence which remains as long as the bread and wine them-selves remain as recognizable food and drink? To ask such ques-tions, naturally, is to ask the question of the theological and litur-gical propriety of eucharistic reservation itself and it is important here to look at this in the context of its early historical develop-ment rather than from the ideological and polemical stances of a later period.

## Eucharistic Reservation and Communion in Historical Perspective

Lutherans (and, undoubtedly, many Roman Catholics), both at the time of the *Formula of Concord* and today, tend to forget that the reservation of the Eucharist and Communion from the reserved Eucharist antedate the thirteenth-century doctrine of transubstantiation by *centuries*. Similarly, the practice of eucharistic reservation is no more intrinsically connected to the doctrine of transubstantiation than transubstantiation is itself intrinsically connected to the doctrine of the Real Presence! Even the Council of Trent said only that transubstantiation was the "most apt" and "most appropriate" way to refer to the change of the bread and wine into the body and blood of Christ![13] And, cer-tainly the long standing traditions of the Eastern Orthodox Churches remind us that it is possible and traditional to acknowledge the real presence of Christ in the Eucharist, to reserve the Eucharist, to celebrate liturgies of the "pre-sancti-fied" (at least in Lent), and to commune the sick from the reserved sacrament without any recourse to the Western medieval doctrine of transubstantiation and without any con-comitant cult of the Blessed Sacrament (e.g., Corpus Christi pro-cessions, Benedictions, etc.).

Thanks to the work of Nathan Mitchell and others,[14] the history of this topic is now easily narrated. Our earliest reference to the distribution and reception of Communion *outside* of the liturgy appears already in the middle of the second century (ca. 150 CE) in Justin Martyr's *First Apology* 65. Herein Justin indicates that, at the conclusion of the liturgy, "deacons" carried the Eucharist to those who were absent from the community's celebration, a practice seemingly consistent with the distribution to the sick and homebound as the "extension of the Sunday worship" in the ELCA today. A short time later in North Africa Tertullian witnesses to the fact that the faithful regularly took the Eucharist home with them from the Sunday celebration for the reception of Communion during the week (at least on the "station" or fasting days of Wednesdays and Fridays).[15] In the middle of the third century, Cyprian of Carthage also refers to this practice and informs us that the consecrated bread was kept in little boxes called *arcae* (or chrismals).[16] These *arcae* were either worn around the neck of believers or kept in their homes.

If Tertullian and Cyprian seem to refer only to the reservation and reception of the body of Christ in this context, rubrics preserved in the so-called *Apostolic Tradition*, ascribed to Hippolytus of Rome (ca. 215 CE),[17] not only corroborate the practice of home reservation and Communion, but make it clear that the ritual of Communion included reception from the cup as well:

> . . . [H]aving blessed the cup in the name of God, you received as it were the antitype of the blood of Christ. Therefore do not pour any out, as though you despised it, lest an alien spirit lick it up. You will be guilty of the blood, as one who despises the price with which he has been bought.[18]

It is quite possible, then, notes Mitchell, that early Christian domestic rituals of Communion from the reserved Eucharist included "blessing the cup" by means of dropping a small portion of the bread into it, i.e., a "consecration by contact." Such a method of "consecrating" the wine, in fact, has continued to the present day in the "liturgy of the pre-sanctified" and distribution of Communion to the sick within various Rites of the Christian East.[19]

That the practice of domestic eucharistic reservation and reception continued into the late fourth century is clearly attested by Basil of Caesarea (+379), who in reference to desert monastics and others, writes:

> All the solitaries in the deserts, where there is no priest, keep the Communion by them and partake of it by themselves. At Alexandria too, and in Egypt, each one of the laity, for the most part, keeps the Communion at home, and whenever he wishes partakes of it himself. For after the priest has completed the sacrifice and distributed it, he who then received it in entirety . . . must believe that he duly takes and receives it from the hand that first gave it. For even in the church, when the priest distributes each portion, he who receives takes it into his complete control, and lifts it to his mouth with his own hand. It comes to the same thing, whether one or many portions at a time are received from the priest."[20]

In light of the contemporary ELCA practice of carrying Communion to the sick and homebound as an "extension of the Sunday worship," it is interesting that Mitchell would comment on the words of Basil noting that:

> quite clearly, Basil regards Communion at home as simply *an extension of the public liturgy in church*; postponing the consumption of some of the bread until a later time is quite inconsequential, since one still 'takes and receives it from the hand that first gave it.'[21]

Nevertheless, if still in the fourth century eucharistic reservation at home and domestic rituals of Communion reception on days when the eucharistic liturgy itself was not celebrated in church were rather common and approved, the custom of taking the Eucharist home came to be discouraged for a variety of reasons. Jerome, for example, expressed his strong disapproval regarding those banned from receiving Communion publicly in church, who yet received privately in their homes.[22] Similarly, the Council of Saragossa (ca. 379–381), perhaps out of fear of the

Eucharist falling into the hands of heretics (i.e., the Priscillianists), decreed that: "If anyone is found guilty of not consuming *in church* the Eucharist he has received, let him be anathema."[23] At the same time, it *is* documented that the practice of home reservation and Communion did continue in some places until the seventh and eighth centuries.

If home reservation and Communion would cease for a variety of reasons, however, the reservation of the Eucharist in churches, especially for the Communion of the sick and for public distribution of Communion on fasting days, certainly continued. Canon XIII of the Council of Nicea refers to the necessity of viaticum being given to the dying but it is the late-fourth century *Apostolic Constitutions* (ca. 381) which contains our first clear reference to the reservation of the Eucharist in the church (i.e., in the sacristy).[24] For several centuries the reserved Eucharist was frequently kept inside an *arca*, chrismal, or pyx within a sacristy cupboard and it is quite possible in some places, as a letter of Chrysostom indicates, that the wine was also reserved.[25] There is no reason to think that these practices were new developments in the fourth century but rather a continuation of what had already been evolving previously. *A Life of St. Basil*, attributed to Amphilochius of Iconium, indicates that Basil had commissioned a golden dove into which he had placed a portion of the Eucharist. This was then suspended over the altar "as a figure of the sacred dove that appeared at the Jordan over the Lord during his baptism."[26]

What is most interesting to note in this overall context, however, is the close relationship that seems to develop in some quarters between the practice of eucharistic reservation and christological orthodoxy. This becomes the case especially within the context of the fifth-century Nestorian controversy.[27] Whatever the eucharistic theology and practice of Nestorius himself might have been in Constantinople, the followers of Cyril of Alexandria apparently interpreted the strict Christological diophysitism of Nestorius and his followers as leading to a eucharistic practice which held that there could be no complete or permanent union between the divine Logos and the bread and wine. Hence, the body and blood of Christ were present in holy Communion but only *temporarily* and limited to the day of the eucharistic liturgy itself. What remained of the eucharistic elements until the next day was no longer considered to be Christ's body or blood. Already Cyril of Alexandria had attacked this approach saying:

> I hear that some people say that the mystical blessing is no longer active to effect sanctification when the Eucharist is left over to the next day. Those who reason this way are insane. For Christ does not become different, and his holy body does not undergo any change. On the contrary, the effectiveness of the blessing and the life-creating grace in It remains unchanged.[28]

Further, for Cyril the very question of the life-giving nature of the Eucharist was at stake in this controversy. That is, for him Nestorius had so separated the divine and human natures in Christ from each other that in the Eucharist itself only the "human" body and blood of Christ could be received.[29] Cyril writes:

> . . . Not as common flesh do we receive it, not at all, nor as a man sanctified and associated with the Word according to the unity of dignity, or as having had a divine indwelling, but as truly the life-giving and very flesh of the Word Himself. For He is life according to his nature as God, and when he became united to his flesh, He made it life-giving.[30]

What Nestorius and his followers might have actually held and taught about the reservation of the Eucharist theologically, however, is difficult to uncover and one must always be cautious of discerning a position based on the critique of opponents. The fact that the ancient Assyrian Church of the East did not historically—and still does not (!)—reserve the Eucharist nor celebrate the liturgy of the pre-sanctified is what undoubtedly has led others to make certain assertions about eucharistic theology in that tradition. For example, according to N. Uspensky and other Orthodox theologians, eucharistic reservation and the liturgy of the pre-sanctified in the Byzantine tradition signify the victory of Orthodox Christology over "Nestorianism" in that both practices presumably safeguard the unity of the person of Christ in the Eucharist as the God-Man whose body and blood are life-giving.[31] The only problem is that they do not produce any hard evidence to support such a claim.

What is most likely the case is that the practice of the ancient Assyrian Church of the East regarding eucharistic reservation is nothing other than a continuation of early Christian liturgical diversity and the survival of one ancient practice. That is, some early Christian communities clearly reserved the Eucharist and regularly communed the sick from the reserved sacrament. Others did not do so but simply carried the Eucharist to the sick on the same day as the celebration. In fact, it may well be that Justin Martyr's own description of deacons carrying Communion to the absent in his *First Apology* is quite consistent with the practice of the Assyrian Church of the East, and that Justin's own (Syrian?) community at Rome did not practice reservation. But only later within the developing homogeneity of liturgical practice across ecclesial boundaries and within the context of a developing christological orthodoxy, would certain practices come to be criticized and even condemned in light of those developments. Indeed, it would be preposterous to assume that prior to the Council of Ephesus (431 CE) East Syrian Christians regularly reserved the Eucharist and then stopped reserving in response to the christological position of the other churches that had now become recognized as the Orthodox position. Does it not make more sense to see non-reservation as one ancient practice which became re-interpreted later on, re-interpreted not by those who followed the practice, but by those who sought to critique and condemn that practice in terms of their own christological position? Even today, according to Mar Bawai Soro, Western California Bishop of the Assyrian Church of the East:

> The Church of the East holds that once the eucharistic elements are consecrated, they become really, truly and permanently, the body and blood of Christ. This theological statement can clearly be seen in Church of the East's liturgical-eucharistic texts, the writings of the Fathers, and in canonical legislation. Church of the East official texts do not dispute or contradict the common orthodox,

catholic faith of the real and permanent presence of Christ in the Holy Qurbana. Now, concerning the practice of eucharistic preservation and the pre-sanctified: At present, we certainly do not preserve the Eucharist, nor am I aware of any such practice in the past. Yet, as recently as the early 1990's, the Holy Synod (not the Patriarch) allowed priests to take the consecrated Holy Qurbana to the sick out in hospitals and homes. Sometimes, it may be through the overnight that the patient receives the Eucharist. But there is still definitively no practice of preserving the Qurbana in our churches.[32]

Hence, in spite of the approaches of Uspensky and others, there is no necessary correlation whatsoever between eucharistic reservation and the theology of Christ's real presence in the Eucharist itself. Those who reserve and those who do not reserve might both assert Christ's real and permanent presence!

Further developments regarding eucharistic reservation and even the developing cult of the reserved Eucharist in the medieval West and at the time of the Protestant Reformation are more widely known than are the practices from the patristic period. Hence, these developments need not be treated in detail here. At the risk of oversimplification, however, it is important to note that the very criticisms of the Lutheran Confessions against late medieval Roman practice (e.g., reservation of the host and Corpus Christi processions) are those which arose because the cult of the Blessed Sacrament outside Mass—including an emphasis on the elevation of the host in Mass—had come to be in practice the practical surrogate for the reception of Communion itself. That is, the desire to see and adore the host ("spiritual" and "ocular" Communion) became, in the words of Joseph Jungmann, the "be all and end all" of eucharistic devotion and the host itself became the supreme relic among many lesser relics.[33] And yet, it was only *after* the Protestant Reformation, and in response to what was perceived to be a denial of the Real Presence on the part of the Reformers, that, increasingly, the Eucharist became reserved in tabernacles placed in the center of the main altar of Roman Catholic churches. Hence, for Roman Catholics the reservation or non-reservation of the Eucharist became most closely associated with the affirmation or denial of Christ's real presence.[34]

Mitchell summarizes the development of the Eucharist outside the eucharistic liturgy *per se* as the story of a significant shift from "Eucharist as meal" to "Eucharist as food," increasingly separated from the context of the "meal" itself.[35] If this is so, then the concern of the Lutheran Reformers for "usus" and "actio" and their suspicion of the external eucharistic cult associated with the reserved sacrament—"nothing can be a sacrament apart from God's command and the ordained use for which it is instituted in the word of God"—might surely be viewed as nothing other than a concern for restoring the very meal character of the Eucharist itself. In other words, without questioning the meaning of the "Eucharist as food," and while strongly affirming the real presence of Christ in, with, and under the "food," the Lutheran Reformers were adamant that such "food" was not an object to be adored *outside* of the overall liturgical *actio* but a gift to be received within that *actio* ("Eucharist as meal") itself. If this seems so obvious to us now, it was surely not so obvious in a late medieval context where Communion was received by the laity at most four times a year, and, at the least, by law, once during Easter as decreed by Lateran IV (1215). What David Holeton has written with regard to the cessation of infant Communion in the medieval West is certainly related to our topic here as well:

> A Christian society that has degenerated to such a state that it becomes necessary to legislate that Christians need receive the Eucharist once a year is fertile for most everything to take place in the context of baptism and the Eucharist. The whole vision of what the Eucharist was, and what its relationship was to the community, had . . . changed.[36]

## Eucharistic Reservation and Lutheranism Today

In light of the previous section, it would seem that the variety of "Lutheran" practices represented by our four contemporary ELCA congregations, with some exceptions, might all be considered somehow consistent not only with Lutheran sacramental theology and practice but with the variety of sacramental practices known throughout the history of the church. That is, the practice of non-reservation of the Eucharist represented by Transfiguration and Faith is surely consistent with the emphasis in both Luther and the Lutheran Confessions as well as with the continuing practice of the ancient Assyrian Church of the East. Indeed, with the concerns expressed both by Luther and the *Formula of Concord* against reservation and about the proper "usus" and "actio" of the sacrament within the context of the eucharistic liturgy itself, one wonders if the early Lutheran movement did not somehow accidentally restore that ancient eucharistic practice still characteristic of the Assyrian Church of the East. Here it is interesting to note that certain polemical Eastern Orthodox theologians, who have condemned "Nestorian" eucharistic practices, have seen in those practices the origins of Protestant "receptionism."[37]

What is very significant, however, is that the lack of reserving the Eucharist in the Assyrian Church of the East has *not* been a factor in the very recent determination of pastoral guidelines for Communion reception between the Assyrian Church of the East and the Chaldean Church, the latter of which is the closely-related Eastern Catholic Church in communion with Rome. Beginning in 1994 with a *Common Christological Declaration Between the Catholic Church and the Assyrian Church of the East*, continued ecumenical dialogue and convergence led in 2001 to a document entitled *Guidelines for Admission to the Eucharist between the Chaldean Church and the Assyrian Church of the East*. While these guidelines are ecumenically significant for a variety of reasons, it is clear that eucharistic reservation was and is not a related issue in this context. That is, even without the practice of eucharistic reservation, the *Guidelines* state clearly that "the Assyrian Church of the East has...preserved a full eucharistic faith in the presence of our Lord under the species of bread and wine."[38] In other words, as this development surely confirms, the reservation of the Eucharist can *not* be a litmus test for determining the orthodoxy of a particular church's theology of the real presence of Christ in the Eucharist. Consequently, in dialogue between Roman Catholics and Lutherans on the question of the Real Presence the issue of reservation might appear to be similarly moot.

At the same time, the apparent careless disregard for the elements remaining after the eucharistic liturgy at Transfiguration and Faith must also be addressed. That is, re-using and mixing consecrated and unconsecrated elements, or using what remains to feed the birds and squirrels, belies an un-Lutheran notion of "receptionism" which cannot be supported theologically. The Lutheran Reformers may well have considered various extra-liturgical practices associated with the Eucharist (e.g., processions and the like) to be abuses, but they did not teach a "receptionism." Hence, if the remaining eucharistic elements are to be reverently consumed or burned in the Lutheran tradition it is because they *are* consecrated and cannot be returned simply to common use, mixed for re-use, or merely scattered on the ground. Indeed, to paraphrase an early Christian document, the *Didache*, "one does not give what is holy to dogs" (or to birds and squirrels).

What then of the practice of eucharistic reservation at both St. Paul's and Christus Rex? While there may be an accidental parallel in the practice of non-reservation and belief in the Real Presence within both the Assyrian Church of the East and the Lutheran churches, this parallel certainly fails when it is remembered that Lutherans chose deliberately in the sixteenth century to stop reserving the Eucharist in their churches. With regard to specific Lutheran-Catholic dialogue and sacramental praxis today, then, the question of reservation is not really so moot at all since the cessation of reservation among Lutherans was a decision consciously directed against Roman Catholic praxis.

But must this still be the case in light of modern ecumenical convergence? That is, can there be a place in Lutheranism for a eucharistic reservation which does not compromise the Lutheran Confessional focus on sacramental "usus" or "actio"? One might surely think so and congregations like St. Paul's and Christus Rex have obviously concluded that eucharistic reservation is an appropriate Lutheran option today.

In an article on eucharistic reservation in contemporary Roman Catholicism Jesuit liturgist Peter Fink has written that:

The food of the Eucharist is reserved after the eucharistic celebration primarily to extend the nourishment and the grace of Christ's table to those unable to participate in the liturgy itself, particularly the sick and the dying. This is clearly stated in the 1967 instruction *Eucharisticum mysterium*: 'the primary and original purpose of the reserving of the sacred species in church outside Mass is the administration of the Viaticum' (*Eucharisticum mysterium*, III, I, A.).[39]

Of course, even the Council of Trent had made essentially the same point saying:

The custom of reserving the Holy Eucharist in a sacred place is so ancient that even the period of the Nicene Council recognized that usage. Moreover, the practice of carrying the sacred Eucharist to the sick and of carefully reserving it for this purpose in churches, besides being exceedingly reasonable and appropriate, is also found enjoined in numerous councils and is a very ancient observance of the Catholic Church. Wherefore, this holy council decrees that this salutary and necessary custom be by all means retained.[40]

Similarly, the significant 1982 ecumenical convergence statement of the Faith and Order Commission of the World Council of Churches, *Baptism, Eucharist, Ministry* suggests:

that, on the one hand, it be remembered, especially in sermons and instruction, that the primary intention of reserving the elements is their distribution among the sick and those who are absent, and on the other hand, it be recognized that the best way of showing respect for the elements served in the eucharistic celebration is by their consumption, without excluding their use for Communion of the sick.[41]

Closely related is the classic statement often attributed to early liturgical movement Belgian pioneer Lambert Beauduin that "the Eucharist is adored *because* it is reserved. It is not reserved in order to be adored." Clearly, the primary motive is for the Communion of the sick and dying. Any other acts of devotion or adoration of the presence of Christ associated with reservation are secondary in nature.

Together with the service called "Distribution of Communion to Those in Special Circumstances," and in light of a renewed Roman Catholic emphasis on eucharistic reservation as an extension of "the nourishment and the grace of Christ's table to those unable to participate in the liturgy itself, particularly the sick and the dying," it should be possible for Lutheranism to re-evaluate and, in some contexts, at least, to embrace a limited practice of eucharistic reservation today. With the relatively rare exception of congregations like Saint Paul's and Christus Rex, the fact that Lutherans have not traditionally reserved the Eucharist has tended to put Lutheranism at odds with what early on became the practice of the *dominant* ecclesial traditions of Christianity in both East and West. Further, reservation of the Eucharist and Communion from the reserved Eucharist, as we saw above in no less than Basil of Caesarea, can be viewed simply as the extension of the distribution of holy Communion from the Sunday Eucharist throughout the week. In this way Lutherans and Lutheran theology could embrace a practice of eucharistic reservation in ways that do not violate the Lutheran confessional stance about "action" and "use." That is, the reservation of the Eucharist for the purposes of the reception of Communion by the "absent" *is* nothing other than the extension of the eucharistic *actio* of the Sunday liturgy itself. Surely such an understanding of reservation for the purposes of Communion reception on the part of the sick, homebound, and dying can be seen today as part of "God's command and the ordained use for which it is instituted in the word of God." At the time of the Lutheran Reformation this focus may well have been obscured by a non-reception piety and a reservation practice viewed primarily for purposes of adoration. But that is hardly a danger today when both Lutherans and Roman Catholics place a similar emphasis on the reception of Communion in the eucharistic liturgy and where both now send out Communion ministers from the Sunday assembly to the sick and dying.

This does not mean, however, that either St. Paul's or Christus Rex are completely off the hook in their reservation and

Communion practices. The previous reservation practice of St. Paul's, with their "tabernacle" kept in the sacristy, was certainly much more consistent with the ancient Christian practice of reserving the Eucharist for the sick, homebound, and dying in sacristy ambries. In fact, it is hard not to interpret the moving of this tabernacle from the sacristy to the former main altar in the church as anything other than an attempt at imitation of (post-Trent) Roman Catholic and/or Anglo Catholic practice. Certainly Christus Rex needs to address its practice of communing the assembly from the reserved Eucharist at the Sunday liturgy. What Robert Taft has said about Roman Catholic practice applies doubly to congregations standing in the Lutheran tradition of the "usus" and "actio" of the meal. Taft writes:

> [I]t is clear that there has to be a better way of narrowing the gap between theory and execution. When one can still now, already generations after Benedict XIV (*Certiores effecti* §3) and Pius XII (*Mediator Dei* §118), go to Sunday Mass in a Roman Catholic parish church almost anywhere—even one whose pastor has an advanced degree in liturgical studies, pastoral theology, or some allied area—and be subjected to Communion from the tabernacle, that monstrous travesty of any true eucharistic symbolism whereby in a single moment common gifts are offered, blessed, distributed, shared—then there must indeed be a better way.[42]

One has to wonder, similarly, why it is that Christus Rex has also embraced the Roman Catholic "Mass of the presanctified" for Good Friday. Indeed, the reception of Communion from the reserved sacrament on Good Friday is itself a rather late development in the history of the Good Friday liturgy. The core of the ancient Good Friday Liturgy, preserved in the current *Lutheran Book of Worship*—and in the Ambrosian Rite of the Roman Catholic Archdiocese of Milan, Italy—is the Passion of St. John 18–19, the Solemn Intercessions, and the meditation, veneration, or adoration of the Cross. In other words, a Communion rite is not an essential part of the Good Friday liturgy and it is difficult to understand why Lutheran congregations would want to embrace something which is so foreign to their tradition. If Lutherans are to embrace the practice of eucharistic reservation, therefore, they need not directly imitate Roman Catholic reservation practices and especially they do not need to imitate "that monstrous travesty of any true eucharistic symbolism" by distributing Communion from the reserved Eucharist at the Sunday liturgy.

## Conclusion

In ecumenical dialogue and conversation, Roman Catholics are absolutely correct in pressing Lutherans on the question of belief in the real presence of Christ in the Eucharist in relationship to the reservation of the Eucharist. But, as I have attempted to demonstrate in this essay, there is no necessary correlation between a firm belief in the real presence of Christ in the eucharistic liturgy and meal and the practice of eucharistic reservation. That is, as the practice of the ancient Assyrian Church of the East indicates clearly, not all churches who hold a high doctrine of Christ's real presence have reserved the Eucharist historically. Further, lack of reserving the Eucharist in the Assyrian Church of the East has *not* been a factor in entering recently into a situation of shared Eucharist with the Chaldean Church. Perhaps, the traditional Lutheran practice of non-reservation could be viewed in the same ecumenical light today.

At the same time, however, I have suggested that Lutherans *could* reserve the Eucharist as but "an extension of the public liturgy in church" (Basil of Caesarea), an understanding toward which the occasional service called "Distribution of Communion to Those in Special Circumstances," already begins to point indirectly. Such a view of reservation, I have argued, does not conflict with the classic Lutheran emphasis of "usus" or "actio." Indeed, if as the "extension of the Sunday worship" the Eucharist can be carried to the sick, homebound, and dying within "a few hours" on Sunday afternoons then certainly the distribution of the Sunday Eucharist can be extended in this way for a "few days" during the week. For, whether "a few hours" or "a few days," the presence of Christ obviously remains somehow beyond the strict confines of the eucharistic celebration *in* church.

Finally, there may yet be another reason why modern Lutheranism might want to reconsider embracing the practice of eucharistic reservation. It is certainly true, as both traditional Lutheran and Assyrian Church of the East practice demonstrates, that belief in the real presence of Christ in the Eucharist does not lead necessarily to eucharistic reservation and, hence, reservation itself cannot be considered a necessity for Lutherans. But it is equally true that in those churches which do reserve the Eucharist there is little question about their belief in the real presence of Christ! It can not be forgotten that in the medieval West, where Communion reception was but an occasional act, it was precisely the practice of reservation along with associated devotional activity, that not only preserved the Eucharist as central in the life of the church, but which safeguarded belief in the Real Presence. If at the time of the Lutheran Reformation the issue was the restoration of the meal character of the Eucharist, perhaps in our own day and age it is the theology of and belief in the Real Presence itself. Indeed, were Lutherans to begin reserving the Eucharist as the "extension of the Sunday worship," consistent with the practices of some in early Christianity, it might put to rest once and for all the erroneous notion that Lutheran theology of the Real Presence is some form of "receptionism." Ironically, Lutheran reservation of the Eucharist today may be one of the best ways to preserve what Lutheranism actually believes, teaches, and confesses about the Eucharist, especially in light of recent ecumenical developments in the ELCA with the Episcopal Church, U.S.A., and various Reformed churches in the United States.

## Notes

1 Although the names of the congregations have been changed, these congregations and the practices described in them do exist and I have experienced them often. Also, while I have indicated that these are all ELCA congregations, I suspect that a similar variety of practices could be found also in congregations of the Lutheran Church–Missouri Synod.

2 *Occasional Services* (Minneapolis: Augsburg Fortress 1982), 82–8.

3 Ibid., 76–81.

4 See below, note 42.

5 Article X of the Augsburg Confession, for example, states that "the true body and blood of Christ are really present in the Supper of our Lord under the *form* of bread and wine . . ." T. Tappert (ed.), *The Book of Concord* (Philadelphia: Fortress Press, 1959), 34 [emphasis added].

6 Tappert, 51. Unfortunately, Melanchthon does not deal with this particular issue further in his *Apology*.

7 Tappert, 588.

8 Herman Sasse, *This Is My Body: Luther's Contention for the Real Presence of Christ in the Sacrament* (Minneapolis: Augsburg Publishing House, 1959), 173–174. In this context one might nuance Sasse's remarks to say that it is only until recently among Lutherans that consecrating new elements was the custom. In the current ELCA statement on sacramental practices, *The Use of the Means of Grace* (Minneapolis: Augsburg Fortress, 1997), 50, for example, the following appears: "in the rare event that more of either element is needed during distribution, it is not necessary to repeat the words of institution." But no clear rationale is given for what amounts to a departure from Lutheran tradition in this context. Sasse (and probably Luther himself) would have found this statement as undoubtedly indicative of a Zwinglian approach to the Eucharist in modern American Lutheranism.

9 Ibid., 174. The Latin phrase quoted above can be translated as: "In this way, therefore, let us define sacramental 'time' or 'action': that it might begin at the prayer of the Lord [*orationis dominicae*] and remain until all will have communed, the chalice will have been drunk, the particles [of bread] will have been eaten, and the people dismissed and left the altar." It is difficult to know here if "orationis dominicae" means the "Lord's Prayer" (Our Father) or is a reference to the institution narrative. Since this definition was given in 1543 it is possible that the reference is to the "Our Father" in the *Deutsche Messe* which actually precedes the institution narrative. But such an interpretation is not likely.

10 Evangelical Lutheran Church in America, *The Use of the Means of Grace: A Statement on the Practice of Word and Sacrament*, (Minneapolis: Augsburg Fortress, 1997), 50.

11 Ibid., 51.

12 *Occasional Services*, 79 [emphasis added].

13 H.J. Schroeder, *The Canons and Decrees of the Council of Trent* (St. Louis: B. Herder, 1941), Session XIII.4.

14 See Nathan Mitchell, *Cult and Controversy: The Worship of the Eucharist Outside Mass* (New York/Collegeville: Pueblo, 1982), 10–19. In addition to Mitchell, the following historical survey is based on Robert Taft, "The Frequency of the Eucharist Throughout History," in Idem. (ed.), *Beyond East and West: Problems in Liturgical Understanding* (Washington, D.C.: Pastoral Press, 1984), 87–110, Edward Foley, *From Age to Age* (Chicago: Liturgy Training Publications, 1991), and, of course, the classic study of O. Nussbaum, *Die Aufbewahrung der Eucharistie*, Theophaneia 29 (Bonn: Hanstein, 1979).

15 See *ad uxorem* 2:5, 2ff., and *De oratione* 19.4.

16 Cyprian, *De Lapsis* 26. See also Foley, 38.

17 *Apostolic Tradition*, chapters 36–38.

18 *Apostolic Tradition*, ch. 38; ET by G. Cuming, *Hippolytus: A Text for Students* (Cambridge: Grove Books, 1998), 28. See P. Bradshaw, M. Johnson, and L.E. Phillips, *The Apostolic Tradition: A Commentary* (Minneapolis: Fortress Press, 2002), 184–185.

19 Mitchell, 12.

[20] Basil, *Letter* 23 as quoted in Mitchell, 17–18.

[21] Mitchell, 18 [emphasis added].

[22] See Ibid., 17.

[23] See Ibid., 18–19.

[24] *Apostolic Constitutions* 8.13.17. See also Foley, 60.

[25] John Chrysostom, *Ep. Ad Innoc.* 3.

[26] Text as quoted by Foley, 60.

[27] See N.D. Uspensky, *Evening Worship in the Orthodox Church* (Crestwood: St. Vladimir's Seminary Press, 1985), 154–56.

[28] Cyril of Alexandria, *A Letter to Calosirius*, as translated in Uspensky, 154.

[29] On this see the classic article by Henry Chadwick, "Eucharist and Christology in the Nestorian Controversy," *Journal of Theological Studies*, New Series (1951), 145–64. Unfortunately, Chadwick does not deal with the question of reservation.

[30] Cyril of Alexandria, *Letter* 17.3. English translation in D. Sheerin, *The Eucharist*, Message of the Fathers of the Church, vol. 7 (Wilmington/Collegeville: Michael Glazier Books, 1986), 276–77. See also W.H.C. Frend, *The Rise of the Monophysite Movement: Chapters in the History of the Church in the Fifth and Sixth Centuries* (Cambridge: University of Cambridge Press, 1972), 124–25.

[31] Uspensky, 155. See also note 38 below.

[32] Email correspondence via Robert Taft, May 20, 2002.

[33] Joseph Jungmann, *The Mass of the Roman Rite*, vol. 1 (New York: Benziger Bros., 1951), 120ff. See also Robert Cabié, *History of the Mass* (Washington, D.C.: Pastoral Press, 1992), 75–84.

[34] See Theodore Klauser, *A Short History of the Western Liturgy* (Oxford/New York: Oxford University Press, 1979), 135–40.

[35] See Mitchell, 19–29.

[36] D. Holeton, "The Communion of Infants and Young Children: A Sacrament of Community," in G. Müller-Fahrenholz (ed.), *And Do Not Hinder Them: An Ecumenical Plea for the Admission of Children to the Eucharist*, Faith and Order Paper 109 (Geneva: World Council of Churches, 1982), 63.

[37] Cf. George Bebis, *Symbolai eis ten peri tou Nestoriou Ereunan (ex Apopseos Orthodoxou)*, Ph.D. Dissertation (University of Athens: 1964), 320–22; and Chrestos Androutsos, *Symbolike*, 2nd edn., (Athens 1930), 285–89ff, and 339ff. I owe these references to Deacon Stefanos Alexopoulos who wrote his Notre Dame doctoral dissertation under my direction on the Liturgy of the Presanctified in the Byzantine Tradition (2003).

[38] Pontifical Council for Promoting Christian Unity, *Guidelines for Admission to the Eucharist between the Chaldean Church and the Assyrian Church of the East* (Rome: 2001), para. 3.

[39] Peter Fink, "Eucharist, Reservation of," in Idem. (ed.), *The New Dictionary of Sacramental Worship* (Collegeville: Michael Glazier Books, 1990), 428.

[40] Session XIII, VI, in Schroeder.

[41] "Eucharist," III., 32, in World Council of Churches, *Baptism, Eucharist, Ministry* (Geneva: World Council of Churches, 1982).

[42] Robert Taft, "A Generation of Liturgy in the Academy," *Worship* 75 (2001), 58.

# PLANNING AND LEADING
# LITURGICAL PRAYER
# IN AN ECUMENICAL CONTEXT

In the past few years two extraordinary documents have appeared which signal a renewed commitment to ecumenism on the part of the Roman Catholic Church, namely, *The 1993 Directory for Ecumenism* (hereafter, *The Directory*) from the Pontifical Christian Unity Council,[1] and the 1995 Encyclical Letter of Pope John Paul II, *Ut Unum Sint*.[2] While both of these documents have a great deal to say about various ecumenical issues in general, one of their major emphases is the necessary place and formative role of common prayer within the ongoing quest for full and visible Christian unity. Indeed, Pope John Paul II couldn't be clearer about this. He writes that:

'. . . change of heart and holiness of life, along with public and private prayer for the unity of Christians, should be regarded as the soul of the whole ecumenical movement and can rightly be called spiritual ecumenism.' We proceed along the road leading to the conversion of hearts, guided by love which is directed to God and, at the same time, to all our brothers and sisters, including those not in full communion with us. Love gives rise to the desire for unity even in those who have never been aware of the need for it. Love builds communion between individuals and between communities . . . Love is given to God as the perfect source of communion—the unity of Father, Son and Holy Spirit—that we may draw

from that source the strength to build communion between individuals and communities or to re-establish it between Christians still divided . . .
. . . This love finds it most complete expression in common prayer. When brothers and sisters who are not in perfect communion with one another come together to pray, the Second Vatican Council defines their prayer as the soul of the ecumenical movement. This prayer is 'a very effective means of petitioning for the grace of unity,' 'a genuine expression of the ties which even now bind Catholics to their separated brethren.' Even when prayer is not specifically offered for Christian unity, but for other intentions such as peace, it actually becomes an expression and confirmation of unity. (*Ut Unum Sint,* 21)

When Christians pray together, the goal of unity seems closer. The long history of Christians, marked by many divisions, seems to converge once more because it tends toward that source of its unity which is Jesus Christ . . . In the fellowship of prayer *Christ is truly present;* he prays 'in us,' 'with us,' and 'for us.' It is he who leads our prayer in the Spirit-Consoler whom he promised and then bestowed on his church in the Upper Room in Jerusalem, when he established her in her original unity. Along the ecumenical path to unity, pride of place certainly belongs to common prayer, the prayerful union of those who gather together around Christ himself. If Christians, despite their divisions, can grow ever more united in common prayer around Christ, they will grow in the awareness of how little divides them in comparison to what unites them. If they meet more often and more regularly before Christ in prayer, they will be able to gain the courage to face all the painful human reality of their divisions, and they will find themselves together once more in that community of the church which Christ constantly builds up in the Holy Spirit, in spite of all weaknesses and human limitations. (*Ut Unum Sint,* 22) [emphasis added]

Finally, fellowship in prayer leads people to look at the church and Christianity in a new way. It must not be forgotten in fact that the Lord prayed to the Father that his disciples might be one, so that their unity might bear witness to his mission and the world would believe that the Father had sent him (cf. John 17:21) . . . It is true that we are not yet in full communion. And yet, despite our divisions, we are on the way toward full unity, that unity which marked the apostolic church at its birth and which we sincerely seek. Our common prayer, inspired by faith, is proof of this. In that prayer we gather together in the name of Christ who is one. He is our unity. 'Ecumenical' prayer is at the service of the Christian mission and its credibility. It must thus be especially present in the life of the church and in every activity aimed at fostering Christian unity. It is as if we constantly need to go back and meet in the Upper Room of Holy Thursday, even though our presence together in that place will not be perfect until the obstacles to full ecclesial communion are overcome and all Christians can gather together in the common celebration of the Eucharist. (*Ut Unum Sint*, 23)

As a Lutheran pastor, who teaches liturgical studies in a Roman Catholic university, this intimate relationship between common prayer and Christian unity expressed by Pope John Paul II is one that intrigues me greatly. And it does so especially as it concerns the formation of (primarily) Roman Catholic seminarians and graduate students preparing for either ordained or lay ministries in which planning for and leadership in prayer, sometimes even "*ecumenical* prayer," will be an essential and on-going component of their ministries. That is, the current ecumenical situation of the churches is such that with varying degrees of frequency and on particular occasions, such as the Thanksgiving holiday or the Week of Prayer for Christian Unity, Christians of differing traditions increasingly find themselves together in common public worship. How, then, does one plan for and lead common prayer in such ecumenical liturgical gatherings?

Some time ago, in an attempt to provide a bit of guidance for intelligent leadership in the area of ecumenical liturgy, I developed a series of five principles intended to serve as kind of checklist either for planning what might be called "intentional" ecumenical prayer services or for evaluating the overall theological and liturgical integrity of those services claiming to be "ecumenical." The remainder of this essay will consist of the presentation of these principles with detailed comments on each one.

Before proceeding with this, however, it must be noted that I offer these as a *Lutheran* liturgist and, therefore, my approach to this subject is very much shaped by the relatively common Western liturgical and sacramental tradition shared by Lutherans and Roman Catholics together. In other words, although members of the Episcopal Church, USA, another ecclesial body sharing the same basic tradition, as well as Christians from the various reformed traditions, might find these principles compatible with their own approaches to this topic, my principles should in no way be construed as applicable to common worship between Roman Catholics and *Protestants* in general. Similarly, only Roman Catholics themselves will be able to judge if what I offer here from an admittedly *Lutheran* perspective is of any assistance to them whatsoever.

**Principle #1. Does the service clearly reflect the liturgical tradition(s) and style(s) of the participating churches, or is one tradition and style overly dominant? In other words, is legitimate liturgical diversity in unity acknowledged and celebrated as mutual gift? Similarly, is the ministry of hospitality intentionally extended, especially toward those who inescapably find themselves in the role of "guest" in someone else's house?**

Since such ecumenical celebrations usually occur in a "host's" liturgical space, the dominance of one ecclesial tradition and style cannot but be visibly and environmentally present. In a Roman Catholic liturgical space, for example, the symbols of Catholicism (e.g., the tabernacle, holy water fonts, and images of the Virgin Mary and/or other saints, symbols not frequently found in many reformation heritage churches in the United States) are naturally present and will certainly signal to participants from other Christian traditions that they are not in their environmental, ecclesial "home." While signs and acts of hospitality and welcome should always be a part of any liturgical community, such signs and acts are thus especially important in ecumenical gatherings.

But, in saying that one tradition and style should not be overly dominant simply means that the service should not convey the notion that members of another Christian tradition are merely "guests" at what is clearly an explicit celebration of another tradition. Rather, as Paragraph 111 of *The Directory* says:

> Representatives of the churches, ecclesial communities or other groups concerned should cooperate and prepare together such prayer. They should decide among themselves the way in which each is to take part, choose the themes and select the Scripture readings, hymns and prayers.
>
> a)  In such a service there is room for any reading, prayer and hymn which manifests the faith or spiritual life shared by all Christian people. There is a place for an exhortation, address or biblical meditation drawing on the common Christian inheritance and able to promote mutual good will and unity.
>
> b)  Care should be taken that the versions of holy Scripture used be acceptable to all and be faithful translations of the original text.

I would hasten to add, however, that this does *not* mean that one should disregard the characteristic *style* of one's own liturgical tradition in favor of a kind of "reductionist" or "lowest common denominator" approach! Instead, it would seem that specific gatherings for ecumenical worship should express synthetically the very *best* of what one's own liturgical tradition has to offer to the ecumenical church. For example, the explicit reverence for the word of God often expressed in solemn Roman Catholic liturgical celebrations by ritual attention to the lectionary or Gospel book through processions, the use of candles and incense, and/or the ritual kiss of the Gospel itself need not and should not be minimized or omitted in such services and may even serve as a fitting reminder to members of so-called "churches of the word" of the important role the word of God as contained in the Scriptures actually plays in contemporary Roman Catholic worship and life. Such traditional "Catholic" emphases upon the importance and sacramentality of gesture, sign, and ceremony should certainly be able to function within "ecumenical worship" as fitting complements to the more so-called characteristically "Protestant" traditions of biblical preaching and corporate hymn singing. Since it has often been my experience in ecumenical services that such customary Roman Catholic gestures and ceremonies tend, in fact, to be absent, I would encourage Roman Catholics to be more willing to share the overall sacramental orientation of their liturgical tradition in these contexts. Indeed, liturgical diversity is not in tension with ecumenicity just as proper understanding of Christian unity does not imply "uniformity" or necessary homogeneity. Legitimate liturgical diversity *should* mean that the rich heritage each tradition brings to what might be called the "ecumenical stew" is not an ecumenical liability but a treasure and gift to be shared openly with other participants.

**Principle #2. Is the service recognizable as a true liturgy of the church with a clearly defined liturgical structure and with equally defined—and well-rehearsed—roles of liturgical leadership and ministry? Is it properly related to, or does it ignore, the particular feasts and seasons of the liturgical year?**

The recognition of legitimate liturgical diversity as a necessary component of the ecumenical context, of course, does *not* mean "anything goes" in ecumenical worship services. Again, for Roman Catholics in particular, paragraphs 111c, 116 and 117 of *The Directory* are especially worth noting:

> It is desirable that the structure of these celebrations should take account of the different patterns of community prayer in harmony with the liturgical renewal in many churches and ecclesial communities, with particular regard

being given to the common heritage of hymns, of texts taken from lectionaries and of liturgical prayers. (111c)

By liturgical worship is meant worship carried out according to books, prescriptions and customs of a church or ecclesial community presided over by a minister or delegate of that church or community . . . (116)

In some situations, the official prayer of *a church* may be preferred to ecumenical services specially prepared for the occasion. Participation in such celebrations as morning or evening prayer, special vigils, etc., will enable people of different liturgical traditions—Catholic, Eastern, Anglican and Protestant—to understand each other's community prayer better and to share more deeply in traditions which often have developed from common roots. (117) [emphasis added]

Simply put, ecumenical worship need not and should not be a "re-invention of the liturgical wheel." And, as the above paragraphs make clear, most of the (Western) *liturgical* Christian traditions today follow a similar Liturgy of the Word in the first place, together with a common three-year lectionary and liturgical calendar (at least for Sundays, Seasons, and most major festivals/solemnities), based on and adapted from the Roman Catholic lectionary and calendar reforms of the Second Vatican Council. Similarly, contemporary liturgical renewal in many of the churches has brought with it a recovery of what has been called the "cathedral tradition" of the Liturgy of the Hours as the prayer of the church for all Christians, with the result that among various churches similar structures and orders already exist at least for the celebration of Morning and Evening Prayer both in official worship books as well as in resources which have been produced ecumenically. In other words, planning for and leading ecumenical worship services with liturgical integrity is already assisted strongly by attending to the guidelines of the liturgical books, materials, and resources which are readily available in one's own tradition and which already display the common ecumenical fruits of the modern liturgical movement.

For Lutherans and Roman Catholics, in particular, however, there is even an *official* Liturgy of the Word explicitly designed for such common worship in the United States, namely, the *Lutheran-Roman Catholic Service of the Word* compiled from Lutheran and Roman Catholic liturgical books under the leadership of both Lutheran bishops and the National Conference of Catholic Bishops.[3] This *official* document, now, unfortunately, out-of-print, was available in both Leader and Pew (i.e., participant) Editions, and provided an excellent model of what an ecumenical service which respects sound liturgical principles should look like. Both Lutherans and Roman Catholics (and others for that matter) can recognize in it the very pattern, language, and flow of the Liturgy of the Word as they know it from their own regular experience of Sunday eucharistic celebrations:

Gathering/Gathering Song
Greeting
Promise of the Word (i.e., a short introductory dialogue)
Penitential Rite (optional)
Prayer
Reading(s)
Psalm Response (or silence)
Acclamation to the Gospel
Gospel
Homily
Silence
Creed (optional)
Prayers (both spoken and sung forms supplied)
Sign of Peace
Lord's Prayer
Offering (optional)
Praise (a lengthy thanksgiving prayer similar in structure
    to the Eucharistic Prayer)
Blessing
Dismissal

In addition to providing this pattern along with specific prayer texts, the Leader Edition[4] also gives lists of suitable readings, hymns, and other suggestions related specifically to various occasions (i.e., during the seasons of Advent, Christmas, Epiphany, Lent, Easter, and Pentecost as well as other times such as Reformation Sunday, the Week of Prayer for Christian Unity, and sanctoral feasts, or emphases such as Justification, Baptismal Renewal, and Thanksgiving) where the use of this joint service would be most appropriate. And, finally, the directions or rubrics at the beginning of the Leader Edition are also quite insistent on the necessity of clearly defined roles of leadership within the celebration.[5]

It is this desirability of clearly defined liturgical roles where I see Roman Catholics making a strong ecumenical liturgical contribution to Lutherans and others. In spite of the so-called Reformation "rediscovery" of the "priesthood of all believers," it has been my experience that it is more often in contemporary Roman Catholic liturgical celebrations where the active "priestly" participation of the whole body of Christ in worship, with specific roles assigned to and filled by *trained* and *rehearsed* ministers, is taken seriously and is most visibly evident and expressed. Here again Roman Catholics can teach the rest of us about our common liturgical and theological heritage by reminding us of, and modelling *for* us, the necessary roles of presider, lector, cantor, acolyte, and other ministries within that *corporate* body known as the liturgical assembly. Quite surprisingly, Lutheran (and some Protestant) patterns of worship leadership can tend to be overly clerical when it comes to leadership roles in the assembly, a problem often magnified when two or more ordained clergy in a given parish either divide up among themselves those sections of the liturgy clearly designated for *one* presider or, what is more serious, usurp the ministry of lay persons by filling those roles clearly assigned to one who is not ordained. Roman Catholics, therefore, have the opportunity in ecumenical worship contexts of teaching the rest of us the liturgical implications of the "royal priesthood of the faithful."

**Principle #3. Is the service sensitive to issues of continued theological and doctrinal division in such a way that the whole assembly may actively participate without compromising the particular and diverse orientations or stances held by different members of the assembly? In**

other words, can those participating experience this service as one which clearly reflects the common ecumenical faith of the church, while at the same time is sensitive to the particular faith expressions of the diverse communities represented?

Among at least Lutherans and Roman Catholics, given the officially approved common service of the word discussed above, this issue is not really as problematic as it might be in other contexts. What I refer to in this principle as the "common ecumenical faith of the church," it should be noted, is not some kind of generic acknowledgement of "Jesus as Lord," but an *explicit* profession of faith rooted in the common ecumenical creeds and confessions (i.e., the Apostles' and Nicene Creeds) of the church—the centrality of the one faith in God, Jesus Christ, and the Holy Spirit which is shared and confessed within the context of particular and traditional faith communities. This is why for Roman Catholics, Lutherans, Episcopalians, and members of the various Reformed churches it tends to be easier to engage in *ecumenical* worship together, where there already is this commonly shared creedal tradition and ecclesial focus, than it is to participate in what might be termed *inter-denominational* worship, where it cannot always be assumed that such traditional confessions of faith are accepted by all the participating communities as constituting a normative statement of their fundamental beliefs.

Nevertheless, even in what I mean by *ecumenical* worship in distinction to *inter-denominational* worship sensitivity to the reality of remaining doctrinal differences should be acknowledged and carefully maintained. And it is here where a particular caution must be raised for Roman Catholic leaders, planners, and participants.

I recently found myself present at Morning and Evening Prayer held as part of the meeting of an ecumenically-constituted professional organization, where the worship planning and leadership for this particular day, August 15, the Solemnity of the Assumption of the Blessed Virgin Mary on the Roman calendar and the lesser festival of Mary, Mother of the Lord on the Lutheran calendar, was the responsibility of Roman Catholic participants. While it is quite possible to celebrate such a feast in honor of the Blessed Virgin Mary together ecumenically, especially in the context of the Liturgy of the Hours, doctrinal issues related to Mary and the Saints certainly represent one of those areas of remaining differences in need of further ecumenical dialogue. But it was abundantly clear here that the hymns, psalm antiphons, prayers, and even the non-biblical readings selected for these offices reflected the specific Roman Catholic dogmatic stance on the Assumption, a stance with which many in that liturgical assembly did not and could not yet agree. Too often this has been my experience in similar contexts where sensitivity "to the particular faith expressions of the diverse communities" gathered for worship has not been maintained in the choice of liturgical materials and so "the common ecumenical faith of the church" was not as clearly reflected as it could have been.

In matters of ecumenical liturgy, however, a little bit of sensitivity can go a long way even in areas where there is not yet full doctrinal agreement. To give but one example, a service of Evening Prayer for the Solemnity of All Saints might be a fitting occasion for an ecumenical worship gathering. If so, then ecumenically sensitive Roman Catholic planners for this would seek to make sure that a prayer *other* than the first option in the Roman liturgical books would be chosen as the prayer of the day. This prayer reads:

> Let us pray (*that the prayers of all the saints will bring us forgiveness for our sins*).
> Father, all powerful and ever-living God, today we rejoice in the holy men and women of every time and place. *May their prayers bring us your forgiveness and love.* We ask this through our Lord Jesus Christ, your Son, who lives and reigns with you and the Holy Spirit, one God, for ever and ever.[6]

Unfortunately, the use of this first option would do nothing other than raise precisely those issues which divide rather than unite the various churches and so polarize the assembly according to individual doctrinal positions. A better prayer choice for such an event obviously would be the second optional prayer provided in the Roman books or a prayer from the books of another tradition. Along these lines, the prayer for All Saints' Day in the American Episcopal *Book of Common Prayer* might be the best choice of all:

> Almighty God, you have knit together your elect in one communion and fellowship in the mystical body of your Son Christ our Lord: Give us grace so to follow your blessed saints in all virtuous and godly living, that we may come to those ineffable joys that you have prepared for those who truly love you; through your Son Jesus Christ our Lord, who with you and the Holy Spirit lives and reigns, one God, in glory everlasting.[7]

To such a prayer an ecumenical liturgical assembly could surely utter an unqualified "Amen" without comprising their specific confessional positions at all.

While this whole issue of "common ecumenical faith" and the importance of sensitivity "to particular faith expressions" may seem so obvious as to require no comment at all, my many experiences tell me that it is precisely this "obvious" issue which too often is neglected. Whether that reflects a lack of ecumenical sensitivity or simply a profound ignorance of the doctrinal positions of other Christian traditions on the part of planners and leaders I cannot say. But in drawing attention to this it is my hope that all might indeed incorporate this rather "obvious" principle into their process of worship planning.

**Principle #4. Is the gift of baptismal identity and unity somehow a central focus of the service either through the choice of texts, hymns, prayers, and ritual acts, or by means of the homily? And, along similar lines flowing from a common baptism, is the lack of common eucharistic participation painfully and prayerfully acknowledged and addressed?**

The "common ecumenical faith of the church," referred to above in Principle #3, is more than a common unitive sharing in the traditional creeds of the church. It is a *common faith* professed in those creeds which has been constituted by "one baptism." Both *The Directory* and *Ut Unum Sint* draw attention to the importance of this fundamental *sacramental* reality for ecumenism. Paragraph 129 of *The Directory* clearly states that:

> The Catholic Church teaches that by baptism members of other churches are brought into a *real*, even if imperfect, *communion with the Catholic Church* and that 'baptism which constitutes *the sacramental bond of unity existing among all who through it are reborn . . .* is wholly directed toward the acquiring of fullness of life in Christ' [emphasis added].

And, near the end of Paragraph 66 of *Ut Unum Sint* Pope John Paul II similarly says:

> . . . the sacrament of baptism, which we have in common, represents 'a sacramental bond of unity linking all who have been reborn by means of it.' The theological, pastoral, and ecumenical implications of our common baptism are many and important. Although this sacrament of itself is 'only a beginning, a point of departure,' it is 'oriented toward a complete profession of faith, a complete incorporation into the system of salvation such as Christ himself willed it to be and, finally, toward a complete participation in eucharistic Communion.'

While the divided churches of the West may not yet be able to participate in a common Eucharist together or even baptize together in a common celebration of Christian initiation, these Roman documents are clear in underscoring the fundamental and basic *sacramental* reality and *bond of unity* constituted by baptism that is shared in common already, a unity which, by definition, is oriented ultimately toward sharing the eucharistic bread and cup. This common baptismal sacramental reality and bond and the implications of that reality and bond must become a focal point for ecumenism in general! And one of the implications of this for ecumenical worship would seem to be that the divided churches should somehow celebrate this fundamental baptismal unity, this *"real communion"* together. Indeed, whether the primary focus of the service is baptismal renewal or not, one of the principal "sacramental" acts of ecumenical worship following the homily well may be a specific re-affirmation or renewal of baptismal vows, complete with a sprinkling rite and exchange of peace. Since we share at least *this* common sacramental reality it is this we should celebrate liturgically in as rich, celebratory, and festive manner as possible. It is sometimes said that if early Christians had known and used the terminology of "Blessed Sacrament" to refer to any of the sacraments their sacrament of choice for this designation would have been *baptism*. And in this sense, therefore, we already share in common the traditional "Blessed Sacrament" of the early Church.

But even more than this can be said. It is well known that in Paragraph 7 of *The Constitution on the Sacred Liturgy* the Second Vatican Council underscored the various modes of the *presence* of Christ in the liturgy:

> . . . Christ is always present in his church, especially in her liturgical celebrations. He is present in the sacrifice of the Mass not only in the person of his minister . . . but especially in the eucharistic species. By his power he is present in the sacraments so that when anybody baptizes it is really Christ himself who baptizes. He is present in his word since it is he himself who speaks when the holy scriptures are read in the church. Lastly, he is present when the church prays and sings.[8]

The ecumenical sharing of common prayer, such as is reflected in the above-discussed *Lutheran-Roman Catholic Service of the Word*, and rooted in the common *sacramental bond* of baptism is, therefore, by no means, a "second-class" or lower form of worship. Rather, it is a celebration of the *presence* of Jesus Christ himself who, if not present by means of the "eucharistic species" in these ecumenical assemblies, nevertheless, is *really* present in such gatherings! Again, in the words of Pope John Paul II, "In the fellowship of prayer *Christ is truly present*; he prays 'in us,' 'with us,' and 'for us.'"[9] Commenting on the ecumenical implications of these multiple presences of Christ in the liturgy, long before anything like the *Lutheran-Roman Catholic Service of the Word* was produced, Roman Catholic theologians Karl Rahner and Heinrich Fries wrote:

> *Pulpit fellowship* is already being practiced in many cases; and it no longer presents a disquieting exception, even to Catholic Christians. But one really should think about this more than ever, *since it is precisely a pulpit fellowship which presupposes a community of faith.* Consider the reality of salvation of the word of God; consider Christ's presence in its various forms, including the form of proclamation; finally consider the theological conformity of word and sacrament—sacrament as visible word (*verbum visibile*), the word as audible sacrament (*sacramentum audible*).[10]

The implications for Christian unity, arising from a common baptismal foundation and "bond," expressed in the common ecumenical creeds of the catholic tradition, and from celebrating together in prayer and word the *real presence* of the crucified and risen Lord among us, are, indeed, many. While the celebration of the Eucharist, "inseparably linked to full ecclesial communion and its visible expression" (*The Directory* 129), is not yet possible in such ecumenical gatherings, and should always be "painfully and prayerfully acknowledged and addressed," it must be underscored that there exists already a basic "communion of faith" between Roman Catholics and certain other Western Christian traditions having their origins in the Reformation period. And in this way, the following words of Pope John Paul II have a special relevance:

> If Christians, despite their divisions, can grow ever more united in common prayer around Christ, they will grow in the awareness of how little divides them in comparison to what unites them. If they meet more often and more regularly before Christ in prayer, they will be able to gain the courage to face all the painful human reality of their divisions, and they will find themselves together once more in that community of the church which Christ

constantly builds up in the Holy Spirit, in spite of all weaknesses and human limitations.[11]

Indeed, it is in such common prayer, in the sharing in the proclamation of the word, and in the thankful celebration and renewal of our "one" baptismal plunge into Christ himself where we will be led ultimately to the eucharsitic banquet together. In the meantime, while our prayer continues to petition God for the unity we seek, there is thus much to celebrate regarding our unity already.

**Principle #5. Does the service somehow challenge the gathered assembly to continue in dialogue, prayer, and action toward greater common and visible unity? And, does the liturgical service make the connection between common worship and common service, witness, and evangelism in the world? In other words, is unity celebrated only for its own sake or for the sake of the church's mission in obedience to the command and will of Jesus Christ?**

Although full and visible Christian unity, expressed in a common Eucharist at some point in the future, is the primary sought after goal of ecumenical worship, the drive toward Christian unity itself is related to, and for the sake of, the credibility of the church's witness, proclamation, and service in and to the world. In John 17, Jesus' own "High Priestly Prayer" to the Father for the unity of the church, it must be remembered, was "so that the world may believe that [the Father] had sent [him]" (John 17:21). Christian unity, therefore, is not simply a good idea. It is, rather, according to the will of Christ, the command, duty, and responsibility of all the baptized. This is undoubtedly why Pope John Paul II asks of all Christians:

How is it possible to remain divided if we have been 'buried' through baptism in the Lord's death, in the very act by which God, through the death of his Son, has broken down the walls of division? Division 'openly contradicts the will of Christ, provides a stumbling block to the

world and inflicts damage on the most holy cause of proclaiming the good news to every creature.'[12]

And, as he further notes:

This unity, which the Lord has bestowed on his church
and in which he wishes to embrace all people, is not
something added on, but stands at the very heart of
Christ's mission. Nor is it some secondary attribute of the
community of his disciples. Rather, it belongs to the very
essence of this community.[13]

This connection between ecumenical worship and the
church's mission probably is best expressed in various kinds of
collaborative ministries of education, witness, and service
among the divided churches.[14] And it is here where excellent
models of, at least, Roman Catholic and Lutheran collaboration
already exist. In 1990 the Roman Catholic Archdiocese of Saint
Paul-Minneapolis (MN), entered into an official covenant relationship with the Minneapolis and Saint Paul Area Synods of the
Evangelical Lutheran Church in America (ELCA). This covenant,
signed both by the Roman Catholic archbishop and the ELCA
bishops, includes a common affirmation of Christian faith and
commits Roman Catholics and Lutherans in that metropolitan
region to several on-going joint liturgical and pastoral ventures.
This covenant states:

WE COMMIT OURSELVES TO:
◆   Confess to God and to each other our past and pres-
    ent prejudice against each other's traditions, practices
    and beliefs, and allow God to forgive our sin against
    each other and God.
◆   Give thanks for the unity God has given us, celebrate
    it in joint services, and pray for the day when we cel-
    ebrate the Eucharist as one community.
◆   Pray for one another in our public worship, that the
    Holy Spirit continue to heal brokenness that now
    exists in doctrine, sacramental life and church order,
    and enable us to work energetically for healing.

- ◆ Listen to the Holy Scriptures and together be instructed by them.
- ◆ Strengthen our common witness to the Christ and our quest for peace and justice.
- ◆ Give special support to those who live a Lutheran-Catholic covenant in their families.
- ◆ Struggle together, and with all other Christians, to resist and transform whatever in our society and culture would erode our common faith.
- ◆ Study jointly the public conversations of the national Lutheran-Catholic Dialogues, and act jointly on recommendations of our respective churches in response to the official dialogues.
- ◆ Urge our congregations, pastors, priests, and lay ministers to cooperate in common matters wherever possible, and encourage joint programs and common use of facilities on all levels of church life.
- ◆ Celebrate and renew this covenant each year.

This particular covenant has born fruit in other areas as well. Not only did the Roman Catholic Diocese of Duluth (MN) and the Northeastern Minnesota Synod of the ELCA sign a similar covenant on October 1, 1995,[15] but the archdiocese and ELCA Synods of Minneapolis-Saint Paul have produced a *Guide For A Lutheran-Catholic Marriage* (June 4, 1995) in response to what is often a difficult pastoral issue facing both of these traditions.

These "Minnesota Models" are excellent examples of the kinds of ecumenical developments in collaborative witness and service that can happen when worship planners and leaders take seriously the emphases of principle #5. For, as paragraph 162 of *The Directory* says:

Christians cannot close their hearts to the crying needs of our contemporary world. The contribution they are able to make to all areas of human life in which the need for salvation is manifested will be more effective when they make it together and when they are seen to be united in making it. Hence they will want to do everything together that is allowed by their faith . . . Their cooperation can help them to overcome the barriers to full communion and at the same time to put together their resources for building Christian life and service and the common witness that it gives, in view of the mission which they share.

## Conclusion

We sometimes hear it said today that "ecumenism is dead" and that the excitement about ecumenism in the immediate aftermath of Vatican II has long since passed away. I would beg to differ. Both *The Directory* and *Ut Unum Sint*, after all, are *recent* documents and both of them show that the commitment to ecumenism on the part of the Roman Catholic Church is as strong as it ever was. I would suggest, then, that far from being dead there has been, instead, a "deepening" of ecumenism in that the ecumenical hopes and dreams of Vatican II have become realized so much that common worship, witness, and service among the divided churches is no longer an exception but approaching the status of a norm. In this we must not lament the perceived lack of ecumenism or excitement about ecumenism but, rather, rejoice in the very fruits of ecumenism among us.

Nevertheless, as long as there is the scandal of Christian division and the lack of full, visible, eucharistic Communion, part of the Church's vocation in the world will be to pray and work that such communion might be finally established. It is, then, my sincere hope that the above principles for planning and leading liturgical prayer in an ecumenical context may be of assistance in this endeavor, especially to those who are charged with the responsibility and privilege of leading us in joining the priestly prayer of Jesus Christ himself that all may, indeed, be one (John 17:21).

## Notes

1 *Origins* 23, (1993), 129–60.

2 *Origins* 25, (1995), 49–72.

3 (Minneapolis: Augsburg Publishing House, 1986).

4 See 21–26.

5 See 7ff.

6 *The Sacramentary* (Collegeville: The Liturgical Press, 1985), 660 [emphasis added].

7 *Book of Common Prayer* (New York: Seabury Press, 1979), 245.

8 A. Flannery (ed.), *Vatican Council II*, vol. 1 (Collegeville: The Liturgical Press, 1975), 4–5.

9 *Ut Unum Sint* 22 [emphasis added].

10 From *Unity of the Churches: An Actual Possibility* (New York/Minneapolis: Paulist Press and Fortress Press, 1985), 125 [emphasis added].

11 *Ut Unum Sint* 22.

12 *Ut Unum Sint* 6.

13 *Ut Unum Sint* 9.

14 See *The Directory* 109, 161–65.

15 See *Catholic Outlook: The Diocese of Duluth* 25 (1995), 4–7.

# FEASTS

# LITURGICAL REFLECTIONS ON THE TRANSFER OF SOLEMNITIES AND FEASTS TO THE FOLLOWING OR NEAREST SUNDAY

There is a traditional Lutheran principle, first enunciated in Martin Luther's 1523 *Formula Missae*, that certain feasts on the sanctoral cycle, if they were important enough to be maintained at all, should be transferred to the nearest Sunday, or, according to later Lutheran liturgical practice, if the date of a particular saint's day falls on a Sunday in a given year its propers and assigned lectionary readings may, in fact, take precedence over those assigned to that Sunday. In light of this principle, Lutherans today regularly celebrate Reformation (October 31) as "Reformation Sunday" on the last Sunday in October, All Saints (November 1) on the first Sunday in November, and often have the option of transferring other saints' days, usually New Testament (e.g., Mary, Mother of our Lord, Aug. 15, and Saint Mary Magdalene, July 22) or apostolic saints, which have the rank of "lesser festival" (the equivalent of "Feast" in the current Roman Calendar) to the Sunday nearest their calendrical date. So much is this both a traditional and contemporary Lutheran custom that even when December 26, 27, or 28 fall on the First Sunday after Christmas, Lutherans will generally celebrate Saint Stephen, Saint John and the Holy Innocents, respectively, instead of the First Sunday after Christmas. With the exception of these December dates, this principle is used only during the Lutheran equivalent of "Ordinary Time" (i.e., the Sundays called "After the Epiphany," where feasts like the Confession of Saint Peter on January 18 and the Conversion of Saint Paul on January 25 may take precedence over Sundays, and during the Sundays called "After Pentecost," where various lesser festivals may take similar precedence as well). But during Advent, Lent, and Easter, calendrical feasts are not transferred to Sundays. As in Roman Catholic practice, when, for example, March 25, the Annunciation of our Lord, falls on a Lenten Sunday it is not celebrated then, and, similarly, Saint Andrew, November 30, is not celebrated on an Advent Sunday, nor is Saint Mark, April 25, celebrated on a Sunday during the Easter season. That is, the priority of the temporal over the sanctoral is maintained during Advent, Lent, and Easter.

Modern Roman Catholic liturgical practice, of course, is rather similar during Ordinary Time, when various solemnities fall on Sundays (e.g., Saints Peter and Paul, June 29, and the Assumption of the Blessed Virgin Mary, August 15) and, in some places, such solemnities are actually transferred to the nearest Sunday for pastoral reasons. In recent history, however, the transfer of various solemnities of the Lord outside of Ordinary Time has also become customary. In several places, where the liturgical books themselves provide such options, it has become quite common to celebrate the Epiphany of the Lord, January 6, on the first Sunday in January (between January 2–8) and, more recently in several dioceses of the United States, to celebrate the Solemnity of the Ascension of the Lord on the Seventh Sunday of Easter.

Such changes have usually been met with a positive response, especially within our changing cultural context, where the level of festivity associated and desired for these solemnities is difficult to achieve or maintain when such celebrations occur on weekdays. Undoubtedly, much is gained pastorally, liturgically, and in terms of spirituality, when these occasions are celebrated on a Sunday, when greater numbers of the faithful may be able to participate than would be able on weekdays and are, thus, more are able to experience through the propers and lectionary readings assigned to them the contents of these important solemnities in the liturgical year.

I wonder, however, if it is time to re-think this practice and to ask whether we have lost, or are losing something, in terms of the priority of Sunday itself as *the* Christian feast day of the paschal mystery, the nature of festivity, and the role of liturgical calendars *vis-á-vis* the cultural context in which we find ourselves today. That is, are the transfers of Ascension "Thursday" to Sunday and of the Epiphany to the first Sunday in January completely positive developments or does this practice need revisiting? What, in fact, is accomplished by these transfers? And if these solemnities can be transferred during the Christmas and Easter seasons then why can't or shouldn't other solemnities during Advent or Lent also be transferred? The following is but an attempt to reflect on these issues and to raise some questions for ongoing consideration and conversation. It is most certainly not meant to call into question the pastoral decisions made by bishops of particular regions to transfer specific solemnities and feasts and should not be read as such.

## I. The Transfer of the Epiphany to the First Sunday in January

Prior to the current reform, the Solemnity of the Epiphany of the Lord on January 6 was not a holy day of obligation and would have been celebrated primarily by those who participated in daily Mass. In the light of the current reform, certainly there is an immense value in having the celebration of the Epiphany on a Sunday in the Christmas Season so that the Epiphany narrative of the visit of the Gentile Magi to Bethlehem, as the sign of Gentile inclusion in the mystery of Christ, is always proclaimed and celebrated as an integral part of the Christmas narrative. Without the Epiphany on a Sunday, this narrative would not be heard in a liturgical context very often, with the exception of those years that January 6 occurs on a Sunday itself.

But what becomes of the *date* of the celebration of the Epiphany itself? Celebrating the Epiphany on January 6, whenever it may occur during the week, brings with it two associations that may be of some importance. First, January 6 brings to a conclusion what we used to call the "Twelve Days of Christmas," a twelve day "season" of the liturgical year which may serve to function counter-culturally in a context which often assumes that those "twelve days" begin eleven days before

Christmas with Christmas Day itself functioning as this "twelfth day." And yet, I know of some Lutheran and Episcopalian parishes for whom the Epiphany on January 6 remains a festive celebration, often concluded by a solemn burning of the Christmas tree each year as the grand finale to the Christmas season. To keep January 6 as the Epiphany, a day even of gift giving in honor of the visit of the "three kings" in some cultures, may be an important sign that, in the words of John Baldovin: "feasts are extraordinary. They lift people out of ordinary chronological time." And, further:

> . . . the antifestal situation of modern society does not demand immediate and unconditional surrender on the part of Christian communities. Faced with an impoverishment of time as well as an impoverishment of cult . . . congregations and their leaders should realize that time need not be shaped by factors which are beyond their control. How individuals and communities order their time is an indication of their priorities. In an increasingly 'de-natured' world, those priorities will have to be fought for. Thus there is something inherently evangelistic about the celebration of Christian feasts.[1]

The transfer of the Epiphany from January 6 to the first Sunday in January may well be a sign of cultural accommodation or "immediate and unconditional surrender." We may have succeeded in transferring the *contents* of the Epiphany to a Sunday but have we succeeded in transferring the "spirit" of Epiphany festivity, if there ever was much, to that Sunday? Or, have we simply exchanged the time-honored tradition of the Epiphany for yet another "ordinary" Sunday celebration, the contents of which may actually matter little, except to us liturgists? That is, since people do not normally go to Mass on January 6 we're going to make sure they receive the contents of this Mass anyway! But in an ecclesial context in which the Solemnity of Mary, Mother of God on January 1 is a holy day of obligation in several places and never transferred to a Sunday, admittedly with the cultural support of it also being New Year's Day, one wonders why priority and more liturgical importance should be given to *this* celebration than to the clearly more central and more fundamental Solemnity of the Epiphany. And, if the Epiphany is *so* important that it should be transferred, then it is certainly important enough to stand on its own, just as the Solemnity of Mary, Mother of God does. Indeed, I doubt that Jews would find the first Sabbath after the first day of the eight days of Hannukah to be a satisfactory conclusion to Hannukah or that the thought of transferring Christmas Day to the Sunday after the Fourth Sunday of Advent would find much support among Christians. But if December 25 and January 1 retain their liturgical importance on their fixed dates, why not January 6 as well?

Second, liturgical historians remind us of the close calendrical associations of January 6 (and December 25) with the early Christian reckoning of the date of Christ's death. The computation hypothesis about the origins of the dates of Christmas and the Epiphany, advanced in recent years especially by Thomas Talley, suggests that these were actually based on a deliberate calculation which sought to correlate the date of Jesus' death (March 25 or April 6; =14 Nisan) with his conception leading to a celebration of his "birth" nine months later on December 25 (possibly celebrated already in third-century North Africa) or January 6 (the date chosen throughout the East). While it is probably true that the principal focus of such feasts was a unitive celebration of Jesus' 'beginnings', i.e., his birth and/or baptism, which later traditions sorted out differently, it remains the case that the very dates themselves have *Paschal* connotations and associations, both of which are somewhat lost by transferring the Epiphany to a Sunday. And the correlation of both Christmas and the Epiphany to the "adult Christ" of Christmas, to use Raymond Brown's phrase, may, indeed, be something we wish to consider seriously.

Another element worthy of our consideration here is what happens to the Feast of the Baptism of the Lord in the context of this Sunday transfer of the Epiphany. As is well known, when the Sunday celebration of the Epiphany occurs on either January 7 or 8, that is, when the Epiphany is actually celebrated *after* the Epiphany, then the regular Sunday *after* the Epiphany, which is the Feast of the Baptism of the Lord, is itself transferred to

*Monday.* In other words, by transferring the Epiphany to a Sunday, the feast of Jesus' baptism which *is* undoubtedly a significant part of the earliest celebration and contents of Epiphany (or "Theophany") itself, is occasionally "bumped" from Sunday in some years and, hence, given less importance. And yet, surely the baptismal-ecclesial focus and implications of the Baptism of the Lord is of similar, if not greater importance liturgically, theologically, and spiritually, than the visit of the Magi. Indeed, the Epiphany, understood as the celebration of Jesus' baptism, was one of the principal occasions, along with Easter, for the celebration of baptism in Christian antiquity. So, in some years we're simply going to transfer that to a Monday, because we transferred January 6 to a Sunday? I'm not sure that the logic of this is all that clear.

## II. The Transfer of "Ascension Thursday" to the Seventh Sunday of Easter

If the transfer of the Epiphany to the first Sunday between January 2 and 8 has been with us for some time, the transfer of the Solemnity of the Ascension to the Seventh Sunday of Easter, while permitted in the current liturgical books for several years, has become more common in dioceses of the United States only recently. It is well known, of course, that, historically speaking, Ascension and Pentecost appear to have constituted a primitive unity. In her late-fourth century pilgrimage diary, for example, Egeria describes a Pentecost Sunday afternoon stational liturgy which commemorated the Ascension and seems to imply as well that any liturgical celebrations on the fortieth day of Easter were not yet celebrations of the Ascension itself. Soon, however, the chronology of Luke–Acts was used to support celebrations of the Ascension on the fortieth day of Easter, always, of course, on a Thursday, and, at least in the United States, Ascension Day is a holy day of obligation. As such, "Ascension Thursday" has become part of our liturgical year vocabulary and one can well imagine people saying that "Ascension Thursday" will now be celebrated on Sunday (similar to the annual question of "What time is Midnight Mass on Christmas?").

But once again, certain questions are raised by this transfer. First, the mere fact that the Solemnity of the Ascension is commonly referred to as "Ascension Thursday" suggests that there is already a firmly ingrained association in the minds of the faithful, an association much more common here than any popular or similar associations readily available with regard to the Epiphany, though, of course, that wasn't always the case.

Second, that this feast occurs, according to Luke–Acts chronology, on the "Fortieth" Day of Easter *does* suggest the strong associations with the biblical significance of the number "forty" both in the Hebrew Bible and the New Testament, a significance readily lost by transferring Ascension to Sunday. So much is this "fortieth day" associated with Ascension in our liturgical tradition that the lectionary readings, chants, hymn texts, and the like aren't as easily transferable to a Sunday as the liturgical contents of other feasts may be. The liturgical contents of the Epiphany, for example, never say that the Magi visit on the "Twelfth Day of Christmas," although I suspect that in some cultures the "three kings" bearing gifts still do and will continue to come on January 6!

Third, I wonder if the integrity of the Easter Season itself is entirely respected by this transfer. That is, what are we saying about Sunday, in general, and the Seventh Sunday of *Easter* in particular, if we allow this Solemnity to take its place? Does not the Easter Season, arranged as it is, have its own particular logic in moving us from Ascension to Pentecost, with that intervening Sunday containing Jesus' High Priestly prayer from John 17 as part of an intended liturgical transition *between* Ascension and Pentecost? As important as the celebration of the Ascension may be, is it so important that it should displace the Seventh Sunday of Easter entirely? Or, is it really of such relative importance to the overall character of the Easter Season that its primary signification may best be served by reuniting it with Pentecost Sunday itself in some way so that the connection between Jesus' "going up" and the Holy Spirit "coming down" is better expressed? Further, if we can transfer a solemnity like this to a Sunday in *Easter*, especially because of its apparent integral connections to the Easter Season, then why not be able either to transfer a solemnity like the Annunciation of the Lord on March 25 to a Sunday in *Lent*, or to allow it to displace a *Lenten* Sunday when March 25 occurs on a Sunday? Is the integrity of Lent more important than the integrity of the Easter Season? In fact, given the historical associations of March 25 with the date of Christ's death in early Christianity, as we saw above in relationship to Christmas and Epiphany, I could well imagine that enough paschal or Easter associations with the date of the Annunciation could be made that might reinforce a similar, integral connection to the focus of Lent. And yet, unlike Ascension, the Annunciation has not been a holy day of obligation.

Fourth, as with the Epiphany on January 6, the connection of Ascension to the fortieth day of Easter, may well be another one of those "extraordinary" feasts, which "lift people out of ordinary chronological time." Indeed, the nature of feasts on particular days tends to interrupt ordinary life with an occasion of festivity and an opportunity to become reoriented and re-grounded in the liturgical tradition. And, as such, "Ascension Thursday," precisely *as* a celebration that does *not* take place on a Sunday can function in a way which is "inherently evangelistic" *vis-á-vis* the numerous challenges of contemporary life. By transferring it to a Sunday, then, we may end up losing many of the classic and traditional associations that Ascension suggests and we may end up missing an "evangelistic" opportunity.

## III. Conclusion: Why Transfer at All?

There are, of course, several pastoral reasons why in our contemporary cultural context it makes great sense to transfer certain important solemnities and feasts, such as the Epiphany or the Ascension, to Sundays and I do find myself in general agreement with many of these: e.g., the difficulty of participation on weekdays; low attendance even for holy days of obligation; difficulties in scheduling weekday celebrations; the mere fact that most feasts become in this way "after work" evening celebrations; and that the notion of any profound sense of festivity is often absent from such celebrations. But whether or not their transfer to Sunday does little more than ensure a larger crowd for the Mass remains to be seen.

In spite of my general support, three things in particular concern me about this practice of transferring feasts: (1) the precedent that such transfers set regarding the priority of Sunday in general; and (2) the notion of festivity; and (3) ecumenical considerations. First, if we wish to maintain the priority of Sunday as *the* Christian feast and the priority of the temporal cycle over the sanctoral cycle, certainly the transfer of both Ascension and the Epiphany, as solemnities integral to both Easter and Christmas, *do* maintain that priority. But if we say that these two can replace either the Second Sunday After Christmas or the Seventh Sunday of Easter then there *is* a precedent being set about the relationship between Sundays and Solemnities even during Christmas and Easter. If these solemnities can replace Sundays in *these* seasons, why, for example, should the Presentation of the Lord on February 2 not regularly be transferred to the first Sunday in February, or, as I noted above, why not transfer the Annunciation to a Lenten Sunday, given the fact that an integral connection with Easter *could* be argued? Similarly, I fully suspect that within some Latino-Hispanic communities there are probably several who would argue that the feast of Our Lady of Guadalupe on December 12 is quite integral to Advent and is an especially powerful symbol or icon of Advent (both incarnationally and eschatologically) in general, just as in some Eastern Christian traditions, Advent itself (though not necessarily called Advent) has a strong Marian dimension and focus. So, why not transfer this feast in Advent? Indeed, a pastoral liturgist working in an Hispanic-Latino context dare not ignore December 12, even when it falls on an Advent Sunday, though such might raise the hackles of liturgists in general.[2] I suspect further that some would argue in a like manner regarding the Solemnity of the Immaculate Conception on December 8. Or, why not, for the same pastoral reasons noted above, simply transfer the distribution of ashes from Ash Wednesday to the First Sunday of Lent, the actual beginning of Lent anyway? I am not advocating any of this! I am simply stating that with the precedent set by the transfers of the Epiphany and the Ascension to Sundays, we may be opening up a liturgical can of worms that needs some careful attention. If we *can* transfer those two solemnities in those seasons, then why not others in other seasons? Are, for example, Sundays in Advent and Lent given higher priority than those in Christmas and Easter? I *do* wonder if by transferring such solemnities we are not in our organization of liturgical time making an "immediate and unconditional surrender" in a modern antifestal context to "factors which are beyond [our] control." And I wonder if in the process we end up overloading Sunday itself or "weekends" with everything having to do with ecclesial life: liturgy, catechesis, parish meetings, and the like. That is, instead of living by liturgical time, occasionally even in a counter-cultural direction, we have allowed other factors to shape our keeping of liturgical time itself. In other words, instead of reflecting careful liturgical inculturation such transfers may actually indicate liturgical accommodation to the prevailing culture, paralleling what some have called "Masses of convenience" on Saturday night with the result that Sunday itself becomes "Family Day" or a day for the pursuit of other non-ecclesial activities, rather than Vigil Masses for Sunday for those whose work makes actual Sunday celebration impossible.

Second, the notion of an obligatory festival, a "holy day" of "obligation" does seem to be somewhat of an oxymoron. One simply cannot mandate an attitude or orientation of festivity, whether on a calendrical date *or* on a Sunday! The real sense of feast and festival is often something beyond our control. In spite of the various pastoral reasons given for the transfer of some solemnities to Sundays, people still come in large numbers to non-obligatory celebrations such as Ash Wednesday, Holy Thursday, Good Friday, and, of course, Christmas and other feasts which have particular and popular religious, often specific ethnic-related, meanings. Among Mexican Americans, for example, the Virgin of Guadalupe *will* be celebrated on December 12 during Advent, even if it occurs on an Advent Sunday, and it *will* be celebrated in grand style because this feast already is an important and defining feast for that community. To ignore it in favor of the official Advent would be to ignore something which is life-giving and life-defining for that community. In other words, if the Epiphany and Ascension were similarly important moments of festival celebration in peoples' lives already, as they are in some cultural contexts, then their regular transfer to a Sunday would be unthinkable. If they are not such moments already, then their transfer to a Sunday is probably inconsequential anyway, for whether the Second Sunday After Christmas or the Epiphany is the content, or the Seventh Sunday After Easter or the Ascension is the content, probably matters very little. It's simply Sunday and those who regularly attend Sunday Mass will be there in either case, regardless of the specific Sunday or Solemnity being "celebrated."

Third, there is an ecumenical consideration that must be raised as well here. I am uncomfortable with individual churches making unilateral decisions about specific solemnities and feasts, which are already shared ecumenically between East and West. That is, the January 6 date of the Epiphany and the celebration of the Ascension on the *fortieth* day of Easter are not simply Western liturgical practices which can be changed arbitrarily to suit pastoral situations and perceived pastoral needs. Rather, in spite of the fact that East and West remain divided on the calculation of Easter itself, there is much in the common heritage of the liturgical year, such as these specific feasts, that remain signs of a fundamental consensus and continuity in the faith. To change such feasts without consultation with the East may inadvertently cause problems.

So, finally, then, what is gained by the transfer of certain solemnities to the nearest Sunday? Other than making liturgical planning easier and less frustrating for those who plan for big celebrations but are then disappointed by minimal attendance and participation I wonder if much at all is accomplished or gained by this. I wonder if the real issue, at least with regard to Ascension, is the fact that Ascension remains a holy day of obligation and several are not taking that "obligation" seriously. And I wonder further, then, if the real answer is to leave the liturgical calendar alone—i.e., let the Epiphany remain on January 6 and Ascension on the fortieth day of Easter—and address both the contemporary meaning of obligation and the wider and more difficult question of liturgical time, feasts, and seasons. What does it mean to live by a particular calendar—with seasons and feasts—in a modern "antifestal" context? Or, to adapt the poignant question of the Passover Seder: "Is this day different from any other day? Should it be? Might it be?"

*Notes*

1 John Baldovin, "On Feasting the Saints," in idem (ed.), *Worship: City, Church and Renewal* (Washington, D.C.: Pastoral Press, 1991) 43, 44, [Maxwell E. Johnson (ed.), *Between Memory and Hope: Readings on the Liturgical Year* (Collegeville: The Liturgical Press/Pueblo, 2001), 375–76].

2 On the relationship between the Feast of the Virgin of Guadalupe and Advent see my "The Feast of the Virgin of Guadalupe and the Season of Advent," elsewhere in this volume, 243–262.

# FROM THREE WEEKS
# TO FORTY DAYS:
# BAPTISMAL PREPARATION
# AND THE ORIGINS OF LENT

In the context of his radical reconstruction of the origins of
Lent (as stemming from the pre-Nicene post-Epiphany forty-day
fast in the Alexandrian Christian tradition) Thomas Talley makes
reference to the much-disputed statement of the fifth-century
Byzantine historian, Socrates, concerning Lenten practice at
Rome.[1] Socrates writes that "the fasts before Easter will be found
to be differently observed among different people. Those at
Rome fast three successive weeks before Easter, excepting
Saturdays and Sundays."[2] This reference, inaccurate for its own
fifth-century context, when combined with the Roman traditions
of the *missae pro scrutiniis* on the third, fourth, and fifth Sundays
in Lent in the *Gelasianum*, the course reading of the Gospel of
John from the third Sunday in Lent to Good Friday,[3] and the
titles *Hebdomada in Mediana* and *Dominica in Mediana* provided by
various *ordines Romani* and lectionaries for the fourth week and
fifth Sunday in Lent respectively, leads Talley to the following
conclusion:

> If it is possible that Socrates' inaccurate description of the
> Roman Lent throws some light on the length of the final
> period of candidacy for baptism in the third century, it is
> no more than possible. In the end, we must be satisfied
> with later data. Nonetheless, in the third century, Pascha

is appearing as the preferred time for baptism in many parts of the Church, and the final preparation of candidates is a concern of the period just preceding the great festival. That preparation for baptism is antecedent at Rome to any extended period of ascetical preparation for the festival itself. That being the case, we can say that the masses *pro scrutiniis* on the third, fourth, and fifth Sundays in the Gelasian Sacramentary point to the older core of preparation for paschal baptism. Around that grew the more extended Lent of 'forty days or more' of which Siricius spoke in 385.[4]

However, on the basis of supporting evidence from other liturgical traditions his conclusion can be made even stronger. In other words, Socrates' "inaccurate description" of a three-week "Lent," as shall be demonstrated in what follows, is indeed *quite* possible, and it is quite possible not only for third-century Rome but also for other liturgical centers prior to the post-Nicene shift to a Lent of forty days.

## I. A Three-Week Lent in Early Rome?

It is Antoine Chavasse who has argued most strongly for the existence of an earlier three-week Lenten pattern in Rome. In a series of related essays,[5] Chavasse interpreted Socrates' statement quite literally as a description of early Roman practice and pointed to a number of factors in support of this. To the "evidence," supplied by the title *mediana*, the John cycle of readings, and the three scrutiny Masses of the *Gelasianum*, Chavasse added: (1) that the Roman tradition of ordination on the Saturday before the *Dominica in mediana* can best be understood if it once came in the context of an original three-week period;[6] (2) that the *Depositio Martyrum* of 354 is an indirect witness to an earlier Lenten period of three weeks, in that the calendar is vacant from March 7th to May 19th, i.e., exactly enough time for a three-week Lent and the fifty days of Easter;[7] and (3) that the Roman year, reckoned as beginning on March 1st, offers only a three-week period before Easter in those years that Easter falls on March 22nd, its earliest possible date. On the basis of all this, therefore, Chavasse concluded that there was an original three-week Lent at Rome which disappeared sometime between 354, the date of the *Depositio Martyrum*, and 384, the date of Jerome's letter to Marcellus in which is the first datable reference to a Roman Lent of six weeks.[8]

Chavasse's speculations on the date of a six-week Lent at Rome, the *Depositio Martyrum*, and the supposed relationship between "Lent" and a (fourth-century?) March 1st Roman New Year can be criticized.[9] His greatest contribution to the question of early Roman Lent, however, is his analysis of the apparent relationship between the Johannine cycle of Lenten readings and the *missae pro scrutiniis* of the *Gelasianum*. Beginning with the oldest surviving Roman lectionary, the *Würzburg Capitulary* (c. 700),[10] Chavasse[11] noted that Gospel readings on the Sundays, Wednesdays, and Fridays of the last three weeks of Lent (which parallel the readings in the Tridentine *Missale Romanum*) produce a rather confusing sequence. The first Johannine reading occurs on the Friday of the current third week in Lent and sets the following course of readings in motion:[12]

**Lent III**

| | |
|---|---|
| Sunday | Luke 11:14–28 |
| Wednesday | Matthew 15:1–20 |
| Friday | John 4:5–42 |
| | (The woman at the well of Samaria) |

**Lent IV**

| | |
|---|---|
| Sunday | John 5:1–15 |
| Wednesday | John 9:1–38 |
| | (The man born blind) |
| Friday | John 11:1–45 |
| | (The raising of Lazarus) |

**Lent V**

| | |
|---|---|
| Sunday | John 8:46–59 |
| Wednesday | John 10:22–38 |
| Friday | John 11:47–54 |

**Holy Week**

| | |
|---|---|
| Sunday | Matthew 26—27 |
| Monday | John 12:1–36 |
| Tuesday | John 13:1–32 |
| Wednesday | Luke 22—23 |
| Friday | John 18—19 |

In analyzing this non-sequential series of readings Chavasse argued that they represented a shift from a pattern that would have placed the John 4:5–42, 9:1–38, and 11:1–45 readings on the

Sundays to which the *Gelasianum* assigns its three scrutiny Masses. Noting that the sermons of Pope Leo the Great indicate that the first two Sundays in Lent already had, respectively, the Matthean pericopes of the temptation and transfiguration of Jesus[13] and that the Matthean Passion was read on Palm/Passion Sunday, Chavasse reconstructed what he considered to be the Roman Lenten series in the time of Leo:[14]

| **Lent III** | | **Lent V** | |
|---|---|---|---|
| Sunday | John 4:5–32 | Sunday | John 11:1–45 |
| Wednesday | Matthew 15:1–20 | Wednesday | John 10:22–38 |
| Friday | Luke 11:14–18 | Friday | John 11:47–54 |
| | | | |
| **Lent IV** | | **Holy Week** | |
| Sunday | John 9:1–38 | Sunday | Matthew 26—27 |
| Wednesday | John 6:1–14 | Monday | John 12:1–36 |
| Friday | John 8:46–59 | Tuesday | John 13:1–32 |
| | | Wednesday | Luke 22—23 |
| | | Friday | John 18—19 |

Such a series of readings, at least for the Sundays, Chavasse found paralleled also in the Milanese and Beneventan liturgical traditions, with the exception that John 4:5–32 was read on the second Sunday in Lent rather than on the third.[15] Similarly, in the Gelasian Sacramentary itself reference is explicitly made to both the John 9:1–38 and 11:1–45 pericopes in the context of the exorcism "over females."[16] Chavasse concluded, therefore, that this particular cycle of readings on the third, fourth, and fifth Sundays was certainly the cycle designed to parallel the three scrutiny Masses themselves.

Nevertheless, even this cycle is still not in sequence; it represented, according to him, a yet earlier shift from a three-week preparation period which must have included a sequential reading from John. He, therefore, reconstructed this "original" series in the following manner:[17]

| Lent I (IV) | | Lent II (V) | |
| --- | --- | --- | --- |
| Sunday | John 4:5–32 | Sunday | John 9:1–38 |
| Wednesday | John 6:1–14 | Wednesday | John 10:22–38 |
| Friday | John 8:46–59 | Friday John 11:[1–45] 47–54 | |

### Lent III (Holy Week) (as above)

Since Holy Week with its Passion readings from Matthew (Sunday), Luke (Wednesday), and John (Friday) had, in his opinion, developed prior to this three-week period, it was necessary to skip over "Passion" Sunday and Wednesday when the Lenten Johannine cycle was formed.[18] This "skip" he found confirmed by the fact that the John 11:1–54 reading is also paralleled on the Friday before Holy Week in the ancient Neapolitan evangeliary, which "has generally conserved the structure of the ancient Roman evangeliary."[19]  On the basis of all this, Chavasse maintained that, in terms of the later development of Lent, two further steps were made. First, when Rome adopted a six-week Lent (sometime between 354 and 384 according to his calculations) the "scrutiny" Gospel readings (John 4:5–32; 9:1–38; and 11:1–45) were each transferred back one week to the Sundays indicated by the scrutiny Masses in the *Gelasianum* (i.e., the third, fourth, and fifth Sundays in Lent). Second, the later shift of the catechetical scrutinies themselves to ferial days caused an "exchange" to take place between the Sunday and ferial Gospel readings. This exchange thus resulted in the rather confusing sequence of Johannine readings in both the *Würzburg Capitulary* and the Tridentine *Missale Romanum.*

Did Rome, then, have a three-week paschal and baptismal preparation period before the post-Nicene development of a six-week Lent? Chavasse's conjectural but reasonable argument, based primarily on the Johannine cycle of readings, may certainly lead one in that direction. In fact, even in the later sources these Johannine pericopes, despite their sequence, are all contained (with the addition of the Friday of the third week) within the time-frame of the final three weeks of Lent. This, combined with the tradition of *mediana*, the scrutiny Masses, and the other possible evidence indicated by him, makes his argument a strong one indeed. In any event, it certainly supports Talley's hypothesis that the scrutiny Masses of the *Gelasianum* "point to the older core of preparation for paschal baptism,"[20] and that Socrates, while inaccurate for the fifth century, may certainly be pointing to what was a well-ingrained and early Roman tradition.

## II. A Three-Week Lent in Early Jerusalem?

Basing his work on the methodology and conclusions of Chavasse, Mario F. Lages argues that a three-week period of Lenten preparation for catechumens existed also in Jerusalem before the end of the third century, a period which is discernible from an analysis of the contents of the Armenian Lectionary.[21] According to Lages, the canon of Lenten readings for the Wednesday and Friday afternoon synaxes at Zion, the canon of readings for Holy Week, and the nineteen biblical readings assigned to Lenten catechesis (which parallel the baptismal catecheses of Cyril of Jerusalem) all constituted independent *libelli* before being incorporated into this important fifth-century liturgical document.[22] Most pertinent to the question of a three-week Jerusalem Lent, however, are his analyses of the psalm series which concluded each of the Wednesday and Friday synaxes and of the nineteen catechetical readings themselves.

Lages claims that the psalm series accompanying the canon of readings at Zion on the Wednesday and Friday stations of the Armenian Lectionary's six-week Lent (excluding Holy Week) fall into two three-week groups as follows:[23]

| LENT I | | LENT IV | |
|---|---|---|---|
| Wednesday | Psalm 50 | Wednesday | Psalm 76 |
| Friday | Psalm 40 | Friday | Psalm 82 |
| | | | |
| LENT II | | LENT V | |
| Wednesday | Psalm 56 | Wednesday | Psalm 83 |
| Friday | Psalm 60 | Friday | Psalm 84 |
| | | | |
| LENT III | | LENT VI | |
| Wednesday | Psalm 64 | Wednesday | Psalm 85 |
| Friday | Psalm 74 | Friday | Psalm 87 |

Noting, however, that weeks four, five, and six appear to indicate the debris of a once continuous psalmody from Psalms 82—87 and the Georgian Lectionary places Psalm 56 on the Friday of the first week while retaining Ps 87 on the Friday of the sixth,[24] Lages seeks to reconstruct the "original" series in the following manner:[25]

| **LENT I** | | **LENT IV** | |
|---|---|---|---|
| Wednesday | Psalm 50 | Wednesday | Psalm 82 |
| Friday | Psalm 56 | Friday | Psalm 83 |
| **LENT II** | | **LENT V** | |
| Wednesday | Psalm 64 | Wednesday | Psalm 84 |
| Friday | Psalm 70 | Friday | Psalm 85 |
| **LENT III** | | **LENT VI** | |
| Wednesday | Psalm 74 | Wednesday | Psalm 86 |
| Friday | Psalm 76 | Friday | Psalm 87 |

Furthermore, the fact that the Georgian Lectionary also assigns Psalm 87 to Good Friday (where the Armenian Lectionary assigns Psalm 22) suggests to him that this "original" series once belonged to an earlier three-week period of preparation before the further development of Holy Week itself.[26] Lages concludes, therefore, that the psalm series in the first three weeks of Lent developed only when the canon of Wednesday and Friday Lenten readings was established, but the psalm series in the last three weeks, given its structural continuity, represents a much earlier development and dates to an original three-week Lenten period.

Further evidence for this conclusion, he claims, is offered by the Armenian Lectionary's nineteen catechetical readings. According to him, these readings served as the basis for Cyril of Jerusalem's pre-baptismal catecheses and belong to the last three weeks of Lent. Yet, prior to the development of Holy Week they would have concluded on Good Friday itself.[27] Lages bases this assumption on two pieces of evidence, namely, the introductory rubric in the Canon of Baptism of the ninth- or tenth-century Armenian liturgy and a reference to catechetical instruction in the Georgian Lectionary. The introductory Armenian baptismal rubric reads in part:

> "The Canon of Baptism when they make a Christian. Before which it is not right to admit him into church. But he shall have hands laid on beforehand, *three weeks or more* before the baptism, in time sufficient for him to learn from the Wardapet [Instructor] both the faith and the baptism of the church."[28]

Because of the similarity in content (i.e., the Creed) between this rubric, the nineteen readings, and Cyril's catecheses, as well as the specification of a "three-week" instruction period, Lages asserts that this rubric is "primitive" and that pre-baptismal catechesis would have been originally given at Jerusalem during the three weeks before Easter baptism.[29] This three-week instruction period may also be indicated by a reference to catechetical training in the Georgian Lectionary. Unlike the Armenian Lectionary, which does not indicate the day on which the nineteen readings are to begin or conclude, a rubric in this lectionary indicates that on the Monday of the fifth week in Lent, that is, exactly *nineteen* days before Holy Saturday baptism, the instruction of catechumens is to begin (*Tertia hora incipiunt legere lectiones instruentes catechumenos ad portas ecclesiae*).[30]

## III. A Three-Week Lent in other Traditions?

*North Africa.* On the basis of the sermons of Augustine and Quodvultdeus of Carthage, I have suggested elsewhere that a three-week final preparation of catechumens prior to Easter baptism might be discernible in fourth-century North Africa as well.[31] In a sermon given on the occasion of the delivery of the Lord's Prayer, Augustine refers to the return of the Creed which had just taken place. Therein he says not only that the Lord's Prayer would have to be returned in a week's time but that those who had not made a "good return of the Creed" still had time to learn it prior to its recitation at baptism itself.[32] Similarly, in a sermon on the Creed, Quodvultdeus of Carthage refers to what seems to have been an enrolment of catechumens on the previous night.[33] By joining these two together one might reasonably conjecture a three-week pattern of final baptism preparation: the *traditio symboli* in week one, its return and the delivery of the Lord's Prayer in week two, the return of the Lord's Prayer in week three, and the final profession of faith in the celebration of baptism.[34] Despite the fact that the scrutinies were on Saturdays in this tradition and that Rome delivered the Creed on a different day, one cannot but be struck by the fact that these three scrutinies offer a curious parallel to the scrutiny Masses in the *Gelasianum*. Consequently, it appears quite possible that, whatever may have taken place in the first three weeks of Lent, it was the three weeks prior to Holy Week in North Africa that were singled out as a special time for catechumenal preparation.

*Spain.* The sources of the Mozarabic Liturgy also seem to point in a similar direction. In both the *Liber commicus*[35] and the *Liber Mozarabicus sacramentorum*[36] a distinction is made between the first three and last three weeks of Lent. While during the first three weeks of Lent weekday Mass is celebrated only on Mondays, Wednesdays, and Fridays, it is celebrated on every day except Thursdays in the final three weeks. Thus, the last three weeks have a different liturgical character and emphasis altogether, with readings and Mass formulas assigned to each day. The reason for this shift and change of emphasis is undoubtedly due to the fact that it was on the Fourth Sunday in Lent (called either *in vicessima*[37] or *in mediante die festo*[38]) that the catechumens were enrolled for Easter baptism. *"En este dia entre los españoles,"* note F. J. Perez de Urbel and A. Gonzales y Ruiz-Zorilla, *"los catecumenos daban sus nombres al sacerdote."*[39] This they support by referring to the first canon of the Second Council of Braga (572) which directs that diocesan bishops:

> ". . . shall teach that catechumens (as the ancient canons command) shall come for the cleaning of exorcism twenty days before baptism, in which twenty days they shall especially be taught the Creed, which is: I believe in God the Father Almighty. . . . "[40]

The evidence for Spain, therefore, would seem strongly to indicate that the final three weeks of Lent, *including* Holy Week in these sources, have a tradition and history which may, in fact, antedate the formation of a later six-week Lenten period itself.

*Naples.* It was to the Neapolitan liturgical tradition that Chavasse appealed for evidence to confirm his argument that John 11:1–54 was originally read on the Friday before Holy Week. Not surprisingly, three weeks of final preparation for Easter baptism seem to be part of this tradition as well. In the Neapolitan evangeliaries studied by Morin it is to be noted that, while the first two Sundays are entitled simply, *Dominica I or II XLgisima paschae*, the three Sundays prior to Holy Week all receive special names obviously related to catechumenal preparation, namely: *Dominica tertia quando psalmi (salem) accipiunt*, *Dominica IIII quando orationem accipiant*, and *Dominica V quando symbulum accipiunt.*[41] Again, the close parallel to the scrutiny Masses in the *Gelasianum* is striking. Morin himself, in fact, was so convinced that this referred to a three-week baptismal preparation period that, as early as 1891, he concluded that: *"à Tolede, à Naples et à Rome il n'y avait que trois semaines entre l'inscription des competents et l'administration du baptême."*[42]

*Constantinople.* It is again Talley who has drawn attention to the fact that in the *typica* of the ninth- and tenth-century Byzantine tradition there is a complete liturgy of initiation on Lazarus Saturday (the day before Palm Sunday) presided over by the patriarch in the little baptistery of Hagia Sophia. He has further noted that a vestige of this liturgy remains on Lazarus Saturday in the current Byzantine rite where the baptismal troparion (based on Galatians 3:27) is sung in place of the entrance chant.[43] What Talley does not note, however, is that the *first* reference to Lenten catechesis and baptismal preparation in the tenth-century typicon edited by Juan Mateos comes on the third Sunday in Lent. On that day an announcement was to be made stating that, because of the necessity of catechesis and examination before baptism, no one would be permitted to enter the catechumenate after this week.[44] Such an announcement certainly looks as though it means that in the Byzantine tradition final preparation for Easter baptism took place during the last three weeks of Lent before Holy Week. M. Arranz, in fact, has argued that, including Holy Week, there was only a four-week period possible for such instruction.[45] Yet, if one maintains the possibility of a baptismal liturgy on Lazarus Saturday, which Talley wants to argue is ancient, then the presence of this rubric on the Sunday which concludes the third week of Lent would leave precisely *three* rather than four weeks for final baptismal preparation.

## IV. Three Weeks of Baptismal Preparation and the Origins of Lent

During the final weeks of Lent in the various liturgical sources of Rome, Jerusalem, Armenia, North Africa, Spain, Naples, and Constantinople it appears that an earlier three-week period of final preparation for baptism has left certain traces or debris. The fact that some of these sources include "Holy Week" within that three-week period, while others conclude this period before the beginning of that week, might also serve to indicate that the tradition itself is older than the various adaptations made of it in these liturgical traditions.

Talley has suggested that the three scrutiny Masses of the *Gelasianum* may reflect the final period of baptismal preparation in the third century, a time when Easter was becoming the preferred baptismal day in many places. However, granted that the indications of this three-week period in the various sources do occur during the final portion of Lent, this period devoted to baptismal preparation need *not* be understood only in relationship to Easter. As Talley himself has shown on the basis of the Alexandrian tradition, there is not a necessary correlation between baptism and the celebration of Easter. Baptism could and did occur at other times of the year. In fact, while paschal baptism is referred to for the West (at least for North Africa) as early as Tertullian in *De baptismo* 19, we simply do not know when it became the preferred day in the East. And, on the basis of the early Armenian and Syrian traditions, Gabriele Winkler has argued that the dominant pre-Nicene interpretation of baptism in the Christian East was that it was a pneumatic ritual of rebirth related to Jesus' own baptism in the Jordan and John 3 rather than a ritual of death and resurrection in Christ along the lines of Romans 6. The latter interpretation makes its full appearance in the East only in the fourth century with the result that the baptismal rite itself becomes transformed.[46]

Nevertheless, whenever baptism was celebrated and however it was interpreted, it is reasonable to assume that it was preceded by some kind of preparation period for the *competentes* or *photizomenoi*. Consequently, it is quite possible that the three-week period reflected in the Lenten materials of later liturgical sources was a very early "free-floating" baptismal preparation period without any *necessary* relationship to the liturgical year at all. Whenever baptism was administered it would have been preceded, as the rubric in the Armenian baptismal liturgy directs, by "three weeks or more" of instruction. And, at least at Jerusalem and Rome, specific biblical readings related to catechesis (e.g., the nineteen catechetical readings of the Armenian Lectionary and the course reading from John) may have been assigned to this period.

In his reconstruction of the Johannine lectionary cycle for Rome, Chavasse argued that the reason for the occurrence of John 11:1–54 on the second (fifth) Friday was because Holy Week (with its Passion readings on Sunday, Wednesday, and Friday) had developed prior to the formation of this three-week cycle. Such an assumption is certainly plausible in that, given the structure of the ancient Christian week and its focus on Sundays, Wednesdays, and Fridays, one might surely expect that this week above all would be organized and receive specific readings rather early in its development. Yet, the first reference to Holy Week at Rome is in the fifth century and we simply do not know what may have characterized the week before Easter prior to then.[47] Because of this, it is just as plausible to assume that the Johannine cycle existed either prior to or independent of the development of Holy Week itself as a series of baptismal preparation readings organized around John 4, 9, and 11 And, if this is the case, there need be no reason to assume that the Lazarus reading from John 11 originally fell on a Friday but, rather, it could have occurred on the third Sunday of this period. Such would certainly better explain the supposed shift of the Sunday readings back one week at that later period presumably indicated by the scrutiny Masses in the *Gelasianum*. Furthermore, reference to Lazarus in the context of "Palm Sunday" is not unknown in other liturgical traditions. In the propers assigned to the *traditio symboli* Mass on Palm Sunday in the Gallican sacramentaries, for example, the raising of Lazarus and the entry into Jerusalem are *both* the object of attention.[48] And, the fact that the early Alexandrian tradition, according to Talley, could conclude its post-Epiphany baptismal preparation period with reference to both a Lazarus-like narrative *and* Jesus' "Palm Sunday" entrance into Jerusalem underscores the fact that neither the raising of Lazarus nor Jesus' entry must necessarily be related to a "pre-paschal" period.[49]

I should like to suggest, therefore, that the three-week period of baptismal preparation indicated in the Lenten portions of various liturgical sources refers originally not to a pre-paschal Lent at all, but to an early and perhaps independent period of final baptismal preparation by itself. Such a hypothesis is admittedly conjectural and speculative but, if correct, would go a long way towards explaining how Lent itself may have developed. When Easter finally became the preferred time for baptism, this independent "free-floating" three-week period would have naturally become attached to it as the final period of catechetical instruction and preparation now in a pre-paschal context. Then, after Nicea, and under the influence of the Alexandrian forty-day post-Epiphany fast, Lent itself came to be created in various ways on the basis of this "core" resulting in the differing lengths calculated in the various traditions. For the East, however, it may be that the post-Nicene adoption of the forty-day Lent also coincided with the adoption of Easter itself as the preferred baptismal day. Yet, even if this is the case, a previously independent three-week period of final baptismal preparation could certainly have been integrated into this new pre-paschal period.

The development of Holy Week also seems to have played a significant role in this process, at least in two places. Contrary to Chavasse, either the further development of Holy Week itself with its Passion pericopes or the merging of this independent three-week cycle with an already established Holy Week could have easily caused the backwards "shift" of the three Sunday readings while, nonetheless, maintaining a Johannine cycle on other days during the final three weeks at Rome. A similar shift may also be conjectured for Jerusalem. It is interesting to note that it is only in the second week of the Armenian Lectionary's seven-week Lenten period (including Holy Week) that readings and psalms are also provided for Monday, Tuesday, and Thursday stations at the Anastasis. According to Lages, such a peculiarity may indicate that this week was originally the first week of a six-week Lent.[50] When Holy Week developed as a separate week altogether in Jerusalem, the beginning of Lent was thereby shifted back one week in order to retain a six-week period of preparation.

## V. Conclusion

Scholars have often concluded that Socrates was mistaken in his claim that the Roman church fasted for three weeks in preparation for Easter at any time in its history.[51] Yet, given the indications of a three-week period in various and unrelated liturgical sources, it may well be that Socrates points us to what was the earliest "core" of Lenten development not only at Rome but, with the notable exception of Egypt, in other traditions as well, a core originally based not on Easter but on final baptismal preparation. Around this baptismal core Lent developed only when Easter became the preferred baptismal day. And, if this is correct, then the forty days of Lent represent a synthesis of two traditions, both of which are baptismal in their origins and orientation: the forty-day Alexandrian post-Epiphany fast, and a three-week baptismal preparation period elsewhere. In its origins, therefore, "Lent" has nothing to do with Easter at all but everything to do with the final training of candidates for baptism.

Further support for a three-week preliminary period before baptism in general *may* also be provided by attention to the origins of the season of Advent in the West. Much of contemporary scholarship on the evolution of the liturgical year itself has tended to discount previously-held theories which claimed that part of the development of the Advent season (often six weeks or forty days in duration), at least in those Western churches outside of Rome, was related to preparation for baptism on Epiphany.[52]

Recently, however, Martin Connell has argued, quite convincingly, that such scholarly discounting may be rather premature. According to him, the fact that, outside of Rome, Epiphany predates the celebration of Christmas, together with an abundance of references to a pre-Epiphany period of preparation in early (fourth and fifth century) and later (early medieval) non-Roman liturgical sources, some which include Christmas itself within this reckoning, others which do not, may provide some circumstantial evidence for speculating still that a pre-Epiphany "Advent," with baptismal connotations, may itself also pre-date the celebration of a December 25 Christmas in those areas of the church. For our purposes here what is most intriguing is that in Spain, according to the Council of Saragossa (380), there was a three-week fasting period prescribed from December 17 to January 6. While baptism is not noted as an Epiphany occasion in this conciliar document, we do know that in Spain Epiphany was, in fact, one of several baptismal occasions. Is it only then when the December 25 feast was adopted, that Advent as we know it would ultimately have become limited in focus as a season of preparation for this new feast on the calendar?[53]

If Connell is correct in his speculations, an earlier understanding and orientation may still appear as traces or remnants in the extant sources and, as such, may help in the assessment that outside of Rome a pre-Epiphany baptismal preparation period may have functioned as a kind of nascent Advent. As with Lent, then, it is possible that "Advent " also owes its origins, in part at least, to a three-week baptismal preparation practice. But the precise evolution of Advent in the West is another topic for another time.

## Notes

1 Thomas J. Talley, *The Origins of the Liturgical Year* (Collegeville: The Liturgical Press, 1986), 165–7.

2 Socrates, *Historia ecclesiastica* V. 22.

3 The fact of the matter is that the "course reading" from the Gospel of John in the Roman books begins on the *Friday* of the third week in Lent, not on the third Sunday.

4 Talley, *The Origins*, 167.

5 See "La préparation de la Pâque, à Rome, avant le Ve siècle. Jeûne et organisation liturgique" in *Memorial J. Chaine* (Bibl. de la Fac. Cath. de Theol. de Lyon, vol. 5), (Lyon: 1950), 61–80 ; "La structure du Carême et les lectures des messes quadragesimales dans la liturgie romaine" in *La Maison-Dieu* 31 (1952), 76–120; and "Temps de préparation à la Pâque, d'après quelques livres liturgiques romains" in *Rech. de Sc. relig.* 37 (1950), 125–45.

6 Chavasse argued that since the Saturdays of the first three weeks of a six-week Lent remained without a proper synaxis until the sixth century and the Saturday of the fifth week remained vacant until the eighth, the presence of ordination on the fourth Saturday may well indicate the remains of an older Lenten structure (See "La préparation de la Pâque," 75). Similarly, he noted a parallel between ordination on this fourth Saturday and the tradition of ordination of the *first* Saturday in Lent which he considered to be a later development (See "La structure du Carême," 83). While he did not go into detail on this question, it is certainly reasonable to assume that the celebration of ordination on the fourth Saturday in Lent *is* an earlier tradition than ordination on the first. That is, it is easy to understand how a celebration on the Saturday of an original "three-week Lent" might be later duplicated and ultimately replaced by one on the first Saturday of a six-week Lent. A development in the other direction is much more difficult to comprehend. If ordinations were celebrated on the first Saturday in Lent prior to their appearance on the fourth Saturday, then why would it have been necessary to add this second celebration after an interval of only three weeks?

7 In this context Chavasse also notes that the *sanctorale* of the Gelasian Sacramentary ceases between March 7th and May 1st and that the Gregorian liturgical documents show that the formulas for Ascension and Pentecost have been inserted into the *sanctorale* after May 12. See "Temps de préparation à la Pâque," 127.

8 See "La préparation de la Pâque," 69 and "La structure du Carême," 83–4. Cf. also P. Jounel, "The Year" in A. G. Martimort, et al. (eds.), *The Church at Prayer*, IV (Collegeville: The Liturgical Press, 1986), 67; Patrick Regan, "The Three Days and the Forty Days" in *Worship* 54 (1980), 5; and Cyrille Vogel, *Medieval Liturgy: An Introduction to the Sources*, translated and revised by William Storey and Niels Rasmussen (Washington, D.C.: Pastoral Press, 1986), 309–10. Vogel even supports Chavasse's attempt to relate a three-week Lent to the secular Roman calendar. He writes (310); "We can deduce the reason for the three-week preparatory fast. Since the Roman year began on March 1, there were exactly three weeks available before March 22, the earliest possible date of Easter. In such a case one would have a beginning of the year fast that would coincide with a fast before Easter . . . In any case, the three week period could not begin before New Year's (March 1) since Easter could not fall earlier than March 22."

9 Talley, for example, has argued (166, 170) on the basis of the Festal Letters of Athanasius that Rome was already observing the fast of forty days in 340. While this may certainly call into question the dates Chavasse assigned to the beginning of the forty-day Lenten observance at Rome, it does not necessarily mean that the *Depositio Martyrum* does not reflect an earlier and authentic Roman liturgical practice. In the supposed relationship of Lent to the Roman New Year, however, there is simply no evidence to support the notion that the Roman church consciously related its pre-paschal fast to the secular

calendar. Therefore, while Chavasse *may* be correct in this, his conclusion is simply too speculative to be accepted uncritically.

[10] For the list of the Lenten Gospel readings from this lectionary see G. Morin, "Liturgie et basiliques de Rome au milieu du VII siècle d'après les listes d'évangiles de Würzburg" in *Revue Bénédictine* 28 (1911), 302–4; W. H. Frere, *Studies in Early Roman Liturgy* II: *The Roman Gospel Lectionary* (London: Oxford University Press, 1934), 8–10.

[11] For the description and discussion which follows see especially "La structure de Carême," 82–4, 89–90, 94–7, and 113–4.

[12] Ibid., 78.

[13] It should be noted, however, that the *Wiirzburg Capitulary* lists the second Sunday in Lent as *Die Dominico vacat*. See Morin, "Liturgie et basiliques . . .", 302.

[14] Chavasse, "La structure du Carême," 78.

[15] Ibid., 113–14. For a list of the Lenten Gospel pericopes in the Milanese liturgical tradition see A. Paredi, "L'evangeliario di Busto Arsizio" in *Miscellanea liturgica in onore di sua Em. il cardinale Giacomo Lercaro* 2 (Rome: 1967), 218; and E. C. Whitaker, *Documents of the Baptismal Liturgy* (Nashville: Abingdon Press, 1970), 133. In his study of the Communion antiphons related to these three Sundays in Beneventan liturgical tradition (*Qui biberit, Lutum fecit,* and *Videns Dominus*) R. J. Hesbert has argued that the original Roman pattern inherited by other Western traditions (e.g., Spain, Gaul, and North Italy) placed John 4:5–32 on the *Second* Sunday in Lent prior to its eventual and final placement on the third Friday. See R. J. Hesbert (ed.), *Graduel bénéventain: Le Codex 10673 de la Bibliothèque Vaticane, fonds latin. XI siecle*, Paléographie Musicale 14 (Tournai: 1931–1936), 219–22, 225–34. Chavasse, however, claimed that the reason for this pericope being on the Second Sunday in Lent in these non-Roman Western rites was that these other churches ignored the Roman tradition of the Ember Days. See Chavasse, "La structure du Carême," 114, and idem., "Le Carême romain et les scrutins prébaptismaux avant le IXe siècle" in *Rech. de. Sc. relig.* 35 (1948), 348–51, 364–5. Hesbert, of course, may be correct in his conclusion. Yet, it would be extremely difficult to explain the shift of this pericope from the Second Sunday all the way to the third Friday if it did not originally belong to that series of Johannine readings which continue to be present exclusively in the last three weeks of Lent. The best explanation, perhaps, is that these other non-Roman Western traditions merely adapted the Roman cycle to their own situations. I am grateful to Dr. Peter Jeffery for referring me to the work of R. J. Hesbert.

[16] "I exorcise you, unclean spirit, through the Father and the Son and the Holy Spirit, that you may go away and depart from these servants of God. For he himself commands you, accursed one, damned one, *who opened the eyes of the man born blind, and on the fourth day raised Lazarus from the tomb*" (DBL, 218) [emphasis added].

[17] "La structure du Carême," 78.

[18] Ibid., 96, 81–2.

[19] Ibid., 96. For the reference to this Gospel reading in the Neapolitan Evangeliary see G. Morin, "La liturgie de Naples au temps de saint Grégoire d'après deux evangeliaires du septième siècle" in *Revue Bénédictine* 8 (1891), 492. Interestingly enough this lectionary refers to this day as *Post. V. dominicas de XLgesima feria. VI. de lazarum.*

[20] Talley, *The Origins,* 167.

[21] M. F. Lages, "Étapes de l'evolution de carême à Jérusalem avant le Ve sièle. Essai d'analyse structurale" in *Revue des Etudes Armeniénnes* 6 (1969), 67–102. See also Maxwell E. Johnson, "Reconciling Cyril and Egeria on the Catechetical Process in Fourth-Century Jerusalem" in Paul F. Bradshaw (ed.), *Essays in Early Eastern Initiation*, (Bramcote/

Nottingham: Alucin/GROW Liturgical Study 8, 1988), 24–6. For the Armenian Lectionary see A. Renoux, *Le Codex armenien Jérusalem 121*, II (Turnhout 1971).

22 Lages, "Étapes . . .", 72–81.

23 Ibid., 81–2. See also Renoux, *Le Codex armenien* . . ., 239–55.

24 See Michael Tarchnishvili, *Le grand lectionnaire de 1'Église de Jérusalem*, I (Louvain: 1959), 68–79.

25 Lages, "Étapes . . .", 82–3.

26 Ibid., 98–9.

27 Ibid., 99–100.

28 DBL, 74 [emphasis added].

29 Lages, "Étapes . . . ", 100.

30 Ibid., 98–100 and Tarchnishvili, 68. John Baldovin, SJ, in *The Urban Character of Christian Worship: The Origins, Development, and Meaning of Stational Liturgy*, Orientalia Christiana Analecta 228 (Rome: 1987), 90–3, and in *Liturgy in Ancient Jerusalem*, (Bramcote/Nottingham: Alucin/GROW Liturgical Study 9, 1989), 13–14, has argued that the catechetical lectures indicated by the nineteen readings in the Armenian Lectionary were delivered *only* on non-stational days in Jerusalem. Hence, according to him, Egeria's description of daily catechetical instruction in both the Bible and the Creed during Lent is either incorrect or must be interpreted rather loosely as referring both to the special catechetical gatherings and to the stational liturgies themselves. Against Baldovin, I have argued elsewhere that Lages' hypothesis is extremely helpful in reconciling the apparent discrepancies between Cyril of Jerusalem's eighteen prebaptismal lectures and Egeria's description of Lent. These eighteen lectures, paralleled by the designated readings in the Armenian Lectionary, can easily be assigned to every day (except Sundays) in the final three weeks of Lent prior to the beginning of Holy Week. Furthermore, if this is the case, then Egeria's statement about the Creed being delivered to the catechumens "after five weeks teaching" is easily squared with Cyril's delivery of the Creed in his fifth catechetical lecture. For, the third week prior to Holy Week in Egeria's eight-week Lenten schema is the fifth week of Lent (see Johnson, "Reconciling Cyril and Egeria," 24–9). A particular problem, however, is that in his fourteenth lecture Cyril refers to the narrative of the ascension which had been read and upon which he had commented during the previous Sunday liturgy. Since the Armenian Lectionary does not list the Lenten Sunday readings it becomes rather difficult to determine the particular Sunday to which he refers. In a recent essay ("A Lenten Sunday Lectionary in Fourth-Century Jerusalem?" in J. Neil Alexander [ed.], *Time and Community* [Washington D.C.: Pastoral Press, 1990], 115–22), Baldovin suggests that Jerusalem may have adopted the Lenten lectionary of Constantinople, in which case the pericopes from Hebrews 4:14—5:6, 6:13–20, and 9:11–14, read respectively on the third, fourth, and fifth Sundays in Lent, may have provided for Cyril the necessary reference or allusion to the ascension. Though Baldovin admits that "it is easier to see a reference to the ascension in the reading from Hebrews assigned to the Fifth Sunday of Lent," he argues that the Sunday in question was the Fourth because: "if the fourteenth lecture followed the Fifth Sunday of Lent there would be too few days left before the beginning of Great Week. A lecture would have to be given every day of that week to conclude before Lazarus Saturday." His argument, thus, continues to stand or fall on his proposed schema of the catechetical lectures themselves. But, if, in fact, it is easier to see a reference to the ascension in the Hebrews reading assigned to the fifth Sunday, then my schema remains equally plausible. For, the Fifth Lenten Sunday in Constantinople and the Armenian Lectionary is the *sixth* Sunday in Egeria (i.e.,

the day before the seventh week of Lent) and it is to *this* Sunday where my schema assumes that the ascension reference was made and it is precisely for "daily catechesis" that I have argued.

[31] Johnson, "Reconciling Cyril and Egeria," 27, note 1.

[32] Sermon 58, in DBL, 146.

[33] "I am to explain to you the sacraments of the past night and of the present holy Creed . . . For you are not yet reborn in holy baptism, but by the sign of the cross you have been conceived in the womb of holy mother Church" (DBL, 150).

[34] In his hypothetical reconstruction of the North African lectionary in the time of Augustine, G. G. Willis comes to a similar conclusion. Yet, he omits any reference to Quodvultdeus of Carthage in this context. See G. G. Willis, *St. Augustine's Lectionary*, Alcuin Club Collection XLIV (London: SPCK, 1962), 63.

[35] F. J. Perez de Urbel and A. Gonzales y Ruiz-Zorilla, *Liber commicus, Edición critica*, I, Monumenta Hispaniae sacra, Series liturgica, II (Madrid: Consejo Superior de Investigaciones Científicas, 1950).

[36] M. Ferotin (ed.), *Liber Mozarabicus sacramentorum,* Monumenta Ecclesiae liturgica 6 (Paris: 1912).

[37] *Liber commicus,* 274.

[38] *Liber Mozarabicus sacramentorum*, 190.

[39] *Liber commicus,* 274, note 1. See also A. W. S. Porter, "Studies in the Mozarabic Office" in *Journal of Theological Studies* 35 (London: Oxford University Press, 1934), 280–2.

[40] DBL, 158. See also *Liber commicus,* 274, note 1.

[41] Morin, "La liturgie de Naples," 530.

[42] Ibid., 535. Actually, by adding Holy Week to this period, there would be four and not three weeks before Easter baptism.

[43] Talley, 188.

[44] Juan Mateos, *Le Typicon de la Grande Église*, II, *Le cycle des fêtes mobiles,* (Rome: Orientalia Christiana Analecta [166], 1963), 38–9.

[45] M. Arranz, "Évolution des rites d'incorporation et de réadmission dans l'Église selon l'Euchologe byzantin," in *Gestes et paroles dans les diverses familles liturgiques* (Rome: 1978), 39. I am grateful to the Rev. Peter Galadza for directing me to this reference.

[46] Gabriele Winkler, *Das Armenische Initationsrituale,* (Rome: Orientalia Christiana Analecta [217], 1982) passim., and idem., "The Original Meaning of the Prebaptismal Anointing and its Implications" in *Worship* 52 (1978), 24–25.

[47] See Vogel, 309.

[48] Cf. L. C. Mohlberg (ed.), *Missale gothicum* (Rome 1961) 53; idem., *Missale gallicanum vetus,* (Rome: 1958), 25; and E. A. Lowe (ed.), *The Bobbio Missal,* Henry Bradshaw Society 58 (London: Henry Bradshaw Society Publications, 1920), 59.

[49] Talley, 194–214.

[50] Lages, "Étapes," 102.

[51] Cf. G. G. Willis, "What is Mediana Week?" in *Essays in Early Roman Liturgy,* Alcuin Club Collections XLVI (London: SPCK, 1964), 101–4; C. Callewaert, "La semaine

'mediana' dans l'ancien Carême romain et les Quatre-Temps" in *Sacris Erudiri: Fragmenta Liturgica* (Steenbruge: S. Petri de Aldenburgo, 1946), 561–89. Neither Willis nor Callewaert, however, deals with the baptismal scrutinies or the Johannine lectionary readings.

52 See Thomas Talley, *The Origins of the Liturgical Year,* 2nd emended edition (Collegeville: Pueblo, 1991), 147ff.; and J. Neil Alexander, *Waiting for the Coming: The Meaning of Advent, Christmas, and Epiphany* (Washington, D.C.: Pastoral Press, 1993), 8–23.

53 See Martin Connell, "The Origins and Evolution of Advent in the West," in Maxwell E. Johnson (ed.), *Between Memory and Hope: Readings on the Liturgical Year* (Collegeville: Pueblo, 2000), 349–74.

# TERTULLIAN'S "DIEM BAPTISMO SOLLEMNIOREM" REVISITED: A TENTATIVE HYPOTHESIS ON BAPTISM AT PENTECOST

In *De baptismo* 19 (ca. 200), influential North African theologian Tertullian provides the following information about the various occasions for the celebration of baptism in the church of his day:

> The Passover [i.e., Easter] provides the day of most solemnity for baptism [*diem baptismo sollemniorem*], for then was accomplished our Lord's passion, and into it we are baptized . . .After that, Pentecost is a most auspicious period [*laetissimum spatium*] for arranging baptisms, for during it our Lord's resurrection was several times made known among the disciples, and the grace of the Holy Spirit first given . . .For all that, every day is a Lord's day: any hour, any season, is suitable for baptism. If there is any difference of solemnity, it makes no difference to the grace.[1]

As is now well known, thanks especially to the work of Paul Bradshaw on initiation and Easter in early Christianity, Tertullian's reference constitutes what is our *first* witness to what will become the nearly universal "ideal" of Easter baptism in the churches of late antiquity and beyond.[2] At the same time, it must be noted that Tertullian's reference "after that" to Pentecost as a "most auspicious period" (*laetissimum spatium*) for baptism (interpreted usually as a reference *not* to the *Day* of Pentecost but to that period between Passover [Easter] and Pentecost, commonly referred to today as the fifty days of the "Easter Season"), is also our *first* witness to baptism at *Pentecost* in the early patristic period. And, together with Easter, the *Day* of Pentecost, but not the *season*, would ultimately be incorporated into and remain a rubrical direction in the liturgical books (especially in the West) as an annual—albeit alternative—solemn occasion for baptism.

Because Pentecost is the "alternative" day for baptism, it has become somewhat of a largely unexamined assumption among liturgical scholars that, whenever baptism was connected historically to Pentecost, this must have functioned as a catch-all occasion for those who were unable to be baptized at Easter in a given year.[3] That is, since Pentecost baptism has been understood as being dependent upon the practice of baptism at Pascha (Easter), the traditional assumption has been that baptism at Pascha must necessarily pre-date the practice of baptism at Pentecost. In part, the wide scholarly acceptance of this interpretation undoubtedly has been due to the presumed necessity of pre-baptismal fasting as part of baptismal preparation (see *Didache* 7), something deemed uncharacteristic of paschal rejoicing during the fifty days. Such an assumption automatically excludes consideration of Pentecost baptism as other than a lesser alternative to Pascha. This interpretation, however, may be anachronistic if it is based on a further assumption that a proscription against fasting *during* Pentecost was a universal characteristic from the beginning. On the contrary, the earliest we know of this proscription is the late second century, from Irenaeus (as quoted by Eusebius), or from the *Acti Pauli* in Asia Minor, during the time in which the *Sunday* Pascha was itself becoming established universally. Furthermore, a general proscription against fasting, even if very early in the history of the Christian Pentecost, need not necessarily imply that those to be initiated at Pentecost would somehow also be excluded from this pre-baptismal requirement themselves. When speaking of pre-baptismal preparation, for example, Tertullian himself in *De Baptismo* 20 nowhere implies that the "frequent prayers, fastings, bendings of the knee, and all-night vigils" of the catechumens only belong to preparation for *Paschal* baptism and not at other times. Indeed, apart from Tertullian's own rationale for baptism *during* Pentecost, the questions still remain: In light of the biblical precedent for connecting Pentecost with baptism in Acts 2:1–42, why does Pentecost (beginning with Tertullian) ultimately emerge as an occasion for baptism ranked lower in preference to Easter? Given the biblical precedent, why is not Pentecost *the* festival occasion *par excellence* in the liturgical year for the celebration of Christian initiation?

There are no references to Christian baptism in relationship to the Jewish feast of *Passover* anywhere in the New Testament, and, *pace* Karl Gerlach, no explicit references to baptism in association with the Quartodeciman Pasch in the early centuries.[4] Luke's account of the first Pentecost in Acts 2, however, certainly suggests that by the end of the first century there was already a strong correlation being made between the Pentecostal gift of the Holy Spirit to the apostles and the baptism of new Christian converts (*three thousand*, in fact!) on the very day of that Jewish feast:

> When the day of Pentecost had come, they were all together in one place. And suddenly from heaven there came a sound like the rush of a violent wind, and it filled the entire house where they were sitting. Divided tongues, as of fire, appeared among them, and a tongue rested on each of them. All of them were filled with the Holy Spirit and began to speak in other languages, as the Spirit gave them ability . . .
>
> . . . But Peter, standing with the eleven, raised his voice and addressed them . . .
>
> . . . "This Jesus God raised up, and of that all of us are witnesses. Being therefore exalted at the right hand of God, and having received from the Father the promise of the Holy Spirit, he has poured out this that you both see and hear . . . Therefore let the entire house of Israel know with certainty that God has made him both Lord and Messiah, this Jesus whom you crucified." Now when they heard this, they were cut to the heart and said to Peter and to the other apostles, "Brothers, what should

we do?" Peter said to them, "Repent, and be baptized every one of you in the name of Jesus Christ so that your sins may be forgiven; and you will receive the gift of the Holy Spirit. For the promise is for you, for your children, and for all who are far away, everyone whom the Lord our God calls to him." And he testified with many other arguments and exhorted them, saying, "Save yourselves from this corrupt generation." So those who welcomed his message were baptized, and that day about three thousand persons were added. They devoted themselves to the apostles' teaching and fellowship, to the breaking of bread and the prayers (Acts 2:1–4; 14; 32–42).[5]

Scholarship on Christian initiation and the liturgical year has not taken seriously into account this biblical text. But well it might. For, indeed, Acts 2 makes it glaringly obvious that, at least for Luke, Christian baptism and the Jewish feast of Pentecost went together. And, as this account states, Pentecost is the only feast day on the Jewish liturgical calendar to which Christian baptism is explicitly connected in the New Testament. Perhaps, then, it is time to revisit anew the feast of Pentecost as *"diem baptismo sollemniorem."*

## I. A Jewish Precedent for Pentecost Baptism?

In two recent essays, "Sinai Revisited" and "The Festival of Weeks and the Story of Pentecost in Acts 2," James VanderKam offers a compelling exegetical analysis of Acts 2 in relationship to how Pentecost was already viewed and interpreted among various sectarian Jewish communities at the time of the writing of Acts. "The fact that an event so momentous as the outpouring of the Spirit on the first disciple band took place on the festival of pentecost," notes VanderKam, "leads one to wonder whether more than mere coincidence of timing might have been involved . . . Was there something about the festival, some associations with it, that led the author of Luke-Acts to couple it with the eschatological gifts of the divine Spirit?"[6] To this might be added the following: Was there also something already "initiatory" in character about Pentecost somewhere in Judaism that would have led the author of Luke-Acts to connect Christian baptism with these eschatological gifts of the Spirit on this particular occasion?

The answer to both questions appears to be a resounding "yes." The recent work on the origins of Christianity by Étienne Nodet and Justin Taylor has underscored not only the importance of the Essene/Qumran community and the writings of the Jewish historian Josephus, but also the ritual practices of the sectarian Jewish community reflected in the *Book of Jubilees*, whose own liturgical calendar was followed by the Essenes. Within those documents, especially within the *Rule of the Community* or *Manual of Discipline* (1 QS 5:8) and *Jubilees* 6:17, the feast of Pentecost occurs annually on a Sunday and always on the 15th day of the third month of the year.[7] Pentecost was not only reckoned as the most important feast of the year, with no apparent connection to Passover (e.g., even Noah had celebrated it), but it also included both an annual covenant renewal ceremony *and* the reception of new members into the community. As Nodet and Taylor write:

> Pentecost, when the Covenant is renewed, is also the day for receiving new members, whose admission into the community is thereby an entry into the Covenant. That is the general setting of the Pentecost of Acts 2, and it is also a cornerstone in the Essene customs . . . ; this likeness is hardly surprising, since we are dealing with circles which originally were alike.[8]

Further, according to VanderKam, there are several notable parallels between the Jewish sectarian practice and interpretation of Pentecost as a celebration of the renewal of the Sinai covenant, and the narrative of Pentecost in Acts 2:

1.  the correlation between the ascent of Moses to Mt. Sinai on 3/15 to renew the covenant, according to *Jubilees*, and the close connection between Christ's own ascension and the outpouring of the Spirit ("Being therefore exalted at the right hand of God,

and having received from the Father the promise of the Holy Spirit, he has poured out this that you both see and hear," Acts 2:33);[9]

2.  the correlation between the coming of the Holy Spirit with "tongues as of fire" (Acts 2:3) enabling understanding among multiple languages and the tradition within Judaism (known early on from Philo of Alexandria and Josephus, and, later, from Rabbinic sources) of Israel itself "seeing" the voices of God *in fiery form* addressed to the "70 nations" of the world at Sinai (Exodus 19–20 and 24); and

3.  the correlation between the ideal Christian community presented in Acts 2:42 ("They devoted themselves to the apostles' teaching and fellowship, to the breaking of bread and the prayers") and the ideal obedient society of Israel constituted at Sinai which accepted the Torah.

The narrative of Pentecost in Acts 2:1–42, therefore, seems to have been influenced decidedly by the ways in which the Jewish Pentecost was already being interpreted and celebrated within some forms of sectarian Judaism during the second and first centuries, BCE, as a commemoration and renewal of the giving of the Law at Sinai. According to VanderKam, this interpretation and celebration is especially to be noted within the *Rule of the Community* or *Manual of Discipline* of the Qumran community. He writes:

The evidence . . . makes it plausible to think that the community . . . fashioned itself to some extent after the Israelite nation at Sinai as traditionally understood. Like Israel then, they, in the wilderness, solemnly agreed to uphold the Sinaitic covenant *on the festival of weeks* [emphasis added] and pledge to obey *all* the divine law mediated through Moses. Like ancient Israel they heard the law and understood it. They too formed a noble unity consisting of those pledged to the covenantal relationship. They organized themselves as ancient Israel had. They established a communal way of life in which much, including property was shared. They too sanctified themselves, separating men from women and thus were in the requisite state of purity for God to appear and reveal his will, as ancient Israel had. All of the measures taken by the community seem to aim at establishing a holy entity unlike what the group saw in others. The Qumran community saw itself as re-creating the camp of Israel in the wilderness.[10]

And, with regard to the early Christian community reflected in Acts 2, VanderKam concludes:

In the New Testament the earliest Jerusalem church, as pictured in Acts, exhibits a number of the same traits. That community was constituted in a new way at Pentecost . . . On that day many new members were welcomed into the fellowship. Those first followers of Jesus also established a unity, an ideal society in which property was held in common, meals were eaten together, and prayers were offered in community. It too was a community that received revelation in this state in a dramatic divine manifestation.[11]

But what specifically of *Christian* baptism in connection to this feast? Whatever the precise relationship between the ritual washings at Qumran and the origins of the Christian practice of baptizing new converts may be,[12] the fact remains that, at Qumran on Pentecost, new members were also received into the covenant community.[13] It is difficult not to see some kind of initiatory correlation between these two events. That is, the baptism of the three thousand converts makes perfect sense in a context shaped by a Qumran-*Jubilees* sectarian interpretation of the festival.

The question, however, is whether the author of Acts has merely used the interpretations and practices of some forms of sectarian Judaism to create what may be called an etiological account of the outpouring of the eschatological Spirit upon the infant church in Acts 2, or if he means to imply that the Christian adoption of the festival of Pentecost itself—even during the late first century (!)—included Christian baptism as a component. In other words, is Luke merely composing a narrative account influenced by some contemporary Jewish practice and interpretation? Or is he actually reflecting in his narrative the liturgical-sacramental patterns employed by the early Jerusalem Christian community leading from repentance to baptism to shared community life, a liturgical-sacramental praxis already connected to a Christianized celebration of the Jewish festival of Pentecost within that early community? Scholars have long held that the New Testament narrative accounts of the so-called dominical "institution" of the Eucharist do not reflect so much a reminiscence of the historical Jesus at *the* Last Supper but, rather, provide glimpses of the eucharistic meal as practiced within various communities at the time of the various writings. If this is true, why, then, would we read the Acts 2 account of Pentecost or, for that matter, the Gospel accounts of Jesus' own baptism in the Jordan, any differently?

In his 2000 Notre Dame doctoral dissertation, "August 15 and the Development of the Jerusalem Calendar," Walter Ray argues that the early Jerusalem Jewish-Christian community represented in Acts employed precisely a Christianized version of the calendar of feasts in *Jubilees* and was decisively influenced by the form of Judaism reflected in that tradition.[14] If Ray is correct, the possibility emerges that what is reflected in Acts 2:1–42 is not simply a narrative structure that uses a distinctively Jewish interpretative or exegetical tradition. Rather, what is reflected may well be the very liturgical and calendrical practice of the early Christian community in Jerusalem, which had inherited and "Christianized" the *actual practice*—on Pentecost itself—of both the renewal of the Sinai covenant (though now explicitly associated with the new covenant sealed by the outpouring of the Holy Spirit of Jesus) and the reception of new members (though now through Christian baptism as the equivalent rite of "reception"). If so, without limiting the celebration of baptism to Pentecost (throughout Acts, obviously, "any hour, any season, is suitable for baptism"), is it not precisely this *Pentecost* correlation between baptism and Holy Spirit that provides the paradigm for the necessary connection between baptism and Holy Spirit in general throughout Acts and, even, with the possible exception of Romans 6, in the overall theology of Paul (see especially

Galatians 3:23—4:7)? Such a practice would go a long way toward explaining why the dominant theological interpretation of baptism in the early centuries of the Church—at least in the East—was precisely adoption or new birth in the Holy Spirit rather than the baptismal death and burial motif of Romans 6.

The major difficulty here, of course, is the fact that our sources for the Christian celebration of Pentecost (unless Acts 2 *is* actually our first witness [!] or unless Paul is already referring to a "Christianized" celebration in 1 Corinthians 16:8) simply do not appear until the late second century, CE (*Epistula Apostolorum* and the *Acti Pauli* from Asia Minor and Irenaeus from Gaul), or at the turn of the second to the third century, CE (Tertullian, *De oratione* 23 and *De baptismo* 19).[15] But, while no reference to baptism (or to much of anything other than a mention of the prohibition of fasting and kneeling during the "period") appears in these late second-century texts, baptism during Pentecost is clear, as we have seen, in Tertullian's *De baptismo* 19. An argument *e silencio* with regard to Pentecost baptism prior to Tertullian cannot, of course, be taken as conclusive. But between Acts 2 and *De baptismo* 19 there are simply no extant clear references to *any* festival day in particular as being more appropriate than another for the celebration of baptism. And yet, with the exception of his clear preference for Paschal baptism as the *diem baptismo sollemniorem* (a practice confirmed elsewhere only in Hippolytus of Rome's early third-century *Commentary on Daniel*), what one sees in Tertullian is in continuity with Acts both in terms of baptism at Pentecost being associated with the "grace of the Holy Spirit first given" and the alternative suitability of "any hour, any season...for baptism." In other words, Tertullian not only refers to Pentecost generally as a period or space (the *laetitium spatium*) but also to the actual thematic focus of what will become associated with the *day* of Pentecost itself.[16]

Might it be the case, then, that baptism on the *day* of Pentecost actually belongs to a much earlier stratum—even an "apostolic" or, at least, early Jerusalem stratum—of the liturgical tradition, which Tertullian himself inherits but now subordinates to Easter, as he appears to do also with the baptismal suitability of "every day," in light of what might be called his own theological-liturgical preference for Pascha? This would suggest that Tertullian himself gave birth to the nearly universal post-Nicene paradigm shift in baptismal theology and celebration toward the "ideal" of Paschal baptism. Furthermore, if this is the case, rather than being a catch-all alternative or newly created occasion for those unable to be baptized at Easter, it is possible that Pentecost does not really "emerge" but, instead, *remains* as a baptismal occasion on the calendar. But it remains as the vestige or remnant of the earlier tradition *now* overshadowed, liturgically and theologically, by Pascha.

## II. Pentecost Baptism and Jesus' "Birth" and Baptism in the Jordan

The primitive Pentecost priority suggested tentatively above might also shed light on the celebration and interpretation of baptism elsewhere in the New Testament and within various early Christian traditions. Adela Yarbro Collins, for example, notes close parallels between the baptism of John and the baptisms occurring on Pentecost and throughout the book of Acts. She argues that:

> . . . the basic function of baptism as reflected in Peter's Pentecost sermon is so similar to the baptism of John. New elements are added, but the starting point is the same. Peter calls for repentance, just as John is said to have done. Peter indicates that the baptism is for the forgiveness of sins. The same association is made in Mark and Matthew. Peter exhorts his Jewish audience, "Save yourselves from this crooked generation." Their response is to submit to baptism. According to Matthew, going to John for baptism was a means of fleeing from 'the wrath to come' (Matthew 3:7) . . . There are two new elements in the function and meaning of baptism in Acts 2. One is that baptism occurs "in the name epi tō onomati of Jesus Christ" (v. 38) . . . The other new element is the association of baptism with the gift of the Holy Spirit (Acts 2:38). In Acts 1:5 the prophecy of John the Baptist is alluded to, that the Coming One would baptize "with the Holy Spirit and with fire" (Luke 3:16). The metaphorical fulfillment

of that prophecy, with regard to the 120 or so followers of Jesus, is narrated in the beginning of Acts 2. Thereafter, the ritual of baptism in the name of Jesus Christ is associated with the gift of the Holy Spirit.[17]

Along similar lines, it is again Walter Ray who has pointed to obvious parallels between what happens at Pentecost in Acts 2 and what happens in the first three chapters of Luke's Gospel with regard to Jesus' conception, birth, and baptism by John in the Jordan. In those chapters the promise of the Holy Spirit and its fulfillment constitute a narrative pattern and provide an *inclusio* linking Luke-Acts together:

> This pattern is repeated several times in Luke-Acts. The first iteration [the Annunciation in Luke 1] puts it into relationship with a narrative pattern which . . . stretches the length of Luke's work: the promises to Abraham and their fulfillment . . . [T]he significance of the Spirit for this promise becomes clearer with each iteration of the pattern, which includes the baptism of Jesus, the Pentecost event, and the account of the coming of the Spirit to Cornelius and his household (Acts 10:1—11:18), which ... is structurally parallel to Luke 1. In this last episode, the Holy Spirit descends on those who hear the words Peter is speaking . . . (Acts 10:44), the words by which they will be saved (Acts 11:14). Peter likens this event to the disciples' reception of the Spirit at Pentecost (Acts 10:47, 11:15–16).[18]

This narrative pattern, however, is more than a literary *inclusio*. According to Ray, what lies behind it is precisely the narrative world of the calendar of *Jubilees*, wherein the festival of Pentecost on 3/15 is simultaneously the celebration of the birth of Isaac (conceived by Sarah on 6/15 = August 15). And, significantly, it is the Isaac-Jesus typology emerging from this tradition that occupies the principal theological attention of St. Paul, especially in his Galatian correspondence (see Galatians 4:21–31). Ray writes:

The Feast of Weeks, understood as the 15th of the third month, had particular meaning for the *Jubilees* calendar as the completion of the fifty days, the time of the ultimate fulfillment of covenant renewal which was both promised and foreshadowed in the birth of Isaac. In its Christian form the final day of the feast would have been remembered as the time of divine adoption of the community and the giving of the Spirit (Acts 2, Galatians 4:5–6), but also the time of particular revelation of the divine sonship of Jesus in the power of the Spirit, first in light of the resurrection/ascension (cf. Romans 1:3, Acts 2:33) but also in light of his special birth (Luke 1:35) . . . We should perhaps add Christ's baptism to the list, where we again find the themes of divine sonship and the coming of the Spirit . . . [I]n Luke-Acts both the birth and baptism of Jesus manifest the same narrative pattern as Pentecost.[19]

Interestingly enough, then, according to Ray, Jesus' own *beginnings*, whether at his conception, his birth in Bethlehem, or at what might be called his "spiritual birth" in the Jordan, have clear Pentecost connotations quite possibly stemming from an early Jerusalem Christian adaptation of this ancient Qumran-*Jubilees* calendrical and narrative tradition.

One wonders further at this point whether this Qumran-*Jubilees* Pentecost tradition is not also somehow closely related to the unique but characteristic emphases of the early Syrian liturgical traditions, theologically focused, as they are, on baptism as adoption and new birth. Unfortunately, Ray does not treat the baptism of Jesus in detail, other than to include it as belonging to the same overall *Jubilees* narrative pattern he attempts to recover at the base of the Jerusalem tradition. But he does state in a tantalizing footnote that if baptism on Pentecost in Acts 2 "represents the practice of the early Jerusalem community, it would explain the early Eastern understanding of baptism as new birth and divine adoption . . . which would fit with the *Jubilees'* narrative world."[20]

In her 1994 essay on the origins of the feast of Epiphany, "Die Licht-Erscheinung bei der Taufe Jesu und der Ursprung des Epiphanie-festes,"[21] Gabriele Winkler draws attention to the numerous references to fire being enkindled in the Jordan itself at the time of Jesus' own baptism. While there are no canonical New Testament references to fire in the Jordan associated with Jesus' baptism, such imagery, as is well known, is a characteristic especially of the early Syrian baptismal tradition.

> Especially in the Syrian tradition (but also in the West), the tradition of the appearance of a fire at the baptism has left a lasting echo. Ephrem, the Acts of John, Jacob of Serug, the Syrian baptismal *ordines*, the Syrian's feast of Epiphany—all these documents are acquainted with the appearance of fire on the Jordan, and they then tie this tradition of Jesus' baptism with their own baptismal usages. That is because, for the Syrians, the Jordan event forms the model for the shape of their baptismal rites.[22]

While Winkler's concern in this essay, admittedly, is not with the particular origins of this imagery in the tradition,[23] others have, in fact, pointed to a possible Pentecost inspiration for it.[24] Indeed, in Luke's Gospel alone does John the Baptist announce that Jesus "will baptize you with the Holy Spirit and *fire*" (Luke 3:16 [emphasis added]), a promise fulfilled on Pentecost. Moreover, according to the important textual variant of Luke 3:22, instead of "You are my Son, the Beloved; with you am I well pleased," the text quotes Psalm 2:7, "You are my son, today I have begotten you." Psalm 2:7 is associated with Jesus' *Ascension* elsewhere in the New Testament (cf. Acts 13:33 and Hebrews 1:1–5), and with divine adoption in the baptismal theology of the early Syrian tradition (cf. *Didascalia Apostolorum* 9).[25] In other words, it seems that the baptism of Jesus provides the precise paradigm for what takes place on Pentecost for the disciples and for the three thousand converts in Acts 2. But, alternatively, it could be that Pentecost provides the interpretative theological paradigm for how the historical event of Jesus' own baptism is narrated. That is to say, a tradition associated with Pentecost itself, or at least the Qumran-*Jubilees* (and early Christian Jerusalem?) tradition reflected in Acts 2, might have provided the framework that makes Jesus' baptism in the Jordan, with its concomitant theology of adoption and new birth in the Spirit, *the* normative paradigm

for Christian baptism in the East. This very Pentecost-Spirit orientation perhaps lies behind Paul's own baptismal theology of
divine adoption and true "sonship" in Galatians 3:26–4:7:

> . . . for in Christ Jesus you are all children [υἱοὶ] of God
> through faith. As many of you as were baptized into
> Christ have clothed yourselves with Christ. There is no
> longer Jew or Greek, there is no longer slave or free, there
> is no longer male and female; for all of you are one in
> Christ Jesus. And if you belong to Christ, then your are
> Abraham's offspring, heirs according to the promise . . .
> [W]hen the fullness of time had come, God sent his Son,
> born of a woman, born under the law, so that we might
> receive *adoption as children* [υἱοὶ]. And because you are
> children [υἱοὶ], God has sent the Spirit of his Son into our
> hearts, crying 'Abba! Father!' So you are no longer a slave
> *but a child* [υἱὸς], and if a child then also an heir, through
> God. [Emphasis added]

In short, liturgical scholarship has been too quick to argue that
the two dominant baptismal theologies emerging from the New
Testament in early Christianity are the "Johannine" imagery of
new birth (John 3:5) and the "Pauline" theology of Romans 6. *Au
contraire*, we really are dealing with two baptismal images that
are *both*, essentially, "Pauline" in character and origin.[26] That is,
already in the middle of the 50s, (long before the Gospels or Acts
were written!), the imagery of divine baptismal adoption *in the
Spirit*, not only in Galatians but also somewhat later in Titus 3:5
("the water of rebirth and renewal by the Holy Spirit"), is also—
and obviously—"Pauline." Hence, the so-called "silence of Paul"
in the early centuries of the Church may well be only a specific
"silence" of Romans 6 theology. And, since Paul's primary concern in Galatians is precisely with the relationship between
Christianity and Judaism—a concern directed against
"Judaizers" within the early Jerusalem community itself—it is
not so surprising that a baptismal theology of new birth and
adoption would emerge as most dominant or characteristic within Semitic forms of early Christianity (e.g., in Syria).

## III. Pentecost and the Eastern Feast of Epiphany

As noted above, Winkler has demonstrated that at the earliest stratum of the tradition, Jesus' baptism is also his pneumatic "birth" in the Jordan. Furthermore, Ray has proposed that, originally, Pentecost celebrated not only the gift of the Spirit, but in light the Isaac typology, "the divine sonship of Jesus in the power of the Spirit." This raises another question: Is the development of the feast of Epiphany in the East, especially when individual Gospels themselves came to serve as the narrative lectionary frameworks for the celebration of the liturgical year beginning on January 6 (at least in Syria and Egypt), merely the separation of one of Pentecost's original components that was increasingly adapted to other calendrical systems? In other words, do both the origins and the interpretation of Epiphany as, originally, that of Jesus' baptism (his "birth" or "beginnings") in the Jordan arise from the earlier Christian celebrations of a unitive Pentecost? It is conventionally held that this kind of separation is precisely what happened with the transfer of the later separate feast of the Ascension from Pentecost to the fortieth day of Easter. Something similar could also have happened with Jesus' birth-baptism.

While admittedly speculative and in need of much more detailed research, a connection between Pentecost and the baptism of Jesus and, ultimately, the feast of Epiphany, stemming originally from the Qumran-*Jubilees* tradition, may well yet produce new scholarly fruits in the study of early calendrical development. An original Pentecost connection would explain a number of early Christian liturgical developments.

## Conclusion: Pascha or Pentecost as the *"Diem baptismo sollemniorem"*?

It is, of course, not necessary to accept the hypothesis suggested tentatively above to argue that Pentecost was or should be a *"diem baptismo sollemniorem"* of, at least, equal rank to Easter (or Epiphany) in the life of the church. In fact, given the biblical precedent for Pentecost baptism in Acts 2, it is nothing short of ironic that Pentecost baptism would be ranked by Tertullian as lower than Easter in baptismal appropriateness and become, as previous scholarship asserts, only an occasion to cover the baptismal overflow from Easter.

Whatever the historical situation may have been in the life of the early Jerusalem Christian community, however, certainly in our own day the feast of Pentecost can be recovered as another prime, and *biblical*, occasion for baptism, even within the context of a full Pentecost vigil at the grand culmination of Easter's fifty days. Pastorally, it would not take much to bring this about.[27]

Indeed, as in the case of the three thousand converts added to the church after Peter's Pentecost homily in Acts 2, perhaps the only proper response to the great mystery of Pentecost is "Brothers [and sisters], what should we do?" And the only answer to that is still: "Repent, and be baptized every one of you in the name of Jesus Christ so that your sins may be forgiven; and you will receive the gift of the Holy Spirit." The celebration of Pentecost, without the celebration of baptism, seems, in this light, to be incomplete and lacking in classic—if not already "apostolic"—focus.

## Notes

[1] Tertullian, *De baptismo* 19, English translation adapted from E.C. Whitaker, *Documents of the Baptismal Liturgy* (London: SPCK, 1970), 9 [emphasis added].

[2] See Paul Bradshaw, "'*Diem baptismo sollemniorem*': Easter and Initiation in Christian Antiquity," in LWSS, 137–47.

[3] See ibid., 144.

[4] See Karl Gerlach, *The Ante-Nicene Pascha: A Rhetorical History*, Liturgia Condenda 7 (Louven: Peeters, 1998), 21–78.

[5] Text quoted from the New Revised Standard Version translation.

[6] James VanderKam, "The Festival of Weeks and the Story of Pentecost in Acts 2," Unpublished paper, University of Notre Dame, 2001.

[7] The *Jubilees* calendar was so constructed that the same day occurred on the same date every year. Such guaranteed the priority of the Sabbath since no festival would ever occur on the Sabbath.

[8] Étienne Nodet and Justin Taylor, *The Origins of Christianity: An Exploration* (Collegeville: The Liturgical Press / Michael Glazier, 1998), 397.

[9] The close relationship between the ascension of Christ and the gift of the Holy Spirit—both celebrated together on Pentecost, as witnessed to by a variety of patristic sources in Palestine and Syria, including Egeria—is well known to liturgical scholars. This relationship, of course, was first brought to light by Georg Kretschmar in "Himmelfahrt und Pfingsten," *Zeitschrift für Kirchengeschichte* 66 (1954–55), 209–53.

[10] James VanderKam, "Sinai Revisited," Unpublished paper, University of Notre Dame, 2001.

[11] Ibid.

[12] On this see Adela Yarbro Collins, "The Origin of Christian Baptism," in LWSS, 39–41.

[13] See Nodet and Taylor, 397ff.

[14] Walter D. Ray, "August 15 and the Development of the Jerusalem Calendar" (Ph.D. Dissertation, University of Notre Dame, 2000).

[15] See Thomas Talley, *The Origins of the Liturgical Year*, second, emended edition (Collegeville: The Liturgical Press, Pueblo, 1991), 60–63.

[16] As Raniero Cantalamessa has demonstrated, "at no point in its development did the *Pentêcostês* have the extended meaning [i.e., as fifty *days*] alone, just as at no point did it have the restricted meaning [i.e., the *Day* of Pentecost] alone." Raniero Cantalamessa, *Easter in the Early Church* (Collegeville: The Liturgical Press, 1993), 22.

[17] Adela Yarbro Collins, "The Origin of Christian Baptism," in LWSS, 50–52.

[18] Ray, "August 15. . .", 220–21.

[19] Ibid., 262.

[20] Ibid., 265, n. 44.

[21] OC 78 (1994), 177–229. This essay appears in English translation by my student David Maxwell as "The Appearance of the Light at the Baptism of Jesus and the Origins of the Feast of Epiphany: An Investigation of Greek, Syriac, Armenian, and Latin

Sources," in Maxwell E. Johnson (ed.), *Between Memory and Hope: Readings on the Liturgical Year* (Collegeville: The Liturgical Press, Pueblo, 2000), 291–347, from where it will be cited in this essay.

22 Ibid., 303.

23 See ibid., 302.

24 See Sebastian Brock, *The Holy Spirit and the Syrian Baptismal Tradition*, *The Syrian Churches Series* 9 (Kottayam, Kerala: Deepika Book Stall, 1979), 11–12, and especially Chapter 8, "Baptism as Pentecost," 134–39; and Joseph Chalassery, *The Holy Spirit and Christian Initiation in the East Syrian Tradition*, Mar Thoma Yogam (Rome: The Mar Thoma Yogam / St. Thomas Christian Fellowship, 1995), 65.

25 In her recent and compelling article, "Initiation by Anointing in Early Syriac-Speaking Christianity," *Studia Liturgica* 31 (2001), 150–70, Susan Myers has sought to demonstrate that in Syria the water-bath of baptism was itself an addition to a more primitive initiatory pattern that included only the anointing (later becoming the pre-baptismal anointing) as the overall pneumatic focus of the rite. It is therefore interesting to speculate that such a pattern may also be dependent upon the apostles' own "baptism" not in water but in the "Holy Spirit and fire" on Pentecost itself.

26 I owe this insight to comments made by Professor M. Daniel Findikyan in a recent conversation.

27 Cf. *Book of Occasional Services* (New York: Church Hymnal Corporation, 1979), 126–27. I have tried to deal with this on a more pastoral level in chapter 3 of my recent *Images of Baptism*, Forum Essays 6 (Chicago: Liturgy Training Publications, 2001).

# LET'S KEEP ADVENT
# RIGHT WHERE IT IS

In the November/December 1991 issue of *Lutheran Partners* Pastor Susan K. Wendorf—"Let's Move Advent"—issued an impassioned plea for the Evangelical Lutheran Church in America (ELCA) to consider moving the Advent Season out of its current pre-Christmas position to a more suitable location in the year. And, judging from the numerous favorable letters her plea engendered (see *Lutheran Partners* March/April 1992), it is clear that her experience, formed by years of continuing pastoral frustration with the difficulties surrounding the celebration of Advent in contemporary American church and culture, is one shared by numerous pastors and other worship leaders throughout the ELCA.

Nevertheless, fully conscious of the risk of being called a "liturgical purist," I have a number of comments and or caveats to offer by way of response. I offer them here not as an "expert" in the field who thinks he has all the answers—although my students may have a different read on this disclaimer—but simply as one who loves Advent (where it is) and wishes to make a contribution to the discussion of this important topic.

The first comment I should like to offer is this. While Lutherans certainly *can* make a unilateral change in the liturgical calendar and so "move Advent" elsewhere in the year, it should always be remembered that Lutherans do not live—or, at least, *should* not live—in a liturgical or ecclesiastical vacuum. That is, while there are specific festivals and occasions unique to our Lutheran tradition (e.g., Reformation Day/Sunday in October and the location of the Transfiguration of Our Lord on the Last

Sunday After the Epiphany), changing one of the Western Christian tradition's ecumenically accepted liturgical seasons—like Advent—would be appropriately accomplished only in direct consultation with these other traditions. To do otherwise would be narrow parochialism—"Luthero-centrism" some might call it today—at its worst. This would be especially true in our contemporary context in which numerous Christian traditions, which have not followed either lectionary or calendar closely in the past, have recently been rediscovering its riches.

Second, we should be extremely cautious about accepting certain assumptions and commonly accepted clichés regarding the origins and celebration of Christmas. According to the most recent scholarship on these origins,[1] the popularly accepted *Religionsgeschichtliche* hypothesis that December 25 was chosen for the celebration of the Nativity of Christ to counter Emperor Aurelian's 274 A.D. establishment of and Constantine's later support for the feast of the *Natale Solis Invicti* (Birth of the Unconquerable Sun) has been shown to be highly questionable.

Yes, an *association* of Christ's nativity with this pagan cult did occur in fourth century Rome *after* Christianity became tolerated. But the birth of Jesus was already associated with the "sun of righteousness" in Malachi 4:2 in a North African document some *thirty years* before Aurelian even established this "sun" feast. It becomes likely then that December 25 was chosen *not* because of a pagan feast already celebrated on this date but in relationship to the fact that quite early in the church's history March 25 was understood to be the actual date of both Christ's Passion and Resurrection *and his conception* so that December 25—exactly nine months later—was originally chosen from a computation based on the assumed date of Jesus' death, resurrection, and conception. And, based on the fact that the Donatists already probably celebrated Christmas in the early fourth century prior to Constantine's victory over Maxentius in 311, its earliest home was possibly North Africa rather than Rome, at a period *before* relationships between church and empire could even make possible or desirable a Christian adaptation of such a pagan feast. J. Neil Alexander, in fact, goes so far as to suggest that Aurelian's "Sun Feast" on December 25 was his attempt to counteract the *Christian* festival among the growing Christian populace of the Roman Empire.

What this suggests, if correct, is that Christmas, contrary to popular assumptions and time-honored explanations, was actually not in origin an adapted "pagan" feast, not the Christian "Birth of the Son" festival chosen to counteract the pagan "Birth of the Sun" festival. Rather, originally dependent upon the presumed date of the events of Jesus' death and resurrection, it receives its content—as does every liturgical celebration—from the Easter focus on the crucified and risen Christ himself. Christmas therefore draws not only its origins but its focus ultimately from Easter! It celebrates the incarnation of the crucified and risen Christ and tells the *whole* story of Christ, *not* just his birth.

The liturgical year, after all, is neither a kind of Hellenistic mystery religions re-enactment of the life of Jesus nor an annual recurring cyclic meditation on and devotion to the historical life of Jesus. Nor is it a time for the church to play "make believe" as though Advent is actually our preparing for a birth that hasn't yet happened but somehow will happen on Christmas. Rather, the liturgical year through feast and fast, through festival and preparation, celebrates the presence of the already crucified and risen Christ among us "Now!" as we remember (*anamnesis*) what he did "once for all" in history (see Hebrews 10:10) and as we await his coming again. But it's always one and the same Christ we remember and expect as we celebrate his abiding presence in the Spirit and as we behold what that presence means for us here and now through the multifaceted prism of Advent, Christmas, Epiphany, Lent, Easter, Pentecost or through the lives of his saints throughout the ages. As the title of Raymond Brown's brief and delightful commentary on the infancy narratives in Matthew and Luke suggests, December 25 celebrates not "Baby Jesus" back somewhere in history, but *An Adult Christ at Christmas*[2] present here and now! The narratives we read tell the story of the *whole* Christ event: birth, life, death, resurrection, gift of the Spirit, and the responses of faith or unbelief to the message of the Gospel by both Jew (symbolized by Mary, Joseph, and the shepherds) and Gentile (symbolized by the Magi and Simeon's Canticle) in a post-Easter context.

Such a "cross-centered" or paschal approach should be readily accepted, especially by Lutherans. To make then what is currently Advent into a kind of "Christmas Season" throughout the entire month of December and to choose another location for Advent would tend to violate not only the holistic theological-paschal integrity of the feast itself but also the reason why this date appears to have been selected in the first place. December 25 as Christmas was chosen, it now increasingly seems to be, for a reason which was ultimately paschal and *not* cultural in orientation. To suggest cultural reasons for a change now, because the "pagans" have taken it *back* is simply not logical. It is the *church's* feast and has always been, in the spite of the cultural associations it acquired both in the late Roman Empire and today.

Third, is it not the case that unless a tradition is reformed or changed by those with authority to do so (e.g., national church assemblies, etc.), members of a particular liturgical or ecclesial family have a *right* to expect that the liturgy in which they participate will reflect and express their tradition, a tradition which is not subject to the passing whims, fancies, or frustrations of a pastor or of certain members who want the liturgy or the calendar to be something other than it is? In other words, as members of a *Lutheran* tradition which joyfully and gratefully accepts the liturgical year, ELCA Lutherans have the *right* to expect that on a given Sunday in Advent (or Lent, or Easter, or whenever) the assigned propers and lectionary readings will be used and the sermon, music, and hymns will reflect that day or season. For example, to have the pastor and others choose a "surprise" day for Christmas each year, as one respondent to Wendorf's essay actually suggested, violates the rights and legitimate ritual expectations of the gathered assembly.

To insist upon the liturgical rights of the assembly is not "liturgiolatry" in a matter which many might consider to be an *adiaphoron* (i.e., something indifferent or unnecessary). It is, rather, the awareness of and respect for the integrity of the liturgical year as the means by which we are allowed, invited, and privileged through various feasts and seasons to celebrate the reality that the Gospel of Jesus Christ, mediated to us by word and sacrament, declares us, forms us, and calls us to be Easter people, Lenten people, Christmas people, and, not least, Advent people who live in hope and expectation for the day of his coming. The issue then is our identity in Christ as his people, his body in the world, and it is precisely this identity we celebrate in the liturgical year. Christmas is about *our* baptismal birth in the adult Christ as he is born anew in us through the Spirit who brings the "glad tidings" of salvation—the one salvation—to us now. Easter and Pentecost are about *our* death and resurrection in Christ, our passover from death to life in his passover, through water and the Holy Spirit in baptism. Lent is about *our* annual retreat, our annual re-entry into the catechumenate and order of penitents in order to reflect on, affirm, remember, and re-claim that baptism—*not* forty days of the Passion narrative or the Seven Last Words (medieval Catholic passion devotions which are perpetuated only by contemporary Protestants it seems) as though Lent were a kind of elongated Good Friday. And Advent is about *our* hope for fulfillment in Christ when "he will come to judge the living and the dead." The liturgical year, then, is about us . . . *in Christ*. In other words, as the great Eastern Rite liturgiologist Robert F. Taft has said on more than on occasion, "We don't plan the liturgy; the liturgy plans *us*!" And, "what we *get* out of it is the inestimable privilege of praising God." If, then, our Christian identity, given in baptism, nourished by word and Eucharist, and continually held before us in feast and season is an *adiaphoron*, then so be it.

This, of course, does *not* mean that liturgy can't be changed or reformed, that ritual forms and hymnody must reflect only one particular culture of the church catholic, or that *Lutheran Book of Worship* must be the only worship resource in use among ELCA Lutherans. But it *does* mean that before liturgical change or reform can be done one must know *what* it is that is being changed so that the particular and essential meanings of a liturgical act, text, or season—in this case Advent itself—can be expressed as clearly as possible. But the Advent liturgy isn't broken and doesn't need reform at this time in history. What is broken, I believe, may be our appropriation of it. What needs change and reform, therefore, is our use and/or abuse of Advent.

Concerning this we may have failed miserably. But in spite of our failure, it is with Advent, perhaps more than with any other liturgical season, where we continue to have the *opportunity* to point beyond our cultural context(s) and, with John the Baptist, proclaim one who is coming—not as an infant at Christmas—but as the crucified and risen one to bring this final age to its consummation, as the crucified and risen one, who by the power of the Holy Spirit in word and sacrament comes to be re-born in *us* at Christmas and always. Therefore, while the world celebrates Christmas from Halloween through December 25 (thus even an early November "Advent" wouldn't quite solve the problem), the church enters the barren wasteland of the Advent desert to focus *not* so much on the coming "birth" of Jesus at Christmas but to prepare the way for the return of the Lord of life and history—for his *parousia* at Christmas. What a wonderful sign of contradiction the Advent liturgy, and by implication the church, can be in today's society, a sign surely to be lost if it were moved and replaced by an extended "Christmas."

Fourth and finally, make some compromises *if you must*. But educate, catechize, and, above all, preach the Gospel. Indeed, is not the question we pastors and other worship leaders are frequently asked—"Why can't we sing Christmas carols in Advent?"—precisely an open door, an invitation for this kind of ongoing catechesis and education? We don't sing Christmas carols in Advent for the same reason we don't sing the Christmas song of the angels (the "Glory the God") or the Easter Hymn of Praise ("Worthy is Christ"), or sell out the Sunday Eucharist in favor of "Sunday School Christmas programs" during Advent. Why? Because it's Advent—not Christmas! It's as simple (and as difficult) as that.

So, attempt to answer the difficult questions but don't sell out Advent in the name of cultural and congregational relevance or from personal pastoral frustration. Part of our Christian identity, part of who we are, is at stake in this question. But as long as we name and continue to experience the tension between a cultural Christmas and a Christian Advent and Nativity the eschatological nature of both liturgy and church is alive and well. Let's keep Advent right where it is. We are doing something right already.

### Notes

[1] See Thomas Talley, *The Origins of the Liturgical Year*, 2nd edition (Collegeville: Pueblo, 1991), 85–103, and J. Neil Alexander, *The Liturgical Meaning of Advent, Christmas, Epiphany: Waiting for the Coming* (Washington, D.C.: Pastoral Press, 1993), 29–57.

[2] (Collegeville: The Liturgical Press, 1988).

# THE FEAST OF THE VIRGIN
# OF GUADALUPE AND
# THE SEASON OF ADVENT

Among Mexican American Roman Catholics and, increasingly, among various Hispanic-Latino Protestant communities as well (especially, but not only, within some communities of Episcopalians and Lutherans[1]), the feast of the Virgin of Guadalupe on December 12 is—or is becoming—an important mid-Advent celebration, important enough in some contexts to challenge even the priority of an Advent Sunday when December 12 itself happens to fall on a Sunday.[2] Surely this is due in large part to the fact that, as John Baldovin has written, "in our own time the Virgin of Guadalupe has served as an effective rallying point for a whole people's hopes for liberation and justice as well as an anchor for their Christian identity."[3] As such, the feast of the Virgin of Guadalupe may well be a rather obvious example of the following primary characteristic of festivity: "[F]easts are extraordinary. They lift people out of ordinary chronological time . . . Feasts are not merely collective visible events but also 'total social facts' . . . Pulling all the stops out for a celebration means having it in a larger social context, something that the entire community can celebrate meaningfully."[4] As a "total social fact," a "fiesta" for some communities that goes well beyond the confines of the specific liturgical celebration of December 12,[5] the feast of the Virgin of Guadalupe and other similar feasts cannot simply be ignored either by contemporary liturgiologists or pastoral liturgists.

It is thus both with the December 12 feast itself—its origins and development—and with the location of this feast within the Advent Season that this essay is concerned. While it is often asserted that feasts such as this point to and underscore an almost irreconcilable tension between "official" liturgy and "popular religion" or "popular piety,"[6] a tension which creates all kinds of local problems in the celebration of the church's liturgy, I want to question whether this tension is more perceived or imagined than necessarily real in the case of Guadalupe. Might, in fact, the December 12 feast in the middle of Advent represent, at least at some level, a synthesis of what our Advent hopes and expectations are all about? Might the Virgin of Guadalupe herself be an indigenous American " icon" of the Advent stance of the church in the world between the "now" and "not yet" of redemption as well as provide a synthesis of the eschatological and incarnational orientations of this liturgical season? Such questions, I believe, can be answered in the affirmative.

## I. The Development of the Feast of the Virgin of Guadalupe on December 12

The origins and development of the feast of the Virgin of Guadalupe on December 12 are as difficult to discern as are the precise historical origins of the Guadalupan narratives and image themselves.[7] No written record of a feast of Guadalupe celebrated on December 12 at Tepeyac, the location of the alleged apparitions to Juan Diego in 1531, exists before 1662, at which time the cathedral chapter of Mexico City requested approval from Rome for the feast on this date, a request that was delayed until 1667. When finally approved by Rome, the response contained the incorrect date of *September* rather than December 12, an error which served to delay the process even further. Earlier, the feast day at Tepeyac was, apparently, September 8, the feast of both the Nativity of the Blessed Virgin Mary on the general Roman liturgical calendar and of the Estremaduran Guadalupe on the local liturgical calendar of the Estremadura region in Spain.[8] In fact, it was not until May 25, 1754, that Pope Benedict XIV finally confirmed both the patronage of the Virgin Mary under the title of the Mexican advocation of Our Lady of

Guadalupe for "New Spain" and approved officially the liturgical propers (i.e., prayers, readings, and chants) for the Mass and
Divine Office for the December 12 feast on the official, local calendar of Mexico.[9] Nevertheless, it is obvious that the feast had
been celebrated in Mexico on December 12 for some time prior
to this confirmation and approval, *at least* from 1662.

Stafford Poole takes this late acceptance of the December 12
date for the feast as further confirmation of his overall thesis
that, directly inspired by the written narratives of Miguel
Sánchez (1648)[10] and Luis Lasso de la Vega (1649),[11] the origins
of Guadalupan devotion itself belong to an overall seventeenth,
and not early-sixteenth, century context.[12] But the lateness of the
"official" recognition of the December 12 date for the *feast* only
confirms either that the choice of this particular date, the date
associated in other narratives with the fourth and final appari-
tion, was inspired possibly by the official written Guadalupan
narratives, or, alternatively, that the date in the narratives was
itself possibly inspired by the growing Guadalupan oral tradition itself. Indeed, in the history of especially Marian feasts in
Western Christianity, the time it takes from the origins of a particular feast in a local church or religious community to when it
becomes recognized officially or incorporated into the general
liturgical calendar can take several centuries! This does not mean
that the feast is not already being celebrated somewhere by some
communities during this period of development but only that
official recognition, approval, or incorporation into the official
calendar is not the same thing as the "origins" of its celebration.
That is, "official confirmation" does not mean the "beginnings"
of a feast itself but it is simply the confirmation, permission, and
approval for what is already taking place. To give but one obvious
example here: the December 8 (now) Solemnity of the
Immaculate Conception of Mary has its origins in an eighth-century Byzantine Christian December 9 feast called "the
Conception of St. Anne," a feast still celebrated today in the
Christian East.[13] This entered the West, via monastic usage in
England, in the eleventh century, and from England it spread
with increasingly popularity throughout Western Europe especially
within various religious orders and communities, most notably
the Franciscans, whose own itinerant life-style contributed to its

wide dissemination. Together with growing theological speculation about Mary's "immaculate conception" (her preservation, or
"redemption by exemption," from original sin), primarily
among Franciscan theologians from the thirteenth century on,
the feast was accepted for Rome itself by a Franciscan pope
(Sixtus IV) only in 1477, and it became a universal feast for the
entire Roman Catholic Church only in 1708. Even so, the particular title of this feast today, "the *Immaculate* Conception of
Mary," did not become its official title until after the promulgation of the dogma of Mary's Immaculate Conception by Pope
Pius IX in 1854.[14] From its eighth-century origins in the Christian
East, then, it took almost *ten* centuries for it to become a universal feast in the West and *eleven* centuries for it to develop into its
current form. Hence, that a local feast like the Virgin of
Guadalupe might take from 1531 until 1662 (or 1754) to evolve
into its final form is actually a relatively short period of time in
the historical development of liturgical feasts.

At the same time, the fact that September 8 may well have
been the original date of the feast, corresponding already to both
the feast of the Nativity of Mary and the Estremaduran
Guadalupe celebrated at Tepeyac, is, again really no indication
whatsoever, pro or con, with regard to the historicity of devotion
to the Mexican Guadalupe herself. Indeed, not only do dates of
feasts periodically change throughout history, but if the
September 8 feast of the Nativity of Mary was already the "titu-
lar feast" of the chapel of Tepeyac, that is, if the feast for the
Estremaduran Virgin of Guadalupe at Tepeyac was the Nativity
of Mary,[15] there is really no reason to expect an alternate date
being sought or established for a separate feast day in honor of
the *Mexican* Guadalupe. The Guadalapan narratives themselves
nowhere call for the establishment of a new liturgical *feast* in her
honor and, in fact, there was really no need for a separate Marian
feast. Had there, in fact, been a call for such an establishment,
this would have been undoubtedly resisted by the early
Franciscan ecclesiastical authorities as much as they were
already highly suspicious and critical of the indigenous
Guadalupan devotion itself.[16]

Furthermore, there is early-sixteenth century evidence for
the existence of the celebration of the feast of the (Immaculate)

Conception of Mary on December 8 in Mexico. If this feast was not yet a universal Roman Catholic feast in the early sixteenth century, it was certainly already being celebrated in the region of Tepeyac, as the existence of a poetic homily of Bernardino de Sahagún for the feast (called by him simply "the Conception of the Blessed Virgin Mary") clearly demonstrates.[17] Even if, then, there *had* been some kind of early indigenous push for an additional Marian feast in close association to December 8 one can only imagine that it too would have been met with resistance and rejection for the simple reason that there already *was* a Marian feast in close proximity to the date.

At the same time, the fact that the liturgical "Propers" (prayers, chants, and lectionary readings) for the September 8 feast of the Nativity of Mary would have been used to celebrate the Virgin of Guadalupe, whether in her Spanish or Mexican advocation, proves nothing about the existence of the feast itself. It only means that, as in the case of the Estremaduran Guadalupe, the liturgical propers of the Nativity of Mary came to be used for the Mexican Guadalupe and that both were associated originally with September 8 in Mexico. Indeed, there is some evidence to suggest that in this time period of history the prayers and readings in what is called the "Common of Feasts of the Blessed Virgin Mary," that is, the collection of prayer texts and readings to be used for feasts not having their own assigned "propers," were identical to those also assigned to the September 8 feast of the Nativity of Mary. Further confirmation of this is supplied by the fact that even when Pope Benedict XIV in 1754 finally approved the specific liturgical propers for the Guadalupe feast on December 12 the Mass for the feast remained, essentially, that of the Nativity of Mary.[18]

As I have argued elsewhere is quite possibly the case with the official Guadalupan narratives of Sanchéz and Lasso de la Vega in the mid-seventeenth century,[19] I suspect that the *official* establishment of the feast of the Virgin of Guadalupe on December 12 is the response of local (Mexican) ecclesiastical authorities to the increasing popularity of Guadalupan devotion itself. Indeed, as long as that devotion was localized at Tepeyac and associated primarily with the indigenous peoples there was no perceived need for a "national" feast. But, what Jean-Pierre

Ruiz has suggested with regard to how the official narratives appear to reflect the "canonization" of the Guadalupan events might also well be related to the development of the feast itself. That is, if by this time, according to Ruiz, "the Virgin of Guadalupe had reached an important breadth of diffusion throughout the various ethnic and socioeconomic strata of colonial Mexico, ranging from the indigenous Nahuas, to the *criollos*, to the Spanish born,"[20] then the establishment of an official feast in her honor may well have been but another concrete expression and confirmation of this wide-spread development and acceptance. This kind of development and acceptance, in fact, has continued well until our own day with a revision of the 1754 liturgy by Pope Leo XIII in 1894,[21] and, more importantly, with new propers for the "Solemnity" of the Virgin of Guadalupe appearing for Mexico in 1974,[22] and for the "Feast" of The Virgin of Guadalupe for the dioceses of the United States appearing in 1987.[23] Prior to this development, the December 12 feast had been permitted for United States dioceses only since 1962 as the equivalent of an "optional memorial."

## II. The Feast of the Virgin of Guadalupe and the Season of Advent

However it was that the feast of the Virgin of Guadalupe came to be celebrated ultimately on December 12, this feast, together with the Solemnity of the Immaculate Conception of Mary four days before it, tends to provide an overall "Marian" focus, especially among Mexicans and Mexican Americans, for the liturgical season of Advent. That is, the popular observance of the season of Advent among Mexican and Mexican American Catholics is organized as follows:

| | |
|---|---|
| December 3–11 | *Novena to the Virgin of Guadalupe* (nine days of special prayer, devotion, and preparation for the December 12 celebration)[24] |
| December 8 | *Solemnity of the Immaculate Conception* |
| December 9 | *Memorial of St. Juan Diego Cuauhtlatoatzin* (Optional) |
| December 12 | *Solemnity or Feast of the Virgin of Guadalupe* |

December 16–24   *Las Posadas Novena* (nine days of special prayer, devotion, and preparation, often celebrated in neighborhoods or in parish communities, consisting especially of festive processions, songs, and ceremonies re-enacting the search of Mary and Joseph for lodging in Bethlehem, followed by joyful celebrations with food and singing at the final designated home or place in the search)[25]

On the popular religious level, then, the first part of the Advent season is oriented to and concerned with prayerful preparation for the December 12 appearance of the pregnant Virgin of Guadalupe. And, after she appears, the rest of the season is devoted to accompanying her and Joseph to Bethlehem for the birth of Christ, an accompaniment often with profound implications for many Hispanic Latinos, especially immigrants, in the United States. As Virgil Elizondo notes:

> The *posada* is easily a *cultic* reminder and reenactment as well, for Mexican Americans who have walked, often at night and through snake infested deserts, to the United States in the hope of finding work. What they have found instead was rejection after rejection. But, like Joseph and Mary, they did not give up; they followed their star . . . The *posada* is a living symbol of a living faith.[26]

Particularly as the Virgin of Guadalupe Mary becomes, then, on the popular religious level the image *par excellence* of Advent expectation and preparation and Advent itself becomes a rather "Marian" season in overall emphasis. Nevertheless, if decidedly "Marian" in emphasis, even this, of course, is oriented, christologically, to Christmas.

The question, however, is whether or not such an obvious "Marian" focus is what the liturgical season of Advent itself is really about. On the official Roman Catholic (and contemporary Protestant) liturgical level the season of Advent is not "Marian" but primarily eschatological and only secondarily incarnational in focus. That is, within the current three-year lectionary used by Roman Catholics and adapted by several contemporary Protestant liturgical traditions today, the lectionary readings assigned to the first three Sundays of this season are all oriented toward the *parousia* or "second coming" of Christ in glory and not to his first coming in Bethlehem at Christmas. The Advent call to "prepare the way of the Lord," then, is a call more related to the church's own eschatological stance in the world as oriented in hope toward ultimate fulfillment in Christ when "he will come to judge the living and the dead" than it is to preparing for Jesus' "birthday." As such, Christmas becomes less a celebration of a past historical event (Christ's birth) and more a kind of anticipated celebration of the *parousia* itself, a celebration of the fullness of redemption and *our* new "birth" by baptism in the One whom the late Raymond Brown referred to as the "adult Christ at Christmas."[27] In fact, it is only on the Fourth Sunday in Advent where the current lectionary readings themselves shift from a clearly eschatological to an incarnational or Christmas focus, with the Gospel pericopes of the Annunciation to Joseph (Matthew 1:18–24), the Annunciation to Mary (Luke 1:26–38), and the Visitation of Mary to Elizabeth (Luke 1:39–45), read respectively in Years A, B, and C of the three-year cycle. Such a shift to an incarnational focus is supported also by the use of the famous "O" antiphons connected to the Gospel Canticle of the *Magnificat* at Evening Prayer beginning on December 17.

It is because of both the strong eschatological character of Advent (assuming its final and current form in the Roman liturgy under Pope Gregory I at the beginning of the seventh century) and its actual location within the classic Roman liturgical books at the *end*—and not at the *beginning*—of the liturgical year that some contemporary liturgical scholars are asserting that the eschatological season of Advent has more to do with the *conclusion* of the liturgical year than with its annual beginning. Historically, its proximity to Christmas, therefore, would have been more accidental than deliberate in Rome, although today it is certainly constructed both as the beginning of the year and as a season of preparation for Christmas.[28] But whatever the historical case, the overall eschatological orientation of Advent toward the *parousia* in the liturgical books today certainly suggests that there is a tension between the "official" Advent liturgy and the "Marian" focus of the season in Mexican and Mexican American popular religion. Elizondo himself refers to this tension when he writes that:

> The entire complex of events at Tepeyac was as mysterious as it was ultimately real. The bishop was disconcerted and his household was disturbed, as theologians, liturgists, and catechists usually are with the ways of God's poor. To this day, liturgists do not want to accept the feast of Our Lady of Guadalupe as the *major feast of Advent*. For them, it seems that God made a mistake in placing the feast of Guadalupe during Advent.[29]

Indeed, related to this, it is interesting to note that the liturgical color of "Royal" or "Sarum Blue," becoming increasingly (and ecumenically) popular as an alternative to the traditional purple or violet Advent color for vestments and paraments during the season, is actually resisted today in several Roman Catholic dioceses precisely *because* blue has traditional Roman Catholic associations with Mary herself (the "lovely Lady dressed in blue").[30] That is, while several contemporary Protestant liturgical traditions have embraced blue as an alternative color for the season, presumably reflecting Advent "hope," Roman Catholics have tended to resist and, in some cases, not even permit its use because Advent is *not*—and is not to be construed as—a Marian season!

But if there is a tension between the "official" eschatological Advent of modern Western Christianity and the "popular" Marian Advent of Hispanic-Latino piety, a more Marian-focused Advent does appear to have some affinities to the pre-Christmas seasons of preparation in some of the Eastern Christian liturgical Rites, to other early non-Roman Western liturgical traditions, and even to some characteristics within the earlier Roman Advent itself. In the Byzantine Rite, for example, beginning with the November 21 feast of The Presentation of Mary in the Temple, multiple Marian images associated with the "Ark of the Covenant," the "Tabernacle," and even as the "heavenly Temple" appear in the various *troparia* and prayers throughout the season.[31] And, two Sundays before Christmas, the Byzantine Rite commemorates "the Holy Ancestors of Christ" (Dec. 24 in the Roman Martyrology), culminating, of course, in Mary, and on the Sunday before Christmas is celebrated "all the Fathers who down the centuries have been pleasing to God, from Adam to Joseph, husband of the Most Holy Mother of God."[32] Among the Syrian Christian traditions, both West Syrian (i.e., Syrian and/or Antiochene Orthodox and Maronite) and East Syrian (i.e, Church of the East, Chaldean, and Syro-Malabar), the assigned Gospel readings on the Sundays for the season of Christmas preparation, called "Weeks of Annunciations," include, in order, the Annunciation to Zechariah, the Annunciation to Mary, the Visitation, the Nativity of John the Baptist, and, finally, the Annunciation to Joseph. Indeed, for these reasons, Eastern "Advent" is often referred to itself as a "Marian" season.

In the ancient liturgies of the non-Roman West there is also some correspondence here. While the precise origins of the March 25 celebration of the Annunciation of Our Lord are obscure,[33] the feast on this date is known to have been celebrated already in the East by the beginning of the sixth century. Before that shift to a calendrical date the Annunciation appears to have been celebrated on the Sunday before Christmas. Interestingly enough, the location of the feast of the Annunciation actually varied as to date in the calendars of other Western liturgical traditions throughout the Middle Ages. In Spain it was celebrated on December 18 and today, within the recently reformed post-Vatican liturgical books of the Spanish or "Mozarabic" Rite, December 18 has remained a solemnity of Mary called, simply, *Sancta Maria*, where the primary focus is still on the Annunciation even though the Annunciation itself is celebrated on March 25.[34] And in Milan, Italy, within the Ambrosian Rite, the Annunciation was and still is celebrated on the last of the *six* Sundays of Advent. Even in the liturgical tradition of Rome, a similar correlation between, at least, Annunciation and Christmas was also true of the more eschatologically oriented *Roman* Advent itself, although Rome had clearly accepted the March 25 date of the feast by the time of Pope Sergius I (CE 687–701). Prior to the post-Vatican II liturgical reform of the calendar, in fact, the Gospel pericopes of both the Annunciation and the Visitation were read, respectively, on the Wednesday and Friday of the third week of Advent, formerly known as the Advent "Ember Days," one of four annual "seasons" of special prayer and fasting throughout the liturgical year.[35] Hence, even with the acceptance of the March 25 date for the feast in the West, a close proximity between the celebration of the Annunciation (and the Visitation) and Christmas remained a traditional characteristic of Western liturgical history in general.

Because in Mary, according to *Sacrosanctum Concilium*, "the church admires and exalts the most excellent fruit of redemption, and joyfully contemplates, as in a faultless image, that which she herself desires and hopes wholly to be,"[36] some today have begun to call for a re-evaluation of not only the current ranking of Marian festivals on the liturgical calendar but for a re-evaluation of their particular dates in relationship to the central mysteries of Christ at the obvious core of the liturgical year. Shawn Madigan, for example, writes:

> The ranking of present festivals gives non-scriptural imagination as great a place, and occasionally, a greater place, than scriptural imagination. When Mary, Mother of God (January 1), the most traditional scriptural festival is not transferred but dispensed with as a 'holy day of obligation' because the clergy are too tired, there is need for liturgical critique. Why not cancel the Immaculate Conception instead? Why are scriptural festivals, such as Visitation and Lady of Sorrows, almost invisible?[37]

And, with particular regard to the appropriateness of Marian festivals and images during Advent, she calls for a kind of re-thinking and re-structuring of the season itself, asking:

> What if the festivals of Annunciation and Visitation were placed early in the Advent season? If the Annunciation were celebrated on the first Sunday of Advent and the Visitation during that week, look at what could be accomplished. Christ the King readings of the end time could stand conclusively as end of the liturgical year without beginning with another set of end times. The

present Annunciation festival (March 25) could be relieved from its non-liturgical presence in the midst of Christ imaging related to Passiontide. This would also lessen the confusion about whether liturgical calendars are planned according to seasons or biological rhythms. Another accomplishment is that the readings for both festivals are appropriate Advent reflections about the church (Annunciation: Isaiah 7:1–14; Hebrews 10:4–10; Luke 1:26–38; Visitation: Zephaniah 3:14–19; Romans 12:9–16; Luke 1:39–56). If the Visitation were placed on a weekday of the first week of Advent, there is logic to John the Baptist appearing on the second Sunday of Advent. Similar to the Annunciation, the present placement of the Visitation has little relationship to the Christ cycle. If the Annunciation and Visitation festivals occurred in early Advent, fitting gospel readings for the last Sunday of Advent could be found by liturgists and exegetes.[38]

If Madigan's proposal, and others like hers,[39] are certainly consistent with the Advent orientations of both the Christian East and various historic traditions in the West, they also make both liturgical and christological sense by intentionally integrating Marian images and festivals into this season of incarnational preparation. December as the "month of Mary" certainly makes a lot more sense than May! But why limit the festival of the Visitation to a weekday? Indeed, if such a suggestion of re-structuring Western Advent is desirable or feasible at all, why not make Advent, as it is in the Syrian East, the celebration of the various "Annunciations" from the opening chapters of Matthew and Luke? That is, why not, for example, celebrate the Annunciation to Zechariah and/or the Birth of John the Baptist on the First Sunday of Advent, the Annunciation to Mary on the Second, the Visitation on the Third, and the Annunciation to Joseph on the Fourth?

It is amazing how the overall "Marian" focus of Advent among especially Mexicans and Mexican Americans already tends to have some affinity to what has been described above both with regard to the focus of Advent within various Christian traditions and to recent proposals for re-thinking the season of

Advent itself. Such a re-structuring of Advent itself, as suggested by Madigan, might offer as well the added advantage of bringing both "official" and "popular" religion closer together within an Advent synthesis. For, indeed, I suspect that within most forms of popular religion and piety, whether Catholic or Protestant, Advent has always been and will continue to be decidedly incarnational in focus and closely related to the people and events surrounding the impending birth of Christ, in spite of what we liturgists and the official liturgy say about eschatology. But whether such a re-structuring of Advent were ever to take place or not, it is significant that the Gospels for the December 8 Solemnity of the Immaculate Conception and now for the Solemnity/Feast of the Virgin of Guadalupe are, respectively, the Gospel readings of *precisely* both the Annunciation and the Visitation in annual proximity to the Second and Third Sundays of Advent already! If the titles of the solemnity and feast are different, the biblical content of both are highly congruent with at least one traditional Advent characteristic even in the Roman West. In other words, the Advent liturgy does not really have to change in order to accommodate either the Annunciation and Visitation since it already does accommodate them. For Roman Catholics, at least, both emphases have actually remained within the season under different names and, as such, both already integrate Mary *and* the principal biblical texts associated with her into Advent itself.

While certainly sympathetic to a re-thinking and re-structuring of Advent in this way, I am not yet prepared to give up either the season's overall eschatological focus or the calls to "prepare the way of the Lord," associated especially with the Second and Third Sundays of the season.[40] But the December 12 festival of the Virgin of Guadalupe, of course, need not be viewed as being inconsistent with even this Advent eschatological focus. Such an eschatological orientation, in fact, certainly appears already in the Prayer After Communion in the Propers for the feast: "May we who rejoice in the holy Mother of Guadalupe live united and at peace in this world *until the day of the Lord dawns in glory*."[41] Similarly, in spite of the fact that modern biblical scholarship would rightly challenge the late medieval Marian exegesis of Revelation 12,[42] an exegesis certainly presumed in the United

States suggestion that Revelation 11:19; 12:1–6, 10 be one of the readings for the feast,[43] the obvious visual correlation between the Guadalupan image and this apocalyptic biblical text does make some kind of, at least, "symbolic" connection possible. That is, even if the woman of Revelation 12 is best understood as personifying both ancient Israel and the New Testament people of God, such personification has certainly come to be embodied symbolically as well in the person of Mary as *the* image *par excellence* of the church itself—the *typus ecclesiae*—an image of "that which (the church) herself desires and hopes wholly to be." If both the pregnant biblical "woman clothed with the sun" and the pregnant Virgin of Guadalupe give birth to the Messiah, both also simultaneously represent the church. At the same time, both the "woman clothed with the sun" in Revelation 12 and the Virgin of Guadalupe are similarly eschatological in orientation, directing attention to the new life and new creation present in the one to whom both give birth. Consequently, if the biblical "woman clothed with the sun" is not really intended to be Mary, she is, nonetheless, like the Virgin of Guadalupe herself, symbolic of the overall Advent stance of the church in the world living in the situation of hope for the ultimate eschatological victory of the fullness of the reign of God over all forms of injustice, oppression, and evil, a victory already revealed in the life, death, and resurrection of her Child.

## III. Conclusion

Whether the liturgical season of Advent is conceived of primarily in incarnational or eschatological ways, it becomes quite easy to understand why for Mexican and Mexican American Catholics "the feast of Our Lady of Guadalupe [is] the *major feast of Advent*." Both traditional orientations associated with the season come to expression in her and, as such, properly understood there is no real need for there to be a tension between the official liturgy of Advent and "popular" faith expressions. The Virgin of Guadalupe and the liturgical season of Advent, thus, can certainly be viewed as belonging together. In the words of Lutheran theologian José David Rodríguez:

The true intent of the (Guadalupe) story is not to bring people to venerate an image of the Virgin. The purpose of the story is to challenge people then as well as today *to join in an ancient biblical tradition*, a very important and popular tradition, that the early Christian community attributed to the Virgin Mary. It is the tradition that is so eloquently presented in the Magnificat. It is the tradition that has a pre-history in the Scriptures with the song of Miriam in Exodus 15, the song of Hannah in 1 Samuel 2, and the song of Deborah in Judges 5. It is a tradition of a God who loves all human beings. But for this love to be actualized, God 'scatters the proud, puts down the mighty from their thrones and exalts those of low degree' (Luke 1:51–52) . . . God's liberation of the poor and oppressed also calls for the liberation of the rich and mighty. The oppressed are not called to take vengeance on the powerful but to liberate them from their own violence. The humble are not raised to dominate over others but to get rid of all forms of domination. Slaves are not liberated to put others in bondage but to rid the world of slavery. God became human in the son of Mary to transform us from arrogant and selfish beings to true 'humanized' beings . . . The story of the Virgin of Guadalupe is part of a broader story of the great saving acts of God in history. The good news for us is that we are invited to be a part of that wonderful and meaningful story.44

Similarly, former executive director of the Women of the Evangelical Lutheran Church in America, Bonnie Jensen, has also drawn attention to the Virgin of Guadalupe saying in a homily:

It is risky for the mighty to sing the Magnificat. It might mean moving from the center to the fringes. It might mean leaving the theologically proper talk to engage in simple, frank discussions. Or it might mean risking tenured positions in our schools of theology, or jobs in the church bureaucracy, as we speak clearly and forthrightly about the implications of our faith. It might mean risking our intellectual credibility as we respect the visions of poor Indians of Guadalupe . . . But we can take the risk! We can sing the Magnificat in faith, knowing that fear can lead us to repentance, and repentance prepares us for the coming reign of God. I was deeply moved by the story of the poor man's vision of the Lady of Guadalupe. I was struck by how lowly, insignificant people have to beg the church to regard them with the esteem with which God regards them. We are not sure whether Mary appeared in a vision to this poor man. Perhaps we have our Protestant doubts. Yet even if we question the vision, the tragic truth remains: the poor and lowly often have to beg the church to proclaim and live out its message of a merciful, compassionate God! Behind the vision's gilded cactus leaves, miraculous roses, and imprinted cloak is the longing for a God who comes, not in the might of military conquest, nor in the ecclesiastical forms and evangelism plans of a mighty church, but in simple compassionate respect and regard for the lowly, the hungry, the women, the poor, the children. We sing the Magnificat to comfort the lowly. We sing to put ourselves in solidarity with the lowly and those who suffer. We sing in order to bring in the reign and community of our Lord Jesus Christ.[45]

Such is the gift and invitation of the mid-Advent feast of the Virgin of Guadalupe.

## Notes

[1] See the various celebrations noted in Chapter 4 of my book, *The Virgin of Guadalupe: Theological Reflections of an Anglo-Lutheran Liturgist* (Lanham, MD: Rowman & Littlefield, 2002), 122–26. Interestingly enough, one of the last official acts of Archbishop George Carey in his capacity as Archbishop of Canterbury was to consecrate Our Lady of Guadalupe Episcopal Church in Waukegan, IL. See *Episcopal News Service* (November 6, 2002) at http://gc2003.episcopalchurch.org/ens/2002-256.html. And for an intriguing essay on Guadalupe from a Mexican American Baptist theological perspective see Nora O. Lozanon-Díaz, "Ignored Virgin or Unaware Women: A Mexican American Reflection on the Virgin of Guadalupe," in María Pilar Aquino, Daisy L. Machado, and Jeanette Rodriguez (eds.), *A Reader in Latina Feminist Theology Religion and Justice* (Austin: University of Texas Press, 2002), 204–16.

[2] See Alex García-Rivera, "Let's Capture the Hispanic Imagination," *U.S. Catholic* (July 1994), 34–35.

[3] John Baldovin, "The Liturgical Year: Calendar for a Just Community," in M.E. Johnson (ed.), *Between Memory and Hope: Readings on the Liturgical Year* (Collegeville: The Liturgical Press, Pueblo, 2001), 436–37.

[4] John Baldovin, "On Feasting the Saints," in M.E. Johnson (ed.), *Between Memory and Hope: Readings on the Liturgical Year* (Collegeville: The Liturgical Press, Pueblo, 2001), 382–83.

[5] On the concept of "fiesta" see Virgil Elizondo, *Galilean Journey: The Mexican American Promise* (Maryknoll, NY: Orbis Books, 1983), 120; and the essays in K.G. Davis (ed.), *Misa, Mesa y Musa: Liturgy in the U.S. Hispanic Church*, 2nd edn. (Schiller Park, IL: World Library Publications, 1997). For a first-hand experience of this Guadalupan fiesta both in Mexico and Los Angeles see the essay by Rubén Martínez, "The Undocumented Virgin," in Ana Castillo (ed.), *Goddess of the Americas/La Diosa de Las Americas* (New York: Riverhead Books, 1996), 106–9. For a description of events at the plaza and basilica in Mexico City on a Sunday outside of December see Erik Hanut, *The Road to Guadalupe: A Modern Pilgrimage to the Goddess of the Americas* (New York: Tarcher/Putnam, 2001), 118–26.

[6] On "popular religion" or popular piety in general see The Congregation for Divine Worship and the Discipline of the Sacraments, *Directory on Popular Piety and the Liturgy: Principles and Guidelines* (Vatican City: 2001). For discussion of various approaches to popular religion in an Hispanic-Latino context see Orlando O. Espín, *The Faith of the People: Theological Reflections on Popular Catholicism* (Maryknoll, NY: Orbis Books, 1997), Roberto S. Goizueta, *Caminemos con Jesús: Toward a Hispanic/Latino Theology of Accompaniment* (Maryknoll, NY: Orbis Books, 1995), Alex García-Rivera, *St. Martín de Porres: The "Little Stories" and the Semiotics of Culture* (Maryknoll, NY: Orbis Books, 1995); and A. de Luna, *Faith Formation and Popular Religion: Lessons from the Tejano Experience* (Lanham, MD: Rowman & Littlefield, 2002). On the resurgence of popular religion in other contexts see Patrick Malloy, "The Re-Emergence of Popular Religion among Non-Hispanic American Catholics," *Worship* 72 (1998), 2–25; and Michael Driscoll, "Liturgy and Devotions: Back to the Future?" in Eleanor Bernstein and Martin Connell (eds.), *The Renewal That Awaits Us* (Chicago: Liturgy Training Publications, 1997), 68–90.

[7] On this see Chapter 2 of my *The Virgin of Guadalupe* (Lanham, MD: Rowman & Littlefield, 2002), 35–61.

[8] On the relationship between the Estremaduran Guadalupe and the Mexican Guadalupe see Richard Nebel, *Santa María Tonantzin Virgen de Guadalupe–Religiöse Kontinuität und Transformation in Mexiko* (Immensee: Neue Zeitschrift für

Missionwissenschaft, 1992) = *Santa María Tonantzin Virgen de Guadalupe–Continuadad y transformación religiosa en México* (México, D.F.: Fondo de Cultura Económica, 1995), 221–27.

9 See the detailed doctoral dissertation of J. Jesús Salazar, *"¿No estoy yo aqui, que soy tu Madre?" Investigación teológica-biblica-litúrgica acerca de La Nueva Liturgia de Nuestra Señora de Guadalupe*, vol. 1 (STD Dissertation, Pontifical Institute of Liturgy, Rome: Sant' Anselmo, 1981), 141–202.

10 Miguel Sánchez, *Imagen de la Virgen Maria, Madre de Dios de Guadalupe: milagrosamente aparecida en la Ciudad de México, Celebrada en su historia, con la profecía del capítulo doze del Apocalipsis* (Imp. Vidua de Bernardo Calderón, Mexico, 1648; reprinted by Cuernavaca, Morelos, 1952).

11 Luis Lasso de la Vega, *Huei tlamahuiçoltica omonexiti in ilhuicac tlatocacihaupilli Santa Maria totlaçonantzin Guadalupe in nican Huei altepenahuac Mexico itocayocan Tepeyacac* (1649). For the very first time a critical edition of the transliterated Nahàutl text with English translation, notes, and introduction has been published: Lisa Sousa, Stafford Poole, and James Lockhart (eds.), *The Story of Guadalupe: Luis de la Vega's Huei tlamahuiçoltica of 1649*, UCLA Latin American Studies, vol. 84 (Los Angeles: Stanford University Press, 1998).

12 Stafford Poole, *Our Lady of Guadalupe: The Origins and Sources of a Mexican National Symbol, 1531-1797* (Tucson: The University of Arizona Press, 1997), 37–41. Poole's study must be read in conjunction with Richard Nebel, *Santa María Tonantzin Virgen de Guadalupe–Religiöse Kontinuität und Transformation in Mexiko* (Immensee: Neue Zeitschrift für Missionswissenschaft, 1992) = *Santa María Tonantzin Virgen de Guadalupe–Continuadad y transformación religiosa en México* (México, D.F.: Fondo de Cultura Económica, 1995), and D.A. Brading, *Mexican Phoenix: Our Lady of Guadalupe: Image and Tradition across Five Centuries* (Cambridge/New York: Cambridge University Press, 2001). See also Magnus Lundberg, *Unification and Conflict: The Church Politics of Alonso de Montúfar OP, Archbishop of Mexico, 1554–1572*, Studia Missionalia Svecana 86 (Lund, Sweden: Lund University, 2002), 197–220.

13 While the date of December 8 for this feast in the West places it exactly nine months before the September 8 feast of Mary's Nativity, the choice of December 9 in the East was made, it appears, for a theological reason. That is, only with regard to Christ can there be a perfect nine-month interval between his conception (the feast of the Annunciation on March 25) and his birth (December 25). In the East, the intervals between the conceptions and births of others, including Mary, are thus symbolically less than a perfect nine months.

14 On the development of this feast see Pierre Jounel, "The Veneration of Mary," in A.G. Martimort (ed.), *The Church at Prayer*, vol. 4: *The Liturgy and Time* (Collegeville: The Liturgical Press, 1986), 139–40; and Kilian McDonnell, "The Marian Liturgical Tradition," in M.E. Johnson (ed.), *Between Memory and Hope: Readings on the Liturgical Year* (Collegeville: The Liturgical Press, Pueblo, 2001), 390–91.

15 See Fidel de Jesús Chauvet, "Historia del Culto Guadalupano," in *Album Conmemorative del 450 Aniversario de las Apariciones de Nuestra Señora de Guadalupe* (Mexico City, D.F.: Buena Neuva, A.C., 1981), 34. Chauvet refers here to a sixteenth-century journal of a Juan Bautista.

16 See M.E. Johnson, *The Virgin of Guadalupe*, 57–8.

17 See Bernardo de Sahagún, *Psalmodia Christiana* (Christian psalmody), trans. A. J.O. Anderson (Salt Lake City: University of Utah Press, 1993), 353–59.

18 On all of this see Salazar, *"¿No estoy aqui, que soy tu Madre?"* vol. 1, 141–202.

[19] See M.E. Johnson, *The Virgin of Guadalupe*, 51–58.

[20] Jean-Pierre Ruiz, "The Bible and U.S. Hispanic American Theological Discourse," in Orlando Espín and Miguel Diaz (eds.), *From the Heart of the People* (Maryknoll, NY: Orbis Books, 1999), 112–13.

[21] On this, see Salazar, vol. 1, 174ff.

[22] See *Misal Romano*, 2nd edition (México, D.F.: Obra Nacional de la Buena Prensa, A.C., 2001), 596–97; and *Leccionario*, vol. III: *Propio de los Santos y Otras Misas*, 1st edn. (México, D.F.: Obra Nacional de la Buena Prensa, A.C., 2001), 172–74.

[23] Bishop's Committee on the Liturgy, *Newsletter* 23: "Feast of Our Lady of Guadalupe," 45; and Idem, *Newsletter* 24: "Feast of Our Lady of Guadalupe and New Liturgical Texts" (Washington, D.C.: National Conference of Catholic Bishops, 1988), 5–6.

[24] For an example of this novena see Celestina Castro, MC-M, *Novena a La Santísima Virgen de Guadalupe, Reina de las Américas* (San Antonio: Mexican American Cultural Center, no date). See also William G. Storey, *Mother of the Americas: A Novena for Our Lady of Guadalupe/Madre de America: Una Novena en Honor a Nuestra Señora de Guadalupe* (Chicago: Liturgy Training Publications, 2003).

[25] For a brief description see *Faith Expressions of Hispanics in the Southwest*, revised edition (San Antonio: Mexican American Cultural Center, 1990), 12–13.

[26] V. Elizondo, "Living Faith: Resistance and Survival," in V. Elizondo and T. Matovina (eds.), *Mestizo Worship: A Pastoral Approach to Liturgical Ministry* (Collegeville: The Liturgical Press, 1998), 11–12.

[27] See Raymond Brown's delightful short commentaries on the Infancy Narratives of Matthew and Luke in *An Adult Christ at Christmas* (Collegeville: The Liturgical Press, 1978).

[28] On this see especially J. Neil Alexander, *Waiting for the Coming: The Liturgical Meaning of Advent, Christmas, and Epiphany* (Washington, D.C.: Pastoral Press, 1993), 7–27. See also Bryan D. Spinks, "Revising the Advent-Christmas-Epiphany Cycle in the Church of England," *Studia Liturgica* 17 (1987), 166–75.

[29] V. Elizondo, *Guadalupe: Mother of the New Creation* (Maryknoll, NY: Orbis Books, 1997), 95 [emphasis added].

[30] The use of blue during Advent and the several erroneous assumptions made about its use historically have been surveyed recently by J. Barrington Bates, "Am I Blue? Some Historical Evidence for Liturgical Colors," *Studia Liturgica* 33 (2003), 75–84. Of particular interest is that in the primarily English sources that Bates discusses blue was used in some places during Lent and other times of the year but *not* during Advent, not even at Salisbury (Sarum) Cathedral, the cathedral where the custom is often thought to have been most characteristic. Lutherans often claim to be following Swedish custom for the use of blue in Advent.

[31] See Mother Mary and Archimandrite Kallistos Ware, *The Festal Menaion* (London/Boston: Faber and Faber, 1969), 164–98.

[32] Pierre Jounel, "The Christmas Season," in A.G. Martimort, *The Church at Prayer*, 93.

[33] In early Christianity March 25 was one of two calendrical dates assigned to the historical date of Christ's Passion as the equivalent to 14 Nisan. In some communities April 6 was recognized as the corresponding date.

[34] Conferencia Episcopal Española, *Missale Hispano-Mozarabicum* (Barcelona: 1994), 34, 136–42.

[35] On "Ember Days," see Thomas J. Talley, "The Origins of the Ember Days: An Inconclusive Postscript," in Paul DeClerck and Éric Palazzo (eds.), *Rituels: Mélanges offerts à Pierre-Marie Gy, OP* (Paris: Les Éditions du Cerf, 1990), 465–72.

[36] *Sacrosanctum concilium* V.103. English translation from A. Flannery, vol. 1: *Vatican Council II: The Conciliar and Post Conciliar Documents* rev. ed. (Collegeville: The Liturgical Press, 1975), 29.

[37] Shawn Madigan, "Do Marian Festivals Image 'That Which the Church Hopes to Be?'" *Worship* 65 (1991), 201.

[38] Ibid., 202.

[39] See also J. Samaha, "Mary in the Liturgical Calendar," *Emmanuel* 100, 1 (1994), 45ff. Bryan D. Spinks also suggests that a couple of Advent Sundays in the West might be devoted to the "Annunciations." See his "Revising the Advent-Christmas-Epiphany Cycle in the Church of England," *Studia Liturgica* 17 (1997), 172–73.

[40] See my essay, "Let's Keep Advent Right Where It is," on pages 237–242 of this volume.

[41] Bishop's Committee on the Liturgy, *Newsletter* 24: "Feast of Our Lady of Guadalupe and New Liturgical Texts" (Washington, D.C.: National Conference of Catholic Bishops, 1988), 6.

[42] On the interpretation of Revelation 12, see Raymond Brown et. al. (eds.), "The Woman in Revelation 12," in *Mary in the New Testament* (New York: Paulist Press and Philadelphia: Fortress Press, 1978), 219–39.

[43] This reading does not appear for the Solemnity in Mexico where the equivalent New Testament reading is Galatians 4:4–7. See *Leccionario*, vol. III: "Propio de los Santos y Otras Misas," 172–74.

[44] José David Rodríguez, Jr., with the assistance of Colleen R. Nelson, "The Virgin of Guadalupe," *Currents in Theology and Mission*, 13, 6 (December 1986), 369 [emphasis added].

[45] Bonnie Jensen, "We Sing Mary's Song," *Word and World* 7/1 (1987), 81–2.

# REFLECTIONS

# FOREVER FLESH

The mystery of the incarnation was not simply an "event" that happened in history once upon a time (*in illo tempore*), but is now over and done with merely as a once-for-all time, historically contingent, and non-repeatable reality. That is, Jesus Christ did not "lose" or "forfeit" his humanity as a result of his passion, death, and resurrection. In the incarnation of the Word, God became a permanent partner in our history; in the resurrection, the humanity of Jesus of Nazareth is glorified. As Xavier Seubert has written, we sometimes forget "that in Jesus Christ God has become a human being, and will remain human forever. The logical consequence of this is that, in becoming irrevocably connected to the human bodiliness of Jesus, God is irrevocably particular in a human way."[1] Further, "Jesus Christ as God-Man cannot enter back into God *in se*, utterly separate from materiality."[2] One must thus speak, quite literally, of God's body, of its fate and future. Having entered into an intimate relationship with materiality, Jesus—as "God-Man"—cannot now retreat from the material, the fleshly, the historical. For Christians believe that "Jesus is God through a relationship that is the substance of God—and this now takes place forever with his bodiliness that is irrevocably one with human history."[3]

This incarnational embodiment, or "enfleshment," of the Word in Jesus the Christ, which happened at a particular place in a particular moment in our historical past (at that moment St. Paul calls the "fullness of time," in Galatians 4:4), is precisely the same Word which is embodied and, hence, continues to be "flesh" for us and for the life of the world not only, of course, but especially within the proclamation of that same Word and the faith-filled celebrations of the sacraments within our liturgical assemblies. In one of his sermons on the Ascension Pope St. Leo I (+461) pointed precisely to the connection between the historically contingent incarnation of the Word and the continual saving encounter with this enfleshed Word now today, when he said: *"Quod itaque Redemptoris nostri conspicuum fuit, in sacramenta transivit."* ("What was visible in our Redeemer has passed into the sacraments").[4] That is, Christ's resurrection and ascension did not remove him from us, but actually made him more available to us, no longer bound by the limitations of space, time, and past historical particularity. What is different is but the modality of his presence, which, as "sacramental," is simultaneously just as "real." Similarly, such an understanding that this same incarnate Word remains and continues to be salvific flesh for us in the present is certainly reflected in *Sacrosanctum concilium* #7, where Christ's multiple and "real" presences are articulated clearly:

> ". . . Christ is always present in his Church, especially in her liturgical celebrations. He is present in the Sacrifice of the Mass not only in the person of his minister . . . but especially in the eucharistic species. By his power he is present in the sacraments so that when anybody baptizes it is really Christ himself who baptizes. He is present in his word since it is he himself who speaks when the holy scriptures are read in the Church. Lastly, he is present when the Church prays and sings."[5]

And, of course, such an emphasis is a primary characteristic of contemporary Roman Catholic ecclesiology and sacramental theology, especially as associated with names like Dominican Father Edward Schillebeeckx, and Jesuit Father Karl Rahner, for whom, just as Christ himself was (and is) the "primordial" or "Ur" Sacrament of God's saving encounter with the world, so too is the church the sacramental continuation of that saving and grace-filled encounter with God in history.[6] Both the church and the sacraments, then, are but the human and embodied extensions of Christ's own incarnation in space, time, and history. The community of grace, the church, expresses its inner being by means of those various sacramental-liturgical actions in which and by which Christ continues to encounter us in saving grace and where we, simultaneously, encounter the presence of Christ *for us*. How we today access, in faith and worship, the Word "made" flesh for us and for the life of the world is, thus, quite clearly stated in Roman Catholic sacramental theology. We do so, primarily, through those grace-filled, embodied encounters and actions called word and sacrament.

If this contemporary Roman Catholic understanding of church and sacrament is well known today, perhaps the very similar emphases in the writings of the great Lutheran theologian, pastor, and martyr, Dietrich Bonhoeffer (+Good Friday 1945) are not as well known, not even among contemporary Lutherans themselves. For, although popularly associated with something called "religionless Christianity," Bonhoeffer's writings on Church, Word, Christ, and Sacrament certainly merit for him some recognition as being a first rate liturgical-sacramental theologian, whose own emphases, in fact, closely parallel and find resonance in much of contemporary Roman Catholic ecclesiological and sacramental thought, and to whom liturgical theologians ought to pay renewed ecumenical attention. Here we can only touch briefly on his theology.

With regard to the word, according to Bonhoeffer, the existence of the Incarnate Christ himself continues to be the bodily Word proclaimed by the church as the very living address and Word of God himself. Christ existing in the flesh as word is

> the personal address of God in which he calls [people] to answer for themselves. In his being as he is and his being there, [humanity] is put in the truth. Christ becomes the address of forgiveness and command . . . Command and forgiveness take place...because the Word of God is the person of Christ . . . Christ is not only present *in* the word of the church but also *as* the word of the church, i.e., as the spoken word of preaching . . . Christ's presence is his existence as preaching. The whole Christ is present in preaching, Christ humiliated and Christ exalted . . . Preaching is the riches and the poverty of the church. It is the form of the presence of Christ to which we are bound and to which we have to keep.[7]

But if this is so, that Christ exists as word, then it is equally true that Christ exists *as* Sacrament. "The word in the sacrament is an embodied word. It is not a representation of the word. Only something which is not present can be represented. But the Word is present . . . The word of preaching is the form in which the Logos reaches the human Logos. The sacrament is the form in which the Logos reaches [humanity] in [its] nature."[8] Similarly:

> "both [baptism and Lord's Supper] flow from the true humanity of our Lord Jesus Christ. In the two sacraments he encounters us bodily and makes us partakers in the fellowship and communion of his Body, and they are both closely linked to his word. Both proclaim the death of Christ for us (Romans 6:3ff; 1 Corinthians 11:26). In both we receive the Body of Christ. Baptism makes us members of the Body, and the Lord's Supper confers bodily fellowship and communion (κοινωνία) with the Body of the Lord whom we receive, and through it the bodily fellowship with the other members of his Body. Thus through the gift of his Body we become one body with him."[9]

Further, if we are encountered bodily today in word, baptism, and Eucharist by the Incarnate Christ, who *is* both "Word" and "sacrament" himself, so also, for Bonhoeffer, the church is nothing other than Christ existing *as* community:

> Just as Christ is present as the Word and in the Word, as the sacrament and in the sacrament, so too he is also present as community and in the community . . . His form, indeed his only form, is the community between the ascension and the second coming . . . What does it mean that Christ . . . is also community? It means that the Logos of God has extension in space and time in and as the community . . . [T]he Word is also itself community in so far as the community is itself revelation and the Word wills to have the form of a created body . . . The community is the body of Christ. Body here is not just a metaphor. The community *is* the body of Christ, it does not *represent* the body of Christ. Applied to the community, the concept of the body is not just a functional concept which merely refers to the members of this body; it is a comprehensive

and central concept of the mode of existence of the one who is present in his exaltation and his humiliation.[10]

And such a corporate-ecclesial body, for Bonhoeffer, is clearly a *visible* body. As he writes,

"the Body of Christ takes up space on earth. That is a con-sequence of the Incarnation . . . Anything which claims space is visible. Hence the Body of Christ can only be a visible Body, or else it is not a Body at all . . . The Church consisting of Christ's followers manifest to the whole world as a visible community...The body of the exalted Lord is . . . a visible body in the shape of the Church."[11]

Futher still, this "visibility" of the church as Christ's body is itself expressed most concretely, according to Bonhoeffer, in the public proclamation and sacramental celebration of the liturgical assembly. "The Body of Christ becomes visible to the world in the congregation gathered round the Word and Sacrament."[12] And, "the whole common life of Christian fellowship oscillates between Word and Sacrament, it begins and ends in worship. It looks forward in expectation to the final banquet in the kingdom of God."[13]

For Bonhoeffer, as for contemporary Roman Catholic ecclesi-ology and sacramental theology, the answer to how we today might have access, in faith and worship, to the Word "made" flesh for us and for the life of the world some two millennia ago, is, therefore, quite similar. If, as a result of his passion, death, res-urrection, and ascension to glory, Christ did not "lose" or "forfeit" his humanity, but rather, God, having become a human being in him, will remain human forever, then it is this human embodiment of God we still encounter salvifically today. That is, Christ is, indeed, "forever flesh," forever embodied in the materiality of his human existence, and it is precisely in his embodiment within the various modes of his existence as word, sacrament, and church where we are continually encountered by him and where, in faith and embodied liturgical activity, we encounter his real and saving presence. Christology, ecclesiology, and sacramentality thus form an inseparable unity in the continued and available saving presence of the Incarnate Christ. The mode of encounter may be different from those who first followed Jesus in the historical past but the reality and availability of his presence and saving gift is the same. Indeed, in the life-giving power, breath, and presence of the Holy Spirit, Christ's embodied existence is not removed from us but made even more available and accessible than it was at that particular moment of his incarnate life in the first century of our common era.

Finally, it should be noted that if Bonhoeffer's theology of word, sacrament, and church appear remarkably congruent with contemporary Roman Catholic thought on these issues, it is because his theology, formed by the classic Greek and Latin Patristic tradition, is, simultaneously and consistently, "Lutheran" to the core! That is, the answer to how we today might have access, in faith and worship, to the word "made" flesh for us and for the life of the world as consisting primarily in word, sacrament, and church, as the multiple but "real" presences of the embodied Christ himself, is nothing other than a sign of our common and ecumenical liturgical-sacramental heritage and tradition. To that end, at least Roman Catholics and Lutherans should be able to speak with one voice about the saving significance of Christ remaining "forever flesh" for us.

## Notes

1 Xavier Seubert, "'But Do Not Use the Rotted Names:' Theological Adequacy and Homosexuality," *The Heythrop Journal* XL (London: Blackwell Publishing, 1999), 65.

2 Ibid.

3 Ibid.

4 Leo I, *De Ascensione* II.

5 Text from A. Flannery (ed.), *Vatican Council II*, vol. 1 (Collegeville: The Liturgical Press, 1975), 4–5.

6 See *Lumen gentium*, 18.

7 *Christ the Center* (New York: Harper & Row, 1966), 51–52.

8 Ibid., 54.

9 *The Cost of Discipleship* (New York: Macmillan, 1955), 280–81.

10 *Christ the Center*, op.cit., 59–60.

11 *The Cost of Discipleship*, op. cit., 277–79.

12 Ibid., 281.

13 Ibid., 285.

# THE PLACE OF SACRAMENT
# IN THE THEOLOGY
# OF PAUL TILLICH

Within post-Vatican II Roman Catholic theology it has become increasingly common to use sacramental language to refer to both the person and work of Christ and to the nature and activity of the church.[1] Generally speaking, Christ is understood therein as the *Ursakrament,* or primordial sacrament, of God's relationship to the world, and the church, which actualizes itself through and by its own sacramental life, is viewed as functioning in a similar fashion because of its identity as the extension of the incarnation in space and time. While such a sacramental approach to christology and ecclesiology is not completely absent in Protestant theology,[2] it has certainly not enjoyed, if acknowledged at all, the dominant position it has achieved within Roman Catholic circles. Ecumenically this is unfortunate but it need not have been so nor need it remain so. For, in the theology of one of the most highly influential Protestant theologians of the twentieth century, Paul Tillich, it is precisely a sacramental approach that is used as the basis for an entire system of thought.

Such a statement may seem rather surprising. Tillich's theology, it is true, is not generally characterized or understood in this manner. His major contributions to theological thought are often considered to be methodology (that is, his apologetic method of correlation between theology and philosophy), his definition of human faith as the state of being grasped by an "ultimate concern," his understanding of God as the "ground of being," or "being itself" which gives the ontological courage to be, and his presentation of Christ as the New Being who, in answer to the question implied in existential estrangement, has restored the essential unity between God and humanity under the conditions of existence. Nevertheless, underlying all of this is a "sacramental principle." While what is traditionally understood as sacramental theology (that is, a theology *of* specific sacraments) plays a relatively minor role in Paul Tillich's theology, "sacrament" itself is, nonetheless, the key to his theological method and its conclusions. This is especially the case in his understanding and presentation of revelation, christology, and ecclesiology. In other words, Tillich does not *have* a sacramental theology; his theology itself *is* sacramental, based on a particular vision of reality ontologically related to that mystery which is the ground and power of being itself.

In defending this thesis it is necessary to begin with Tillich's theology of symbol. It is, after all, only from this starting point that his systematic thought can be properly understood as expressing a clear sacramental approach. It is this that provides the overall consistency to his thought. And, as will be seen, it is this which is synonymous with sacrament itself.

## I. Tillich's Theology of Symbol

According to Tillich, everything that is said about God—other than that God is being-itself and, as such, determines the structure of everything that has being—is symbolic in character.[3] Both in his *Systematic Theology*[4] and in an essay on the symbols of faith in his *Dynamics of Faiths*[5] Tillich lists six characteristics of symbol in general. First of all, while a symbol shares with a sign the characteristic of pointing beyond itself to something else, a symbol is not a sign but *more* than a sign. That is, secondly, a symbol, unlike a sign, "participates" in the reality to which it points. Thirdly, by participating in that reality it "opens up levels of reality which are otherwise closed for us."[6] Hence, there is an intrinsic or ontological relationship between the signifier and the signified (or, in classical sacramental terminology, between the *sacramentum* and the *res sacramenti*). The fourth characteristic is that the symbol also opens up dimensions of reality *within us* to that reality being symbolized. Fifthly, the symbol grows and develops out of particular situations. It cannot be arbitrarily created. And, finally, because it grows and develops it can also die when the situation changes. In a changed situation the symbol is no longer able to communicate.

What is said about symbolic character and function in general applies as well to religious symbols. If everything that is said about God is symbolic then "the language of faith is the language of symbols."[7] A true symbol, however, cannot draw ultimate attention to itself. If it does, if the finite symbolic expression is perceived to be the ultimate reality itself, then the result is demonic distortion and idolatry. Tillich writes that "Holiness cannot become actual except through holy 'objects.' But holy objects are not holy in and of themselves. They are holy by negating themselves in pointing to the divine of which they are the mediums. If they establish themselves as holy, they become demonic."[8] Nevertheless, he continues, "the holy needs to be expressed and can be expressed only through the secular, for it is through the finite alone that the infinite can express itself."[9]

Religious symbols, therefore, are the media by which the infinite is expressed in finite objects and categories. This is possible, says Tillich, because everything finite participates in being and so in the ground of being, being-itself, or God. This is clearly a sacramental approach! It is through finite symbols (or sacraments) that the reality of God, the power of being, is mediated. In fact, as Tillich states:

> "Religious symbols are double-edged. They are directed toward the infinite which they symbolize *and* toward the finite through which they symbolize it. They force the infinite down to finitude and the finite up to infinity . . . If 'Father' is employed as a symbol for God, fatherhood is seen in its theonomous, sacramental depth . . . If a segment of reality is used as a symbol for God, the realm of reality from which it is taken is, so to speak, elevated into the realm of the holy. It no longer is secular. It is theonomous."[10]

This theology of symbol expressed primarily in its character of participatory mediation and necessary self-negation becomes a crucial aspect in every section of Tillich's theology. It is most clear, however, in his treatment of revelation, christology, and ecclesiology. And it is with these three areas that this essay is concerned.

## II. Revelation

Alexander McKelway accurately describes Tillich's theology of revelation by saying that "Revelation, which is essentially mysterious and remains so, occurs when either nature or history becomes for someone 'transparent' to the divine ground of all being. Some part of reality is used by the divine in such a way that through it the divine is manifest."[11] By presenting such an interpretation Tillich indicates that all of reality is, at least potentially, "sacramental" in that all of reality can become a medium through which the divine is manifest. "There is no reality, thing, or event," he writes, "which cannot become a bearer of the mystery of being and enter into a revelatory correlation."[12] Such a view, however, must be distinguished from what is traditionally understood as "natural revelation" or "natural theology." It is not that nature itself has an independent revelatory character but that it can be used *for* revelation. It is to this possibility, claims Tillich, that the scholastic term *analogia entis* refers. It is not the task of natural theology then to abstract the infinite from the finite but to point to the necessity of using finite symbols for the infinite. Similarly, history, groups, and individuals can likewise become transparent to the divine presence if they "point to something that transcends them infinitely, to the self-manifestation of that which concerns us ultimately."[13] It is interesting to note in this context that Tillich calls for a rethinking of the question of sainthood in Protestant theology. "Saints," he says, "are persons who are transparent for the ground of being which is revealed through them and who are able to enter a revelatory constellation as mediums."[14]

It must be emphasized, however, that the basic medium for revelation is the "word" both in its denotative and expressive functions or powers. Revelation, in fact, cannot be understood without the interpretative word. Yet, in a revelatory situation the normal functions of words carry with them and convey a transcendent power. Words of revelation do not give divine teachings, information, or impose laws. Rather, "In the situation of revelation, language has a denotative power which points through the ordinary meanings of words to their relation to us. In the situation of revelation, language has an expressive power which points through the ordinary expressive possibilities of language to the unexpressible and its relation to us."[15] Such language is thus transparent. "Something shines (more precisely, sounds) through ordinary language which is the self-manifestation of the depth of being and meaning."[16] The word, therefore, as *the* medium of revelation is itself, like nature or history in the same correlation, a symbolic or sacramental reality.

However, as was seen above in relationship to symbols in general, there is the danger of demonic distortion and idolatry in the context of revelation as well. The finite media of revelation, that is, the events, natural objects, people, and words (for example, bibliolatry) through which revelation occurs, can be elevated above their function and take the place of that which is mediated through them. There is, thus, a need for some criterion by which revelatory situations and experiences (which are general and universal) might be evaluated. For Tillich that criterion is the event of Jesus as the Christ which he calls "actual" or "final" revelation. Only this event is final revelation because "a revelation is final if it has the power of negating itself without losing itself."[17] And this is what the Christ event is all about. Jesus, *united* with the ground of being and meaning under the conditions of existence, refused to become an idol. That is, Jesus, as a "medium of revelation," refused to make himself equal to that revelation itself (Philippians 2:5–11). He remained transparent for and ultimately sacrificed himself to this revelation itself. Jesus therefore "is the Christ as the one who sacrifices what is merely 'Jesus' in him. The decisive trait in this picture is the continuous self-surrender of Jesus who is Jesus to Jesus who is the Christ."[18]

This, as will be seen in more detail below, is precisely Tillich's theology of the symbol now applied in the context of final revelation or christology. Jesus as the Christ is the final revelation and criterion of all revelation because the Christ is the ultimate symbol or medium of revelation both in participation and self-negation.

As final revelation the Christ is most appropriately called the "Word of God." Tillich, in fact, gives six different meanings to this term. The Word of God is "the principle of divine self-manifestation in the ground of being itself."[19] It is the medium of creation, the manifestation of the divine life in both the history of revelation and in final revelation. It is the Bible in a derived sense as the document of final revelation, and, again in a derived sense, it can be the message, proclamation, or teaching of the church. That Tillich understands this "Word" to be more than speech or language is clearly stated. For, as he writes,

> "The Word is a name for Jesus as the Christ. The Logos, the principle of all divine manifestation, becomes a being in history under the conditions of existence, revealing in this form the basic and determinative relation of the ground of being to us . . . The Word is not the sum of the words spoken by Jesus. It is the being of the Christ, of which his words and his deeds are an expression. Here the impossibility of identifying the Word with speech is so obvious that it is hard to understand how theologians who accept the doctrines of the Incarnation can maintain this confusion."[20]

In his discussion of revelation the word is the necessary element or medium. But this word is not to be identified with speech or language. The Word which "speaks" in all revelation, *the* necessary element, is the Logos as either the medium of creation (revelation through nature), the medium of history (revelation through history, events, or persons), or, as the medium of final revelation, the incarnate Logos himself. It is this symbolic/sacramental principle of divine self-manifestation that gives revelation, through its various media, its power, depth, and meaning.

## III. Christ as Symbol – Christ as Sacrament

Because of his insistence that Jesus is the Christ as the one who sacrifices what is merely Jesus in him *to* the Christ, Tillich's christology has been criticized as being heterodox in an Adoptionist or Nestorian manner.[21] In fairness to this criticism it must be stated that Tillich does see some form of adoptionism as necessary for a correct interpretation of Jesus' identity. An isolated incarnational view as a kind of metamorphosis or transmutation of a divine being is inadequate by itself. For Tillich, then,

> The Incarnation of the Logos is not metamorphosis but his total manifestation in a personal life. But manifestation in a personal life is a dynamic process involving tensions, risks, dangers, and determination by freedom as well as by destiny. This is the adoption side, without which the Incarnation accent would make unreal the living picture of the Christ. He would be deprived of his finite freedom; for a transmuted divine being does not have the freedom to be other than divine.[22]

Is such a view necessarily heterodox?

The answer to this, and, indeed, the very key to his christology, is precisely his theology of symbol. It is this that appears to be ignored by his critics. If a symbol, by his definition, participates in that to which it points, opens up levels of reality which are otherwise closed, is transparent to those realities and denies its own ultimacy in the process of signifying, then Jesus as the Christ is *the* symbol *par excellence.* And, as a symbol which functions as the mediation of New Being, then Jesus *as* Jesus is never really separated from Jesus as the Christ. The person, words, and works of Jesus remain indissolubly bound to the reality of the Christ. If the New Being (or final revelation) is to be received *as* revelation then the medium itself remains essential. There is no revelation without some kind of finite medium. The "two natures" of Christ are thus maintained in a rather "orthodox" manner even if Tillich's language sounds heterodox.

That symbol is the key to his christological understanding is made especially clear in a 1953 essay entitled "Die Judenfrage— ein christliches und ein deutsches Problem." Herein, Tillich says that "Mount Golgotha is the center of places for Christian thought. What happened on this mount in approximately the thirtieth year of our era determines all of the future. In this event the 'Holy' appeared. It achieved presence (*Gegenwart*) and sacramental reality. Christ can be called the *Ursakrament* of the Christian faith. He is the source of all the sacraments in the church."[23] Furthermore, he says elsewhere that the Christ is not determined "as a religious person," but as "the underlying sacramental reality, the New Being."[24] Christ therefore is *the* ultimate symbol but it is highly significant that Tillich uses not the word symbol but "sacrament" in this context. If Christ fulfills all of the requirements necessary for a symbol and, as such, is *the* medium of final revelation, then he is also the *Ursakrament*, the primordial sacrament of New Being which mediates this reality. To participate in the New Being is to participate through the medium, symbol, and sacrament of New Being which has appeared under the conditions of existence as the concrete representative of the essential unity between God and humanity (that is, essential God-manhood).

Such an understanding of Christ makes it clear that, from the very beginning of his theological system, Tillich is dealing with and presenting what is essentially a sacramental view of reality. Ulrich Reetz is thus correct when he says that Tillich uses "the concepts 'sacramental' and 'symbolic' as synonyms. Every symbol has a sacramental character insofar as the Absolute becomes transparent in it. By the same token every sacramental reality is always also symbolic, insofar as it refers to the Absolute."[25] His christology, therefore, is only adequately understood on the basis of this sacramental-symbolic approach. It is, in fact, the clearest expression of this fundamental orientation in his thought.

## IV. Ecclesiology

A similar sacramental-symbolic perspective is also operative in his understanding of the church which, for him, is an integral part of christology itself. There is a necessary relationship between the reality of Jesus as the Christ and the believing community which recognizes him as such. For, without the believing reception of Jesus as the Christ, Jesus would not be the Christ. "The receptive side of the Christian event is as important as the factual side. And only their unity creates the event upon which Christianity is based . . . They are necessarily interdependent."[26]

Yet, this "receptive side of the Christian event" is not identical with a particular church or the churches in general. Rather, it is to be understood as the spiritual community (that is, the invisible body of Christ) which is determined by the appearance of Jesus as the Christ. It is this spiritual community which is both latent and manifest under the conditions of historical existence. It is latent before an encounter with the final revelation of Jesus as the Christ and manifest after this encounter. In relationship to the church and the churches "the churches represent the Spiritual Community in a manifest religious self-expression."[27] As such, "the Spiritual Community does not exist as an entity beside the churches, but it is their Spiritual essence, effective in them through its power, its structure, and its fight against their ambiguities."[28]

The New Being as Spirit ("God Present" or "Spiritual Presence") in the spiritual community, therefore, corresponds both to Tillich's theology of revelation (universal and final) in terms of latency and manifestation, and to his christology (the distinction between Jesus and the Christ) in terms of essence and form or expression. It also, of course, directly corresponds to his understanding of symbol. For, an identification of the historical existence or sociological reality of the church(es) with its essence (spiritual community) results in demonic distortion and idolatry. When such identification happens the finite again takes the place of the infinite. In other words, the church participates in and points to the reality of spiritual community but it is not this reality itself! The church is a manifest "symbol" of the spiritual community and, if symbol and sacrament are synonyms, it is then a sacrament of that community.

This distinction between church and spiritual community is extremely important for understanding both the sacraments themselves as well as the sacramental principle. He writes:

The Christian churches, in their controversies over the meaning and number of the particular sacraments, have disregarded the fact that the concept 'sacramental' embraces more than the seven, five, or two sacraments that may be accepted as such by a Christian church. The

largest sense of the term denotes everything in which the
Spiritual Presence has been experienced; in a narrower
sense, it denotes particular objects and acts in which a
Spiritual community experiences the Spiritual Presence;
and in the narrowest sense, it merely refers to some
'great' sacraments in the performance of which the
Spiritual Community actualizes itself.[29]

In relationship to the specific Christian sacraments, then, it is
not the church as an historical/sociological reality which is acting but the spiritual community manifest in the church which
acts and whose essence is here thus actualized and becomes concrete. Though he does not refer to it here, Tillich is obviously
echoing article 7 of the *Confessio Augustana* which says that the
church, understood as the assembly of the saints or believers,
exists where "the Gospel is preached in its purity and the holy
sacraments are administered according to the Gospel."[30] Where
the gospel is preached and the sacraments rightly administered
there the essence of the church—the "invisible church," or, in
Tillich's language, the spiritual community—is concretely
present and manifest.

Such a narrow specific view of sacrament, however, cannot
be adequately understood without attention to the broad sacramental principle undergirding this view. The loss of this principle is, according to Tillich, "*the* Protestant pitfall," in its traditional understanding of the Word of God as a spoken or written
word.[31] It is the reason why the "great" sacraments have lost
their meaning within Protestantism. Human nature therein is
reduced to "conscious self-awareness of intellect and will," with
the result that "no Spirit-bearing objects or acts, nothing sensu-
ous which affects the unconscious, can be accepted."[32] It is
against this view that Tillich argues, and it is because of this that
one might read his entire theology as a sacramental approach
and as an attempt to save the sacramental principle and the
sacraments themselves for Protestant Christianity.[33] For, as he
says, "a Spiritual Presence apprehended through the consciousness alone is intellectual and not truly Spiritual. This means that
the Spiritual Presence cannot be received without a sacramental
element, however hidden the latter may be. In religious

terminology, one could say that God grasps every side of the human being through every medium."[34]

Furthermore, the sacramental element or material through which this spiritual presence is mediated is a symbol and, as such, is intrinsically/ontologically related to that which it expresses. Sacramental elements then "have inherent qualities (water, fire, oil, bread, wine) which make them adequate to their symbolic function and irreplaceable. The Spirit 'uses' the powers of being in nature in order to 'enter' man's spirit. Again, it is not the quality of the materials as such which makes them media of the Spiritual Presence, it is their quality as brought into sacramental union."[35]

It is from this perspective—the ontological relationship between nature and the ground of being—that Tillich could discuss the specific sacraments of the church. Unfortunately, he does not do so in his *Systematic Theology*. In a related essay entitled "Nature and Sacrament," however, he does make some attempt to do so in relationship to the two Protestant sacraments of baptism and the Lord's Supper. So, in baptism, for example, there is a "special character or quality, a power of its own" that makes water necessarily suited for and intrinsically related to this ritual washing.[36] Similarly, in the Lord's Supper, bread and wine are viewed by him as "representing the natural powers that nourish the body and support in the human body the highest possibility of nature. They point to the presence of the divine saving power in the natural basis of all spiritual life as well as in the spiritual life itself."[37]

It is clear, nevertheless, that Tillich is more interested in the sacramental principle than in the sacraments themselves. Because this is so, there is a kind of sacramental "relativism" in his thought. Sacraments as symbols, after all, are not arbitrarily created (even by dominical institution) and they can both grow *and* die. Indeed, the only criterion is that sacramental acts which mediate the New Being "must refer to the historical and doctrinal symbols in which revelatory experiences leading to the central revelation have been expressed, for example, the crucifixion of the Christ or eternal life."[38] No medium, symbol, or "sacrament" is thereby excluded as inadequate on this basis. But *the* question or determining factor is the extent to which *any* sacramental act or object possesses and conveys the power of the spiritual presence in order to grasp the members of the spiritual community.[39] It is the experience of the community which is the key. If sacraments, as symbols, can grow and die this means that baptism and the Lord's Supper *could* become obsolete. They *could* lose their symbolic power of mediating the spiritual presence. It also means that in the case of four or five of the traditional seven sacraments of Western Catholicism this is precisely what happened in the churches of the Reformation. But it can also mean, especially for Protestantism, the recovery of the sacramental principle in general and with it the possibility of "new sacraments" or the rediscovery of the depth and power of the other four or five "traditional" ones. In any event, it is the sacramentality itself which remains essential in some form or another both for the mediation of the New Being as Spirit and for the actualization of the spiritual community manifest within the church(es).

## V. The Church and the Kingdom of God

As the concrete (though fragmentary) manifestation of its essence, that is, the spiritual community, the church also has a particular relationship to the kingdom of God which Tillich understands as the goal, *telos*, or inner aim of history itself.[40] Again, not surprisingly, Tillich's symbolic-sacramental principle is operative in describing this relationship. For, not only in terms of the spiritual community is the church "the anticipatory representation of a new reality, the New Being as community,"[41] it is also the representative of the ultimate universal unity of matter and Spirit in the kingdom.[42] While spiritual community refers to human beings who are grasped by the power of the New Being as their ultimate concern, the kingdom of God includes all elements of reality.

"The kingdom of God embraces all realms of being under the perspective of their ultimate aim. The churches represent the Kingdom of God in this universal sense."[43]

The church itself, of course, is not the kingdom anymore than it is the spiritual community. Both kingdom and spiritual community are independent of the church and are at work within history outside of, as well as inside the church. Yet the church is a special manifestation of them both. And it is this representative of manifestation primarily in its *sacramental life*.

"To the degree in which a church emphasizes the sacramental presence of the divine, it draws the realms preceding spirit and history, the inorganic and organic universe into itself . . . The sacramental consecration of elements of all of life shows the presence of the ultimately sublime in everything and points to the unity of everything in its creative ground and its final fulfillment. It is one of the shortcomings of the churches of the 'word,' especially in their legalistic and exclusively personalistic form, that they exclude, along with the sacramental element, the universe outside man from consecration and fulfillment."[44]

As the concrete manifestation of the kingdom, therefore, the church represents the ultimate and final "essentialization" of all being (nature, history, and persons) in the ground of being itself.[45] In other words, the church is the sacrament, the symbol of the ultimate unity of all things in God, a final panentheism. In this manner, Tillich has not only brought revelation, christology, and ecclesiology into a synthesis but he has also included creation and eschatology as well. For "creation is creation for the end: in the 'ground,' the 'aim' is present."[46]

## VI. Conclusion

The theological synthesis presented by Tillich is achieved on the basis of a sacramental-symbolic view of reality. It may be argued that every element analyzed in his system functions on a concrete sacramental level as a medium of the absolute. There is no universal or final revelation without sacramental media, Jesus as the Christ is *the* ultimate symbol or *Ursakrament* which mediates the power of New Being, and the church is the manifestation of that New Being as Spirit or spiritual community and the eschatological kingdom whose essence is actualized sacramentally. Tillich can articulate his theology in this way because the sacramental principle itself is present and operative within the divine Trinity itself.[47] This principle, of course, is that of the divine self-manifestation of God in the Logos who is both the rational structure of the universe and the Logos incarnate in Jesus of Nazareth who as the Christ, the New Being, is the final revelation himself. Tillich, therefore, does not *have* a sacramental theology. His theology is sacramental in its method, its conclusions, and, one might say, in its very "ground."

Finally, it should be noted that throughout his work Tillich is consciously making use of the necessary dialogue between an interdependency of what he calls the "Catholic substance" and the "Protestant principle."[48] Whether in his theology of symbol, revelation, christology, or ecclesiology, he is always aware of the danger of identifying the "signifier" with the "signified." Such identification happens and has often happened in the history of the church resulting in what he calls demonic distortion and idolatry. Therefore, to avoid this, while retaining the necessary concreteness of sacramental media (the "Catholic substance"), some critical or prophetic principle is necessary. This criterion Tillich finds in the "Protestant principle," the Reformation doctrine of justification by grace through faith. It is on the basis of this principle that Tillich subjects the whole Christian tradition to a radical critique in the name of the ultimate who uses but, nonetheless, transcends all forms of sacramental/symbolic manifestation. By correlating this principle with the concrete "Catholic substance" Tillich attempts to achieve what may be called an "Evangelical Catholic" synthesis which is both sacramentally concrete and absolutely universal at the same time. The ecumenical implications of this approach, especially in terms of Lutheran-Roman Catholic dialogue on the sacraments, have not been, but should be obvious.

## Notes

1 Cf. Edward Schillebeeckx, OP, *Christ the Sacrament of the Encounter with God* (New York: Sheed and Ward, 1963), and Karl Rahner, *The Church and the Sacraments*, tr. W. J. O'Hara (New York: Herder and Herder, 1963).

2 Cf. André Birmelé, "La sacramentalité de l'Église et la tradition luthérienne," *Irenikon* 4 (1986), 482–507.

3 *Systematic Theology* (Chicago: University of Chicago, 1951), 1:238–39. Hereafter all references to his *Systematic Theology* will be abbreviated S.T., volume number, and page.

4 S.T., 1:239–41.

5 *Dynamics of Faith* (New York: Harper & Row, 1957), 41–54.

6 Ibid., 42.

7 Ibid., 45.

8 S.T., 1:216.

9 Ibid., 218.

10 Ibid., 240–41.

11 *The Systematic Theology of Paul Tillich* (New York: Dell, 1964), 256.

12 S.T., 1:118.

13 Ibid., 121.

14 Ibid., 121. The calendar of Lesser Festivals and Commemorations in *Lutheran Book of Worship* (Philadelphia: Board of Publication, Lutheran Church in America, 1978), 10–12, is a recent example of this "rethinking" of sainthood in at least one Protestant denomination.

15 Ibid., 124.

16 Ibid.

17 Ibid., 133.

18 Ibid., 134.

19 Ibid., 157.

20 Ibid., 158.

21 These criticisms have come primarily from the Barthian school. See McKelway, *The Systematic Theology of Paul Tillich*, 168.

22 S.T., 2:149.

23 ". . . der Berg Golgotha ist die Mitte des Raumes für christliches Denken. Was auf diesem Berg etwa im Jahre 30 unserer Zeitrechnung geschah, bestimmte alle Zukunft. In diesem Ereignis ist das Heilige erschienen. Es hat Gegenwart und sakramentale Realität gewonnen. Christus kann das Ursakrament des Christentums genannt werden. Er ist die Quelle alles Sakramentalen in der Kirche." Quoted in Ulrich Reetz, *Das Sakramentale in der Theologie Paul Tillichs* (Stuttgart: Calwer Verlag, 1974), 100–101. The translation is my own.

24 "Entscheidend ist nicht der Christus 'als eine religiöse Person' sondern 'die zugrundeliegende sakramentale Wirklichkeit, das neue Sein.' " Quoted in ibid., 101.

[25] "die Begriffe 'sakramental' und 'symbolisch' sogar synonym gebrauchen kann. Jedes Symbol hat einen sakramentalen Charakter, sofern in ihm das Unbedingte transparent wird. Umgekehrt ist jede sakramentale Wirklichkeit immer auch symbolisch, sofern sie auf das Unbedingte verweist."

[26] S.T., 2:99.

[27] S.T., 3:153.

[28] Ibid., 163.

[29] Ibid., 121.

[30] *The Book of Concord,* ed. Theodore Tappert (Philadelphia: Fortress, 1959), 32.

[31] S.T., 1:157.

[32] S.T., 3:121.

[33] Cf. his essay "Nature and Sacrament," in *The Protestant Era,* tr. James Luther Adams (Chicago: University of Chicago, 1957), 111–112.

[34] S.T., 3:122.

[35] Ibid., 123.

[36] "Nature and Sacrament," 96.

[37] Ibid., 98.

[38] S.T., 3:123.

[39] See ibid., 124.

[40] See ibid., 350.

[41] Ibid., 243.

[42] See ibid., 201.

[43] Ibid., 375.

[44] Ibid., 377.

[45] See ibid., 408–09.

[46] Ibid., 398.

[47] See ibid., 283–94.

[48] See ibid., 245.

# THE ONE MEDIATOR,
# THE SAINTS, AND MARY:
# A LUTHERAN REFLECTION

In *The One Mediator, the Saints, and Mary*,[1] the recently published statement of the results of the eighth official dialogue between Lutherans and Roman Catholics in the United States, members of both Christian traditions, in order to "make greater progress toward fellowship,"[2] are challenged to address themselves to two further questions. This statement asks whether it is possible that:

1. "Lutheran churches could acknowledge that the Catholic teaching about the saints and Mary as set forth in the documents of Vatican Council II . . . does not promote idolatrous belief and is not opposed to the gospel? and
2. "the Catholic Church could acknowledge that, in a closer but still incomplete fellowship, Lutherans, focusing on Christ the one Mediator, as set forth in Scripture, would not be obliged to invoke the saints or to affirm the two Marian dogmas?"[3]

With all due respect to the participants of this round of bilateral dialogues, these results are rather puzzling. Is this all that can be hoped for from the past almost thirty years of American Lutheran-Roman Catholic dialogue in general and the past ten years on this issue alone: that Lutherans might finally recognize that Roman Catholics who venerate and invoke Mary and the saints are not idolaters; and that Lutherans need not venerate and invoke Mary and the saints in order to be in closer communion with Roman Catholics?[4] Indeed, more than once in this document is the fear expressed on the part of Lutherans that at events such as ordinations and baptisms celebrated according to the Roman Rite (where either the litany of the saints or another series of sanctoral petitions is used) Lutherans might be forced to compromise their confessional position and identity.[5]

What is most surprising, however, is that Lutherans are nowhere challenged in this text as to whether or not the invocation of Mary and the saints might have something *positive* to contribute to liturgical, ecclesial, and spiritual life. In other words, Lutherans are simply not asked whether some form of sanctoral invocation might be compatible with a Lutheran theology of justification and therefore indeed be acceptable (although not *required*) among those who understand their ecclesial identity as both evangelical and catholic. Nor are Lutherans asked how their theology of Mary as *Theotokos*[6] and *laudatissima virgo*,[7] as well as their confessional affirmation that blessed Mary, the angels, and saints in heaven "pray for the Church in general,"[8] might be more clearly affirmed and reflected in Lutheranism today. Along with clear and precise statements of current Roman Catholic theology on Mary and the saints supported by the documents of Vatican II and *Marialis cultus* of Pope Paul VI,[9] Lutherans are simply allowed to repeat their sixteenth-century protests, fears, and reservations.

## I. Luther and some Lutherans on the Invocation of Mary and the Saints

That a different approach to this issue could have been taken by Lutherans and a different challenge thus issued to Lutherans is demonstrated by some of the earlier writings of Martin Luther himself.[10] In his *Sermon on Preparing to Die* in 1519, for example, Luther advocates the invocation of Mary and the saints in order that true faith in God might be created and preserved

... let no one presume to perform such things [i.e., faith] by his own power, but humbly ask God to create and preserve such faith in and such understanding of his holy sacraments in him. He must practice awe and humility in all this, lest he ascribe these works to himself instead of allowing God the glory. *To this end he must call upon the holy angels, particularly his own angel, the Mother of God, and all the apostles and saints,* . . . However, he dare not doubt, but must believe that his prayer will be heard. He has two reasons for this. The first one is that he has just heard from the Scriptures how God commanded the angels to give love and help to all who believe and how the sacrament conveys this. . . . The other reason is that God has enjoined us firmly to believe in the fulfillment of our prayer and that it is truly an Amen.[11]

More important, however, is his 1521 *Commentary on the Magnificat.* In this work Luther not only asks that a proper understanding of Mary's hymn of praise be granted by Christ "through the intercession and for the sake of his dear Mother Mary,"[12] but he also provides an evangelical interpretation of the *Regina caeli,* the Marian antiphon still sung during the fifty days of Easter at the end of Compline in the Roman office. He writes:

The words [*quia quem meruisti portare*] are to be understood in this sense: In order to become the Mother of God, she had to be a woman, a virgin, of the tribe of Judah, and had to believe the angelic message in order to become worthy, as the Scriptures foretold. As the wood [of the cross] had no other merit or worthiness than that it was suited to be made into a cross and was appointed by God for that purpose, so her sole worthiness to become the Mother of God lay in her being fit and appointed for it; so that it might be pure grace and not a reward, that we might not take away from God's grace, worship, and honor by ascribing too great things to her. For it is better to take away too much from her than from the grace of God. Indeed, we cannot take away too much from her, since she was created out of nothing, like all other creatures. But we can easily take away too much from God's grace, which is a perilous thing to do and not well pleasing to her. It is necessary also to keep within bounds and not make too much of calling her 'Queen of Heaven,' *which is a true-enough name* and yet does not make her a goddess . . . She gives nothing, God gives all. . . .[13]

He continues later in this same commentary, saying:

Mary does not desire to be an idol: she does nothing. God does all. *We ought to call upon her, that for her sake God may grant and do what we request. Thus also all other saints are to be invoked,* so that the work may be every way God's alone.[14]

While such statements on the part of Luther have often been seen as mere remnants of late medieval piety, Eric Gritsch notes that this orientation "is quite consistent with [Luther's] view of the praise of God by the saints on earth and the saints in heaven. The emphasis is on the work of salvation done 'in every way [by] God alone.'"[15] These statements thus give *some* place to the invocation of Mary and the saints within an evangelical theological perspective. Indeed, the implication seems to be: as Mary and the saints have been redeemed solely by the grace of God in Christ and have thus become embodied examples of God's justifying grace, so we—in a baptismal solidarity with them not broken by death—may continue to call upon them for their prayer that we too might be faithful to *God* and, consequently, learn, like them, to ascribe all honor and glory to God *alone*.

Furthermore, it is well known that in his *Personal Prayer Book (Betbuchlein)* of 1522 (appearing in various editions through 1545), Luther retained the traditional Hail Mary.[16] In so doing, of course, he did not intend this as a prayer *to* Mary or even as an invocation of her, but rather as a meditation on God's grace bestowed *upon* her. He writes:

Let not our hearts cleave to her, but *through her* penetrate to Christ and to God himself. Thus what the Hail Mary says is that all glory should be given to God. . . . You see that these words are not concerned with prayer but purely with giving praise and honor. . . . Therefore we should make the Hail Mary neither a prayer nor an invocation because it is improper to interpret the words beyond what they mean in themselves and beyond the meaning given them by the Holy Spirit. . . . But there are two things we can do. First we can use the Hail Mary as a meditation in which we recite what grace God has given her. Second, we should add a wish that everyone may know and respect her [as one blessed by God].[17]

Although interpreted in an evangelical sense, this traditional western Christian (and biblical) salutation of Mary thus continued to hold a place within early Lutheran devotional life both as a meditation on the incarnation and as an ascription of honor to Mary herself.

These indications of at least *some* devotion to Mary and the saints within the early Lutheran tradition, however, find little place in the recent Lutheran-Roman Catholic statement. Although Eric Gritsch's background essay referred to above brought out some of these concerns,[18] the statement itself makes no reference to them. At the very least, one might have expected that the statement would have challenged Lutherans as to whether the "traditional" form of the Hail Mary, as retained, interpreted, and defended by Luther himself, might be reappropriated among Lutherans today.

Other Lutherans have been less fearful and cautious concerning this issue. The late Arthur Carl Piepkorn (d. 1971), himself a participant in some of the earlier Lutheran-Roman Catholic dialogues, suggested in 1967 that a consensus could at that time be reached on a number of mariological themes. According to him, there could be agreement on

a place for Mary in prophecy (although it would probably be somewhat more restricted than a Marian maximalist would rejoice at); the virgin conception and birth; the rightfulness of the title *theotokos*; the Virgin's place in the Church as the first of the redeemed; her role as the *kecharitomene* par excellence, uniquely endowed with God's favor; her paradigmatic piety, patience, humility, and faith; her status as the most blessed of women; her *fiat mihi* as the typical divinely empowered response that God elicits from all those of His children whom He calls to be in freedom workers together with Him; the analogy between the Blessed Virgin Mary and the Church that makes it possible for a Lutheran to use the Magnificat as the canticle at vespers and to say the first, pre-Counterreformation part of the *Ave Maria . . .* as memorials of the Incarnation; the probability of her intercession for the Church; the paradoxical parallel between the obedient Virgin Mary and the disobedient Virgin Eve that theologians have noted since the second century (although originally the thrust was Christological rather than Marian); St. Mary's virginity certainly *ante partum* and *in partu* and fittingly *post partum*; the legitimacy of apostrophes to her in hymns and in the liturgy; the propriety of celebrating the Annunciation, the Visitation, and Purification for what they really are, feasts of our Lord, to which some non-Roman-Catholics, following the Church's example in the case of St. John the Baptist, would be willing to add her Nativity on September 8 and Falling Asleep on August 15; the devotional value of good, unsentimental representations of her in the arts, especially after the earliest surviving models which always show her with the holy Child; and the legitimacy of naming churches and church institutions after her and after the mysteries of her Annunciation, Visitation, Birth, and Falling Asleep.[19]

Similarly, in a sermon entitled "Ave Maria, Gratia Plena," noted Lutheran theologian Joseph Sittler once said that

if . . . the figure of Mary articulates in her song and demonstrates in her quiet life powers and dimensions of the action of God and the response of men, both our thought and our worship are the poorer for neglect of her. It is not strange, but right and proper, that her meaning should be declared and her praise sung from a Protestant pulpit. If we can find it in our competence in this place to hail the witness to the faith of Augustine, of Luther, of Calvin, of Wesley, how grudging before the gifts of God never to utter an *Ave Maria*—Hail Mary![20]

Such statements go far beyond the questions addressed by the current Lutheran-Roman Catholic dialogue and offer a much greater challenge to Lutherans. Cannot a more positive assessment of Mary and the saints (including an appreciation for some form of Marian devotion) be called for from a Lutheran perspective instead of a simple recognition that Roman Catholics are not idolaters in invoking them[21] or that Lutherans won't be *required* to invoke them in a situation of greater unity? Had a statement like Piepkorn's been incorporated into the document, for example, *The One Mediator, the Saints, and Mary* would have been hailed as a much more positive (although controversial) ecumenical statement and as a greater sign of Lutheran-Roman Catholic convergence on this issue. Apparently, something happened between 1967 when a Lutheran like Piepkorn could speak as he did and 1992 when these concerns are hardly to be found.

## II. Mary and the Saints in Lutheran Liturgy

In another background essay included in the document, John Frederick Johnson provides a brief survey of the place of Mary and the saints in both the *Lutheran Book of Worship* (LBW) and *Lutheran Worship*.[22] In so doing, he draws attention to the retention of some traditional Marian festivals (Presentation/ Purification, Annunciation, Visitation, and the newly added Mary, Mother of Our Lord, on August 15[23]); the rather full (and ecumenical) sanctoral cycle of Lesser Festivals and Commemorations in especially LBW (including All Saints on November 1); the commemorations of the saints in the funeral rite and the litany of evening prayer;[24] and to particular hymns related to the Lesser Festivals and Commemorations. In the hymn "Ye Watchers and ye holy Ones" (Hymn 175 in LBW), the second verse addresses Mary directly:

"O higher than the cherubim, More glorious than the seraphim, Lead their praises; 'Alleluia!' Thou bearer of the eternal Word, most gracious, magnify the Lord. . . ."

He describes this second verse in the following manner:
After *invoking* seraphim, cherubim, archangels, and
angelic choirs, it *invokes* Mary as higher than the cherubim and more glorious than the seraphim. As bearer of
the eternal Word and the most gracious, she is *petitioned*
to magnify the Lord (as she once did on earth). For some
unknown reason *Lutheran Worship* . . . omits the invocation of Mary. *The Lutheran Hymnal*, replaced by *Lutheran
Worship*, contains the verse of invocation.[25]

According to at least this hymn, therefore, Lutheran liturgy
*does* invoke Mary and the saints! Even if they are not explicitly
petitioned to do anything *for* us, they are nonetheless addressed
directly by the liturgical assembly. There are, however, other
examples in LBW not mentioned in Johnson's admittedly "non-
exhaustive overview."[26] The traditional Marian hymn, *Stabat
Mater*, "At the Cross, Her Station Keeping" (retained as Hymn 110
in LBW but omitted from *Lutheran Worship*[27]), is nothing other than
a devotional hymn commemorating Mary as the *Mater Dolorosa* in
which the faith and devotion of Mary serve to inspire the worshiper on to a greater faith and trust in Christ crucified:

Who, on Christ's dear mother gazing,
Pierced by anguish so amazing,
Born of woman, would not weep?
Who, on Christ's dear mother thinking,
Such a cup of sorrow drinking,
Would not share her sorrows deep?

Jesus, may her deep devotion
Stir in me the same emotion,
Source of love, redeemer true.
Let me thus, fresh ardor gaining
And a purer love attaining,
Consecrate my life to you.

Furthermore, Eucharistic Prayers I and II specifically refer to
receiving "our inheritance with all your saints in light" and ask
that the prayers of the assembly may be joined "with those of

your servants of every time and every place."[28] Along similar lines, all of the eucharistic prefaces refer to the union between the church's praise on earth and that of the "hosts" or "whole company" of heaven, with the preface for Easter mentioning Mary Magdalene and Peter as part of this "company,"[29] and the preface for Apostles making provision for the insertion of the particular Apostle(s) being commemorated on a given day.[30] Most intriguing, however, is the preface for All Saints, where not only is the praying community to be "moved" by the past witness of the saints but is also presently *"supported by their fellowship"* as it continues to "run with perseverance the race that is set before us."[31]

The propers for the festivals of the Annunciation and Mary, Mother of our Lord are also illuminating. The Gospel verse for both festivals is: "Hail, O favored one, the Lord is with you! The Holy Spirit will come upon you"; and the psalm response for Mary, Mother of Our Lord is: "Hail, O favored one, the Lord is with you."[32] No matter how one might interpret these passages from Luke 1:28, 35, the fact remains that where these feasts are celebrated and where these propers are used an entire Lutheran congregation *at public worship is* addressing Mary by giving voice to the opening phrase of the Hail Mary. Similarly, as Johnson notes, in *The Lutheran Hymnal,* but not in *Lutheran Worship,* the gradual for the Visitation reads: "Blessed art thou, O Mary, among women, and blessed is the fruit of thy womb. Behold, there shall be a performance of those things which were told thee from the Lord."[33]

The saints also play a role in *Lutheran Book of Worship* rites and prayers other than the Eucharist or the propers assigned to particular festivals. Included in the intercessions of the baptismal rite is a thanksgiving for all who have gone before us in the faith, where "St. John the Baptist, Mary, mother of our Lord, apostles and martyrs, evangelists and teachers" are specifically mentioned.[34] In the final petition of the litany of evening prayer, the assembly, "rejoicing in the fellowship of all the saints," commends itself to Christ the Lord.[35] And, in the concluding collects of responsive prayer I and II (used respectively for morning and at various times throughout the day) God is asked to "let your holy angels have charge of us, that the wicked one have no power over us."[36]

If Mary, the saints, and the angels are referred to and occasionally addressed in these ways in Lutheran liturgy, this focus becomes even more pronounced in the confessional rites attached to both the office of compline and the eucharistic liturgy for Ash Wednesday. In compline confession is made to God "before the whole company of heaven,"[37] and in the Ash Wednesday liturgy, confession is made to God, to one another, "and *to* the whole communion of saints in heaven and on earth."[38] While neither this "whole company of heaven" nor "whole communion of saints" is asked for their intercession, in a manner consistent with traditional Roman forms of the *Confiteor*, the saints are, nevertheless, directly addressed by the praying community.

Like the early period of the Lutheran Reformation itself, therefore, contemporary Lutheran liturgy gives a larger place to Mary, the angels, and the saints—including the possibility of some direct address to them—than the Lutheran-Roman Catholic statement would seem to indicate. Lutheran liturgy expresses itself as the worship of God which is indeed united with both that of Mary, the *Theotokos* and the *laudatissima virgo*, the one who is "higher than the cherubim and more glorious than the seraphim,"[39] and with the whole company of the angels and saints in heaven. To this company or communion of saints Lutheran liturgy does on occasion make confession. This company is sometimes addressed in hymnody, and in every celebration of the Eucharist the church's praise of God is consciously united with theirs, just as the eschatological hope expressed in the eucharistic prayer is to "receive our inheritance with all [God's] saints in light." And, this "great cloud of witnesses" (Hebrews 12:1) is understood as those who by their continued "fellowship" with us somehow "support" the pilgrim church in its earthly journey. One might say, therefore, that the contemporary Lutheran *lex orandi*—as reflected primarily in LBW—is more open to the ecumenical question of Mary and the saints than the received Lutheran *lex credendi*—as reflected in the Lutheran-Roman Catholic statement—would seem to allow.

## III. Conclusion

So where does this leave us? Where, indeed. Lutherans and Catholics in Dialogue VIII, *The One Mediator, the Saints, and Mary* is a good beginning. One can only express a profound sense of gratitude that the issue of Mary and the saints, properly understood and explained in the light of the sole mediatorship of Christ, need no longer be church-dividing.[40] But between Lutherans and Roman Catholics there is much that remains to be done.

It is true, of course, that Lutheran liturgy nowhere asks Mary and the saints for their intercession on our behalf before God. But it is equally true that more than mere commemoration of the saints or following their example is implied in those places where direct address *to* them does occur. Given this, Roman Catholics would be remiss in not pushing Lutherans further on whatever distinction may be implied between direct address *to* and invocation *of* the saints. If Mary and the saints can be addressed, why might they not be asked for their prayerful intercession, especially as that intercession was related to the creation and preservation of faith itself in the early writings of Luther?

While Luther himself eventually came to reject any invocation of Mary and the saints as "nothing but human twaddle,"[41] and while the Lutheran Confessions similarly reject any such practice,[42] Lutheranism, unlike the Reformed tradition, has always taught that whatever is not explicitly forbidden by Scripture is permissible. Consequently, as the recent statement notes: "Saints on earth ask one another to pray to God for each other through Christ. They are neither commanded nor forbidden to ask departed saints to pray for them."[43] If, then, from at least a Lutheran perspective, the invocation of Mary and the saints belongs to the realm of Christian freedom, it becomes quite possible today for a Lutheran Christian to move beyond the charges of Mari- or hagiolatry made against Roman Catholics, and to both view and *appreciate* the contemporary Roman Catholic theology and practice of invocation as one legitimate liturgical expression of Christian faith in the one mediator, and, without any quirks of conscience, to participate in such expressions within an ecumenical context. Indeed, if such practices, properly understood, are not to be seen any longer by Lutherans as idolatry, then for the sake of "greater progress toward fellowship," could not Lutherans also view the litany of the saints (where the petitions ask only for the prayer of the saints *in general*, i.e., "pray for us"), simply as a concrete liturgical expression of the Lutheran confessional affirmation that blessed Mary, the angels, and "the saints in heaven pray for the Church in general?"[44] This could not be done in the sixteenth century. But can it not be done today? Theologically prepared with Luther's interpretation of the *Magnificat* and his *Personal Prayer Book* of 1522, may not the Lutheran Christian even sing the *Regina caeli* (including the words *quia quem meruisti portare*) and recite an *Ave Maria* (or two) to the glory of God's inexpressible grace shown to this woman who, because of that unmerited grace alone, is indeed *Theotokos, laudatissima virgo*, and, according to the theology of at least one hymn sung by Lutherans, reigns above the cherubim and seraphim and leads the praises of the heavenly chorus around the throne of God?

## Notes

[1] *One Mediator, the Saints, and Mary* (Minneapolis: Augsburg Fortress 1992). Hereafter this text will be referred to by OMSM and page number.

[2] One wonders why "fellowship" rather than "full communion" was the term chosen in this context. Both Lutherans and Roman Catholics use the terminology of "full communion" to refer to the desired goal of ecumenical dialogue.

[3] OMSM, 62.

[4] Reflections on the dogmas of the Immaculate Conception and Assumption of the Virgin Mary are beyond the scope of this essay. For a recent Protestant treatment of these and other related issues, however, see John MacQuarrie, *Mary for All Christians* (Grand Rapids: Wm. B. Eerdmans, 1990).

[5] Cf. OMSM, 58, 123. However no mention is made of some recent versions of the litany of the saints where, rather than direct invocation (i.e., St. N., pray for us), the petitions read: "In union with St. N., let us pray to the Lord" and the response is either "Lord, hear our prayer," or "Lord, have mercy." See also the ecumenical Litany of the Saints in *Welcome to Christ: Lutheran Rites for the Catechumenate* (Minneapolis: Augsburg Fortress, 1997), 70–71, where, in response to petitions like "For Mary, mother of our Lord," the congregation sings "Thanks be to God."

[6] "We believe, teach, and confess, that Mary did not conceive and bear a mere and ordinary human being, but the true Son of God; for that reason she is rightly called and in truth is the Mother of God" (Formula of Concord: "Epitome" VIII, 12 in Theodore

Tappert, *The Book of Concord*, (Philadelphia: Fortress, 1959), 488, and "Solid Declaration" VIII, 24 in Ibid., 595.

[7] OMSM, 61.

[8] *Apology of the Augsburg Confession*, XXI, Tappert, 230.

[9] See OMSM, 102–15.

[10] Cf. Eric Gritsch, "The Views of Luther and Lutheranism on the Veneration of Mary," in ibid., 235–48. See also idem., "Embodiment of Unmerited Grace: The Virgin Mary according to Martin Luther and Lutheranism," in Alberic Stacpoole (ed.), *Mary's Place in Christian Dialogue* (Wilton, CT: Morehouse-Barlow, 1982), 133–41.

[11] *Lutheran Worship* (St. Louis, MO: Concordia Publishing House, 1986) 42, 113.

[12] *The Magnificat*, trans. A.T.W. Steinhauser (Minneapolis: Augsburg, 1967), 77.

[13] Ibid., 44–45 [emphasis added]. Note also the contemporary paraphrase of the *Regina caeli* in Thomas McNally and William G. Storey, eds., *Day by Day: The Notre Dame Prayerbook for Students* (Notre Dame: Ave Maria Press, 1975), 49: "Joy fill your heart, O Queen most high, alleluia! Your Son who in the tomb did lie, Alleluia! Has risen as he did prophesy, alleluia! Pray for us, Mother, when we die, alleluia!"

[14] Ibid., 46 [emphasis added].

[15] Gritsch, 381, n. 37.

[16] *Lutheran Worship*, 43, 39–41. The "traditional" Hail Mary, of course ends at the words "blessed is the fruit of your womb, Jesus." The second half ("Holy Mary, Mother of God, pray for us sinners now and at the hour of our death"), though in use in various places at the time of the Reformation, did not achieve its current form until the *Breviarium Romanum* of Pope Pius V in 1568. See Josef Jungmann, *Christian Prayer through the Centuries* (New York: Paulist Press, 1978), 109. For a contemporary Roman Catholic suggestion regarding this "traditional" and christological form of the Hail Mary, see McNally and Storey, *Day by Day*, 147–51.

[17] *Luther's Works*, 43, 39–40 [emphasis added].

[18] See above, n. 10.

[19] Arthur Carl Piepkorn, "Mary's Place Within the People of God According to Non-Roman-Catholics," *Marian Studies*, 18 (1967), 79–81. I owe this reference to the excellent essay by Gregory Paul Fryer, "Mary as Archetype of the Church: An Essay in Generosity Toward Mary," *Currents in Theology and Mission* 12/6 (1985), 361–70.

[20] Joseph Sittler, *The Care of the Earth and Other University Sermons* (Philadelphia: Fortress, 1964), 55–56, 63.

[21] Certain forms of Roman Catholic popular piety as well as some of the literature (presumably published with ecclesiastical permission) regarding Marian apparitions and the claims (both salvific and political) concerning the messages of these apparitions, however, will continue to give Lutherans (and others) pause.

[22] John Frederick Johnson, "Mary and the Saints in Contemporary Lutheran Worship," OMSM, 305–10.

[23] While it is ecumenically laudable to have a festival in honor of Mary on August 15, this particular festival, new to both *Lutheran Book of Worship* (LBW) and *Lutheran Worship*, is confusing. A feast called "Mary Theotokos" on August 15 is the earliest Marian feast anywhere, and appears already in the Jerusalem liturgy of the late fourth-early-fifth centuries. But a Marian festival under *this* title would be more appropriate on January 1, the

traditional commemoration of the title *Theotokos* of the Council of Ephesus (431), not August 15, the traditional date of her Dormition, Falling Asleep, or Assumption. Furthermore, the title itself is puzzling. Lutherans strongly affirm Mary's title as *Theotokos*, i.e., "Godbearer," or "Mother of God," in order to safeguard the personal identity of the God-Man, but even Nestorius of Constantinople would have been satisfied with the title "Mother of our Lord" because of its ambiguity. This, therefore, is one of those places where we Lutherans need to be challenged further concerning the liturgical reflection of our confessional theology about Mary.

24 He refers here, however, only to the thanksgiving for the faithful departed in the litany of evening prayer. See Johnson, 308.

25 Ibid., 309 [emphasis added]. That this verse was Athelstan Riley's poetic reference to the assumption of Mary is noted by Reginald Fuller, *Preaching the Lectionary* (Collegeville: The Liturgical Press, 1984), 557.

226 Johnson, 306.

27 Although it is nowhere stated why the second verse of "Ye Watchers and Ye Holy Ones" was omitted from *Lutheran Worship,* the reason for omitting the *Stabat Mater* was that "this hymn directs the worshiper to Mary and her response to Christ's suffering rather than to Christ in His suffering." See *Report and Recommendations of the Special Hymnal Review Committee* (St. Louis: Concordia, n.d.), 31. If there is a correlation intended between the omission of both the second verse of "Ye Watchers and Ye Holy Ones" and this entire hymn, the implicit logic can only be that it is permissible for the Lutheran worshiper to be directed to the praise of God offered by the angelic host, the patriarchs and prophets, the apostles and martyrs, and the souls in "endless rest," but not that offered by Mary herself.

28 *Lutheran Book of Worship* (LBW), *Minister's Edition* (ME), (Minneapolis: Augsburg, 1978), 223.

29 Ibid., 213.

30 Ibid., 219.

31 Ibid., 220.

32 Ibid., 174, 178.

33 Cited by Johnson, 310.

34 LBW/ME, 189.

35 Ibid., 68.

36 Ibid., 81, 84.

37 Ibid., 72.

38 Ibid., 120 [emphasis added].

39 Verse two of "Ye Watchers and Ye Holy Ones" (LBW, Hymn 175).

40 OMSM, 57ff.

41 See *On Translating: An Open Letter,* LW, 35, 199.

42 Cf. *Augsburg Confession,* XXI, Tappert, 46ff, *Apology of the Augsburg Confession,* XXI, Tappert, 229–36, and *The Smalcald Articles,* Part II, III, Tappert, 297.

43 OMSM, 61.

44 *Apology of the Augsburg Confession,* XXI, Tappert, 230. See also 232.

# LITURGY AND THEOLOGY

In his conflict with Semi-Pelagianism over the necessity of divine grace throughout the entire process of human salvation, the monk Prosper of Aquitaine (c. 390–463), who was a product of Augustinian theology, argued that:

> in inviolable decrees of the blessed apostolic see, our holy fathers have cast down the pride of this pestiferous novelty and taught us to ascribe to the grace of Christ the very beginnings of good will, the growth of noble efforts, and the perseverance in them to the end. In addition, let us look at the sacred testimony of priestly intercessions which have been transmitted from the apostles and which are uniformly celebrated throughout the world and in every Catholic Church; so that the law of prayer may establish a law for belief [*ut legem credendi lex statuat supplicandi*]. For when the presidents of the holy congregations perform their duties, they plead the cause of the human race before the divine clemency and, joined by the sighs of the whole church, they beg and pray that grace may be given to unbelievers; that idolaters may be freed from the errors of their impiety; that the Jews may have the veil removed from their hearts and that the light of truth may shine on them; that heretics may recover through acceptance of the catholic faith; that schismatics may receive afresh the spirit of charity; that the lapsed may be granted the remedy of penitence; and finally that

the catechumens may be brought to the sacrament of regeneration and have the court of the heavenly mercy opened to them.[1]

Although Prosper's argument on the basis of the *lex orandi* is an addition to one based on the teaching of the apostolic see, liturgical theologians have tended to latch on to this principle as the primary one for discerning a principal source for the church's faith and theology. How is liturgy a 'source' for theology? What is the relationship between the church's prayer and its faith and doctrinal formulations? How does liturgy shape believing?

The answers to the above questions are not easy. In fact, the answers given to them—as well as the precise interpretation and methodological weight of Prosper's principle—vary from one theologian to another. The definitions of liturgy and theology and the presence or absence of a verb in the use of Prosper's phrase are important keys in attempting to answer the question of the precise relationship between liturgy and theology in the writings of various theologians. Does the theologian supply a verb (*lex orandi lex est credendi*), omit the verb in favor of the principle's popular shorthand formulation (*lex orandi, lex credendi*), or keep the verb as it appears in Prospers own text (*ut legem credendi lex statuat supplicandi*)?

In order to illustrate both the complexity of this problem and the lack of consensus in liturgical theology today, this essay focuses on the relation between liturgy and theology in three contemporary and highly influential liturgical theologians from three different Christian traditions: Alexander Schmemann (Russian Orthodox), Geoffrey Wainwright (British Methodist), and Aidan Kavanagh (Roman Catholic). All three subscribe to Prosper's phrase as a fitting methodological principle. But all three offer different definitions of liturgy and theology. All three use different verbs (or no verb) in their appropriation of Prosper's principle. And, consequently, all three provide different understandings of the relationship between *lex orandi* and *lex credendi*.

# I. Alexander Schmemann:
## *lex orandi lex 'est' credendi*

The late Alexander Schmemann devoted a number of his writings to the question of the relationship between liturgy and theology.[2] According to him, neither 'liturgical theology' as a sub-discipline within the broader theological curriculum nor the attempt to develop a 'theology of liturgy' from which one might deduce the correct norms to which a program of liturgical reform must conform are adequate approaches to this question Rather, theology as the "orderly and consistent presentation explication and defense of the church's faith" must be rooted in the very experience of the faith itself, an experience which is "given and received in the church's *leitourgia*—in her *lex orandi*."[3] In other words, for Schmemann the *lex orandi* 'is' (*est*) the church's *lex credendi*, and the theological task is ultimately an interpretative and descriptive process which attempts "to grasp the 'theology' as revealed in and through liturgy."[4] He maintains that if theology is

> the attempt to express Truth itself, to find words adequate to the mind and experience of the church, then it must of necessity have its source where the faith, the mind, and the experience of the church have their living focus and expression, where faith in both essential meanings of that word, as Truth revealed and given, and as Truth accepted and 'lived,' has its *epiphany*, and that is precisely the function of the *'leitourgia.'*[5]

There is therefore no need for specific kinds of theology called either 'liturgical theology' or 'theology of liturgy.' Although theology should not be reduced to liturgy, all Christian theology should somehow be 'liturgical,' in that it has "its ultimate term of reference in the faith of the church, as manifested and communicated in the liturgy."[6]

But what is it in liturgy that makes the liturgical experience this 'epiphany' of the church's faith in such a way that it is the ultimate source for theological reflection and discourse? For Schmemann it is not a particular liturgy with its given texts, rubrics, ritual acts, and interpretations that does this. It is rather, what he calls the liturgical *Ordo,* the basic underlying structure and theology of liturgy enshrined, even hidden, with the various Byzantine *ordines* and *typica.* It is "the unchanging principle, the living norm or "logos" of worship as a whole within what is accidental and temporary."[7] And the unchanging principle, norm, or 'logos' presented by this *Ordo,* having apostolic and Judeo-Christian origins, is a particular understanding and revelation of the co-relation of a normative eschatology, cosmology, and ecclesiology which are manifested in the very core of the church's liturgical act and experience, especially in the Eucharist (a manifestation of the eternal kingdom of God) celebrated by the church within time. Indeed, the principle of the *Ordo* is the "co-relation and conjunction of the Eucharist with the liturgy of time in which we recognize the fundamental structure of the church's prayer, as having existed from the very beginning in her 'rule of prayer'."[8] Thus, within the *lex orandi* of the early church there was, in his opinion, an "organic . . . self-evident connection and interdependence of the Lord's Day, the Eucharist, and the Ecclesia (the coming together of the faithful as 'church'),"[9] manifesting an eschatological, ecclesial, and cosmological vision. He continues:

> It is clear that on the one hand, this connection still exists liturgically, but it is equally clear that on the other hand, it is neither understood nor experienced in the way it was understood and experienced in the early church. Why? Because a certain theology and a certain piety shaped by that theology, by imposing their own categories and their own approach changed our understanding of the liturgy and our experience of it.[10]

Since this organic connection between world, church, and kingdom 'still exists liturgically,' it is within the liturgy above all that

> the church is *informed* of her cosmical and eschatological vocation, *receives* the power to fulfill it and thus truly *becomes* 'what she is'—the sacrament, in Christ, of the kingdom. In this sense the liturgy is indeed 'means of

grace' . . . in the all-embracing meaning as means of always making the church what she is—a realm of grace, of communion with God, of new knowledge and new life. The liturgy of the church is cosmical and eschatolog-ical because the church is cosmical and eschatological; but the church would not have been cosmical and escha-tological had she not been given, as the very source and constitution of her life and faith, the *experience* of the new creation, the experience and *vision* of the kingdom which is to come. And this is precisely the 'leitourgia' of the church's cult, the function which makes it the source and indeed the very *possibility* of theology.[11]

Because the church's *lex orandi is* the church's true *lex creden-di,* the task of theology is merely to explicate, explain, and defend this liturgically received vision and experience. Although Schmemann nowhere says this, he seems to imply that theolo-gy—if not a 'reduction' to liturgy—is, nevertheless, synonymous with catechesis or mystagogy, that is, an explanation of the vision and experience mediated in and by the liturgy.

Thus, one does not seek a 'reform' of the liturgy. Rather, the liturgy is allowed to remain as it is, while the critical task of the theologian is to articulate and make clear the unchanging apos-tolic theological principle of the *Ordo* contained and expressed therein. Schmemann's theological model, therefore, is much clos-er to preaching than it is to lecturing, more at home in the patris-tic pulpit than in the medieval or modern theological academy.

Schmemann's overall concern, of course, was more with the-ology itself than it was with liturgy. What he sought was the rein-tegration of liturgy, theology, and piety within his own Eastern Orthodox tradition, a tradition in which he saw theology as hav-ing become captive to (Western) scholastic categories cut-off from the living liturgical tradition, and in which the essential eschatological, cosmological, and ecclesiological vision and prin-ciple of the liturgical structure or *Ordo* had been obscured (from the time of Constantine onwards) in favor of an increasingly 'mysteriological piety.' Though well aware of the historic and current problems in Eastern liturgy, Schmemann saw the solu-tion not in changing the liturgy, but in restoring both theology and piety to their original and organic connection with the *lex orandi* itself. What needed changing was not the liturgy, but a theology and piety divorced from the unchanging (but often hidden) principle of the church's fundamental and constitutive 'rule of prayer.' With those bent on reforming the Orthodox liturgy Schmemann claimed that

> no meaningful discussion . . . *is* possible because . . . any interest in precisely the *meaning* of the liturgy as a whole, of the 'lex orandi' in its relationship to 'lex credendi' is absent, because the liturgy is viewed as an end in itself and not as the 'epiphany' of the church's faith, of her experience in Christ of herself, the world and the kingdom.[12]

The way in which Prosper's principle is appropriated in the approach of Alexander Schmemann is clear. It is within the liturgy itself, at least within what Schmemann identified as the unchanging principle of the liturgy, that the church's faith is revealed and expressed and so becomes the 'source' for theological reflection and discourse, even if that discourse is limited to the explanation, explication, and defence of that 'liturgical' vision.

This is a strong argument. Indeed, *lex orandi lex est credendi* reminds us that what the church believes, teaches, and confesses will certainly be reflected and expressed within its worship. Consequently (and this is true not simply for Eastern Orthodoxy), if one wants to understand a particular religious tradition one must not only read its theological texts but experience and consciously study its worship, a fact which seems so obvious that it should make the study of liturgy a required part of every academic curriculum of theological or religious studies.

It is also true, however, that Schmemann's theological interpretation of the unchanging eschatological, cosmological, and ecclesiological principle of the *lex orandi* is precisely that, a *theological* interpretation. And, whether one agrees with this interpretation or not, the fact remains that this, ultimately, is Schmemann's own interpretation and vision of what the liturgy is, reveals, and what its role should be in theological reflection and discourse—a vision supported in large part[13] by the now outdated work of both C. W. Dugmorex[14] on the normative character of Jewish synagogue worship for early Christian worship and Gregory Dix[15] on the so-called primitive and universal 'shape' of the liturgy and the post-Constantinian decline and shift from an eschatological to a historical focus. In other words, in spite of his own reluctance to offer a 'theology of liturgy,' it is precisely a theology of liturgy that Schmemann provides, an elucidation of the 'correct' theological vision, norms, and principles which not only govern the liturgical celebration but function as the sources for theology itself.

If this is a correct reading of Schmemann's approach, then his hesitation to embrace a program of reform of Orthodox liturgy does not appear as a logical corollary. To this Western Christian at least, it would seem that if Schmemann is right in noting that the underlying, unchanging, and fundamental principle of the *Ordo* has been so obscured by a scholastic theology and concomitant mysteriological piety such that it has changed not only the understanding but also the 'experience' of liturgy, then the recovery of this principle might indeed provide the basis of a liturgical reform which would allow the church's true *lex orandi* to function in a clearer fashion as 'source' for both theology and piety. In other words, could it not be said that not only should the organic connection of theology and piety with liturgy be rediscovered, but that the liturgy itself should also be reformed today according to the true *lex orandi*, so that whatever gets in the way of and obscures this principle in the liturgical act itself is suppressed? Contrary to the romantic and popular myth of the unchanging Christian East, Eastern Christian liturgy has changed, can change, and is being changed today in various ways. Byzantine liturgical history teaches us that.[16] What Schmemann offers, however, in spite of his protests to the contrary, is a theological vision which might provide some substance and rationale for guiding such a program of reform and renewal among those in the Christian East who find it desirable and necessary.

## II. Geoffrey Wainwright:
### lex orandi, lex credendi

In the last two chapters of the second part of his now classic systematic theological study *Doxology*, Geoffrey Wainwright presents both a critical study of the relation between *lex orandi* and *lex credendi* and a brief survey of the use of this formula in the history of doctrine. If *lex orandi lex 'est' credendi* is the key to Schmemann's approach, it is the absence of a verb altogether which characterizes Wainwright's appropriation and use of Prosper's principle. For Wainwright it is clear in this context that by *lex orandi* he means the liturgy primarily as liturgical 'text' or 'feast' and by *lex credendi* he means faith or believing primarily as 'doctrine' or 'dogma.' He says that

> the Latin tag *lex orandi, lex credendi* may be construed in two ways. The more usual way makes the rule of prayer a norm for belief: what is prayed indicates what may and must be believed. But from the grammatical point of view it is equally possible to reverse subject and predicate and so take the tag as meaning that the rule of faith is the norm for prayer: what must be believed governs what may and should be prayed.[17]

Wainwright notes further that in the history of Christian doctrine the *lex orandi* has played a more normative role within the Roman Catholic tradition than it has within Protestantism. While particular doctrines have certainly shaped liturgy and liturgical practices in various historical periods within Roman Catholicism,[18] it is particularly in Protestantism that the *lex credendi* has exercised almost absolute control over liturgical life:

> Roman Catholicism characteristically appeals to existing liturgical practice for proof in matters of doctrine. There *lex orandi, lex credendi is* most readily taken to make the (descriptive) pattern of prayer a (prescriptive) norm for belief, so that what is prayed indicates what may and must be believed. Protestantism characteristically emphasizes the primacy of doctrine over the liturgy. The

phrase *lex orandi, lex credendi is* not well known among Protestants, but they would most easily take the dogmatic norm of belief as setting a rule for prayer, so that what must be believed governs what may and should be prayed.[19]

As an ecumenically minded and orientated Protestant theologian, however, Wainwright attempts to take seriously the historically authoritative character of the *lex orandi* in shaping doctrine. In support of this, at least in the patristic period, he draws attention to Ignatius of Antioch's equation of the Docetists' abstinence from the Eucharist with a denial on their part of the reality of Christ's incarnation; Tertullian and Irenaeus invoking Christian sacramental practice against the Gnostic devaluation of matter; the arguments of Athanasius and Basil for the divinity of the Holy Spirit based on the baptismal formula against the Pneumatomachian denial of the Spirit's divinity; Basil of Caesarea's dispute with those same Pneumatomachians on the proper interpretation of both the uncoordinate and co-ordinate forms of the trinitarian doxology; the witness of liturgical practice supporting the clause "with the Father and the Son he (i.e., the Holy Spirit) is worshipped and glorified" in the third article of the Creed of Nicea-Constantinople; and, among other possible examples from this period, Ambrose interpreting the interrogative form of the baptismal formula in use at Milan as teaching orthodox trinitarian doctrine.[20] In all of these cases it is the liturgy which has shaped doctrine, the *lex orandi* which has established the *lex credendi*, and not the other way around.

However, because Wainwright is concerned about "worship getting out of hand"[21] and about the mutual and conjunctive interplay between worship and doctrine, he offers further both a particular definition of liturgy in relation to doctrine and a number of theological criteria or tests for determining whether or not a liturgically originated doctrine is consistent with that definition. "Worship . . . is a source of doctrine," he writes, "in so far as it is the place in which God makes himself known to humanity in a saving encounter. The human words and acts used in worship are a doctrinal locus in so far as either God makes them the vehicle of his self-communication or they are fitting responses to

God's presence and action."[22] And the criteria he suggests are three tests of origin, spread, and ethical correspondence. Each of these calls for additional comment.

## The test of origin

According to Wainwright, the more that ideas and practices can be traced back to Jesus himself, the more authoritative weight they are to be given. However, since this is extremely difficult—if not impossible—to determine, it is the post-Easter church "which must be credited with an authority of historical origination second only to Jesus himself."[23] And since Jesus and this post-Easter church have as their primitive witness the writings of the New Testament, the test of origins is whether a particular liturgical text or practice conforms to that of the primitive church as it is reflected in the canonical New Testament. The canon of scripture, therefore, is the primary criterion to be applied in determining whether a given liturgical text or practice is authoritative for doctrine, and "Protestants in dialogue with Catholics must not give up their insistence on the need for a scriptural test to be applied to Christian worship and doctrine, however difficult the application may be."[24]

## The test of spread in time and space

Conformity to scripture is not the only criterion for determining the authority of the *lex orandi*. "Theology draws, too," he writes, "on the tradition of the church, in which certain elements or periods impress themselves as more authentic and hence serve as standards."[25] By this he means that "the closer a liturgical item comes to the universality of the Vincentian *quod semper, quod ubique, quod ab omnibus*, the greater will be its importance as a doctrinal locus." Indeed, "it is hard to believe that any practice approaching universality in the Christian tradition should be so far removed from the divine truth as to lack suitability as a source of doctrine."[26] Therefore, both scripture and the 'universal' Christian doctrinal tradition (i.e., primarily the golden age of the patristic writers and the great ecumenical councils of the fourth and fifth centuries) appear to function as criteria in a complementary fashion.

But having said this, Wainwright is quick to point out exceptions to the applicability of this Vincentian canon. While the practice of infant baptism, for example, may correspond to this canon, the fact that many have questioned its appropriateness throughout Christian history and others have even abandoned it altogether not only calls into question Augustine's use of it "as 'proof' for his doctrine of original sin" but also advocates the doctrinal significance of "repentance, faith and personal commitment" to God in relation to baptism. Similarly, Wainwright sees further exceptions to this canon in that traditional Protestant rejections of both the sacrificial nature of the Eucharist and the cult of the Virgin Mary seriously call into question the claim of their universal acceptance in the church.[27]

It is within the Marian cult and the related Marian dogma of the Roman Catholic tradition, in particular, where Wainwright especially emphasizes the need for a necessary conjunctive linkage between *lex orandi* and *lex credendi*. As one example of this, the dogma of the immaculate conception of Mary can be considered. According to Wainwright, the argument of Pius IX in *Ineffabilis Deus* that the establishment of the feast and of propers for the Conception of the Virgin by previous popes constituted the *lex orandi* and was itself evidence for the dogma's traditional acceptance is actually "a new *lex orandi* . . . seen by Pius to have been deliberately introduced by his papal predecessors in order to promote . . . a particular doctrine."[28] It is at this point that Wainwright suggests that Protestants, accustomed as they are to the normative character of the *lex credendi* over the *lex orandi*, might well ask "why the Roman magisterium did not curtail, rather than sanction and even encourage, popular devotion (to the Virgin Mary) when it took an aberrant turn."[29]

To call such a process an 'aberrant turn,' however, says more about Wainwright's own theological position than it does about the *lex orandi* principle itself. In fact, it makes one wonder whether Wainwright's use of the principle is not ultimately a specific apologetic for Protestant doctrine alone. That is, Wainwright allows the *lex orandi* to function as a source for the *lex credendi* only if it supports those dogmas with which he finds himself in doctrinal agreement. But a Roman Catholic historian of doctrine might surely respond by noting that (a) both popular and liturgical devotion to Mary is at least as old as the third- or fourth-century Greek prayer *Sub tuum praesidium*, which contains the phrase 'holy Mary, Mother of God'; (b) the earliest datable Marian feast—'Mary the Mother of God' on 15 August—is already included in the fifth-century Armenian Lectionary reflecting (presumably) the fourth-century Jerusalem liturgy; (c) the doctrinal title *Theotokos*, officially defined at Ephesus in 431, is shaped precisely by the popular liturgical practice which invoked her under that title; (d) Mary is commemorated in the *Communicantes* of the Roman eucharistic prayer from at least the fifth century; and (e) by the seventh century Rome had already instituted a feast of Mary on 1 January and adopted the earlier Eastern Marian feasts of 2 February, 25 March, 15 August, and 8 September.[30]

Whether a dogma of the immaculate conception of Mary can or should be deduced from the *lex orandi* is, of course, a debatable topic. But, in a general sense, the existence of a Marian *lex orandi* shaping a Marian *lex credendi* within the Christian tradition would certainly seem to fit the test of the Vincentian canon, at least within a universal patristic and pre-Reformation context in both the East and the West. Moreover, current ecumenical discussion of the principal Roman Catholic dogmas of Mary's immaculate conception and assumption may yet find a way to make possible an even more 'universal' acceptance of their theological intent. The Anglican theologian John Macquarrie writes:

> I believe that these two dogmas, when purged of mythological elements, can be interpreted as implications of more central Christian teaching. Theologically, of course, their significance does not lie in anything they say about the private biography of Mary but as pointing to moments in the life of the community of faith, for here . . . there is an intimate parallel between Mary and the church.[31]

To cite but one example of these implications, Macquarrie suggests elsewhere that the dogma of the immaculate conception may in fact parallel the *sola gratia* principle of the Reformation tradition.[32] Even in the case of the ecumenical church today, therefore, the *lex orandi*, in so far as it concerns the Marian cult, may yet serve as a source for shaping faith and doctrine in those issues which currently serve as dogmatic symbols of division.

## The test of ethical correspondence

While recognizing that there is no clear one-to-one relationship between liturgy and ethics, Wainwright claims that "a liturgical practice which is matched with some directness by holiness of life makes a weighty claim to be treated as source of doctrine; and any link that could be traced between a liturgical practice and moral turpitude would to that extent disqualify the liturgical practice as a source of doctrine."[33] But this is a difficult test to apply to either liturgical practice or doctrine, and Wainwright does not offer any concrete examples. Liturgical acts that promote or serve merely to bless the *status quo* of political and economic systems, racism, or sexism might surely fall into this category. Yet, as he notes, "in so far as the sacraments, or any form of worship, fail to produce appropriate fruit in the lives of the participants, the failure is due to a lack or refusal on the human side of the encounter with God."[34] In other words, while a particular liturgical text, practice, or feast may be ethically inappropriate, generally speaking, unethical behavior is more often the result of the (mis)appropriation, (mis)use, or (mis)understanding of the text, practice, or feast on the part of the worshipping community. Instead of a clear test to be applied to the liturgy in relation to doctrine in general, this criterion of ethical correspondence seems to be a call for an ongoing prophetic critique of the liturgy in order to draw out and underscore its ethical implications.

However, one might apply this test of ethical correspondence to what Wainwright cited above as the other Roman Catholic example of a liturgical practice—generally lacking in Protestantism—from which doctrinal conclusions have been made: the sacrificial Eucharist. In spite of his noting this as lacking universal acceptance, and so presumably failing the test of the Vincentian canon, the fact of the matter is this: although a sacrificial understanding of the Eucharist may not be explicitly formulated in scripture (the first test), the history of Christian eucharistic celebration, anaphoral texts, and interpretation from the late first-century *Didache* up to (but not including) Luther's

*Formula Missae* of 1523 certainly understands the Eucharist in sacrificial terms and categories. If anything meets the problematic criterion of the Vincentian canon, at least up to the Reformation period, certainly a sacrificial understanding of the Eucharist does. Again, therefore, Wainwright's overall Protestant theological orientation receives more weight than the *lex orandi* principle itself. Nevertheless, it is Wainwright himself who argues for the possibility of an ecumenical theological interpretation of eucharistic sacrifice:

> Could not the contentious notion 'we offer Christ' paradoxically be seen as antipelagian? It could be an acknowledgement that we have nothing else to offer . . . To say 'we offer Christ' may then become a bold way of acknowledging the transforming presence and work of Christ within us. Again, paradoxically, it could thus be the very opposite of pelagianism.[35]

But does a sacrificial theory of the Eucharist issue in a particular ethic or holiness of life? While a *do-ut-des* approach (i.e., the principle of reciprocity) to religious ritual is always a danger, a community which is formed by such a sacrificial understanding may well perceive that its life of ministry and service in and to the world is to be one of sacrificial self-offering in union with Christ, into whose own pattern of self-offering, celebrated and actualized in the Eucharist, they have been and are to be conformed. A sacrificial Eucharist, therefore, may indeed meet Wainwright's criterion of ethical correspondence and so function, according to his own definition, as an authoritative source of dogma.

The use and appropriation of Prosper's principle in Wainwright's approach is also clear. But the role he assigns to the *lex orandi* in the development of doctrine is a very limited one. Although he calls for the mutual or conjunctive interplay of both *lex orandi* and *lex credendi*, it is clear that his overall preference is for the *lex credendi* as the dominant of the two principles. Even the above three tests or criteria are theological doctrinal tests, not specifically liturgical ones.[36] Like Schmemann, Wainwright's primary concern is with theology more than it is with liturgy. And, while he claims that reflective theology "can and should draw on the experience of the church in worship for its reflection" rather than relegating such experience to 'practical theology,' it is clear that this plays a secondary role to other theological tasks. That is, theology "has the task of reflectively expounding the worship of the church in order to facilitate an intelligent participation in it," but its task also includes "the responsibility, where necessary, of criticizing particular acts of worship and the formulations and practices of the liturgy."[37] In other words, it might be said that what Wainwright ultimately offers is not a liturgical theology but a particular (Protestant) theology of liturgy or theological approach to the liturgy, in which it is not the *lex orandi* but the *lex credendi* that has the final authoritative say in the worship, doctrine, and life of the church, even if all three of these are to have the doxological praise of God as their goal.

## III.  Aidan Kavanagh:
### *Ut legem credendi lex statuat supplicandi*

In distinction from both Schmemann and Wainwright, it is precisely Prosper's use of the third-person subjunctive form of the Latin verb *statuo* which serves as the methodological key in Aidan Kavanagh's approach to the relationship between liturgy and theology. In direct response to Wainwright, Kavanagh says that *lex orandi, lex credendi* can only become what Wainwright calls a Latin 'tag' in modern usage

> when the two laws are allowed to float free from each other by the removal of the verb which originally united them. That verb was *statuat*, as in *lex supplicandi legem statuat credendi*: The law of worshiping founds the law of believing. So long, I think, as the verb stays in the sentence it is not possible to reverse subject and predicate any more than one can reverse the members of the statement: the foundation supports the house. Having said that, one cannot really say that the house supports the foundation . . . Similarly, I think, one cannot first say that the *lex orandi* or *supplicandi* founds or constitutes the *lex credendi*, and then add that, of course, the latter also

founds and constitutes the former. The verb blocks this. The old maxim means what it says.[38]

It is this understanding of the constituting function of the *lex orandi* for the *lex credendi* which characterizes the major section of his book, *On Liturgical Theology*.[39]

Instead of looking at liturgy either as a 'text' (i.e., a *locus theologicus* for the drawing out of specific doctrinal conclusions) or as an *Ordo* in which the church's faith and vision of reality make their 'epiphany' so as to be expounded theologically, Kavanagh is concerned with the foundational character for all theology of the liturgical *act* itself:

> If theology as a whole is critical reflection upon the communion between God and our race, the peculiarly graced representative and servant of the cosmic order created by God and restored in Christ, then scrutiny of the precise point at which this communion is most overtly deliberated upon and celebrated by us under God's judgment and in God's presence would seem to be crucial to the whole enterprise.[40]

According to Kavanagh, it is the liturgical act which founds the faith of the church and makes theological reflection possible. This is because, in his opinion, believing is consequent to the constitutive function of the liturgical act:

> Belief is always consequent upon encounter with the Source of the grace of faith. Therefore Christians do not worship because they believe. They believe because the One in whose gift faith lies is regularly met in the act of communal worship—not because the assembly conjures up God, but because the initiative lies with the God who has promised to be there always. The *lex credendi* is thus subordinated to the *lex supplicandi* because both standards exist and function only within the worshipping assembly's own subordination of itself to its ever-present Judge, Savior, and unifying Spirit.[41]

And what occurs in a liturgical act, in this encounter with the One regularly met in the act of communal worship, is the beginning of a continual Hegelian dialectic of thesis, antithesis, and synthesis worked out within the worshipping community. In a liturgical act a given community (thesis) is, in his words, "brought to the brink of chaos," i.e., changed by this liturgical encounter with God in word and sacrament (antithesis). It then goes away to 'reflectively adjust' to this change (synthesis) until the next liturgical encounter when the process begins all over again. "It is the *adjustment* which is theological in all this," he writes. "I hold that it is theology being born, theology in the first instance. It was what tradition has called *theologia prima*."[42]

The distinction between *theologia prima* and *theologia secunda* is, of course, an extremely important one for Kavanagh. If *theologia prima is* 'theology being born' in the worshipping community's reflective adjustment to its experience of and encounter with God in the liturgical act, *theologia secunda* is second order (systematic) theological study done by the professionally trained academic theologian, even within that sub-discipline called 'liturgical theology.' It is the primacy of this *theologia prima* that Kavanagh advocates in and for the overall theological task. For, according to him,

the liturgical dialectic of encounter, change, and adjustment to change amounts to a reflective and lived theology which is native to all the members of the faithful assembly. This is *theologia* which is constant, regular, and inevitable as these people encounter God in worship and adjust to the changes God visits upon them. The liturgical assembly is thus a theological corporation and each of its members a theologian . . . Mrs. Murphy and her pastor are primary theologians whose discourse in faith is carried on . . . in the vastly complex vocabulary of experiences had, prayers said, sights seen, smells smelled, words said and heard and responded to, emotions controlled and released, sins committed and repented, children born and loved ones buried, and in many other ways . . . [Their] vocabulary is not precise, concise, or scientific. It is symbolic, aesthetic, and sapiential . . .

Nowhere else can that primary body of perceived data be read so well as in the living tradition of Christian worship.[43]

It is thus this encounter between God and the world, an encounter enacted in the rite of the liturgical assembly, about which *theologia secunda* "forms propositions."[44] From this primary theological act of liturgy "other acts of secondary theology take their rise within that life of right worship (*orthodoxia*) we call the liturgical assembly, the community of faith, the church."[45] *Lex orandi,* therefore, constitutes, establishes, or founds *lex credendi.* Prosper's principle cannot be accurately construed in any other way.

Because it is the liturgical act and experience of the assembly which is primary, it is from the critical reflective adjustment to this act and experience that, in Kavanagh's opinion, the church develops its canonical norms. These are: (1) the canon of holy scripture, which regulates what should be read and heard, and thereby "keeps the assembly locked into the fundamental relationship that gives it is unique character . . . , namely, its relationship to the presence in its midst of the living God;" (2) the canon of baptismal faith, that is, the trinitarian-baptismal creeds, which "distill the substance of revealed Gospel into baptismal form" and so "keep the assembly's worship firmly rooted in relationship to a divine presence which is . . . communitarian and personal;" (3) the canon of eucharistic faith, contained in the eucharistic prayers, which "distill the substance of revealed Gospel and its baptismal creeds into strictly euchological forms of thanksgiving and petition within the corporate person of him whose Gospel is in motion for the life of the world;" and (4) the collection of canon laws, "which regulate the daily living and the due processes of assemblies of Christians in conformity with the foregoing canons of scripture, creed, and prayer."[46] These various canons are not the result of *theologia secunda,* not the result of an imposed or legislated doctrinal control from the outside, but the fundamental way in which the liturgical assembly as a social group comes to govern its liturgy and its life so that the liturgical encounter with the Source of the grace of faith remains, indeed, primary for its faith and life.

As is the case with both Schmemann and Wainwright, Kavanagh's use and appropriation of Prosper's principle is quite clear. His firm insistence on the use of the proper verb, however, makes it serve a quite different function than it does in either Schmemann or Wainwright. If both of them are primarily concerned with theology, Kavanagh's overriding concern is with liturgy. Thus he attempts to present what might truly be called a *liturgical* theology. By focusing not on liturgical 'text' or 'principles' but on the foundational character of the liturgical act itself, Kavanagh has provided a great service for liturgiologists and theologians alike. It is the liturgical act which must be studied and analyzed—by whatever methodological disciplines—because it is the first and ongoing act and experience by which Christians encounter the Gospel in their midst. The primacy of the liturgical act, event, and experience therefore must be kept primary, and theological attention must be given to the symbolic, mythical, and ritual language of this event, as this is the primary 'theological' language of the liturgical community's 'experience.'

Kavanagh's approach, however, is not without its problems. The first of these may be called the lack of evaluative criteria. As Geoffrey Wainwright notes in a review of Kavanagh's book,

> it needs to be asked, by what criteria a particular pattern or act of worship is to be discerned as truly Christian. How do we know that when "something vastly mysterious" transpires (p. 76), it is an effect of the Holy Trinity? How do we know that an "experience of near chaos" (pp. 73–75) is a tryst with the God of Jesus Christ? How do we know that "the flow of liturgical worship, 'like the current of a mighty river'" (p. 87), is in fact borne along by the Holy Spirit?[47]

In other words, the ongoing dialogue between 'Mrs. Murphy and her pastor' may well be an imprecise, unconcise, and non-scientific *theologia prima* conversation formed by years of experiencing a variety of liturgical acts and events, but there would seem to be a need for some kind of criterion in determining whether or not either of them has adequately and accurately perceived the meaning of those acts. Is there not at least the possibility in their conversation not only of different interpretations but of 'wrong' interpretations (held and expressed by either one), shaped not by *the* Gospel but by some other gospel, value, or religious orientation? After all, both Mrs. Murphy and her pastor could be imprecise, unconcise, and non-scientific heretics.

A second, but closely related, problem is this. Although the liturgical act and experience may always be primary in shaping the faith of the community, has there ever been a liturgical act, since the Last Supper itself, which has not also been the result of, and hence shaped by, what Kavanagh calls *theologia secunda*? Indeed, the very liturgical act and canons by which the assembly seeks to govern its worship and life are also the result, at least in part, of second-order theological reflection on the part of the teaching authority in the church. While it may be that the liturgical experience of the community is what gives birth to the various forms of liturgy and its canonical norms in its continual reflective adjustment to the encounter with God in the first place, the history of liturgy demonstrates that the liturgy itself, and hence the content of a particular liturgical *act*, which certainly includes the *texts* read and performed, is also shaped and 'constituted' by secondary theology. Thus, the distinction between *theologia prima* and *secunda*, writes the Anglican liturgiologist Paul Bradshaw,

> can be used only with caution. While it may be true that liturgical rites may on occasion manifest the immediate and intuitive turning of human beings toward God, and so may offer a different perspective from that of the academic theologian, yet equally both in the past and in the present liturgical texts and rubrics are often themselves the products of *theologia secunda*, compositions deliberately intended to reflect some previously articulated doctrinal position.[48]

Finally, focusing on the liturgical act and experience as the saving encounter with the source of the grace of faith and claiming that Christians "believe because the One in whose gift faith lies is regularly met in the act of communal worship" runs the risk of isolating and absolutizing the liturgical act in relation to other possible encounters with this one who is the source. Kavanagh does not mean, of course, that the liturgy 'produces' faith or that the liturgy is some kind of Pelagian guarantee that those worshipping will automatically receive faith. Rather, it is the church's *lex supplicandi* which nourishes, strengthens, clarifies, and perhaps brings to expression a developing faith.[49] Nevertheless, the danger of this kind of language may be, ultimately, to bind the proclamation and hearing of the Word to its liturgical forms. And, for that matter, if it is *not* the liturgical act which Kavanagh intends as primary for both faith and theology, then it becomes very difficult to understand how the liturgical act can be *theologia prima* at all. Thus, one is led to ask whether there is not something else which is even more primary than this liturgical act, some kind of *lex credendi* perhaps which comes to expression in, is continually nourished by, but, nevertheless, in some fundamental primordial way 'constitutes' the *lex orandi*? And might not this 'something else' be the living address of the word of God spoken and responded to in faith, which is indeed present in, experienced by, and celebrated in the liturgical act, but in no way bound to that act but bound instead to the Spirit of God?

## IV Conclusion

Vatican II's Constitution on the Sacred Liturgy says that the liturgy is both 'fount' or source and 'summit' of the church's life. That there exists in general an intimate relationship between liturgy and theology, that the prayer of the church is related to its faith and doctrine, and that what the church does in liturgy shapes what it believes all seem self-evident. But beyond this general statement that liturgy and theology are companions, the precise nature of that relationship is allusive and obscure. The meaning of that relationship, as the above survey of our three liturgical theologians has demonstrated, depends more on the particular interpretation and weight given to it in an individual theologian's approach. Consequently, the three variations of the *lex orandi* principle tell us more about the particular theologies of Schmemann, Wainwright, and Kavanagh than they do about whatever meaning and weight Prosper of Aquitaine may have originally intended by the enunciation of this principle.

Nevertheless, it is fair to ask which (if any) of them is the closest to the usage of Prosper himself. In this regard, Kavanagh says that

> *Lex supplicandi* is something much more specific than the broad and fuzzy notion of the 'practice of the church' . . . It is a law of supplicatory prayer—not prayer or worship in general, but of prayer which petitions God for the whole range of human needs in specific, a law of eucological petition. This is the nub of the reason why the *lex supplicandi* founds and constitutes the *lex credendi* and is therefore primary for Christian theology. The way Christians believe is, somehow, constituted and supported by how Christians petition God for their human needs in worship.[50]

But is this what Prosper actually implies? As noted at the beginning of this essay, Prosper's use of this principle is another argument against Semi-Pelagianism made by him *in addition to* one based on the "inviolable decrees of the blessed apostolic see." Furthermore, it seems quite clear that what gives the *lex orandi* any authority whatsoever in this context is that: (1) this "sacred testimony of priestly intercessions" has been, in Prosper's opinion, "transmitted from the apostles" themselves; and (2) it is "uniformly celebrated throughout the world and in every Catholic church." Since this is the case, the *lex supplicandi* also can be said to 'constitute' the *lex credendi*, not in isolation but because it conforms to the traditional and biblical *doctrinal* teaching of the church. In other words, Prosper's argument is a doctrinal one which uses liturgical evidence in addition to other factors because that liturgical evidence is consistent with those other sources.[51] It would be extremely difficult not to see the parallel here with Wainwright's criteria of both the canon of scripture and conformity to the *quod semper, quod ubique,* and *quod ab omnibus* of Vincent of Lerins. Indeed, both Prosper and Wainwright are concerned principally with orthodoxy (understood correctly not as "right worship" but as "right belief"[52]). In spite of the absence of a verb, therefore, it is the overall *approach* of Wainwright which most closely approximates that of Prosper himself.

This does not, however, make Wainwright's Protestant doctrinal conclusions or his implied insistence on the supremacy of
the *lex credendi* over the *lex orandi* correct. After all, liturgy does
shape, found, or constitute the faith, believing, and doctrinal
teaching of the church. It did not do this only in the so-called
golden age of the fourth- and fifth-century patristic period, but it
has done so throughout history and continues to do so today,
especially in a contemporary context of ecumenical liturgical
renewal and reform. Nevertheless, both principles must be
allowed to function complementarily in the pursuit and articulation of doctrinal truth. While Wainwright certainly intends this
to happen, his focus on the superiority of the *lex credendi* over the
*lex orandi* actually inhibits their complementarity in favor of a
particular theological and doctrinal orientation to which the *lex
orandi* must conform, just as Kavanagh's insistence on the constituting superiority of the *lex orandi* does the same in an opposite manner and Schmemann's equation of the two actually, if
not intentionally, reduces theology to a doctrinal explication and
defense of an irreformable liturgy.

The Jesuit theologian Edward Kilmartin, concerned like
Wainwright with the relation between liturgy and doctrine,
offers a much more balanced approach to this question, an
approach which holds *lex orandi* in dialectic tension with *lex credendi*. According to Kilmartin, to focus on either the *lex orandi* or
the *lex credendi* to the exclusion of the other threatens to obscure
the unique value of two different kinds of expression of faith:

> The slogan 'law of prayer–law of belief' leaves in sus-
> pense which magnitude might be the subject, and which
> the predicate, in particular instances. Consequently, it
> seems legitimate to state the axiom in this way: *the law of
> prayer is the law of belief, and vice versa* . . . On the one hand,
> the law of prayer implies a comprehensive, and, in some
> measure a pre-reflective, perception of the life of faith. On
> the other hand, the law of belief must be introduced
> because the question of the value of a particular liturgical
> tradition requires the employment of theoretical dis-
> course. One must reckon with the limits of the liturgy as
> lived practice of the faith. History has taught us that

forms of liturgical prayer and ritual activity, however orthodox, often had to be dropped or changed to avoid heretical misunderstanding. Moreover, in new historical and cultural situations, the question of the correspondence between the community's understanding of Christian truth, and its expression in the liturgy and that of the authentic whole tradition, must continually be placed. To respond responsibly to this problem, other sources of theology must be introduced along with the liturgical-practical grounding of the knowledge of faith.[53]

All three variations of the one principle of Prosper of Aquitaine summarized in this essay find their echo in Kilmartin's synthetic statement. The law of praying is the law of believing (Schmemann) and the law of praying *constitutes* the law of believing, providing a kind of *theologia prima*, "prereflective perception of the life of faith" (Kavanagh). But, just as importantly, the law of believing cannot be allowed to function in isolation from other legitimate theological principles without distorting the theological quest for and articulation of truth (Wainwright). Therefore, whether any verb, even Prosper's own verb of choice, is used or not in particular formulations of the *lex orandi* principle, both the *lex orandi* and the *lex credendi* must and do function together in the development of doctrine and in the theological reflection, discourse, and self-interpretation of the church catholic.

## Notes

1 *Capitula Coelestini* 8 (Migne, *Patrologia Latina* 51, 205–12). English translation from Geoffrey Wainwright, *Doxology* (London: Epworth Press; New York: Oxford University Press, 1980), 225–6.

2 See his *Introduction to Liturgical Theology,* 2nd edn. (Crestwood, NY: St. Vladimir's Seminary Press, 1975); *For the Life of the World* (Crestwood, NY: St. Vladimir's Seminary Press, 1973); "Liturgical Theology, Theology of Liturgy, and Liturgical Reform," *St. Vladimir's Theological Quarterly* (1969), 217–24; and "Liturgy and Theology," *The Greek Orthodox Theological Review* 17 (1972), 86–100. Thomas Fisch has recently edited a collection of Schmemann's essays on this topic in *Liturgy and Tradition: Theological Reflections of Alexander Schmemann* (Crestwood, NY: St. Vladimir's Seminary Press, 1990).

3 "Liturgy and Theology," 89–90.

4 "Liturgical Theology, Theology of Liturgy, and Liturgical Reform," 218.

5 Ibid., 219.

6 "Liturgy and Theology," 95.

7 *Introduction to Liturgical Theology*, 32.

8 Ibid., 70.

9 "Liturgical Theology, Theology of Liturgy, and Liturgical Reform," 219.

10 Ibid., 219–20.

11 "Liturgy and Theology," 92.

12 "Liturgical Theology, Theology of Liturgy, and Liturgical Reform," 222.

13 See *Introduction to Liturgical Theology*, 40–71.

14 *The Influence of the Synagogue upon the Divine Office* (London: Oxford University Press, 1944).

15 *The Shape of the Liturgy* (Westminster: Dacre Press, 1945).

16 See Robert Taft, "How Liturgies Grow: The Evolution of the Byzantine Divine Liturgy," in idem, *Beyond East and West: Problems in Liturgical Understanding* (Washington, D.C.: Pastoral Press, 1984), 167–92; and *The Byzantine Liturgy: A Short History* (Collegeville: The Liturgical Press, 1992).

17 *Doxology* (London: Epworth Press; New York: Oxford University Press, 1980), 218.

18 See ibid., 259–63.

19 Ibid., 252.

20 Ibid., 228–9, 232–4; "The Praise of God in the Theological Reflection of the Church," *Interpretation* 39 (1985), 42.

21 "The Praise of God," 42.

22 *Doxology*, 242–3.

23 Ibid., 243.

24 Ibid., 242.

25 "The Praise of God," 44.

[26] *Doxology*, 243.

[27] Ibid., 244.

[28] Ibid., 238.

[29] Ibid., 240.

[30] See P. Jounel, "The Veneration of Mary," in A. G. Martimort (ed.), *The Church at Prayer*, vol. 4 (Collegeville: The Liturgical Press, 1986), 130ff.

[31] *Principles of Christian Theology*, 2nd edn. (New York: Charles Scribner's Sons, 1977), 397.

[32] See *Mary for All Christians* (Grand Rapids: Eerdmans, 1990), 75.

[33] *Doxology*, 245.

[34] Ibid., 403.

[35] *Doxology*, 272–3.

[36] On this, see David Power's review of Wainwright's *Doxology* in *Worship* 55 (1981), 64.

[37] Wainwright, "The Praise of God," 43–4.

[38] "Response: Primary Theology and Liturgical Act," *Worship* 57 (1983), 324.

[39] New York: Pueblo, 1984. See especially 73–150.

[40] Ibid., 78.

[41] Ibid., 91–2.

[42] Ibid., 74, 76.

[43] Ibid., 146–7.

[44] Ibid., 145.

[45] Ibid., 96.

[46] Ibid., 141–2.

[47] *Worship* 61 (1987), 183–4.

[48] "The Reshaping of Liturgical Studies," *Anglican Theological Review* 72 (1990), 482.

[49] *On Liturgical Theology*, 99.

[50] Ibid., 134.

[51] On the original doctrinal use and meaning of this phrase in Prosper of Aquitaine, see the important essay by Paul de Clerk, '"Lex orandi–Lex credendi". Sens origenel et avatars historique d'un adage equivoque,' *Questions liturgiques* 59 (1978), 193–212.

[52] In spite of· recent popular attempts to argue the contrary, 'orthodoxy' means 'right belief.' It does not come from *orthodoxologia*, 'right worship' or 'right glory,' but from *orthodoxeo*. See G. W. H. Lampe, *A Patristic Greek Lexicon* (Oxford: Clarendon Press, 1965), 971. It is thus a doctrinal, not a liturgical-doxological word.

[53] *Christian Liturgy I. Theology* (Kansas City: Sheed & Ward, 1988), 97.

# CAN WE AVOID RELATIVISM IN WORSHIP? LITURGICAL NORMS IN THE LIGHT OF CONTEMPORARY LITURGICAL SCHOLARSHIP

In its call for contemporary liturgical reform and renewal the Second Vatican Council's *Constitution on the Sacred Liturgy* distinguished clearly between what the Council Fathers saw as "unchanging" and "divinely instituted," and, therefore, "irreformable" in liturgy, and what was changeable and, hence, reformable.[1] Recent studies of the origins of Christian worship,[2] however, make it increasingly difficult to argue in favor of much of anything that might, in fact, be considered "normative" from the church's "classic" tradition for liturgy today. That is, contemporary scholarship appears to be demonstrating that it is, precisely, those so-called "unchanging" and "divinely instituted" elements themselves that are subject to critique and revision. Similarly, contemporary challenges to historic worship patterns in the United States, e.g., the increasing phenomenon of megachurches, the church-growth movement, the development of "seeker services," have also led increasingly to the notion across ecclesial lines that the church's historic and traditional liturgy is merely but "one" of several options for "worship" today and can be easily dispensed with for "pastoral reasons." That is, in spite of the growing contemporary ecumenical convergence in liturgy (e.g., *Baptism, Eucharist, and Ministry* [Geneva: World Council of Churhes, 1982]), it is becoming quite difficult to maintain that there is much of anything which is constant and unchanging in the liturgical traditions of the churches of the early Christian period. What we see, instead, seems to be the great tradition in constant flux and development with no single discernable common pattern, ritual contents, or theological interpretation. Therefore, when someone like Geoffrey Wainwright states that "rather than present *experience* being allowed to hold sway over the inherited tradition," we should let "the inherited *tradition* shape and govern present experience,"[3] I want to ask immediately, "*which* inherited tradition and from what *church* in that 'tradition?'"

Where, then, does that leave us? Is liturgy today absolutely "relative" and so to be based on the subjective criteria of personal (or ecclesial) taste, preference, or choice? Or can a case still be made for some kind of "normativity" based on the inherited traditions? In other words, can we avoid "liturgical relativism" and still take seriously the growing scholarly critique of ancient liturgical traditions, the assumptions that have been made for liturgical reform based upon earlier readings of those traditions, and the challenges offered to historic liturgy today? These questions are especially relevant not for liturgical history or ritual studies but for the construction of contemporary liturgical theology. The remainder of this essay will attempt to provide, at most, a preliminary answer.

## I. Some Recent Attempts at Articulating Liturgical Theology

In recent years, three notable approaches to the issue of liturgical theology have been suggested by Gordon Lathrop, James White, and Paul Bradshaw. In their individual ways each has tried to take account of the immense variety existing both historically and today in Christian liturgy and each has tried to articulate possible avenues in which the contemporary discussion might proceed further. Although none of these use the terminology of "model" in their work, it is precisely different models for conceptualizing liturgical theology that they attempt to provide. Since any model itself is necessarily limited in its focus to particular features which always means the suppression of other features that don't fit the model, none of these three should be taken in any kind of comprehensive way as the *only* way to envision liturgical theology. Some models in liturgical theology, for example, will be more "explanatory" or "descriptive" in nature and others more "exploratory" or "prescriptive" in nature. But it is precisely because any given model does not present the "whole picture" of a particular phenomenon that a model can become a useful tool in illuminating significant aspects of the entire, in this case, liturgical theological process, aspects that another model might necessarily suppress. Hence, like symbols themselves, models are most useful because they give rise to thought and invite further reflection.[4] In what follows here, the models for the study of liturgical theology suggested by Lathrop, White, and Bradshaw are summarized briefly and, in the next section, a critique of all three and my own further suggestions, based on the kind of thought and reflection that these models invite, are offered as a few observations oriented toward ongoing discussion.

## A. Gordon Lathrop and the Ordo of Christian Worship

In two recent and highly influential books, *Holy Things: A Liturgical Theology*[5] and *What Are the Essentials of Christian Worship?*,[6] Gordon Lathrop has suggested that what is essential, and therefore, central and "normative," for Christian worship is a liturgical *"ordo"* or overall "pattern" for the scheduled ritual of Christian worship which is both ecumenical and transcultural. This *"ordo,"* in part, is based on the post-resurrection appearances of Jesus in the New Testament (especially the Emmaus account in Luke 24), the description of baptismal and Sunday worship provided by Justin Martyr in his *First Apology*, as well as traditional confessional documents and current ecumenical convergence in liturgical practice and interpretation within a variety of churches. According to Lathrop, this *"ordo,"* expressing a juxtaposition between various elements, such as word/table, Sunday/week, teaching/bath, praise/intercession, year/Pascha, old/new, reflects not only the pattern of how God actually relates to humanity but is easily discernable as the very common "core" of Christian worship throughout the ages.[7] "So these are the essentials of Christian worship," he writes:

A community *gathers in prayer* around the scriptures *read* and *proclaimed*. This community of the word then tastes the meaning of that word by keeping the meal of Christ, *giving thanks* over bread and cup and *eating* and *drinking*. It is this word-table community, the body of Christ, which gathers other people to its number, continually *teaching* both itself and these newcomers the mercy and mystery of God and *washing* them in the name of that God. All of these essential things urge the community toward the world—toward prayer for the world, sharing with the hungry of the world, caring for the world, giving witness to the world . . . Around these central things, which will be most evident in Sunday and festival worship, other gatherings of Christians may also take place.[8]

Other elements of the liturgical assembly, according to Lathrop, flow from this central core as well. He continues:

The very centrality of bath, word, and table, and the very reasons for their centrality . . . do begin to give us some characteristics of the mode of our celebration. These characteristics . . . are corollaries which ought not be easily ignored. A list of such characteristics should include *ritual focus*, a *music which serves*, the importance of *Sunday* and other festivals, a *participating community, many ministries*, and a *recognized presider* who is in communion with the churches.[9]

Lathrop's *ordo* has certainly contributed to the overall perspective of the recent Evangelical Lutheran Church in America statement on sacramental practices, *The Use of the Means of Grace*.[10] Even more, it has had ecumenical implications for how various churches might think in common about the centrality of baptism, word, and Eucharist in their liturgical assemblies[11] and for questions related even to liturgical inculturation and adaptation in diverse contexts as well.[12]

However one might assess Lathrop's overall model for articulating a liturgical theology, he has provided a great service to the ecumenical church in providing a model, vision, and a language by which the immense variety of Christian worship past and present might be evaluated along theological lines. Even within those churches who have most directly inherited such an *ordo* it still serves for "renewed religious intensity and renewed religious critique"[13] among them. Hence, for those who are not ready or able to abandon the search for norms which might govern Christian worship, Lathrop's suggestion of an *ordo* provides a clear, historically and ecumenically sensitive model for how some kind of liturgical normativity might still be advocated today. For Lathrop, clearly all is not relative in Christian worship. Some "holy things" are absolutely essential and central. And those on the periphery are oriented toward the center.

## B. James White and the Principal of "Survival"

If Lathrop's influential work has pointed decidedly toward the normativy of a classic *ordo* for Christian worship which is both transcultural and universally ecumenical, a very brief critique of liturgical theology by James F. White, "How Do We Know It Is Us?"[14] offers a strong rationale for a much more relativist model in approaching the topic. While expressing admiration for Lathrop's attempt as achieving "the finest available description of classical Christian worship,"[15] White asks:

> Do we want to say that what happens in most churches in the United States on a Sunday morning is 'baby worship,' since it does not match some ecumenical or historical standard? Do we want to say that a preaching service each week and Thirteenth Sabbath Lord's Supper (as among Seventh Day Adventists) is not authentic Christian worship? Do we disqualify those for whom the major events in the liturgical year are Children's Sunday, Homecoming, Revival, and Rally Day (none of which, as yet, has been commercialized)? . . . We face a basic problem in ignoring the worship of most North American Christians . . . Any scheme that totally ignores the worship life of about sixty percent of American Christianity is highly questionable. To imply that the *ordo* of Christian worship is missed by all those for whom the Eucharist is an occasional service, for whom the pragmatic Christian

year makes more sense than the traditional Christian year, is indeed risky business.[16]

In his own attempt to provide a model for doing liturgical theology which respects a more objective and empirical approach, White offers several criteria that might be used to assist in determining what it is that constitutes or elucidates "authentic" Christian worship. The first of these criteria, and indeed the primary and governing criterion for White, is that of "survival." That is, "if a form of worship survives more than the original generation, it must have some validity as a means of humans relating to God." Hence, for him "the consequence is that we need to spend much more time in *describing* rather than *prescribing*."[17]

Three other "universal" and "constant" criteria follow for White on this first one. The second is that an "essential of authentic Christian worship is *coming together in Christ's name.*"[18] That is, the assembly or gathering of the *ecclesia* itself to *do* liturgy is primary and what is actually *done* by those assemblies in a variety of different forms and orders is secondary. The third criteria of such "authentic" liturgy is "*expectation of encounter with the divine*" in whatever form(s) of worship a particular liturgical assembly may embrace. And, the fourth and final criteria suggested by him is that "authentic Christian worship can take *an enormous variety of forms*, some of which we have experienced in the past and many more that we may discover in the future."[19]

By means of these four criteria, White seeks to do justice not only to the observable existence of the immense variety and denominational richness and diversity of liturgical practices within (especially North American) Christianity today, but to other forms and patterns (mega-churches, seeker-services, and the like) increasingly being developed and which may, indeed, survive in the coming years. Since in this model almost any surviving form of public worship in any Christian tradition is quite easily evaluated as constituting "authentic" Christian worship, *what* any Christian community actually *does* in its public worship is really quite relative to its own "gathering" in "expectation" of an encounter with the divine. Hence, for White, there are really no universal liturgical "norms," no universal *ordo*, which may be abstracted or deduced which *prescribe* what it is that *the* church *should* do as normative and regular practice in its liturgical assemblies (even the proclamation of the word or celebration of *any* sacrament, if the Quaker tradition is also included as part of the ecumenical mix), other than, perhaps, particular tradition-based norms in and for *specific churches* themselves. Apart from these criteria, all is relative since all are equally "authentic."

## C. Paul Bradshaw and Difficulties in Liturgical Theology

Paul Bradshaw's recent essay, "Difficulties in Doing Liturgical Theology,"[20] raises issues somewhat similar to those in White's approach. First, Bradshaw critiques the all too common assumption in various liturgical theologies that there is such a thing as *the* liturgy of *the* church, a divinely instituted *"sacred liturgy,"* an assumption which treats the role of historical research into the actual state of liturgical development as largely irrelevant to the faith-based conviction that there is a fundamental continuity of the church's liturgy through the ages. Such a liturgical fundamentalist approach is based on a rather romantic vision of what has been assumed to be *the* liturgical practice of *the* early church. And the result of this vision is that it has fostered a mentality in approaches to liturgical theology which tend either to ignore practices that obscure this romantic vision or seek to "restore" the "true pattern" by writing off "Reformation developments as being the death of the authentic Christian liturgy . . . seen essentially as the work of fallible humans in contrast to the divine character attributed to the shaping of . . . worship."[21] He writes:

> [N]ot only is the fundamental continuity of liturgical practice assumed without historical research, but historical research itself does not give us grounds for concluding that there is any fundamental continuity, except in the very broadest of terms. The 'deep structures' running through liturgy are very few indeed if we apply the test of universal observance to them. There are very few things that Christians have consistently done in worship at all times and in all places.[22]

Second, Bradshaw looks critically at the use of the Latin formula *lex orandi, lex credendi* in liturgical theology in its original and classic sense of the relationship between liturgy and *doctrine*. As such, Bradshaw reminds the reader that Prosper of Aquitaine's use of *legem credendi lex statuat supplicandi* in the context of the semi-Pelagian controversy, was one argument among several about the need for divine grace in human salvation. Nor was it even his basic argument in this context, since, for Prosper himself, the actual intercessory prayer *for* grace that he cites is but an added illustration of the doctrinal authority of the "Apostolic See" in the first place. Hence, the principle of *lex orandi* ought not be invoked as a kind of liturgical "proof text." He notes, similarly, that the application of *lex orandi* has often been "highly selective," with "certain features of liturgical practice . . . highlighted as authentic, while others are disregarded as aberrations from the norm."[23] As examples of this selective approach, he points to the fact that although modern liturgical reform has given a theological priority to the early Christian period in general, it has not always regarded several equally evidenced liturgical practices or intepretations as having equal weight for the renewal of the church's worship today (e.g., episcopal elections by the people, and the abandonment of other baptismal rites and images in favor of the "paschal mystery" priority of Romans 6). Although the claim is often made in such contexts that the liturgy itself is the "source" for Christian theology, doctrine, and/or renewal, the fact of the matter is that doctrine itself tends not only to shape liturgy but how people actually "read" liturgical texts and practice. In his words, *lex orandi, lex credendi* is "always a two-way street."[24]

Third, Bradshaw draws upon Jewish liturgiologist Lawrence Hoffman's helpful categories of ritual or liturgical meaning: *private*, what meaning individuals give to rites; *official*, the interpretations of experts; *public*, the shared meaning about certain rites in spite of their "official" interpretations; and *normative*, how people see the world and themselves as a result of celebrating a rite. To these Bradshaw not only calls for a distinction to be made further between the intentions for meaning held by the original compilers of a rite and the different meanings attached to the same rite by future generations (e.g, the *Book of Common Prayer*), but he notes that the concern of liturgical theologians has almost always been with "official" meanings, "even though it is the other meanings that may very well be the real forces that motivate people to engage in the ritual."[25]

Fourth, as an illustration of these various levels of meaning engendered by liturgy, Bradshaw offers a strong critique of Aidan Kavanagh's popular methodological distinction between *theologia prima*, based on the liturgical assembly's direct liturgical experience, and *theologia secunda*, arising from secondary theological reflection upon that experience.[26] "Even if we were to grant the premise . . . that it is possible to distinguish primary theology from secondary reflection, the problem is not thereby resolved." He continues:

> Aidan Kavanagh's writings have introduced his readers to the figure of 'Mrs. Murphy,' who represents the ordinary person in the pew and who is therefore understood to be the authentic exponent of 'primary theology.' . . . [But], it is precisely the expressions of natural piety of the putative Mrs. Murphy and countless other churchgoers—devotions to the sacred heart of Jesus, for example, or sentimental nineteenth-century hymns—that are usually denigrated by the professional liturgical theologian and swept away by the liturgical reformer on the grounds that they fail to conform to the inherent spirit of the liturgy! Where is the value attached to *theologia prima* here?[27]

Therefore, although there is no question but that continual participation in the liturgical experience is formative of faith and life, the liturgy that is actually experienced in Christian assemblies has itself also been shaped and conditioned by several factors (doctrinal, canonical, and catechetical, all three the products of *theologia secunda* in Kavanagh's categories). And, for that matter, Mrs. Murphy and others who regularly participate in liturgical celebrations have likewise been "formed" by similar ecclesial-specific doctrinal, canonical, catechetical and other sources already and may certainly attach various "private" and "public" meanings to the rites in which and on account of which they participate. The liturgical theologian needs to pay attention to all possible meanings in interpreting a "rite."

If, finally, like White, Bradshaw also can say that "there is a much too ready tendency to move from *description* to *prescription*" in liturgical theology,[28] his overall model appears somewhat less "relativist" than does White's. Rather, Bradshaw's suggestion is for liturgical theology:

> ... to abandon its tendency to rest upon bad history or no history at all, and instead to take the fruits of historical research much more seriously indeed ... And it needs to acknowledge that liturgy is as much a human artifact as a divine creation and that belief in the one God does not demand that there be only one way of worship or one theology.[29]

Such a statement, however, is not a call to abandon altogether the search for liturgical "norms" or for the very broad "deep structures" that might run through the history of Christian worship. Instead, Bradshaw reminds us that the task is actually more complex, messier, and much more difficult than has often been assumed. Nevertheless, while in his opinion Lathrop's more "minimalist" attempt to determine an *ordo* for Christian worship "may be a little too neat and tidy," it *does* offer, he says, "a promising avenue for future exploration."[30]

## II. The Search for Normativity and Authenticity in Christian Worship Today

All three of these liturgical scholars make significant contributions not only to the question of liturgical theology but to whether or not there are, in fact, any norms whatsoever to be deduced which might establish, govern, and critique the celebration of Christian worship in the various churches today. Before addressing this latter question directly in my conclusion, I wish in what follows to provide an assessment of each of these models.

### A. Gordon Lathrop and the Ordo for Christian Worship

Along with the fact that Lathrop's suggestion of an *ordo* may be "a little oversystematised to fit the full facts of history,"[31] it must be stated that there is probably no such thing as a pure *ordo* existing anywhere in some idealized form apart from its very concrete, cultural, ecclesial, and linguistic ritual expressions.[32] That is, the deducing of an *ordo*, in large part, is a logical construct, an abstraction made on the basis of very minimal descriptions of the patterns of Christian liturgy in the early period. Even Justin Martyr in his *First Apology*, it must be noted, is not necessarily giving us an *ordo* for Christian liturgy for all times and all places but a brief outline for the Roman Emperor, Antoninus Pius, of what, perhaps, *one* Christian community at Rome was doing in its baptismal and Sunday worship in the middle of the second century.[33] To abstract some kind of transcultural, timeless, and ecumenical *ordo* for Christian liturgy from such brief descriptions, in which all the precise details the historian would actually need or want are lacking, may indeed be rather risky business if the overall attempt is to find a normative pattern for what the church *should* do in its liturgical assemblies as a result.

Nevertheless, if only in "the very broadest of terms," the mere fact that this overall *pattern* for Christian worship, to use White's primary criterion, obviously "survives" and is quite easily discernable throughout the distinct rites of the first Christian millennium and beyond, *does* grant a certain legitimacy to Lathrop's attempt. That is, even if we do not know from the earliest period what exactly constituted Christian liturgy in exact detail, the fact remains that all our evidence from, at least, Justin Martyr on through the Reformation indicates the existence of some kind of "baptismal" rite of incorporation, the existence of the Christian churches assembling, their coming *"together in Christ's name,"* on Sundays and other feasts to hear the word and share in some form of eucharistic meal with its great *eucharistia*, the existence of patterns for daily prayer (whether private or communal), some form of "order," and some form of ministry to the poor. All of this points, indeed, to some kind of universal pattern or *"ordo"* of worship that the diverse churches of Christian antiquity *did* see as constituting a type of universal norm which determined "authentic" Christian worship and transcended local diversity and variety. The diversity we encounter in the churches of the first few centuries, then, is, precisely, a diversity in *how* baptism and its various encompassing rites are celebrated, *how* Sunday and festival observance is structured (e.g., whether Pascha is on a calendrical date or a Sunday), *how* the meal is celebrated and its gifts gathered and distributed, *how* the meal prayers are to be prayed and what their various structural components were, and *how* the various ministries of *episkope* and *diakonia* might be ordered. But no one, to my knowledge, actually questioned the very existence, structure, and contents of Christian worship as having to do with these "holy things." These, it seems, were givens and are constitutive parts of the inherited Tradition, which may indeed serve to "shape and govern present experience." To that end, Lathrop's model of the *ordo* remains not only one of "the finest available description[s] of classical Christian worship," but commends itself as a most fruitful model in the contemporary search for some kind of ecumenical-liturgical "norm."

## B. James White and the Criterion of "Survival"

Both White and Bradshaw lament the fact that various attempts to write liturgical theologies have tended to be more *prescriptive* than *descriptive*, but only White has drawn from this the conclusion that "we need to spend much more time in *describing* rather than *prescribing*" in the actual construction of liturgical theology today.[34] While granting this need as an absolutely crucial step in the study of *any* liturgy past or present, I wonder whether there isn't a tendency here to equate two distinct methodologies. That is, *descriptive* analyses of any phenomenon are not necessarily the *primary* task of the *theologian*, who may well be required to make *prescriptive* statements as well for the sake of the life of the church here and now as it seeks to appropriate, even selectively, various elements from that tradition in its own practice and interpretation today. Robert Taft has written of these methodological distinctions, saying that:

> As one who is basically an historian in method, my point of departure is usually the *history* of the tradition. This step precedes *theology* which is a reflection on the tradition in its intersection with contemporary experience.

*Pastoral practice* should be in continuity with this tradition, and both mirror and shape our reflection on it.[35]

If, therefore, "history can only help us decide what the essentials of [a] tradition are, and the parameters of its adaptation,"[36] then *description* either of an historic or contemporary rite in the construction of a liturgical theology can only be a first, albeit absolutely crucial and indispensable, step in the process.

For that matter, however, White himself actually goes beyond a mere descriptive methodology. Apart from his criterion that "authentic Christian worship can take *an enormous variety of forms,*" his other three criteria are, precisely and already, *theological* criteria applied to the phenomenon of worship in general, and, with the exception of "in Christ's name" in the "gathering" criterion, need not apply to *Christian* worship alone. One must ask, in fact, if beyond the need for objective and empirical description, these criteria alone actually help us much in arriving at precise theological interpretations of worship. Those churches which approach the question of liturgical theology on the additional basis of canon, creed, and confession in some kind of continuity with the churches of the first millennium, I should think, would find these criteria somewhat lacking in their applicability. Within Roman Catholicism, for example, several popular devotions might certainly fit the criterion of *surviving* "as a means of humans relating to God," a gathering "in Christ's name" to perform an act of worship, and, similarly, those who participate in them might surely expect some kind of "divine encounter" with God. But even if recognized as legitimate and authentic "forms" of Christian worship, are such devotional practices to be viewed by Roman Catholics, then, as being on par with the Sunday Eucharist? That is, although Mrs. Murphy and her companions might see some of these devotions as being at the very center of their Catholic spirituality, are they, in fact, *at* the center of Catholic spirituality and life, or, are they actually on the periphery? Or, with regard to several Protestant traditions, especially those with clear historic and/or confessional norms or preferences regarding the Sunday Eucharist, are the surviving patterns of Sunday Services of the Word alone to be accepted as "authentic" representations of those traditions or are there criteria by which a liturgical theologian might conclude that they are, in fact, departures from a traditional "norm?" While surely no one wants "to say that what happens in most churches in the United States on a Sunday morning is 'baby worship,'" it would seem that the burden of proof actually falls *not* on those churches who defend an inherited *ordo* of some sort but on those who, for whatever reason, have chosen to separate themselves from that "ecumenical or historical standard."

Of course, several things have "survived" which the historian and social scientist will need and want to study and describe, but survival itself does not necessarily provide the only data upon which the liturgical theologian constructs a theology. Other criteria, such as the actual historical development of certain forms, the reasons for their particular development, and their relationship with other existing forms, must also play a role in the theological process. But the liturgical theologian also has the obligation to draw theological conclusions from such descriptions about whether or not the developed practice and interpretation is consistent with or a departure from the norm. History by itself may not be normative here, but it is certainly instructive for those who seek to reform contemporary liturgical practice in a manner and spirit consistent with what is known of the pristine shape and history of any given rite.[37] Indeed, not to allow such a theological evaluation in service to the church makes any liturgical reform or renewal next to impossible.

The value of White's criteria, then, are that they assist us in seeking to pay attention to the diverse experiences of what constitute Christian worship today, especially within a North American context. As a way to account for the manifold ways of worship that do and may come to exist in several Christian traditions, White has done us a great service in reminding us that liturgical theologies have often been, at best, "minority reports," reflecting but one Christian liturgical tradition. What White's contribution to this question actually does is to remind us of the great difficulties in constructing *any* comprehensive liturgical theology in which Eastern Orthodox Christians, Roman Catholics, Lutherans, Anglicans, Reformed, and Protestants, including even Seventh-Day Adventists and Quakers, might see themselves represented and reflected. When faced with such a daunting task, one can probably do no more than develop the sorts of non-specific and general criteria that his model suggests.

The question must be asked, however, if that is the task of liturgical *theology* and, if so, whether the construction of such a comprehensive liturgical theology not only *can* but whether it even *should* be attempted. If, in White's own words, "large segments of North American Christianity have no interest in ecumenism and are doing quite well without us,"[38] this might *not* mean that the rest of us can afford to ignore their worship practices in our own theological reflection upon liturgy. But it also does not mean that the task of constructing an *ecumenical* liturgical theology for those historic churches, who certainly see themselves both in doctrinal and liturgical continuity with the church of the first millennium, should also not continue to be attempted. To that end, some kind of ecumenical *ordo* does seem to suggest itself as a common inheritance. That is, if, on the level of "reception," there is still no ecumenical consensus on several issues it remains the case that this lack of consensus is not about the existence of a liturgical *ordo* itself but comes about precisely because there may be legitimately different ways in which the churches seek to follow and be guided by that inherited "*ordo*" in the first place. The ecumenical liturgical theologian, therefore, may well conclude "that the *ordo* of Christian worship *is* missed by all those for whom the Eucharist is an occasional service." But this does not mean that those who have kept (or restored) the *ordo* cannot learn volumes about Christian worship and life from these other traditions, just as those traditions can and *should* be challenged by such traditional churches to embrace the *ordo* in their own attempts at renewal.

Nevertheless, what is at stake here for the ecumenical liturgical theologian is not simply the need for the recognition of greater liturgical diversity and heterogeneity even among those who accept the classic "*ordo*," but a particular theological understanding of God and how God acts incarnationally and *sacramentally* in history and the church. The ecumenical liturgical theologian can no more view that foundational understanding of how God is believed to act as "one" option among several than s/he can fly in the face of canon, creed, and confession without thereby denying his/her own identity and separating him/herself from the historic orthodox Christian faith. Such a basic theological perspective about the very nature of God's encounter with humanity can certainly *not* be abandoned in the name of a more inclusive or heterogenous approach. In such a context, *prescriptive* statements have always been and will continue to be necessary, even if, in the process of constructing a theology they might certainly often benefit from more comprehensive understandings of history. "How do we know it is us?" asks White. "We know it is us," the *ecumenical* liturgical theologian might respond, "because the liturgy we celebrate bears the trinitarian-christological orthodoxy of the historic Christian tradition and proclaims and expresses that understanding of God who acts by means of word *and* sacrament in our Sunday and festal assemblies."

## C . Paul Bradshaw and Difficulties in Liturgical Theology

It would be hard to disagree with Bradshaw's challenge that liturgical theology needs to pay greater attention to the actual contributions of historical research on the origins and evolution of Christian worship and, thus, to avoid either a kind of "liturgical fundamentalism" or sweeping and romantic generalizations about historical development. Similarly, Bradshaw's critique of the use of *lex orandi, lex credendi*, his call to attend to what Hoffman has identified as several diverse possible "meanings" (official, private, public, and normative) in any liturgical rite, and his critical challenge to the use of the category of "*theologia prima*" in the construction of liturgical theology are all, in my opinion, right on target and important contributions that need to be taken seriously.

If, however, neither his critique of *lex orandi, lex credendi* nor of "*theologia prima*" needs further comment, the difficulties come in attempting to envision what a contemporary liturgical reform and theology would look like: (1) if the actual contributions to historical research were to be taken seriously; and (2) how it is, especially in other historical contexts, that one arrives at different levels of meaning and what their implications for liturgical theology may actually be. Both of these call for additional exploration here.

If contemporary liturgical reform and theology were to take more seriously the contributions of historical research on the origins of Christian worship and its sources, I suspect that the worship books of several Christian traditions today would reflect a much greater diversity in form, contents, and style than what actually appears. In particular, I would imagine that the anaphora of the so-called *Apostolic Tradition*, would not have suggested itself as the "model" anaphora finding itself incorporated and adapted in some form into almost every modern worship book across ecclesial lines. Nor would the Syro-Byzantine anaphoral shape known to us from the Orthodox East necessarily have been accepted as *the* normative pattern for constructing all other modern eucharistic prayers. Instead, we would have a variety of diverse anaphoral patterns in our books, some bi-partite, some tri-partite, some which incorporated an institution narrative, others which did not, some which incorporated the *Sanctus*, others which concluded with the *Sanctus*, some which reflected a more Alexandrian model of prayer and others certainly reflecting the Syro-Byzantine shape. I would imagine that together with Easter baptism, interpreted along the lines of Romans 6, other feasts in the liturgical year, such as Epiphany or the celebration of Jesus' baptism on the Sunday after the Epiphany, would have been accorded equal weight as suitable times to conclude an adult catechumenal process and that our baptismal theologies themselves would attend more closely to other biblical and traditional images. I would imagine further that a variety of baptismal rites would co-exist today, that a recovery of the catechumenal process leading to adult baptism would not have been such a slavish imitation of the so-called *Apostolic Tradition*, that the Roman rite would have merely "restored" confirmation to its immediate and integral postbaptismal location with presbyteral confirmation more widely employed, that modern versions of the liturgy of the hours would be less monastic and less centered in psalmody, that easier recognition of the various ministries of oversight, leadership, and service and differing rites of ordination as they exist in the various churches would have been made in the light of the unclear history of episcopal and apostolic succession in the first few centuries, that bishops themselves would be elected by the people, that Ignatius of Antioch's preference for the monarchical episcopacy would be more often juxtaposed to Jerome's description of Alexandrian practice some three centuries later, and, among probably several other changes, that the liturgical year would have *ended* with Advent rather than beginning with Advent.[39]

Some kind of *ordo*, however, would still be discernable. The contemporary church would *still* be gathering in Christ's name at various intervals, on Sundays and feasts, to hear the word, celebrate the meal with its great thanksgiving prayer, and be sent forth into the world to be the body of Christ it receives and is. Still there would be ordered ministries. Still the church would be praying and singing in its daily prayer, and seeking to incorporate others into its life through catechumenal processes. How this was all done might be more diverse, but the "core" would still be done.

But at the same time, the liturgical theologian cannot afford the luxury of pretending that s/he lives in the ante-Nicene period or that the first few centuries are any more of a "Golden Age" than any other age or period. Some of the diverse practices we encounter in early liturgical history die out, in fact, precisely because they did not meet the criterion of the developing "orthodoxy" of a later period. The classic Christian doxology, "Glory *to* the Father, *through* the Son, *in* the Holy Spirit," for example, became, against Arianism and semi-Arianism, the orthodox form of "Glory *to* the Father, and *to* the Son, and *to* the Holy Spirit" for good trinitarian reasons, even if the loss of Christ's role as active mediator may have been downplayed in the process. Epiphany baptism itself may have been suspect and so challenged in the name of orthodoxy because of possible adoptionist or Arian christological overtones, a reason also occasionally given for the establishment of the December 25 feast of Christmas in some places in the East. Do not postbaptismal rites which emphasize the gift of the Holy Spirit in baptism or explicit epicleses of the Holy Spirit in the anaphora develop, in part at least, because of doctrinal concerns for the Spirit's divinity in the context of the Council of Constantinople and its aftermath? Do not written anaphoras themselves come to express this concern for orthodoxy in a context in which the orthodoxy of extemporaneous prayer could no longer be assumed? Does not the catechumenate itself, as we know it from the great fourth- and fifth-century mystagogues, develop from some very real pastoral reasons as the church sought to incorporate converts with some integrity and authenticity in a changed socio-political-economic context? Does not the very shape of the Syro-Byzantine anaphora come to function as the doxological profession of orthodox trinitarian faith long before there was an actual creed recited in the eucharistic liturgy? And, for that matter, does not the fact that all the churches of the ancient world came to embrace the historic episcopacy as a "sign" of communion with each other and of orthodox continuity with the apostolic faith against Gnosticism and other challenges to the church's identity, at least serve as challenge to the ordering of ministries in the church today, especially among those who have chosen to separate themselves from this historic office?

In spite of the fact that liturgical theologians *need* to pay attention to what can be known of the whole sweep of liturgical history, and in spite of the fact that the results of solid historical research do challenge several "selections" made for liturgical renewal today, the liturgical theologian also cannot pretend that history did not develop the way it did and that something called "orthodoxy" with its liturgical implications never happened.

Hoffman's categories of several meanings, embraced by Bradshaw, is an important criterion to which liturgical theologians need to pay attention. But how? Today it might be relatively easy to determine what different levels of private, public, or normative meanings are actually held by people through the use of surveys, questionnaires, and other instruments. The task becomes quite difficult, however, in trying to get at this in the liturgies of the past. The examples of Augustine being moved by Ambrosian chant outside of the cathedral in Milan, Egeria's description of the pilgrims' weeping during the reading of the Passion at the Sunday resurrection vigil in fourth-century Jerusalem, or John Wesley's heart being "strangely warmed" upon hearing Luther's commentary on Romans read in a liturgical context might be historical examples of differences in meaning accorded to liturgical acts. We might assume further that a largely non-communicating attendance at the eucharistic liturgy from the late-fourth century on, including the development of various allegorical liturgical commentaries (e.g., the Western *expositiones missae*), would also reveal multiple meanings accorded to the Eucharist and its celebration. And, we might get a strong sense of a difference in meaning accorded to confirmation in the medieval west through the abundance of legislation about its official importance when it appears that no one, neither parish priest nor faithful, were taking it all that seriously. But while we can assume some things, we do not know exactly *what* meanings were actually held or accorded such liturgical celebrations, whether private, public, or normative, by these people. If then, liturgical theologians have tended to base their theologies on official meanings alone it is, in part, because often it is only the official meaning that is clearly available and, in the absence of video recordings and other modern ways of assessing meaning in other historical periods, official liturgical texts have been the primary source of information.

At the same time, the modern celebration of confirmation in the Roman Rite or what some Protestant traditions refer to as "Affirmation of Baptism" might be one of the best examples where Hoffman's approach is most fruitful. The "official" meaning of confirmation or affirmation of baptism is clear. For those baptized in infancy it is either, as confirmation, the initiatory *seal* of the Holy Spirit or, as in affirmation, the affirmation of what is believed to have been given as a gift already in baptism. But on the private, public, and normative levels a host of other meanings may be and are held: entrance into adulthood; mature faith commitment and decision; graduation from a religious education program; assumption of adult responsibilities in church and society; a time for family reunions; reception of gifts; and, undoubtedly several others. The official meaning might play a quite minimal role in all of this even in terms of motivation for participating in such a rite.

Knowing these several meanings accorded to a liturgical rite, of course, is important for the construction of liturgical theology. But, what, exactly, is the liturgical theologian to do with this knowledge other than merely *describe* these various meanings? Even if confirmation and affirmation rites themselves might be able to bear all of these meanings in some kind of harmless synthesis in the life of the church, what happens in other rites when there is serious dissonance between official and other meanings? In such cases it would seem that the liturgical *theologian* cannot be content with mere *description* but would want to accord still some kind of "normativity" to the "official" meanings of the rites and the continual need for ongoing catechesis in those meanings. Indeed, if on some levels of meaning, Advent is about Christmas shopping, infant baptism about avoiding Limbo, adult baptism about making Pelagian choices, the Mass about manipulating a wrathful and vindictive God or "buying" it on behalf of departed loved ones, devotion to Mary about her holding back her son's destructive arm before he crushes the world, or various ritual acts (e.g., rites of reception into full communion and the Good Friday Reproaches) interpreted as ecclesial triumphalism or religious bigotry, then there is no other recourse for the liturgical theologian but to the "official" theological and doctrinal meanings themselves. Knowing and describing the various meanings even of rites which have "survived" gets one little further than laying out the data. And, unless liturgical theologians are to be nothing other than chroniclers of history, or sociological and/or anthropological "observers," there must be some room for theological *prescription* as well. If not, the study of liturgy itself might just as well be moved out of theology departments altogether and into those of history, anthropology, sociology, and/or psychology, and even the very question of liturgical "reform" ultimately becomes moot.

## III. Conclusion

So, where, then, does all of this leave us, indeed? At several places throughout this essay I have attempted to argue that, no, not all is relative in terms of what the church does in liturgical celebrations and, yes, there still is a case to be made for some kind of "normativity" based on the inherited traditions, at the very least, a case based on the kind of ecumenical and transcultural *ordo* that Lathrop suggests. In such an *ordo*, centered in Sunday, assembly, baptism, word, meal, year, and some kind of ministerial ordering, together with the orthodox doctrinal heritage of the church of the first millennium, there should be plenty of room for a diversity of practices and interpretations, past and present, in which the gifts of several differing Christian churches might find a welcome place. Along with the helpful models of White and Bradshaw, certainly the results of critical historical research on Christian origins and sources and the actually existing wide variety of liturgical practices today can serve as well to express further the great and often neglected riches of the wider Christian tradition. No, there does not need to be only *one* homogenous liturgical practice nor one theological interpretation of that practice, nor one model for how liturgical theologians go about their craft. Of course not! But the elements of what constitutes the ecumenical *ordo* do seem to be a given and are, thus, non-negotiable, an *ordo* which still serves to "renewed religious intensity and renewed religious critique" not only for those churches who have separated themselves from an "*ordo*" but perhaps especially for those who claim continuity with the catholic doctrinal and liturgical tradition.

What is at stake in this question of liturgical "relativism" or "normativity," however, is not simply *how* one does worship, how one attends to the diverse patterns of worship existing today, or even how liturgical theologians *think* about worship, whether descriptively or prescriptively. What appears to be at stake is the very identity and liturgical self-expression of classic orthodox Christianity itself. Goeffrey Wainwright has written that: "Without the heartbeat of the sacraments at its center, a church will lack confidence about the Gospel message and about its own ability to proclaim that message in evangelism, to live it out in its own internal fellowship, and to embody it in service to the needy."[40] And, elsewhere he writes that: "[a] deeper replunging into its own tradition will . . . be necessary if the church is to survive in recognizable form, particularly in our western culture."[41] If, thanks to historical scholarship, such "deeper replunging into its own tradition" is a much more complex endeavor than it has ever been, thanks to that same scholarship, the treasures to be uncovered there for Christianity and its worship life are richer than we may have so far imagined. But the goal in all this, of course, is not simply survival but faithfulness, fidelity to the God who acts and works for human salvation through sacraments, people, and communities and to the sacramental worldview that continues to define and characterize classic Christianity. No, all is not merely "relative" in questions of liturgical practice and theology today. The articulation of what is to be "normative," however, is a much more difficult task than the

Fathers of Vatican II or other contemporary liturgical reformers have assumed it to be.

## Notes

[1] *Constitution on the Sacred Liturgy*, 21.

[2] See especially P. Bradshaw, *The Search for the Origins of Christian Worship*, 2nd edn. (New York/London: Oxford, 2002).

[3] G. Wainwright, "Divided by a Common Language," in idem, *Worship with One Accord: Where Liturgy & Ecumenism Embrace* (New York/Oxford: Oxford University Press, 1997), 156 [emphasis added].

[4] The first chapter of A. Dulles, *Models of the Church* (Garden City: Doubleday, 1974) still provides an excellent description of the use of models in theology.

[5] G. Lathrop, *Holy Things: A Liturgical Theology* (Minneapolis: Fortress Press, 1993).

[6] G. Lathrop, *What Are The Essentials of Christian Worship?* (Minneapolis: Augsburg Fortress, 1994).

[7] Lathrop, *Holy Things*, 33–83.

[8] Lathrop, *What Are The Essentials of Christian Worship?*, 22.

[9] Ibid., 23.

[10] Evangelical Lutheran Church in America, *The Use of the Means of Grace: A Statement on the Practice of Word and Sacrament* (Minneapolis: Augsburg Fortress, 1997).

[11] See "Towards Koinonia in Worship: Report of the Consultation on the Role of Worship Within the Search for Unity," *Studia Liturgica* 25 (1995), 3–31.

[12] See the Lutheran World Federation, *Nairobi Statement on Worship and Culture: Contemporary Challenges and Opportunities* (Geneva: 1996); and S. Anita Stauffer (ed.), *Worship and Culture in Dialogue* (Geneva: Lutheran World Federation, 1994).

[13] G. Lathrop, *Holy Things*, 224.

[14] J. White, "How Do We Know It Is Us?" in E. Anderson and B. Morrill (eds.), *Liturgy and the Moral Self: Humanity at Full Stretch before God* (Collegeville: Pueblo, 1998), 55–65.

[15] Ibid., 57.

[16] Ibid., 57–8.

[17] Ibid., 63 [emphasis added].

[18] Ibid., 64 [emphasis is original].

[19] Ibid., 65 [emphasis is original].

[20] P. Bradshaw, "Difficulties in Doing Liturgical Theology," *Pacifica* 11 (June 1998), 181–94.

[21] Ibid., 185.

[22] Ibid., 184–5.

[23] Ibid., 187.

[24] Ibid., 188.

25 Ibid., 190. The article in which Hoffman suggests these various levels of meaning is "How Ritual Means: Ritual Circumcision in Rabbinic Culture Today," *Studia Liturgica* 23 (1993), 78–97. Hoffman, however, was not the first to argue that liturgical theologians need to pay attention to multiple meanings in ritual performance or to suggest various meanings to which attention should be given. See especially Margaret Mary Kelleher, "Liturgy: An Ecclesial Act of Meaning, " *Worship* 59 (1987) 482–97; idem, "Liturgy and the Christian Imagination," *Worship* 66 (1992), 125–47; and idem, "Hermeneutics in the Study of Liturgical Performance," *Worship* 67 (1993), 292–318.

26 See A. Kavanagh, *On Liturgical Theology* (New York: Pueblo, 1984).

27 Ibid., 192–3.

28 Ibid., 186.

29 Ibid., 194.

30 Ibid., 186.

31 Ibid., 186.

32 I owe this insight to a statement made by John Baldovin, S.J., in his June, 1998, address to the conference, *Church and Eucharist: The Many Presences of Christ*, sponsored by the Notre Dame Center for Pastoral Liturgy, at Notre Dame, IN.

33 There are several things, for example, we simply do not know clearly from Justin's description: (1) the shape and contents of the baptismal rite in actual use; (2) whether Sunday worship took place on Sunday *morning* or if the rite he knew actually took place in the evening; (3) whether the prayer of thanksgiving prayed extemporaneously by the *proestos* was a single *eucharistia* over the bread and cup or, like other surviving examples from the pre-Nicene time period (e.g., the *Didache*, and *Didascalia Apostolorum*), was a series of prayers accompanying an actual meal with bread prayers at the beginning and cup prayers at the end; (4) the actual state of the various "orders" (*proestos* and deacons) throughout the church in this period; and (5) whether the collection for the poor actually took place at the end of the eucharistic rite or at some other point during the rite.

34 J. White, "How Do We Know It Is Us?", 63 [emphasis added].

35 R. Taft, "Introduction," in Idem, *Beyond East and West: Problems in Liturgical Understanding*, 2nd revised and enlarged edition (Rome: Edizioni Oriental Institute, 1997), 13–14.

36 R. Taft, *The Liturgy of the Hours in East and West* (Collegeville: The Liturgical Press, 1986), xv.

37 See Ibid., xv.

38 J. White, "How Do We Know It Is Us?", 58.

39 See J. Neil Alexander, *Waiting for the Coming: The Liturgical Meaning of Advent, Christmas, Epiphany* (Washington, D.C.: Pastoral Press, 1993), 7–28.

40 G. Wainwright, "The Sacraments in Wesleyan Perspective," in idem, *Worship with One Accord: Where Liturgy & Ecumenism Embrace* (New York: Oxford, 1998), 106.

41 G. Wainwright, "Renewing Worship: The Recovery of Classical Patterns," in idem, *Worship with One Accord: Where Liturgy & Ecumenism Embrace*, 138.

# Schwenkfelders in America:
## Papers Presented at the Colloquium
## on Schwenckfeld and the Schwenkfelders

# Schwenkfelders in America:

Papers Presented
at the Colloquium
on Schwenckfeld
and the Schwenkfelders

Pennsburg, Pa.
September 17-22, 1984

edited by

Peter C. Erb

Pennsburg, Pa.
Schwenkfelder Library
1987

ISBN 0-935980-06-7

©Copyright 1987 by
Schwenkfelder Library

# Table of Contents

# Preface

In September, 1984, Schwenkfelder Library sponsored a week-long Colloquium on Schwenckfeld and the Schwenkfelders to celebrate the 250th anniversary of Schwenkfelder life in America and the 100th anniversaries of the initiation of the *Corpus Schwenckfeldianorum* project and the beginning of formal collection of Schwenkfelder books and manuscripts, now Schwenkfelder Library.

Of the papers presented at the Colloquium or stimulated by it, twenty-one generally dealing with the life and thought of Schwenckfeld and his sixteenth-century followers have already been published by Schwenkfelder Library in a companion volume, *Schwenckfeld and Early Schwenkfeldianism*. Papers treating a second theme of the Colloquium, Schwenkfelder life and culture in America, are presented here.

Schwenckfeld was a vigorous protagonist in the religious controversies of the Protestant Reformation, frequently writing to defend his beliefs against virulent attack. After his death the next generation of his followers energetically sought to collect, preserve, and publish his writings. By the time of the emigration to Pennsylvania in 1734, Schwenkfelder leaders carried on this tradition by laboriously copying, binding, and preserving theological treatises in manuscripts running to five or six hundred pages. The article by W. Kyrel Meschter and myself describes the time, labor, and devotion, almost beyond our present day comprehension, of the writers of some 200 bound and 1500 unbound manuscript volumes, mostly copied before the year 1800, now extant in Schwenkfelder Library. Preservation of the theological tradition moved later generations to persevere in the seventy-five year effort to present to scholars a critical edition of Schwenckfeld's works, the nineteen volume *Corpus Schwenckfeldianorum*, completed in 1961. The

availability of reliable texts produced among scholars a broad
reinterpretation of Schwenckfeld and his seminal role in the
Protestant Reformation in Silesia and South Germany, which
continues to this day.

But it is not alone their theological traditions that draw
attention to the Schwenkfelders. They are a unique social
phenomenon, surviving almost 200 years in Europe and another 150 years in America without the support of institutional structures, which Schwenckfeld shunned. Following the
emigration Pennsylvania Schwenkfelders strove to maintain fellowship with co-believers in their homeland until the decline
of Schwenkfeldianism there broke off contact. The emotional
attachment to their homeland, however, endured, to be periodically revived by the residence of the *Corpus* staff in Wolfen-
buttel, Germany, from 1902 to 1918, the 1934 Bicentennial
Pilgrimage to Silesia, the relief efforts on behalf of the Silesian
exiles following the close of World War II, and several more
recent group visits to the old homeland.

A broad interest in the colonial origins of the American
people generally, and intensive study of the ethnic streams
of immigration which blended in the melting pot of colonial
America, has lately directed attention to the Pennsylvania Germans, the Schwenkfelders prominently among them, and their
material, social and political culture. Here care is in order.
Although Schwenkfelders, for instance, retained their founder's
concern for religious toleration, the religious freedom which the
Schwenkfelders found in early eighteenth-century Pennsylvania
was for them the possibility of continuing their lives without
interference from established religious and political authority
rather than acceptance of the late eighteenth-century Enlightenment ideals enunciated in the heat of the American revolution.

Schwenkfelder Library archives house a wealth of source materials chronicling the circumstances leading to the Schwenkfelder emigration, the conditions of the voyage, and the experience of arriving and settling in a new land, which await
organized presentation by an author steeped in theology, sociology, and modern colonial historiography. The papers in
this volume, however, throw valuable light on elements of this
experience.

The context of Schwenkfelder life in America is well set out by Professor Horst Weigelt's analysis of the primary emigration. Lee C. Hopple has kindly provided a geographic survey of the Germanic homeland of the movement. A most valuable demographic study of eighteenth-century Schwenkfelders is provided by Rodger C. Henderson. William T. Parsons' review of Schwenkfelder indentures gives us material for further consideration of the circumstances surrounding immigration in the eighteenth century. The study by Monica Pieper on the Schwenkfelder poet, Daniel Sudermann, and L. Allen Viehmeyer on the development of Schwenkfelder hymnology in the eighteenth century help us better to understand the nature of the social continuity between the Schwenkfelders on the two continents.

Papers by Don Yoder, John B. Frantz and John L. Ruth enlighten the interaction between colonial Schwenkfelders and the Quakers, Moravians, and Mennonites respectively. Alan G. Keyser provides us with fine insights into the nature of early Schwenkfelder architecture. Elizabeth R. Gamon introduces us to Schwenkfelder production of textiles, and Thomas S. Eader to Schwenkfelder builders of organs and organ making. Kathleen Manolescu reviews techniques of dairy farming, a prominent occupation of early Schwenkfelders.

The papers offer only a sampling of important aspects of Schwenkfelder culture in colonial Pennsylvania. Time did not permit studies in such significant areas as Schwenkfelder artistic expression, development of educational institutions, political activities, particularly in Indian relations, and technological innovation, nor scientific, primarily medical, contributions to colonial development by prominent Schwenkfelders.

The Colloquium papers presented in these two volumes by no means exhaust the creative energies stimulated by the 1984 anniversary celebrations. W. Kyrel Meschter was moved to publish his *Twentieth Century Schwenkfelders*, surveying Schwenkfelder institutions, personalities, and activities during the present century. The celebration provided the impetus for the Library to develop computerized indexes of its Fraktur, Newspaper, Almanac, and Bible collections, bringing these collections to the attention of scholars generally engaged in the study of the history of culture, particularly that of southeastern Pennsylvania. It provided opportunity for Francis Blase to gather the results of his collection of Heebner Farm machinery into his *Heebner and Sons: Pioneers of Farm Machinery in America, 1840-1926.* In 1985 the translation of Horst Weigelt's important study *Schwenkfelders in Silesia* appeared, offering the English reader a full view of the changes occurring within the Schwenkfelder movement in Silesia from the early 1520s to the early nineteenth century. And in 1986 R. Emmet McLaughlin's *Caspar Schwenckfeld, Reluctant Radical; His Life to 1540,* published independently by Yale University Press, offered scholar and lay reader alike important new insights into the early life of Schwenckfeld and the reformation background against which his thought developed.

Without the dedication and industry of a number of people the Colloquium and the publication of the papers resulting from it would have been impossible. Some comments in *Schwenckfeld and Early Schwenkfeldianism* bear repeating. We are especially grateful for their role in supporting and organizing the Colloquium itself, to Dr. Claude A. Schultz, Jr., W. Kyrel Meschter (who also provided helpful editorial suggestions for the publication of the papers), Dr. Ruth Harris, and Mrs. Lib Dewey. Dennis Moyer, Director, and Claire Conway, Secretary, of the Library, worked diligently throughout the presentation of the Colloquium and the publication of these papers. In the preparation of the present volume special thanks are due Alice Croft for care in the editorial process and, above all, to Dennis Moyer for useful comments and oversight of the photography work and final printing of the volume. Typesetting for the volume was done on the computer facilities made available through the Computing Centre at Wilfrid Laurier University, Waterloo, Ontario.

Peter C. Erb,
Associate Director,
Schwenkfelder Library

# The Emigration of the Schwenkfelders from Silesia to America

## Horst Weigelt

The history of the Schwenkfelders has not yet been fully written. Some parts of their history are fairly well known, but there are others of which we have no certain knowledge. Without doubt this is true of the period during which the Schwenkfelders left their Silesian homeland to emigrate to America.

In the paper which follows we approach this problem in three succeeding steps. First it is necessary to give a brief account of the emigration of the Schwenkfelders from their Silesian homeland. Regarding this we have to ask two questions: why did they leave Silesia and why did they turn to the Oberlausitz in the kingdom of Saxony to live? The next problem relates to the religious, social, and economic situation of the Schwenkfelders in the Oberlausitz region, primarily on the estates of Count Zinzendorf where most of the Schwenkfelder refugees found a temporary home. The third problem is to discover the reasons for a further emigration from Saxony after a stay of nearly eight years. We shall show that they had by no means envisaged America as a place of refuge, but made several attempts to settle in Germany before they finally decided to attempt a settlement in America and to try to find a new homeland there.

## The Attempts of the Schwenkfelders to Find a New Home

The Schwenkfelders had settled in the region of Glatz, but from the middle of the sixteenth century they also had established communities of a considerable size in the Bober-Katzbach Mountains.[1] They settled in several villages built along the road which belonged partly to the principality of Liegnitz, and partly to the principality of Schweidnitz-Jauer. Initially they enjoyed the open or covert sympathy of their landlords. However, as soon as they separated themselves openly from the

Lutheran church and quarreled with Lutheran doctrine, opposition from the local Lutheran ministers arose. Urged by these Lutheran ministers several landlords finally proceeded against the Schwenkfelders. Their books and writings as well as their property were repeatedly confiscated; they were thrown into prison and even exiled.

However, these periods of persecution alternated with more peaceful periods. During the Thirty Years' War there were hardly any repressive measures against them, nor did the persecution strike all Schwenkfelder communities with the same intensity. The reason was that the Schwenkfelders lived in villages which belonged partly to the principality of Schweidnitz-Jauer and partly to the duchy of Liegnitz.

Until the beginning of the eighteenth century the Schwenkfelders had been persecuted only by Lutheran ministers and their landlords. This, however, changed completely when, in the course of the Counter Reformation, a Jesuit mission[2] was opened in Harpersdorf in 1719. At first the Jesuits attempted their conversion by friendly persuasion; thereafter they resorted to increasingly repressive measures.

The Schwenkfelders tried to avoid the influence of the Jesuit mission in various ways. Eventually they sent a delegation to the court at Vienna in 1721 to ask for toleration.[3] During their extremely costly stay in that city for several years, they succeeded in submitting seventeen petitions[4] to the Emperor Charles VI, but their request for toleration was not granted. They were bitterly disappointed when, in a rescript[5] dated July 30, 1725, the Emperor decisively rejected their plea for toleration. He refused to accept any further submission and introduced even sharper measures against them. For example, it was decreed that Schwenkfelders who stayed away from catechetical instructions without giving sufficient reason were 'on a first offense to be fined according to their means, on a second offense the fine was to be doubled, and if they further disobeyed they were to be punished with imprisonment or hard labour. Schwenkfelder minors were to be looked after by Catholic guardians and sent to Catholic places to be reared in the true Catholic religion.'[6]

When the Schwenkfelders' attempts to gain toleration failed, they sought help from the Amsterdam Mennonites[7] on October 16, 1725, hoping that they would, once again, come

**Illustration 1**

Illustrations 1-5 are of Schwenkfelder houses built at Bertelsdorf on the estates of Count Zinzendorf following the Schwenkfelders' emigration there from Silesia after 1726.

to the aid of the persecuted as they had done in 1660 and 1661 in the case of the Bernese Anabaptists.[8] They requested that the Mennonites seek the assistance of the British and Dutch ambassadors to the Viennese court, asking either for toleration or for the right to emigrate—a right which they did not possess because they belonged to an illicit religion as defined by the Treaty of Westphalia. When the answer from the Dutch Mennonites was delayed and persecution was growing,[9] they found themselves forced to leave their homes secretly, leaving all their goods behind. Now their problem was to find a place to go. According to their statements King Friedrich Wilhelm I had invited them three times in 1724 to settle in the thinly populated area around Berlin and to establish a linen factory there. They did not, however, accept his invitation 'for certain grave reasons.'[10] Apparently they feared military conscription.

Since at the time Holland appeared to be the promised land for all religiously persecuted peoples, the Schwenkfelders decided to emigrate there. On December 3, 1725, they asked the Amsterdam Mennonites whether they might come and build up a new livelihood there.[11] Once again to their 'consternation and surprise' no answer came, while 'the persecution daily increased and the adversaries became fiercer and fiercer.'[12]

Now they turned to the Oberlausitz area which was only about ten hours distance by foot to the west. They contacted Johann Christoph Schwedler who was pastor in Nieder-Wiesa. This Pietist pastor immediately turned for assistance to Melchior Schäffer, pastor of Holy Trinity in Görlitz, who was also closely allied to Halle Pietism and who was to intercede for them with the magistrate of Görlitz and ask for asylum.

About the same time, on December 9, 1725, they asked Count Nicolaus Ludwig von Zinzendorf whether he would allow them to spend at least the winter months in Herrnhut.[13] They had become acquainted with the count in August 1723 when, together with his two friends, Friedrich von Wattenwyl and Pastor Melchior Schäffer, he had made his first journey to Silesia. He wanted to visit a relative on his mother's side, Otto Conrad van Hohberg, in Zobten.[14] Having had first-hand experience of the unfortunate situation of the Schwenkfelders, he drafted several petitions to the Imperial Court on their behalf. One month later he interceded for them in an audience at the Imperial Court which stayed at that time at Brandeis.[15]

He applied to the imperial minister Rudolph Siegmund Count von Sinzendorf and to the director of the supreme royal office of Silesia, the privy councillor Johann Anton von Schaffgotsch, to obtain the right of emigration for the Schwenkfelders, but he was not successful. When Zinzendorf received the request from the Schwenkfelders mentioned above, he immediately gave them permission to settle in his territories.[16]

## The Exile of the Schwenkfelders in the Oberlausitz.

On February 14, 1726, the first six or seven Schwenkfelder families fled under cover of darkness from Harpersdorf.[17] During this month and the months of March, April, and May more than one hundred and seventy families escaped and fled to Oberlausitz. Some fled to Görlitz, but most of them found shelter in Berthelsdorf. We will first look at the Schwenkfelders who fled to Görlitz.

The city of Görlitz gave temporary asylum to the Schwenkfelders under the condition that 'they live peacefully and quietly.'[18] Two days later the city fathers asked their regent, Friedrich August I, elector of Saxony, 'how they were to deal with the present emigrants and those who were still to come.'[19] On May 2 an answer was received through the privy councillor, Gottlieb Friedrich von Gersdorff, stating that the privy council had decided to tolerate the Schwenkfelders for the time being, but not to allow them to practise their beliefs publicly or to buy houses or estates.[20] Some remained in the city of Görlitz.[21]

Most of the Schwenkfelders took shelter in Berthelsdorf with Count Zinzendorf.[22] Since they all wished to reside in one place, however, for a short time they considered moving on. On the suggestion of the Amsterdam Mennonites they sent a delegation to Altona in the spring of 1726 to look there for a settlement.[23] When this came to naught, there arose a growing desire among many Schwenkfelders to emigrate to Pennsylvania.[24] The Amsterdam Mennonites discouraged this vigorously, both because of the political and economic situation in that British colony and the danger of the voyage, and refused all aid.[25] When all these attempts failed, the Schwenkfelders decided to stay in Berthelsdorf,[26] which the Count had bought in 1727 from his uncle Gottlieb Friedrich von Gersdorff.

In Oberberthelsdorf the Schwenkfelders lived in a row of houses which they built themselves and which even today are known as the Schwenkfelder houses. Much financial assistance came from the Haarlem Collegiants for the establishment of their new existence.[27] Here the Schwenkfelders lived unmolested until 1734. But during these eight years Zinzendorf was anxious to convert them. He thought that the separation of the Schwenkfelders was only caused by the ignorance, foolishness, and frivolity of the Lutheran pastors. But all his attempts to convert them were in vain. In particular the Silesian emigrants took offence at Zinzendorf's Christocentrism. There was no inner relationship between the doctrine of the Schwenkfelders and the Pietism of Zinzendorf as is sometimes suggested.

In Oberlausitz, as in Silesia, the Schwenkfelders maintained an industrious and quiet life in passive obedience to the political authorities.[28] They held conventicles for edification directed by Balthasar Hoffman[29] but sometimes they also attended Lutheran worship services, particularly funeral orations. They went to Lutheran pastors for baptism, marriage, and burial.[30] However, they did not attend the Lord's Supper and fiercely opposed all attempts to get them to accept the Lutheran confession. Consequently, some Lutheran pastors, especially Johann Adam Schön and Johann Daniel Geissler in Görlitz, began to preach against them and to act against them with measures of church discipline.[31]

The Schwenkfelders' stay in Oberlausitz was to be a short one. At the beginning of August, 1731, Emperor Charles VI protested to the Elector of Saxony, Friedrich August I (who was also King of Poland), through Leopold von Waldstein that Count Zinzendorf had accommodated some of his imperial subjects from Moravia.[32] He demanded their expulsion. He was, however, referring to the Bohemian Brethren from Kunwald and Zauchtental, not to the Schwenkfelders. On the proposal of the privy council,[33] the King in turn ordered that the Count be informed that he would no longer be allowed 'to attract more emigrants through letters or messengers.'[34] In addition he ordered Georg Ernst von Gersdorff as officer of Görlitz to submit information concerning the emigrants.[35] Since Gersdorff maintained that this was possible only after a detailed study,[36] he was appointed to carry it out.[37] The commission met in Herrnhut on January 19, 1732.[38] During the stay the commission became aware of the Schwenkfelders, who hitherto had not been noticed by the political authorities of Saxony. On

January 22 the commission departed. One day later Zinzendorf wrote once again to the privy council and spoke for the frightened Schwenkfelders.[39] He requested the privy councillor to reassure them that there was nothing to be apprehensive about.

The final report of the commission—the text of which is no longer available—was not unfavorable to the Schwenkfelders. However, the upper consistory, which was to give its opinion on the report,[40] issued a negative judgement against them.[41] It expressed the opinion that it might have been well if Count Zinzendorf had not taken them in, since it might have been known from the beginning that it would be difficult to win them over or to bring them on the right path.

On the direction[42] of the privy council to the supreme officer of Bautzen, Friedrich Caspar von Gersdorff, issued on April 29, 1732, Zinzendorf sent a report on the Schwenkfelders in August, 1732.[43] In this letter he defended them once again. He wrote: 'In the community they are good honest people. They work untiringly, trade diligently and successfully, and are generally active and skillful. They are intelligent officials and farmers, correct payers, equitable businessmen, and very elegant spinners. In morals they are good theorists and practicians; they serve everyone, and never let others serve them in vain; they lead, in general, a quiet, secluded, honorable, pure, humble, unaffected life.' Zinzendorf made mention of the possible trading advantages. On January 26, 1733, he went on to point out to Count Gersdorff that the Schwenkfelders would gladly pledge loyalty to the constitution.[44]

But on January 5, 1733, the privy council advised Friedrich August I to command the Schwenkfelders in Berthelsdorf to leave the country one by one since they did not belong to any of the three religions tolerated by the Treaty of Westphalia.[45] Friedrich August II, who succeeded his father Friedrich August I on February 1, 1733, agreed.[46] On April 4, 1733, the supreme officer of Bautzen was instructed by a decree,[47] which was signed by Alexander von Miltitz, to order the Schwenkfelders in Berthelsdorf 'to leave the country, but to give the command to each of them individually.'[48] Since the Schwenkfelders had not been pleased with their new home because they had been under constant pressure to accept the Lutheran confession, they did not protest. They only requested Zinzendorf's permission to be allowed to leave as a single body.[49]

### The Schwenkfelders' Search for a New Settlement and their Emigration to America.

There are some indications that the Schwenkfelders attempted to gain permission to settle in Hamburg, Brandenburg, Isenburg in Wetterau, and elsewhere, although it was to no avail.[50] In the meantime, Count Zinzendorf was negotiating with the British ambassador in Copenhagen to find a place for the Schwenkfelders in Georgia.[51] On the recommendation of their friends in Holland the Schwenkfelders declared themselves prepared to go to Georgia if the Count was successful in gaining a promise for them of the free passage, free land, and tax abatement as given to other settlers.[52] Probably in November, 1733, Zinzendorf submitted an anonymous request through Christoph Karl Ludwig von Pfeil, member of the Württemberg delegates in Regensburg, to the trustees for Establishing the Colony of Georgia,[53] but according to the Schwenkfelders' records,[54] not all their demands were met. Finally, the Schwenkfelders, probably already in Berthelsdorf, decided to emigrate to Pennsylvania. In any case they had received good reports from some Schwenkfelder families who had already gone there.[55] Not all of the Schwenkfelders left. Some continued to live peaceably in Berthelsdorf. The Schwenkfelders in the Görlitz area also remained in the country for the time being.

Between April 20 and 28, 1734, forty Schwenkfelder families —one hundred and eighty persons—left and started their journey to America. The emigrants wrote a culturally and historically interesting account[56] of their five-month journey. According to this account the Schwenkfelders set out in small groups on April 20, 1734, as ordered by the authorities. Apparently the authorities wanted to prevent their emigration causing too much sensation.

The emigrants gathered in Pirna and there boarded a boat which took them down the Elbe to Altona, passing Dresden and Magdeburg. On May 17 they arrived in Altona where the famous Mennonite family van der Smissen supported them for eleven days in a house which had been especially prepared for them; the family even catered for them free of charge. On May 29 they sailed for Haarlem on three Dutch ships. However, heavy sea dispersed the ships, thus preventing the Schwenkfelders from gathering in Haarlem before June 6. In Haarlem

they also found well-furnished lodgings, provided by the van
Buyschanse brothers, Abraham, Isaak, and Jan.  Eventually
the brothers not only arranged a passage on the British ship,
the *Saint Andrew,* for them, but paid all the fees. The fare for
adults was 30 Reichstalers; adolescents under fifteen paid half-
price. Children under the age of four were transported free of
charge but they could not claim a bed or food. The Buyschanse
brothers, however, requested the wealthy Schwenkfelders to
give the same amount of money to a fund for the poor after
they had happily arrived in America. The brothers themselves
contributed 224 Reichstalers as a financial base for the fund.
After fifteen days the Schwenkfelders left Haarlem and travelled to Rotterdam where they boarded the *Saint Andrew* on
June 21. After the ship had spent a week in harbor, they sailed
to Plymouth along the south coast of England. Apart from the
Schwenkfelders there were some other passengers aboard, for
the most part emigrants from the Palatinate. On July 29 they
put to sea from Plymouth.

After a passage lasting fifty-six days during which they repeatedly experienced storms and extreme calms, they arrived
in Philadelphia and went ashore on September 22. Since they
refused to take an oath for religious reasons, the authorities
complied and declared it sufficient for all male Schwenkfelders
over sixteen to certify their allegiance to the British king by a
handshake.

The amount of pain and want the Schwenkfelders had to
suffer is plain from the written account. On the passage two
adults and seven children died, in most cases babies and infants.  While the hymn 'Ach, wie elend ist unsere Zeit' was
sung, the dead bodies were buried in the sea. The first verse
of this hymn reads in German:

> Ach! Wie elend ist unsere Zeit
> Allhie auf dieser Erden!
> Gar bald der Mensch dernieder leit:
> Wir müssen alle sterben.
> Allhie in diesem Jammerthal
> Ist Müh' und Arbeit überall,
> Auch wenn es wohl gelinget.

Storms and heavy seas repeatedly forced the passengers to stay
below decks in closed holds. Food was a big problem; it lacked
vitamins although the menu was fairly well balanced. According to the account they had beef on Sunday; on Monday it was

rice and syrup, on Tuesday salted pork and peas, on Wednesday pastry, on Thursday beef and peeled barley, on Friday stockfish, and on Saturday stewed peas and syrup. For the first two weeks there was a daily ration of a pint of beer and a pint of water for everyone, but later only foul tasting water was left. The foul taste could not be removed by adding coffee. Fresh rainwater, which they gathered, became a great refreshment.

In America, too, the Schwenkfelders initially sought a single tract of land to settle on, 'to be for all others a praiseworthy example of Christian concord and union and not to be so easily infected by the common disease of covetousness.'[57] But when this was found to be impossible, they eventually settled in small groups about fifty miles north of Philadelphia near the Moravians and Mennonites, in Berks County, in Northhampton County, in Goshenhoppen, and Skippack. These areas were climatically and geographically similar to that of their Silesian homeland. As already mentioned, not all of the Schwenkfelders left Silesia. The majority of them remained in their homeland. The Jesuits continued their work with great zeal. Although the Schwenkfelders stubbornly opposed the Jesuits, the latter induced a significant number of them to convert. For example, in their report of 1732 the missionaries listed 324 persons who had been converted.[58] The growing number of Catholics naturally led the Jesuits to desire a church of their own in Harpersdorf. Finally, in spring of 1732 they obtained the administration of the parish, thereby hoping to convert even more of the Schwenkfelders and to reinforce the faith of those whom they had already converted. Together with the Lutherans the Schwenkfelders attempted to hinder the work of the Jesuits or to make it at least more difficult. They did not shrink from using strong-arm tactics. At the end of February, 1736, to the great displeasure of the Jesuits, more Schwenkfelder families from Harpersdorf and Armenruh fled to Görlitz.[59]

But in October 1740 Emperor Karl VI died unexpectedly at the age of 55, whereupon Friedrich II of Prussia, citing an ancient legal claim, marched a small army into Silesia. Perhaps made aware of the Schwenkfelders' situation by the Schwenkfelders themselves, a decree[60] for their protection was issued by the King's order. According to that decree, the execution of the former decrees was stopped. But, as the correspondence between the Silesian Schwenkfelders and their fellow believers in Pennsylvania clearly indicates, the edict of May, 1741, was intended to return them to the same status they had had before the arrival of the Jesuit mission. They were once again placed under the parochial jurisdiction of the Lutheran church, but not to be tolerated or recognized as a separate denomination. Not incorrectly did they characterize this as an individual freedom of conscience, not as a general toleration.[61]

The king of Prussia also called upon the Schwenkfelders who had fled to return to Silesia. They were assured that they could live and work and move about in peace. Although the Silesian Schwenkfelders urgently wished their fellow believers to return, the Pennsylvania Schwenkfelders did not comply. As pacifists they feared military conscription after their return. They regarded military service as belonging to the kingdom of the devil. Moreover, it is also important to note that they had no material need to take up the invitation.

The toleration that the Silesian Schwenkfelders enjoyed was broad enough so that a new period of growth could have started among them. But renewal did not come; instead the Schwenkfelders declined in number and their theological ideas became obsolete. During the last period of their history, from 1741 to 1826, the Silesian Schwenkfelders did not compose a single book; their only publication was the *Vindication for Caspar Schwenckfeld* of 1771, prepared in Pennsylvania by Christopher Schultz, Caspar and Christopher Kriebel, Balthasar Hoffman, and others.[62] This book was dedicated to Friedrich II of Prussia.

The reason why Schwenkfeldianism in Silesia was unable to renew itself lay primarily in the social structure of its adherents. They were, for the most part, old, single, or widowed persons.[63] The number of families with children was very small. Young Schwenkfelders had to marry Lutherans or remain single. When they married Lutherans, they almost always became Lutherans and broke their ties with the Schwenkfelders.

Vocations were changing as well during this period. Whereas the first generation had been nobles, theologians, or physicians, and the second often farmers, landowners, craftsmen, and independent employers, many of the remaining Schwenkfelders were day-laborers or tenant-farmers, earning their living

Illustration 2

Illustration 3

mostly by spinning. A cultural decline went along with this social decline. Whereas earlier some Schwenkfelders even knew
Latin, Greek, and Hebrew, these people could now hardly read
or write their native language.

Lastly, there is also a theological background to the absence of renewal among the Schwenkfelders. In the many letters which the Silesian Schwenkfelders wrote to Pennsylvania,
one looks in vain for the distinctive mark of later Schwenkfeldianism: the realization of the new man. Even the ethically-
motivated exclusiveness had been given up.

Finally, the correspondence from Silesia to Pennsylvania became rarer and rarer. In October 1857, having received no mail
for many years, the Schwenkfelders in Pennsylvania wrote to
Probsthain asking whether Schwenkfelder congregations still
existed is Silesia. They were immediately answered by the
Lutheran pastor there, Oswald Kadelbach, who informed them
that the last Schwenkfelder, the farmer Melchior Dorn, had
died in Harpersdorf in 1826.[64] Thus, exactly one hundred years
after the flight of the Schwenkfelders from Silesia, Schwenkfeldianism had there come to an end.

Compared to that of the Silesian Schwenkfelders the development of the Schwenkfelders in Pennsylvania took a different
course. Besides sociological and cultural reasons the most important factors were theological in nature. The earlier isolation of the Schwenkfelders was abandoned and they came to
know other theological movements and forms of piety. This
caused them, on the one hand, to give consideration to their
own spiritual tradition. On the other hand, they received a
new impetus from other theological positions and from other
forms of Christian life.

## Notes

[1] For this and the following see H. Weigelt, *Spiritualistische Tradition im Protestantismus. Die Geschichte des Schwenckfeldertums in Schlesien*, (Berlin, 1973), 195-260. [English translation: *The Schwenkfelders in Silesia* (Pennsburg, 1985)].

[2] On the Jesuit mission see the studies of A. F. H. Schneider, whose manuscript notes are in SchLP [Schwenkfelder Library, Pennsburg] and Berlin SB [Staatsbibliothek Preussischer Kulturbesitz]. Unfortunately Schneider never completed evaluating his work other than in a summary of his studies in an 1862 publication of the Elisabeth School in Berlin

*(Uber den geschichtlichen Verlauf der Reformation in Liegnitz und ihren späteren Kampf gegen die kaiserliche Jesuiten-Mission in Harpersdorf*, Abtheilung II, [Berlin, 1862]).

3  For this and the following see Christoph Schultz to Anton N., April 6, 1768, SchLP, VC 3-7,8-9; Christoph Hoffmann, *Kurze Lebens-Beschreibung Balthasar Hoffmans*, 1777, SchLP, VR 22-9; Wroclaw DA [Diozesan-Archiv], Harpersdorf 3, Gravamina, 10, and SchLP, VN 73-7 (JAH [Jesuiten-Archiv Harpersdorf], Gravamina), 569-70. Cf. Chr. Schultz, *Erläuterung für Herrn Caspar Schwenckfeld, und die Zugethanen seiner Lehre, wegen vieler Stücke, beydes aus der Historie und Theologie, welche insgemein unrichtig vorgestellt, oder gar übergangen werden*, Jauer 1771, 59; A.F.H. Schneider, *Jesuiten-Mission*, 11-12.

4  Christoph Hoffman, *Kurtze Lebens-Beschreibung Balthasar Hoffmans*, 1777, SchLP, VR 22-9 (these petitions are no longer extant).

5  Karl VI to the Breslau Royal Upper Council, July 30, 1725, SchLP, VN 73-6 (JAH, Instrumenta ad Modum Operandi), 19-24.

6  Ibid., 22-23

7  Schwenkfelders to the Mennonites in Amsterdam, October 16, 1725, Amsterdam BD [Bibliothek der Verenigde Doopsgezinde Gemeente, Universiteitsbibliotheek], No. 2908.

8  K. Guggisberg, *Bernische Kirchengeschichte* (Bern, 1958), 365.

9  Adam Wiegner to Daniel Hoovens, December 3, 1725, Amsterdam BD, No. 2909.

10  Ibid.

11  Ibid.

12  Adam Wiegner to [Daniel Hoovens], January 14, 1726, ibid., No. 2911.

13  Schwenkfelders to Nikolaus Ludwig von Zinzendorf, December 19, 1725, printed in part in A. G. Spangenberg, *Das Leben des Herrn Nicolaus Grafen und Herrn von Zinzendorf und Pottendorf*, Teil II, n.d., 326-27. Cf. N. L. v. Zinzendorf, 'Kurze Relation von Herrnhut und Berthelsdorf seit der Abreise des Herrn Heitz,' *ZBG* 6 (1912), 56. See also A.G. Spangenberg, *Zinzendorf*, Teil II, 324; E. Beyreuther, *Zinzendorf und die sich allhier beisammen finden* (Marburg/Lahn, 1959), 152.

14  See N.L. von Zinzendorf, 'Die Geschichte der verbundenen vier Brüder,' *ZBG* 6 (1912), 99. Cf. Spangenberg, *Zinzendorf*, II, 262.

15  On this and the following see Zinzendorf, 'Kurze Relation von Herrnhut,' 46. Cf. Spangenberg, *Zinzendorf*, Teil II, 266-67; Beyreuther, *Zinzendorf und die sich allhier beisammen finden*, 1.

16  Nikolaus Ludwig von Zinzendorf to the Schwenkfelders, December 25, 1725, excerpted in Spangenberg, *Zinzendorf*, Teil II, 327. Cf. Zinzendorf, 'Kurze Relation von Herrnhut,' 56; Beyreuther, *Zinzendorf und die sich allhier beisammen finden*, 152.

17  The magistrate of Görlitz to August II, February 23, 1726, Dresden SA [Staatsarchiv], loc 5861, Vol. I, fol. 11r; excerpts are printed in Chr. G. Jahne, *Dankbare Erinnerung an die Schwenckfelder in Nordamerika* (Görlitz 1816) 27-28. Cf. Adam Wiegner to [Daniel Hoovens],

March 16, 1726, Amsterdam BD, No. 2914; Adam Wiegner, Melchior Kriebel, Balthasar Jäckel und Georg Wiegner to the Mennonites in Amsterdam, April 3, 1726, ibid., No. 2915.

[18] The magistrate of Görlitz to August II, February 23, 1726, Dresden LA, loc 5861, Vol. I., fol. 12v.

[19] Ibid.

[20] Gottlob Friedrich von Gersdorff to the magistrate of Görlitz, May 2, 1726, ibid., fol. 15r. (in summary).

[21] Gottlob Friedrich von Gersdorff to the magistrate of Görlitz, July 9, 1727, ibid., fol. 29r.

[22] Friedrich Caspar von Gersdorff to August II, September 13, 1732, Dresden LA, loc 5854, fol. 57v-58r.

[23] [Christian Hanisch] to the Mennonites [in Haarlem], June 17, 1726, ibid., No. 2920 (incomplete).

[24] Adam Wiegner to Ameldonk Leew, Jan Schalle and Cornelius van Putten, September 12, 1726, ibid., No. 2921; Adam Wiegner to the Mennonites [in Amsterdam], January 6, 1727, ibid., No. 2923.

[25] Ameldonk Leew, Jan Schalle and Cornelius van Putten to the Schwenkfelders, April 1, 1727, excerpted in O. Kadelbach, *Ausführliche Geschichte Kaspar v. Schwenckfelds und der Schwenckfelder in Schlesien, der Ober-Lausitz und Amerika, nebst ihren Glaubensschriften von 1524-1860, nach den vorhandenen Quellen bearbeitet* (Lauban, 1860), 59-62.

[26] Cf. Friedrich Caspar von Gersdorff to August II, September 13, 1732, Dresden LA, loc 5854, fol. 58r.

[27] Isaak Crajesteijn to Christian Hanisch, May 10, 1726, partially printed in Kadelbach, *Ausführliche Geschichte*, 58-59.

[28] Cf. Nikolaus von Zinzendorf to Friedrich Caspar von Gersdorff, n.d. [about August 1732], Herrnhut ABU [Archiv der Bruder-Unität], R 5 AN 20, 40, printed in E.S. Gerhard and S.C. Schultz, 'The Schwenkfelders and the Moravians in Saxony, 1723-1734,' *Schwenckfeldiana* 1 (1944), 8-10; Friedrich Caspar von Gersdorff to August II, September 13, 1732, Dresden LA, loc 5854, fol. 58v; Friedrich Caspar von Gersdorff to August II, December 19, ibid., fol. 74r (original).

[29] Cf. E.S. Gerhard, 'Balthasar Hoffmann (1687-1775), Scholar, Minister, Writer, Diplomat,' *Schwenckfeldiana* 1/2 (1914), 35-52.

[30] On this and the following see Friedrich Caspar von Gersdorff to August II, September 13, 1732, Dresden LA, loc 5854, fol. 58v-59r.

[31] Kadelbach, *Auführliche Geschichte*, 63.

[32] Karl VI to Leopold von Waldstein, n.d. [before August 15, 1731], Dresden, LA, loc 5854, fol. 3r-v; excerpted in F. Korner, *Die kursächsische Staatsregierung dem Grafen Zinzendorf und Herrnhut bis 1760 gegenüber. Nach den Acten des Hauptstaatsarchivs zu Dresden dargestellt* (Leipzig, 1878), 16. Cf. Leopold von Waldstein to Karl VI, August 17, 1731, SchLP, VN 73-6 (JAH, Instrumenta ad Modum), 528-31.

33 Privy Council to August II;, August 16, 1731, Dresden LA, loc 5854, fol. 5v-6r.

34 August II to the Privy Council, August 20, 1731, ibid., fol. 8r.

35 August II to Georg Ernst von Gersdorff, August 20, 1731, ibid., fol. 7r.

36 Georg Ernst von Gersdorff to August II, September 15, 1731, ibid., fol. 12r-v.

37 Privy Council to Georg Ernst von Gersdorff, November 8, 1731, ibid., fol. 17r-v.

38 Georg Ernst von Gersdorff to August II, March 15, 1732, ibid., fol. 41r-50v. On the investigations see 'Konflikt der kursächsischen Regierung mit Herrnhut und dem Grafen von Zinzendorf. 1733-1738,' *Neues Archiv für sächsische Geschichte* 3 (1882), 5-10.

39 Nikolaus Ludwig von Zinzendorf to the Privy Council, January 23, 1732.

40 Privy Council to the Upper Consistory, n.d. Dresden LA, loc 5854, fol. 54r-55r.

41 Upper Consistory to August II, November 1732, ibid., fol. 61r-65v (original). A copy is found in loc 1892, fol. 13r-15r.

42 Privy Council to Friedrich Caspar von Gersdorff, April 19, 1732.

43 [Nikolaus Ludwig von Zinzendorf to Friedrich Caspar von Gersdorff, n.d. [about August 1732], Herrnhut ABU, R 5 AN 20, 40.

44 Nikolaus Ludwig von Zinzendorf to Friedrich Caspar von Gersdorff, January 26, 1733.

45 Privy Council to Friedrich August II, January 5, 1733, Dresden LA, loc 6854, fol. 78r.

46 Friedrich August II to the Privy Council, March 31, 1733, ibid., fol. 83r.

47 Friedrich August II to Friedrich Caspar von Gersdorff, April 4, 1733, Herrnhut ABU, R 5 A 5, 18 u. Dresden LA, loc 6854, fol. 82r-v; printed in N.L. v. Zinzendorf, *Büdingische Sammlung*, Bd. III, in N.L. v. Zinzendorf, *Ergänzungsbände zu den Hauptschriften*, hrsg. von E. Beyreuther und G. Meyer (Hildesheim, 1966), Bd. 9, 12-13.

48 Ibid., fol. 82v and p. 13, respectively.

49 Nikolaus Ludwig von Zinzendorf to N.N., n.d. [about autumn 1733], Herrnhut ABU, R 5 A 2a; partially printed in English in Gerhard and Schultz, 12.

50 H. W. Kriebel, *The Schwenkfelders in Pennsylvania. A historical sketch* (Lancaster, 1904), 29-30.

51 Spangenberg, *Zinzendorf*, Teil IV, 803-804; G. Reichel, *August Gottlieb Spangenberg, Bischof der Bruderkirche* (Tübingen, 1906), 97-98.

52 [Schwenkfelders] to Nikolaus Ludwig von Zinzendorf, n. d. [after October 23, 1733], Herrnhut ABU R 14 AN 2,2a (R 6 A 5, 20); Melchior Kriebel, Georg Weiss, Balthasar Hoffman, Balthasar Jäckel and others to Nikolaus Ludwig von Zinzendorf, n.d. [after October 23, 1733], ibid., R 14 A 2,2c (R 14 N 2,2e; R 5 A 5,21), printed in English in Gerhard and Schultz, 11-12.

53 [Nikolaus Ludwig von Zinzendorf] to N.N., n.d. [before November 1733], Herrnhut ABU, R 5 10. Cf. A.G. Spangenberg, *Zinzendorf*, IV, 803.

54 Kriebel, *Schwenkfelders in Pennsylvania*, 31.

55 Schultz, *Erläuterung*, 64. Cf. Christoph Schultz to Anton N., April 6, 1768, SchLP, VC 3-7, 4.

56 Christoph Schultz, 'Reise-Beschreibung von Altona bis Pennsylvanien,' printed in Schultz, *Erläuterung*, 450-61.

57 Joh. Ph. Fresenius, *Bewahrte Nachrichten von Herrnhutischen Sachen*, Bd. III, Frankfurt und Leipzig 1748, 112.

58 For this and the following see Weigelt, *Spiritualistische Tradition*, 262-63.

59 Cf. Kadelbach, *Ausführliche Geschichte*, 65-66.

60 The decree is printed in J.A. Hensel, *Protestantische Kirchen-Geschichte der Gemeinen in Schlesien* (Leipzig und Liegnitz, 1768), 738; Kadelbach, *Ausführliche Geschichte*, 49. For this and the following see H. Weigelt, 'Friedrich II. von Preussen und die Schwenckfelder in Schlesien. Ein Beitrag zum Toleranzverständnis Friedrichs II,' *Zeitschrift für Religion in Geschichte und Gegenwart*, 22 (1970), 230-43.

61 Karl Ehrenfried Heintze to Christoph Kriebel, February 11, 1722, SchLP, VC 3-7, XXXIX.

62 On this and the following see S. G. Schultz, 'History of the Erläuterung,' *Schwenckfeldiana* 1 (1940), 21-24.

63 According to the list of persons which accompanied the letter of Georg Fleigner, Christoph Groh and Karl Ehrenfried Heintze to the Schwenkfelders in Pennsylvania (February 15, 1768, SchLP, VC 3-7, 37) 17 of the total of 44 Schwenckfeld adherents in 1760 were single.

64 Oswald Kadelbach to the Schwenkfelders in Pennsylvania, December 2, 1857, SchLP, VOD-K, 2b2.

Illustration 4

Illustration 5

# The Geography of Schwenkfeldianism

## Lee C. Hopple

Caspar Schwenckfeld converted to Lutheranism in 1518. Because of a gradually evolving disappointment with the scope and direction of Luther's Reformation, Schwenckfeld developed a set of religious beliefs which resulted in his breaking away from the mainstream of the Reformation.

Between 1526 and 1527 Schwenkfelder groups were firmly established in a number of Silesian communities, the principal ones being: Liegnitz, Ossig, Luben, Raudten, Steinau, Wohlau, and Neisse (Figure 2). Except for the last named all are clustered around the Oder River in northeastern Silesia. A number of extenuating circumstances beyond Schwenckfeld's control, the most important being publication of certain personal documents without his consent, caused him to leave Silesia in 1529, never to return. During the period from 1527 to his departure in 1529, the faith expanded to a number of other cities and towns, the primary centers being Goldberg, Jauer, and Breslau. Thus, by 1529, Schwenkfeldianism was firmly entrenched in ten major centers. and a number of small Silesian towns.

## Schwenckfeld's Exile

Upon leaving Silesia in 1529, Schwenckfeld probably did not remotely anticipate he would never return. Throughout his long exile, he was continually on the move. He spent varying periods at five primary centers of refuge: Strassburg, Augsburg, Ulm, Esslingen, Justingen, and again Esslingen (Figure 3).

After leaving Silesia he went directly to Strassburg at the invitation of the Magisterial reformers there. While in Strassburg he travelled a circuit from Rappoltsweiler, and Hagenau through Landau, to Speyer (Figure 3). Then, in 1533, following a number of debates ending with refusal to accept the religious precepts of the Magisterial theologians, Schwenckfeld was forced to leave Strassburg. He decided to seek refuge in Augsburg.

From Augsburg he travelled widely and frequently. Various sojourns took him to Mindelheim, Kempten, Isny, Memmingen, Stettin, Ulm, Kongen, and Frankfurt. During his stay in the Augsburg area Schwenckfeld returned to some of these cities and smaller centers several times. In 1534 he fled to Ulm (Figure 3).

During his years in Ulm and vicinity, Schwenckfeld visited Geislingen, Esslingen, Kirchheim, and several smaller cities. Because of religious disagreements with local leaders and adverse publicity from some publications he was expelled from Ulm in 1539. Schwenckfeld then moved from Ulm to Esslingen, his fourth primary center of refuge (Figure 3).

During his residency in and around Esslingen and some cities he visited previously, he journeyed through Wageg and Justingen. Schwenckfeld left Esslingen in 1542, accepting an invitation by the local prince to enjoy his protection at Justingen Castle. From his home at Justingen Castle Schwenckfeld secretly journeyed to Baden, Cannstatt, Blaubeuren, and Kaufbeuren and returned to some cities he visited in earlier times (Figure 3).

Religious wars erupted between Catholics and Protestants in the 1540s, the Catholics gradually emerging the victors. Consequently, Schwenckfeld was no longer safe in Justingen and he fled back to Esslingen in 1547.

During his second stay in Esslingen he visited Nürnberg, Oepfingen and other towns (Figure 3). Schwenckfeld was forced to leave Esslingen in 1550. Over the years a number of synods promulgated edicts outlawing him. These edicts engendered fear even in his most ardent supporters. Hence, after leaving Esslingen, Schwenckfeld never found a permanent refuge.

For the next eleven years, until 1561, Schwenckfeld traversed and circled southern Germany in what appears an aimless path. The period 1550-1561 is a story of excruciating privations. Little is known of this final era of Schwenckfeld's life. However, he is known to have passed through Heidelberg, Leeder (Figure 3), and smaller cities. It was in Ulm, in

1561, that Schwenckfeld completed his life in the home of some friends who buried him secretly.

By 1561, there were Schwenkfeldian 'congregations' in many of the aforementioned cities (Figure 3) and smaller communities visited by Schwenckfeld during his many journeys across south Germany. Although Schwenkfeldianism was widely dispersed across south Germany, the number of adherents probably never surpassed 1500. Persecution by the state churches, the atrocities of war, especially those of the Thirty Years' War, completely annihilated Schwenkfeldianism in southern Germany by the 1650s.

## Schwenkfeldianism in Silesia and Saxony

After Schwenckfeld's departure and despite several periods of moderate persecution the movement in general enjoyed relative peace and prosperity for some 150 years. By the close of the sixteenth century the faith had diffused westward; from the major 'congregations' around the Oder River established by 1529 and across Silesia to the border of Saxony. Together with some smaller cities, sizeable 'congregations' were established in Harpersdorf, Hirchberg, and Landshut (Figure 2). The Schwenkfelder population in and adjacent to Silesia is estimated to have been between 4,000 and 4,500 at the close of the sixteenth century, but was reduced to between 500 and 600 by the closing years of the century.

In the 1720s the Schwenkfelders commenced secret negotiations with the authorities of Saxony for purposes of obtaining permission to settle in that principality. The discussions were successful and about 400 of the remaining Schwenkfelders migrated across the border from Silesia to Saxony and established communities at Bertelsdorf, Görlitz and Herrnhut (Figure 2). In less than a decade, because of religious tumult the Schwenkfelders were ordered to leave Silesia. Following considerable debate among themselves and lengthy deliberations with the British, the Schwenkfelders reached the decision to emigrate to Pennsylvania. In April, 1734, following careful planning and substantial preparation, 181 Schwenkfelders began the frighteningly long, arduous journey to Pennsylvania.

The Schwenkfelders travelled up the Elbe River from Pirna to Hamburg-Altona, stopping for various reasons and for varying intervals at sixteen Elbe ports along the way (Figure 4).

Following unavoidable delays in Altona, they sailed to the
Netherlands in three ships. Some arrived at Haarlem, some
at Amsterdam, others at Rotterdam (Figure 4). The philan-
thropic Dutch Mennonites stocked their vessels and provided
for their needs while in the Netherlands. After a number of
long frustrating delays, they set sail for Plymouth England
(Figure 4). Sailing from Plymouth on July 29, they arrived
in Philadelphia on September 22, 1734, experiencing all the
hardships characteristic of an eighteenth century transatlantic
voyage.

In all (including several minor migrations) 219 Schwenk-
felders set sail for America, and 206 completed the crossing.
The last descendant of those deciding to remain in Silesia or
Saxony passed away in 1828, thus ending the movement in
Europe.

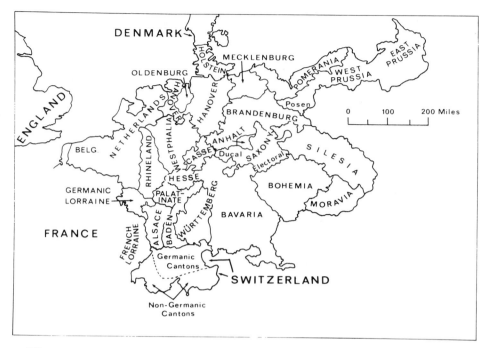

Figure 1: Principal Pre-eighteenth Century Germanic States

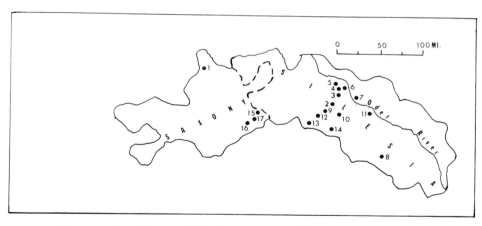

Figure 2: Schwenkfeldianism in Silesia and Saxony

| | |
|---|---|
| 1. Wittenberg | 10. Jauer |
| 2. Liegnitz | 11. Breslau |
| 3. Ossig | 12. Harpersdorf |
| 4. Luben | 13. Hirchberg |
| 5. Raudten | 14. Landshut |
| 6. Steinau | 15. Görlitz |
| 7. Wohlau | 16. Herrnhut |
| 8. Neisse | 17. Bertelsdorf |
| 9. Goldberg | |

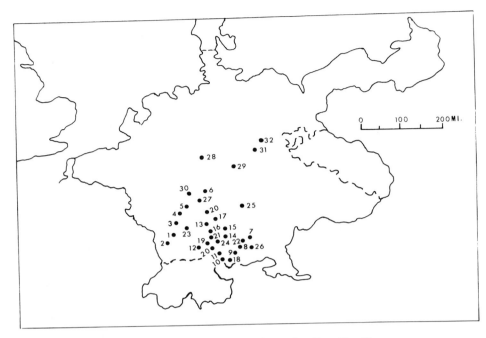

**Figure 3: Schwenkfeldianism in South Germany**

| | | |
|---|---|---|
| 1. Strassburg | 12. Stettin | 23. Baden |
| 2. Rappoltsweiler | 13. Kongen | 24. Oepfingen |
| 3. Hagenau | 14. Ulm | 25. Nürnberg |
| 4. Landau | 15. Geislingen | 26. Leeder |
| 5. Speyer | 16. Kirchheim | 27. Heidelberg |
| 6. Frankfurt | 17. Esslingen | 28. Marburg |
| 7. Augsburg | 18. Wageg | 29. Schmalcald |
| 8. Mindelheim | 19. Justingen | 30. Worms |
| 9. Kempten | 20. Cannstatt | 31. Weimar |
| 10. Isny | 21. Blaubeuren | 32. Naumburg |
| 11. Memmingen | 22. Kaufbeuren | |

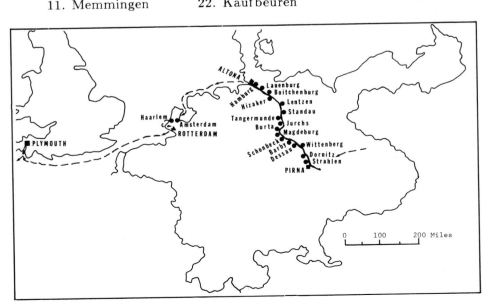

**Figure 4: Schwenkfelder Migration**

# Eighteenth-Century Schwenkfelders:
# A Demographic Interpretation

Rodger C. Henderson

Using various methods and sources of the social historian, recent scholarship has studied numerous groups of inhabitants
of eighteenth-century Pennsylvania and extended our knowledge of the nature of community. Some historians have approached their subject by focusing on religious groups in order to examine changing communities[1] or alterations in family
life.[2] One scholar, in a broad and sweeping study of southeastern Pennsylvania from a geographical perspective, searched
for knowledge of the crucial features of the 'Best Poor Man's
Country.'[3] Other historians have drawn attention to the social
and economic life of families in urban centers.[4] The county has
also served as an organizational device as investigators have
systematically scrutinized materials helpful in understanding
economic change in Chester,[5] demographic and family structures in Lancaster,[6] and inheritance patterns in York.[7] One
researcher has found 'community' embedded within the confines of the township.[8] A number of problems emerge from
the diverse conclusions reached by scholars who have, in these
various ways, attempted to understand the mentalité of early
Pennsylvanians. Despite the vigorous outpouring of scholarship, the Schwenkfelders have gone nearly unnoticed.[9] Their
experience sheds light on some of the problems of community
confronting historians.

Controversy over the extent and direction of demographic
changes and disagreement about the value system and normative order in eighteenth-century Pennsylvania require further
consideration. Some historians argue that patriarchal, familial, and communal values predominated among Pennsylvania's
early settlers. Traditional patterns of thought shaped family
decisions and governed economic and social behavior in the
colony and state. Patriarchs arranged marriages for their offspring, curbed sexual expression by the young, and wielded

economic power over family members. Elders asserted their rights over property transfers to control marriage ages and the domestic lives of their children.[10] There is, however, disagreement with this assessment of community in Pennsylvania. Other scholars take the position that Pennsylvanians lived in an open society characterized by liberal, individualistic, competitive values. In general, these settlers took action appropriate to maximize self-interest in a market economy. The bonds of lineage and European custom disintegrated in this unconfined country where private ambitions, personal competitiveness, and market-oriented desires of individual mobile, nuclear families took hold. In Pennsylvania, the settlers exhibited weak bonds of patriarchal authority, communal values gave way to individual freedom, and people planned and worked for their own material well-being more than community concerns.[11]

One purpose of the following essay is to evaluate, in the light of new evidence discovered for Pennsylvania's Schwenkfelder pioneers, the relative strengths of the arguments offered by those who see a familial, communal society as opposed to others who perceive an individualistic competitive community. Additionally, the present study seeks to fill in some gaps in the knowledge of population patterns and family life among the Schwenkfelders during the eighteenth century. Another objective is to measure the degree of change over time in demographic patterns and family structure as Schwenkfelders adjusted to their new home in Pennsylvania.

Reconstitution of 188 Schwenkfelder families furnished answers to a number of questions about marriage ages, family sizes, and life expectancy.[12] Techniques developed by European historical demographers assisted in the collection of the families' vital data and stimulated the analysis of the statistical compilations.[13] Three transitional periods of the Schwenkfelders' and Pennsylvania's economic and social evolution guided the sorting of these reconstituted families into three marriage cohorts.[14] Nuptials contracted before 1741, from 1741 to 1770, and from 1771 to 1800 defines membership in the groups. The first cohort embraces people who migrated to and settled in southeastern Pennsylvania and who married before 1741. The second cohort comprises couples who wedded between 1741 and 1770 and lived in the region during a period of remarkable growth and expansion in population, wealth, and institutions. The third cohort consists of husbands and wives who took vows from 1771 to 1800 and who felt the tensions that brought on the Revolution. They lived through the War years, the Confederation period, and the Federalist era.

Between 1731 and 1737 probably 219 Schwenkfelders emigrated from Europe but only 206 set foot in Pennsylvania.[15] Three remain unaccounted for and ten are known to have perished during the journey to the Quaker Colony. The newcomers proved unsuccessful in their efforts to obtain one large tract of land on which they wished to establish the entire group. In consequence they individually acquired smaller scattered parcels of land clustered in an area about fifty miles northwest of Philadelphia in parts of the present day Montgomery, Bucks, Berks, and Lehigh Counties. Most of the original fifty-one immigrant families had obtained land by the 1760s. They joined other pioneer settlers and engaged in general mixed farming to supply their daily bread. While the majority farmed others plied their trades as spinners, weavers, carpenters, and surveyors. Because they were few in number and lived in a dispersed farm settlement pattern, Schwenkfelders mixed into an already existing diverse social and economic system. They kept faithful records of births, deaths, and marriages, and that fact makes possible this more detailed account of their daily lives through the first three generations after migration to Pennsylvania.

Since the average age at first marriage is an economic and social barometer for any community, historians must pay close attention to this suggestive measuring device. The matrimonial age and shifts in the 'most important single demographic variable in the study of pre-industrial societies'[16] over time may betoken some crucial changes that developed in the neighborhood. The marriage rate influences fertility and family sizes and reflects mortality and life expectancy. Moreover, the timing of wedlock reveals social customs and discloses trends in the economy, such as the quality of harvests and the availability of land. Without a doubt, marriage is highly significant 'whether it be considered in regard to the community or to the individuals of mankind.'[17]

Contemporary observers overwhelmingly concluded that in eighteenth-century Pennsylvania men and women married young, and ascribed the cause to the favorable state of the economy and the expansive liberty that residents enjoyed. Benjamin Franklin thought that wedlock 'is greater in proportion to the ease and convenience of supporting a family.' More people joined in matrimony, 'and earlier in life,' when men obtained land to farm, learned crafts useful to the society, or found employment as laborers. He conjectured that 'our marriages are made, reckoning one with another, at twenty years of age... and... marrying early is encouraged from the prospect of good subsistence.'[18] Franklin was not an isolated voice commenting on Pennsylvania marriage practices. Since such information was of vital concern to all members of the community, others echoed the common knowledge that Franklin expressed. Pennsylvanians wedded early and the reasons for such youthful matrimoral ties, according to contemporaries, stemmed directly from the web of the advantageous economic and social circumstances of the community.[19]

Schwenkfelders who married before 1741 became husbands and wives at ages and in configurations that have been described as a 'European Marriage Pattern.'[20] Men found wives when they reached an average age of 29.3 years and women became wives at a mean age of 24.4. Over three-fourths of the husbands took vows when they were between 25 and 34 years of age.[21] According to the European pattern men wedded at average ages between 25 and 30 and women above 23 and generally 24. But change occurred between 1741 and 1770 as both brides and grooms married younger than the members of the first cohort.

The average age at first marriage for brides and grooms wedded between 1741 and 1770 shifted downward in response to changes in the Schwenkfelders' economic and social circumstances.[22] After the initial period of disruption and migration, more members of this religious group obtained land, found work, and began to act according to the 'custom of the country' to 1770. More women wedded when less than 20 years old and very few delayed matrimony past age 30. Consequently, the mean age at first marriage for brides registered 22.8. At the same time more men wedded when under 25 and fewer postponed vows past age 35. Thus, the average age at first marriage for grooms declined to 26.5 for those who found wives between 1741 and 1770. The trends established by the members of the first two cohorts persisted into the period after 1770.

In the Revolutionary era Schwenkfelder couples took vows at ages even younger than their parents and grandparents and wedded in patterns that reflect a further shift away from European customs but toward the adoption of American standards.[23] After 1770 about one-fourth of the women who married did so when they were not yet 20. This change is reflected in an average age a first marriage of 22.1 years. For men, the mean age at first marriage declined further, to 25.7 years, in part, a consequence of the fact that greater proportions of Schwenkfelder males found wives when less than 25 years old. By 1800 Schwenkfelders entered matrimony at ages very similar to those discovered to prevail among Lancaster County men and women. There, brides entered first matrimonial unions when 22.6 years old and grooms when 26.5 years of age.[24]

The temptation is to see the shift in mean age at marriage as part of the process of Schwenkfelder assimilation into the daily life of the Pennsylvania colony. European customs changed under the influence of new economic and social circumstances found in the colony. Whereas men once married near age 30, and women above 24, they began to marry younger because of relaxation of traditional familial and communal standards. A different view of the matter, taken in light of considerable evidence of tightened economic opportunities in the form of higher land prices and reduced availability of suitable arable land, suggests another plausible explanation.[25] People holding strong familial and communal attachments made diligent efforts to locate and provide land for their offspring, thus assuring them a modicum of economic success, and encouraging earlier marriages, in an agricultural society.[26]

Eighteenth-century Schwenkfelder couples, once married, generally lived long lives together as husbands and wives. That the marriage institution was particularly durable is evident from the fact that the mean length of marital bonds measured 28.2, 29.5, and 34.2 years across three cohorts.[27] Marriages lasted until death intervened to dissolve them; divorce, separation, and abandonment remained unheard of. Marriage was for life or, 'Till death us do part.' The proportion of marriages lasting less than 25 years decreased from 47.7 to 38.5 to 26.0 percent by 1800. Conversely, the percentage of couples whose marriages endured 25 or more years improved from 52.4 to

74.1 percent during the century. The statistics indicate that for those people who survived to at least age 20 and who married, life could, indeed, be long and fruitful. The numbers have significance not only as indicators of life expectancy but also for patterns of remarriage and family sizes.

Because long life and religious values encouraged lengthy, durable marriages, over 80 percent of all weddings united never-married men and women.[28] Remarriage was relatively infrequent except during the second cohort when 20 percent of all marriages included at least one partner entering a second matrimonial union. This configuration perhaps emerged as the aftermath of the period of migration and early settlement. By the 1740s widows and widowers from the first cohort formed new relationships. Another contributing factor may have been the more frequent visitation of epidemic diseases as population density increased in the 1750s and 1760s. These factors, working in conjunction with the usual loss of life among women in childbirth or its complications, produced more remarriages between 1741 and 1770. Very few men marrying for the first time sought widows as partners. However, when they remarried for a second or third time, widowers frequently thought widows attractive mates, but they expressed a stronger preference for never-wedded brides to bereft women. Widows remarried less frequently than men. Fewer Schwenkfelder women remarried because their first husbands penalized them if they did. Abraham Kriebel willed 500 pounds in gold and silver coin 'as long as she remains my Widow. But if she should marry again then she shall only have two hundred and Fifty Pounds Money aforesaid.'[29] Males who entered wedlock two or more times fathered larger families than those who wedded only once, and they created much larger domestic units than those produced by couples whose unions ended before the conclusion of the wives' childbearing years.

Marital fertility among Schwenkfelders gave concrete expression to the facts that brides married young, life expectancy encouraged lengthy unions, and durable marriage bonds resulted in large families. The average size of Schwenkfelder families increased considerably over the century. Travelers, diarists, and residents alike thought of Pennsylvania wives as exceptionally fecund, as generating families in excess of ten to fifteen children. Gottlieb Mittelberger, for example, considered 'the females… very fertile. For one marries young…. Whenever one meets a woman, she is either pregnant, or carries a child in her arms, or leads one by the hand. Every year, then, many children are born.'[30] Examination of 188 Schwenkfelder families supports this testimony. During the century the average births per marriage increased from 5.5 to 6.0 in the second cohort and then rose sharply to 7.3 after 1770.[31] Fewer parents had less than six children and increasing numbers of couples formed families in excess of ten. These figures give dramatic expression to the improved quality of life Schwenkfelders enjoyed. Readily available productive land yielded plentiful harvests of nutritious food. Improved diet, more than medical advances, contributed to the health, long life, and large families of Schwenkfelders. The proportions of men and women who married earlier in life and the increasing numbers who had children in the first year of wedlock kept premarital pregnancy and illegitimacy rates to a minimum. Strong religious values reinforced this tendency.

The Schwenkfelders consistently abided by a code of acceptable sexual behavior before married life. Social norms and religious values discouraged premarital sex and encouraged the practice that consenting adults wed before they had children. Moreover, the community expected that partners had made preparation to enter adult society in religious matters, had reached responsible age, and established economic security.[32] Some aberrations from these regulations occurred and change manifested itself in the second half of the century. But only 7.1 and 4.9 percent of the parents in the second and third cohorts had their first children before nine months of wedlock elapsed.[33] Trends in premarital pregnancy and in illegitimacy paralleled one another as in other areas.[34] These findings strongly imply that parental influence, social norms, and religious values deterred sexual expression by the young. The data bolster the interpretation of historians who argue that familial and communal values, rather than individualism and competitiveness, prevailed in the social development of early Pennsylvania.

The power to enforce standards concerning premarital sex and illegitimacy depended to a great extent on the duration of marriages. Likewise, parental presence in the family over long periods of time enhanced elders' ability to regulate youngsters' choices of marriage partners and their timing of wedlock.

Long life added to adults' authority to control property transfers and thus regulate these behaviors. Enforcement of familial
and community values rested on the foundation of survivorship.
Consideration of diseases, death rates, and life expectancy for
Schwenkfelders indicates that parents had relatively long lives
and, therefore, the potential to insist upon and receive childrens' compliance with these rules.

The social and physical environment in which Schwenkfelders lived not only encouraged earlier marriages for women
and facilitated larger families but sustained the members of a
growing community through increasingly longer lives. Children
born to Schwenkfelder parents married before 1800 enjoyed
good prospects of survival through infancy and childhood, attained adulthood in great numbers, married and raised sizable
families, and in surprising proportions, endured to an advanced
age. But mortality differences between the sexes crucially influenced the members of the Schwenkfelder faith. Male children born before 1800 suffered higher rates of mortality than
females from infancy through the various stages of life.

Variations in life expectancy by sex materialized from differences in male and female death rates.[35] Female children born
to Schwenkfelder parents married before 1800 could expect to
live for an average of 41.2 years. Having endured the first, most
dangerous year of life, young women living to age 20 had life
expectancies of 43.4 years. Male babies, however, could anticipate an average future lifetime of 38.9 years at birth. Young
men who survived to age 20 lived 1.4 less years on average
than females who attained the same age. Futures for men and
women converged at age 50 since there was only a 0.7 year
difference in favor of females. The female advantage in life
chances at birth and through youth diminished between ages
20 and 50 due in part to the dangers inherent in childbearing
or its complications. Nevertheless, Schwenkfelders, representing a hardy strain of survivors of migration and pioneering,
enjoyed greater longevity than other Pennsylvanians. Female
expectation of life in Lancaster County after 1770 at birth, 20,
and 50, measured 35.8, 35.2, and 20.4 years respectively. Male
futures for the same stages of life after 1770 computed to 35.2
36.2, and 19.3 years, respectively.[36]

Schwenkfelder demographic patterns shifted during the
eighteenth century. Marriage ages for brides and grooms declined steadily over the century as larger numbers of men and

women wedded at earlier periods of life in response to improved economic conditions. The duration of marriages lengthened considerably by 1800, indicating improved life chances for both adult males and females, and the working of the powerful force of religious values that sanctified marriage. Remarriage rates remained relatively low due to the duration of first marriages. Births per marriage increased from an average of 5.5 before 1741 to 6.0 between 1741 and 1770. This figure rose to 7.3 in the third cohort. Premarital sex and illegitimacy occurred only infrequently and reflected the force of familial and religious values. Male and female life expectancy improved during the course of the century, and so by 1800 women at birth anticipated future life times of 41.2 years, and men, 38.9 years.

Several discoveries from the Schwenkfelder study support the interpretation that familial and communal standards rather than competitive individualism and market-oriented values governed peoples' lives. The duration of marriages and long life made possible parental control of childrens' behavior. Life expectancy for men and women at age twenty measured more than forty years. Thus, parents lived to rear most of their children to adulthood. Large proportions of elders in families and in the community strengthened the hand of those empowered with authority to enforce customary behaviors. Patriarchal, familial, and communal norms guided daily behavior among Schwenkfelders. Marriage ages for brides and grooms shifted downward by 1800 in response to economic changes and as parents continued to have their say in such matters as the timing of marriages and choice of partners. They remained able to assert themselves and willing to assist youngsters just so long as their children did not try to wed when they were too young. Premarital sex rates remained low throughout the period. Low rates of illegitimacy paralleled this tendency and thus reaffirmed the community's values concerning such behaviors. Parental enforcement of these regulations remained vigorous to 1800. As the economic structure tightened, parents perhaps became less able to demand and receive compliance with strict rules. Outmigration also weakened the power of parental supervision, as did marriage outside the religious faith.

# Notes

1  G. L. Gollin, *Moravians in Two Worlds: A Study of Changing Communities* (New York, 1967).

2  J. William Frost, *The Quaker Family in Colonial America: A Portrait of the Society of Friends* (New York, 1973); Barry Levy, 'Tender Plants': Quaker Farmers and Children in the Delaware Valley, 1681-1735,' *Journal of Family History*, 3 (1978), 116-35; Robert V. Wells, 'Quaker Marriage Patterns in a Colonial Perspective,' *William and Mary Quarterly*, 29 (1972), 415-42; Jack D. Marietta, *The Reformation of American Quakerism, 1748-1783* (Philadelphia, 1984).

3  James T. Lemon, *The Best Poor Man's Country: A Geographical Study of Early Southeastern Pennsylvania* (Baltimore, 1972).

4  Stephanie G. Wolf, *Urban Village: Population, Community, and Family Structure in Germantown, Pennsylvania, 1683-1800* (Princeton, 1976); Jerome H. Wood, Jr., *Conestoga Crossroads: Lancaster, Pennsylvania, 1730-1790* (Harrisburg, 1979); Sam Bass Warner, Jr., *The Private City: Philadelphia in Three Periods of its Growth* (Philadelphia, 1968).

5  Duane E. Ball, 'Dynamics of Population and Wealth in Eighteenth-Century Chester County, Pennsylvania,' *Journal of Interdisciplinary History*, 6 (1976), 621-44; Duane E. Ball and Gary M. Walton, 'Agricultural Productivity Change in Eighteenth-Century Pennsylvania,' *Journal of Economic History*, 36 (1972), 102-17.

6  Rodger C. Henderson, 'Community Development and the Revolutionary Transition in Eighteenth-Century Lancaster County, Pennsylvania' (Ph.D. dissertation, SUNY-Binghamton, 1983).

7  Daniel Snydacker, 'Kinship and Community in Rural Pennsylvania, 1749-1820,' *Journal of Interdisciplinary History*, 13 (1982), 41-61.

8  Lucy Simler, 'The Township: The Community of the Rural Pennsylvanian,' *Pennsylvania Magazine of History and Biography*, 106 (1982), 41-68.

9  Selina G. Schultz, 'The Schwenkfelders of Pennsylvania,' *Pennsylvania History*, 24 (1957), 293-320.

10  Frost, *Quaker Family*; Levy, 'Tender Plants'; Wells, 'Quaker Marriage Patterns'; James A. Henretta, 'Families and Farms: Mentalitè in Pre-Industrial America,' *William and Mary Quarterly*, 3d Ser., 35 (1978), 3-32.

11  Lemon, *Best Poor Man's Country*; Wolf, *Urban Village*; Wood, *Conestoga Crossroads*; Warner, *Private City*; Syndacker, 'Kinship and Community'; Gary B. Nash, 'Social Development,' in Jack P. Greene and J. R. Pole, (eds.), *Colonial British America: Essays in the New History of the Early Modern Era* (Baltimore, 1984), 238-342.

12  The basic source which provided the vital data necessary for reconstitution of the families was Samuel Kriebel Brecht (ed.), *The Genealogical Record of the Schwenkfelder Families, Seekers of Religious Liberty Who Fled From Silesia to Saxony and Thence to Pennsylvania in the Years*

*1731 to 1737* (New York, 1923). All tables presented in the following essay derived from this source.

13 E. A. Wrigley (ed.), *An Introduction to English Historical Demography: From the Sixteenth to the Nineteenth Century* (New York, 1966), 96 159.

14 Schultz, 'The Schwenkfelders'; Henderson, 'Community Development.'

15 This paragraph draws on material presented in C. Lee Hopple, 'Spatial Development of the Southeastern Pennsylvania Plain Dutch Community to 1970: Part II,' *Pennsylvania Folklife*, 21 (1972), 39-42; Schultz, 'The Schwenkfelders,' 293, 304-05, 311; 'Narrative of the Journey of the Schwenkfelders to Pennsylvania, 1733,' *Pennsylvania Magazine of History and Biography*, 10 (1886), 167-79; Howard Wiegner Kriebel, *The Schwenkfelders in Pennsylvania: A Historical Sketch* (Lancaster, 1904), 35-54.

16 Wrigley (ed.), *Introduction to English Historical Demography*, 150.

17 *Pennsylvania Chronicle*, September 14, 1767; Jim Potter, 'Demographic Development and Family Structure,' in Greene and Pole, *Colonial British America*, 127-32.

18 Benjamin Franklin, *Observations Concerning the Increase of Mankind, Peopling of Countries, etc.* (Boston, 1755), 3, 4, 8.

19 Israel Acrelius, *A History of New Sweden; or, The Settlements on the River Delaware* (Philadelphia, 1874), 356-57; Gottlieb Mittelberger, *Journey to Pennsylvania in the Year 1750 and Return to Germany in the Year 1754*, edited by Oscar Handlin and John Clive (Cambridge, Mass., 1960), 81; Peter Kalm, *Travels in North America*, edited by Adolph B. Benson (2 vols.; New York, 1966), 1: 211, 223; Henry D. Biddle (ed.), *Extracts From the Journal of Elizabeth Drinker, From 1759 to 1807* (Philadelphia, 1889), 218.

20 J. Hajnal, 'European Marriage Patterns in Perspective,' in D. V. Glass and D. E. C. Eversley (eds.), *Population in History: Essays in Historical Demography* (Chicago, 1965), 108-09.

21 See Table I.

22 See Table II.

23 See Table III.

24 Henderson, 'Community Development,' 449, 454.

25 Henderson, 'Community Development,' 127-40, 258-85, 481-93; Wolf, *Urban Village*, 52, 85-88, 108-09, 120-24; Wood, Jr., *Conestoga Crossroads*, 166-80; Lemon, *Best Poor Man's Country*, Table I, 11; James T. Lemon and Gary B. Nash, 'The Distribution of Wealth in Eighteenth Century America: A Century of Change in Chester County, Pennsylvania, 1693-1802,' *Journal of Social History.*, 2 (1968), 1-24; Ball, 'Dynamics of Population and Wealth,' 637; Gary B. Nash, *The Urban Crucible: Social Change, Political Consciousness, and the Origins of the American Revolution* (Cambridge, MA, 1979), Table 3, 395 and Table 4, 396.

26  Gregorius Schultz, Will, May 4, 1770; Christopher Schultz, Will, October 24, 1788; Abraham Kriebel, Will, March 12, 1792. These wills are located at the Schwenkfelder Library, Pennsburg, Pennsylvania. Among Moravians stricter regulations led to demands for abandonment of communal structures. Economic success promoted individualism. (Gollin, *Moravians in Two Worlds.*) Rigorous enforcement of Quaker regulations influenced more exogamous marriages. (Jack D. Marietta, 'Quaker Family Education in Historical Perspective,' *Quaker History*, 63 (1974), 3-16).

27  See Table IV. The duration of marriages in Lancaster County measured 24.8, 27.1, and 23.9 years across three cohorts. (Henderson, 'Community Development,' 143, 287, 495).

28  See Table V. In Europe as many as 25 to 30 percent of widowed first marriage partners entered second unions. (Jacques Dupaquier, et. al., eds., *Marriage and Remarriage in Populations of the Past* (London, 1981), 7, 31, 56, 212, 284, 335-46, 593; E. A. Wrigley and R. S. Schofield, *The Population History of England, 1541-1871: A Reconstruction* (Cambridge, 1981), 258). About 25 percent of Lancaster County first marriage partners eventually took second spouses. (Henderson, 'Community Development,' 151, 324, 510). Brides and grooms marrying for the first time composed 88.1 percent of Quaker marriages so 'remarriage was not too common.' (Wells, 'Quaker Marriage Patterns,' 422-25). At Germantown, however, men 'frequently had second families by marrying younger women when their wives... died.' (Wolf, *Urban Village*, 263, 273-75).

29  Abraham Kriebel, Will, March 12, 1792.

30  Mittelberger, *Journey to Pennsylvania*, 81.

31  See Table VI. The mean births per marriage in Lancaster during the same years registered 7.2 7.3, and 7.1 respectively. (Henderson, 'Community Development,' 169, 349, 523).

32  Kriebel, *The Schwenkfelders in Pennsylvania*, 91-94, 221-25.

33  See Table VII. The rates are comparable for Lancaster County where 4.6, 6.4, and 4.3 percent of the parents in three cohorts had their first children before nine months of wedlock. (Henderson, 'Community Development,' 171 173, 357-59, 525-28). Some Pennsylvanians showed 'a good deal of toleration for premarital conception.' (Wolf, *Urban Village*, 260-61). Perhaps they did in Germantown, where premarital conception approached a rate touching one of four marriages. (Ibid., 261). But among Quakers 'both bridal pregnancy and illegitimacy were rare.' (Robert V. Wells, 'Family Size and Fertility Control,' *Population Studies*, 25 (1971), 76). Other data, however, show that many Quakers married out of the discipline of family and Meeting 'often after sexual intimacy.' (Levy, 'Tender Plants,' 121, 127-30).

34  Daniel S. Smith and Michael S. Hindus, 'Premarital Pregnancy in America, 1640-1971: An Overview and Interpretation,' *Journal of Interdisciplinary History*, 5 (1975), 539, 561-64.

35 See Tables VIII and IX. The tables have been constructed using concepts and techniques outlined in E. A. Wrigley, 'Mortality in Pre-Industrial England: The Example of Colyton over Three Centuries,' *Daedalus*, 97 (1968), 546-80; Lorena S. Walsh and Russell R. Menard, 'Death in the Chesapeake. Two Life Tables for Men in Early Colonial Maryland,' *Maryland Historical Magazine*, 69 (1974), 211-27; James M. Gallman, 'Mortality Among White Males in Colonial North Carolina,' *Social Science History*, 4 (1980), 295-316; Mortimer Spiegelman, 'Life Tables,' in David L. Sills (ed.), *International Encyclopedia of the Social Sciences* (1968), 9: 292-99; George W. Barclay, *Techniques of Population Analysis* (New York, 1958), 93-122.

36 Henderson, 'Community Development,' Table 118, 566, and Table 119, 569.

## Table I
### Age at First Marriage, Brides and Grooms Wedded before 1741

| | Women | | Men | |
|---|---|---|---|---|
| Age | No. | % | No. | % |
| 15-19 | 5 | 14.3 | 0 | 0.0 |
| 20-24 | 11 | 31.4 | 5 | 14.7 |
| 25-29 | 16 | 45.7 | 14 | 41.2 |
| 30-34 | 3 | 8.6 | 12 | 35.3 |
| 35-39 | 0 | 0.0 | 3 | 8.8 |
| Totals | 35 | 100.0 | 34 | 100.0 |
| Mean | 24.4 | | 29.3 | |

## Table II
### Age at First Marriage, Brides and Grooms Wedded 1741-1770

| | Women | | Men | |
|---|---|---|---|---|
| Age | No. | % | No. | % |
| 15-19 | 9 | 20.0 | 1 | 2.0 |
| 20-24 | 19 | 42.2 | 10 | 20.4 |
| 25-29 | 16 | 35.6 | 30 | 61.2 |
| 30-34 | 1 | 2.2 | 7 | 14.3 |
| 35-39 | 0 | 0.0 | 1 | 2.0 |
| Totals | 45 | 100.0 | 49 | 99.9 |
| Mean | 22.8 | | 26.5 | |

## Table III
## Age at First Marriage, Brides and Grooms Wedded 1771-1800

| Age | Women No. | % | Men No. | % |
|-----|-----------|-----|---------|-----|
| 15-19 | 21 | 24.4 | 5 | 5.7 |
| 20-24 | 46 | 53.5 | 37 | 42.1 |
| 25-29 | 15 | 17.4 | 33 | 37.5 |
| 30-34 | 4 | 4.7 | 9 | 10.2 |
| 35-39 | 0 | 0.0 | 3 | 3.4 |
| 40-44 | 0 | 0.0 | 0 | 0.0 |
| 45-49 | 0 | 0.0 | 1 | 1.1 |
| Totals | 86 | 100.0 | 88 | 100.0 |
| Mean | 22.1 | | 25.7 | |

## Table IV
## Duration of Marriages

| Years | Before 1741 No. | % | 1741-1770 No. | % | 1771-1800 No. | % |
|-------|-----------------|-----|---------------|-----|---------------|-----|
| 1-4 | 2 | 4.8 | 8 | 12.3 | 7 | 7.9 |
| 5-9 | 5 | 11.9 | 3 | 4.6 | 2 | 2.3 |
| 10-14 | 1 | 2.4 | 4 | 6.2 | 2 | 2.3 |
| 15-19 | 6 | 14.3 | 2 | 3.1 | 4 | 4.5 |
| 20-24 | 6 | 14.3 | 8 | 12.3 | 8 | 9.0 |
| 25-29 | 4 | 9.5 | 5 | 7.7 | 6 | 6.7 |
| 30-39 | 7 | 16.7 | 19 | 29.2 | 24 | 27.0 |
| 40-49 | 6 | 14.3 | 7 | 10.8 | 18 | 20.2 |
| 50-59 | 5 | 11.9 | 7 | 10.8 | 17 | 19.1 |
| 60-69 | 0 | 0.0 | 2 | 3.1 | 1 | 1.1 |
| Totals | 42 | 100.0 | 65 | 100.1 | 89 | 100.1 |
| Mean | 28.2 | | 29.5 | | 34.2 | |

## Table V
## Remarriage Patterns

| Rank | Before 1741 No. | % | 1741-1770 No. | % | 1771-1800 No. | % |
|------|-----------------|-----|---------------|-----|---------------|-----|
| 1-1 | 36 | 87.8 | 56 | 80.0 | 81 | 88.0 |
| 1-2 | 0 | 0.0 | 3 | 4.3 | 0 | 0.0 |
| 2-1 | 3 | 7.3 | 5 | 7.1 | 10 | 10.9 |
| 2-2 | 1 | 2.4 | 6 | 8.6 | 1 | 1.1 |
| 3-2 | 1 | 2.4 | 0 | 0.0 | 0 | 0.0 |
| Totals | 41 | 99.9 | 70 | 100.0 | 92 | 100.0 |

## Table VI
### Births per Marriage

| Births | No. | Marriages Before 1741 % | No. | Marriages 1741-1770 % | No. | Marriages 1717-1800 % |
|---|---|---|---|---|---|---|
| 0 | 4 | 10.0 | 5 | 9.6 | 4 | 4.2 |
| 1- 5 | 14 | 35.0 | 16 | 30.8 | 23 | 24.0 |
| 6-10 | 21 | 52.5 | 27 | 51.9 | 54 | 56.3 |
| 11-15 | 1 | 2.5 | 4 | 7.7 | 14 | 14.6 |
| 16-20 | 0 | 0.0 | 0 | 0.0 | 1 | 1.0 |
| Totals | 40 | 100.0 | 52 | 100.0 | 96 | 100.1 |
| Mean | 5.5 | | 6.0 | | 7.3 | |

## Table VII
### Premarital Sex and Birth of First Child

| No. | Before 1741 % | No. | 1741-1770 % | No. | 1771-1800 % |
|---|---|---|---|---|---|
| $\leq$ 9 mo. | 0 | 0.0 | 4 | 7.1 | 4 | 4.9 |
| 9-12 mo. | 18 | 54.6 | 29 | 51.8 | 53 | 64.6 |
| 2nd yr. | 10 | 30.3 | 19 | 33.9 | 22 | 26.8 |
| 3rd yr. | 2 | 6.1 | 2 | 3.6 | 2 | 2.4 |
| 4th yr. | 2 | 6.1 | 1 | 1.8 | 0 | 0.0 |
| 5th yr. | 1 | 3.0 | 1 | 1.8 | 1 | 1.2 |
| Totals | 33 | 100.1 | 56 | 100.0 | 82 | 99.9 |

## Table VIII
### Abridged Life Table, Female Children Born Before 1800

Of 100,000 born

| Year of Age x | Rate of Mortality Per 1000 $1000q_x$ | Number Surviving to Exact Age x $l_x$ | Number Dying Between Ages x and x+1 $d_x$ | Number of Years Lived By Cohort Between x and x+1 $L_x$ | Total Years Lived by Cohort From Age x on Until All Have Died $T_x$ | Average Years Lived After Age x per Person Surviving to Exact Age x $e_x$ |
|---|---|---|---|---|---|---|
| 0- 1 | 263.2 | 100,000 | 26,320 | 86.840 | 4,117,326 | 41.2 |
| 1-4 | 89.6 | 73,680 | 6,602 | 281,516 | 4,030,486 | 54.7 |
| 5- 9 | 16.4 | 67,078 | 1,100 | 332,640 | 3,748,970 | 55.9 |
| 10-14 | 13.4 | 65,978 | 884 | 327,680 | 3,416,330 | 51.8 |
| 15-19 | 20.6 | 65,094 | 1,341 | 322,118 | 3,088,650 | 47.5 |
| 20-24 | 40.0 | 63,753 | 2,550 | 312,390 | 2,766,532 | 43.4 |
| 25-29 | 61.1 | 61,203 | 3,740 | 296,665 | 2,454,142 | 40.1 |
| 30-34 | 37.7 | 57,463 | 2,166 | 281,900 | 2,157,477 | 37.6 |
| 35-39 | 54.1 | 55,297 | 2,992 | 269,005 | 1,875,577 | 33.9 |
| 40-44 | 29.6 | 52,305 | 1,548 | 257,655 | 1,606,572 | 30.7 |

| | | | | | |
|---|---|---|---|---|---|
| 45-49 | 81.1 | 50,757 | 4,116 | 243,495 | 1,348,917 | 26.6 |
| 50-54 | 54.5 | 46,641 | 2,542 | 226,850 | 1,105,422 | 23.7 |
| 55-59 | 114.1 | 44,099 | 5,032 | 207,915 | 878,572 | 19.9 |
| 60-64 | 152.7 | 39,067 | 5,966 | 180,420 | 670,657 | 17.2 |
| 65-69 | 83.3 | 33,101 | 2,757 | 158,613 | 490,237 | 14.8 |
| 70-74 | 244.9 | 30,344 | 7,431 | 133,143 | 331,624 | 10.9 |
| 75-79 | 310.8 | 22,913 | 7,121 | 96,763 | 198,481 | 8.7 |
| 80-84 | 451.0 | 15,792 | 7,122 | 61,155 | 101,718 | 6.4 |

## Table IX
### Abridged Life Table, Male Children Born Before 1800

| Year of Age x | Rate of Mortality per 1000 $1000_{qx}$ | Of 100,000 Born Number Surviving to Exact Age x $l_x$ | Number Dying Between Ages x and x + 1 $d_x$ | Number of Years Lived By Cohort Between x and x + 1 $L_x$ | Total Years Lived by Cohort From Age x on Until All have died $T_x$ | Average Years Lived After Age x per Person Surviving to exact Age x $e_x$ |
|---|---|---|---|---|---|---|
| 0- 1 | 287.0 | 100,000 | 28,700 | 85,650 | 3,888,803 | 38.9 |
| 1- 4 | 89.5 | 71,300 | 6,381 | 272,438 | 3,803,153 | 53.3 |
| 5- 9 | 21.1 | 64,919 | 1,370 | 321,170 | 3,530,715 | 54.4 |
| 10-14 | 7.2 | 63,549 | 458 | 316,600 | 3,209,545 | 50.5 |
| 15-19 | 25.2 | 63,091 | 1,609 | 311,433 | 2,892,945 | 45.9 |
| 20-24 | 60.2 | 61,482 | 3,701 | 298,158 | 2,581,512 | 42.0 |
| 25-29 | 44.7 | 57,781 | 2,583 | 282,448 | 2,283,354 | 39.5 |
| 30-34 | 52.2 | 55,198 | 2,881 | 268,788 | 2,000,906 | 36.3 |
| 35-39 | 46.5 | 52,317 | 2,433 | 255,503 | 1,732,118 | 33.1 |
| 40-44 | 75.8 | 49,884 | 3,781 | 239,968 | 1,476,615 | 29.6 |
| 45-49 | 46.5 | 46,103 | 2,144 | 225,155 | 1,236,647 | 26.8 |
| 50-54 | 63.3 | 43,959 | 2,783 | 212,838 | 1,011,492 | 23.0 |
| 55-59 | 48.3 | 41,176 | 1,989 | 200,908 | 798,654 | 19.4 |
| 60-64 | 136.4 | 39,187 | 5,345 | 182,573 | 597,746 | 15.3 |
| 65-69 | 250.0 | 33,842 | 8,461 | 148,058 | 415,173 | 12.3 |
| 70-74 | 216.9 | 25,381 | 5,505 | 113,143 | 267,115 | 10.5 |
| 75-79 | 384.6 | 19,876 | 7,644 | 80,270 | 153,972 | 7.8 |
| 80-84 | 525.0 | 12,232 | 6,422 | 45,105 | 73,702 | 6.0 |

# Schwenkfelder Indentures
# 1754-1846

## William T. Parsons

In the manuscript collections of the Schwenkfelder Library, are located eighteen indentures from the Upper Perkiomen Valley area, which is also sometimes also called Goshenhoppen. Perkiomen is undoubtedly an Indian name, although the precise meaning has been debated for two hundred years. Goshenhoppen is most likely of Indian origin as well, although some have tried to locate it in German Europe, or to say it is a corruption of a biblical place name. At any rate it has defied precise definition. Whatever the derivation of the name, people and places in these indentures are to be found in that rough quadrangle which is the meetingpoint of Montgomery, Berks. Bucks, and Lehigh Counties today, although early items among these indentures speak of Philadelphia County before Montgomery County was erected from its northern reaches in 1784.

The local saying that Schwenkfelders did not believe in binding out an essentially free people, has been the source of local wonder and skepticism for years.[1] Initially, I thought the eighteen indentures among the records here disproved the saying. In reality, however, only about twenty percent of names in these documents are of Schwenkfelders. Indeed the majority of those members of the then peace-testimony church members are to be found among the witnesses to the indenture of Lutheran, German Reformed, and Mennonite young persons. This paper, then, does not destroy the common saying but serves to reinforce it.

These indentures are in many ways typical of the colonial and early national indenture. It was then a legal means of training apprentices for life occupations, giving them shelter and guidance all the while. Within the last several years some students of economic development have made distinctions between servant indenture and apprenticeship, based chiefly on age.[2]

It is important for us to define terms which relate to this legal process, since vast differences exist between popular assumptions and Pennsylvania English law definitions. Terms for these particular local processes developed for us in early eighteenth century usage, although contract indentures are a part of English Common Law. Location away from the English labor market and scarcity of all laborers made indentured bondage in Pennsylvania a different matter than in England. 'A bound servant enjoyed all rights, whether political or legal, except those specifically denied him by law or contract. His mobility, his freedom of occupational choice, and certain personal liberties were curbed merely for a term of years.'[3]

Among the indentures below all but two are work indentures. Numbers 4 and 13 are passage indentures, whereby Christina Wieand was bound to Abraham Kriebel and John Schaller was indentured to Andrew Schultz for monies due him for payment of passage money to the ship captain or his agent. Tendencies for a gradual inflation of fares is seen, from 1765 (c.$60.00) to 1817 ($100.00). We have few details on Christina; she was both female and minor. She is not to be found in the Philadelphia port records which normally are the source of our information. Eventually family records, a Wieand genealogy, family tree, or church or local records in Freinsheim or in Pennsylvania may furnish more clues.

It was the always observant Benjamin Franklin who noted the endemic labor shortage as early as 1740. 'Labor will never be cheap in Pennsylvania,' he said. 'No man continues long a Labourer for others, but gets a plantation of his own.'[4] The lure of land brought many of the Pennsylvania Germans to the Quaker province in the first place. One would be quite surprised if they suddenly ceased their search for land of their own when here.

But for many the effort to come to the New World had cost them all that they had. The obvious alternative was work indenture to pay passage money and to get their children started in a gainful trade while at the same time assuring a roof over their head and at least some food on the table.

For all the others, indenture is work or apprentice indenture, that is, minor persons are bound out for a period of time, varying from six months to eighteen years, while passage indentures were usually of three, five, or seven years' duration. Most recent scholarship reveals that indentures in late colonial Pennsylvania usually ran four or five years.[5]

During their time under indenture servants learned the particular trade of their master, ranging from farming or housewifery to carpenter/cabinetmaker or blacksmith. Virtually all were enabled to pay travel costs from a trade which was then their own.[6] Ordinarily it was orphan children or those with a single surviving parent who were put into a position of unfree worker. To their great surprise German immigrants, accustomed to the feudal law of the old German states, found themselves protected by English contract law.

Arrangements were made by parents, guardians, or overseers of the poor who most often held responsibility for minors.[7] A local historian recently noted that the work indenture refered to a status rather than a simple contract relationship.[8] In the eighteenth and nineteenth centuries the indentured servant stood under a shadow but the position was a way up the ladder of work status. Stevenson Fletcher elaborates further: 'Apprenticeship was not merely a system of labor, it was a method of education, especially for the poor. Although abused at times, it trained good workmen.'[9]

Boys were normally apprenticed at twelve and served until their twenty-first year. Girls went into service at twelve or earlier and served to eighteen.[10] Parents did threaten children with the warning that 'they would bind them out.' Indenture did not always carry a negative connotation. Many times the community regarded it as a positive means to teach and to protect. This type of status was not free from discrimination since women served longer for the same passage debt than did men.[11]

In William Penn's benevolent Quaker Province of Pennsylvania, the law required that every master furnish the man completing his apprenticeship with a new axe and more than one of several types of hoe.[12] It became a fixture in these arrangements which were actually contracts under English and then American law that the worker was entitled to his 'freedom dues' at the end of his work term, assuming good and faithful service.

Pennsylvanians considered work a God-given blessing and one of the normal rights of Englishmen in British North America; in contrast, voluntary idleness was considered not only an evil but sin. Labor was always in short supply in colonial Pennsylvania and as a result was usually expensive.[13] Family labor was very important among Pennsylvania's working population. That served the double purpose of keeping German children in line and built a new family esprit-de-corps.[14] Scotch-Irish people objected that their German neighbors worked their wives in the field at harsh labor, but German wife and growing children proudly worked to hold up their share of a family responsibility.[15]

Occasionally in Pennsylvania, Black, Indian, convict, and felon labor was used or considered. That rarely worked; the German never liked to hold Blacks in bondage. On the other hand, many German independent farmers and landowners made their beginning in Pennsylvania as indentured persons. In turn, they offered the same sort of opportunity to fellow Germans who came over later. North and South Carolina were similar, especially where German settlers were concerned.[16]

A perfect case in point of that idea was the example of the Griesemer brothers who first arrived in Pennsylvania in 1730. In Northampton, Berks, and Lancaster counties, they began to farm under indenture to landholders. By the time those workers had earned their own lands and position, they gave the same chance to more recent arrivals. While it is true that not every work contract was productive, the majority were. The resulting relationship and comraderie contributed to the continuing strength of the ethnic community.[17]

It is not an exaggeration to say that men who began their relationship as master and servant were found side by side on the patriot side of the War of the American Revolution. After all, apprentices were job trainees.[18] They not only learned their trade from the master who was surrogate parent, but they absorbed values and character traits as well.

More formally, masters owed instruction, protection, room and board to the servants under their care. That applied not only to the servants who worked out their passage money in eighteenth century America, but to the sons, daughters, and orphans who were put to service in the nineteenth century.[19] They promised the worker to see to his welfare and to furnish the work tools of his apprenticeship trade. In many ways, the indentured apprentice became a part of the master's family.

In virtually every apprenticeship indenture, the master saw to it that they were trained to read and write, that they learned the scriptures or catechism and attended church or parochial school. If the master failed to carry out his promises, he was held liable in court and the apprentice might well gain his freedom immediately. 'The master was assured of the servant's labor.'[20] But, that meant that when a youngster was put out at very early age, the master had to carry him without productive return until he grew old enough to work. It often took years.

The apprentice had his meals, a roof over his head, and a home to live in. 'It was a guarantee for him.'[21] He promised to mind his morals, not to get out of line and often promised not to frequent taverns or ale-houses or other houses of ill-repute. By contract, he agreed not to fornicate nor to get married while under service. On completing his indenture he became a free man, legally equal to any other in the province; he had a right to church membership and with it a right to vote.[22]

## Documents

1 ADS. Upper Hanover Township, Philadelphia County [now Montgomery County]. 23.5x19.5cm. 2pp. 20 March 1754.

This Indenture Wittnesseth That Adam Hiligas and Buckhart Hoffman, Overseers of the poor of the township of Upper Hanover, County of Philada., For Good Consideration hath put and bound and by those presents hath put and bound WILLIAM UNDICHMAN Apprentice unto John Hood, of the sd. Township, Weaver, To Serve him, the said John Hood, Exec[utor]s or Assigns, for Eighteen years from ye First of January Last, and during all wch Term, the said Apprentice his sd Master, Execr. or Assigns faithfully Shall Serve and that Honestly and Obediently in all things as a Good and Dutifull Apprentice ought to do, and the Said Master, Execr. or Assigns during the Said Term. Shall Teach or Cause to be Taught or Instructed the said Apprentice in the Art or Mystery of Weaving and Teach ye sd. Apprentice to read and at Expiration Shal Give him Two Pounds Currency and Customary Freedom dues with Good Apparel, meat, drink, Washing and Lodging during ye term.

In Wittness where of The said parties to these presents have Hereunto Set their Hands and Seals Interchangably, ye 20th day of March Anno Dom: 1754.

Executed with ye Approbation                              Johannes Huth
of us the Subscribers, two of
the Justices of the Peace:

Row[lan]d Evans
Henry Pawling
Endorsed on rear: Indenture Wm Undichman      Deed

2 Broadside, signed. data inserted. Philadelphia. 19 x 21cm. 1p. 22
April 1765. [Form printed by Andrew Steuart, Second Street, Phila.]

This Indenture Witnesseth, That ELIZABETH SOWER, in Con-
sid[eration] of Twenty Two two shillings [22 s.?] paid for her by Lewis
Farmer, as also for other good Causes, She, the said Elizabeth hath bound
and put her self, and by these Presents doth bind and put her self Servant
to the said Lewis Farmer, to serve him, his Executors and Assigns, from
the day of the date hereof, for and during the Term of Four Years and
Six Months thence next ensuing. During all which Term, the said servant
his said Master his Executors, or Assigns, faithfully shall serve, and that
honestly and obediently in all things, as a good and dutiful Servant ought
to do. AND the said Master his Executors and Assigns, during the Term,
shall find and provide for the said Servant sufficient Meat, Drink, apparell
Washing and Lodging, and freedom dues.

And for the true Performance hereof, both Parties bind themselves
firmly unto each other by these Presents. IN Witness whereof they have
hereunto interchangeably set their Hands and Seals. Dated the 22nd Day
of Aprill in the 5th Year of his Majesty's Reign; and in the Year of our
Lord, one thousand, seven hundred and sixty-five.
Signed, sealed and delivered
in the Province of: Phila. PA                              Lewis Farmer
Bound before Tho[mas]Lawrence
    May[o]r

3 ADS. Philadelphia. 19x21cm. 1p. 1 May 1765.

Hiermit Ver-spreche, zur, zu mir Verbundenen Dienst Magd, anstatt
ihres frey A[rb]eides, Sechs Pfund Pensilvanier Geld zu bezahlen, nach Ver-
fliesung ihres Zeith. Solte sie aber in wahrender Zeit sterben, so ist das Ver-
sprochenen aufgehoben, und nicht zu bezahlen. Solches bezeichnet meine
Hand und unterschrift, gegeben Philadelphia, May the 1st 1765
6 = 0 = 0                                          Abraham Kribel
Witness: Lewis Farmer

[3a] Philadelphia 1 May 1765. [translation by William T Parsons]

Herewith I promise [bind myself for] my indentured servant girl instead
of having her work for free, to pay her Six Pounds, Pennsylvania money,
at the expiration of her time. Should she, however, die in the meantime
[before her time of service is completed, ] then the obligation is terminated,
and no payment shall be made. To that I set my hand and seal. Done at
Philadelphia, 1 May 1765.
£ 6. 0. 0                                         Abraham Kriebel
Witness: Lewis Farmer

4 Broadside, Signed. data inserted. Philadelphia. 29x21cm. [Printed
and Sold at the New Printing office, Philadelphia.] 1p. 6 October 1765.

This Indenture witnesseth, That CRISTENE WIANT, Daughter of Elies Wiant, with the Consent of her father and in for and in Consideration of the Sum of Twelve Pounds to her sd Father in hand, Paid for her Passage by Abraham Creble as also for other good Causes She the said Cristene Wiant hath bound and put her self Servant to the said Abraham Creble to serve him his Executors and Assigns, from the Day of the Date hereof, for and during the full Term of nine years 8 months and 3 weeks thence next ensuring. During all which Term, the said Servant her said Master his Executors and Assigns, faithfully shall serve, and that honestly and obediently in all things, as a good and dutiful Servant ought to do.

AND the said Master his Executors and Assigns, during the said Term, shall find and provide for the said Servant sufficient Meat, Drink, apparril Washing and Lodging and at the Expiration thereof to give her five Pounds Lawful money in Consideration of her Freedoms.

AND for the true Performance whereof, both the said Parties bind themselves firmly unto each other by these Presents. In Witness whereof, they have hereunto interchangeably set their Hands and Seals. Dated the Sixth Day of October in the Year of his Majesty's Reign. Annoque Domini 1765.

Sealed and Delivered
in the Presence of                                                Abraham Kreeble
Befor Jno Bull

5 Broadside, signed. data inserted. Philadelphia. 19x21cm. 1p. 6 August 1768.

This Indenture Witnesseth, That PETTER HENDERSON, with the Consend of his father, Jeames Henderson, Hath put himself, and by these Presents, doth voluntarily, and of his own free Will and Accord, put himself Apprentice to Christian Stetler, to learn his Art, Trade and Mystery, and after the Manner of an Apprentice to serve him, his Exctrs and Assigns from the Day of the Date hereof, for and during, and to the full End and Term of fourteen yers next ensuing. During all which Term, the said Apprentice his said Master faithfully shall serve, his Secrets keep, his lawful Commands every where readily obey. He shall do no Damage to his said Mastor, nor see it to be done by others, without letting or giving Notice thereof to his said Mastor. He shall not waste his said Mastors Goods, nor lend them unlawfully to any. He shall not commit Fornication, nor contract Matrimony, within the said Term: At Cards, Dice, or any other unlawful Games, he shall not play, whereby his said Mastor may have Damage. With his own Goods, nor the Goods of others, without Licence from his said Mastor, he shall neither buy nor sell. He shall not absent himself Day nor Night from his said Mastors Service without his Leave: Nor haunt Ale-houses, Taverns or Playhouses; but in all Things behave himself as a faithful Apprentice ought to do during the said Term. And the said Mastor shall use the utmost of his Endeavour to teach or cause to be taught and instructed the said Apprentice in the Trade or Mystery of a Courd winder and procure and provide for him sufficient Meat, Drink, apparril, Lodging and Washing, fitting for an Apprentice, during the said Term of fourteen years and Teach or Cause to be Taughd to Read and write in said Term and it is further agreed by both partys that the said apprentice is to have a Sheep whan he Shall be Nineteen years of age for his yuse and at the Expiration of said Term to give him a good sued of apperil, besides his ould ones and Tools Suffitiond to work.

AND for the true Performance of all and singular the Covenants and Agreements aforesaid, the said Parties bind themselves each unto the other firmly by these Presents.  IN WITNESS whereof the said Parties have interchangeably set their hands and Seals hereunto. Dated the sixth Day of August in the Eighd Year of the Reign of our Sovereign Lord George the Third, King of Great-Britain, andc. Annoque Domini One Thousand Seven Hundred and Sixty Eighd.

Sealed and delivered in                                   Christian Stetler
the Presence of us:
    FDk [Frederick] Antes

6 Broadside, signed. data inserted. Philadelphia. 34.5x21.5cm. 1pp. 27 April 1772.

This Indenture Witnesseth. that FRIEDRICK SWARTZ Hath put himself, and by these Presents, with the Consend of his father, doth Voluntarily, and of his own free Will and Accord, put himself Apprentice to Christian Stetler to learn his Art Trade and Mystery, and after the manner of an Apprentice to serve him, his Assigns from the Day of the Date hereof, for, and during, and to the full End and Term of Eliven years 7 days next ensuing; During all which Term, the said Apprentice his said Master faithfully shall serve, his Secrets keep, his lawful Commands every where readily obey. He shall do no Damage to his said Mastor, nor see it to be done by others without letting or giving Notice thereof to his said Mastor. He shall not waste his said Mastors Goods, nor lend them unlawfully to any. He shall not commit Fornication, nor contract Matrimony, within the said Term; At Cards, Dice or any other unlawful Games he shall not play, whereby his said Mastor may have Damage. With his own Goods, nor the Goods of others, without Licence from his said Mastor, he shall neither buy nor sell. He shall not absent himself Day or Night from his said Mastors Service without his Leave: Nor haunt Ale-houses, Taverns or Play-houses; but in all Things behave himself as a faithful Apprentice ought to do, during the said Term.  And the said Mastor shall use the utmost of his Endeavour to teach, or cause to be taught and instructed the said Apprentice in the Trade of Mystery of Courd weinder, and procure and provide for him sufficient Meat, Drink, apparril, Lodging and Washing, fitting for an Apprentice, during the said Term of Eleven Years and Nine Days and Teach or Cause to be Taught to Read and Write in Said Term and at the Expiration to have freedum and Seven Pounds teen Shillings in Mony.  AND for the true Performance of all and singular the Covenants and Agreements aforesaid, the said Parties bind themselves each unto the other firmly by these Presents.  IN WITNESS whereof the said Parties have interchangeably set their hands and Seals hereunto. Dated the twenty Seventh Day of

April in the Twelveth Year of the Reign of our Sovereign Lord George the
third, King of Great-Britain, andc. Annoque Domini One thousand Seven
Hundred and Seventy Two 1772.
Sealed and delivered in
the Presence of us
Fdk[Frederick] Antes                                        Christian Stetler

7 ADS. Plymouth Townwhip, Montgomery County. 35x21.5cm. 1p. 2
June 1788.

This Indentur Witnesseth that Henry Gilinger of the Township of Plim-
moth in the County of Montg[omer]y, has bound his Daottor MACK-
DALENA GILINGER, with her consent, a Sarvind unto Melchor Reinewald, of the Township of Toamencin County as afrsaid, to Twell from the
Day of the Date herof for and During the full Term of Ten Years and five
Month and Ten Days next Insuing, During all Which Term the Said Sarvend
hir sd Master faithfully Shall Serve and That Honestly and obedently in
all Things as a Good and Dutifull Sarvent ought to Do and the sd Melchor
Reinewald During the Said Term Shal Instruct the Said Servend to Raet-
ting the Byble and Write a ledgeble hand and the Said Master is to Geat
the Sarvend in Instruit to Receve the Ceckerment and find and Provide for
Said Sarvend Sufficient Meat Drink apparel Washing and Lodging Suiting
for and a sarvent and at the Expiration of Said term to Give Hear five
Pount of Good and Law full monny in Silver or Goold and a New Spenning
Weell and a good New freedom [suit] and for the true Performance therof
and each of the Said parties Bind themselves firmly unto Each other by
these Presents. In Witness Where of the[y] have interchangeably Set there
Hands and Seale, Dated the Secont Day of June Anno Dom onethousand
Seven hundred and Eighty Eight [Signed the interlining with her cosent of
the Township of Towamencin whas done before.]
Bound before me                                        Henrich Geilinger
Christian Weber                                                      har
                                                    Makdalena Gilinger
                                                               Mark

8 Broadside, signed. data inserted. Lower Salford Township. 34x21cm.
1p. [Printed by Joseph Crukshank.] 16 December 1797.

This Indenture Witnesseth, That ABRAHAM GERKES, son of William Gerkes, late of Lower salford township Deceased, by and with the
consent of his Mother Philippina Gerkes, Hath put himself, and by these
Presents, he the said Abraham Gerkes with the said Mothers consent, doth
voluntarily, and of his own free Will and Accord, put himself Apprentice to
Christian Bergy of the Township of Lowersalford aforesaid, blacksmith, to
learn his Art, Trade and Mystery, and after the Manner of an Apprentice
to serve the said Christian Bergy his heirs and Assigns from the Day of the
Date hereof, for, and during, and to the full End and Term of Two years and
nine months next ensuing. During all which Term the said Apprentice his
said master faithfully shall serve, his Secrets keep, his lawful Commands

every where readily obey.  He shall do no Damage to his said Master, nor see it to be done by others, without letting or giving Notice thereof to his said master.  He shall not waste his said Master's Goods nor lend them unlawfully to any.  He shall not commit Fornication, nor contract Matrimony within the said Term.  He shall not play at Cards, Dice, or any other unlawful game, whereby his Master may have Damage.  With his own Good, nor with the Goods of others, without Licence from his said Master, he shall neither buy nor sell.  He shall not absent himself Day nor Night from his said Master's Service, without his Leave: Nor haunt Ale-houses, Taverns, or Play-houses; but in all things behave himself a[s a] faithful Apprentice ought to do, during the said Term.  And the [said] Master shall use the utmost of his Endeavour to teach or cause to be taught or instructed the said Apprentice in the Trade or Mystery of a Blacksmith and procure and provide for him sufficient Meat, Drink mending of Cloaths and find him Shows, Lodging and Washing fitting for an Apprentice, during the said Term of two years and nine months, and at the expiration of one year and six months, to pay said apprentice the sum of six pounds, and the like sum at the expiration of said Term and allow Said apprentice two weeks each year in haymaking and one week in second crop mowing and to find him as good Shoes when free as be broaght.  AND for the true performance of all and singular the Covenants and Agreements aforesaid, the said parties bind themselves each unto the other, firmly by these Presents.  IN WITNESS whereof, the said Parties have interchangeably set their Hands and Seals hereunto.  Dated the sixteenth Day of December Annoque Domini, One Thousand Seven Hundred and Ninety-seven.
Montgomery Countyss
Bound Before me the Subscriber,                          Abraham Gerges
one of the Justices of the Peace
in and for the County abovesaid.
Witness my hand and Seal –
    Fred[eric]k Conrad
Endorsed on reverse: Indenture Abraham Gerkes to Christian Bergey

9 ADS. Macungie Township, Norhampton County. 17x21cm. 2pp. 25 March 1799.

This Indentire Witneset That ANNA RITTER aged about five years by and with the Consent of her Mother Susana Ritter of Macungy Township and County of Northampton, widow, and Michael Neihart and Peter Neihart Administrators bound and put herself and by these presents Doth bind and put herself Servant to Henry Christman in the Township and County aforesaid for and during the full term of Thirteen Years and two weaks from the date hereof thence next ensuing during all which term the said Servant his said Master his executors or assigns faith fully shall serve and that honestly and obediently as a good and dutifull Servant ought to do.  And the said Henry Christman his Executors and assigns during the said term shall find and provide for the said Anna Ritter Sufficient meat drink appearal lodging and washing and at the expiration thereof shall give

# This Indenture

**WITNESSETH, THAT** Catharina Hystrud, Daughter of Jacob Hystand of Hereford Township, Berks County Labourer,

hath put her self, and by these presents doth voluntarily and of her own free will and accord, put herself apprentice to Jacob Stauffer of Upper Milford Township Northampton County Farmer of House wifery — to learn the — art, trade and mystery, and after the manner of an apprentice, to serve him, from the day of the date hereof, for and during the full end and term of Ten Years, four Months & 14 days ——— next ensuing. During all which term, the apprentice her — said master faithfully shall serve, his — secrets keep, his lawful commands every where gladly obey. She shall do no damage to her said master nor see it done by others, without letting or giving notice thereof to her said master. She shall not waste her said master's goods, nor lend them unlawfully to any. She shall not commit fornication nor contract matrimony within the said term. At cards, dice, or any other unlawful game she shall not play, whereby her — said master may have damage. With her own goods nor the goods of others, without licence from her said master shall neither buy nor sell. She shall not absent her self day nor night from her said master's — service, without his leave; nor haunt ale-houses, taverns or play-houses; but in all things behave her self as a faithful apprentice ought to do, during the said term, and the said master shall use the utmost of his deavour to teach, or cause to be taught or instructed, the said apprentice in the trade or mystery of House wifery and procure and provide for her sufficient meat, drink, Apparrel — lodging and washing, fitting for an apprentice, during the said term & also to teach her, or cause to be taught, to read in the German Language And at the Expiration of said Term to give her, a Customary new Suit of Cloathing (besides her Wearing Apparrel) Also One ~~Chest~~ Cow, One Bed & Bedstead with Curtains — One Spinning Wheel — And one Chest, either Poplar & painted, or one of Walnut boards. —

And for the performance of all and singular the covenants and agreements afore-said, the said parties bind themselves each unto the other firmly by these presents. IN WITNESS whereof the said parties have interchangeably set their hands and seals hereunto. Dated the first — day of June — in the twenty third year of American independence, &c. Annoque Domini one thousand seven hundred and ninety nine ——

Sealed & Delivered
In the presence of
Jacob Finster
Bound before me
Peter Richards

Catharina Hystand

the Customary freedom duse One Cow and a good new bet and a Speenet weel and sufficient Close for Everyday and Sunday Close and the same tim sent it to the Minister to take the Sacrament and to sent it the said Servent to school and teach or cause him the said servant to be thaught in reading and wrighting. In witness whereof I have set my Hand and Seal this twenty fifth Day of March in the year of our Lord one Thousand seven Hundred and Ninety Nine.

Anna Ritter          My Hant und Seal                             her
Witnessed before me                                         Anna Ritter
Year and Day abovesaid Peter neihart                          merck
Henry Jarrett                                            Susana Ritter
                                                           her merk

Endorsed on rear: Indenture from Anna Ritter to Henry Christman

10 Broadside, signed. data inserted. Hereford Township, Berks County. 33x20.5cm. 1p. 1 June 1799.

This Indenture WITNESSETH THAT CATHARINA HYSTAND, Daughter of Jacob Hystand of Hereford Township, Berks County Labourer, hath put her self and by these presents doth voluntarily and of her own free will and accord, put herself apprentice to Jacob Stauffer of Upper Milford Township Northampton County Farmer to learn the art, trade and mystery of House Wifery and after the manner of an apprentice, to serve him from the day of the date hereof, for and during the full end and term of Ten Year's four Months and 14 days next ensuing. During all which term, the apprentice her said master faithfully shall serve, his secrets keep, his lawful commands every where gladly obey. She shall do no damage to her said master nor see it done by others, without letting or giving notice thereof to her said master. She shall not waste her said masters goods, nor lend them unlawfully to any. She shal not commit fornication nor contract matrimony within the said term. At cards, dice, or any other unlawful game She shall not play, whereby her said master may have damage. With her own goods nor the goods of others, without licence from her said master, shall neither buy nor sell. She shall not absent herself day nor night from her said master's service without his leave; nor haunt ale-houses, taverns or play-houses; but in all things behave her self as a faithful apprentice ought to do, during the said term, and the said master shall use the utmost of his endeavour to teach, or cause to be taught or instructed, the said apprentice in the trade or mystery of House Wifery and procure and provide for her sufficient meat, drink, apparrel, lodging and washing, fitting for an apprentice, during said term, As also to teach her, or cause to be taught, to read in the German Language. And at the expiration of said Term, to give her a Customary new Suit of Cloathing (besides her Wearing Apparrel). Also One Cow, One Bed and Bedstead with Curtains, One Spinning Wheel, And One Chest, either Poplar and painted, or one of Walnut boards. And for the performance of all and singular the covenants and agreements aforesaid, the said parties bind themselves each unto the other firmly by these presents. IN WITNESS whereof the said parties have interchangeably set their hands and seals hereunto. Dated the first day of June in the twenty third year of American independence, andc. Annoque Domini one thousand seven hundred and ninety nine.

Sealed and delivered                                      Catharina Hiestand
In the presence of Jacob Hiestand
Bound before me Peter Richards

11 ADS. Colebrookdale Township, Berks County. 32.5x20cm. 4pp. 24 December 1813.

This Indenture Witnesseth That CATHARINA SPRINGER, Daughter of John Springer of Colebrookdale Township Berks County hath put herself, and by these presents doth voluntarily and of her own free will and accord, put herself apprentice to Jacob Stauffer of Upper Milford Township Lehigh County Farmer, to learn the Art, Trade and Mystery of Housewifery and after the Manner of an Apprentice, to serve him from the Day of the Date hereof, for and during the full End and Term of Three Years, Nine Month, and four Days next ensuing, During all which Term, the apprentice her said Master faithfully shal serve, his secrets keep, his lawful Commands every where gladly obey. She shall do no Damage to her said Master nor see it done by others, without letting or giving Notice thereof to her said Master. She shall not wast her said masters goods, nor lend them unlawfully to any, she shall not commit Fornication nor contract Matrimony within the said Term. At Cards, Dice, or any other unlawful Game She shall not play whereby her said Master may have Damage. With her own Goods nor the Goods of others, without licence from her Master, shall neither buy nor sell. She shall not abscent herself Day nor night from her seid Masters service, without his leave; not haunt Ale houses, taverns or playhouses; but in all things behave herself as a faithful apprentice ought to do, during the said Term, and the said Master shal use the utmost of his endeavour to teach, or cause to be taught or instructed, the said Apprentice, in the Trade or Mistery of house wifery and procur and provide; for her sufficient meat, drink, apparrel lodging and washing, fitting for an apprentice, during the said term, as also to teach her or cause to be taught, to write and read in the german Language, and at the expiration of said Term, to give her a customary new suit of Cloathing (besides her wearing Apparrel.) Also one Cow, One Bead and beadstead with Curtains and in place of that, a good planket which she may choose, One Spinning Wheel, and One Chest or the Value thereof in Cash. And for the performance of all and singular the Covenants and agreements aforesaid, the said parties bind themselves into each other unto the other firmly by these presents. In Witness whereof the said parties have interchangeably set their Hands and Seals hereunto. Dated the twenty-fourth Day of December Anno Domini One Thousand Eight Hundred and Thirteen.

Sealed and delivered                                          her
in the presence of                                  Catarina Springer
John Springer                                           marke
Jacob Oberholser                                    Jacob Stauffer

Endorsed on reverse: Indenture with Catharina Springer Along with many separate calculations, stands what appear to be financial matters concerning an estate (Possibly Stauffer's):

| | | |
|---|---:|---:|
| Abraham Stauffer is due to 10 Bonds pr his Land, | | amt $2218.73 |
| Due to Bond dated May 19th 1835 | | amt 950.00 |
| For the 37'8th 25 day theron at 5 per cent | | amt 177.46 |
| | | 3346.19 |
| Due in vondue paper | | 4.81 |
| | | 3351.00 |
| Peter Stauffer to 5 bonds ech 100 or 501.11.1 | | 1337.47 |
| Daniel Stauffer to 7 bonds amt | | 1116.00 |
| Susanna Stauffer widow of Jacob sen | | 500.00 |
| Peter must give out | 297.63 | |
| Abraham must give out | 2265.80 | |
| Daniel must have yet | 78.– | |
| Susann must have yet | 694.– | |
| John must have | 1394.– | |

12 ADS Upper Milford Township, Lehigh County. 28x21mm. 1p. 11 February 1814.

Dieser Indentur bezeuget, dass sich HENRICH TRUMP Jacob Trumps Sohn von Uppermilford Township in Lecha County (bey, und mit dem Rath und Zustimmung seines besagten Vaters, der es mit der Unterschrift als Zeuge bezeuget) an Caspar Schultz von Upperhanover Township Montgomery County Bauer als Knecht (Lehrjung) verbunden hat und begiebet, und durch dieses gegenwärtige verbinden Thut und giebt um besagtem Caspar Schultz seinen Executoren Administratoren oder an wen er dieses ubermacht nach Art eines Knechts zu dienen und beÿ ihm zu bleiben, von dem Tag dieses Datums an während der Zeit durch bis zu dem vollen Ende von Neun Jahr uns Sechs Monath voll angehalten und geendiget. Während dieser gantzen Zeit soll besagten Knecht seinem besagten Meister treulich dienen und Das in allen Dingen ehrlich und gehörsamlich, als einem fleissigen Knecht zuständig ist, Und besagter Caspar Schultz seine Executors Administrators oder an wen er dieses übermacht soll besagten Knecht lernen, oder machen dass er in der Kunst, Handel und Wissenschaft eines Bauren gelernt und unterrichtet werde, desgleichen lernen oder machen dass er gelernt werde im Lesen und Schreiben, und soll besagten Knecht auch während besagter Zeit mit hirnlanglichem Essen, Trincken, Kleidung, Waschen und Beherbergung versehen; und soll auch am Ende dieser Zeit besagtem Knecht, benebst seiner gemeinen Kleidung, einen gantz neuen Anzug von Kleidung; oder aber Acht Pfund in Geld geben, wie es etwa etwa [sic] besagter Knecht erwählen möchte.

In Zeugniss dessen haben die besagten Partheyen ihr Hand und Siegel darunter gesetzt den 11ten Tag February 1814.

12a ADS. Upper Milford Township, Lehigh County. 31x20cm. 2pp. 11 February 1814. [Same as No. 12, but in English.]

This Indenture Witnesseth That HENRY TRUMP the son of Jacob Trump of Upper Millford Township in the County of Lehi (by and with the advice and consent of his said father testified by his signing as a witness hereto) hath bound and put himself and by these presents Doth bind and put himself apprentice to Casper Shultz of Upper Hanover Township in the County of Montgomery, Farmer after the manner of an apprentice to dwell with and serve the said Casper Shultz his executors administrator and assigns from the day of the date hereof for and during the full end and term of nine years and sixmonths thence next ensuing and fully to be complete and ended, During which term the said apprentice his said Master faithfully shall serve and that honestly and obediently in all things a dutifull apprentice ought to do. And the said Casper Shultz his executors administrators or assigns shall teach or cause to be taught and instructed the said apprentice in the art trade and mystery of a Farmer and teach or cause him to be taught to read and write and shall and will find and provide for said apprentice sufficient meat drink apparel washing and lodging during said term, and at the expiration thereof shall and will give his said apprentice beside his common apparel one new suit of Clothes or the sum of eight pounds in money as said apprentice may choose.

In Witness whereof the said Parties have hereunto set their hands and seals the 11th day of Feb'y 1814.

Witness present                                               his
   his                                        Henry Trump
Jacob Trump                                                  mark
  mark
W Thompson                                                 Casper Schultz
Done the 11th Feb'y 1814 before me
   John Thompson
Endorsement on rear: Indenture Henry Trump to Casper Shultz

13 Broadside, signed. data inserted. Hereford Township, Berks County. 29x21cm. [Printed by J. Bioren Co.] 1p. 1 September 1814.

This Indenture WITNESSETH, That John Schaller of his own free will and with the consent of his Father, hath bound him Self Servant to Andrew Schultz of Hereford Township Berks County, Farmer, for the Consideration of One Hundred Dollers paid to C. L. Manhart, for his passage from Amsterdam as also for other good causes, he the said John Schaller hath bound and put him self and by these Presents doth bind and put him self Servant to the said Andrew Schultz to serve him, his Executors, Administrators and Assigns from the day of the date hereof, for and during the full Term of Three Years and Six months from thence ensuing. During all of which term the said Servant his said Master, his Executors, Administrators and Assigns faithfully shall serve, and that honestly and obediently in all things, as a good and faithful Servant ought to do. AND the said Andrew Schultz, his Executors, Administrators and Assigns, during the said term shall find and provide for the said Servant sufficient Meat, Drink, Apparel, Washing and Lodging. And at the Expiration of his term, to have Two complete

Suits of Clothes, one thereof to be new, and if he conducts him self to the satisfaction of his master, he shall have Thirty Dollers as a preasent.

And for the true performance hereof, both the said parties bind themselves firmly unto each other by these Presents. IN WITNESS whereof they have interchangeably set their Hands and Seals. Dated the first day of September, Annoque Domini one thousand eight hundred and Seventeen. Bound before

Andrew Leinau                                                    Andrew Shultz
Register

14 Broadside, signed. data inserted. Colebrookdale Township, Berks County. 32x20.5cm. [Printed by Ritter and Co., printers, Reading.] 2pp. 3 May 1823.

THIS INDENTURE WITNESSETH, That DANIEL EHST of Colebrookdale township in the county of Berks and State of Pennsylvania by and with the Advice and consent of his Guardians Jacob Gaubel and John Ehst bothe of the township and county aforesaid hath put himself, and by these presents doth voluntarily and of his own free will and accord, put him self Apprentice to John Hoch of Colebrookdale township in the county of Berks aforesaid to learn the art, trade and mystery of a Farmer and after the manner of an apprentice, to serve the said John Hoch from the fifteenth day of April last past for and during and to the full end and term of two years and six month thence next ensuing, and fully to be complete and ended: during all which term the said apprentice his said Master faithfully shall serve, his secrets keep, his lawful commands every where readily obey; he shall do no damage to his said Master nor see it done by others without giving notice thereof to his said Master; he shall not waste his Masters goods, nor lend them unlawfully to any; he shall not commit fornication, nor contract matrimony during the said term; at cards, dice or any other unlawful game he shall not play, whereby his said Master may have damage: with his own goods or with the goods of others, without licence from his said master he shall not buy nor sell; he shall not absent him self day or night from his said Masters service without his leave: nor haunt ale houses, taverns or play houses; but in all things behave him self as a faithful apprentice ought to do during the said term.

AND the said Master shall use the utmost of his endeavours to teach or cause to be taught and instructed, the said apprentice, in the art, trade and mystery of a Farmer and procure and provide for him sufficient meat, drink, apparal, lodging and washing, fit and convenient for such an apprentice, during the said term and send the said Apprentice six months to School during said term and also pay the teacher and at the expiration of said term Shall and will give his said Apprentice One new suit of apparel besides his old suits of Apparel.

IN TESTIMONY WHEREOF, the said parties have hereunto interchangeably set their hands and seals, the eighth day of May in the year of our LORD one thousand eight hundred and twenty three.
SEALED and DELIVERED

in the presence of us,                                            Daniel Ihst
Abraham Ihst        John High                                     Jacob Gabel
Iohannes Ihst                                                     Johannes Ihst
Endorsed on reverse: Indenture of Apprenticeship
Daniel Ehst to John Hoch
Free 15th October Anno Dom 1825

15 ADS. Longswamp Township, Berks County. 20x19cm. [irregular indenture cut] 2pp. 16 April 1828.

Aprill denn 16den 1828 Hatt Sich Ein Accort Zugetragen Zwischen Dem kind dem heit Dato denn 25ten Aprill 18– Hatt Sich Ein Accort Zu GETRA FRITSCH [ESTHER FRITSCH]

Langen Schwam                                    Henry Christman
Taunschipp Bercks Caunty                                     Getr
Hatt sich Ein birgen zu Getra                    Aprill den 25ten
die zwaeilte Barty                        Hatt sich Ein Acort Zu Getragen
                                            Zwischen den wid [beid ?]

[On reverse:] Solte Es aber der fall sein Dass ich nicht mehr beym leben were, so soll sie ihre Dinst Zeit bey Meinmen gelibten Ehweib aus stehen wan sie zueinem nahmen fuhren Thut biss die Maria frei ist so, und dann Soll mein gemeltet Ehweibe der gemelten Maria die Gemelten Artickel Alle geben wie sie gemelt sind von Meinen Hinterlassenem Guth.

[15a] Longswamp Township, Berks County. 16 April 1828.

16 April 1828. We have both reached an agreement between ourselves from this date forward to 25 April 18–. Made an agreement with GETRA FRITSCH.

Longswamp Township, Berks County               Henry Christman
Made a bargain with                      Getra or Esther Fritsch
Gertrude as the other party.                Reached an agreement
                                               between the two

[Codicil:] But if by chance I do not remain alive for the term, then she shall remain with [serve] my dear Wife, who shall honor my promises to the servant, and if Mary keeps her part of the bargain, until she shall be free, then shall my said widow give to Mary all the promised articles, as she ought to do, from my own estate.

16 ADS. Rockland township, Berks County. 17x20cm. 2pp. 30 March 1833.

Mertz den 30 Jar 1833 Hatt sich Ein Acord oder Bergen Zu getragen Zwischen Abraham Oswalt Von Rockland Taunschip Bercks Caunty, einer Seit, und Ester Lang Von langen Schwamm Taunschip ob gemelten county andere Seit Von Wegen dem gemelten Oswalt seiner Tochter Ester Auff Ihr Elt, dass ist Zu Sagen biss sie Achzehen Jahr alt ist. Weiter so ver Stricht die gemelte Ester Lang der ESTER OSWALT. Zu geben ordenliche Gleidung Vor Sonntage wie auch vor Wertag welegis schon frau Kleid, und auch Zum Pfarren schicken und mass ihren ein guth Bett geben und Bett Cath Mehr muss sie ihr geben ein Pirs Mehr ein neu Spinrath.

Solches bezeign wir beide Mitt unsere Eigene Handen Bey Zeigen zu unserer gegenwarth.

Henrich Christman

Abraham Oswalt
ihr
Ester Lang
merck

Endorsed on rear: Acord Zwischen Abraham Oswalt und Ester Lang.

[16a] Rockland Township, Berks County. 30 Mar 1833.

30 March 1833. An agreement or bargain is herewith undertaken between Abraham Oswald of Rockland Township, Berks County, party of the first part, and Esther Long of Longswamp Township of the said County, of the second part, on behalf of the said Oswald's daughter, ESTHER OSWALD, [who shall serve] until she is of age, that is to say, until she becomes 18 years old, and thus that the said ESTHER OSWALD shall serve Esther Long. [At the end of her term] she shall give ESTHER OSWALD a proper suit of Sunday clothes as well as work clothing for a woman; and also to send her to the Pastor [to learn to read the Bible]; she [Esther Long] shall also give her a good bed and bed clothes; secondly she shall give her a purse; and further, a new spinning wheel. To all this we agree and sign our hand and seal for this matter.

Abraham Oswald Esther Long Henry Christman

17 ADS. Douglass Township, Montgomery County. 29x22cm. 3pp. 24 June 1846.

This Indenture witnesseth, That JACOB HUBER of Douglas Township in the County of Montgomery (a son of Jacob H. Huber) (by and with the advice and consent of his Guardien John Hoffman of the same Township and County, testified by his signing as a witness hereto) hath bound and put himself Apprentice to Absalon Huber of Upper Hanover Township in the said County of Montgomery Carpenter and Cabnitmaker, after the Manner of an Apprentice to dwell with and serve the said Absalon Huber his executors, Administrators and Assigns from the first day of April next ensuing the date hereof, for and during, and untill the full end and term of Two Years, thence next ensuing, and fully to be completed and ended: During all which term the said Apprentice his said Master faithfully shall serve. and that honestly and obediently in all things, as a dutifull Apprentice ought to do. And the said Absalon Huber (his Executors, Administrators or Assigns) shall teach and instruct, or cause to be taught and instructed, the said Apprentice the art, trade and mystery of a carpenter and cabinetmaker, and shall and will find and provide for the said Apprentice, sufficient meat, drink, washing and lodging and mending his wearing apperal except shoes or Boots, during the said term; and at the expiration thereof, shall and will give his said Apprentice one fore plane, one Jack plane and one smoothing plane one hand saw, one hatchet and square all to be new and of good quality and shall pay unto the said Apprentice the sum of Twelve Dollars Lawfull money, one half thereof to be paid during te first year an the other half thereof during the second year, and shall also pay unto his said Guardien the sum of three Dollars like money as aforesaid at the expiration of the first year to be applied by said Guardien for mending said Apprentices' shoes; In witness whereof the said parties have hereunto set their hands and seals, the twenty fourth day of January in the Year of our Lord One Thousand eight hundred and forty Six. (1846).

Witness present at Signing                              Jacob Hover
Amos Schultz                                          Absalohn Huwer
Elizabeth Schultz                                   Johannes Hoffman

    [Endorsed on rear:]
Indenture of Jacob Huber and Absalon Huber for to learn said Jacob Huber the art of Carpenter and Cabinetmaker during the term of 2 years from the 1st day of April 1846 till Ap. 1st 1847 [sic].

18 ADS Douglass Township, Montgomery County. 32x20.5cm. 3pp. 5 December 1846.

This Indenture witnesseth, That WILLIAM HOFFMAN of Douglass Township in the county of Montgomery and state of Pennsylvania (by and with the advice and consent of his Father, of the same place testified by his signing as a witness hereto) hath bound and put himself and by these presents, doth bind and put himself, Apprentice to George Edelman of New Hanover Township in the county and state aforesaid Shoemaker, after the manner of an apprentice to serve the said George Edelman from the first day of October next ensuing the date hereof for and during , and untill the end of six months hence next ensuing, during all which term the said apprentice his Master faithfully shall serve, and that honestly and obediently as a dutifull apprentice ought to do. And the said George Edelman shall teach and instruct or cause so to be done the said apprentice the art, trade and mystery of a Shoemaker at all times when the said Geo. Edelman has any work to be done and shall and will during the said term wash and mend the clothing of said apprentice the said John Hoffman to find his boarding for the said apprentice and the said John Hoffman shall have the one moiety or half part of all the work which the said apprentice may earn for the said Edelman at shoemaking during said term in cash to be paid by said Edleman unto said John Hoffman or to his heirs or assigns; It is hereby agreed by and between the said parties that if in case the said John Hoffman and Geo. Edelman shall agree that the said Edelman will dwell on the premises of the said Hoffman after the first day of april A. D. 1848 for a term of two years more than they have agreed upon this day, by certanes articles of agreement entered upon, then and in that case the said apprentice shall serve the said Edleman eighteen months longer as above said and his said master shall instruct him as aforesaid in the art of a shoemaker and Jo. Hoffman shall find his board and finally in every respect as specified for the said six months. In witness whereof the said parties have hereunto set their hands and seals this fifth day of December in the Year of our Lord one thousand eight hundred and forty six. 1846.

Witness present at signing                            William Hoffman

Isaac Schultz jr                                           Johannes Hoffman
Amos Schultz                                               George Edelman
Endorsed on rear: Indenture for Wm. Hoffman as apprentice to Geo Edelman

## Personalities in Schwenkfelder Indentures

These alphabetized names of personalities who appear in the previous indentures, attempt to provide historical and genealogical information so as to identify persons found here. Sometimes data about additional generations have been included where it is of use for researchers' identifications. All indentured persons are indicated by listing them in upper case letters: JACOB HUBER.

Spelling stands as in the original. When obscure words are present, a correct form follows. All indentures are in the collection at the Schwenkfelder Library, Pennsburg, PA. As it turns out, very few of the names involved, servants or masters, proved to be Schwenkfelders. In fact, most of the Schwenkfelders whose names do appear on the documents, are witnesses or officials.

In attempting to sort out actual persons whose names do in fact appear on the indentures, I have tried to give as complete data as possible, that is to be accurate yet helpful. Still the readers will not be surprised to find that this researcher cannot state with absolute certainty which of four Johannes Huths is in the document cited. Suggested answers will appear. Signatures have been compared where that process is possible.

I offer profound thanks to Claire Conway, Holly Green, Mrs. James Young, Mrs. William Smith and Dennis Moyer for their help in locating and accumulating pertinent data on the many personalities encountered above. Since research is never really complete, I invite additions and corrections from our readers. Some few incorrect assumptions may eventually have to be changed or deleted but for that a we shall have to await those suggestions and comments. Time is a great ally.

Frederick Antes was born 2.07.1730. His father and a brother both emigrated to Pennsylvania from Freinsheim, Pfalz. He resided in New Hanover Township and was a member of Goshenhoppen Reformed Church. Justice of the Peace for Philadelphia County from 1754 to 1756, he also witnessed indentures in 1768 and 1772. Served as an officer in the Patriot Army of George Washington. Mention in McMichael American Revolution diary. Antes died 20.07.1801.[23]

Christian Bergey was probably Mennonite and was born about 1776. He was a blacksmith who resided in Lower Salford Township and took ABRAHAM GARGES as apprentice in 1797; it is not clear how long after 1797 Bergey died.[24]

John Bull was born 1.06.1731 and became a farmer, business man and land speculator in Philadelphia County. Chosen a judge in the colonial government, he signed the indenture of CHRISTINE WIEAND to Abraham Kriebel in 1765. Married on 13.08.1752 to Mary Phillips, Bull was a colonel who served on the War Board under General George Washington in the American Revolution. Member of the Episcopal Church, he also became a Mason. Bull was elected to the Pennsylvania Assembly from Northumberland County in 1805. John Bull died 9.08.1824.[25]

Henry Christman, a farmer and merchant, lived in Longswamp Township from 1805 to 1833. His date of birth was about 1776. Christman was a member of Longswamp German Reformed Church, where he married Barbara [ ]. They stood sponsors 1.01.1806 for four week old Jacob Christman, son of Jacob and Susanna Christman. While master of a servant girl in 1828, he was concerned that he might die. Bilingual, he signed one indenture in German script and another in English. Henry Christman died sometime after 1833. Confusing the issue no little is the existence of a second near contemporary Henry Christman [actually Johann Heinrich Christman] in nearby Hereford Township, Berks County. This second Henry, a son of Philip Christman, was born 3.02.1777 and died 17.04.1852.[26] Henry from Longswamp married Evan and included her in his will in 1828.

Frederick Conrad was born in 1767 near Center Point, Worcester Township, Montgomery County, a descendant of Henrich Cunrath who arrived in Philadelphia on the Ship *Lydia* 29.09.1741. Frederick Conrad was a farmer and a blacksmith; he was a member of Wentz Reformed Church, quite near to his home. He married Catharine Schneider, a member of Swamp Reformed Church in 1821. Conrad served 'as clerk of vendue' in 1784 as noted in the Melchior Schultz Account Book. Elected to the Pennsylvania Assembly in 1798, he served until 1801; then elected to two terms in the House of Representatives to 1807. Frederick Conrad was chosen justice of the peace in Worcester Township where he was known as 'Squire Conrad' from 1807 until his death in 3.08.1827. Prothonotary of Montgomery County from 1821 to 1827. A letter from Daniel Yost to Frederick Conrad 24 Jul 1805, dealt with '*der erwehlung des Simon Schneider zum Gover[nor]s*' (electing Simon Synder to be Governor of Pennsylvania).[27]

George Edelman, born 2.11.1807 in New Hanover Township, Montgomery County, was the son of Johannes and Mary [Fried] Edelman, members of New Hanover Lutheran Church. George, one of eleven children, was baptised 29.11.1807, and confirmed in 1815. He married Melina Hauk 23.10.1831. A master shoemaker with WILLIAM HOFFMAN as his apprentice in 1846, Edelman set up as shoemaker at John Hoffman's 1846 to 1848. He died between 1848 and 1850.[28]

Abraham Ehst was born 9.12 1794 and farmed in Colebrookdale Township, Berks County. The son of Samuel and Maria Ihst, he had a brother John and sisters Dinah and Christina. Abraham was Lutheran, the descendant of Nicholas Ish (born 1711) who arrived in Philadelphia on the *Pink Plaisance* 21.09.1732. Abraham Ihst signed DANIEL EHST'S Indenture in German script. Died 25.10.1891 just seven weeks before reaching the age of ninety-seven.[29]

DANIEL EHST, son of Daniel (1771-1815) and Catharine [Keller] Ehst (1781-1862), was born in Colebrookdale Township, Berks County in 1811.

He was a Lutheran farmer who also worked as gunsmith. He married Susanna K. Stauffer. EHST was indentured in 1823 to a relative, John Hoch [High], who 21.12.1821 had married Christina Ihst. DANIEL signed his own indenture IHST in German Script. John Gabel and John Ehst, both Mennonites, were his guardians in 1823. DANIEL EHST is in the 1860 Census; he died in Reading, June 1889.[30]

John Ehst (born 12.04.1782 and died 25.03.1869) was a Mennonite farmer of Colebrookdale Township, Berks County. Married 1) Anna Weiss circa 1806 and they had two children; 2) Elisabeth Swartley about 1812: they had three sons and five daughters. John Ehst a guardian of DANIEL EHST in 1823, signed in German script. Buried in Boyertown Mennonite Cemetery.[31]

John Ehst (born 5.11.1805, died 9.12.1886) was also a farmer in Colebrookdale Township, Berks County and was Mennonite also. At age eighteen he acted as witness on the 1823 DANIEL EHST indenture, which he signed Iohannes Ihst in German script. He is buried in the Bally Mennonite Cemetery.[32]

Rowland Evans was born before 1724 and resided in Gwynedd Township, Philadelphia County. In 1754, he served as Justice of the Peace and later was Judge in Philadelphia County. Identified in a 1756 Huebner land transaction. A member of the Society of Friends, he served in the Pennsylvania Assembly, 1761-71, where he stood in opposition to Benjamin Franklin. Evans died in 1789.[33]

Lewis Farmer, born before 1740, was an innkeeper in Philadelphia County. He held one indentured servant and witnessed a second indenture. A colonel on the staff of George Washington in the American Revolution in 1781; he served as sheriff in Philadelphia County in 1782. Farmer was married 2.02.1786, most likely a second marriage. Farmer died in the same county in 1805.[34]

GETRA [ESTRA or ESTHER] FRITSCH was bound to Henry Christman Longswamp Township in 1828, when she was already twenty-two years of age. Signed her indenture g e t r in German script. If Henry Christman died, ESTHER should serve the widow, who shall honor the girl's freedom dues. ESTHER was German Reformed, born 6.04.1808 (baptised 22.05.1808), and was the daughter of Henry and Maria [ ] Fritsch; her sponsors were Esther Butz and John Schwartz. ESTHER FRITSCH lived in Macungie Township, Lehigh County, also.[35]

John Gabel, Mennonite farmer of Colebrookdale Township, Berks County, was born 25.07.1776. He married Catharina Hoch (born 19.12.1784, died aged 101 24.05.1886). Gabel served as guardian for DANIEL EHST in 1823. Listed as John Gaubel on the indenture, he signed Gabel in English letters. Died 21.08.1830.[36]

ABRAHAM GERKES [GARGES] was born in 15.09.1779 in Lower Salford Township, Philadelphia [later Montgomery] County. Son of William and Philippina Garges, Mennonites, he was apprenticed to Christian Bergey (same township) when eighteen in 1797. His contract allowed time off for haymaking and for second crop each summer. Signed his name GERGES in German script on 1797 indenture. Married Elisabeth [ ] (born 1778) after 15.09.1800. ABRAHAM GARGES died 10.07.1859 and was buried in Salford Mennonite Cemetery.[37]

Philippina [ ] Garges was born about 1745 and married William Garges before 1769. By 1797, when her son ABRAHAM was bound to Christian Bergey, she was widowed. A Mennonite housewife resident in Lower Salford Township, she died after 1798.[38]

William Garges was a Mennonite farmer, born in Lower Salford Township before 1740; by 1769, he married Philippina. Their son ABRAHAM GARGES was indentured in 1797 after the father's death. William Garges was Lower Salford Tax Collector in 1776.[39]

Henry Gilinger, farmer in Plymouth Township, was born before 1752. He was the father of MAGDALENA GILINGER, who was indentured in 1788, while Henry still lived. He signed the indenture Geilinger in German script. He must have died after 1788.[40]

MAGDALENA GILINGER was born 10.12.1780 in Plymouth Township. She was apprenticed to Melchior Reinwalt of Towamencin Township for housewifery in 1788, with service to end in 1798. Date of death is not known.[41]

James Henderson, a farmer in Philadelphia County had his son PETTER HENDERSON bound out to Christian Stetler in 1768.

PETTER HENDERSON, was born in 1761 in Philadelphia County. At age seven, he was indentured to Christian Stetler to learn to be cordwainer. Was free of his indenture by 1782.[42]

Catherine Hiestand, see Catarina Hystand.

Jacob Hiestand, see Jacob Hystand.

John High, see John Hoch.

Adam Hillegas, a German Reformed tanner, was born in 1708. He immigrated into Pennsylvania on the Ship *Samuel* 11.08.1732 at age twenty-four. Arrived in Goshenhoppen in 1737 and joined Goshenhoppen German Reformed Church. He married Anna Schultz, a daughter of Melchior Schultz, 14.10.1757. Lived in Upper Hanover Township and sold land to John Yeakel for Schwenkfelder use. This Adam served as Overseer of the Poor for Upper Hanover Township in 1754. He died in 1786.[43]

Adam Hilegas [Hillegass] of Upper Hanover Township was born 5.01. 1717 and died 12.03.1779. He was also a member of Goshenhoppen Reformed Church.

John Hoch [High] was a Mennonite farmer from Colebrookdale Township, Berks County, born 2.07.1795. On 17.01.1821 he married Christina Ihst (24.04.1800-21.02.1843), daughter of Samuel and Maria Ihst, and the Hoch's had eleven children. A second marriage, this time to Hannah Cleaver, took place 30.03.1850. She outlived him. He trained DANIEL EHST as farmer in 1823. John Hoch died 23.06.1852 and was buried in Boyertown Mennonite Cemetery.[44]

Burckhardt [Buckhart] Hoffman, born before 1702, was a German Reformed farmer of Upper Hanover Township. He had arrived in Philadelphia on the Ship *Molly* 30.09.1727, and signed the oath *Burckhardt Hoffman* in German script. His son, Andreas Hoffman, was born 16.04.1732 and is listed in the New Goshenhoppen Church records. In a Deed Poll for land sold by Jacob Fisher to Herman Fisher, deeded lands abutting the Fisher lands include those of Burgert Hapman [Burghart Hoffman,] Michael Ziegler and Leonard Ox [Ochs]. In 1754, Hoffman was one of two Overseers of the Poor in Upper Hanover Township. His date of death is not clear.[45]

John Hoffman, a Lutheran farmer in Douglas Township, Montgomery County, was born 24.11.1802. A Lutheran, he married Catharina Miller (12.07.1808 to 22.03.1894) and they had a son, WILLIAM M. HOFFMAN, shoemaker apprentice, and seven other children alive in 1850. Neighbors of Amos Schultz and Henry Huber, mentioned in other indentures. John Hoffman died 19.07.1868.

At Goschenhoppen Folk Festival, East Greenville, 9.08.1985, a visitor showed two Lutheran hymnbooks to the author. One was inscribed: *Johannes Hoffman seim Gesang-Buch, Geschrieben den 28ten Januarius A.D. 1820*; the other: *Dieses Gesang Buch gehort Catharina Miller, Geschrieben d. 28te Octobris Im Jahr unsers Herrn Jesu Christi* 1824. They were undoubtedly confirmation hymnbooks for the two, who were married a few years later.[46]

WILLIAM M. HOFFMAN was born 22.11.1827 in Douglas Township, the son of John and Catharine [Miller] Hoffman. He was bound for six months to George Edelman, to learn shoemaking while Edelman lived and worked at John Hoffman's. Lutheran, he was buried in Huber's Church, (Christ Lutheran Church) Cemetery, Niantic, PA, after his death 9.03.1907.[47]

John Hood, *see* Johannes Huth.

Absalohn Huber, carpenter/cabinetmaker of Upper Hanover Township, was born before 1820. JACOB HUBER was bound to him in 1846. Probably died before 1850.[48]

JACOB [D.] HUBER, Lutheran was born on his father's farm in Douglas Township, Montgomery County, 13.05.1829. The son of Jacob D. Huber, and Elisabeth M. Huber, he married Catherine [ ] (12.03.1827-21.01.1903). After the death of his master, Absalohn Huber, JACOB D. in 1850, lived on the farm of his brother, Henry Huber (22.06.1816-15.01.1900). JACOB D. HUBER died 24.12.1905.[49]

Jacob H. Huber was a Lutheran farmer/laborer from Douglas Township, who was born 18.06.1789, son of Michael (14.11.1755-8.10.1836) and Elisabeth Hillegas Huber (8.03.1761-20.01.1839). Jacob H. Huber married 1) Elisabeth Mumbauer (16.10.1789 to 24.04.1843) on 23.01.1814 and they had two sons and three daughters; married 2) Hannah Eschbach on 19.08.1849. In 1850, Jacob H. and new wife Hannah, lived in the *grossdaadi haus* on the farm of his son Henry Huber. Jacob H. Huber died 12.02.1859.[50]

Johannes Huth, Junior [John Hood] was born in the Rhineland and immigrated into Philadelphia as a minor on the Ship *William and Sarah* 18.09.1727. This Johannes Huth was a German Reformed weaver in Upper

Hanover Township by 1754, when he signed as master to an indentured servant in German script. This Johannes appears to be Junior, for his signature in 1754 is quite different from the signature of Johannes Huth [Senior] on the 1727 oath. On arrival at the port of Philadelphia, there were three persons over sixteen in the family and one (Johannes, Junior) under sixteen. They had all moved to Goshenhoppen by 1731. 'Old Mrs. Huth,' the wife of Johannes, Sr., was born in 1707, died 04.1776 and was buried 9.04.1776, 'aged about 76.' A son of Johannes, Jr., named Johannes [III], married Barbara Zimmerman in 1748. Johannes and Barbara had a fourth Johannes, born in 1749, who married in 1776. They had five children in seven years. The Huths all belonged to New Goshenhoppen Reformed Church. Johannes Huth, Jr., died 1770.[51]

CATARINA HYSTAND [CATHERINE HIESTAND] of Hereford Township, Berks County, probably Mennonite, was born 17.09.1791. She was bound to Jacob Stauffer, farmer in Upper Milford Township, Northampton County [later Lehigh] to learn housewifery. Upon completion of her service, she was to get a chest, either painted poplar or solid walnut wood, as freedom dues. The signature on the indenture is *Catharina Histand*, in German script, but might be that of the daughter or of her mother.[52]

Jacob Hystand [Histand] was a Mennonite laborer from Hereford Township, Berks County, born before 1776. In 1790, the family numbered just three. Father of the girl bound in 1799 when his wife had already died, he signed his name in German script.[53]

Abraham Ihst, *see* Abraham Ehst.

Daniel Ihst, *see* Daniel Ehst.

Iohannes Ihst, *see* John Ehst.

Johannes Ihst, *see* John Ehst.

Henry Jarrett, farmer and Justice of the Peace for Macungie Township, Northampton County in 1799, was born before 1769 and died sometime after 1799.[54]

Abraham Kriebel was born 18.10.1736 and married Susanna Schultz (21.08.1740-10.10.1820). Abraham was a farmer and storekeeper in Philadelphia and Towamencin Township. He was Schwenkfelder. Signed two indentures as master in German script. An acquaintance of Wendel Wieand of Goshenhoppen, he paid the passage money for CHRISTIAN WIEAND. Wife SUSANNE recalled Indian visits to Towamencin in 1765. Abraham Kriebel was fined for non-service 1777 to 1780. He died 30.01.1801.[55]

'DIENST MAGD' 'MAID SERVANT GIRL' for Abraham Kriebel did indentured service for him in 1765, but her actual name is not indicated. She was born circa 1752 and probably lived nearby.[56]

Ester Lang [Esther DeLang], a free single woman farmer who was born 7.12.1797 of German Reformed parents David and Barbara [ ] DeLang. She was baptised 25.03.1798, when Adam and Catarina Helwig served as her sponsors. On the indenture contract by which ESTHER OSWALT became her servant, DeLang signed with her mark. Esther DeLang died sometime after 1833.[57]

Thomas Lawrence II, born about 1720, lived in Philadelphia where he served as Mayor in 1765. He has an Episcopalian who moved in leading Philadelphia society. Mention by Jacob Hiltzheimer and James Allen; the latter graphically described the death of Thomas Lawrence, 21.01.1775.[58]

Andrew Leinau, who was born before 1790, served as Register of Port Arrivals for Philadelphia in 1817. In that position, he validated JOHN SCHALLER's 1817 indenture. He died after 1817.[59]

C. L. Manhart, passenger agent for an unidentified shipping line in 1817, received passage money from Andrew Schultz for JOHN SCHALLER's voyage from Germany. Manhart was born before 1790, lived in Philadelphia and died sometime after 1818.[60]

Michael Neihart [Newhard], gunsmith in the Lehigh Valley, was born 11.07.1778. He was a member of the German Reformed Church; lived near Laury's Station, North Whitehall Township, Northampton [later Lehigh] County. He was named guardian for ANNA RITTER in Macungie Township. Michael Newhard died 10.03.1842.[61]

Peter Neihart [Newhard], born 7.02.1781, near Allentown, was a blacksmith and a member of Zion Reformed Church, Allentown. At age 21 and 18 respectively, Michael and Peter Newhard served as co-administrators of a Ritter estate; Peter signed his name on the ANNA RITTER indenture in 1799 in German script. Peter Newhard died 13.03.1844.[62]

Jacob Oberholser [Oberholtzer, Junior] was born 5.12.1773 and lived in Colebrookdale Township, Berks County. he farmed and worked as a blacksmith. In 1790, the family of Jacob Oberholtzer, Senior, included two males over sixteen, two under that age and five females. Jacob Junior married Esther Moyer. Oberholtzers, Stauffers and Springers were all interrelated and were neighbors as well. Oberholtzer was a Mennonite; he signed the SPRINGER indenture as witness in 1813. Jacob Oberholtzer died 3.04.1859 and is buried in Bally Mennonite Cemetery.[63]

Abraham Oswalt was born about 1790 and lived in Rockland Township, Berks County. He was a farmer and signed an 1833 indenture in German script. His father, John Oswalt, lived in that township with his wife in 1790; Abraham was born after the census was taken. How long after 1833 Abraham Oswalt died is unclear but on an 1876 map, Oswaldt land is shown in School District 6, bordering on Maxatawny Township.[64]

ESTER OSWALT [Esther Oswald], of Rockland Township, Berks County, who was bound to Esther Lang in 1833, was born after 1815 and was most likely Mennonite.[65]

Henry Pawling [II] was born in 1713 and was baptised Episcopalian 1.11.1713. Henry II was a farmer and land speculator at Pawlings Ford, Providence Township, Philadelphia [later Montgomery] County. His father, Henry I of Padsbury, England, had bought land from William Penn in 1681; he was on the first vestry at St. James Episcopal Church, Perkiomen Township in 1701. Henry II owned 1200 acres in Perkiomen Township along with his Providence Township holdings near Perkiomen Junction. He was Justice of the Peace in Philadelphia County in 1754 and in Montgomery

County 1789-1792. He dated his will 18.11.1791, so he died after that date.[66]

Melchor Reinewald [Melchior Reinwalt] was born 1.04.1744. He was a Schwenkfelder farmer who married Mary Anders 5.05.1767. Mary Anders Reinwalt was born 25.04.1738 and died 11.07.1768, less than seventeen months after their wedding. Almost twenty years a widower, he took as second wife, Rosina Snyder, thirteen years his junior, 5.04.1785. Melchior Reinwalt is mentioned in the Melchior Schultz Account Book, 6.06.1787: 'for digging the graves of Catharina and Barbara Heebner.' In 1788, a bound servant girl came to help his thirty-year-old wife and stayed for ten years. Melchior Reinwalt died 5.12.1812. He is buried in the Towamencin Schwenkfelder Cemetery.[67]

Peter Richards of Hereford Township, Berks County, was born 22.07. 1755, as recorded in New Hanover Lutheran Church Records. He kept store and was a surveyor; he owned land in Maxatawny Township. Richards owned the Upper and Lower Mt. Pleasant Forges along Forgedale Road above Barto in 1791. He served as Justice of Peace in Hereford Township in 1795 and still lived there in 1799. By 1808, he was living in Pottsgrove. Richards died before 1831.[68]

ANNA RITTER was born about 1794, since she was five years old when indentured in 1799 to Henry Christman of Macungie Township, Northampton County. She was the daughter of [ ] and Susanna [ ] Ritter, a widow in that year. Peter and Michael Newhard served as administrators for her in 1799. How many years after that year ANNA RITTER died, has not yet been found.[69]

Anna [Anna Barbara] Ritter, born about 1754, lived in Macungie Township, Northampton [later Lehigh] County. She signed as a witness on the indenture of her granddaughter in 1799. She may well have been the mother-in-law of Susanna [ ] Ritter. She died sometime after 1799.[70]

Susanna [ ] Ritter, of Macungie Township, was born before 1778, was a widow by 1799 and signed ANNA RITTER's indenture with her mark. Some still undetermined time after 1799, she died.[71]

JOHN SCHALLER was born 1.04.1800 and served as apprentice farmer under Andrew Schultz of Hereford Township, Berks County, in 1817, for three years and six months. His father was still alive in 1817. JOHN SCHALLER was still alive in 1850, when two men by that name lived in Lehigh County, one in Weissenberg, the other in Lynn Township.[72]

Amos S. Schultz was born 11.05.1809, in Upper Hanover Township, Montgomery County. He was Schwenkfelder, a farmer, the son of Isaac Schultz (born 21.03.1778, died 15.10.1867) and Susanna S. Schultz (7.05.1782-17.09.1834). Amos S. Schultz also farmed in Washington Township, Berks County, until he married Elizabeth Kriebel (23.12.1812-29.03.1891) on 16.04.1833. He ran both farm and grist mill in Washington Township and a grist mill near Niantic in Douglas Township, Montgomery County. An unmarried brother Isaac Schultz (1811-1874) worked as hired hand for him. Amos S. Schultz served as Justice of the Peace in Douglas

Township from 1840 to 1850. Two of his neighbors were John Hoffman and Henry Huber. Amos S. Schultz' portrait is in the Schwenkfelder Collection today. He died 10.05.1895.[73]

Andrew Schultz [Shultz] was born 28.06.1771 in Hereford Township, Berks County. A Schwenkfelder farmer, he married Rosina Snyder (13.09.1785-27.09.1823) and they had four daughters and two sons. JOHN SCHALLER was bound to him in 1817, a year before Andrew's death, which occurred 9.05.1818.[74]

Caspar Schultz was born 20.12.1781. He was a Schwenkfelder farmer of Upper Hanover Township, Montgomery County. He had a twin named George who died in 1851. On 7.06.1810, Caspar married Christina Yeakel (30.03.1790-9.04.1862). When HENRY TRUMP was bound servant to Schultz in 1814, Caspar signed with his mark.[75]

Elizabeth K. Schultz, wife of Amos S. Schultz, was born 23.12.1812 in Worcester Township, the daughter of Samuel and Christina Kriebel. She signed the indenture of JACOB. D. HUBER in German script. Elizabeth Schultz died 29.03.1891. The portrait of Elizabeth Kriebel Schultz is in the Schwenkfelder Collection.[76]

Isaac Schultz, [Jr.], born 8.06.1811, was a Schwenkfelder, younger brother and hired man for Amos S. Schultz in Douglas Township between 1840 and 1874. He never married. He signed the WILLIAM HOFFMAN indenture as witness in 1846. Died 2.01.1874.[77]

ELIZABETH SOWER, an inhabitant of Germantown or Philadelphia, was born 22.10.1751. She was indentured to Lewis Farmer in 1765. Her date of death has not yet been located.[78]

CATHARINA SPRINGER, born 28.09.1796 in Colebrookdale, Berks County, was bound to Jacob Stauffer for housewifery in 1813. She was Mennonite, daughter of John Springer of Colebrookdale Township, Berks County. An older brother John (22.03.1794-18.09.1866) married Mary Reinwalt (5.08.1808-23.07.1895) in 1829. CATHARINA's date of death remains elusive.[79]

John Springer [Johannes] was a Mennonite who was born in Colebrookdale Township 10.08.1765. He was a farmer who married Catherina Kungle (26.04.1769-29.12.1851), the daughter of Peter and Anna Kungle. Their daughter, CATHARINA SPRINGER, was indentured in 1813. John Springer and Jacob Stauffer both married Kungle women. Springer died 18.02.1830.[80]

Abraham Stauffer was Mennonite. He was born in Colebrookdale Township about 1788. He married Anna Clemmer. On 24.04.1887, Abraham died and is buried in the Bally Mennonite Cemetery. On the reverse of the CATARINA SPRINGER indenture of 1813, is a post-1835 reference to Jacob Stauffer's estate. Abraham died in 1853.[81]

Daniel Stauffer, born before 1813, was a Mennonite who lived in Colebrookdale Township, Berks County. He is also mentioned in the estate reference on the back of the 1813 indenture. Probably died after 1835 and is buried in Upper Milford Township.[82]

Jacob Stauffer, Senior, Mennonite born in Colebrookdale Township 2.08.1754 then to Upper Milford Township, Northampton County, where he farmed with his family. Listed in 1790 as Jacob Tapher with a wife and five sons. Jacob Stauffer had married 1) Barbara Oberholtzer, and after her decease, married 2) Susanna Yoder. The widow, Susanna Y. Stauffer is included in a post-1835 reference on the reverse of an 1813 indenture. Jacob Stauffer died 20.03.1839.[83]

Peter Stauffer was born 17.08.1790 and lived in Upper Milford Township, Lehigh County. He was of Mennonite faith. 1835 reference to him on an 1813 indenture. Died after 1850.[84]

Susanna Yoder Stauffer, 'widow of Jacob sen[ior, ]' was born 28.10.1782. She married Jacob Stauffer about 1800. They had at least six children; her husband died in 1834. The family lived in Colebrookdale and Upper Milford Townships. As widow, Susanna was apportioned the same amount as the younger children. Susanna died 5.04.1852 and is buried in Bally Mennonite Cemetery.[85]

Christian Stetler (1743-1812), a Lutheran cordwainer in New Hanover Township, Philadelphia County. In 1763 he had property surveyed by David Shultze. In indentures of 1768 and 1772, he promised to teach HENDER-SON and SWARTZ to be cordwainers, signing his name in German script both times. In 1790 Census, he appears in Montgomery County listing, with eight members in his family; in 1800 Census there were four males and four females in the family. A 1799 assessment listed 'Stetler's Tavern on the Swamp Road'. By will (12.02.1812), he gave land for a church and a school.[86]

FRIEDRICK SWARTZ was born 16.04.1762. By indenture, he served eleven years as cordwainer apprentice to Christian Stetler in Philadelphia County. At least one parent was alive in 1772. The bound service of FRIEDRICK SWARTZ was completed in 1783.[87]

John Thompson was born in 1780. He was Lutheran, a surveyor and ironmaster in Hereford and Washington Township, Berks County. He owned the parcel of land on which Dale Forge stood; in fact he was part owner of Dale Forge in 1811. Justice of the Peace in 1814. Both William and John Thompson are supposed to have been born in Chester County. John Thompson died 17.06.1819.[88]

William Thompson, a Lutheran in Hereford Township, farmer, surveyor, land agent and ironmaster, who may well have been born in Chester County before 1763. William may have been either brother or father of John Thompson. William did outlive John. William witnessed the indenture of HENRY TRUMP, which John Thompson legally approved as Justice of the Peace. William was also concerned with the estate of John Thompson. William died after 1819.[89]

HENRICH TRUMP [HENRY] was born 11.08.1802 and lived for some time in Upper Milford Township, Northampton [later Lehigh] County. He was the son of Jacob Trump, who still lived in 1814. The young man was bound for nine years and a half in 1814 to Caspar Schultz as knecht, to become farmer by 1823. TRUMP signed the indenture with his mark. HENRY TRUMP died sometime after 1814.[90]

Jacob Trump, who was born before 1787, lived in Upper Milford Twp, Lehigh County. He was the father of the indentured HENRY TRUMP and signed his son's indenture with his mark. Died some time after 1814.[91]

WILLIAM UNDICHMAN was born in 1751 in Upper Hanover Township, Philadelphia County. In 1754 he was apprenticed to a weaver for eighteen years. He did not sign his indenture, though hardly a wonder, since he was just three years old when bound out. There is no definite indication that he did not die before completing his indentured service.[92]

Christian Weber, Jr., (1743-1815), lived in Towamencin Township, Philadelphia County. Farmer and innkeeper, he was named Justice of the Peace by Governor Thomas Mifflin in 1788. His father, Christian Weber, Sr., (1696-1778) had arrived in Philadelphia on the Ship *James Goodwill* with 4 others in his family 27.09.1727. Taxes in 1776 were based on 52 acres for Christian Sr., and 100 acres for Christian Jr., all in Towamencin Township. The family of Christian Jr. in 1800 consisted of four males and four females. After 1800, Christian, Jr., also served as County Commissioner.[93]

CHRISTENE WIANT [CHRISTINE WIEAND] was born in Freinsheim in 1759, the daughter of Elias and Christiana Wieand. Arrived in 1765 with the Elias Wieand family, she was indentured 'with the consent of her father, Elias Wieand' at age six, for a term of nine years, eights months and twenty-one days, in payment of the twelve pounds passage money paid for her at the port. She had arrived in the Goshenhoppen region by October 1765. Clear of her service, she joined New Goshenhoppen German Reformed Church when she was confirmed in 1775 by Reverend John Theobald Faber. Her marriage and death dates have eluded this researcher.[94]

Elies Wiant [Elias Wieand] was born at Freinsheim, Pfalz, before 1742 and arrived in Philadelphia with his family 24.08.1765 aboard the Ship *Polly*. By October of that year, they were all in Goshenhoppen. A son, David, was born 17.08.1769 and 13.03.1772, another daughter, Anna Maria Elisabetha Wieand arrived. All these persons appear in the New Goshenhoppen Church Records. In 1779, Elias Wieand was the schoolteacher [*schulmeschder*] at Goshenhoppen; in 1790 his family was composed of four males, (2 over sixteen) and two females. Date of death is after 1790.[95]

## Notes

[1] Conversation, William T. Parsons and Martha B. Kriebel, Collegeville, Pa., 24 June 1984.

[2] Robert O. Heaver, *Economic Aspects of Indentured Servants* (Ann Arbor, 1976), 45-46.

[3] Richard B. Morris, *Government and Labor in Early America* (New York, 1965), 500.

[4] Stevenson Fletcher, *Pennsylvania Agriculture and County Life 1640-1840* (Harrisburg, 1950), 107.

[5] Sharon V. Salinger, *Labor and Indentured Servants* (Ann Arbor, 1980), 314.

[6] Robert Bushong, 'Pennsylvania's Old Apprenticeship Law,' *Goschenhoppen Newsletter* (July 1985), 2.

[7] William T. and Phyllis V. Parsons, 'Be It Remembered That These Indentured Servants...' *Pennsylvania Folklife* 28 (1979), 10-12.

[8] Bushong, 2.

[9] Fletcher, 115.

[10] Bushong, 2.

[11] Heaver, 100.

[12] Fletcher, 115.

[13] Cheeseman Herrick, *White Servitude in Pennsylvania* (Philadelphia, 1926), 293.

[14] Salinger, 105-11.

[15] Parsons, 'Be It Remembered,' 12.

[16] Warren B. Smith, *White Servitude in South Carolina* (Columbia, S. C., 1961), 38-41, 70-71.

[17] Parsons, 'Be It Remembered,' 21-22; Ella Griesemer Martindale, *Griesemer Family* (Reading, 1981).

[18] Parsons, 'Be It Remembered,' 21.

[19] William T. and Phyllis V. Parsons, 'Indentured Servants in Pennsylvania,' [Joint Lecture] Green Lane, Pa., 17 April, 1980.

[20] Abbott E. Smith, *Colonists in Bondage* (Chapel Hill, N. C., 1947), 7, 16-17.

[21] Bushong, 2.

[22] Parsons, 'Indentured Servants.'

[23] Theodore Bean, *History of Montgomery County* (Philadelphia, 1884), 179, 849-53; William Egle, 'Constitutional Convention of 1776,' *Pennsylvania Magazine of History and Biography* 3 (1879), 98.

[24] Information from Indentures.

[25] William Buck, *History of Montgomery County* (Norristown, 1859), 88-89; James H. Bull, *Record of the Descendants of John and Elizabeth Bull, 1674-1919* (San Francisco, 1919), 6-16.

[26] William J. Hinke, 'Church Records of Longswamp Reformed Church,' (1938), 25, 32, 45; John B. Stoudt, *Christmas in Pennsylvania* (Collegeville, Pa., 1977), 17.

[27] MS Letter, Daniel Yost to Frederick Conrad, 24.07.1805, Historical Society of Montgomery County; Moses Auge *Lives of the Eminent Dead* (Norristown, 1879), 34-36; Edward Matthews, *Sketches of Worcester* (Skippack, 1934), 78-81.

[28] J. J. Kline, *History of New Hanover Lutheran Church* (New Hanover, 1910), 316, 586.

[29] Ralph B. Strassburger and William J. Hinke, *Pennsylvania German Pioneers* (Norristown, Pa., 1934), I, 79; Tombstone Reading.

[30] Federal Census of 1860: Colebrookdale Township.

31 Jesse Bechtel, 'Boyertown Mennonite Burying Ground,' *Perkiomen Region* 7 (1929), 51.

32 'Tombstone Readings, Bally Mennonite Cemetery' (Bally, 1960), 47.

33 Howard Jenkins, 'The Welsh Settlement at Gwynedd,' *Pennsylvania Magazine of History and Biography* 8 (1884), 179-80; Samuel Foulke, 'The Pennsylvania Assembly in 1761-62,' *Pennsylvania Magazine of History and Biography* 8 (1884), 407, 409.

34 William P. McMichael, 'Diary of Lieutenant James McMichale,' *Pennsylvania Magazine of History and Biography* 16 (1892), 131, 143-46; Jacob Parsons, *Diary of Jacob Hiltzheimer* (Philadelphia, 1893), 77, 78, 207.

35 Hinke, 'Church Records,' 36.

36 Bechtel, 29; On-site visitation by the author.

37 Census of 1850, Lower Salford Township; Wilmer Reinford, 'Burials in Salford Mennonite Cemetery, Creamery,' 37; Bean, 954.

38 Ibid., 158, 172.

39 Identification from Indenture.

40 Identification from Indenture.

41 Identification from Indenture.

42 Identification from Indenture.

43 William J. Hinke, *The Goshenhoppen Union Church Records* (Lancaster, 1929), 14, 175, 221, 269, 275, 283; Strasssburger and Hinke, I: 60, 64, 65; II: 54, 57; Samuel K. Brecht, *Genealogical Record of Schwenkfelders* (New York, 1923), 61, 68.91, 92, 103.

44 Bechtel, 50.

45 Hinke, *The Goshenhoppen Union Church Records*, (Lancaster, 1929), 18, 278; Strassburger and Hinke, I: 12, 13; II: 3.

46 Federal Census of 1850, Douglas Township; Roxanna Gebert, 'Tombstone Inscriptions, Christ Lutheran, Niantic,' 1980, 3, 8; Private Collection.

47 Federal Census of 1850, Douglas Township; Gebert, 3.

48 Identification from Indenture.

49 Federal Census of 1850, Douglas Township; Gebert, 2.

50 Federal Census of 1850, Douglas Township; Gebert, 1.

51 Strassburger and Hinke, I: 7; II: 1.

52 Identification from Indenture.

53 Federal Census of 1790.

54 Information from Indenture.

55 Brecht, 350-51.

56 Identification from Indenture.

57 Hinke, 'Church Records of Longswamp Reformed Church,' 24.

58 'Diary of James Allen,' *Pennsylvania Magazine of History and Biography* 9 (1885), 183-84; Parsons, *Diary*, 27, 29, 32.

59 Identification from Indenture.

60 Identification from Indenture.

61  Charles R. Roberts, *History of Lehigh County* (Allentown, 1914), III:
    954-58. The entire Ritter-Neihart relationship remains somewhat un-
    clear, though Roberts, as historian of the Newhard Family, is the obvi-
    ous authority.

62  Roberts, III: 953.

63  Federal Census of 1790, Berks County, Pennsylvania; 'Tombstone Read-
    ings, Bally Mennonite Cemetery,' (1960), 12, plot 3-52.

64  *Atlas of Berks County, 1876* (Philadelphia, 1876).

65  Identification from Indenture.

66  Bean, 1022, 1027, 1047-48; A. J. Barrow, 'St. James, Perkiomen,' *Penn-
    sylvania Magazine of History and Biography* 19 (1895), 87-88, 91-92.

67  Bean, 1088; Brecht, 56, 630-33; 'Plan of Towamencin Schwenkfelder
    Cemetery,' blueprint, (1934): Lot M-14.

68  ADS: Peter Richards, Surveyor's Plot Plan, 'The Draught of Two Lots
    of Land Situate in Hereford Township,' 2.04.1798 /s/Peter Richards.
    Land Deeds and Estate Papers, Berks County, Private Collection of
    Holly K. Green; Andrew Berky, *Journals of David Shultze* (Pennsburg,
    1952), II: 112, 132; Alfred Gemmell, *The Charcoal Iron Industry in the
    Perkiomen Valley* (Allentown, 1949), 38.

69  Identification from Indenture.

70  Roberts, III: 1054.

71  Ibid., III: 1054-58. Precise identity of ANNA RITTER is not known.
    Unlike Hoffman, Staufer and Schultz data, which fell right into place,
    Anna, Anna Barbara and Susanna Ritter continue to be elusive.

72  Federal Census of 1850, Lehigh County.

73  Federal Census of 1850; Brecht, 946, 948, 953-54.

74  Federal Census of 1790; Brecht, 1191. ¡75Brecht, 1187, 1189.

76  Federal Census of 1850; Brecht, 946, 948, 1200.

77  Federal Census of 1850; Brecht, 946, 948.

78  Identification from Indenture

79  Bally Mennonite Cemetery Records, 59.

80  Federal Census of 1800; Bally Mennonite Cemetery Records, 59; Hinke,
    *The Goshenhoppen Union Church Records*.

81  A. J. Fretz, *Genealogical Record of Descendants of Henry Stauffer*
    (Harleysville, 1899), 267, 268.

82  Ibid., 275.

83  Ibid., 260, 267.

84  Ibid., 267, 273.

85  Ibid., 267.

86  Federal Census of 1790; Frederick Sheeder, 'East Vincent Township,'
    *Pennsylvania Magazine of History and Biography* 34 (1910), 199. It
    seems there was a 'Stetler's Tavern' in Vincent Township, Chester
    County, as well as along the Swamp Pike in Montgomery County.

87  Identification from Indenture.

88  ADS: John Thompson, Surveyors Plot Plan, 'Land Situate in Here-
    ford Township, Berks County Surveyed for Henry D. Overholtzer (who

purchased the same from Jno Thompson,' 23.02.1818 /s/ John Thompson; 'Draught of a Tract of Land in Hereford Township, Surveyed for John Bechtel, Lawful Guardian of John Thompson's Heirs, 17.06.1819,' Land Deeds and Estate Papers, Berks County, Private Collection of Holly K. Green; Gemmell, 238-39.

89 Land Deeds and Estate Papers, Berks County, Private Collection of Holly K. Green.

90 Identification from Indenture.

91 Identification from Indenture.

92 Identification from Indenture.

# Domestic Architecture of the Schwenkfelders in Eighteenth-Century Pennsylvania

## Alan G. Keyser

In 1767 David Schultze, a Schwenkfelder surveyor who had come with the second migration of the Schwenkfelders in 1733,[1] prepared a map of their settlement in Pennsylvania for his co-religionists in Europe. The map accompanied a letter by Melchior Schultz who commented on the building arrangements of the group: "Here everyone builds according to his own plan and circumstance on his own land, which is commonly laid out square so that he has water, and meadow, cleared land and woods around him."[2] It is somewhat unusual for a group which had come from the same geographic area and had such close genealogical ties as did the Schwenkfelders that each would 'build according to his own plan.' This paper examines the pre-1800 domestic architecture of the first Schwenkfelder immigrants and of their descendants in Pennsylvania.

After the 1734 migration Christopher Wiegner, the would-be leader of the group, hoped to purchase a large tract of land on which they could settle as a community. They were not successful in buying a tract of two thousand or more acres, however, and in 1735 they decided to purchase land wherever conditions seemed most favorable. The decision had two results. It put them into an already established community where settlers of Germanic origins had begun architectural patterns fifty years earlier. It also put them into an area which was no longer solid isolated wilderness, and thus they avoided some of the extreme hardships experienced by the earlier frontier settlers.[3]

## The House of the Immigrant Generation

Some of the earliest settlers in the area which was to become Montgomery County built 'settlers' huts' as their first structure on the farm. Evidence indicates that the Schwenkfelders had no need for such buildings and put up more permanent cabins as the first improvement on their properties. Caspar Kriebel's "ancient dwelling stood... on the lower slope of the hill. It... bore the date of 1734."[4] Kriebel came to Pennsylvania on September 12, 1734, and must have built the house almost upon arrival. He had apparently made some sort of agreement to buy this farm before the actual purchase date of May 13, 1735, or he would not have begun improvements.

George Schultz of Goshenhoppen may also have built his house before he legally owned the property. In his diary Christopher Wiegner records, 'George Schultz came to me and asked if I would build the foundation to the cellar for the new house and set up the chimney.'[5] This request was made on October 20, 1734. Schultz did not buy his tract in New Goshenhoppen until August 4, 1736, but a number of settlers made improvements on their tracts before legally buying them. From the amount of stone work required by Wiegner it is clear that it was a log house with a stone cellar and chimney. George Schultz's tract of 260 acres later came to be the Markley farm and mill at the covered bridge across the Perkiomen Creek in Upper Hanover township.

Later George Schultz bought the tract in Upper Hanover which was subsequently bought by the three Schultz brothers: George, Melchior, and Christopher. The house on this tract, according to tradition, was built in 1737 by the three brothers and was 'the first two-story dwelling in a wide area—there were no others on this side of the Blue Mountains.'[6] The latter part of the assertion is unlikely. But the former is possible, because the two-story house in Pennsylvania was a rarity before 1740. The drawing of this house made by Amos Schultz in 1830 shows it to have been more a tall one-and-one-half-story house than a two-story one. (Illustration 1) It had a central chimney for the kitchen fireplace.

Another typical Pennsylvania German log house was built by Balthasar Krauss, a Schwenkfelder immigrant of 1733. (Illustration 2) He purchased the tract on which the house stood in 1749. Tradition states that he resided there from 1735 and built the house in 1743. The story was that this two-and-one-half-story central fireplace house came to be known as 'The Krauss Palace,' because it was much larger than the neighboring houses in the period. It measured thirty-one feet long by

Illustration 1A. This drawing was made in 1830 by Amos S. Schultz of the farm which his great-grandfather settled. The house on the left was reportedly built in 1737 by carpenter Melchior Neuman for the Schultz brothers. The one near the barn was the one to which Eva Heydrich moved in 1771. (Courtesy Schwenkfelder Library).

Illustration 1B. This is a photograph of the farm in Illustration 1A. The only building remaining from the 1830 period is the two story log house on the far right, which was occupied by Eva Heydrich in 1771. Photograph by H. Winslow Fegley

Illustration 2A. The Balthasar Krauss 'Palace,' according to tradition, was built in 1743 and is typical of the architecture of the immigrant generation. Photograph by H. Winslow Fegley (Courtesy (Schwenkfelder Library).

Illustration 2B. A photograph of the Krauss 'Palace' on the left showing the rear and gable end opposite the one in Illustration 2A. Photograph by H. Winslow Fegley.

twenty-three feet across the gable and was the second house on the site.

Sadie Krauss Kriebel[7] was born on the Balthasar Krauss farm and as a girl was often in the house. She described it thus. It had two rooms on the first floor—a narrow kitchen with one outside door, a door to the room, one window, a stone floor, a stairway to the second floor, and a fireplace. (Illustrations 3, 4) The kitchen had a wooden tub or barrel into which water flowed from a spring several hundred feet from the house. This room in the early twentieth century was used by her mother for doing the family laundry. The other room on the first floor was the stove room. It had two windows on the front, and one window on the gable end. The walls were of round logs inside and out. The second floor had three rooms. All that remains of this house is the fireplace lintel which Elmer E. S. Johnson put into the house he built in the mid 1920s, and three side-lap red oak shingles, twenty-four inches long, which were found in the house but appear never to have been used.

Several houses built by members of the first generation were recorded by photography during the final decades of the nineteenth century. The 'Captain Baltzer Heydrick house' was probably built by Baltzer's maternal grandfather, Christopher Yeakel. In the direct tax of 1798 it is listed as occupied by tenant Baltzer Heydrick, owned by Abraham Heydrick (Baltzer's father), and described as '1 old log house 20 x 20.'[8] By the time it was photographed (Illustration 5) it no longer had a chimney, but from the front door and cellar door placement it would seem to have been one of the typical Germanic type log houses with a kitchen inside the front door and a stove room over the half cellar.

The house sometimes referred to as the 'Christopher Yeakel house' appears to have been inhabited and owned by an entirely different Schwenkfelder immigrant, Susanna Krauss Neiss, wife of the Mennonite Cornelius Neiss. This house stood at the corner of Germantown Avenue and Mermaid Lane in present day Chestnut Hill. It was typical of the one-and-one-half story log houses built by Pennsylvania Germans between 1725 and 1775.[9] (Illustration 6)

Another house, part of which was recorded by camera, stood in Lower Salford township, Montgomery County. It is likely that Christopher Wiegner and his wife Anna built the house in the late 1740s on what has been long known as the Kriebel farm. In 1806 a new house was built and the kitchen of the old one-and-one-half story log house was cut off and reassembled as a stable elsewhere on the farm.[10] The half remaining (Illustration 7) stood until the early twentieth century. Some of the logs from this house are catalogued in the collection of the Schwenkfelder Museum, and the Dutch door with its wooden locks and pulls is still on the farm.

Surveyor David Schultze's house was photographed some time in the last two decades of the nineteenth century. But the house was so far from the camera that little can be learned about it other than it was a moderately large two-and-one-half story house which stood near the Schwenkfelder Library on State Street in East Greenville.

Christopher Schultz settled in Hereford township, Berks County next to the Washington Cemetery in 1741, and built a house and other farm buildings on the land he cleared. His house no longer stands, but between the present house and the barns on the site stands a summer kitchen/wash house which was built of materials from an eighteenth-century house. The old hand-hewn joists, doors, and hinges in this wash house may be remnants from Christopher Schultz's house.

## Meeting Room

In addition to the features commonly found in Pennsylvania German houses the Schwenkfelders had at least two of their own, the meeting room, and the *Stüblein*.

Several religious denominations in German Pennsylvania held their meetings for public worship in private homes during the eighteenth century. The Schwenkfelders were among them. But unlike the Amish, Mennonites, Brethren, and River Brethren where all the families took turns as host to the congregation, the Schwenkfelders had designated meeting homes. The denomination had divided their geographical area into the 'Upper District' (the area in northern Montgomery County, southeastern Berks County and southwestern Lehigh County), and the 'Lower District' in central Montgomery County. The Upper District was larger, had more families, and eight meeting homes. The Lower District was smaller and had six meeting places.

Illustration 3. The kitchen of the Balthasar Krauss house showing the fireplace with mantle shelf and crane. The Germanic houses in Pennsylvania had no cellar under the kitchen and for that reason some had a stone kitchen floor. Photograph by Jos. S. Powell (Courtesy Schwenkfelder Library).

Illustration 4. After the 'Palace' had been dismantled the fireplace and chimney stood for some years. The back wall of the fireplace near the right jamb still contains the opening for firing the jamb stove. (Courtesy Schwenkfelder Library).

Illustration 5. The house once occupied by Balzer Heydrick was probably built around mid-century by Christopher Yeakel. This house stood near Flourtown. (Courtesy Schwenkfelder Library).

Illustration 6. The Susanna Krauss Neiss house which was long known as the Christopher Yeakel house stood in Chestnut Hill at the corner of Mermaid Lane and Germantown Avenue. Photograph by H. Winslow Fegley (Courtesy Schwenkfelder Library).

Christopher Schultz listed these fourteen meeting homes in
1767[11]—the Lower District: Caspar Kriebel, Hans Christoph
Heebner, Caspar Seipt, George Kriebel, Christoph Kriebel, and
Christoph Hoffman; the Upper District: George Schultz, Melchior Schultz, Christoph Schultz, Christopher Krauss, Christ.
Jaeckel, Hans Jaeckel Sr., Gregorius Schultz and his cousin
George Schultz Sr. Of these fourteen houses only one or perhaps two are now standing (1985). Melchior Schultz's two-
story stone house is still standing in Hereford township, Berks
County although somewhat altered and enlarged. The religious
meetings were held in the stove room which was twenty-four
feet four inches long and seventeen feet two inches wide. The
room was divided in two, sometime during the nineteenth century.

Hans Christoph Heebner's stone house may still be standing in Worcester township, Montgomery County. The present
house on the site is in the form of an ell having been built in
several sections. The eastern-most wing has some architectural
features which could place it in the pre-1780 period, but it is
a small house and quarters would have been cramped if more
than thirty people attended meeting there. The interior of the
house has been heavily remodeled in the twentieth century and
retains none of the eighteenth-century partitions. As a result
it is difficult to determine the original floor plan of the house
without extensive architectural archeology.

Over the years as meeting home hosts became older or
died, members of the next generation took up the duties
of hosting the worshipping Schwenkfelders. Those in the
Upper District—-Goshenhoppen—were George Kriebel, Balthasar Krauss, Balthasar Schultz, Barbara Yeakel, Jeremiah
Yeakel, and Peter Gerhard; in the Lower District were Abraham Kriebel, Christopher Dresher, Balthasar Yeakel, George
Anders, George Heydrich, and Andrew Kriebel.[12] As new hosts
took over, the meetings were moved to their houses. Several
of these houses in the later listing were like those used in the
1760s. Two described elsewhere in this paper were those of
Balthasar Krauss and Jeremiah Yeakel. Both of these had
only two rooms on the first floor—a kitchen and a *schtubb*.

The meeting room was not a separate room built just for religious meetings in any of these houses, but it was the long stove
room of the type built by nearly all immigrant Schwenkfelders.

The difference between these stove rooms and those of the majority of the Schwenkfelders' neighbors was the shape. Most eighteenth and early nineteenth-century Pennsylvania German stove rooms were nearly square and had the master bedroom adjoining. The Schwenkfelder head of the immigrant generation nearly always slept in his high posted bedstead at one end of the stove room.

Eighteenth-century Pennsylvania Germans including the Schwenkfelders lived in their living room which they called a *Stube* in High German and a *Schtubb* in the Pennsylvania Dutch dialect. Here they pared and cut fruit and vegetables in preparation for cooking, rolled and dried their noodles and pot pie, and gathered around the 'dining table' to pray and eat. This room with its five-plate iron stove was, in winter, the only heated room in the house; as a result the family sat here to read and write, and to spin and sew. On baking day the dough trough stood next to the stove and contained the rising bread sponge. According to eighteenth-century Schwenkfelder remembrances many of these functions were carried on in another room of the house by the elder family member or members.

## Stüblein

More than a few Schwenkfelder immigrants seem to have built houses with a *Stüblein* or small room. The *Stüblein* seems to have been a 'small living room,' or small stove room.

Unfortunately none of the houses which contained this distinctively Schwenkfelder trait have survived. The most often mentioned example was the *Stüblein* or *Stubel* built by the minister, teacher, copyist, and bookbinder Christopher Hoffman. He bought his farm in Lower Salford township in 1752 and in 1753 he married Rosina Drescher. By May of 1754[13] Christopher and Rosina were living in their new house with Christopher's parents, Baltzer and Ursula Hoffman. In a letter to Europe Christopher said, 'My parents moved onto the place with us, and because we had to build a new house I built a small room' for them. 'Here they lived until it pleased God to take mother from us by death on May 25, 1767. Father is still in the *Stüblein*, but eats at our table.'[14] 'For his age he is always pretty well. The majority of his work consists of spinning and along with that singing and reading.'[15] Another writer notes that Baltzer Hoffman 'in the last years... remained almost entirely in his little room.'[16] Baltzer Hoffman died July 11, 1775, and his *Stüblein* apparently stood unused for several years

In October of 1777 his *Stüblein* was again pressed into use. The American Army encamped in the area east of the present village of Mainland and was a heavy burden on the farmers there. Christopher Hoffman's house was taken over by General Pulaski. Hoffman recorded 'the heaviest burden of the war was in October of 1777 when the American Army set up encampment around us. For nine days we had the general of the cavalry and his body guards with us. They were crowded times. The general and his company took over the living room, and we had to move into the *Stubgen* [sic] (little room) where my father had lived.'[17]

Near Christopher Hoffman in Lower Salford lived Christopher Kriebel who also had a *Stüblein*. It is reported that 'Eva Heidrich lives with Christopher Hoffman in a *Stüblein*. She is well and passes her time spinning. She is quite cheerful in her widowhood... '[18]

About three and one half miles south of these two houses was still another, that of George Drescher. In 1766 he wrote, 'Mother died four years ago.... Since that time I have been pretty well, although granted age brings problems with it. I am still in the *Stüblein*....'[19]

And still another reference to this institution comes from Helena Heidrich living some three thousand miles east of the areas just mentioned. In reference to Eva Heidrich who was living with Christopher Kriebel, Helena wrote in a letter, 'I especially greet Eva Heidrich.... I too am alone in a *Stüblein* and earn my bread and firewood by spinning.'[20] Although this is the only European reference found, it would seem proper to conclude that this method of housing elderly members of the Schwenkfelder families probably derived from traditions of some age in Europe.

Not all widows and widowers lived in the *Stüblein*. Some came to live in the more usual small house on the farm. Eva Heidrich who lived with Christopher Kriebel in the *Stüblein* from 1765 moved to George Schultz's in Upper Hanover in

1771. 'There she lives in a small house near his dwelling. She is 72 years old.... Her work is to spin stocking yarn with the spindle which is commonly the occupation of our old people.'[21]

Another reference to a little house for a widow comes from the 1797 will of Baltzer Yeakel[22] where he gave his wife the privilege to continue to live in 'the same house wherein I now live, as long as it pleaseth her. But if she should choose to live in a house alone, then my son David... shall build a house for his mother.' (The house was apparently never needed nor built, for there is no evidence of the house described on the property today.) It shall be built 'on a convenient place not far from the spring, six and twenty feet by Eighteen, The logs to be flatted on two sides, one story and a half high, a cellar under the Stove room, the lower floor double boarded, and above the said room and kitchen also a good floor laid sufficient windows in whole house, and a good Shingle roof put on it.' This description would have fit many of the houses in the neighborhood and is a listing of the major features of many Pennsylvania German houses.

Like most early Schwenkfelder houses there were only two rooms on the first floor, a kitchen and stove room. The cellar was under the stove room only, another common feature of the Pennsylvania German house. The logs were to be squared on two sides only, the inside and the outside. This was the most common finish. Many houses had a double-boarded floor to provide added insulation against dampness and cold from the cellar under the room. Although some log houses had clay tile roofs the great majority had Baltzer Yeakel's prescribed shingle roof.

It appears that the earliest houses built by the immigrant generation were log and were one-and-one-half or two-and-one-half stories high with the 'Continental type' floor plan, having a kitchen with central fireplace for cooking and a stove room with a jamb stove for heat. The exterior was of round or squared logs with wood or stone chinking filling the interstices. Some had casement windows and all had a Dutch door for the front door. For many the front door into the kitchen was the only exterior one. These modest houses were the dwellings of the Schwenkfelders who were adults at the time of immigration.

Illustration 7. The Christoph and Anna Wiegner log house in Lower Salford. The kitchen was sawed off the right side of the house in 1806 and was put up as a stable elsewhere on the Kriebel farm. Photograph by H. Winslow Fegley (Courtesy Schwenkfelder Library).

Illustration 8. Jeremiah Yeakel built this house near the Hosensack Meetinghouse in the late 1770s. Photograph by Jos. S. Powell (courtesy Schwenkfelder Library)

## Houses of the Second Generation

Those who immigrated as children or were born in the first twenty years after immigration could be considered the second generation. It is their houses we will examine next.

These were built between the years 1750 and 1790 and for the most part differed little from those of the immigrant generation. The most notable exception was their size. They were usually two rather than one story and were somewhat larger. Many still built with logs, but more used some stone. This was more durable, although it was more expensive and took longer to build a home with stone. But the second generation had more money than their fathers; they had more time, and were looking to build more durable improvements on the family farm.

Several houses built by this generation survived into the second half of the twentieth century. One of the most notable was the Jeremiah Yeakel house which stood near the Hosensack Meeting House in Lower Milford township, Lehigh County. Distinctive architectural details on the interior trim and doors of this house would seem to indicate that it was built in the late 1770s. This two-and-one-half story log house was twenty-seven feet long and nineteen feet across the gable. The logs were squared on two sides only and had pointed native stone chinking. As in many Schwenkfelder houses the first floor had only two rooms—the kitchen with central fireplace and the stove room. The 'room' never had a jamb stove but a six-plate stove with rivited stove pipe. This was a departure from long standing tradition. (Illustrations 8-10)

Jeremiah Yeakel hosted the traditional Schwenkfelders' Gedächtniss-Tag (Memorial Day) Services in his home in 1781, 1785, and 1789.[23] These meetings were probably held in the stove room. The interior walls were originally the exposed logs and white coated chinking, but in the early nineteenth century many inch-long pegs were driven into holes in the logs and used instead of lath to hold the new plaster coat for the walls. The ceiling was of open beams. The interior doors, door trim, paneling, and window trim had a single coat of red lead paint.

The kitchen had a front and back door, a door to the stove room, one to the second floor and one to the stone cellar steps. The second floor had only two areas, a large bedroom and a hallway. The attic was one large room with the stack from the fireplace in the middle. The cellar was under the stove room. The area under the kitchen was unexcavated.

The house built by Jeremiah Yeakel's brother, Balthasar, in 1766 still stands one-half mile northwest of the house site just described. Balthasar Yeakel built his house of stone thirty-six by twenty-six feet, one-and-one-half stories with a knee wall of about three feet on the second floor. According to the assessment for the Direct Tax of 1798 the house was owned by Balthasar's son, David Yeakel, and was noted as being two stories high. It was not a full two stories, but since it was more than one, it was so listed for tax purposes. This house faced south and had a kitchen with central fireplace on the east end. On the west end were two rooms—a large square stove room and behind that a long narrow *Kammer* or master bedroom. Few Schwenkfelder homes of the 1760s had a separate bedroom adjoining the stove room. But most of the non-Schwenkfelder neighbors had a *Kammer* in the same period. This is another change included by the second generation. The second floor of this house was heavily altered in 1838 when the roof was removed and the walls extended to a full two stories so it is now impossible to determine its room arrangement.

Another house built by a member of the second generation bore a date stone with the inscription 'D. Schultz 1787.' It is not clear what this means because the house stood on land owned and farmed by Gregory Schultz from 1779 to 1820.[24] The construction details confirmed the 1787 date, and since Gregory Schultz owned it at that time it is probably safe to assume that he was the builder. It was built on the plan of the 'continental house type' and was about thirty-eight feet long and twenty-six feet wide. (Illustration 11) It was a two-story house of which the first was pointed native brown stone and the second was of oak planks mortised, tennoned, and pegged into vertical posts. It had two rooms on the first floor, a kitchen with a fourteen-foot-wide central fireplace for cooking, and a stove room.

This stove room was about seventeen feet wide and about twenty-four feet long. It had a narrow-board white oak floor and an open beam ceiling nine feet high. The living room was entered through a single interior door next to the fireplace in the kitchen. The room had five double hung windows of six

Illustration 9. The kitchen of the Jeremiah Yeakel house showing the central cooking fireplace. (Courtesy Goschenhoppen Historians).

Illustration 10. The upstairs hall with the ladder-like stairs leading to the attic of the Jeremiah Yeakel house. ( Courtesy Goschenhoppen Historians).

Illustration 11. Gregory Schultz owned the farm in Upper Hanover township where this house was built in 1787. The date stone to the left of the door was marked 'D. Schultz 1787.' (Courtesy Robert C. Bucher).

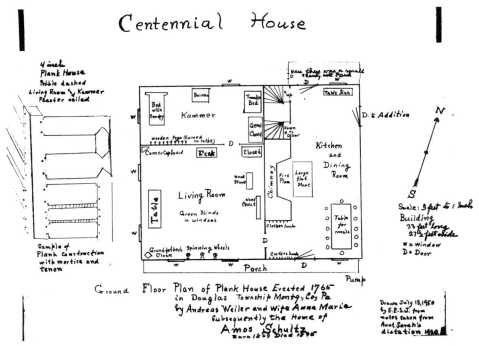

Illustration 12. The first floor of the Amos S. Schultz house in Douglass township, Montgomery county as it appeared about 1850. Dr. Elmer E. S. Johnson recorded the information from Amos S. Schultz's daughters between 1900 and 1910. Dr. Johnson shows no cook stove in the kitchen, but Amos S. Schultz surely had one by this time. (Courtesy Schwenkfelder Library).

over six sash with eight by ten lights. The gable wall contained two wall cupboards with three shelves and two doors on each. The doors were hung on hand forged hinges that had 'rat tail' pintles. The walls were plastered and white-washed. It was a large, bright, well-lit room.

The house was old fashioned when new in 1787 and was probably the last large house of its type to be built for many miles in any direction. The reason for building a house with the old floor plan may have been that it was intended for use as a meeting home, although no records show that it was. It may also have been that Gregory Schultz had a conception of a larger dwelling house. This notion soon changed for just ten years later the Krauss brothers, John and Andrew, built a Georgian house east of Gregory Schultz.

Before we examine the dwellings of the third generation we will look at how the first two generations might have furnished their houses.

## Furnishing the Schwenkfelder House

The best document on the placement of furniture in the Schwenkfelder home comes not from the eighteenth century, but some fifty years after the period. It was recorded by Elmer E. S. Johnson in his notebooks shortly after 1910 and rewritten in 1950 on large sheets of corrugated board.[25] (Illustrations 12, 13) These notes Dr. Johnson recorded from interviews with his maternal aunts, the daughters of Amos Schultz, who recalled the period of the late 1840s.

Until then many of the living patterns had remained unchanged from the eighteenth century with one major exception. The dining area had been moved from the *Schtubb* to the kitchen. Tighter housing construction and the use of the cook stove permitted this change. In the early period the drafts blew through the cracks between the logs, around the doors and windows, along the floors and up the chimney of the cooking fireplace, making the kitchen only marginally habitable in the coldest weather. This all changed with the advent of the kitchen stove. Although Dr. Johnson does not show a stove in the drawing of his grandparents' kitchen, they most surely had one by mid-century. The date 1850 is not on the drawing, but the youngest child who is listed with a bed upstairs was

Luciana Schultz, born in 1845. And since the *Kammer* shows a trundle bed where undoubtedly the youngest family member slept, it is likely that this was occupied by Edwin Schultz who was born in 1848.[26]

Although Amos S. Schultz lived in the Upper District seventy-five years after Caspar Seipt died in the Lower District, it would still be safe to use Amos Schultz's furniture placement as a guide for locating much of Caspar Seipt's furniture of 1773.[27] The inventory lists the contents of Caspar Seipt's two houses. His mother-in-law, Mary Yeakel, lived in a small house on the property.

| | |
|---|---|
| 1 bedstead, beddings 2 chaf bags | £ 6-5-0 |
| a red painted cloth press | £ 2-10-0 |
| a small cupboard | £ 0-2-6 |
| a chest | £ 0-10-0 |
| a red painted chest and a small painted do | £ 1-0-0 |
| a painted box | £ 0-1-6 |
| a wax press and old doe trough | £ 0-6-0 |
| an old cradle and old chest | |
| 2 small pails 1 old chest old cards | £ 0-3-3 |
| a doe trough and mortar | £ 0-5-5 |
| a dresser and small cupboard red painted | £ 1-10-0 |
| a iron stove and pipe in the little dwelling house | £ 3-15-0 |
| a red painted table | £ 0-11-0 |
| a meal chest (page torn here) | |
| a spinning wheel, 2 Stubels (?), 1 chair 1 Reel | £ 0-10-0 |
| a dresser and cradle | £ 0-8-0 |
| a small bedstead with beddings | £ 3-4-0 |
| a clock case | £ 0-7-6 |
| an Iron stove and Long pipe | £ 3-15-0 |
| a looking glass | £ 0-2-0 |

This is only an extract, listing the wooden furniture and stoves. The complete inventory contains cooking utensils, farm equipment, and many other items typically found on the middle class Pennsylvania German farm of the time. Some of the items listed in the 1773 estate inventory are again listed in a German document recording the moveable goods of Caspar Seipt's widow which she gave her children in 1789.[28] Only the lists for the eldest daughter, Elisabeth, and the youngest son, Abraham, survive. Among Elisabeth's items are the red painted wardrobe, the little flowered chest, and the small bedstead with mattress in the bedroom above the stove room. Abraham received the high posted bedstead with the bedding in the new bedroom, and one flax chest in the new bedroom. Both listings mention rooms associated with furniture in a Schwenkfelder house—the guest bedroom above the stove room and the master bedroom, *die Kammer*.

This is one of the few times a separate master bedroom is designated, and here it is listed as a recent addition to the Seipt house. Caspar Seipt's house of 1773 probably had no separate master bedroom, and he and his wife slept in the high posted bedstead located along the back wall of the stove room.

In the kitchen, as mentioned earlier, one would have found the greatest difference between the 1773 patterns and those of 1850. Caspar Seipt's 1773 estate inventory lists only four items which would have been in a kitchen—'a small cupboard, a dresser and small cupboard red painted and a dresser.' The dresser was probably what was more properly called a kitchen dresser or what is now termed a Dutch cupboard. The small cupboards were possibly small hanging wall cupboards which could have hung in either the kitchen or the stove room. Since Caspar Seipt's farm had a main farm house and a small grandmother's house for his mother-in-law, it would be safe to assume that one dresser and one small cupboard were in each house. Thus, the only wooden furniture which would have been in the kitchen of the main house was a kitchen dresser and possibly a small hanging cupboard.

Seipt's red painted dining table would have been in the stove room as it was in Melchior Yeakel's house in December of 1777 when two robbers 'broke into his house and stove room. They both sat at his table with gleaming sword and pistols and forced him to give them a large sum of money."[29] As on the Amos S. Schultz plan the clock case, stove, and spinning wheel would have had their place in the stove room.

The furniture placement on the second floor would have been similar to the Amos Schultz home since only bedsteads and chests are mentioned as second floor furniture in the Seipt estate inventory.

## Houses of the Third Generation

The third generation of Schwenkfelders in Pennsylvania had just begun to build on their farms by the close of the eighteenth century (the termination date of this study). As an example of the architecture used by this generation we will look at the house built by the grandsons of Balthasar Krauss who built the 'Krauss Palace' in 1743. Their father, Balthasar Krauss, Jr., was born in the log 'palace,' November 7, 1743 and when married he continued to live in the 'palace' and there reared his family. The two eldest sons, John and Andrew, were also born there only fifteen months apart and apparently had close ties. In 1797 they entered into a partnership to build a house where both could live under one roof. John had married in 1795 and had one daughter at the time they began building. Andrew was not yet married, but he would marry in November of 1797 before the house was finished. (Illustration 14)

Because it was a joint venture with one-half the cost being paid by each brother, John kept a running account of the building of the house.[30] The John Krauss journal is preserved in the collection of the Schwenkfelder Library. Because it is one of the most complete records about building a house kept by any Pennsylvania German during the eighteenth century it would be helpful to give all the entries concerning the house. The first entry appears unceremoniously on February 9, 1797.

'I and Andrew, my father and Father-in-law, Solomon Yeakel, Andrew and David Yeakel did cart wood for rafters into the sawmill at Henry Stroh and John Gery

Feb 11. On the same day we went up to our wood land to fetch our wagon which got broke on the 9th.

March 8. i rode in Chester County for to bespoke masoners and was all night by Mr. Shuler in said county.

9. I Kriebel was a hauling stones and on the 10th likewise. Andrew Boyer did 2 days load and unload stones. Peter Weber did one day break stones. Also Andrew Yeakel and David Yeakel and Jeremiah Meschter and Caspar Riser did the same gratis.

19. I made agreement with Mr. Glinger, masoner for building a house.

23. We and Seybert and Solomon Yeakel were digging stones.

29. I made settlement with Andrew Boyer for working.... Likewise for 2 days loading and unloading stones for 3/9 per day which I had to pay my share 3/1/6

May 8. I went to town. At the same time I bought from Keyser and Gorges, Philadelphia 2000 undressed shingles for the consideration of 13/6/3/.

12. I rode to Michael Fackenthal for bespoke boards on which Journey I spent about 9 pence.

15. Jacob Kriebel did cart stones in Free.

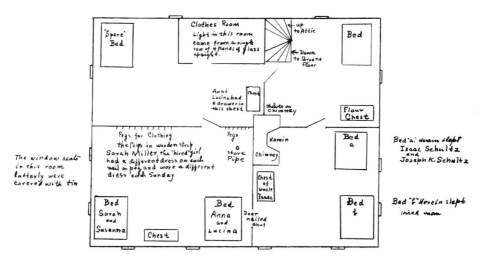

Illustration 13. The second floor of the Amos S. Schultz house showing the furniture placement and listing who occupied what. (Courtesy Schwenkfelder Library).

Illustration 14. This house was built by John and Andrew Krauss between 1797 and 1799. It is a Georgian house with a kitchen ell to the rear.

17. Jacob Kriebel, George Hilligas and Samuel Reder did cart stones this day a gratis.

19. We and Jacob Kriebel did cart blocks in Sawmill a gratis.

20. We begun to dig cellar

22. On this day I paid to George Heilig for boards bought on the vendue 1/12/3 and for sawing boards 2 dollars.

July 28. This week Caspar Riser carted 2 days and Abraham 1 and George Hillig 1 day stones. Fred Grisemer load 3 days (1 day a gratis) and Sol Yeakel 2 days stones.

August 1. Two masoners (John Wager and Will Alloe) begun to work at our house.

7. This day evening the three ohter [sic] masoners, viz: Peter and Jacob Gelinger, George Chrestman did come and begun the next day to work.

9. We layed the first Joists for the new house. [It appears that John and Andrew did all the carpentry and cabinet work on the house themselves. They never once mention paying a carpenter.]

10. We set up the staffel posts. On the 7th and 8th we fetched 124 bushels of lime from Mr. Philip Wind in Saucon at the rate of 1 schilling per bushel of which we fetched 2 loads from Jacob Stauffer 1 load and Adam Hilligas the other. For this lime I paid. Frederick Griesemer helped 10 and Hillig 8, Sol Yeakel 3.

14. I fetched veal at Conrad Breys. This day Andrew Krauss, Christopher Yeakel and Christopher Schultz fetched boards from Eastown 0-19-0

17. We set up the lower Window frames.

18. We layed the middle Joists.

19. I fetched 29 1/2lb of Veal from David Yeakel. Solomon Yeakel—3 1/2 days he helped the masoners.... This Day morning Peter and Jacob Glinger went home.

22. The two masoners came again.

23/ I been in Allentown and brought some yarn to the weaver for a carpet 7 3/4lbs. This day the upper window frames were set up.

26. I fetched meat from my father-in-law, 76 lbs. at 4 pence per lb.=1/5/4. This week did John Hilligas help 6 days, Fred Grismer 6 days and Sol Yeakel 5 days.

28. We put in the upper Joists and on the next day the roof timber. This two days did John Grismer help instead of Fred.

Sept 1, 1797 This day at about nine o'clock did the masoners finish up the new house when they have worked twenty-two days with five hands. Andrew paid sixteen dollars to said masoners. This week did John Hilligas help four days tenting and 1 day a threshing and Solomon Yeakel 4 days tenting and 1 day threshing.

3. This evening I went to the city of Philadelphia for fetching shingles for which I borrowed money from my father-in-law -fifty dollars. I paid for 2000 shingles 39 dollars 14/12/6... glass 1 4 1/2.

11. I fetched 48 1/2 ponds of nails from Adam Schultz

20. Jeremias brought us 1000 shingles from Germantown for 18 dollars of which I paid 4-2-6

Oct. 8. This day evening our masoners came again for pointing the house.

9. I and Andrew Yeakel went to John Shell and bought 21 pounds spain white 2 pence per lb = 8 Shillings 15 lbs. of white lead 13 pence per lb = 16 sh.3. 6 lbs of rice at 2 pence per lb 2 sh 1 lb of coffee... This day I borrowed 2 bushels of wheat from my father.

13. This day about breakfast our masoners finished pointing and measured the house and found it to contain 418 perches at 2/6 per perch = 52 pounds 5 shillings.Five dollars we paid them for coming over = 54/2/6 my share 27/1/3 of which I paid 23/0/6 for the remaining 3/2/0 I gave a note. Paid to Peter Weber for loading stones 1 day 0/3/9.

Perches which the house contained viz

| | |
|---|---:|
| 2 chimneys as far as the bricks | 14.8 |
| 2 chimneys on the garret | 20.75 |
| 2 gable ends on the garret | 20.95 |
| 2 sides on the second story | 62.3 |
| 2 gable ends on the second story | 41.8 |
| 2 chimneys on the second story | 36.9 |
| 2 sides on the lower story | 56.4 |
| 2 gable ends on the lower story | 44.3 |
| 2 chimneys on the lower story | 26.9 |
| The house total | 325.1 |
| Cellar | 77.5 |
| 2 chimneys | 15.6 |
| total amount | 418.2 |

Masoner and tenters have been here about 199 (working) days.

26. I and Jeremiah Krauss went to Easton for fetching boards where I paid for boards 9/3/9

November 3. I was at John Shells and bought one box of glass at £ 4-12

24. I went to Allentown and fetched a carpet made for us, paid for weaving 0-16-0 and for dying yarn 0-8-10/

30. I and my wife been on my brothers wedding and on the next day he removed into the new house spent 0-2-11

Jan. 6, 1798 Paid unto John Gery for sawing joists

Sept 17. Our Plasterers begun to work this day. This evening went I and Solomon Yeakel to Pottstown for plaster nails and fetched 53 lbs at 15 pence per pound. For this we borrowed from Andrew Schultz 10 dollars.

19. I fetched 5 lbs of plaster nails from John Shell Andrew fetched 20 bushels of hair from Ludwig Graber.

20. Jacob Kriebel fetched one load of Sand.

21. Christopher Schultz was carting 2 load of Sand.

22. I borrowed 5 dollars from George Hilligas for plaster nails which Mr. Lutz went to get for us.

25. I balanced an account between us and J.D. Danneberger. For 8 weeks his labor came to £ 12/14 for which I paid him money as may be seen above 5/5/1 and a half. He had bread for 7/6 milk for 7 soap 3 yarn 11 meat 6 is £ 6/4/0. Andrew Paid him in brandy 7/6 bread 2/6 butter 11/ meat 3/9 flour 17/6 money 1/10 and a half = 2/4/1

27. I went to Plymouth for lime, but came to Thomas Lancaster where I been all night. Get 17 bushels of lime, paid him 14 per b = 1/2/6 Spent 2/7 and a half, paid for 6 lbs of rice 2/ This week Philip Brey 6 days.

30. This evening Philip Brey went to Thomas Lancaster and fetched 25 bushels of Lime, this lime Andrew Paid 15 pence per bushel.

Oct 1. This evening 3 plasterers and the tender went home.

4. Andrew fetched 40 bushels of lime at Mr. Winds. This day 1 balanced again our account with Danneberger.

6. On the 5th we agreed with Danneberger for work at 7/6 per day and 4 quarts of whiskey per week.

17. This day our plasterers finished our house since they had worked about 78 days. I paid to Peter Hollowbush 12 dollars and to John Bride 8 dollars for Plastering 7/10/0.

20. This day the masons began to mason our kitchen Paid to J. David Danneberger 5 dollars.

22. Did I and Andrew settle our accounts between us... Since building the house we had about 712 boarders of which were carpenters about 300 and masons and tenders 180, plasterers 112.

23. Paid for bricks 2 dollars 15/

26. Paid 50 cents to George Krauss for work.

Nov 6. today our masons get done the kitchen and the walls up. 192 perches at 2/6 per p = 64 dollars.

7. Paid to Danneberger 3 shillings

9. I fetched a stove from David Yeakel bought on Vendue and 600 oak shingles from my father-in-law.

April 24, 1799 We moved in the new house

Oct 21-23 I been plastering our Kitchen.

Dec 31. Concerning the new house I paid in all £ 129. The rest Andrew answered me so we are even concerning the new house until this date.

The house, the building of which is described in these accounts, is still standing, and has been little altered. Its style is a departure from the old central fireplace 'continental type' log house in which the builders were born. Rather it is squarely in the middle of late eighteenth-century Pennsylvania farm architecture, a central hall Georgian house, with the kitchen as an ell to the rear of the house. Both the first and second floors have four rooms—two on either side of the hallway. The kitchen was originally divided into two rooms each having a walk-in cooking fireplace with a wooden crane and a beehive bake oven attached to the back wall. The dividing partition has been removed, but the fireplaces and ovens are intact, as well as one of the original wooden cranes.

The Krauss brothers apparently did the cabinet work for the house because there is no record in the journal of payment for this type work. All the other labor on the house is carefully noted along with the costs. The expertly crafted woodwork on the outside consists of window frames worked with crown molding planes, the front door way with paneling and dentil moldings, and the cornice with elaborate dentil moldings. Inside the woodwork is more conservative, but the hall and stairway are good examples of Georgian finish work; so too are the mantles over the four heating fireplaces in the front section of the house and the trim around the windows and doors.

The house built by the Krauss brothers at the close of the eighteenth century was typical of what the Schwenkfelder descendants and other Pennsylvania Germans were to build for themselves for the next few decades. Although other Pennsylvania Germans had built this style of house as much as forty years earlier, the Schwenkfelders finally yielded to this more spacious structure.

## Houses Not Built By Schwenkfelders

Certainly not all Schwenkfelders lived in houses built by members of their own society. They bought houses built by other Pennsylvania Germans and builders with British background. This phase of Schwenkfelder history will not be examined here other than to mention a few. The Peter Wentz house (built 1758), which was George Washington's headquarters before and after the Battle of Germantown, was owned by Melchior Schultz and his descendants from 1794 until it was purchased by Montgomery County in 1969. This house is a fine example of Pennsylvania German Georgian architecture.

In 1760, Melchior Wagner bought a farm in Worcester township, Philadelphia County. On this farm there were already buildings put there by former owners. There was a smoke house with a datestone inscribed 1680 and the house built by Welsh Quaker William Roberts in the 1720s. Melchior Wagner took residence there and shortly added a stone section to the eastern end of the 1720s brick house. Wagner's addition, which nearly tripled the size of the house, had Germanic features such as ladder type stairs leading to the attic. Wagner's primitive improvements stand in contrast to the more refined woodwork of the door trim and mantle in the earlier part. This house with Wagner's addition is still standing on his tract in the eastern corner of Worcester township.

## Schwenkfelder Barns

Many Schwenkfelders in Pennsylvania earned their living from farming, and most lived on farms during the eighteenth century—those in Germantown excepted. All Schwenkfelder farms had a barn, but since they were good farmers and firmly followed the practice of tearing down the old barns and building greater, none of their eighteenth century barns survive intact. Not one was even clearly recorded on film or in an accurate drawing. As a result we are left with the task of arranging the fragmentary evidence to form a somewhat hazy picture of their barns.

The Schwenkfelders borrowed the house architecture from their neighbors, and it would be safe to assume that they borrowed the neighboring barn styles too. In the geographical area of Schwenkfelder settlement, the predominant barn used

by the Pennsylvania Germans was the *Boddam Scheier*.[31] This
is a barn in which the cow stable is on one side of the central
threshing floor and the horse stable is on the other. The bank
barn with its threshing floor above the stabling, so typical of
the Pennsylvania Dutch country, was little used in Montgomery
county and adjoining areas before 1800. The prosperous members of the third generation may have built a few bank barns
just before the turn of the century.

Two photographs of Schwenkfelder farms exist with a hint
of an eighteenth-century barn on each. (Illustrations 16, 17)
One shows just the corner of a log *Boddam Scheier*[32] with the
'V' saddle notch. The other[33] shows the barn on the Christoph
Wagner farm (since 1810 the Heebner farm ) in Worcester
township, Montgomery County. It appears to be covered with
vertical weather boarding, but since it is behind a large tree, it
is not possible to say much else about the building. It too seems
to be a one-level barn, but this one seems to have an 'overshoot'
on the stable-door side. The hand-wrought iron weathervane
from this barn still survives and has the date 1755 and initials
'CW' incised in the monster head of the vane. Also stamped in
four places on the piece are the supposed maker's initials 'IK.'
Christoph Wagner bought this farm in 1754 and a new barn
was apparently one of his first improvements.

The best document on the barns of the Schwenkfelders is
the assessment list for the Direct Tax of 1798. Although the list
does not exist for much of the Schwenkfelder area, the records
for a few townships have survived. The barns or stables were
not large and the median barn covered only about 700 to 927
square feet of ground area. About half were of native stone
and would have been pointed with a lime and sand mortar in
either ridge or flat pointing.

In Lower Salford township two important relics of these
small stone bottom barns still survive on the original farms.
One is now set into the front wall next to the stable doors on
the mid-nineteenth-century bank barn on immigrant Christoph
Kriebel's farm. It is part of the wooden lintel which was once
over the threshing floor doors on the front of the barn. The
piece has the initials 'CK' and the date 1748. The later barn
also contains some of the hand-hewn structural members as
well as some of the sheathing for the threshing floor doors of
the 1748 structure.

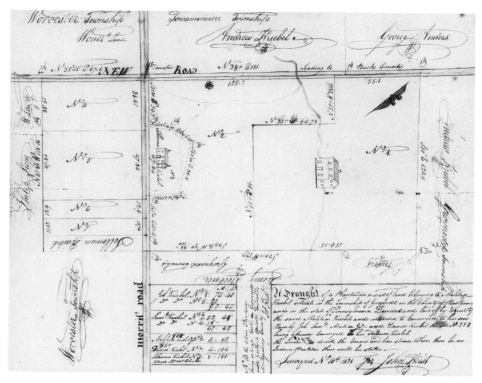

Illustration 15. This draught of the Melchior Kriebel farm in Gwynedd township shows the old central chimney house at the original location and the Georgian house of the 1820s along Morris Road. Drawn by John Heist. 1821. (Courtesy Schwenkfelder Library).

Illustration 16. At the extreme right edge of this photograph is a corner of the old log stable on the Balthasar Yeakel farm near the Hosensack Meetinghouse. Photograph by H. Winslow Fegley (Courtesy Schwenkfelder Library).

Illustration 17. The building in the center of the photograph is probably Christoph Wagner's 1755 barn. The stable doors open toward the southeast for protection against the winter winds. (Courtesy Schwenkfelder Library).

Illustration 18. This bank barn with cantilevered forebay was built in Hereford Township, Berks county by David and Anna Schultz in 1803. It is typical of the early bank barns of the northern Montgomery and southeastern Berks county areas. (Courtesy Dennis Moyer).

On a neighboring farm much of Christoph and Anna Wiegner's 1748 barn still exists. The tradition is that in 1837 the owner wanted a larger more modern bank barn and tore the old bottom barn down. He built a stone foundation stable-high and put the frame work of the old barn on this with 'CW ANNO 1748 AW' over the threshing floor of the bank barn where it remains. Some of the 1748 door hardware and mow-wall sheathing are still in place on this barn. One of the stable doors has a wooden pull on the exterior which seems to have been from the 1748 barn. Relating to this the two halves of the Dutch door from the log house of the 1740s on this farm have been preserved and have similar wooden door pulls.

The predominant roofing material for eighteenth-century Pennsylvania German barns was rye straw grown on the farm. A 1753 rental agreement of immigrants Christopher Hubner and his son, John Christopher Hubner, refers to the barn roof. 'Further it is agreed, that the aforesaid tenants shall also keep the Straw roofs in repair upon the Barn and Stables in Case any Damage Should be done to them by the winds or storms."[34] Here the owner recorded the usual barn roofing material and the reasons for repairing it. It was necessary to replace these roofs about every ten to twelve years, but that was not specified in the agreement. Toward the end of the century wood shingles, laid side-lap fashion in vertical and horizontal courses, came into use on the more substantial barns in the area. Schwenk-felders were certainly never the last to adopt improvements in agriculture, and it would be safe to assume that they also began putting the same wood shingle roofs on their barns that they had long used on their houses.

Another bit of information which may indicate relative size of the Schwenkfelder barns can be gleaned from the township tax records. The number of horses and cattle are given, because these animals were once annually taxable property. Given the assumption that the greater the number of animals the larger the barn, and that the stables were almost never filled to capacity, it would be possible to arrive at relative size for the barns.

The information drawn from the 1769 tax records published in the Pennsylvania Archives yielded this information.[35] Schwenkfelders had from zero to four horses, but about eighty per cent had at least two and more than one-third had three or four. They had from one to eight cows with about half holding five or more. This is not much of a dairy herd by modern standards, but it produced enough butter, cheese, and cream for a family. It also produced butter which the housewife could market as a cash crop. The average Schwenkfelder farmer in 1769 had about seven head of livestock in the barn. Large barns were not necessary for housing horses and cattle but for the protection of crops.

## Outbuildings

During the period under study the Schwenkfelders certainly built and used the same farm outbuildings their neighbors did. Only one has survived. The spring house on the Abraham Beyer farm in Worcester township. Beyer bought the property in 1737 and apparently built the spring house within a few years. There is no date on the building, but the style and construction of both the second floor door frame and batten door would indicate a pre-1745 date. The ceiling of the spring room has the original paling in place between the joists. The roof timbers and second floor walls have been reworked so that it is now impossible to determine the original shape of the building, but it is clearly a remnant from the settlement period, and perhaps the oldest Schwenkfelder building remaining. (Illustration 19)

Another outbuilding recorded only by photograph was the weavershop (Illustration 20) on immigrant Christoph Rinewald's tract just west of Kulpsville.[36] The photograph shows a log building with a door in the center of the front and a window on both sides. This building is usually listed as the 'Rinewald cottage,' but it has none of the features typical of dwellings in the period. In one photograph the outline of part of the loom appears inside the left window. The construction seems to be of the late eighteenth-century period and was probably built by Christoph Reinwald who belonged to the third generation.

## Conclusion

This paper is a catalogue of most of the recorded eighteenth-century Schwenkfelder domestic buildings. It does not attempt to compare those buildings remaining and those recorded verbally or by photograph with the larger body of Pennsylvania German buildings of the same period and area. If one

Illustration 19. This spring house on the original Abraham Beyer farm in Worcester township is probably the oldest surviving Pennsylvania Schwenkfelder structure. It contains a number of architectural features of the 1740s.

Illustration 20. Christopher Reinwalt of the third generation and his children earned their livings by weaving. This log building once stood on their farm in Towamencin township near Kulpsville, and appears to be a weaver shop rather than the 'Rinewalt Cottage' as it was called at the end of the last century. Photograph by H. Winslow Fegley (Courtesy Schwenkfelder Library).

were to make that comparison it would be readily apparent that the Schwenkfelders were heavily influenced by the building practices already in use when they arrived in the mid 1730s. The immigrants immediately took on the 'continental type' log house as their own. As housing styles changed the Schwenkfelders were not among the innovators, but waited about forty years to try a new style.

Their barns were ground barns like their neighbors' and when their neighbors took up building bank barns around 1800 the Schwenkfelders too saw the benefits of this two-story structure.

Had Christopher Wiegner been successful in locating his group of 1734 Schwenkfelder immigrants in an isolated religious colony, perhaps the story of their domestic architecture would have been one of transplanted forms from Silesia. Wiegner failed, and the Schwenkfelders borrowed their building forms from their neighbors.[37]

## Notes

[1] For details on the Schwenkfelder migration to America see Samuel Kriebel Brecht, *The Genealogical Record of the Schwenkfelder Families....* (Pennsburg, Pa., 1923), 10-18, 34-43.

[2] Ibid., 84 and Plate 12.

[3] Ibid., 60.

[4] Edward Mathews, *History of Towamencin Township* (Skippack, 1897), 13.

[5] Peter C. Erb (ed.), *The Spiritual Diary of Christopher Wiegner* (Pennsburg, 1978), 96, 97.

[6] *The Life and Times of Amos Schultz 1809-1895.* (The Amos Schultz Family Union, 1953), 2.

[7] This information was obtained in an interview with Sadie Krauss Kriebel in March 1984.

[8] 'The Direct Tax of 1798 Springfield Township,' *Bulletin Of The Historical Society of Montgomery County* 23 (1982), 262.

[9] Brecht, 65, 72

[10] James Y. Heckler, *The History of Harleysville and Lower Salford Township* (reprint; Schwenksville RD, 1958), 194, 195.

[11] Letter Christopher Schultz June 16, 1767, catalogue number at Schwenkfelder Library Lit. 11 page 18.

[12] Selina Gerhard Schultz, 'The First One Hundred Schwenkfelder Memorial Days 1734-1834,' *Schwenckfeldiana* 2 (1952), 34-36, 38, 40, 42, 47, 50, 51, 55, 57, 59-61, 63, 67, 70; 2 (1954), 5, 11, 17, 22, 27, 31, 41.

13  Letter Rosina Hoffman to Barbara Wiegner May 21, 1754. Schwenkfelder Letter File, VK 1-10, No. 3299.

14  Letter Christoph Hoffman to Melchior Teichman [1769]. Schwenkfelder
Letter File, VK 1-9, No. 2846.

15  Letter Christoph Hoffman to George Jäckel June 12, 1767. Schwenkfelder Letter File, VK 1-9, No. 2835.

16  Letter Christoph Schultz to Christoph Groh July 1, 1779 from manuscript Joshua Schultz volume, 235-36. Schwenkfelder Library.

17  Letter Christoph Hoffman April 22, 1785. Schwenkfelder Letter File,
VK 1-9, No. 2933; *The Perkiomen Region* 5 (1927), 490, 91.

18  Letter Christoph Hoffman to Melchior Teichman [1769]. Schwenkfelder
Letter File, VK 179, No. 2846.

19  Letter George Drescher to N. and N., July 9, 1766. Schwenkfelder
Letter File, VK 1-10, No. 3428.

20  Letter Helena Heidrichen in Ober Harpersdorf to Christoph Hoffman
Schippach February 1770. Schwenkfelder Letter File, VC 2-6 27.

21  Letter Christopher Kriebel [c. 1772]. Schwenkfelder Library. Letter
number VK 1-11, No. 3747.

22  Baltzer Yeakel's will October 2, 1797 copy on file at Schwenkfelder
Library. VS 16-83.

23  'The First One Hundred Schwenkfelder Memorial Days,' *Schwenckfeldiana* 2 (1952), 61; 2 (1954) 5, 27.

24  Deeds on file at Recorder of Deeds office Norristown, Pa. DB 16260:
George Schultz and wife Anna to Gregory Schultz March 16, 1779; DB
42485: Gregory Schultz to son Daniel Schultz September 9, 1820.

25  This set of drawings is on file at the Schwenkfelder Library.

26  Brecht, 948.

27  Estate inventory of Caspar Seipt of Towamencin township, Philadelphia county taken December 23, 23, 1773. Schwenkfelder Library File
number 11-1-178.

28  These papers are on file at the Schwenkfelder Library File number 11-1
178.

29  Letter Christoph Schultz to Schlesien December 27, 1777. Schwenkfelder Library VC 3-7229.

30  The John Krauss Journal typescript made in the 1950s on file in the
Schwenkfelder Library was used for the quotes in this sections.

31  Alan G. Keyser and William P. Stein, 'The Pennsylvania German Tri-
Level Ground Barn,' *Der Reggeboge* IX, 3, 4, 1-25.

32  Schwenkfelder Library Photograph FA-2 of the Baltzer Yeakel farm near
Hosensack.

33  Schwenkfelder Library Photograph FB-43.

34  Andrew S. Berky (ed.), *The Journals and Papers of David Schultze*
(Pennsburg, 1952) 1: 141.

35  William Henry Egle (ed.), *The Pennsylvania Archives*, 14, Third Series
(1897) 20, 23, 30, 33, 56, 58, 68, 85.

36 Schwenkfelder Library Photograph HOM 55.
37 I would like to acknowledge the assistance of Dennis Moyer and Anne Heebner in the many hours of touring the eighteenth-century Schwenkfelder territory, of Claire Conway for ferreting out the information at the Schwenkfelder Library and of Ellen Gehret for typing the manuscript of this paper.

## Appendix

This information was drawn from the Direct Tax of 1798 and shows the type domestic buildings used by the Schwenkfelders in 1798. Some assessors were more thorough and recorded more details than others. Microfilms of these tax lists are available from the National Archives, Washington D.C.

*Dwelling Houses*

| Location | Owner | Occupant | House Size | Materials | Story |
|---|---|---|---|---|---|
| 5 | Andrew Beyer | | 26 x 18 | Log | 1 |
| 3 | Abraham Heebner | | 35 x 30 | Stone | 2 |
| 3 | Christopher Heebner | | 30 x 18 | Stone | 2 |
| | | | 1 springhouse | Stone | |
| 4 | Abraham Heydrick | | 40 x 19 | Stone | 2 |
| | | | 1 frame shop 22 x 17 | Wood | |
| 4 | Abraham Heydrick | Baltzer Heydrick | 20 x 20 | 1 old log house | |
| 2 | George Heidrick | | 40 x 25 | Frame | 1 |
| 1 | Abraham Harris | Baltzer Hoffman | 25 x 15 | Stone | 1 |
| 5 | Balthasar Krauss | | 31 x 23 | Log | 1 |
| | | | 1 springhouse | | |
| 5 | Jeremiah Krauss | Michael Weber | | Log | |
| 5 | John Krauss | | 40 x 30 | Stone | 2 |
| | | | 1 Joiners Shop springhouse | | |
| 2 | Abraham Kriebel | | 30 x 26 | Stone | 1 |
| 5 | Abraham Griebel | | 48 x 28 | Log | 2 |
| 5 | George Griebel | | Log | | |
| 5 | Jacob Griebel | | 34 x 28 | Stone | 2 |
| | | | 1 springhouse | | |
| 2 | Jeremiah Kriebel | | 39 x 20 | Frame | 1 |
| 1 | Melchior Kriebel | | 38 x 25 | Stone | 1 |
| 5 | Widow Orfers | | 28 x 20 | Log | 2 |
| 5 | Baltzer Schultz | Henry Stroh | 26 x 18 | Log | 1 |
| 4 | Abraham Yeakel | | 26 x 23 | Stone | 2 |
| | | | 1 kitchen 25 x 18 | Stone | |
| 5 | David Jaeckel | | 36 x 26 | Stone | 2 |
| 5 | George Jaeckel | | 36 x 24 | Frame | 2 |
| 5 | Jeremiah Jaeckel | | 34 x 24 | | 2 |
| 5 | Melchior Jaeckel | Peter Smyer | | Log | 2 |
| 5 | Melchior Jaeckel | C. Neiss | | Log | 1 |

| Location | Owner | Occupant | Type | Size | Materials | |
|---|---|---|---|---|---|---|
| 5 | Melchior Jaeckel | | | 42 x 34 | Log | 2 |

*Barns and Outbuildings*

| Location | Owner | Occupant | Type | Size | Materials |
|---|---|---|---|---|---|
| 5 | Andrew Beyer | | Stable | | |
| 3 | Abraham Heebner | | Barn | 56 x 30 | Stone and Frame |
| 3 | Christopher Heebner | | Barn | 33 x 28 | Stone |
| 4 | Abraham Heydrick | | Barn | 36 x 22 | Stone |
| 4 | Abraham Heydrick | Baltzer Heydrick | Barn | 18 x 14 | Frame |
| 1 | Abraham Harris | Baltzer Hoffman | Barn | 28 x 18 | Stone |
| 3 | Jacob Hoffman | | Barn | | Log |
| 5 | Balthasar Krauss | | Barn and stables | | |
| 5 | John Krauss | | Barn | | Old Log |
| 1 | Abraham Krieble | | Barn | 40 x 20 | Wood |
| 5 | Abraham Griebel | | Barn | | Stone and Frame |
| | | | Gristmill | | |
| 5 | George Griebel | | Stable | | |
| 5 | Jacob Griebel | | Barn | Stone | Frame |
| | | | Smith Shop | | |
| 1 | Melchior Kriebel | | Barn | 33 x 22 | Stone |
| | | | Stable | 37 x 22 | Log |
| 4 | Abraham Yeakel | | Barn | 40 x 30 | Stone |
| 5 | David Jaeckel | | Barn | | |
| | | | Shop | | |
| | | | 2 Stables | | |
| 5 | George Jaeckel | | Barn | | Frame |
| 5 | Jeremiah Jaeckel Barn | | Frame | | |
| 5 | Melchior Jaeckel | Peter Smyer | Barn | | Frame |
| 5 | Melchior Jaeckel | C. Neiss | Barn | | Very Old Log |
| 5 | Melchior Jaeckel | | Barn and Stable | | Frame |

**Key to Locations**

1. Gwynedd Township, Montgomery County

2. Lower Salford Township, Montgomery County (did not record barn details)

3. Norriton township, Montgomery County

4. Springfield Township, Montgomery County

5. Upper Milford Township, Northampton County

# Schwenkfelders and Moravians in America

## John B. Frantz

Unlike several other topics that are treated in this volume, this one is not new. Indeed, Howard W. Kriebel included a chapter on 'The Relation Between the Schwenkfelders and Zinzendorf...' in volume 13 of the Pennsylvania-German Society's *Proceedings and Addresses* that appeared in 1904.[1] Forty years later, Elmer S. Gerhard and Selina Gerhard Schultz devoted an entire issue of *Schwenckfeldiana* to this theme.[2] Selina Schultz and Lester K. Kriebel collaborated in an earlier edition of *Schwenckfeldiana* on 'George Weiss and the Moravians....'[3] Other authors also have alluded to the subject.[4] It would be impossible to discuss it without drawing on their good works.

Nevertheless, what follows is a different interpretation of the relationship between the Schwenkfelders and Moravians. Most previous writers have been more negative than positive. Although there certainly were some unpleasant and even harsh episodes, there was at least for the Schwenkfelders a positive dimension in America as well as in Europe. It may be that the Schwenkfelders would not even have survived as a distinctive group of Christians had it not been for the Moravians.

Schwenckfeld differed from Luther, Zwingli, Calvin, and others in emphasizing to a greater degree the spiritual aspects of Christianity, including Christology, sacramentology, and ecclesiology. Schwenckfeld taught that the church was exclusively spiritual, indeed, 'ethereal.' He even recommended that administration of the sacraments be suspended until Christians understood more clearly their spiritual significance.[5] Their followers in general maintained this approach.

The Moravians' concern for the Schwenkfelders became evident when the Schwenkfelders felt it necessary to seek asylum outside of their native Silesia. Having suffered discrimination for scores of years from local Lutheran authorities because of their religious non-conformity, the Schwenkfelders in 1719 became the objects of a Jesuit mission to convert them to Roman Catholicism. Petitions to the imperial court failed to secure toleration. Rather than conform or suffer persecution, some Schwenkfelders decided to escape to other territories. Count Ludwig von Zinzendorf agreed to accept Schwenkfelder refugees on his estate in Saxony to which more than 400 emigrated in early 1726.[6] Here, under the Count's protection, the Schwenkfelders lived relatively undisturbed for eight years.[7]

Zinzendorf was a pietistic Lutheran who had been trained in law for service at court but his religious inclinations eventually prevailed. He had as one of his godparents at baptism Philip Jacob Spener, an early leader of German Pietism, and had studied under Spener's successor, August Herman Francke, at the University of Halle, the center of Lutheran Pietism. There he deepened his sensitivity to the pietistic emphases on religious feeling that produced spiritual rebirth and pious living rather than sterile theological dogma that seemed to result in mere scholastic controversy; he learned to stress ecumenicity instead of distinctive and divisive ecclesiastical institutions; and he became more aware of the need to spread the gospel into the uttermost parts of the world.[8] Although Zinzendorf claimed to the end that he was Lutheran, he carried these concepts further than many and combined them with his emphasis on Christ's suffering and death in what was called for a time the 'blood wounds' theology.[9]

Consistent with Zinzendorf's piety, ecumenism, and evangelism in the early 1720s he had previously granted asylum to a remnant of the *Unitas Fratrum*, spiritual descendants of the fifteenth-century reformer John Hus, who became known popularly as Moravians. With the Moravians he realized many of his religious aspirations by becoming their leader and by having them accept his understanding of Pietism. Like Spener's pietistic societies in parish churches, the Moravians were to be a society of truly converted people within the church at large, bringing in others of whatever ecclesiastical affiliations. Zinzendorf did not ask converts to leave their churches but to act as leaven among their co-religionists.[10]

The Schwenkfelders' longstanding familiarity with Moravian hymns and their understanding of Schwenckfeld's priority on the personal piety of the newborn Christian over the complex theology of highly organized ecclesiastical bodies caused them initially to feel comfortable among the Pietists;[11] nevertheless, in time, they began to suspect that, as Balthasar Hoffman put it, this 'benevolent lord' wanted them to 'join his church and become a part of its congregation.'[12] A few, such as Christopher Wiegner, responded favorably; others, especially George Weiss and Balthasar Hoffman, remained aloof.[13] Consequently, when the imperial authorities in 1734 forced them to leave Saxony, they declined Zinzendorf's advice that they go to Georgia, and nearly 300 went instead to Pennsylvania, in British America, financed by Dutch merchants, in Hoffman's words, as 'a way of getting away from the Count.'[14]

If going to Pennsylvania was the Schwenkfelders' way of avoiding the Moravians' influence, it did not work. Zinzendorf seemed determined to maintain and even enhance his influence over them. Christopher Wiegner recorded in his diary several months before the Schwenkfelders' departure that the Count wanted him to prepare himself for service as a commissioner, presumably in America. A short time later the Moravian, August Gottlieb Spangenberg, asked Wiegner if he could accompany him to Pennnsylvania.[15] Although Spangenberg delayed his journey until 1736, Moravians George Boehnish and Christopher Baus did go with the Schwenkfelders in 1734. Boehnish hired out as a mason and helped Schwenkfelder David Schultze to build his new house. Spangenberg worked in Wiegner's fields, and his biographer commented that a 'visitor might have seen Spangenberg threshing in the barn.'[17]

Never far from the Moravians' minds, however, was their goal of forming a pietistic ecumenical society of converted people from the various religious groups in Pennsylvania. This province seemed an ideal location with its consequent ecclesiastical pluralism. Francis Daniel Pastorius observed that the diversity was so great that the settlers must have come on Noah's ark. Governor George Thomas charged that the German colonists brought with them what he called 'all the religious whimsies of their country' and subdivided even further after their arrival. The English evangelist George Whitefield noted fifteen different religious groups in Germantown alone. Spangenberg counted forty-five in southeastern Pennsylvania. Wiegner identified, in addition to Schwenkfelders, Lutherans,

Reformed, Dunkards, Sabbatarians, Anabaptists, and Inspira-
tionists, but his list was incomplete. Later Zinzendorf likened
Pennsylvania to the tower of Babel.[18]

The ecumenically-minded Wiegner and the Moravians associated with people of diverse religious affiliations and back-
grounds.  In Philadelphia they listened to a sermon by a
Seventh-Day Baptist, possibly Michael Wohlfahrt, and observed their baptismal service. Several residents of the clois-
ter at Ephrata later visited Wiegner at his plantation, and
the Moravians returned the call.  They conferred with 'Anabaptists,' presumably Mennonites or Baptist brethren.[19] After Spangenberg arrived in 1736, they formed an informal ecumenical group known as the Associated Brethren of the Skippack that included the Inspirationist John Adam Gruber, the
Reformed Henry Antes, and additional Pietists.[20]

Despite the Moravians' concern for other groups, they did
not lose sight of the Schwenkfelders. For a time the Moravians
even adopted the Schwenkfelders' peculiar garb and joined
them in worship.  At one service, 'Spangenberg spoke and
Boenisch [sic] prayed.'[21] Although the Schwenkfelders normally
received Spangenberg favorably, most did not become converts. At one point Spangenberg was so discouraged concerning
the Schwenkfelders that he advised Zinzendorf to forget about
them.[22] At another time, however, he urged Zinzendorf to come
to America to evangelize among them and others. Zinzendorf
took up his suggestion late in 1741.[23]

Shortly after Zinzendorf arrived, he convened a series of ecumenical meetings to develop his Community of God in the
Spirit.  Zinzendorf, through Henry Antes, issued a circular
inviting members of numerous religious groups.[24] Wiegner and
two other Schwenkfelders attended the first session that was
held in Germantown on January 1, 1742. Because they quickly
concluded that 'they were wanted only that it might be noised
abroad that they too were represented,' they left. Except for
Wiegner, the Schwenkfelders were not represented at any of
the later assemblies.[25]

According to the Schwenkfelders Zinzendorf was outraged
by their refusal to acknowledge his leadership. After he had
preached on January 6, 1742, at Christopher Wiegner's home,
several called on him to pay their respects and were castigated
for their efforts, as he condemned their practices and beliefs.

He charged that Schwenckfeld and George Weiss also 'taught error' in putting aside the church's outward 'ceremonies,' such as administration of the sacraments. He added that if he had realized that they were not going to organize as a congregation, he never would have permitted them to leave Saxony. Their theology, he charged, included too much of the mysticism that he and the Moravians had rejected and did not stress sufficiently the 'suffering of Christ' and what Zinzendorf called Christ's 'glorious death.'[26] In Zinzendorf's evaluation of Pennsylvania's religious denominations that he presented to the third ecumenical conference at Oley on February 10-12, 1742, he described the Schwenkfelders as being in what he considered a 'lamentable condition.'[27]

Zinzendorf claimed that Christ had appointed him 'the reformer of the Schwenkfelder religion' and that the Schwenkfelders also had given him authority over them, facts which he could prove from written documents. In a letter Zinzendorf mentioned that their move to Pennsylvania had displeased him but had not ended his power over them. He went on to say that he would give them three months to dismiss those whom he labelled their 'false teachers,... unconverted elders and... and blind leaders' and to replace them with 'someone who,' as he put it, 'comprehends the cross of Christ,' who 'would convert some of you, introduce the Sacraments and thus make you capable of bearing the name of a church.'[28] If the Schwenkfelders refused to heed his admonition, he promised that he would 'persecute' them as long as he lived, even taking their children from them to teach the youth what he considered more valid doctrine.[29] In an attempt to give legal force to his threat he went to the civil authorities with his claim to power over the Schwenkfelders; however, he was advised that because he had not paid for their passage to America, he had no power to coerce them.[30]

The Schwenkfelders denied Zinzendorf's claims and rejected his leadership.[31] No doubt their ability to maintain their independence contributed to the reservation that Zinzendorf expressed in his 'Pennsylvania Testament' about the province's religious freedom that, as he said, made this country quite different from other countries in the world.[32] Zinzendorf left Pennsylvania in late 1742 with what he called reconciliation in his heart, feeling that he and the Moravians were not liked in this country. He charged that neither the authorities nor the citizens could be considered friends.[33] As Andrew Berky stated in his biography of Abraham Wagner, Zinzendorf took a 'long look' at his year in Pennsylvania and saw nothing but 'rotten wood.'[34]

Most earlier writers on this topic concluded on a similar negative note. Schwenkfelders, such as Howard W. Kriebel, were highly critical of Zinzendorf. He commented concerning the Moravian leader that 'A heart of charity will not impugn the motives or his life, but perchance may see in him one of God's lambs wrapped in wolf's clothing, and actuated by a fuedalistic spirit entirely foreign to the genius of the church and state in Pennsylvania.'[35] Lester K. Kriebel and Selina Gerhard Schultz observed that the Moravians 'finally retreated beyond the sea, having been routed by the scholarly pen and powerful theological arguments of the meekest man in Pennsylvania, George Weiss.'[36] Elmer S. Gerhard and Selina Schultz noted that it had taken 'the Schwenkfelders sixteen years to shake off their would be reformer.'[37]

These assertions are not incorrect. Certainly to some Schwenkfelders, as well as to some members of other German religious groups in Pennsylvania, the Moravians' evangelism seemed to constitute harassment, however pure their motives might have been. 'Pioneer... Pastor' John Philip Boehm of the early Reformed congregations and Henry Melchior Muhlenberg, patriarch of German Lutheranism in Pennsylvania, complained frequently about what they considered the intrusions of the Moravian missionaries and were pleased to drive them from their midst.[38]

Despite the apparent failure of the Moravians, especially Spangenberg, Zinzendorf, and their sympathizers, such as Wiegner, to convert the Schwenkfelders to Moravianism or even to bring them into the 'Community of God in the Spirit,' the Moravians made a vital contribution to the Schwenkfelders and to other groups also. As Andrew Berky explained, 'Zinzendorf's attempt to subvert [as he put it] Schwenkfelders' beliefs... opened a new period of soul searching and questioning' from which they as well as other 'sectarian and churched groups' emerged 'more mindful than ever of their own indigenous and peculiar tenets.'[39]

Throughout the association between the Schwenkfelders and Moravians Schwenkfelder leaders attempted to deepen their people's understanding of their heritage. They began this effort in Silesia in response to the Jesuit mission, continued it somewhat in Saxony, and intensified it in America.

Shortly after the Schwenkfelders settled in Pennsylvania, they chose George Weiss as their leader. A linen-weaver by trade, he was born of well-educated parents and was extraordinarily well-read, especially in theology, including Schwenckfeld's writings. He learned 'Hebrew, Greek, and Latin, and used them to advantage in his scriptural exegesis.' As a young man, he had helped his poor but learned father to 'transcribe and compile' a Schwenkfelder hymnal. This knowledge and experience enabled him to remind Schwenkfelders frequently and profoundly of their heritage. He compiled formal responses to challenges posed by the Jesuits in Silesia, including a 'Glaubens-Bekenntnisz' or 'Confession of Faith' that Schwenkfelders presented in Saxony in 1726 and that later was printed in America in 1772. While still in Saxony, he began the compilation of a lengthy catechism in which he set forth basic Christian teachings from a Schwenkfelder perspective. He compiled lengthy answers to the questions that Spangenberg posed. His 'Gedächtnisstag' or Memorial Day addresses also called back his followers to their spiritual foundations. For the services of worship he led, Weiss composed not only sermons but also hymns.[40]

Weiss was a practical as well as a theoretical leader. Although the Schwenkfelders were widely scattered from just beyond Philadelphia, in the Skippack region, Goshenhoppen, to Macungie and Oley,[41] Weiss visited in their homes and conducted services in different neighborhoods. He seemed especially concerned about instructing the youth in the teachings of Schwenckfeld. Indeed, he agreed in a covenant with the people to do this. Apparently a humble and gentle man, Weiss could be sharp when he believed that the occasion demanded it. At one point in his controversy with Spangenberg he implemented sound pedagogical technique and answered the latter's several questions with another eighty-four of his own. On another occasion he told Wiegner and Spangenberg to stop disrupting the Schwenkfelders' meetings and to stay away from them.[42]

When Weiss died in 1740, Balthasar Hoffman was selected to succeed him. Like Weiss, he too was a weaver but also

had acquired, as Elmer S. Gerhard noted, 'knowledge of the
ancient languages' and of theology. Hoffman was one of three
Schwenkfelders who had gone in 1721 to the Emperor's court
in Vienna to plead for tolerance. In America he had travelled
with Weiss and so was familiar with his role. He too catechized
the young people, conducted services, and composed serious
hymns and theological tracts. A bibliography of his works
occupies more than two full pages in volume 1, number 2 of
*Schwenckfeldiana*.[43]

It became Balthasar Hoffman's responsibility to respond
to Zinzendorf when the Moravian leader came to Pennsylvania in late 1741. Humbly but clearly Hoffman informed the
Count that the Schwenkfelders would not attend the conferences of his 'Community of God in the Spirit.' He explained
that 'we [the Schwenkfelders] shall not part with the knowledge
and convictions we possess, nor let anything go thereof.' In reply to Zinzendorf's accusation that the Schwenkfelders ignored
his authority Hoffman said, 'we do not concern ourselves' but
'commend the matter to the Triune God.'[44]

'The Triune God' did not inspire all Schwenkfelders to support Weiss, Hoffman, and other Schwenkfelder leaders during
the 1730s and early 1740s, George Hübner was host to Zinzendorf's second synod. Christopher Wiegner continued to associate as much as possible with both Schwenkfelders and Moravians. Abraham Wagner went his own separatistic way.[45] In
fact there were times when resistance, dissension, and indif-
ference were so widespread as to depress the leaders. Weiss
stopped going to Macungie and Goshenhoppen for a time in
1737. Hoffman actually resigned in 1741 and again in 1745,
before his health forced him to give up leadership permanently
in 1749.[46]

Nevertheless, the Schwenkfelders coalesced, consolidated,
and survived during this period as a distinctive people of God.
Perhaps they would have done so under any circumstances. It
may be that effective leadership would have emerged in the religiously free environment of Pennsylvania even without external
stimulation. That is not the way it happened, however. The
Schwenkfelders maintained their separate identity in the context of vigorous efforts by another group to have them become
what they had not been. It is likely that the Moravian missionaries and their leader failed only in that they did not bring

the Schwenkfelders to an appreciation of particularly Moravian positions. In order to reject the Moravians, the Schwenkfelders had to identify themselves, define their own positions, and renew their adherence to the teachings of Caspar Schwenckfeld. In that the Moravians forced the Schwenkfelders to do that, the Moravians contributed significantly to the Schwenkfelders' survival in the difficult years that followed their settlement in America.

## Notes

1 Howard Wiegner Kriebel, 'The Schwenkfelders in Pennsylvania,' *The Pennsylvania-German Society Proceedings and Addresses* (Lancaster, 1904), 103-19.

2 Elmer S. Gerhard and Selina Gerhard Schultz, 'The Schwenkfelders and the Moravians Two Hundred Years Ago (1723-1742),' *Schwenckfeldiana* 1 (1944), 5-51.

3 Lester K. Kriebel and Selina Gerhard Schultz, 'George Weiss,' *Schwenckfeldiana* 1 (1941), 5-33.

4 G. K. Meschter, 'Zinzendorf and the Schwenkfelders,' paper read at 'Gedächtnisstag,' September 24, 1898, Towawencin, Pennsylvania; C. Z. Weiser, 'Caspar Schwenckfeld and the Schwenkfelders,' *The Mercersburg Review* 17 (1870), 360; Andrew Berky, *Practitioner in Physick: A Biography of Abraham Wagner 1717-1763* (Pennsburg, 1954), 50-54; and Norman Dollin, 'The Schwenkfelders in Eighteenth Century America' (Columbia University, unpubl. Ph.D., 1972), 62-77.

5 Peter C. Erb, *Schwenckfeld in His Reformation Setting* (Pennsburg, 1978), 87. See also 77-88 and Martha B. Kriebel, *Schwenkfelders and the Sacraments* (Pennsburg, 1968), 20.

6 Balthasar Hoffman, 'A Short and Thorough Report of the Schwenkfelders,' trans. by L. Allen Viehmeyer, *The Tumultuous Years: Schwenkfelder Chronicles 1580-1750* (Pennsburg, 1980), 34-46; Kriebel, *Schwenkfelders in Pennsylvania*, 21-26; Weiser, 'Schwenkfelders,' 364-68; and Lee C. Hopple, 'Germanic Origins and Geographical History of the Southeastern Pennsylvania Schwenkfelders,' *Pennsylvania Folklife* 32 (1982-83), 86-90.

7 Hoffman, 'Short and Thorough Report,' 46-47.

8 August Gottlieb Spangenberg, *The Life of Nicholas Lewis Count Zinzendorf...* , trans. by Samuel Jackson (London, 1838), 1-3, 5-10; and John Weinlick, *Count Zinzendorf: The Story of His Life and Leadership of the Renewed Moravian Church* (Nashville, 1956), 14-15, 23-30. See also David Allen Stattschneider, " 'Souls for the Lamb:' A Theology for Christian Mission According to Count Nicholaus Ludwig Von Zinzendorf and Bishop Augustus Gottlieb Spangenberg' (University of Chicago, unpublished Ph.D., 1975), 47-52.

9   Weinlick, *Zinzendorf*, 198-206; J. Taylor Hamilton and Kenneth G. Hamilton, *History of the Moravian Church: The Renewed Unitas Fratrum, 1722-1957* (Bethlehem, 1967), 154-59; and Levin Theodore Reichel, *The Early History of the Church of the United Brethren...* (Nazareth, 1888), 178-182.

10  Weinlick, *Zinzendorf*, 67-82; and Hamilton and Hamilton, *History of the Moravian Church*, 23-29.

11  Allen Anders Seipt, *Schwenkfelder Hymnology* (Philadelphia: America Germanica Press, 1909), 41, 58-61, 65-66, 71, 98, 100, 104; *The Spiritual Diary of Christopher Wiegner*, trans. and ed. by Peter C. Erb (Pennsburg, 1978), xxiv; and E.J. Furcha, 'Key Concepts in Caspar von Schwenckfeld's Theological System,' *Church History* 37 (June 1968): 161-70.

12  Hoffman, 'Short and Thorough Report,' 46-48.

13  Wiegner, *Spiritual Diary*, xxv-xxvi; Kriebel and Schultz, 'George Weiss,' 6-8; and Hoffman, 'Short and Thorough Report,' 47.

14  A few Schwenkfelders went to Pennsylvania as early as 1731; others followed until 1737. See Kriebel, *Schwenkfelders in Pennsylvania*, 28-33, 29; Hoffman, 'Short and Thorough Report,' 48; and Dollin, 'Schwenkfelders in Eighteenth Century America,' 423.

15  Wiegner, *Spiritual Diary*, 62-63, 78-79.

16  Ibid., 80, 85-86; and Kriebel, *Schwenkfelders in Pennsylvania*, 103.

17  *The Journals and Papers of David Schultze*, trans. and ed. by Andrew S. Berky (Pennsburg, 1952), vol. 1, 56; Reichel, *Church of the United Brethren*, 70; and Karl F. Ledderhose, *The Life of Augustus Gottlieb Spangenberg...* (London, 1855), 39-40.

18  Weinlick, *Zinzendorf*, 157; Nicholas Ludwig Zinzendorf, 'Wahrer Bericht an seiner liebe Teutsche,' in *Authentische Relation...* (Philadelphia, 1742), 6-7; Wiegner, *Spiritual Diary*, 114-15; Francis Daniel Pastorius, 'Positive Information from America,..., March 7, 1684,' in *Narratives of Early Pennsylvania, West New Jersey, and Delaware, 1630-1707*, ed. by Albert C. Myers (New York, 1912), 396; 'Governor Thomas to the Bishop of Exeter, April 23, 1748,' in *Historical Collections Relating to the American Colonial Church*, ed. by William S. Perry, II (New York, 1969), 256; and *George Whitefield's Journals* (London, 1960), 357; August Gottlieb Spangenberg to the Congregation at Herrnhut, April 5, 1736, MS. in Archiv der Bruder-Unitat, Herrnhut/Oberlausitz, People's Republic of Germany (photo-copies in the Manuscript Division of the Library of Congress); Weigner, *Spiritual Diary*, 133-34; and Berky, *Abraham Wagner*, 53.

19  Wiegner, *Spiritual Diary*, 96.

20  Georg Neisser, *A History of the Beginnings of Moravian Work in America*, trans. by William N. Schwarze and Samuel H. Gapp, ed. by Samuel H. Gapp (Bethlehem, 1955), 23-24.

21  Gerhard and Schultz, 'Schwenkfelders and Moravians,' 19-20; and Weigner, *Spiritual Diary*, 106-16, 119, 124-25, 135.

22  August Gottlieb Spangenberg to Nicholaus Ludwig von Zinzendorf,
    May 21, 1738, MS. in Moravian Archives, Herrnhut.
23  Reichel *Church of the United Brethren*, 92-93; and Neisser, *Beginnings
    of Moravian Work*, 34.
24  Neisser, *Beginnings of Moravian Work*, 35.
25  Gerhard and Schultz, 'Schwenkfelders,' 21, and Kriebel, *Schwenkfelders
    in Pennsylvania*, 112.
26  Gerhard and Schultz, 'Schwenkfelders,' 21-22.
27  Ibid., 24.
28  Nicholaus Ludwig von Zinzendorf to the Schwenkfelders, in ibid., 26-27.
    See also 27-28.
29  Balthasar Hoffman to Nicholaus Ludwig von Zinzendorf, April 12, 1742;
    and Zinzendorf to the Schwenkfelders, in ibid., 27-28. See also 28-29.
30  Ibid., 24.
31  Ibid., 24-25, 27-29.
32  Nicholaus Ludwig von Zinzendorf, 'Pennsylvania Testament,' in *Die
    Büdingsche Sammlung...*, Das XIII Stuck (Leipzig: D. Korte, 1742),
    224.
33  Ibid., 225.
34  Berky, *Abraham Wagner*, 53.
35  Kriebel, *Schwenkfelders in Pennsylvania*, 118.
36  Kriebel and Schultz, 'George Weiss,' 28-29.
37  Gerhard and Schultz, 'Schwenkfelders and Moravians,' 28.
38  See John B. Frantz, 'John Philip Boehm: Pioneer Pennsylvania Pastor,'
    *Pennsylvania Folklife* 31 (Spring 1982), 129; *The Life and Letters of
    the Rev. John Philip Boehm*, ed. by William J. Hinke (Philadelphia,
    1916), 102-07, 348-53, John Philip Boehm to the Classis of Amsterdam,
    November 17, 1742, on 370-72, 'Second Faithful Warning of Mr. Boehm,
    May 19, 1743,' on 373-84; and Leonard R. Riforgiato, *Missionary of
    Moderation: Henry Melchior Muhlenberg and the Lutheran Church in
    English America* (Lewisburg, 1980), 85-102.
39  Berky, *Abraham Wagner*, 54-55.
40  Kriebel and Schultz, 'George Weiss,' 5-15.
41  Kriebel, *Schwenkfelders in Pennsylvania*, 39-49.
42  Kriebel and Schultz, 'George Weiss,' 17-18; Gerhard and Schultz,
    'Schwenkfelders and Moravians,' 20; Wiegner, *Spiritual Diary*, 119-20;
    and Balthasar Hoffman, 'A Report of the Trials and Tribulations of the
    Schwenkfelders in America...,' in *Tumultuous Years*, 73-83.
43  Elmer S. Gerhard, 'Balthasar Hoffman (1687-1775)...,' in *Schwenck-
    feldiana*, 1 (1941), 35-38, 40, 42-46, 48-52. See also Hoffman, 'Report
    of the Trails and Tribulations,' 73-74, 78, 83-90.
44  Balthasar Hoffman to Nicholaus Ludwig von Zinzendorf, April 12, 1742,
    in Gerhard, 'Balthasar Hoffman,' 40-41.
45  Kriebel, 'Schwenkfelders in Pennsylvania,' 114; Wiegner, *Spiritual Di-
    ary*, 108-55; and Berky, *Abraham Wagner*, 38-44, 54-60.
46  Kriebel and Schultz, 'George Weiss,' 8; Hoffman, 'Report of the Trials
    and Tribulations,' 80, 84, 86, 89-90; and Gerhard, 'Balthasar Hoffman,'
    38.

# The Schwenkfelder-Quaker Connection: Two Centuries of Interdenominational Friendship

## Don Yoder

The earliest printed reference to the term Schwenkfelder in America located by the editors of the *Dictionary of Americanisms* comes from Jedidiah Morse's *American Geography* of 1789. There we learn that among the 'Germans' in Pennsylvania was a group known as 'Swingfelters, who are a species of Quakers.'[1] Yankee Morse, in his attempt to relate the unknown to the known, had jumped to a common fallacious American conclusion. Even so he was not completely in error, since the two movements share a spiritual heritage.

The spiritual worlds of Schwenkfelders and Quakers were related in that both represented the radical left-wing phase of the Protestant Reformation, the Schwenkfelders growing out of German, particularly Silesian, mysticism and Quakers arising out of what Hugh Barbour has called Spiritual Puritanism in the British Isles.[2] While both movements became American denominations, in the eighteenth century both of them preserved a transatlantic base. The Quaker ministry traveled back and forth across the Atlantic, and the Schwenkfelders preserved their ties with their spiritual kinsmen in Silesia and elsewhere in Europe through correspondence. The Schwenkfelder and Quaker worlds impinged upon each other in three geographical arenas—Protestant Germany, Puritan England, and Colonial Pennsylvania.

After Quaker missionaries had invaded the German states in the 1650s and 1660s, Quakerism and Schwenkfeldian thought were linked in the popular theological press. An anti-Quaker tract of 1661, the 'Quaker Abomination' (*Quäcker-Grewel*), linked the Quakers in series with earlier 'deceitful and malicious' spirits who despised the stated ministry and adhered to outmoded heretical errors. Listed here, along with Schwenkfeld, are Storch, Carlstadt, Müntzer, Knipperdolling, and

Weigel. The minister who wrote the tract bitterly complained
how 'this Quaker cancer has already eaten around itself in such
a way that divers persons attached to our evangelical religion
have been seduced by them and plunged into Quakerish error.'[3]

The interplay of English theology and Schwenkfeldian
thought in the seventeenth century has been discussed by Rufus M. Jones in his *Spiritual Reformers in the 16th and 17th
Centuries*. In looking for the roots of Quakerism he made a
thorough study of similar groups and individuals on the continent and in the British Isles.

The earliest evidence he was able to locate at the time was
Wyllyam Turner's tract *A Preservative or Treacle against the
Poyson of Pelagius* (1551), which mentions the 'Swengfeldians'
along with the 'furious secte of the Annabaptistes.' But although he found little evidence of the spread of Schwenkfeld's
views in sixteenth-century England, they were 'clearly in evidence in the seventeenth century.'

> One of the most obvious signs of his influence in the seventeenth
> century, both in England and in Holland, appears in the spread of
> principles which were embodied in the 'Collegiants' of Holland and
> the corresponding societies of 'Seekers' in England. The cardinal
> principle of these groups in both countries was the belief that the
> visible Church had become apostate and had lost its divine author-
> itative power, that it now lacked apostolic ministry and efficacious
> sacraments and 'the gifts of the Spirit' which demonstrate the true
> apostolic succession. Therefore those who held this view, 'like doves
> without their mates,' were *waiting* and *seeking* for the appearing
> of a new apostolic commission, for the fresh outpouring of God's
> Spirit on men, and for the refounding of the Church, as originally,
> in actual demonstration and power.[4]

The thinkers that he dealt with in his book—in addition to
Schwenkfeld, Denck, Franck, Castellio, Coornhert, Weigel,
Boehme and others—were ethical and spiritual reformers
rather than founders of new sects and churches. As a Quaker
historian he saw Quakerism not as a radical innovation, but
rather as an historical articulation of this seeking and searching of the previous centuries, which 'gave the unorganized and
inarticulate movement a concrete body and organism to express itself through.'[5]

Quaker interrelationships with Schwenkfelders in Britain include two converts to Quakerism who migrated from Silesia to
England in 1674. These were Hilarius Prache (Prachius), the
learned pastor of the parish of Goldberg, and his son-in-law

John George Matern, schoolmaster at Goldberg and candidate for the ministry. Matern became a schoolmaster in Quaker schools, for which he prepared a textbook for teaching Latin, Greek, and Hebrew. Both Prache and Matern had been influenced by Schwenkfeldian as well as Boehmist thought in Silesia and were close friends to the Schwenkfelder leader, Martin John, Jr. (1624-1707), with whom they kept up a correspondence after their emigration.[6] These German Friends with their Schwenkfelder connection also had a connection with Pennsylvania. After the death of Prache and Matern, their widows, Barbara Prache and her daughter Rosina Matern, now the wife of John Bringhurst of London, emigrated in 1694 to Philadelphia, where they took their place in American Quakerism.[7]

While British Friends were aware of the Schwenkfelders on the Continent, the two groups, Quakers and Schwenkfelders, came to know each other most intimately in Pennsylvania, following the Schwenkfelder migration to North America. Drawn together through spiritual kinship and facing common political dangers on the local scene, leading members of both groups formed personal friendships with each other in the colonial period. The common moral concerns with slavery, with the Pennsylvania Indians, and the threats to religious and political liberty during the French and Indian and Revolutionary war periods drew the two pacifist groups together for political action.

This joint political concern and activity led to an unusual and important correspondence between leading Schwenkfelders and their Quaker counterparts, who met now and then and corresponded with each other through several decades of the eighteenth century. On the Schwenkfelder side the principal correspondents appear to have been Christopher Schultz and Caspar Kriebel, on the Quaker side, Israel Pemberton and Anthony Benezet.

Christopher Schultz (1718-1789) was the undoubted leader of the Schwenkfelders in Pennsylvania during the middle and latter part of the eighteenth century.[8] According to Elmer E.S. Johnson, he was 'peculiarly fitted for eminent leadership among his people during the formative period of their establishment in America.' He settled at Hereford in the so-called Upper District, across the Berks County line, and for many years was the leading pastor and spiritual adviser of his fellow believers

from the Hereford Hills in Berks County to Whitemarsh and
Chestnut Hill in the Philadelphia area. His classical education
in Latin and Hebrew and his extensive collection of Schwenkfeld's writings in book form and manuscript prepared him for
mediating Schwenkfelder theology both to his own group and
the outside world. For example, he compiled the first Schwenkfelder hymnal, the *Neu-Eingerichtetes Gesangbuch* of 1762, the
Schwenkfelder Catechism of 1768, and wrote the historical and
doctrinal compendium, the so-called *Erläuterung*, which was
published in Silesia in 1771.

In addition to his position within the church as chief
spiritual adviser, he became the Schwenkfelders' principal
spokesman and liaison to the outside world, particularly with
the allied Quaker and other pacifist denominations. Soon after
his arrival in America he mastered the English language and
carried on much of his American correspondence in English.
His cooperation with the Quakers at the time of the French and
Indian War and later is detailed in what follows, but it should
be noted that during the revolutionary period he was one of the
leading citizens of Berks County and was chosen as a member
of that county's Committee of Observation. In this capacity
he attended the provincial convention held in Philadelphia in
January, 1775, which adopted resolutions against the arbitrary
acts which Parliament was attempting to force on the colonies.
During the war, however, he adhered to the pacifist position
and aided his brethren as well as his colleagues in the Mennonite and other pacifist groups to maintain their testimony
for peace and nonviolence. The material that follows demonstrates the key position that Christopher Schultz occupied in
colonial Pennsylvania as liaison between the secular and ecclesiastical forces and as shaper of the Schwenkfelder tradition in
America.

Caspar Kriebel (1700/1701-1771) emigrated in 1734 and
settled in what is now Montgomery County. According to *The
Genealogical Record* he 'was a well educated man and took an
active part in the affairs of the Schwenkfelders.' For example, he joined his cousin Christopher Schultz in establishing
a school system for the Schwenkfelder communities and became an administrator and trustee of these schools. In December, 1756, he and Christopher Schultz attended the meeting
of the Friendly Association for preserving peace with the Indians, held at the Friends' Schoolhouse in Philadelphia. He

was a hymnist as well, and a number of his hymns were included in the first American Schwenkfelder hymnal published by Christopher Saur in 1762.[9]

Israel Pemberton (1715-1779) was a wealthy merchant in Philadelphia and patron of the colonial city's charitable institutions, as, for example, the Pennsylvania Hospital, of which he was a founder. His wealth earned for him the title 'King of the Quakers,' but his political skills and insights drew him more and more into the leadership of Delaware Valley Quakerism. He was the leading organizer of the Friendly Association at the time of the French and Indian War. During the Revolution he and his brothers were unfortunately exiled to Virginia by the revolutionary government of Pennsylvania. The correspondence of Israel Pemberton and his brothers, John and James, fills forty volumes of the Pemberton Collection at the Historical Society of Pennsylvania.[10]

Anthony Benezet (1713-1784) was a French convert to Quakerism in England. Emigrating in 1731 to Pennsylvania, he served for many years as a schoolmaster among Friends, and carried on trade with the West Indies, the British Isles, and the New England colonies. He had close contacts with the Pennsylvania Germans, particularly with the Moravians, since his sister Susan Benezet was the wife of the Moravian missionary, Johann Christopher Pyrlaeus. Anthony Benezet was one of the winsome spirits of early Pennsylvania Quakerism. He is remembered for his aid to the exiled Acadians who came to Philadelphia in 1755, for his pioneer antislavery tracts, for his friendship with and advocacy of the Indians, and for his work in behalf of temperance. His biographer sums it up by calling him a 'model Quaker.'[11]

This correspondence, parts of which are preserved in the Pemberton Papers at the Historical Society of Pennsylvania, the Schultz and other collections in the Schwenkfelder Library, and the Haverford College Library, reveals an exciting exchange of ideas, spiritual and moral support, and projects for the mutual information of one group about the other through the translation of key German books and tracts into English and English works into German. Let us look at a few examples.

The first phase of this Quaker-Schwenkfelder connection was, in fact, that of a united political front, with the Schwenkfelders supporting the Quaker party in the assembly and

Schwenkfelder participation in the so-called 'Friendly Association' established in the 1750s by Israel Pemberton and other prominent Quakers.

The organization was called 'The Friendly Association for regaining and preserving peace with the Indians by pacific measures.' In 1756 the Schwenkfelders formed a union among themselves to support the program of the association and raised money for it.[12] Christopher Schultz and Caspar Kriebel attended the meeting of the association in Philadelphia (held in the Friends' School House). Christopher Schultz noted the reasons for Schwenkfelder participation in the following account:

> The Quakers as well as we and others who have scruples of conscience against taking up arms against an enemy were accused of not being willing to bear their due share of the common burdens. They took pity on the miserable condition of the inhabitants along the frontier and felt that the Indian war arose on account of the unjust treatment of the Indians and was carried on under unholy purposes to the serious detriment of the province. With these things in mind they formed a union among themselves and invited others to join them with the purpose of doing what was possible to restore peace with the Indians and to preserve the same in the future, knowing that such effort and object could only be accomplished by heavy labors and expense.[13]

Part of the money contributed by the Schwenkfelders was applied toward the release of prisoners and the rest left 'for further purposes, necessities and considerations.' In connection with this cooperative venture of the peace churches before the Revolution one of the Schwenkfelders wrote a paper on 'Why should citizens attend the treaties with the Indians?' and in 1762 George Kriebel and Christopher Schultz both attended the Indian treaties at Easton and Lancaster.[14]

Schwenkfelder concern for religious liberty was expressed in a letter of April 4, 1764, from Christopher Schultz to Israel Pemberton (Appendix, No. 8). Unrest in the upcountry areas following the close of the French and Indian War had led to the possibility of a revocation of Pennsylvania's charter. Schultz expresses the fear that in the case of Pennsylvania the fundamental freedom of conscience might be lost, with the citizenry subjected to the rule of Anglican bishops and forced to serve in military units.[15] The Quakers and Moravian Brethren were protected in their liberties by the laws of Great Britain. But, he asks, 'what should be our [i. e., the Schwenkfelders'] Case and other Societies of the like Principles, who have so far trusted themselves under the Wings of this Government erected and constituted for the best time by Quakers?' The letter reveals thoroughgoing political awareness by the Schwenkfelder leader. In his pro-toleration concern he was, of course, following the model created by earlier leaders of his people in Europe who in 1721-1726 had literally 'stood before kings' in pleading the Schwenkfelder cause at the imperial court at Vienna.[16]

Another theme of the Quaker-Schwenkfelder correspondence is that of furnishing each other information on each party's religious beliefs. Because of the German-English linguistic barrier, translations of key documents and tracts were proposed, to enlighten the Quakers and others in the English-language world on Schwenkfelder beliefs, as well as to spread Quaker testimonies among the German population.[17]

This mutual interchange of letters on the nature of the beliefs and principles of the two groups even reached the British court. In a lengthy letter of 1769 from Christopher Schultz to his Silesian correspondent Carl Ehrenfried Heintze, dealing with the proposed publication in Germany of his *Erläuterung für Herrn Caspar Schwenkfeld, und die Zugethanen seiner Lehre*,[18] Schultz tells how a plea for Schwenkfelder liberty reached the ears of the new Hanoverian queen in London, Charlotte of Mecklenburg-Strelitz, wife of George III.[19] It all happened through the amazing Schwenkfelder-Quaker transatlantic network of correspondence and friendship.

The story is as follows. Anthony Benezet reported to Schultz that Jacob Hagen, a wealthy Quaker merchant of London, had contacted him asking him to send him books by Schwenkfeld.[20] Schultz referred Benezet, among other things, to Arnold's *History of Hereticks*, sent along Schwenkfeld's tract on *The Three-Fold Life*, (*Von dreierlei Leben*), and himself prepared a 'brief compendium, in English, of Caspar Schwenkfeld's life and teachings.' John Hunt, a Quaker minister visiting Philadelphia from London, a friend and neighbor of Hagen's, took the materials back to London with him.[21] Hagen as representative of the Quakers paid a formal visit to Queen Charlotte on her arrival in England, addressing her in German, with 'orders to mention the Friends in Pennsylvania, and amongst others, to name also the Schwenkfelders.' It appears that the queen already knew of Schwenkfeld and asked to have copies of

his writings. Schultz confesses that had he known at the time
that the Jesuits in Liegnitz in Silesia still had copies of 'our
books,' he would have urged the English authorities to take
action toward getting the books to England. Again Christopher Schultz aided in international understanding and reveals
his perceptive knowledge of the European situation and his
awareness of the transatlantic networks of communication.

Obviously connected with this international interchange of
information is the letter dated at Hereford, April 15, 1768,
and addressed to 'Dear Friend Israel' (Appendix, No. 10);
in it Christopher Schultz calls his correspondent's attention
to the materials on Caspar Schwenkfeld in Gottfried Arnold's
*Kirchen und Ketzer-Historie* and sends with the letter a 'Book
of Caspar Schw[enckfeld]'s Works, to be send [sic] to London
if you can think proper.' He mentions having sent to Anthony
Benezet 'some short account of the Historie of C.S. and his
Followers, which if thou pleases, I hope he will let thee see.'[22]

The correspondence even gives us hints of the importance
of the Schwenkfelder-Quaker connection for the book business
in the colonies. A letter from Pemberton to Schultz dated '7th
month 9th,' 1757, mentions receiving Schultz's translation of
Hopkins' Address (a tract on Indian missions in New England),
but unfortunately Christopher Sauer 'has gott it translated &
printed already.'[23] Secondly, 'the Abridgement of Sergeant's
Memoirs is in the press & will I expect be printed next week,
when it is done I purpose to send thee some of them' (Appendix, No. 5).[24]

Another joint project appears to have been the German
translation of the key Quaker text, Robert Barclay's *Apology*.
Schultz's letter to Pemberton, dated Hereford, March 29, 1773
(Appendix, No. 13), reports Schultz's progress in examination
of the German translation of Barclay's *Apology* 'to near the
End of the eleventh Proposition,' and promises to finish checking it.[25] The same letter was accompanied by a 'little Treatise
of Caspar Schwenkfeld' translated into English by a 'friend' in
view of a 'willingness' among the English population, which
Schultz several times thought he had observed, 'to See Something in the English language of his Works.' The Schwenkfelder
wished 'the grace of much heavenly Light to all who *read* it,'
and asks his correspondent in a P.S. to 'Remember my Love to
Anthony Benezet.'

A letter dated Philadelphia, '7th month [July] 14th, 1783,' from Anthony Benezet to 'Dear Friend Christ^r Schultz' (Appendix, No. 14) mentions the project of publishing a German translation of Elizabeth Webb's letter and other Quaker tracts.[26] The value of the Webb letter was in Benezet's opinion that it gave the reader 'a prospect of y^e simplicity & plainness of Christianity & tends to remove that partial orthodoxy & proud conceit in favour of y^e particular opinions & practices to[o] prevelant amongst the sects, which annex a holiness to opinions, even such as are right in themselves rather than those pious practices which change the heart.' Benezet mentions the plans for translating the Webb tract in a letter to 'Dear Friend John Pemberton' dated May 29, 1783, preserved in the collections of the Historical Society of Pennsylvania. 'There is also Elizabeth Webb's letter, which I find is particularly acceptable to feeling tender minds of all denominations. Besides the number friends had printed, I got fifteen hundred on my own acc[oun]t which are near all gone. At the request of our Friend Elisha Kirk of York town we are getting it translated in German, to print it in that language if we answer the charge the Germans from several quarters having call for it.'[27]

The Schwenkfelder correspondence with European fellow-believers and friends in the faith as preserved in the Schwenkfelder Library has turned up some unusually important items not only for American but also for European church history. Some of the correspondence mentions Dr. George de Benneville (1703-1793), Huguenot physician and preacher in Oley in Berks County who was one of the founders of Universalism in America.[28] It appears that he was the link between the Schwenkfelder, Abraham Wagener, and the Reformed Pietist, Gerhard Tersteegen of Mühlheim on the Ruhr, who exchanged letters in the 1750s. Tersteegen's letter of May 15, 1753, comments on mystical movements in Europe and America ('I myself believe that we do not need so many mystical books...'). He thanks his Pennsylvania correspondent for the books he has sent, as well as for his two letters of 1752, answered via Dr. de Benneville. The letters to Tersteegen have not turned up, but they must have mentioned the Quakers. Tersteegen in his reply mentions that 'in Amsterdam I have been acquainted with the English or so-called Quakers among whom are some devout hearts; I spoke a number of times in their church there in the

Dutch language.' He closes with the wish to be remembered in his correspondent's prayers.[29]

A final theme of the correspondence was education. In their noblesse oblige to their German brethren, Quakers on occasion even paid for the education (in English) of needy Schwenkfelder youth.[30] A letter from Israel Pemberton to Christopher Schultz, dated Philadelphia, July 15, 1765 (Appendix, No. 9) refers to the boarding and schooling of Abraham Hartranfft's son and asks his correspondent, 'If thou can'st find another such poor child that is likely to be benefited by it, I will in like manner pay for his maintenance at a School a year.' He also inquires on the state of the school among the Schwenkfelders, the number of 'scholars' and the subjects the 'master' is capable of teaching.

In addition to their major relations in the eighteenth century, Schwenkfelders and Quakers encountered each other after the Revolution in the form of a fringe group which involved both ex-Quakers and ex-Schwenkfelders. Jemima Wilkinson (1752-1819), the radical ex-Quaker and Rhode Island prophetess, the self-styled 'Universal Friend' who created a Shaker-like community in the Genesee country of Western New York State in the 1780s, worked the Philadelphia area in 1782 and 1783. She made Quaker and other converts in Eastern Pennsylvania. She was invited to Worcester Township in the Schwenkfelder country by an ex-Quaker, Abraham Supplee, now a Methodist preacher, whose sister had married the Schwenkfelder, David Wagener, the son of Melchior Wagener.[31] The 'Universal Friend' made a convert in David Wagener, who wrote at the time:

> 1782, October ye 19. Came ye New England Friends to my House first, the same evening a meeting: next morning on ye first day of the week had a Great and powerful meeting to the communing and embellishing of my Soul—the same at my house again next day or second day, again at Bethel; meeting rather more powerful than the day before, at the Same Meeting House. That day afternoon they took their leave from me and I and my father conducted them to Chris Funk that evening, lodged there that night, next day I went with them to Bethelem [Bethlehem].
>
> The Publick Friends' Names (the Universal Friend) or by name Chimima Wilkenson, Thomas Hathaway, Alice Hasard, William Potter, Arnold Potter, Sarah Brown, William Furniss [Turpin], all of New England, and Jehue Eldridge public friend from Philadelphia.

With her followers from New England the Universal Friend again visited Philadelphia in 1784, finding a welcome at the home of Christopher Marshall, Jr., where huge gatherings were held that were noted by various Philadelphia diarists of the time. David Wagener again welcomed 'Chimima' to his farm in Worcester, whence she went on to New Jersey. When she was unable to visit Pennsylvania herself in the next years, she sent her lieutenants who included the Wagener farm on their itinerary.[32]

According to Jemima Wilkinson's latest and best biographer, Herbert A. Wisbey, Jr., David Wagener's religious pilgrimage began with his Schwenkfelder upbringing, and his membership for a time in the Methodist movement, which gave him his wife, Rebecca Supplee, sister of Abraham Supplee, Methodist preacher. But he had not yet found what he wanted. He was attracted to Quakerism itself when Jemima Wilkinson entered his world. He wrote on the occasion of her first visit, 'When I heard the Gospel Trump's sound, I knew it was the true sound, and that it was with great power from on high, even to the convincing and converting of souls that heard and obeyed the counsel delivered.' Also converted were David's sisters, Anna and Susanna Wagener, and their brother, Jacob. When the Universal Friend founded her 'New Jerusalem' in New York State, David and the other ex-Schwenkfelders settled there and remained her faithful followers until their deaths were recorded in the 'Death Book of the Society of Universal Friends.'[33]

There are of course two sides to every question. A manuscript history of the Schwenkfelders written in 1838 gives the story in judgmental fashion, stating that while Dr. Abraham Wagener and his brother Melchior were sound in the faith, the latter's 'silly children' ran after Jemima Wilkinson and her 'singing, praying and teaching companions,' who 'seized' the Wageners' property. Leaving Pennsylvania for the Genesee Country, these defectors, in the opinion of the historian, 'abandoned truth and fatherland.'[34]

Judging from the wider American viewpoint these ex-Schwenkfelders made solid contributions to the history and development of their adopted 'fatherland.' In the lengthy sketch devoted to this branch of the Wagener family in *The Genealogical Record*, we learn that the Wageners founded the town of Penn Yan, New York. And they are even remembered by American farmers and orchardists for developing the

Wagener Apple, long a favorite in New York State and other fruit-growing areas of the nation.[35]

In the nineteenth century the Schwenkfelder people went their quiet way in the Schwenkfelder homelands of Perkiomen, Goshenhoppen, Bally, and Hosensack. Unlike most other Pennsylvania German groups, the Schwenkfelders did not increase, nor did their ecclesiastical organization spread to other areas by migration. In their home area the Schwenkfelders made the quiet transition from a religious society to a church, an American denomination, readopting the outward sacraments and in a sense doing what some American Quaker groups did in the midwest with the development of pastoral meetings, thus moving closer to the dominant Protestant patterns of worship and ministry.

Like Quakerism, Schwenkfelders lost many members though migration to other parts of the country, although unlike the Quakers, they did not plant Schwenkfelder outposts in the areas where they settled.[36] They also lost members, as did Quakers, through intermarriage with non-members, as well as through conversion to the more active Pennsylvania German evangelistic movements such as the Evangelical Association in the days before the Civil War.[37] Nevertheless, the testimony of the Schwenkfelder society and the impact of its group culture continued to influence the area of Schwenkfelder settlement.

Because of their small numbers, Schwenkfelders were little known outside their area of original settlement, and unlike the Moravians, the Harmonites, and the Ephrata Community, they never attracted the attention of travelers, ecclesiastical visitors, and just plain tourists.

After the Civil War the writings of three Pennsylvanians, one of them a Quaker, brought to the outside American world a knowledge of Schwenkfelder life and thought. The first of these was the Reverend Clement Z. Weiser (1830-1898), Reformed pastor and publicist in the area, who wrote an influential article in the *Mercersburg Review* in 1870, describing the Schwenkfelders and their religious views and practices.[38] The second was the Philadelphia lawyer, later Governor of Pennsylvania, Samuel W. Pennypacker (1843-1916), who attended the *Gedächtnistag* celebration in 1883 and wrote a much copied article about it in the Philadelphia newspapers.[39] In the article he linked Schwenkfeld and Quakerism in the following way: 'Anticipating George Fox, the founder of the Quakers, by a century and a half, he taught that baptism was a spiritual washing. that the supper was a spiritual feast, that the outward ceremonies and observances were in vain and that to take an oath, to bear the sword and to be luxurious in dress or living was to offend against the injunctions of Christ.'

But the most important of the three was the Pennsylvania Quakeress, Phebe Earle Gibbons (1821-1893), whose book, *'Pennsylvania Dutch,' and Other Essays*, really introduced the wider American world to the Pennsylvania Germans in her chatty, housewifely, neighborly style.[40] Since her perceptive essays on the Mennonites, Amish, and Moravians, based on first hand 'field work,' as we may as well call it, proved such a success, she added to the second edition of her book (1874) a lengthy chapter on the Schwenkfelders, based on personal visits. She writes of her experience:

> I had before seen the Schwenkfelders mentioned as a people who, like the Mennonites, Quakers, etc., are opposed to war, but I never became personally acquainted with them until the spring of 1873. At that time, a gentleman of West Chester advised me to inform myself concerning them, speaking of them as a delightful people. On arriving at Norristown, I therefore made inquiry about them from citizens of that borough, and was kindly furnished with several letters of introduction to members of the Schwenkfelder community living about seven miles north of the town.
>
> It was about noon when the stage left me at the house of one who had formerly been a preacher in the society. Here I dined, conversed with my host about his people, and looked at various large. old volumes which he showed to me. Then, having been supplied with an escort, I went to a house in the same neighborhood, the dwelling of an elderly brother, who had learned my errand, and had expressed a wish to meet me.
>
> Under his hospitable care, I remained until Sunday evening; and he took me to the meeting-house, and to other places. Through him I also received a present of several books, giving the history and doctrines of the society.
>
> On Sunday evening he took me to the house of another member. whose kindly care did not cease until he had conveyed me—on Monday morning—again to the borough of Norristown.[41]

In the course of her Schwenkfelder weekend she attended services, read German inscriptions in the cemeteries, made notes from printed and manuscript tomes, and wrote a long sympathetic account of the life and teachings of Schwenkfeld, the history of his followers in Europe and their emigration to

Pennsylvania. She even describes the 'Anniversary or Yearly Meeting,' that is, the *Gedächtnistag*, the account of which she conflated from her own inquiries about it and Pastor Weiser's written report.

Her accounts of Schwenkfelder doctrines and practice accent the similarities with Quakerism.

> In plainness of speech, behaviour, and apparel, in opposition to war, to oaths, and to a paid ministry, in a belief in the teachings of the Divine Spirit and in the inferiority of the written word to the indwelling Spirit, in discarding religious forms, in opposition to priestcraft or a hierarchy, and although not practicing silent worship, yet in their desire to live 'in the stillness,' the Schwenkfelders resemble the Quakers. We might almost say that they are Quakers of an older type (Quakers it may be of whom George Fox had never heard?).[42]

There were differences from Quakerism too—they employ stated prayers, they elect their preachers, they do not acknowledge the spiritual equality of women.

She cited a 'recent writer' (evidently Weiser) who makes the statement 'that it is no misnomer to call these people the Pennsylvania German Quakers,' adding the caveat 'that they are more ancient than George Fox.' But the pastor's statement that 'Caspar Schwenkfeld has been the George Fox of Silesia' went too far. This was, says Phebe, 'an instance of the looseness of language.'[43]

There were other nineteenth-century contacts between the two groups. At the same time that Phebe Earle Gibbons visited the Schwenkfelder communities as a sympathetic observer from Pennsylvania's Quaker community, rural Schwenkfelder leaders from the Upper District—the same area where Christopher Schultz had lived and worked in the eighteenth century— were carrying on a correspondence with an English Quaker historian, Robert Barclay (1833-1876), part of which was included in his book, *The Inner Life of the Religious Societies of the Commonwealth* (London, 1876). For details, see Appendix, No. 15.

Finally I have included two articles on the Schwenkfelders which appeared in Philadelphia's Orthodox Quaker periodical, *The Friend: A Religious and Literary Journal*, in 1904 and 1923. These, two out of many such journalistic encounters which could be cited from the twentieth century, reflect the

ongoing interest that each group found in the other, and the
recognition of spiritual kinship over the centuries. For these
two testimonies to the Schwenkfelder-Quaker connection, see
Appendix, Nos. 16 and 17.

The story of the Schwenkfelder-Quaker relationship is part
of a larger framework, the relationship of Quakers to the Pennsylvania Germans as a whole, and to the Pennsylvania German 'peace churches' in particular. In the colonial period
the Quakers, as founders and shapers of early Pennsylvania,
served in a sense as a spiritual 'big brother' to the Mennonites, Brethren, Amish, and other sectarian groups including
the Schwenkfelders.[44] The spiritual kinship of these groups in
Europe and the practical concerns of peace, antislavery, Indian
affairs, and education drew them together. The Friends, with
their international, transatlantic horizon, especially sought out
brethren of the spirit on both continents. William Penn's visits to Holland and Germany had brought him in contact with
a variety of pietist, spiritual, and radical seekers of truth.[45]
The strong interrelationship of Quakers and European Mennonites continued in the nineteenth century. For example,
when Stephen Grellet visited Russia, he sought out the Mennonite communities and with them those of the Doukhobors,
spiritual dissenters from the Russian Orthodox Church.[46]

The story of the Schwenkfelder-Quaker relationship, one
of smaller compass, is nevertheless of great historical importance for Pennsylvania. The colonial friendships that brought
the Schultzes, Yeakels and other Schwenkfelders into correspondence and visits with leading Friends like Pemberton and
Benezet had longlasting effects, not only in the spiritual development of both groups and in the growth of mutual awareness
of each other's traditions and writings, but also issued in practical results in the defence of religious and political liberties.
This friendship, mutual spiritual irradiation, and practical concern for peace, human rights, and dignity have continued.[47]

Perhaps in the last analysis the Schwenkfelder-Quaker connection can be viewed as a grassroots Pennsylvanian phase of
the ecumenical movement. While the relations between the
two bodies did not lead to union, each side came to honor and
respect the other's understanding of the spiritual life. Let me
close with three quotations reflecting this ecumenical outreach

on the part of the Pennsylvania Quakers and the Pennsylvania Germans.

In a letter written to a friend in Scotland, Anthony Benezet gave his testimony as follows:

> Though I am joined in church fellowship with the people called Quakers, yet my heart is united in true gospel fellowship with the willing in God's Israel, let their distinguishing name or sect be as it may. My soul longs to be a possessor of that gospel charity, even the love of Christ, which embraces the whole universe,—flowing for every individual, let his name, or even erroneous opinion, be what it may, if so be his heart is but sincere toward God. That this spirit of charity, which is christian love, may more and more prevail, is my earnest desire, that so the divers sects of christians may not only be so in name, but may, by the love they bear to one another, show that they are Christ's disciples in deed and in truth.[48]

Christopher Schultz, that sagacious spokesman for the Schwenkfelders, reveals in the following statement his recognition of the practical ecumenicity that came from living together in the religious pluralism that Pennsylvania more than any other British colony in America represented. He describes this pluralism and this ecumenical laissez-faire in a letter to the Silesian Schwenkfelders in 1768:

> You can hardly imagine how many denominations you will find here when you are attending a big gathering like that at Abram Heydrich's or Abraham Jaeckel's funeral.... We are all going to and fro like fish in water but always at peace with each other; anybody of whom it would be known that he hates somebody else because of his religion would be immediately considered a fool; however, everybody speaks his mind freely. A Mennonite preacher is my next neighbor and I could not wish for a better one; on the other side I have a big Catholic church. The present Jesuit Father here comes from Vienna and his name is Johann Baptista Ritter. He confides more in me than in those who come to him for confession, when he has a problem he comes to me. These gentlemen have learned perfectly to adapt to the tempo. Next to them the Lutherans and Reformed have their congregations and churches here, the latter are the most numerous here. On Sundays we meet all of them, coming to and fro, but it does not mean anything.[49]

And for the final note, I close with a statement from one of my favorite Pennsylvania Quakers, Phebe Earle Gibbons. She closes her essay on the Schwenkfelders with these friendly words:

> And now may we not also rest our souls upon these expressions from the constitution of the Schwenkfelder society, translated almost literally?

'In the nature of God, we first perceive love as that noble and outflowing power which binds God and men together.... If the society build upon this fundamental part of the divine nature, namely, love, then their only immovable aim will be, first, the glory of God, and second, the promotion of the common weal of every member.'[50]

## Notes

[1] Jedidiah Morse, *The American Geography* (Elizabethtown, N.J., 1789), quoted in Mitford M. Mathews (ed.), *A Dictionary of Americanisms on Historical Principles* (Chicago, 1951), 1472.

[2] Hugh Barbour, *The Quakers in Puritan England* (New Haven, 1964), 25-28. For the influence of 'spiritual Puritanism' on other groups in America, see Don Yoder, 'The Spiritual Lineage of Shakerism,' *Pennsylvania Folklife*, 27 (1978), 2-14.

[3] Wilhelm Hubben, *Die Quäker in der deutschen Vergangenheit* (Leipzig, 1929), 93-94; see also 21.

[4] Rufus M. Jones, *Spiritual Reformers in the 16th and 17th Centuries* (New York, 1914), 84-86.

[5] Ibid., 337.

[6] For the Matern-Prache connections with the Silesian Schwenkfelders as well as with English and American Quakers, see 'Letters of Hilary Prach and John G. Matern,' *The Journal of the Friends Historical Society*, 16 (1919), 1-9. Two letters of the above, addressed to 'Beloved Friend Martin John at Laubgrund,' were translated from *Unschuldige Nachrichten von Alten und Neuen Theologischen Sachen* (Leipzig, 1706), 8th section, 432-46. See also Horst Weigelt, *The Schwenkfelders in Pennsylvania*, trans. by Peter C. Erb (Pennsburg, 1985). For John Matern's work among English Quakers, see 'John Matern, Schoolmaster,' *The Journal of the Friends Historical Society*, 10 (1913), 149-52.

[7] Josiah Granville Leach, *History of the Bringhurst Family with Notes of the Clarkson, De Peyster and Boude Families* (Philadelphia, 1901), 21-22, 32, 95-96. The Journal of John Bringhurst, Jr., states, 'My Mothers Father Hilerias Prache was a Priest in orders in Garmina [Germany] & my Mothers first Husband John Matern was a School Master there. was both convinced of the Truth Profest by the people called Quakers in the year 1671, not having any to join with there, writ to frds in Holland & London and Received sattisfactory answers to com over accordingly my Grandmother & Mother being also convinced they all left Germoney went to Holland & from thence to London where John Matern Kept School at Christopher Taylors at Edmonton where he died the 5th 7mo 1680.' John Bringhurst Sr., printer and publisher of Quaker books in London, married the widow Rosina Matern in 1682. After the death of 'Grandfather Prache' his widow with a daughter and granddaughter came to Pennsylvania, and after John Bringhurst's death in 1701 the Bringhursts joined them in Philadelphia.

8   For biographical materials on Christopher Schultz, see 'Christoph Schultz,' *The Pennsylvania-German*, 11 (1910), 649-58; Elmer E. S. Johnson, 'Christopher Schultz in Public Life,' *Schwenkfeldiana*, 1 (1940), 15-20; and *The Genealogical Record of the Schwenkfelder Families*, edited by Samuel Kriebel Brecht (Pennsburg, Pa., 1923), 964-68.

9   For Caspar Kriebel, see *The Genealogical Record*, 348-49.

10  For Israel Pemberton, see Theodore Thayer, *Israel Pemberton: King of the Quakers* (Philadelphia, 1943); and *Dictionary of American Biography*, 14: 412.

11  For Anthony Benezet, see George Brookes, *Friend Anthony Benezet* (Philadelphia, 1937); *Dictionary of American Biography*, 2: 177; and 'Biographical Notices of Anthony Benezet,' *Friends' Miscellany*, 3 (1832), 97-109.

12  Howard Wiegner Kriebel, *The Schwenkfelders in Pennsylvania: A Historical Sketch* (Lancaster, Pa, 1904), 144.

13  Ibid., 146.

14  Ibid., 146-48.

15  For the colonial reactions to the threat of assigning Anglican bishops to the colonies, see Arthur L. Cross, *The Anglican Episcopate and the American Colonies* ( New York, 1902).

16  The Schwenkfelder delegation in Vienna remained there several years. The negotiations for tolerance were, however, unsuccessful. When the actual persecutions began in 1725, with forced baptisms of Schwenkfelder children, the Schwenkfelder leaders wrote to the Amsterdam Mennonites asking them to use their influence to help them to obtain their rights, and to Count Zinzendorf for shelter at Herrnhut. See Kriebel, 22-24. For firsthand accounts of the delegation, see *The Tumultuous Years: Schwenkfelder Chronicles 1580-1750 - The Reports of Martin John, Jr. and Balthazar Hoffman*, translated by L. Allen Viehmeyer (Pennsburg, Pa., 1980).

17  On the Quaker side, there was in the 1780s, if I recall correctly an unlocatable note on the subject in my papers, interest in Philadelphia Yearly Meeting to issue translations of Quaker books for distribution to the 'sober Germans amongst us.' That the production was considerable is evident from Charles R. Hildeburn, *A Century of Printing: The Issues of the Press in Pennsylvania, 1685-1784* (Philadelphia, 1885).

18  The *Erläuterung* was published at Jauer, Silesia, by Heinrich Christ. Müller in 1771. A revised edition appeared at Sumnytown, Pennsylvania, in 1830, from the press of Enos Benner, publisher of the *Bauernfreund*, the major German newspaper in the Schwenkfelder area.

19  The bilingual character of the English court in this period was underscored in the letters of the baroness von Riedesel, who mentions that George III spoke excellent German. See *Baroness von Riedesel and the American Revolution: Journal and Correspondence of a Tour of Duty 1776-1783* (Chapel Hill, 1965), 140.

[20] Jacob Hagen is described in a letter from Dr. John Fothergill to (Israel) Pemberton, April 9, 1759, as follows: 'He is about 44 or 5, in the mercantile way, acquainted with the nature of Parliamentary and public business, cool, friendly and judicious. His name is Jacob Hagen, and I believe he will be nominated one of your correspondents. As he is a man of considerable property, he would have some weight in proportion...' (*Chain of Friendship: Selected Letters of Dr. John Fothergill of London, 1735-1780* (Cambridge, Mass., 1971), 211. The editor identifies him as Jacob Hagen (1715-1795), a Quaker merchant whose family, of German origin, had established themselves as stave-makers in Mill Street (Ibid., 213, note 5).

[21] John Hunt (1712-1778), an English Quaker preacher, made several ministerial visits to the American colonies before emigrating to Pennsylvania in 1769. In 1756 he and Christopher Wilson were sent from London Yearly Meeting to investigate the question of the alleged mismanagement of Indian affairs in the colony. This investigation was one of the causes which led to the Quakers leaving the Assembly and founding the Friendly Association. In Pennsylvania Hunt settled at Darby. He was one of the leading Quakers exiled in 1778 to Virginia, where he died in that year. John Pemberton called him 'a great, wise and experienced minister and elder.' For biographical materials, see the *Dictionary of Quaker Biography* (typescript), Quaker Collection, Haverford College Library.

[22] Schultz in a previous letter had misinformed Pemberton as to the publication place of the copy of Arnold's work which he was citing. In this letter he corrects it from Basel to Schaffhausen, and gives the date as 1740. It is of interest to note that a copy of this Schaffhausen edition of Arnold, recently (1984) sold at auction in Pennsylvania, may have been Schultz's copy.

[23] For the title of this volume, see Appendix, Document 5.

[24] For the title of this volume, see Appendix, Document 5.

[25] For the title of this German translation of Barclay's *Apology*, see Appendix, Document 13.

[26] For the complete titles of the Webb tract in English and German, see Appendix, Document 14.

[27] Brookes, 393-95. Elisha Kirk (1757-1790) was a member of York Monthly Meeting who traveled widely in the Quaker ministry. York County was one of the many areas where Pennsylvania Germans came in contact with Quakers. It appears from this letter that Elisha Kirk was one of the leaders in providing Quaker literature for Pennsylvania's German-speaking population. For his memoirs and journal, see *Friends' Miscellany*, 6 (1834), 1-75.

[28] For Dr. George de Benneville, see Albert D. Bell, *The Life and Times of Dr. George de Benneville (1703-1793)* (Boston, Mass., 1953); and DeB. R. K[eim]., 'The De Benneville Family,' *Notes and Queries*, Annual Volume 1898 (Harrisburg, Pa., 1899), 181-83.

29  For additional light on this correspondence, see Peter C. Erb, 'Gerhard Tersteegen, Christopher Saur, and Pennsylvania Sectarians,' *Brethren Life and Thought*, 20 (1975), 153-57. For Abraham Wagener, see below, n. 31.

30  The Pennsylvania Germans often sent their sons to English schools, and very often Quaker schools, to learn English. Another method for learning English, recorded from Northampton County, was to hire the sons out on a New Jersey farm where they were forced to speak English.

31  For the Wagner (Wagener) family, see Andrew S. Berky, *Practitioner in Physick: A Biography of Abraham Wagner, 1717-1763* (Pennsburg, Pa., 1954), and *The Genealogical Record*. Note the accounts in ibid., 1440-53 for David Wagener, the Supplees, and Jemima Wilkinson.

32  The best biography of the 'Universal Friend' is Herbert A. Wisbey, *Pioneer Prophetess: Jemima Wilkinson, the Publick Universal Friend* (Ithaca, N.Y., 1964). See also *Dictionary of American Biography*, 20: 226-27, and the earlier biography by David Hudson, *Memoir of Jemima Wilkinson, A Preacheress of the Eighteenth Century: Containing an Authentic Narrative of Her Life and Character, and of the Rise, Progress and Conclusion of Her Ministry* (Bath, N.Y., 1844).

33  Wisbey, 88-89.

34  *Freund Baltzer Hübners Abschrift, und Auskunft von den ersten Ansiedelungen der Schwenckfelder Hier in Amerika, und nebst andern beyläufigen Interessanten Berichten von Begebenheiten unter u. mit ihnen; Auch Etwas von ihren Grund-Regeln, Predigern, Erziehung, gottesdienstl. Häusern, u.s.w. hie in Pennsylvanien.* It appears from a note at the end of this 20-page manuscript in the Schwenkfelder Library, which I have translated for publication, that it was written by Isaac Schultz, Sr., and copied by 'Friend Baltzer Hübner' December 16, 1839, from Schultz's manuscript of 1838, and further revised by Schultz in 1858.

35  The Wagener apple was named for Abraham Wagener who initiated his nursery at Penn Yan in 1796. The earliest published reference is in the Report of the New York State Agricultural Society for 1847. By 1892 it was offered by nurserymen throughout the country except for the North Mississippi Valley, the Rocky Mountain region, and the plains states from Nebraska to Texas. It is in the Northern Spy group, and crossed with the Northern Spy it produced the Ontario Apple. For details, see S.A. Beach, et al., *The Apples of New York* (Albany, N.Y., 1905), I, 21, 24, 354-56.

36  That there was some intermarriage with Quaker families in Montgomery County and elsewhere is clear from *The Genealogical Record*. Examples include, among others, the Brinton, Coates, Cloud, Foulke, Hicks, Johnson, Lippincott, Lukens, Mendenhall, Pusey, Rhoads, Shoemaker, Supplee, Tyson, and Updegrove families.

37  The Evangelical Association (*Evangelische Gemeinschaft*), a Methodist-like denomination founded among the Pennsylvania Germans about

1800 and now a part of the United Methodist Church, converted a considerable number of Schwenkfelders in the Upper Milford area in the 1820s and 1830s. See R[euben]. Yeakel, *History of the Evangelical Association* (Cleveland, 1894), 1: 189-191, 223-25, et passim. Reuben Yeakel (1827-1904) became a leading bishop of this denomination, editor of its German and English periodicals, and president of its theological seminary.

[38] Clement Z. Weiser (1830-1898) was a Reformed clergyman in Montgomery County remembered for his contributions to local and church history of the area. His article, 'Caspar Schwenkfeld and the Schwenkfelders,' appeared in *The Mercersburg Review*, 17 (1870), 347-73.

[39] Governor Pennypacker had Germantown Quaker family background although he was not himself a Friend. He had a large collection of Schwenkfelder literature, bought at country sales in the Schwenkfelder area. In discussing this collection in his autobiography, he makes the following statement: 'Of the Reformers, Luther was a charcoal burner; Calvin was a peasant; and among them all the only man of long lineage and high culture was Caspar Schwenkfeld von Ossig, a nobleman of Silesia. He taught a system of sweet and pure theology which, carried through the Mennonites of Holland to England, led to the origin of the Quakers' (*The Autobiography of a Pennsylvanian*, Philadelphia, 1918), 161-64.

[40] Phebe Earle Gibbons was a Philadelphian married to the Quaker anti-slavery leader, Dr. Joseph Gibbons of Lancaster County. For her biography, see Alfred L. Shoemaker, 'Phebe Earle Gibbons,' *The Pennsylvania Dutchman*, 4/7 (1952), 5. Her book went through three editions. We have used the third (1882) edition here.

[41] Ibid., 231-32.

[42] Ibid., 265.

[43] Ibid., 231, 265.

[44] While Schwenkfelders and Quakers were similar in the ways in which they expressed religion in life, the Quakers appear to have had some direct influences upon the Schwenkfelders in meetinghouse architecture, the use of plain speech, and the choice of the name for their denomination when it was first incorporated in 1782 as a 'society' of Schwenkfelders rather than a 'church,' modeled probably on the Quaker usage, Society of Friends. The denomination took the name Schwenkfelder Church in 1908.

[45] Penn's journal of his mission in Germany in 1677 has recently been reedited in the definitive edition of the Penn Papers, *The Papers of William Penn*, ed. by Mary Maples Dunn and Richard S. Dunn (Philadelphia, 1981), 1 (1644-1679), 425-508.

[46] Benjamin Seebohm (ed.), *Memoirs of the Life and Gospel Labours of Stephen Grellet* (Philadelphia, 1860). For his visit to the 'Duhobortzi' and other 'spiritual Christians,' as he calls them, see 1, Chapter 32, also 447-52 and 455-57. The Philadelphia Friends along with London

Yearly Meeting offered moral and monetary assistance to the Doukho-
bor group when after long decades of persecution in Russia they decided
to migrate to Canada in 1898. In their outward history they were thus
similar to the Schwenkfelder exiles of the eighteenth century. For the
Quaker-Doukhobor connection, see Joseph Elkinton, *The Doukhobors*
(Philadelphia, 1903).

[47] The twentieth century has brought renewed contacts between Quakers
and Pennsylvania's other peace churches, including the Schwenkfelders.
See W. Kyrell Meschter, *Twentieth Century Schwenkfelders: A Narrative History* (Pennsburg, Pa., 1984).

[48] 'Biographical Notices of Anthony Benezet,' *Friends' Miscellany*, 3/3
(1832), 101.

[49] Dietmar Rothermund, *The Layman's Progress: Religious and Political
Experience in Colonial Pennnsylvania, 1740-1770* (Philadelphia, 1961),
190-91. The original, in German, is in the Kriebel Letterbook in the
Schwenkfelder Library.

[50] Gibbons, 42, 270.

## Appendix

**Doc. 1. Letter of the Schwenkfelder Subscribers to the Friendly
Association, November 13, 1756.**

During the French and Indian War, when due to international intrigues
Indian incursions on the white settlements were increased, the Quakers initiated the so-called Friendly Association for Regaining and Preserving Peace
with the Indians. The Schwenkfelders and other pacifist sects supported
this effort with contributions. Caspar Kriebel and Christopher Shultz were
liaison between the Schwenkfelder subscribers and the Quaker Trustees of
the Association, with whom they met on occasion. Responding to Israel
Pemberton's call for aid, the Schwenkfelder fathers met at Skippack on
November 13, 1756, and pledged their financial support to the project.
David Schultz, Christopher Schultz's cousin, was appointed an auditor to
check the accounts of the funds collected. A copy of the letter sent to the
Friendly Association appears in full in *The Journals and Papers of David
Shultze*, trans. and ed. by Andrew S. Berky (Pennsburg, 1952), 1: 187-89.
It was republished in part in Richard K. MacMaster et al., *Conscience in
Crisis: Mennonites and Other Peace Churches in America, 1739-1789—
Interpretations and Documents* (Scottdale, Pa., 1979), 140-41.

It is the will of the within subscribers, that it may be known that they
are a few families of a dispersed people in Silesia, who have always, under
God's blessing, maintained themselves by the labors of their hands only, and
have been forced to leave their estates behind in Silesia, on account of their
confession, and who have already here, partly suffered by the incursions of
Indians, in relieving their poor, distressed neighbors. Therefore, they hope
that their contributions, small as it is, will not be contempted, for it may

well be compared with the two mites which the poor widow in Evangelio cast in, for they have cast in their living. Nevertheless, they do it with cheerfulness and delight, to be assisting in the intended salutary endeavors, as also they are ready to satisfy their true loyalty to the King's government to which they have submitted.

Know all men by these presents, That, whereas, some of the principal members of the people called Quakers, within this province of Pennsylvania, do intend to raise a considerable sum of money by way of a public and voluntary subscription, to lay a fund in order to be thereby enabled to do some satisfaction to those Indians who have already done terrible damage and disturbances to the frontier inhabitants of this province, and therewith, if possible, to procure a peace to this country; and as the said members have also communicated their said scheme to us, the hereunto subscribers, so late emigrants of Silesia, and desired of us to assist them in the above mentioned purpose.

So know ye, therefore, that in consequence thereof, we whose names are hereunto subscribed, do, in the name of God, hereby voluntarily and of our own free will and accord, promise to pay and contribute to the above said fund, which is to be employed to so salutary an end, consistant with the Gospel of our Saviour, and with principles of the doctrine we profess, every one of us, all the respective sums of money as every one shall hereby promise and subscribe, on or before the twenty-seventh day of November next ensuing, after the date hereof, unto Caspar Kriebel and Christopher Schultze, as this day by us chosen and appointed trustees, for the term of two years from hence next ensuing, either in ready payment, or in case of non-payment, every one of us shall be at liberty to keep the principal sum in his hands, and to pay the interest for the same, after the said twenty-seventh day of November next. To the true and punctual payment whereof, we do hereby oblige and bind our heirs, executors, and administrators, and every of us and them, in the penalty of double the sum, as every one hereunto shall subscribe, firmly by these presents.

In witness and confirmation and for the true performances thereof, we have hereunto set our hands, together with the respective sums of money, as every one hereby promises to pay and contribute, to the purposes above mentioned.

Done at Lower Salford Township, in the county of Philadelphia, on this thirteenth day of November, Anno Domini, 1756.

George Anders
George Kriebel
Beyer's Estate
George Heydrick
Balthazar Heydrick
Hans Christopher Heebner
George Hoffman
Christopher Heebner
David Heebner

George Heebner
Caspar Heydrick
Melchior Hartranft
Christopher Hoffman
Balthazar Hoffman
Christopher Yeakle
Abraham Yeakle
Balthazar Yeakle
Caspar Kriebel
Balthazar Krauss
Christopher Kriebel
Melchior Kriebel
Christopher Krauss
George Dresher
Christopher Dresher
Melchior Meisther
Christopher Meisther
David Meisther
Christopher Neuman
Christopher Reinwalt
Christopher Reinwalt
Melchior Scholtz
Gregorius Scholtz
David Scholtz
George Scholtz (2nd)
Christopher Scholtz
Caspar Seipt
Johannes Yeakle
Christopher Yeakle
Maria Yeakle
Christopher Wagner
Hans Weigner
Melchior Weigner

**Doc. 2. Caspar Kriebel and Christopher Schultz to the Friendly Association, December 2, 1756.**

This letter, evidently delivered in person to the Trustees of the Friendly Association by the Schwenkfelder representatives, expressed concern for the complete understanding of the project and the management of the monies involved. The original, as transcribed here, appears in *Papers Relating to the Friendly Association, Etc.,* Volume I, 243, Quaker Collection, Haverford College Library. A variant transcription appears in *Conscience in Crisis,* 141. The verso of the original includes the address: 'Direct to Caspar Kriebel near Jacob Wenns in Towamensing,' and the label: 'From Caspar Kribel & Ch.ʳ: Schultz 3 Decr 1756 Concerning the subscriptions made by the Swingfelders.'

That we the Subscribers were sent and come to Phil.[a] to got [get] ourselves better informed about the Fundamental Views and Measures and Managements of the Known Subscription, of which the Subscribers in the Paper of yesterday by us communicated to the general Meeting, has hitherto been partly much in the dark: So we must now in discharge [of] our Duty confess, that by what we have been able to learn as well in open Meeting as private Conversation, we are fully Satisfyed, about the good Intents and Purposes as well [as] Management of the Affair concerned, and that therefore we on our own Part were readily willing to join our Subscription, to have it entered by the Treasurer, but Since it is now our Duty to look back upon our People whom we at present represent in this Matter, we find that the Manner of Application [of] the money is somewhat otherwise, as a Report prevailed amongst us at the Time of Subscription, that a Fund Should be laid by of the said Money, and the Interest which from Time to Time should arise of the Said Money, Should be applied to Such Uses as is by and would be by the pacific minded Friends intendet, and on these Terms some poor Subscribers were induced to Subscribe more readily, whilst they apprehended the Money would not so directly be demanded, and could by paying Interest keep it as long as were convenient for them in their own Hands, therefore as we find the Matter otherwise, it will be but prudent to inform them of the Circumstances wherein we find the Matter, and convince them of the good Purposes of applying the Money as well as we are convinced, before we enter their Subscription in the Treasurers Hand.

2d. Dec:[r] 1756

Casper Kribel

Christopher Shultze

**Doc. 3. Caspar Kriebel and Christopher Schultz to Israel Pemberton, May 23, 1757.**

Here the Schwenkfelder subscribers, through their representatives Kriebel and Schultz, propose to split their payments into two portions. As a voice from the upcountry areas closer to the Indian raids that were a constant threat at this time, the letter expresses a cautious realism over the situation and the prospects of peace. On the verso: 'To Israel Pemberton at Philadelphia. Towamensin 23. 5 m.[o] 1757. From Caspar Kribel & Christopher Shulze.' The original appears in *Papers Relating to the Friendly Association, Etc.* Volume I, 343, Quaker Collection, Haverford College Library. A variant transcription appears in *Conscience in Crisis*, 143-44.

Dear Friend Isr.[l] Pemberton

Several of you will remember that we was in Decemb.[r] last with you at your Meeting and notifyed our Concurrence to your Scheme for the pacifick Measures with the Indians; now the most part of the Subscribers amongst us are resolved to pay in at present the half Part of their respective Sums, and if Affairs can be Settled with the Delawares they will Pay the Rest about Next Fall, therefor we the hereunto Subscribers have resolved to come down to Philad.ᵃ at next Quarter Session C[o]urt and will consult with you, wether this and other like Resolves, will Suit your Plan and Measures, that then we might do accordingly. And you will please to inform us with the Bearer hereof wether the said mentioned Time will be convenient on your Part, that we can meet one or other of you, that the Money which we then should have with us, could properly be accepted and received. We have a While Since heard of Severall Murders committed on our Frontiers, we hope you Shall better know, what Prospect there is, of any Hopes, towards a well grounded Pacification than we do. Please to let us also Somewhat know, and we Shall allways continue your hearty Friends

Casper Kriebel

Christ.ʳ Sholtze
Towamenson
May 23.ᵗʰ 1757

### Doc. 4. Receipt for the Schwenkfelder Subscription to the Friendly Association, June 7, 1757.

This receipt for funds subscribed for the Friendly Association by the 'Swingfelders' in Towamencin and Goshenhoppen is found in copy form (without the signature of Israel Pemberton) in *Papers Relating to the Friendly Association, Etc.*, Volume I, 355, Quaker Collection, Haverford College Library.

Philadelphia the 7th day 6 mo. 1757

Received from Casper Krebel and Christopher Schultz the Sum of One hundred and five pounds twelve Shillings lawful money of Pennsylvania being part of several sums subscribed by the said Casper & Christopher and their Brethren Members of the Congregations of the Swingfelders in Towamenson and Cowissihoppen Townships in the County of Philadelphia, and I promise and oblige myself to employ the said Sum of one hundred and five pounds twelve shillings & such other or further Sums, as may hereafter be collected and paid to me by the said Casper & Christopher & their Brethren towards regaining and preserving Peace with the Indians in such manner, as they may think proper to direct or in Case they should not give me any particular Directions concerning the same, before the said Money may be wanted for the use Aforesaid then in such manner as the Trustees of the people called Quakers members of the Association for regaining & preserving Peace with the Indians by pacific measures may advise and direct

witness my hand

**Doc. 5.    Israel Pemberton to Christopher Schultz, July 9, 1757.**

The original letter, addressed 'To Christopher Shultze in Hereford township[,] Philadelphia County,' is preserved in the manuscript collections of the Schwenkfelder Library (VOC P⁴). The books referred to in the letter are: (1) Samuel Hopkins, *An Address to the People of New-England. Representing the very great Importance of attaching the Indians to their Interest; not only by treating them justly and kindly; but by using proper Endeavours to settle Christianity among them. By Samuel Hopkins, A.M. Pastor of a Church in Springfield. Printed in Boston, 1753. Being a Conclusion to the Historical Memoirs relating to the Housatunnuk Indians; with an account of the Methods used for the Propagation of the Gospel among the said Indians, by the late reverend Mr. John Sergeant. Now recommended to the serious Consideration of the Inhabitants of Pennsylvania, and the Other Colonies.* (Philadelphia: Reprinted by B. Franklin, and D. Hall. 1757). (2) [Samuel Hopkins]. *An Abridgment of Mr. Hopkins' Historical Memoirs, relating to the Housatunnuk, or Stockbridge Indians; or, A brief Account of the Methods used, and Pains taken, for civilizing and propagating the Gospel among that Heathenish Tribe, and the Success thereof, under the Ministry of the late Rev. Mr. John Sergeant.* (Philadelphia. Printed and Sold by B. Franklin and D. Hall. 1757).

Philad:ᵃ 9. 7 mo. 1757


Loving ffriend

I have just rec.ᵈ thy Letter with the Translation of Hopkins' address; I am told Christ:ʳ Sowr has gott it translated & printed already, but have not Seen any of them, intend to write to him abᵗ it. the Abridgement of Sergeant's Memoirs is in the press & will I expect be printed next week, when it is done I purpose to send thee some of them.

Several of us intend to sett out for Easton next fourth day—how long yᵉ Business will Keep us there is uncertain but I think not less than two or three weeks. I shall be glad to see thee there.

I am tho' in hast[e] Thy real ffr.ᵈ
Isr: Pemberton


**Doc. 6. Christopher Schultz to Israel Pemberton, August 29, 1760.**

Like other letters in this correspondence, this document reflects the deep interest Christopher Schultz had in Pennsylvania's Indians and their religious beliefs. The Indian Settlement on the Susquehanna referred to here was evidently Wyalusing, as clarified in the following letter, which also refers to Pemberton's account of the Indians' visit, which Schultz expressed an interest in. The letter was located in *Papers Relating to the Friendly Association, Etc.*, Vol. IV, 11, Quaker Collection, Haverford College Library.

Hereford Aug[ust]. 29. 1760.

Worthy Freind Isr.[l]

Thy Favours of the 15. Instant by Bern.[d] Wannemaker are much oblig-
ing, as I was thereby informed of some Proceedings of the Indians. And as
thee was further pleased, to make me a promise, if I would call on Thee
in such a Time as now 'to endeavor to furnish me with a more particular
Account of them Indians and their Religious Sentiments who lately visited
you at Philad.[a] & appeared to be a sober people & of good Conduct having
a lively Sense of Religion' Which Account would be acceptable to several,
as also to know whereabout on Susquehana River they live, if a Place on
Lewis Evans Map of the middle Settlements could be indicated that would
also gratify my Curiosity. Therefore I pray now to pardon my Impunity in
taking the Liberty to desire now such an Account, if it conveniently can be
delivered to the Bearer hereof.

And as Thee also formerly was pleased to give me some Detail of what
had happened with the Indian Goods, thee hast conveyed the other Year to
Pittsburg, in which it was likely there would be some Discount on thy Side,
though as I perceived the Affair was first begun and happened to be in
Reality for the Commun Service: But the Accounts were then not settled,
nor any Application made, to the General of any Funds for Recovery of
such Damage: Therefore I would also fain know how Thee came off with
the same, whereas I presume we could not indifferently look upon it but
equally bear some portion of the same, as being for the general Good.

I remain with true Love and

Affection thy Friend
Christ.[r] Schultze

### Doc. 7. Christopher Schultz to Israel Pemberton, December 1, 1760.

During the French and Indian War hundreds of Pennsylvanians were
taken captive by the Indians. In this letter Schultz speaks for his Schwenkfelder brethren asking that half of their contributions to the Association
treasury be used for redeeming captives. The letter speculates on what
may happen if the Cherokees return to their alliance with the British, and
offers Friends a German translation of a document entitled 'Remarks on
the Behaviour of Pawpunahoak.' Papoonhank, as his name is more frequently spelled, also known as 'Munsee John,' was a Moravian convert to
Christianity. He settled a village of the Munsee (Muncy) clan, a branch of
the Delawares, at Wyalusing in 1758, later moving to the Moravian mission
stations in Ohio, where he died in 1775. The letter was sealed with a red
wax seal, unfortunately broken, and includes Pemberton's notation: 'Hereford Dec:[r] 1760 From Chris:[r] Shul[t]ze signifying that the Swingfelders are
willing to Contribute £ 100 out of their Mon[e]y towards the release of the
Captives am.[g] y[e] Ind.[ns]. The address is given as: 'M.[r] Israel Pemberton
at Philadelphia.' The original appears in *Papers Relating to the Friendly*

*Association, Etc.*, Volume IV, 59, Quaker Collection, Haverford College Library. A variant version appears in *Conscience in Crisis*, 150-51.

Hereford Dec. 1, 1760.

Beloved Friend!

Having consulted our Friends, concerning the Proposals lately made to us, for laying out of our Money now in thy Hands: They give these for their Opinion, as the Relief of the Poor Captives amongst the Savages, is a Matter of immediate Necessity to which Humanity as well as Christianity obliges [us] to contribute: They are willing that in Conjunction [with] what other Friends do contribute about the half part of the said Money be applied towards the Release of Such poor Prisoners late our fellow Inhabitants, if it shall be found meet, that something shall and may be done, and the future Circumstances continue to be such, that the Release of them be retarded, and not effected by the Measures of our Government.

As there is now a Prospect of the Cherokees returning to their Alliance with the English it is probably [probable] our northerly Indians shall not so much hesitate as they hitherto have done, to accomodate themselves to reasonable Terms, especialy as there is the giving up their Prisoners. Nevertheless as we trust the Friends will act in that Affair with all due Circumspection, that when they have the immediate Relief of the Captives at Heart to effect the same, they will be not less cautious to prevent unnecessary Charges upon private Contributors as they are themselves.

The other part of the said Money of about a Hundred pounds could be left for further Purposes, Necessity's or Considerations as Time and Occasion will furnish and bring on.

With these presents I do return the Remarks on the Behaviour of Pawpunahoak having copied and translated the same into High Dutch, it hath been very acceptable to several of my Friends, who rejoice in perceiving the hand of Grace to operate so strongly on the poor Heathens[.] I thank [thee] for the Communication of that Relation as well as for the Inquiry presented to me. If a high dutch Copy of the said Remarks should be of Service to thee, to shew them to some Friend, I would upon Notice willingly furnish Thee with one. I remain Thy most affectionate Friend

Christ.$^{r}$ Shultze

### Doc. 8. Christopher Schultz to Israel Pemberton, April 4, 1764.

After the war was concluded in 1763 the local political scene in Pennsylvania was far from calm. As this letter informs us, the threat of the loss of the civil and religious rights granted by the Penn Charter of 1681 raised its head in the assembly, and there was talk of establishing the Church of England in the colony. Here Schultz speaks not only for his Schwenkfelder brethren but for all emigrant groups who came to Pennsylvania to enjoy the freedoms and liberties promised by Penn. A copy of the original is preserved in the manuscript collections of the Schwenkfelder Library (VOC-S$^{9}$). It has been published in Dietmar Rothermund, *The Layman's Progress: Religious and Political Experience in Colonial Pennsylvania, 1740-1770* (Philadelphia, 1961), 181-82.

Hereford in Berks County

Beloved Friend Israel Pemberton!

I have been hindered by several circumstances to see Philadelphia (this last winter)) and pay Thee a Visit, to inform myself how Friends bear up with the care, Insurrections, and Diffamations from an unruly wicked People in the Country who neither know nor understand what they do or say, acting in both parts against the Rules of God and Man.

And now we hear that such a misunderstanding breaks out in our Legislature as threaten[s] a Revolution in our Constitution that our Charter should be delivered up in the Kings hands in which case if such as have transported themselves with their Families hither, in hopes for a full and free Enjoyment of the celebrated Privileges of the said Charter should be deprived of the same especially of the First Article of the Freedom of Conscience and instead of that be subjected to Episcopal Jurisdiction and Military Actions it would be very hard and striking to the Heart. It is true Quakers and Unitas Fratum are protected in their Religions by the Laws of the Realm of Great Brittain but what should be our Case and other Societies of the like Principles, who have so far trusted themselves under the Wings of this Government erected and constituted for the best time by Quakers? ... Therefore we earnestly desire and admonish you in brotherly love to use all possible means to prevent the Destruction and depriving of religious Liberty in any Respect, so laudably planned by your Fathers, for the Benefit of all Settlers, whose whorty [worthy] Followers we hope you will approve [prove] yourselves, in taking care that their Intention be not violated, and what alteration should be made or agreed to it may be with Safety of Conscience for every Individual in this Province. And since you are the people who made the first Agreement for the Settlement of this Province, your consent or non-consent to any alteration must conservently be of very great weight. And though we trust your best Endeavours in this critical circumstances will not be wanting, nevertheless we thought to encourage you a little in the same with this few Words, the freedom of which you will indulge from your Fellows in Sufferings.

Israel be so good and let me have some account how the above mentioned affairs stand, if it can be. I am with true love thy obliged friend.

C.S.

April 4, 1764.

### Doc. 9. Israel Pemberton to Christopher Schultz, July 15, 1765.

Quaker relations with the Schwenkfelders included the education of some Schwenkfelder children at Quaker expense. Here Israel Pemberton reports his willingness to support the schooling of one of Abraham Hartranft's sons. The school is not mentioned, but since boarding was involved, it was probably one of the Friends' institutions in Philadelphia or Germantown. It would be interesting to know which of the sons of Abraham Hartranft (d. 1766) was involved here, and whether he was the ancestor of General John Frederick Hartranft (1830-1889), Governor of Pennsylvania 1870-1879, or of Dr. Chester David Hartranft (1839-1914), father of the *Corpus Schwenkfeldianorum* project at Wolfenbüttel in Germany. The original, addressed 'To Christopher Shultze in Hereford township,' is part of the manuscript collections of the Schwenkfelder Library (VOC-P$^3$). A German postscript on the verso, addressed to 'bru[der]. Chri[stoph].,' reads 'Wenn etwas allgemeines in diesem ist so lasse michs wissen aber anders nicht.' There follows news of the correspondent's dealings with Michael Röder, Juncken, and Michael Bauer, which, however, appears not to deal with the subject of the letter.

Philad.$^a$ 15. 7 mo: 1765

Dear Friend

I have lately been to Abram Hartranft's & have seen his Son& am very willing to pay for his boarding & Schooling a year, being in hopes he will be capable & dilijent in the improvement of his time in learning, & if Thou can'st find another such poor Child that is likely to be benefited by it, I will in like Manner pay for his Maintainance at a School a year. I shall be pleas'd to hear that your Master is skilful & industrious in his Business & that the School prospers. I Suppose this Boy will be sent up in about two weeks time.

When thou has't a Convenient opportunity after the School is Settled, an Account of the Number of Scholars & of what the Master is Capable of teaching them will be acceptable to me,

Thy Loving Friend

Isr: Pemberton

& if Thou mentionest the Expence of Boarding & Schooling it may be in my way to inform others of it, who may incline to Send Children, if there be room for any.

### Doc. 10. Christopher Schultz to Israel Pemberton, April 15, 1768.

From his well-stocked library of church history and theology, Schultz was able to respond to Pemberton's request for information on Schwenkfeld's works and the history of his followers. This was part of the larger task of informing Queen Charlotte and the British court of the Schwenkfelders and the defence of their liberties. See also the following document. The letter is addressed 'For Israel Pemberton at Philadelphia,' and bears the notation: 'April 15, 1768[:] Mem.$^o$ from Chr.$^r$ Shultz for Jacob Hagen.' The original of the letter here transcribed is in the Pemberton Papers, Volume XX, 16a-b, Historical Society of Pennsylvania, and is printed with the Society's permission.

Hereford April 15.<sup>th</sup> 1768

Dear Friend Israel!

In the Account I gave Thee this Week, of Godfried Arnolds Historie of Church and Hereticks, I put down in the last Line printed at Basel, *Gedruckt zu Basel*, but have been mistaken, I find now it is Schafhousen, which I desire may be corrected and the Year 1740 added to the same; the Historie of Caspar Schwenkfeld is to be found there in Part II. Lib. XII. Cap. XX. pag. 836 seq. Item in Appendice Num. LXIX from pag. 1246. to 1249. where several of his Letters are inserted, as also large Extracts of his Works, and part of the Acts of his Colloquio with Blaurer, Butzer and Frecht at the Palace of Tübingen before the Commissioners of Duke Ulrick of Wurtenberg An. 1535. And his End, written by Jacob Hoh of Dieffenau a Nobleman. I send [sent] Anthony Benezet some short Account of the Historie of C.S. and his Followers, which if thou pleases I hope he will let thee see, I remain with much Love, Thy Sincere Friend

Christ.<sup>r</sup> Schultz

P.S. I also send a Book of Caspar Schw.<sup>s</sup> Works, to be send [sent] to London if you can think proper

[Appended to the letter:]

Gottfried Arnold in seiner Kirchen und Ketzer-Historie im XVI. Seculo giebt eine feine Nachricht von Caspar Schwenkfeld von Ossing seines Lebens, Lauffs und Lehre, allwo auch feine Extracts seiner Schriften und Nachricht von seinen Werken zufinden sind, imgleichen Extracts aus August Saligs Historie wegen besagten Autor und Nachricht von seinen Manuscripts aufbehalten in der Wolfenbittelischen Bibliothek Gedruc[k]t zu Basel.

### Doc. 11. Christopher Schultz to Anthony Benezet, April 13, 1768.

This essay, 'The origin of the So-called Schwenkfelders,' preserved in the Schwenkfelder Library, was directed as a letter to Anthony Benezet by the Schwenkfelders' principal spokesman to the outside world, Christopher Schultz. The text was corrected by the author himself, and I have followed his corrected text. The document is remarkable evidence of the ready acculturation of an emigrant on the part of an individual who was accustomed to reading, writing, and speaking German daily. A nineteenth-century notation written on the document informs us of its provenance: 'Dieses gegenwärtige ist der Aufsatz und eigne Handschrifft dess Christoph Schultzen von einem brief den er an den Anthony Benezet ums Jahr 1754 geschrieben, weil derselbe und andere Quaker gern Nachricht gehabt hätten vom Ursprung der sogenannten Schwenkfelder.' It would seem, however, on the evidence from Schultz's correspondence with Carl Ehrenfried Heintze (See below, No. 12), and the Schultz letter to Pemberton of April 15, 1768 (see above, No. 10) that the date of this item is 1768. A German translation of this English original is dated April 16, 1768 and bears the notation: 'Copia und Translation einer Schrifft, welche auf Veranlassung

eines gehaltenen Gesprächs mit etl[ichen]. freunden in Philad: in Englis-
cher sprache an einen derselben übersandt worden: Als ein fürnehmer Herr
in London, Jacob Hagen nach Schwenckfelds Schrifften, durch seine Corre-
spondenten allhie hatte nachfragen lassen.' The final paragraph, omitted
from the English original, has been added thereto in translation. The German translation of this missing paragraph reads as follows: 'Mit diesem
empfehle ich dich, mein werther Freund! Der Gnade unsers Herren Jesu
Christi, Mit Begehren, dass du diese meine Relation in Guttem aufnehmen
wollest, und dabey meine Defects in der Sprache entschuldigen; Der ich
bin mit vieler Liebe dein aufrichtiger Freund Christoph Schultze Hereford
Township April 16 1768.' Appended to the German copy of this letter is a
second part giving details on the treatment of the Silesian Schwenkfelders
by the Lutherans and the local nobility. Relations there were not what
they were to be in Pennsylvania. One Lutheran minister in conducting a
Schwenkfelder burial said in his sermon that he saw the Schwenkfelder's
soul 'already burning in a pool of hellish fire.' Schultz adds an amusing
story of what some people must have considered 'judgment by lightning.'
When a Schwenkfelder house was struck by lightning, the Lutheran minister (Schultz names him) remarked from the pulpit the Sunday following:
'Here one can see how God struck hard with thunder and lightning.' Soon
afterwards lightning struck the parsonage, which completely burned down.
Then the minister said: 'Whom the Lord loveth, he chasteneth.'

Dear Friend Anthony

Remembering our late Discourse, concerning Caspar Schwenkfeld, and
the Continuance of the Followers of his Doctrine untill this Time, which was
but imperfect, I thought to give Thee a Short but more consistent Account
of that Matters, in the following lines[:] Caspar Schwenkfeld of Ossing was
a Nobleman of a good Family in Nether-Silesia in the Principality of Lignitz
born An. 1490. Was never married, in his young Years he was in the Service
of several Princes, and had an unblamed Character and was in high Favour
with his Prince Frederick Duke of Lignitz Brieg and Wolau, but [when]
his Hearing became to fail him Some what, he declined such Service and
Dedicated himself entirely to the Service of Christ, and followed him in such
a Christian Life and true Virtue that even his bitterest Enemies could not
find to blame him in. When Luther and the Wittenbergers had abolished
the papistical Mass and Transsubstantiation and where [were] introducing
the Use of the Lords Supper according to their own Opinion Schwenkfeld &
Valentine Crautwald could not conform with them, especialy concerning the
Words, This is my Body, which Schwenkfeld construed My Flesh (Body) is
meat indeed John VI, 55 and that to the Soul of Believers, for the Disciples
had eat of the Bread and had drunk of the Cup. Mark XIV, 2. But Luther:
This Bread/ by, under or with the Bread/ is my Body, and that the Body
of Christ could be eaten both by believers and unbelievers. He at the
direction of his Prince then personally conferred with Luther Anno 1525,
and the Wittenbergers in a friendly Manner, and left his Papers with them
concerning the S.[d] Article, 2 months after his Departure, Luther send [sent]

him a very rough and unfriendly Declaration testifying that they differed So far that either himself or Schwenkfeld must belong to the Devil. and so the Breach being made, Schwenkfeld began to write, and laid his Confession open to the World, wherein he also contradicted the then most prevalent Opinions of External Things being effectual Means to Salvation, as there is: The External Word & Absolution, the Use of the Sacraments, Forms of Worship & Religion, etc. as also The Imputation of Justification by a historical Faith: The Regeneration by Water Baptism; The Denying the human Nature of Christ now in his exalted Estate[;] the Adoration and coequal Glory of Divinity; which were especially done by the Zwinglians now called Calvinists, of which Article he wrote his Confession of Jesus in three parts, full of the Strongest Evidenc[es] of holy Writ (and the Fathers for the Glory of Christ, to be the true God and eternal Life, the Man Act. 2, 22 in whom dwelleth all the undivided fulness of the Godhead bodily, Col. 2, 9 to be the true Mediator 1. Tim. 2, 5 and Head of his Body, the Church. Col. 1, 18, of his fulness the Members receive and he imparts unto them by the Emanation of his Spirit Life and Grace, by living Faith, t[h]rough the Channel of external or terrest[r]ial Things whatsoever, Such Knowledge of Christ he reckoned the Treasury of all Wisdom and Knowledge, and the fundamental Norm of all his Doctrine which he also highly recommanded to every One, in a most devout pleasant Manner, Shewing that his heart, Tongue, and Pen were full of the same as he also defended the Same in Several publick Disputations and Colloquies with the Predicants before the Magistrates, at Strassburg, Tübingen and other Places. he died Died (sic!) Dec. 10, 1561, his Symbolum was: Nil Christo triste recepto, which very well agreed, with his whole Life, as a modern Historian Says: For he was persecuted and condemned and his writings confiscated most every where, We have about 90 boocks or Treatisies of him, and as he had an extended Correspondentz all over the Empire, with all Ranks of People his Letters are of a vast Number, and some of them of a number of Sheets and were after his Death by his Friends collected, and ordered to print in five folio Volumes, of which 3 have appeared in publick, the Rest have been Suppressed by the Adversaries. The Followers and Lovers of his Doctrine were soon called Schwenkfeldians, and it is true they were generally not ashamed of the Name of that Servant of Christ, under Ignominy for his Lords sake, and are so denominated until this Day. He never intended to have a Sect, but Send [sent] every one unto Christ, he gave them no Forms of Worship, but exhorted the Lovers of Christ to meet together in all Simplicity, to pray, exercise and exhort themselves in Godliness, Love and Knowledge of the Lord, etc. Some of them have been preserved till this Time in Silesia, but their Number has from Time to Time very much declined having been pressed and Suppressed with great Rigour especially at different Times as towards the End of the 16th Cent[ury]. and about 1660. An. 1719 two Missionarys of the Order of Jesuits were Send [sent] to the imperial Court to convert them to the roman Catholik Religion, first to Use tender Means, and on Refusal to make Use of Force and the Magistrates were commanded to Assist them, in such Execution, they Send [sent] Deputyes to the Court of Vienna, to Supplicat[e] a further Toleration, but by the Craftiness of the Jesuits, it was all in vain, though the Emperor Charles VI. at an Audience declared, that all Should remain in Statu quo[.] A rescript came out, that Parents must send their Children to the Information of the Jesuits, and such as Disobeyed were to be send to Fortresses to be chained to the Wheal borrows for ever, and the Children taken. Which obliged them to take to flight in the Night, leaving their Estates behind, and to seek Shelter in Saxony, which began An. 1726, and continued from Time to Time, till 1733 when the Elector King of Poland died, then at the Instigation of the Jesuits they were demanded of [by] the Young Elector who more hearkened to the Priests then [sic] his Father did, to be delivered up, but the Ministers of the Court of Dresden, gave them the Hint of it, and advised them to go, unto Some other Dominions, they heard of proposals of Toleration of Several States in the Impire (as also in Poland) but considering, that the Princes of Such States are Souvereigns of an arbitrary Power, such Toleration might be only during Pleasure or of One Man's Life, and hearing of the full Freedom of Conscience established in Pennsylvania by the Quackers, Founders of that Province, under the Sanction of the British Crown and Constitution, and the mild Government of the House of Hannover they resolved to go to that Place, and accordingly embarked at Pirna on the River Elb for Altona, 1734, and are by the good Providence of the Almighty and the never Seeked for but truly Christian Assistance of good Friends indeed, in Holland, whom they never knew before freely and happily arrived here, and made partakers of the Enjoyment of the said Freedom, which God further grant and preserve, and that his holy Name may be known and praised from Children to Childrens Children. Amen. We are but a Small Number here, and dont call unto us, Seeing our Noughtiness [nothingness], wishing that Christ and his Kingdom may be revealed in the Hearts of Us and of all Men.

With this I commend thee, my worthy friend, to the Grace of our Lord Jesus Christ, desiring that you will receive this my account amicably, and at the same time excuse my defects in language. I am with much love thy sincere friend

Christoph Schultze
Hereford Township

April 13 1768

## Doc. 12. Christopher Schultz to Carl Ehrenfried Heintze, February 3, 1769.

This lengthy letter was written to Heintze, a Schwenkfelder sympathizer and correspondent in the old Schwenkfelder homeland of Silesia, to accompany Schultz's manuscript book, the *Erläuterung für Herrn Caspar Schwenckfeld, und die Zugethanen seiner Lehre*. The purpose was to give a true and correct account of Schwenkfelder teachings and history for the

American-German public. Heintze had it published at Jauer in Silesia in 1771, at the printing establishment of Heinrich Christ. Muller, in an edition of 500 copies, which were received in Pennsylvania in 1772, and bound by the Schwenkfelders for general circulation. The long inscription of the title-page can be translated: 'A Vindication of Caspar Schwenkfeld and the adherents of his faith relating to many points in history and theology which commonly are presented incorrectly or passed entirely over, in which their history to 1740 is briefly told, their confessions of faith are summarized and the true conditions of the disputes concerning the ministry, the holy Scriptures and the glory of the humanity of Jesus Christ are unfolded; truthfully and simply described from approved, credible and many hitherto unpublished documents and from personal experience, offered to the service of all seekers after and lovers of the truth by a few of those who sometime ago migrated from Silesia and now reside in Pennsylvania in North America.' The final section of the letter tells the intriguing story of how Schultz, through the Quaker-Schwenkfelder network, sent materials on the Schwenkfelders to the British court in London. A copy of the entire letter is in the manuscript collections of the Schwenkfelder Library.

Grace, salvation, and life in Christ Jesus our Saviour first of all! In Christ highly esteemed friend and brother, Carl Ehrenfried Heintze! My sincere greeting to you, the mother, Eva H. (whom we consider to be your mother) and all the brothers of the Heintze family, including neighbor Teichmann, and no less to each and every old familiar relative in the faith in Harpersdorf, Armenruh, Langneundorf, and Lauterseiffen, wishes for all that is good in body and soul.

It shall be a heartfelt joy at all times to learn that all is well with all of you. May our dear Lord and God, Jesus Christ draw and direct the hearts of all of us to the One and Only. Amen.

Dear brother!

Since together with this message we are sending a written book called *A Vindication of Caspar Schwenkfeld*, I want first of all to give a necessary account of this book. Some years ago, as we were at one time assembled at Skippack and several copies of the Preussische Helden und Staats-Geschichte Fr. II, had come to hand, in which the Schwenkfelders are mentioned, it was proposed, considered, and decided that a true narration be written as a service to the public because the accounts were found to be so very incorrect everywhere. It was expected of me to do this, but at that time there seemed to be no way open whereby it could be brought before the public appropriately, although we were confident that if it could be brought before a Christian publisher, they would undoubtedly publish it. Publisher Marchen in Görlitz was mentioned. If he were still living, he would, it was hoped, be a promoter. Examples of what this good man did are known. However, the matter came to a standstill and nothing was done. But when providentially by correspondence a good prospect opened, the matter was again brought under discussion last fall and was strongly urged. I was again approached to undertake it and finally I resolved to do so, hoping that the dear Lord will have a gracious eye upon it, if we devote ourselves to give a hand to the truth which has been suppressed for almost 200 years (during this long time no one came forth to champion it in print), and to commend it to God wholly, to do as it pleases Him and to provide ways for its publication. And so, shortly before Christmas I began with it, in God's name, and have since then been busy with it in addition to my ordinary, necessary duties. About Christmas time a considerable head and eye weakness, which are still with me, caused me not a little inconvenience. But since I had news through the old [Moravian] bishop David Nitschmann (who visited me in Advent) that in the beginning of March there would be a good opportunity to send it to you, I did everything possible to reach the goal. By the help of God this has now happened. The Lord be praised for his support. My cousin, Caspar Kriebel of Towamencin, in his old age contributed to it by copying and was glad to see this work go forward for the advancement of truth, and pursued it as well as possible by copying. It is his copy which we are transmitting. Others inspected it, especially the first half, as did the aged Balthasar Hoffman who very willingly gave his approval to this undertaking, and when I recently again discussed it with him, he had a very favorable opinion of it and confirmed all my narrations. As you may know, his knowledge cannot be scant.

We hope that when you, dear friends, read it, you will not find it unpleasant, but in many things be useful for accuracy, And if you find the contents of it good, we have our thoughts fixed upon you, dear brother Heintze, God granting you grace and courage, you who are accustomed to associate with people, that you consider it with the counsel of good friends (whoever they may be) and make inquiry whether there might not here or there, among the great publishers, be found one who would put this book into print, as such people are accustomed to do with all kinds of books. For this reason also an address to bookdealers has been placed in the front of the book. We cannot doubt that there are such people, as also that it would not sell. It is at least something new and quite remarkable, the like of which the curious histories and the learned do not have. They may make of it afterwards what they will. And if God be gracious and will let it please Him that from the perception of the suppressed Schwenckfeld, or rather from the knowledge of His Son, some power should come to light, He will give grace to understand. Yea, may He strengthen you thereto and go before you and open a path that you may find a way pleasing to Him. For traveling expenses and loss of time you are to make satisfaction from the enclosed sum and not cut yourself short. You are burdened without that.

Furthermore, since it is a matter which concerns our confession in common, you shall have the right and power, wherever you find anything objectionable or obstructive to the course of the work, to do whatever is most conducive to the progress of truth, be it in changing, omitting, or adding, as the case may call for, in order that the great and important may not suffer because of the small and trifling. For, since we have been away [from Silesia] for so long a time, and great changes have taken place with you, we may perhaps not be able to surmise exactly what today is feasible with you. Therefore, dear brother, fix your eyes upon Christ and His revealed truth and abide by that truth. Afterwards one must of course bend and duck under all kinds of circumstances in order to get through. One must not incautiously or wantonly invite suffering. Hence, because we mention many things by name, out of recent times, and you [...] that it would cause you suffering for which you would not be prepared (and wherein we would not want to be burdensome to you), omit it or do as you think. And furthermore, should you find positively that there was an error in the narration of an historical event, correct it, so that naught but truth be promoted. If you wish to add something or continue it, do as you please. We deliver it as it is and commend it to God's holy will and pleasure and to your faithful hands and care. Be especially careful when you give it out of your hands, that (as there are many examples) it may not be dealt with treacherously, or that you perchance lose it and the enemies perhaps carve a piece out of it.

It was also our thought and purpose that Caspar Schwenkfeld's departure from this life should be added in the back of the book as an appendix and be printed as it was described by Jacob Held and as Arnold has it in the History of Heretics. It is extant also in octavo with his picture, and a brief sketch of his life. Hence this is to be left out and only that which Jacob Held wrote, namely, the summary, be included, and after that the more detailed account. We did not want to write it into the book, thinking and hoping that you would arrange that it be included either in printed or in written form.

Furthermore, since it is not unusual on such occasions that there be some stipulation, I would like to say that if it be printed, you see to it that a few dozen copies be allowed free, of which we would like to have a few. We will take under consideration how they might be gotten here. I think at present that if only they were once in England, we are acquainted with merchants here who have friends and acquaintances in London. I know they would willingly serve us. But if you find that it could be done through the Moravian Brethren, if it be not too burdensome to them, no other provision would be necessary. One more thing I would like to say, since I mentioned Marchen, that it might be most advisable to have it published and distributed in Prussia or by its subjects because liberty is maintained better there than elsewhere. In other places a publisher might have inconvenience on account of it [....] However, you will consider these things yourself, because time is getting too short for us and we will have to hasten with everything, it may be that many errors in writing which have not been corrected will be overlooked, even though we are now running through it. If you notice anything, correct it.

Since we see in the newspapers that a big mass of dark clouds is gathering in the East, over Turkey, Russia, Poland, we are in great anxiety whether the unrest might also spread out over you. May the Lord be near you with his protection. There are also considerable disagreements between these American colonies and Great Britain, but we hope they will abate.

Dear esteemed friend, C.E.H., I and Caspar Kriebel are together here at my house these days and to the last hour are very earnestly engaged in making corrections and an index for the *Vindication* (day before yesterday the letters were gathered together here). Because we must hurry so, it may be that we will make mistakes here and there in the index and elsewhere, be so good as to make corrections wherever or whatever it be in order that distinctness and accuracy be promoted, and add it thereto. One of these will be that the paragraph number in the headings be also placed to the chapter number, because the paragraphs in many cases got too long, etc. We give it out of our hands with resigned spirit into the faithful hand of divine providence and hope to have done in good faith what was possible at this time. May the sovereign king of heaven dispose of it according to his pleasure. I do not doubt that if he delivers it into your hands, you will deal faithfully with it. Afterwards, having done that, let us not fret at all or be unduly anxious about what he will do with it. Martha 's work must be done too, but in our part we would not forget Mary's part. Lord Jesus grant us mutually that we choose Mary's part wholeheartedly.

Christ.Schultz

Dear Brother, I must tell you one thing more. Count it among my follies, if you deem it proper. But there are some supporting me for whose names you would have esteem if you should recount them. It is that all of us who are called Schwenkfelders, wherever we dwell, owe his majesty, the King of Prussia deep thanks. He is the first sovereign, prince and crowned head who so praiseworthily was pleased to grant very graciously, through a public, royal mandate, our religion free, unhindered exercise. We here in America feel cheerfully moved to sincerest thanks toward his Majesty and wish that the All-Highest bless him. The like of it has not happened in the 200 years of the existence of this name. If it should happen that a publisher for our *Vindication* be found, this is what I wanted to say, that he be consulted whether he would approve of it or think it feasible to address a brief dedication (or in what name or form it be put) to his Majesty and print the same in the front, wherein such an expression of humble thanksgiving presented by his subjects would be the chief purpose, and whereby those of us here might also be remembered. You would be intent only on the content of a short draft and would go to a lawyer who would put it into the shape agreed upon by you and the publisher, and you would pay the lawyer his fee. What more would be involved in the presentation to his Majesty, you will be able to find out.

The account of the four citizens of Goldberg is pleasing to me. May the Arch-Shepherd rise and take charge of his lambs. In return I must tell you this: Anthony Benezet, my old, well-known, and very devout friend, a Quaker in Philadelphia, asked me to come to him. He told me that Jacob Hagen, one of the greatest merchants in London, wrote to him asking him to secure the books of Caspar Schwenkfeld for him. He asked my advice and assistance. Soon after that I came to Israel Pemberton who is one of the wealthiest and greatest in this Province, with whom I have been well acquainted for more than twelve years, through Indian affairs. He told me the same with more details. He was about to write to me, and told me that Hagen had inquired in Hamburg and Frankfurt but could obtain nothing. I acquainted them with the nature of the books and wrote directions to our old correspondent in Frankfurt-on-the-Main, referring to Gottfried Arnold's *History of Heretics* which I knew was in London. When I got home I wrote in English, to these gentlemen in Philadelphia, a brief compendium of Caspar Schwenkfeld's life and teachings and sent them at the same time Schwenkfeld's tract *The Three-fold Life* which, white inside and neatly bound, I had previously received from Frankfurt. All of this they sent to London. As I was at table with Israel Pemberton and we were speaking of the matter, in came John Hunt who also is such a merchant in London and one of the foremost Quaker preachers. He has been on a visit in America for the third time. I heard him preach and learned to know him ten years ago at Easton at the Indian Peace Conferences. Israel Pemberton at once told him what we were discussing, for Hagen and Hunt are special friends and neighbors in London. On the Saturday before Whit-Sunday, Hunt set out for London together with another from Philadelphia, arrived there safely, and took the things with them. When our queen arrived in the kingdom for the first time, the Quakers' Meeting of London through this man Hagen, paid her a formal visit. He had orders to mention the Friends in Pennsylvania, and amongst others, to name also the Schwenkfelders. Owing to the fact that all other colleagues had to speak through interpreters because the princess did not yet know English, and this man Hagen spoke German, he, before others, won the favor of the princess and since then stands in high regard. The Queen has since then spoken of Schwenkfeld, that she had heard of this man at home and would like to see his books. This was the reason for the inquiry.

So you can see for yourself what wonderful things happen where one would not expect. Had I at that time known that the Jesuits in Liegnitz have our books, I would have pointed precisely to that place. At the Court they would have found a way thither. the above happened three weeks before last Whitsuntide. Time must yield the result.

### Doc. 13. Christopher Schultz to Israel Pemberton, March 29, 1773.

Schultz reveals his unusual erudition in this letter, where he turns up as proofing the German translation of Barclay's *Apology*, and in his offer to send to Philadelphia for use in the schools there, a New Testament in the Syriac language, and a Lexicon and Grammar of Syriac and Latin. The 'little Treatise of Caspar Schwenkfeld' referred to in the second paragraph has not been identified. The translation is No. 3333 in Hildeburn (2:242): *Robert Barclays Apologie oder Verteidigungs-Schrift der wahren Christlichen Gottesgelahrtheit, Wie solche unter dem Volk, so man aus Spott Quaker, das ist, Zitterer nennet, vorgetragen und gelehret wird. Oder Völlige Erklärung und Rettung ihrer Grundsätze und Lehren, durch viele aus der Heil. Schrift, der gesunden Vernunft, und den Zeugnissen so wohl alter als neuer berühmten Scribenten gezogene Beweissthümer. Nebst einer gründlichen Beantwortung der stärksten Einwürffe, so gemeiniglich wider sie gebraucht werden. Anjetzo nach der zweyten Lateinischen und neunten Englischen Herausgebung gantz von neuem ins Deutsche übersetzt.* (Germantown: Gedruckt bey Christoph Saur, dem Jüngern, 1776.) 797 (25).

The letter is part of the Pemberton Papers, Volume XXIV, 140, Historical Society of Pennsylvania, and is printed here with the Society's permission.

Hereford March 29th 1773.

Dear Friend Israel Pemberton!

I have proceeded in the Examination of the Translation of Rob.[t] Barclays Apology to near the End of the Eleventh Proposition. I am Sorry to detain you So long from Seeing it finished, being hindered by many Occurrencies and Business which I could not prevent, I shall give it the best Dispatch as I shall be able to bring it to End.

The Reason of Sending these Lines, is concerning the Inclosed little Treatise of Caspar Schwenkfeld; me thought I had Several Times observed a Willingness to See Something in the English Language of his Works, and lately I Spoke to One of my Friends who is a little acquainted, with the Said Language, to try to translate that little Treatise, which he hath done, in the Manner as it is now presented to Thee. It is true I See and confess it falls much Short of the Propriety of Sense and Language, nevertheless I trust the Meaning can be understood which is not perverted. I wish the grace of much heavenly Light to all who read it, I remain in Love under divine Protection thy Friend

Christopher Schultze

P.S. Remember my Love to Anthony Benezet

[Appended to the letter:] I have the New Testament in the Syrish Language as also a Lexicon and Grammar Syrish and Latin and many Texts of Scripture in the Same Language written with Hebrew Letters being willing to part with the Same, I shall bring the s.[d] Books along with me, when I shall happen to come to Phild.[a] which I dont know when it will be, perhaps they could be of Service to Some Body there or about the Schools.

## Doc. 14. Anthony Benezet to Christopher Schultz, July 15, 1783.

Here again, in a letter preserved in the manuscript collections of the Schwenkfelder Library, we find Christopher Schultz in his role of proofreader of a German translation of a Quaker tract. The 'friend at York Town' who had it translated was Elisha Kirk. The translator, 'J.M.' or 'I.M.' of York according to the printed German edition (see below) has not yet been identified. Elizabeth Webb (d. 1726) was a distinguished Quaker minister from Gloucester in England who emigrated with her husband Richard Webb, settling in Philadelphia in 1700 and at Birmingham

in Chester County in 1704, where the first Birmingham meetinghouse was
built on her land. In 1710 she made a ministerial visit to England, and there
meeting Anthony William Boehm, court chaplain, she sent him a letter de-
tailing her conversion and call to the ministry. The German translation referred to is: *Einige Glaubens-Bekentnisse und göttliche Erfahrungs-Proben,
in einem Send-schreiben von Elisabetha Webb an Anton Wilhelm Böhm,
Capellan zum Prinzen Georg von Dänemark, Im Jahr 1712. Aus der Englischen Sprache übersetzt von J.M. Jorck [York], Im Jahr 1783. Philadelphia,
gedruckt bey Carl Cist, in der Markt-Strasse, 1783.* The English original
had appeared in 1781: *A Letter from Elizabeth Webb to Anthony William
Boehm, with his Answer.* (Philadelphia: Printed and Sold by Joseph Crukshank, in Market-Street 1781). Copies of both German and English editions
are in the collections of the Historical Society of Pennsylvania. If the 'observations' in Benezet's P.S. are in book form, they can possibly be located
in either (1) *An historical account of Guinea... with an inquiry into the
rise and progress on the slave trade,* or (2) *Notes on the slave trade* (1780).
Finally, George Wiegner (1721-1784) was one of the Schwenkfelder exiles of
1734 who settled in Upper Hanover Township, Philadelphia County. The
Benezets had known the Wiegners for almost a half century. According to
the Christopher Wiegner (Jr.) diary for January 21, 1738, 'Benezet bought
the 200 acres. His son expects to settle among us,. For this reference, see
*The Spiritual Diary of Christopher Wiegner,* trans. and ed. by Peter C.
Erb (Pennsburg, Pa, 1978), 150.

Philadelp$^a$ the 15$^{th}$ 7$^{th}$ Mon July 1783

Dear Friend Christ$^r$ Schultz

I received in due time the translation of Elizab$^t$ Webb's letter which
thou sent back from thy account of its imperfections. I thought it not
worth while troubling our friend Waggoner or any other & intirely laid it
aside. But as it continues to be the desire of some wel disposed people
amongst the Germans to have it in their language and a friend at York
Town who is strongly of that mind has undertood [undertook] to cause it
to be translated there which when done must be submitted to some good
judge, We are endeavouring to raise money to bear the charges but as I
fear this will be difficult to compleat, if thou, my Friend G. Weigner or any
other well disposed people were willing to assist we should kindly accept of
your help & send you books to the amount of your subscription or more if a
profitable use can be made of them. I am strong in the belief that this book
will be of service in giving the reader a prospect of y$^e$ simplicity & plainness
of Christianity & tends to remove that partial orthodoxy & proud conceit in
favour of y$^e$ particular opinions & practices so prevelant amongst the sects,
which annex a holiness to opinions, even such as are right in themselves
rather than those pious practices which change the heart. The Bearer is
going so that I must conclude in haste thy affectionate friend.

Anthony Benezet

Inclose[d] send some observations on y$^e$ Slavery practiced amongst us
which calls for y$^e$ notice of every lover of Mankind & requires our particular

notice in its proposal by y$^e$ Southern Colonies to open a new the trade for Slaves to Guinea. Please to communicate it to my friend George Weigner with my best love

### Doc. 15. The Barclay Correspondence, 1875-1876.

One of the classics on English religious patterns of the seventeenth century and the origins of Quakerism is Robert Barclay, *The Inner Life of the Religious Societies of the Commonwealth* (London, 1876). Robert Barclay (1833-1876) was a Quaker preacher and scholar who in his search for Schwenkfelder influences on Quakerism and the history of Schwenkfeld's followers corresponded with the Pennsylvania Schwenkfelders. The first letter reproduced here was directed to him by George Meschter, William Schultz, and Jacob Meschter, as spokesmen for the group, and forwarded by Daniel S. Schultz, and was published in Barclay's book (1876 edition), 243-44. The authors of the letter were the Reverend George Meschter (1808-1887), a progressive who in the controversy over the introduction of the outward sacraments advocated their adoption; the Reverend Jacob K. Meschter (1818-1891), elected a minister of the Schwenkfelder Society in 1854 and served for 37 years, a farmer and eloquent preacher who, it was said, 'prepared his sermons behind the plow'; and the Reverend William Schultz (1806-1890). These three as leaders of the Society had renewed the Schwenkfelder correspondence with Silesia in 1857; hence it was appropriate that they joined forces in the Barclay Correspondence. Daniel S. Schultz (1816-1886), under whose name a copy of the second letter is filed in the Quaker Collection at Haverford College Library, was a surveyor and justice of the peace in the Upper District, secretary of the Upper District Conference, a denominational leader, and a leading Schwenkfelder historian of the nineteenth century. For these Schwenkfelder correspondents, see *The Genealogical Record*, 931,949-50. and 1192. For the Barclay correspondence, see *The Schwenkfeldian*, 2:60; 3:8, 19, and 24.

Colebrookdale, Berks County, Pennsylvania,

November 22nd, 1875.

To Robert Barclay, England.

Dear Friend, — We have the honor to acknowledge the receipt of your letter of the 2nd of August. and regret that we cannot more satisfactorily reply to your inquiries as to the differences (if any) between the teachings of Caspar Schwenkfeld and that of George Fox. The 'Journal' of the latter is not in our possession, neither have we any evidence that, as early as 1630, or earlier, any of the followers of Schwenkfeld emigrated to Amsterdam; nor that at any time Hans de Rys's Congregation existed there; neither do we have any information to the contrary.

Judging from the brief notices of the teachings of George Fox in our possession, we have reason to believe that they did not differ materially from those of Schwenkfeld; and among the followers of both, here in America, there is a striking similarity, in the almost total absence of formalities and ceremonies in their religious practices. Both are discarding judicial oaths, carnal weapons, and are unostentatious in dress.

Notwithstanding the fact that the Friends are of English descent, having their books, worship, and conversation in the English language, and the followers of Schwenkfeld here all of it in German, yet there always existed a lively sympathy, love, and esteem between the parties.

You wish to obtain some work that would show the religious practices and principles we have adopted in America. For that purpose we send [you our] 'Compendium of Christian Doctrines of Faith,' which, together with the 'Catechism and Constitution' contained in 'Kadelbach's History' in your possession, may suffice. It is, however, proper to mention the fact that *neither in Europe nor here, have the followers of Schwenkfeld at any time administered Baptism and the Lord's Supper.*

Owing to the persecutions which prevailed from 1630 to 1640, the religious practices of our ancestors in Germany about that period, were chiefly confined to meeting in private houses for prayer and admonition, and in endeavours in the daily walk of life to imitate as much as possible the example of the Heavenly Master.

In the love of Christ, sincerely your friends

George Meschter,
William Schultz,
Jacob Meschter.

December 17th, 1875, Colebrookdale, Penna. Per Dan. S. Schultz.

This letter was written in English. In a subsequent communication, D.S. Schultz states that their actual membership is 500, and that these constitute two congregations, principally located in Montgomery County, Pennsylvania. Each congregation has three ministers, and they have three meeting-houses. Both congregations are under one Church government. At their Annual Conference and elections, all male members have a voice.

Colebrookdale, Penn^a
March 13, 1876

Robert Barclay
Surrey, England

Esteemed friend:

Your kind favor of the 19th January reached us: and in reply we will inform you that there are not quite 500 actual members of the followers of Caspar Schwenkfeld in America. These constitute two congregations located principally in Montgomery County, Pennsylvania. Each of these congregations has 3 ministers and three meeting houses or places of public worship, in which worship is held alternately.

Both congregations are under one church government. At their annual conferences & elections all male members have a voice. As yet, public worship is conducted exclusively in the German language, and inasmuch as the membership is of German descend [descent], & always received its religious instructions in that language, it is not likely that this method will be departed from in the near future. It may seem strange to you that we are conducting our religious affairs in the German language, & the temporal in the English; but there are numerous other religious denominations in the rural districts of Eastern Penn[a] and elsewhere in our Northern & Western States in the same predicament.

The number of professed Schwenkfelders in America has remained nearly Stationary for the last decade or longer. It is difficult to assign the Cause of this; perhaps it is our own fault. We have never made any special efforts to make proselites or to obtrude Schwenkfeld's doctrines upon any one, or engaged in any missionary work exclusively our own; yet all sincere followers of Schwenkfeld would be rejoiced to know that sooner or later his doctrines will be taught in different languages & beli[e]ved by thousands. God, in His wisdom may so order it yet.

It is indeed gratifying to us now, to receive across the Atlantic your very favorable testimony to the principles & doctrines of that 'most worthy man Caspar Schwenkfeld.' But in speaking of Schwenkfeld's doctrines, let us bear in mind that he did not claim them as his own, but repeatedly declared that they were the teachings of his most gracious Lord and Master, Jesus Christ. And any impartial mind prayerfully studying his writings and contemplating his deathbed declarations and victorious passage hence ought to be convinced that it was *no boast* in Schwenkfeld making the declaration aforesaid.

I fear I have not replied as fully to your inquiries as you wish. We have in course of preparation a short historical sketch of the Schwenkfelders in America for a friend in Western Penn[a], that will be too late for your book but when printed you shall have one. Our Catechism (which you find in German in Kadelbach's Hist[ory]' is printed in English also. In case you prefer it in English we will gladly send you one.

We are anxious to see your forthcoming work when ready.

On pages 72-73 [of] Kadelbach's Hist[ory] you find our Confession of Faith in a condensed form.

With high regards

Your friend
Dan[iel]. S. Shultz

### Doc. 16. The 'Friend' and the Schwenkfelders, 1904.

Quakers continued to recognize their spiritual kinship with the Schwenkfelders throughout the nineteenth and twentieth centuries. This sympathetic report on the Schwenkfelders and their history in Europe and Pennsylvania, which appeared originally in the *Philadelphia Bulletin*, was reprinted with approval in Volume 77 of *The Friend: A Religious and Literary Journal*, the leading periodical of Philadelphia's Orthodox Quakers, on Sixth Month 25, 1904, 395-396.

The Schwenkfelders

The place which the Schwenkfelders hold in our religious population is not conspicuous. They have only one church in Philadelphia and their existence is confined for the most part to two or three of the eastern counties of Pennsylvania. Their number too probably does not now much exceed a thousand persons. Yet the money which they spend on the literary and educational as well as spiritual concerns in their organizations is believed to be greater relatively than is produced for those purposes by any other sect in the United States. The name which they long ago adopted is often mentioned in Pennsylvania, and every once in a while it furnishes a theme for inquiry or speculation among the ill-informed.

The name of the Schwenkfelders is derived from that of Caspar Schwenkfeld, one of those German zealots who broke away from the Roman Catholic Church in the days of the Reformation, but who could not reconcile himself to the doctrines of Luther. Although he never gathered his followers together as a formal organization, the influence of his teachings were widespread. With much tolerance and with a personal esteem for most of his opponents, he declared in substance that the Bible itself does not furnish the internal power of spiritual enlightenment, but that this must come from that inner realization of Christ Himself. It was thus that he preached a set of principles from which were deduced the broadest rights of individual conscience in spiritual affairs, the separation of Church and State, the reduction of ecclesiastic rule, simplicity of personal conduct, and the worthlessness of merely external forms in either worship or behavior. Although his teachings were regarded as mischievous by Catholics and Lutherans, and he was subjected to much humiliation as a reformer, it has been the habit, it is said, of most German historians to ascribe to him a high standard of morality and self-denial in his government of his own life. Then and long afterward his followers underwent much punishment at the hands of the law for their firmness in adhering to their opinions in matters which brought them in conflict with the civil authorities; and in this respect their experience was not unlike that of the English Quakers, whose own principles were largely the same as those that had been formulated by Schwenkfeld.

But that reformer had been in his grave for five generations before the first of the people in Silesia who had adopted his name arrived in this country. They came to Philadelphia in 1734 at a time when the representatives of almost every ism or shade of an ism that religious thought or religious ecstasy can produce were finding their way from Germany to Pennsylvania. Governor Pennypacker has commended them as the one sect fleeing from European oppression to maintain steadily to this time the custom of a Memorial Day in honor of their advent in the land of promise. In the company of exiles which landed here were to be found many names that have since been notable in the life of the Commonwealth—Weiss, Schulz, Hartranft, Heydrick, Anders, Kriebel, Hoffman, Reinwald, Yeakel and Wiegner. The places which were settled by the men thus named, and their associates, were chiefly in the outskirts of what is now Philadelphia and in Montgomery County, and even to-day there are many traces of the agricultural life to which they once betook themselves. It was remarkable that, without a regular clergy, indifferent as they were to the making of converts by solicitation, and long organized more by tacit than by written agreement, they were able to keep up their religious identity in a community where they were often looked upon as heretical or foolish. Yet they have succeeded in perpetuating their unity to this day by marrying among themselves, their rules which govern the contract of matrimony being exceedingly strict to the end that there may be no doubt of the fitness of the couple to marry, that they shall hold the same religious opinions and that everybody interested in them shall have full opportunity to show, if they see fit, why the marriage should not take place. It seems that whenever a young Schwenkfelder wishes to marry outside of his religion he was likely to be told by his father that this would be a 'mixed marriage,' and that such a marriage was like the nesting of the crow and the dove.

In their methods of discipline as to habits and morals there is much that suggests the practices and the principles of the Society of Friends. For a long time a Schwenkfelder in Montgomery County could usually be distinguished from the rest of the community for the home spun simplicity of his garb, intended as it was to promote his purity and humility. The plainness of their meeting houses, the absence of all costly markings in their grave yards and the discouragement of any thing in their homes which tends to foster the spirit of luxury, bear ample testimony to their zeal in keeping down the promptings of vanity. It has been their policy so far as possible to settle among themselves those private contentions which ordinarily become matters of public litigation. Their moral system, severe as it is and searching among themselves, is apparently free of that spirit which grows restless, irritable or intolerant, because other people may not think and act likewise. They were early interested in education and unlike many other sects they did not employ dubious schemes such as lotteries, for example, for its support. It may have been that they were not numerous enough to make it profitable to have recourse to that once popular means of raising money for religious purposes, but there is more reason to believe that their repugnance to it arose from an inner perception of the ultimate immoral effects of the thing itself.

The Schwenkfelders, like the Quakers, the Dunkers and the Mennonites are opposed to wars and warring or the bearing of arms. They were unwilling in the Colonial days to contribute money that would be used in the military movements against the Indians. They soon found, after the opening of the Revolution that the man who was reluctant to take up arms because his conscience could not permit him to do so was to be treated by his neighbors as a public enemy. In an early stage of the war, they adopted a declaration in which it was said that those who adhered to the 'apostolic doctrines of the sainted Caspar Schwenkfeld and who seek to maintain the same by public services and by instruction of the young,' had pledged themselves to stand by one another in the payment of all fines that might be imposed upon them for refusing to 'render military service in case deadly weapons are carried and used,' although they were ready to bear their due share of the common civil taxes and burdens. They were subjected to a pressure too hard for the steadfastness of many of their number.

### Doc. 17. The 'Friend' and the Schwenkfelders, 1923.

On Eighth Month 2, 1923, Philadelphia's Orthodox Quaker organ, *The Friend: A Religious and Literary Journal*, Volume 97, pp. 52-53, published an article by Ann Sharpless entitled 'Schwenkfelders.' As the article informs us, Schwenkfelders along with Quakers and representatives of other peace churches met at Bluffton, Ohio, August 4-7, 1922, at the Bluffton Peace Conference, or, as it was called in a report in *The Friend*, Eighth Month 31, 1922, The National Conference of Religious Bodies who hold that Peace Between Nations can be maintained by following the teachings of Jesus. The committee organizing the conference was made up of the Philadelphia Quaker Wilbur K. Thomas, the Schwenkfelder, Elmer E.S. Johnson, and the Mennonite, Samuel K. Mosiman, President of Bluffton College, which hosted the gathering. Dr. Johnson spoke at the opening session, and the Schwenkfelder presence was deeply felt. The author of the article reproduced here, Ann Sharpless (1850-1944), was a Friends' minister from Chester County, Pennsylvania, a longtime teacher at the Westtown School, and co-editor of *The Friend*.

Schwenkfelders

Ann Sharpless

Among the delegates to the Bluffton Peace Conference last summer were two Schwenkfelders. One of them presided at two or more of the sessions, having served on the Committee that called the Conference.

Schwenkfelders—who are they? They stand for peace, but what else? What is their history? Where are they located? These questions so wrought upon my mind that I began to investigate, and was rewarded by finding out some curious and interesting facts:—

1st—That their founder, Caspar Schwenkfeld, a Silesian nobleman, held views surprisingly like those of George Fox, though antedating Fox some one hundred and thirty years.

2nd—That all the Schwenkfeld congregations in the world are to be found in Southeastern Pennsylvania, until recently in the three Counties of Montgomery, Berks and Lehigh. I think a church now exists as well in the city of Philadelphia.

3rd—That they number at present about 1370 members.

4th—That these people came to Philadelphia in 1733-4-5-6 and 7, most of them in the good ship *Andrew* in 1734.

5th—That yearly on Ninth Month 24th, they hold Thanksgiving services in memory of their escape from persecution in Germany, and of their happy finding of freedom in Pennsylvania.

6th—That, though meeting in private houses for worship with zeal and faithfulness, they formed no system of church organization until 1780, nearly three hundred years after the birth of their founder.

7th—Evidences of culture are found in their early writings, showing that they came from an educated class. That as early as 1764 they set up schools which, visited monthly by trustees, were maintained until Pennsylvania established her own public school system. Earlier than 1764, however, they had First-day schools. In their secular schools, the course included Latin, Greek and Higher Mathematics.

Caspar Schwenkfeld was born in 1489 or 1490. He studied at various German centres of learning, and afterward entered on the life of a courtier. But Luther was just then arousing Germany against the existing Church evils and the young nobleman shared in the general awakening. He took his stand as a reformer, but went further than Luther in his appreciation of the inward and spiritual nature of Christianity. The Lord's Supper and Baptism were cases in point. These he regarded much as Friends regard them, saying, 'As often as a man receives Divine sweetness in Christ, so often does he keep the Lord's Supper with Christ.' He did not, however, entirely reject the outward rites, but thought them of little importance. Judas, he said, ate the Supper with the other apostles; if that rite had uplifting power, why did he commit the evil deed? Schwenkfeld emphasized the work of the Holy Spirit, the New Birth, the quietness and stillness of regenerative power, and its continued work.

His followers formed little meetings, 'in every respect,' says Rufus Jones in his *Spiritual Reformers*, 'like a Seventeenth Century Quaker Meeting,' although now they do not have silent worship, and do have set prayers and singing. They believe in simple religious forms and in a plain and simple life. They oppose a paid ministry, and their preachers may be farmers or mechanics, but not women. It is possible in some of these respects, as will appear, that changes have occurred. They oppose war and oaths, support their own poor, and are 'just in the payment of their debts.'

Schwenkfeld met the usual fate of those who are ahead of their time—persecution. Both Papists and Lutherans were against him. He was an exile and a wanderer thirty years. 'He lay concealed in hedges, in outhouses, in hidden caves.' But those thirty years were not fruitless. As he went up and down the fatherland he animated little groups of followers with his spirit, and led them into his way of thinking. 'It is reckoned that Schwenkfeld's followers numbered during his life from four to five thousand scattered over all Germany.' He died in 1561, and though later many of his people joined the Lutherans, the truths he taught went marching on ever to other lands, and 'Schwenkfeld,' says Rufus M. Jones 'was a living force in the period of the English Commonwealth.'

One of the questions that come up is how far do these people still cling to the doctrinal views and devotional practices of their founder? One of their well-informed members makes answer as follows:—

'I might say that the Church today is endeavoring to follow the ideals set by our leader, but it has become much modernized; so that the similarity between the services and organization of the Schwenkfelder Church and that of the Friends is not what it was in the early history of our organization in Pennsylvania. When the Schwenkfelder Church was organized in 1780, and even prior to that time, Christopher Schultz, the leader of our people, had many conferences with Pemberton and other Quakers, and the Schwenkfelder Society was organized on the basis similar to that of the Society of Friends. As a matter of fact, when the Schwenkfelders started their school system in 1764, some Quaker boys attended these schools, and we know that during at least one year two Quaker boys lived in the home of Christopher Schultz, and he translated for them one of Schwenkfeld's tracts into English. There are many other instances when the Quakers and Schwenkfelders acted together during the eighteenth century.'

The first Thanksgiving services were held in 1734 on the day they disembarked, somewhere outside the built-up part of the city of Philadelphia, under the autumn sky. There they ordained that every autumn should witness a similar observance, and never since has it been omitted. This introductory ceremony over, they made a short journey to the northward. They are now particularly numerous in the farm lands around Norristown and other parts of Montgomery County. Until 1790 these anniversary services were held in private houses, sometimes with one 'House Father,' and sometimes another, who acted as host, and led the meeting. At present they meet in their places of worship. The aged and infirm make special effort to come, the youths and maidens are there too. They have a simple meal, but grateful and peaceful hearts make a good accompaniment.

From some examination of their organ, *The Schwenkfeldian*, I gather that they are an earnest, forward-looking people, awake to the spiritual cry around them, laboring for temperance, and sending workers to the foreign mission-field. Their chaplains and Y.M.C.A. workers came home from the Great War 'impressed with the fact that Christianity is the only remedy for war.'

To perpetuate the good name and fame of their ancestors, they have formed the Society of the 'Descendants of the Schwenkfelder Exiles.'

It seems fitting that we as Friends should know more of this fine little sect, whose history is interwoven with our own, and with whose beliefs ours have much in common.

# Mennonite Reflections
# on Schwenkfelders

John L. Ruth

Appearing in the midst of a series of professional historians, I feel out of place since I have never made a serious study of the history of either denomination I've been asked to discuss here. My own training was in literary rather than historical studies. Yet, because I am a loyal (and local) Mennonite, because Schwenkfelder neighbors have always been a part of my Mennonite consciousness, and because it has been my lot to write some amateur history, I can say something about how Schwenkfelders look to Mennonites of my orientation. I should like to use the words of the Apostle Peter, slightly modified: 'Professional background on this topic have I none, but such as I have I will give.'

There are many varieties of Mennonites. My own variety stems largely, ethnically speaking, from origins in Zurich and Bern, just after the peasants' uprisings of 1524. When I read of the first baptisms of the 'Brothers,' as the 'Anabaptists' of Switzerland called themselves, and their subsequent contacts with people of similar persuasion in the reforming city of Strasbourg, it isn't long until I hear references to Caspar Schwenckfeld. If I read the works of the Anabaptist Pilgram Marpeck, one-time city engineer for Strasbourg, I run across a sharp interchange he had with Schwenckfeld, and I'm made aware that in those times of acrid debates the Reformers sometimes had as much trouble with each other as with the Catholics who tried to suppress them. What catches my attention, as a non-expert in the field, is the Anabaptist objection to what they feel is the 'spiritualism' of Schwenckfeld. And after all these years I would still tend to feel that Schwenkfelder theology, something like that of the Quakers, lacks a certain minimal coarseness of fiber that, as a down-to-earth common Christian, I need to function in this world.

Yet I feel, historically, a commonness, too. It is confirmed by several developments involving our two peoples in
the seventeenth century. My Swiss ancestors in Bern found
prayers that they liked in Schwenckfeld's *Deutsches Passional*,
and borrowed them when they finally came to printing their
own prayerbooks. Actually, in being drawn to Schwenckfeld's
more spiritualistic language, they were departing somewhat
from their own people's original agenda: living a separate,
ordered life as a church under the cross, stressing obedience
and the Kingdom of God rather than a primarily inner realization. Their genius, as I tend to view it, lay in applying
the gospel of Christ to concrete communal life. In enjoying
Schwenckfeld's type of devotion, which certainly has both intensity and integrity, they show an inclination toward what is
often called Pietism. This indeed was common ground not only
for Schwenkfelders and Mennonites, but for the soon-to-emerge
Dunkers or Brethren, as well, and it is no accident that they all
eventually found themselves living here in Pennsylvania with
the benevolent Quakers.

There were elements in the other great wing of my people—
the Dutch Mennonites—that were analogous to some of Schwenckfeld's emphases. Menno Simons' idea of Christ could fit
Schwenckfeld's notion of the 'celestial flesh.' I recall how my
uncle, the local ice-man, startled me, a young Mennonite minister, by telling me that Menno Simons thought that Jesus,
though born of a woman, had no navel. The man for whom
our fellowship was named, my uncle reported, believed that
Jesus was brought into the world *through* the body of Mary,
passing through like a bullet through a gun without taking
its substance from the gun. It was fascinating for me to realize later that nearly four centuries after Menno Simons had
imbibed some of Melchior Hoffman's spiritualistic ideas, they
could be the subject of conversation on a folk level in my own
Lower Salford Township.

I might interject here a comment on an irony of history
regarding the Dutch Mennonites. It seems, from the point of
view of a matter-of-fact Pennsylvania 'Old' Mennonite of Swiss
origin, that the assemblage of Christians who were variously
called Mennonites or *Doopsgezinde* in what we call Holland
today, were not necessarily an inherently stable group. The
white heat of Reformation dynamics welded them together at

first, but not long after they developed serious internal polar-
izations. These lasted for decades and longer. When my own
ancestors here in Philadelphia County answered a letter from
several Dutch Mennonite leaders in 1773, they asked how the
Dutch Mennonites were doing with their factions. One of the
factors in the general variety or instability of Dutch and Lower
Rhenish Mennonitism was precisely the issue of spiritualism.
It was never fully resolved since the fellowship had multiple
origins never fully intergrated. I felt this in the Mennonite congregation at Krefeld in 1983, as I noticed the devout expression
on the faces of the people as they sang Gerhard Tersteegen's
'Gott ist gegenwärtig,' but also heard them telling the newspaper reporters, with expressions of dubiousness, that nonresistance was no longer much of a factor in their present thinking.
On another topic, my Swiss Anabaptist ancestors could not
become enthusiastic about Menno's christology (it was a matter of debate among the Dutch themselves). And we probably
forget that before the Schwenkfelders even wrote to the Dutch
Mennonites for help around 1725, citing the Europe-wide reputation of Holland and its Mennonites for toleration and benevolence, the Mennonites had gone into a serious numerical decline. Like the Schwenkfelders of the twentieth century they
had succeeded beyond their earlier dreams—culturally and
economically—but had become ambivalent about their original theological bases. Many of their children were reverting to
main-line Christianity, both Reformed and Catholic, where the
cultural life was richer. At their apogee the Dutch Mennonites
had produced *Martyrs' Mirror*, a written monument to their
suffering ancestors, analogous to the later *Corpus Schwenckfeldianorum*. There had then been affluence to pay for its
publication—by 1685 in an impressively illustrated two-volume
set. Yet when my Swiss-Palatine ancestors of Lower Salford
and Franconia wanted the use of it for their sons and daughters half a century later (1742), the Dutch themselves had lost
their enthusiasm for it. One recalls Jesus' words about our
readiness to build monuments to prophets whose courageous
truths we are hardly willing to live out.

However, I haven't finished with the eighteenth century developments I alluded to a moment ago. It strikes me, in reading through the letters sent to the Dutch Mennonites by Adam
Wiegner in 1725 (which reflect a tradition going back before

1700), that the poor, persecuted conventicles of Schwenkfelders *knew about* the Mennonites in a special way. They mention not only Mennonites of Danzig, and Hutterites from near Vienna (whom a Schwenkfelder visited), but my greatly harassed ancestors in the Canton of Bern, Switzerland, and the aid that the wealthy Dutch Mennonites had given them. All this suggests a kind of common awareness, difficult to define precisely, and yet very important. The European groups who maintained their faith without benefit of the magisterial, state-ratified churches knew about each other and shared an attitude of faithfulness and humility that fostered a sense of a fraternity. They *sympathized* with each other, whether they were wealthy Mennonites whose peoplehood was declining (like that of Philadelphia Quakers) while they were doing the most energetic and international relief work, or a tiny group of spiritualists like the Schwenkfelders whose fellowship was so strong, spiritually, that it had been able to survive without printing or meetinghouses or sacrament.

The Schwenkfelders insisted repeatedly to the Dutch Mennonites that there was no one in the world to their knowledge with whom they were 'so nearly and harmoniously allied as with the Mennonite Churches.' The Dutch Mennonites didn't completely buy this; they called the Schwenkfelders, after some prodding, 'fellow-believers,' but not 'fellow-members.' They checked with Count von Zinzendorf on the Schwenkfelders' spiritual authenticity. Of course, this was a bit like sending the goat to bring the cabbage since Zinzendorf would have dearly loved to add the devout Schwenkfelders to his fellowship-to-end-all-denominations. Fifteen years later in Pennsylvania Zinzendorf would be unsuccessfully wooing both Schwenkfelders and Mennonites in several climactic attempts to merge all the Pennsylvania sects into the brotherhood he envisioned.

But my main interest here is to recall how (1) both Dutch Mennonites and Swiss *Täufer* had spiritualistic leanings, growing at the beginning of the eighteenth century, that led them to common ground with the Schwenkfelders, and (2) the Schwenkfelders had an instinctive trust in the charitable Mennonites, whose faith was demonstrated less in meditation on the inner Christ than in works of charity.

We're all familiar with the story of how wealthy Mennonites of Hamburg and Haarlem supported and outfitted the 1734 emigration of Schwenkfelders from Saxony to Pennsylvania. Interestingly, the large collection taken up by the Mennonite Committee in Amsterdam for the Schwenkfelders was carried out after the Committee had flatly refused to pay the ocean passage of any more Mennonites from the Palatinate to Pennsylvania. In 1732 some Oberholtzers, Gehmans, and Derstines had still gotten help, but there would be, said the Amsterdamers sternly, no more such handouts.

Had my own ancestors in a 1717 migration—Kolbs, Landises, Lederachs, Meyers, and Ruths—not already snapped up the best acreage of the Lower Salford and Franconia township landscape, the Schwenkfelders might have settled there in a body. As it was, they reported that Caspar Wistar's still vacant land there was now pretty much surrounded with other people. Still, as they dispersed from the Neshaminy to the upper reaches of the Perkiomen, a pocket of them settled in at one corner of my native Lower Salford, and also in Methacton, Towamencin, and Hereford, Mennonites got new Schwenkfelder neighbors. Here they lived together in a kind of non-intercommuning peace that made European observers incredulous.

It was the local Mennonites' good fortune to have living in their community a remarkably gentle and spiritual teacher of European provenience unknown to us, named Christopher Dock. He seems to have taken a liking to the Mennonites and taught in two of their schools. Regarded by the Lutheran pastor at Goshenhoppen as himself a Mennonite, he probably did become a member of the congregation at Salford. He was an early proponent—perhaps the main one—of the use of *Fraktur* art to motivate his pupils. Only in the 1980s is the sheer volume of *Fraktur* output among our local Mennonites being discovered, and it will take some serious study for its sensitivities to be adequately assayed. I would like to thank all involved with the Schwenkfelder Library for its role in the preservation and collection that make Mary Jane Hershey's extensive present *Fraktur* research a possibility. Here you have performed a community and a spiritual service.

No *concerted* effort was forthcoming among the Mennonites for the education of their children; it was a Pietist or Dunker editor from Germantown who saw to it that Dock's ideas came out in print. But the Schwenkfelders, inheritors of the thought

of a man who had done an incredible amount of publishing, set
up a little school program in Lower Salford and Towamencin
in the last decade of Christopher Dock's life. In 1790 they had
a little academy up at Hosensack. In these efforts we see symbolized a difference between Schwenkfelders and Mennonites of
this old Pennsylvania community. The Mennonites have paid
a price for neglecting the life of the mind. The Schwenkfelders
got into schooling and libraries and record-keeping (and celebrating the past) well before the Mennonites. Although now we
too have waked up to these activities, in the meantime, while
our attention was on other things, it was often the Schwenkfelders who saved for our community a goodly number of our
books and *Fraktur*. The result, when I look from my Mennonite community across at the Schwenkfelder one, is that I feel in
our ethos an aesthetic crudeness set off by the foil of the greater
Schwenkfelder sensitivity to these things. At the same time I
muse on the fact that the Mennonite secret weapon has always
been peoplehood and connectedness. Though, like the American Indians, the Mennonites didn't write down their story, they
passed on a set of convictions simply through oral and familial continua. Only since World War II is this communication
taking institutional shape in the manner of the Schwenkfelders,
and the question is, will the growth of our institutions, delayed
so long by the tendency of the Mennonites to distrust worldly
mechanisms and arrangements, be a sign of our own acculturation and loss of communal focus? Pound for pound, there's
no one in our region as energetic or successful in preserving the
records and artifacts of a culture, as the Schwenkfelders. But
with us Mennonites, the emerging story must needs include the
fostering of our original heritage, not the shifting, in practice,
to a main-line Protestant ethic. In this we have the historic advantage of a greater peoplehood mass than the Schwenkfelders
have had for the last quarter-millennium. One hopes that this
communal integrity will translate into the creativity necessary
for the facing of new historical challenges.

Just as once the Dutch Mennonites helped the Schwenkfelders through a difficult geographic transition, so the Schwenkfelders helped us Mennonites of southeastern Pennsylvania, by functioning as a means of preserving local history before
we ourselves woke up to the responsibility as it takes shape in
the late twentieth century. Thank you.

I hope and pray the Mennonites do not abandon their historic understanding of and commitment to what they used to call 'the church under the cross.' One of the most deeply felt tenets of a Mennonite of Swiss origin (and for many of Dutch origin, too) is the belief in the cross of Christ as the paradigm of reality. This has important relevance to the use of force. Generally, with success and acculturation comes a rapid waning of any beliefs in this vein that are regarded as non-standard by the macroculture. This happened among the European Mennonites beginning around 1800. Is it only the Pennsylvania Mennonite cultural lag that has allowed the teaching of non-resistance to survive until 1986? Back in 1756 the Schwenkfelder men gathering in Lower Salford decided to endorse the aims of the Quaker-sponsored 'Friendly Association,' designed to assuage the alienation between whites and Indians of our colony. The Mennonites agreed to do the same thing. Already at that time, on the other hand, and in the Revolutionary years ahead, the Schwenkfelders evinced an orientation to the exigencies of warfare that was not the same as that of the Mennonites. Here, from a Mennonite point of view, the inwardness of the Schwenkfelder devotion gave a latitude in external behavior that the Mennonite did not share. For the latter, the laying down of force was an essential part of the 'experience' of Christ's cross, more crucial even than the sensing of a profound subjective emotion. Yet the Schwenkfelders knew something of this too, and it was their sharing of such feelings that had directed their attention toward the Mennonites already in Silesia and Saxony.

Mennonites married Schwenkfelders, and vice versa, often without a serious culture-clash, here in Pennsylvania. We Mennonites got a spate of Anderses, Heebners, and Kriebels that way. My great-grandfather informed one of his sons in no uncertain terms that there would be no horse from his stable available for the courting of a Baptist girl, but when the same son drove all the way from Bucks County to Center Point to court a Kriebel, there seems to have been no objection. Another point of frequent contact was the annual Harvest Home Service, where Mennonite preachers would hold forth in Schwenkfelder meetinghouses, and vice versa, even into my own time.

I wouldn't want the Mennonites to follow the logic of organization as easily as the Schwenkfelders increasingly did. Back in 1847 a wing of our more progressive people organized a new Conference, and since then they have accepted more readily than the older body a parliamentary procedure and constitutional structure. This—and it has its advantages, to be sure— is both the glory and the weakness of their approach to doing church. But we older Mennonites do not feel that more streamlined ways are necessarily more spiritual, or even humane ways of dealing with our issues. Several years ago I was in a meeting of the Franconia 'Conference Council,' when a rather weighty issue arose. Some men had brought a proposal for the disposition of an important piece of property owned by the Conference. We somewhat hesitantly voted to endorse their proposal and tell them to proceed. But after a half hour some doubts began to be raised, and finally sentiment swung in a direction opposite from what we had first approved. The moderator began a parliamentary procedure in an attempt to rescind our earlier action. Things became technical and complicated, and no one knew what move to make next. After some delay the moderator simply threw up his hands and said, 'Look, we know what we want; we don't want to do what we said we wanted to a little while ago. Isn't that right?' Everybody agreed, and we stopped trying to make a rational procedure out of what we were agreeing on. In that throwing up of the moderator's hands I felt a deliverance and a happiness. As an old-line Mennonite I do not look for the attainment of the goals I seek for our church in some improved 'method' which the 'world' may offer. On the other hand, I hope to be open-minded enough to allow church-proceedings every spiritual advantage.

Regarding your and our experience with the evangelicals of our last twenty decades—you as a Schwenkfelder fellowship were hurt more that we. The same thrust of the 1830s that may have taken a good third of your people and caused the rest to debate hard about kneeling for prayer and whether or not your people were born again, took parts of several of our congregations after 1856. These good people, seeking more life than they could find among their more sober relatives, have generally built devout congregations—although at the price of forgetting a part of their heritage—particularly the mutual aid and nonresistance parts. We tend to think the spiritualism of your Schwenkfeldian heritage made you more vulnerable, and that the more unimaginative, communal-oriented and disciple-expressed ethos of the Mennonites had more innate resistance to novelty and 'excitement.' Nevertheless, I must acknowledge that I recognize in the loyal Schwenkfelders of today a depth of respect for their heritage that is a testimonial to its power.

Our more liberal group, founded in 1847, got Sunday School when you did, as well as things like missionaries, Christian Endeavour, and the use of English. In all these culturally related matters we were hanging back, and only gained momentum a half-century after you did. On some of these things we're still getting our act together. Will it be that we too will have senators and cabinet members in another several decades? We're less likely to do so than you for the same reasons that we are less likely to erect a church with a large steeple or replace meetinghouse with gothic decor. Our traditional teaching on simplicity and 'nonconformity' will hold us back from centering our hopes in the political process. Yet, it's quite obvious, our businesses are succeeding to a remarkable degree in these boom times, and to what lengths the next generation will carry its cultural expression remains to be seen. We're earnestly discussing the issue of ordaining women in our Conference. We want to deal with this, not in the cheap way of splitting over it, but, debating scriptural teaching, walking consciously and as a community over whatever threshold we agree to cross. Jesus said that Heaven would back us in what we bind and loose in his name. This is not the same thing as simply joining what we can't lick, culturally speaking.

We'll certainly never do as good a job on our genealogy as you did in 1923; by now, in any case, there are too many non-ethnic names coming into our fellowship for that, and we enjoy having that problem.

In the 1950s, when John Falter painted your Central Church for the cover of the *Saturday Evening Post*, the Mennonite he painted for the cover of another issue was an auctioneer from Bucks County. The artist had no idea the man was a Mennonite, I'm sure, so his representing him as a rather folksy, slightly uncouth personage was simply innocent fun. Yet in the contrast between the gracious statement of the architecture of Central Church and the grizzled auctioneer lies a fairly accurate comparison of where our two communities were three decades ago. Now, the grandchildren of that auctioneer are at the universities and in the professions along with yours.

While the auctioneer was selling off John Souder's irreplaceable notebooks, representing his collections of local Mennonitica from half a century, your Elmer E. S. Johnson was greedily—and most fortunately—snapping them up and stashing them safely in your emerging library. Again, thank you. But now we too are building museums and libraries, and some of the items that have been flooding in from our Mennonite homes, where even Abraham Harley Cassel and Governor Pennypacker didn't find them, are Schwenkfelder things. We can now help each other in this great work of storing our community's spiritual treasure. In this, you will be our elder and superior sibling, as you were when we first began to look hard at our local background, in the fall of 1971, and you lent us the carefully archived *Fraktur* of our old schoolmasters, that we ourselves had failed to preserve.

Now both Mennonites and Schwenkfelders explain their heritages at the Kutztown Folk Festival. We descendants of persecuted enclaves can now, like other Americans, be 'proud' of our forbears—perhaps doubly so. You've had your major pilgrimages to what used to be Silesia and Saxony, and some of our people go to Anabaptist country from Friesland to Zurich every year. Scholars from Vancouver to Strasbourg dutifully articulate and edit the teachings and debates of our founders. What will be the fruit of this renaissance of what we both hope is spiritual awareness? Will our monuments, literary and architectural, bespeak a genuine spiritual dialogue? Or will they function primarily as celebration of our American success stories—yours first, and then, after a decent interval, the Mennonite one?

History suggests that we'll have our work cut out for us, distinguishing between sociologically and spiritually understood 'realities.' In this regard, I think, in closing, of the comment of an observant Quaker woman from Lancaster County, who looked around in our community. The peaceable sects, she said, tended to have uniform political tastes. Though some had communion, and some didn't, and they all had their own church fellowships, there was something else that must have run to the core of who they were. Was it, at bottom, a spiritual identity? One hopes so. The editors of a Montgomery County newspaper told her, she wrote, 'that he does not know a Mennonite or Schwenkfelder who is not Republican.'

# Sudermann
# in America

## Monica Pieper

In the 'Silesian Room' of the Schwenkfelder Library in Pennsburg hangs the painting entitled 'The Landing of the Schwenkfelders from the St. Andrew.' In it the painter, Adolf Pannash, sought to convey an impression of the arrival of the Silesian emigrants to Pennsylvania 200 years after the historical event took place. Conspicuous in Pannash's presentation are the many books which, along with the usual household effects, the artist has assigned to his little group. By such a means Pannash sought to mark a phenomenon which was to remain characteristic of the Schwenkfelders: The careful maintenance of the written basis of their confession brought along from Europe as well as the extensive literary activity growing out of this.

In addition to Schwenckfeld's own writings numerous texts of his disciples also found their way into the New World. Here, the religious life of the Schwenkfelders, blossoming anew, secured a continued spiritual existence for several poets in a way that would have been unthinkable in Europe at that time. A vivid example of this is afforded by the texts of the Schwenkfelder hymnist Daniel Sudermann (1550-ca.1631), whose influence has remained more distinct in Pennsylvania than in his European homeland. From the sources of the Schwenkfelder Library in Pennsburg it is obvious how highly the Schwenkfelder religious community esteemed Sudermann's work and in what way it made use of it for religious life.

This esteem can be traced back to the immigration of 1734 when the 'luggage' of the Silesians contained some works of Sudermann as well. The first step in making fertile use of his poems for religious life was taken soon after by those members of the community who, with industry and diligence, produced handwritten copies of the texts in order to increase their utility for edification and instruction. For the same reason melodies were added to poems and prayers and these were integrated with biblical passages and hymns selected for worship on Sundays and religious holy days. As a result Sudermann's original works were extensively supplemented. Such editions of Sudermann's poetry reached their climax when forty-seven of his hymns were incorporated into the first Schwenkfelder hymnal printed in America.[1] The reprint of Sudermann's texts in a hymnbook used by a community is unique—in post-Reformation Germany none of his hymns or poems were reprinted after the poet's own initial publication.

Other traces of Sudermann in Pennsylvania are secondary to this in importance, but are of great interest. Thus, many Sudermann prints reached America in the years following the emigration of 1734, but their origin and acquisition cannot be documented with any certainty. Some found their way into the Schwenkfelder Library through the passionate book collector and subsequent governor of Pennsylvania, Samuel W. Pennypacker. Others were probably purchased from Germany as part of the preparations for the *Corpus Schwenckfeldiano-rum* between 1895 and 1918. In this regard it should be noted that Schwenckfeld's Bible, which has been part of the library since 1890, also went through Sudermann's hands and was annotated by him.

Thus, the attention which posterity paid to Daniel Sudermann grew first and foremost out of the needs of the religious life. Scholarly attention was not initially directed to him. Of the notebooks which A. F. H. Schneider made during his work on Schwenkfelder hymnists and which are preserved in the Schwenkfelder Library, one is on Sudermann. Schneider's volume is a collection of data and personal names which were used in the printing of his essay on the subject.[2] A 700-page collection which reached Pennsburg via Hartford Theological Seminary in the course of the gathering of Schwenckfeldiana has similar contents.[3]

Significant scholarly interest in Sudermann was aroused when the work on the *Corpus Schwenckfeldianorum* was begun. Probably between 1880 and 1919, a number of transcriptions of Sudermann manuscripts were made under the direction of Dr. Elmer E. S. Johnson. They are for the most part based on the extant pieces in the Staatsbibliothek Preussischer

Kulturbesitz in Berlin.[4] The transcriptions are very careful reproductions of the original texts of the poems, as well as the sketches for Sudermann's copper-etchings. It is likely that the work was so extensively undertaken since the editors of the *Corpus* hoped to devote space to the poet in their publication. The collection of loose sheets, subdivided into thirty-four chapters, is likewise kept in the archives of the Schwenkfelder Library.

Finally, there is the work of Joachim H. Seyppel. In the early 1960s Seyppel worked in Pennsburg and in the course of his study he discovered three poems which were no longer to be found in Germany.[5]

## The American Transmission of Sudermann's Poetry

The discovery of three Sudermann poems which are no longer traceable in mid-European libraries, throws some light on the importance of the American tradition at this point. Of course, the literary value of Sudermann must not be overestimated, but if one takes seriously his intention to contribute, not to art, but to spiritual exaltation, one immediately recognizes that his purpose found delightfully fertile soil among the Schwenkfelders in America. It is possible to add a fourth poem to the list of Sudermann's printed texts, beside the three rediscovered by Seyppel. The first line of this poem runs: 'Man sagt, es waren zwen Studenten' ('Tis said there were two students). The text is found on page 119 of a Sudermann collection which contains the exposition on the Song of Songs as well as 120 poems that were taken from *Schöne Auserlesene Figuren* and other printed works. The collection is catalogued in the Schwenkfelder Library as VN 33-12. The page was printed by Jacob von der Heyden in Strassburg and shows the typical division for Sudermann. There is first a large header which makes known the contents of the poem (*Von zweyerley Studenten und unterscheyd ihrer beyden Geschickligkeiten* 'Of two Students and their different fortunes'). This is followed by an illustration which presents the dramatic climax of the occurrences in the text, as well as a picture and a subtitle in Latin (the latter is not typical in Sudermann's work). The poem tells of the two students who have concluded their studies and are returning home. One of them is leading a donkey loaded

with books.  While crossing a bridge, the donkey, together
with all the books, falls into the water and drowns.  After the
owner has lamented the loss of his property, the second student
speaks and in his voice Sudermann presents the moral of the
poem: the printed 'outer' word does not enrich a person; only
that knowledge which God has placed in the human heart and
which one cannot lose is helpful.  The conception and content
of the poem correspond to that of a text from the third part of
*Schöne auserlesene Figuren* which begins 'Zween Brüder in ein
Kloster kamen.'[6] Here as well, the contrast between two persons with different values about the printed word is followed by
the instruction that the only person who can become 'divinely
blessed' is the person who has internalized Christian teaching.
In both poems, Schwenckfeld's thoughts about the inner and
outer Word of God are obvious.

Although all other poems in the collection VN 33-12 are
contained in the well-known Sudermann prints, it seems that
there is really one issue of the poem 'Man sagt, es waren zwen
Studenten.' The collection in which it is found was in the possession of Matthias Yeakle, originally from Ober-Harpersdorf,
who came to Pennsylvania with his family in 1734.[7] The collection is one of the few Schwenkfelder Library volumes here
under discussion whose transmission can be traced back almost directly to its Silesian origin.  In 1778 the book shows up
on the booklist of Christopher Yeakle (1718-1810).[8] During the
next three generations it remained in the possession of the same
family.[9] In 1894 it was bought by Andrew Anders, and through
his descendants it reached the Schwenkfelder Library in 1908.
As already noted we are not so fortunate in being able to trace
the transmission of most of the other Sudermann prints in the
Schwenkfelder Library and thus to reconstruct the use of such
works for worship and teaching among the Schwenkfelders.

Dissemination and use of Sudermann's poetry can, however,
be traced from the numerous copies which were increasingly
produced prior to and during the early years of the immigration.  The oldest of these volumes, VB 2-3, was produced in
1734 and consists of two parts: the first contains Sudermann's
*Hohelied Auslegung* which is supplemented by an alphabetic
index and a designation for readings on Sundays and holidays.
The second part is a collection of poems, entitled 'Medita-
tiones,' which is probably the work of George Weiss.[10] To this

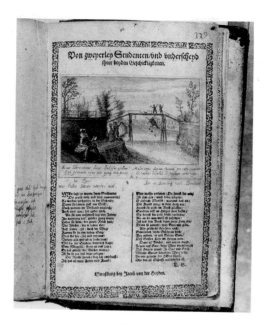

Daniel Sudermann
'Man sagt, es waren zwey Studenten'
Schwenkfelder Library, VN 33-12, p. 119

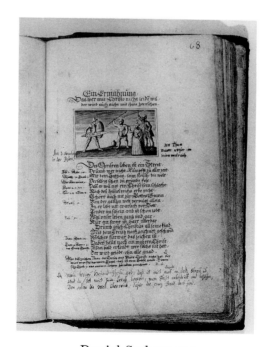

Daniel Sudermann
'Des Christen leben ist ein streit'
Schwenkfelder Library, VN 33-12, p. 68

part the two registers previously mentioned are added. On the back of the titlepage, the copyist gives some hints as to his method: 'The reader shall know that the author Dan. Sudermann has not written all these poems as hymns, but only those which are entitled hymns; the others were divided into hymns by G. Weiss not long ago, and furnished with melodies and also with refrains, after which this has been transcribed. Where Sudermann's work ends and G. Weiss' addition begins, a red line has always been drawn.' According to the 'Guide to Manuscript Volumes' of the Schwenkfelder Library the copyist of this volume is unknown. A script comparison with the volume VR 11-15 could, however, allow one to conclude that the copyist was Abraham Wagner whose extensive abilities are outlined in Andrew S. Berky's biography of his life as 'pietist,' 'physician,' and 'poet.'[11] Even if the copy stems from Wagner, however, it originated in Europe since the family did not leave Saxony until 1737. In this way, as well, the collection of Sudermann texts produced in 1726[12] by George Weiss found its way into the New World.

A later copy of Sudermann made by Abraham Wagner marks him as an important representative of the Schwenkfelder community. The volume VR 11-15, which was already mentioned, contains the *Hohelied Auslegung* in Wagner's hand and is dated 1742. At that time Wagner was 'Medicus Practicus of Norriton in the county of Philadelphia,'[13] having spent the first years of his stay in Pennsylvania in the house of his medical teacher, Dr. Melchior Heebner. Wagner, who must be regarded as one of the most educated men of the Schwenkfelder community according to the *Genealogical Record*, did not occupy himself with the literary tradition of the Schwenkfelders alone, but became familiar with the works of numerous Protestant theologians. Thus, he had read among others, Christian Hohberg, Johann Arndt, and Gottfried Arnold. He established a correspondence with Gerhard Tersteegen, and prepared a Spener biography shortly before his death.[15] His interest in religious poetry was not merely a passive one. In his youth he had already begun to write poems and hymns, thirty-four of which found their way into the Schwenkfelder hymnal of 1762. In his poetry he gave expression to his innermost feelings, as the twelve-verse hymn on the death of his niece, Rosine Yeakel, in 1743 shows.[16] From Berky's evaluation of Wagner's poetry it

becomes clear how close his spirituality was to that of Sudermann: 'It was a form of devotional literature that held a peculiar appeal for men who invited martyrdom, gladly endured the
persecution and quite rightly felt themselves set apart from the
main currents of life. It was the personal expression of what
was exclusively a personal religion and its roots were firmly
imbedded in the Christian tradition of the Psalmists, the Saints
and the Reformers.'[17] One cannot do justice to the poetry of
either author if one measures them with classical artistic standards: 'It is rather like discussing the merits of a cake recipe
without taking into consideration the real purpose of the eating
which in the final analysis is nourishment and not taste.'[18] The
volume VR 11-15 was later to be found among the possessions
of Samuel W. Pennypacker, who wrote a few reflections on the
contents on an empty page of the book. His thoughts spring
from a book-lover's interest in religious literature, but show no
extensive familiarity with the theological currents which fed
Sudermann's poetry.

In the work of later copyists the *Hohelied Auslegung* received most attention. The volume VC 3-3, again divided into
two parts, contains the *Hohe geistreiche Lehren* in a transcription of 1744, which was made by Maria Yeakel (1799-1781).[19]
The two registers which were contained in a transcription of
1734 are adopted in this copy as well. But there are differences between it and earlier copies; it stems from the year
1749 and was possibly produced by Melchior Schultz, one of
the 1734 immigrants.[20] The copyist of this volume not only
confined himself to reproducing the texts and dispensing with
the illustrations which are part of the printed original, but in
place of the picture he has set a description, in order to provide
some impression of the original. How meticulous his information is may be seen in his words: 'Here stands the groom,
beneath the brightly shining name JHS, set up very royally. In
his right hand he holds a sceptre, and the bride stands facing
him, dressed in beautiful garments, her hands folded across
her breast, and holding a beautiful necklace. It is as if she
were approaching her groom, regarding him with the friendli-
est countenance and the loveliest mouth. Meanwhile he has his
eyes directed towards her, stretching forth to her his left hand,
as if to receive her (Cant. 1:16).'

With a transcription which points to the broader processing of traditions from the sixteenth and seventeenth centuries

by subsequent Schwenkfelders this inventory can be concluded.
VR 13-22 consists of a postscript to the *Catalogus oder Register der Bücher Herrn Caspar Schwenckfelds*, produced in 1561.
Besides Schwenckfeld's own writings it ennumerates also those
of his best-known followers. Thus, Daniel Sudermann is mentioned in the following short description: 'Daniel Sudermann, a
well-established Theologus Mysticus, has written many highly
illuminating pieces about the Song of Songs of Solomon, as
well as having put into verse much from the old teachers of the
church, and has published these, supplied with his instructive
symbols. His writings are printed at Strassburgh' (129). The
basis for this description was doubtlessly the *Hohelied Auslegung* itself from whose titlepage, content, and dates are taken
almost verbatim.

Besides this prose-article about Sudermann, his name is
found in a lyric which commemorates the most important
Schwenkfelder authors and leaders from the Reformation to the
early eighteenth century. The copy does not give any information about the author of this lyric, alongside which a second,
similar one is placed. Berky demonstrates that Abraham Wagner was the author and introduces two further poems of this
kind, which were written by Balthasar Hoffman and Christopher Kriebel in imitation of Wagner.[21] Although Sudermann
appears in those two lyrics at the same place as in Wagner's,
he is no longer mentioned in the second text in volume VR 13-
22. The poetic appraisal of Schwenkfelder authors is there put
under the motto: 'Warning not to despise faithful witnesses
to the truth and their writings' (116). That this warning was
taken seriously is demonstrated in the further dissemination of
Sudermann's texts.

## The Editing of Texts for Use in the Congregation

Daniel Sudermann himself saw the collection and transmission
of hymns as his most important task, when he began to collect
and edit Christian literature generally for the purpose of edification. Adam Reissner had worked in a similar fashion, and so
the point of departure was set for a century-long collection and
supplementation of hymns among the Schwenkfelders, the climax of which came with their first printed hymnal, published
in Germantown, Pennsylvania in 1762. The preparatory work

for this is marked by the unbroken activity of collecting, organizing, and improving which began in Sudermann's own day
in Alsace, was carried on by the Schwenkfelder communities of
Silesia, and was finally completed in America.

Two manuscript collections complied by Caspar Weiss in
1709 also contain hymns by Sudermann.[22] However, the final shape of the collections was left to his son George, who
extended the collection in 1726.[23] The impact of this work
is first noted in the collection-edition which Matthias Yeakle
brought to Pennsylvania in 1734. In both parts of that volume
manuscript supplements to the printed texts follow the same
pattern: the part in Sudermann's text—usually the end of a
poem—is marked at the side with a letter which is repeated
on the lower part of the sheet or on the opposite page, where
the supplementing, new text also appears. In the same handwriting remarks on melody or assignment to certain Sundays
or religious holy days are noted on the upper edges of the text.
These supplements to the text are found in VB 2-3 of 1734,
discussed above, in which the copyist has integrated the additions into the texts of Sudermann, setting them off from the
original by a red line. New in this volume is the marking of
the beginning of each stanza by numbers. Sudermann had all
texts which were not meant as hymns printed in blocks of up to
ninety lines. The subdivision into stanzas, as Weiss understood
it, is not yet noted in the volume VN 33-12.

Concerning Weiss' intentions in supplementing the work,
Allen Anders Seipt writes: 'His revision of the hymns of Daniel
Sudermann... consisted of a restrophicizing of a number of the
Sudermann hymns, and the addition, to the majority of hymns,
of one or more strophes intended as prayer.'[24] The examples
which follow serve to illustrate this intention. In the poem 'Des
Christen Leben ist ein Streit,' Sudermann calls upon the Christian to combat his three worst enemies—the world, the flesh,
and the devil. He then describes the complacent individual
who avoids this battle and concludes with the threat of mer-
ciless death for the person who is unwilling to struggle. All of
this is done in impersonal description and neutral statements.
The revision of the text, which is attached directly to Sudermann's version, undertakes a marked turn to the personal:
Christ is directly addressed and asked for help and strength
for this battle. The four line supplement to the

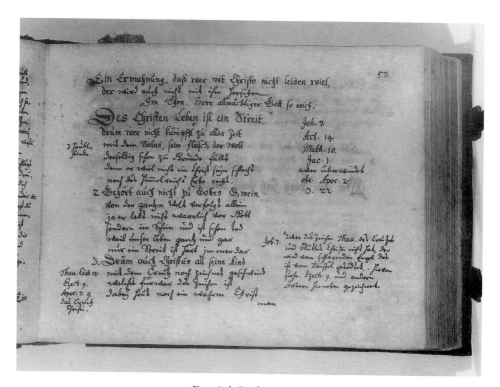

Daniel Sudermann

'Des Christen leben ist ein streit'

Schwenkfelder Library, VN 2-3, pp.57-58

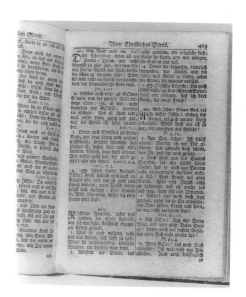

Daniel Sudermann

'Des Christen leben ist ein streit'

Schwenkfelder Library, 289.2 Sr (Sciver, 1762), p. 413

poem 'Die Seel thorecht greifft in der Zeit' (48), becoming the eighth verse, presents itself in a similar fashion:

Behütt mich Jesu dass ich nicht,
viel ohn dich begehr drin such mich,
sondern mich verlass dass dein Geist
in mir wohn und würck allermeist.

(Protect me, Jesus, that I may not covet much without thee, seeking myself therein, but trust that thy Spirit dwell in me and work most thoroughly.)

Here too the impersonal observation, meant for instruction, has been transformed into an address to Christ; the reader of the poem has turned into one who prays. It is in harmony with this, that the soul, as bride of Christ, no longer occupies the center of the text, but the personal 'I' facing Jesus does. Thus, the connection with mysticism, to a large degree only formal in Sudermann, falls away entirely. The revision of the poem 'Nun höret, was Christi Braut rein' (1-4) indicates that George Weiss intended to soften the break between the original and the new edition. He divides the poem of fifty-three lines into stanzas of four lines each and uses the remaining last line as beginning for the fourteenth stanza:

Durch ihn glaubs nur des lebens Cron
Denn er hat sie erworben schon
und will sie jedem teilen mit
der ihn von Hertzen darum bitt

(Through him one may believe the crown of life, for already he has obtained it and wants to share it with everyone who petitions him for it with all one's heart.)

With this stanza he remains faithful to the position of Sudermann, establishing however, the key-word 'petition,' which is then added in the fifteenth and sixteenth stanzas. In summation it may be said that in his revisions Weiss not only wanted to make existing texts available but that in doing so he redirected their intentions in his final verse: the objective observations on Christian virtues end in a subjective petition for the grasping of these virtues.

Only in a few poems are the revisions not undertaken at the end, but interposed into the text itself. Sudermann's warning to patient endurance of slander ('gegen der zunge Schwerdt') provides an example of such textual insertions. The manuscript revisions in the printed text VB 2-3 were used in the manner already described. However, the copyist thought it wise to set

the initials of the author 'G. W.' on the edge of the revised parts
of the text in order to avoid confusion. In terms of content,
the sense of these insertions is hardly justifiable; indeed, they
have a very disruptive effect on the original sentence structure.
The dialogue between the patient Christian and his attacker
which as presented by Sudermann is interrupted several times
in this way, so that it is difficult to follow the thought structure
of the poem. Possibly these insertions were made for musical
reasons, that is, the text had to be 'stretched' for the sake
of the melody. The two sources, however, mention different
melodies. Further study of the development of this hymn in
the Schwenkfelder community is limited by the fact that it was
not incorporated into the 1762 printed hymnal.

That hymnal, the *Neu-Eingerichtetes Gesang-Buch* published by Christopher Saur in Germantown in 1762 was the
highpoint of the Schwenkfelder hymnic tradition. If one considers not only the century-long, increasingly intensified work
of collecting and editing, but also takes a look at the situation
of the Schwenkfelders in Pennsylvania barely thirty years after
the immigration, one recognizes immediately that printing was
carefully considered. Around 1760 the community had already
established itself in its new home, at least insofar as the initial
difficulties in struggling 'intensively for the barest necessities
of daily living'[25] can be said to have been overcome. The members of the community were now in a position to focus their
attention more directly on the development of their spiritual
life. When the first 'Schwenkfelder General Conference' gathered in 1762, an important mark of this changed attitude was
set by Christopher Kriebel (1724-1800). He called on his fellow believers 'to consider their present status and the need for
cooperation in an effort to create unity of life and action, and
to remember and consider gratefully many past events in their
lives as well as the rich blessings they are now enjoying.'[26]

The results of his appeal were a strengthened communal
conscience and the formation of unified worship and catechetical practices. Near the end of the same year the hymnal was
published.[27] In its preface praise of God and spiritual edification were mentioned as the purposes of communal singing. As
already mentioned, the hymnal made use of forty-seven of Sudermann's poems in the form established by George Weiss, the
distribution of the texts being concentrated in the first half of

the second part, 'Von der Oeconomie und Regierung Gottes.' Knowing the themes preferred by Sudermann, the reason for their inclusion in this section is obvious, since the chief concern of this part is primarily with questions of faith, of the loving longing for God, and of the prerequisites for the imitation of Christ. The chapters with themes on ecclesiastical life, set in the second part, contain markedly fewer texts by Sudermann. The same is true of the first part, which is concerned with the nature of God and the life of Christ.

These observations again make it clear that the Pennsylvania Schwenkfelders not only grasped Sudermann's intention, but continued it. In all this, however, not merely were contents of preaching considered, but there was a clear concern with the faithful transmission of the original sources of the European poets. This is evident in the manuscript annotations which mark the original text and the supplementation, a practice continued in the Saur hymnal. Instead of the 'red line' of the copy, the picture of a hand pointing to the textual supplementation appears in the printed work. The same sign was used by Sudermann himself 150 years earlier when he wanted to direct a reader's attention to a peculiar feature in the text. In almost all cases, the Saur edition took over the Weiss additions to Sudermann's poems; other divergencies from the original text are isolated and insignificant.

One poem in the Saur edition has, however, been significantly changed. The piece begins 'Das heylige Evangelion' and was extended by four lines in handwriting in the printed version of 1734. The lines were added in the copy (VB 2-3) as well.[28] Their author is George Weiss who concluded the poem in the form of a personal prayer in a manner typical for him. In the printed 1762 hymnal, however, forty-two additional lines were added to the original fourteen line piece. The additions have nothing in common with Weiss' additions. The lines added in the 1762 hymnal contain a description of the soul and its virtues in strongly mystical language which culminates in an eulogy on Christ, the bridegroom, and his merits. With this, the tenor of the *Hohelied Auslegung* is precisely continued. There are likewise close parallels with the original poem's sentence structure and rhyme scheme, indicating that the author has carefully considered Sudermann's own thought. Unfortunately, there are no traces indicating the author of this revision.

The Saur hymnal organizes the subdivision of the songs, 917 in all, according to key points of content. At the same time, it takes into account the attempts made after George Weiss to organize the pieces according to content and melody and to allocate them according to reading and preaching themes. Beside the alphabetical register, the hymnal contains a melody register and appendix, as well as a register for use on Sundays and major feast days.

Sudermann himself never undertook such a division of his poems, but as early as the manuscript revision of the printed volume, which came to Pennsylvania in 1734 through Matthias Yeakle, the Schwenkfelders had begun to arrange the pieces according to the events of the church year. The practice was followed closely in subsequent editions. The initial subdivision was likely the work of George Weiss, whose activity in this area Balthasar Hoffman discussed in 1753.[29]

The registers were in all likelihood based on those of the Silesian, Erasmus Weichenhan (died 1594). His sermon collection was first printed in 1672, and was reprinted in 1741 in Germantown and in 1842 in Allentown, Pennsylvania.[30] The collection was extremely popular among Schwenkfelders who read his sermons on the particular days of the church year according to which the sermons were arranged. The Sudermann hymns were intended to be read in association with these sermons on the specified days. Thus, in his sermon for Maundy Thursday Weichenhan cites John 13:1-15 and divides his address into four points; the last of which is entitled 'on footwashing.'[31] The Sudermann prints designate Sudermann's hymn on the same theme as one of the pieces to be used on this day. Likewise, on the fifteenth Sunday after Trinity the sermon theme treats the difference between the service of God and Mammon, and the Sudermann texts assigned to this day condemn worldly desires.[32] Many Sudermann hymns were possible for a sermon theme such as the one Weichenhan treats on the twentieth Sunday after Trinity, 'of the king who arranged a marriage for his son.'[33] In this case the hymn registers cite twelve poems from Sudermann's commentary on the Song of Songs and thus present the relationship between Christ and the human soul as a bond of love.[34]

This method of allocation indicates a very pragmatic treatment of the religious poetry. If, however, one realizes that

Sudermann—and many other hymnists of his time—wrote with the intention of rendering the fundamentals of their Christian convictions in an accessible form, it is clear that such treatment of earlier hymns do justice to the original intentions of the authors. Their first concern was that their texts be utilized in the life of the community. Because of this any scruples in respect to the conservation of artistic originality would be misplaced, since Sudermann did not consider himself an artist, but a teacher whose works were meant to be used according to the religious requirements of posterity. He never demanded awe-struck distance for his work. He treated the sources he used in the same way. They too were shaped according to later purposes for developing Christian perfection.

## Sudermann and Schwenckfeld's Bible

Sudermann treats Schwenckfeld's personal Bible in the same way as he did earlier poetic texts. This volume was discovered some 250 years after Sudermann's day and provides valuable insights into the theological interests of Schwenckfeld and early Schwenkfeldianism. The inscriptions on the inside cover provide information concerning the Schwenkfelders through whose hands this historically and artistically valuable volume passed after Schwenckfeld's death.[35] Schwenckfeld himself indicated that the volume was to be passed on to 'the virgin Catharine Streicher of Ulm.' Thereafter, it came into the possession of Johann Heyd and Daniel Friedrich and finally reached Sudermann. He also placed importance on the fitting preservation of the volume after his own death, committing it to Samuel Friedrich or the communities of Marckirchen and Rappoltzweiter. From 1632, however, the ownership of the Bible is unknown until it reappeared in 1890 at an auction in London and, through Harrassowitz, a bookseller in Leipzig, finally came into the possession of the Schwenkfelder Library.

The edition, known as the 'Worms Bible,' was published by Johann Denck and Ludwig Hätzer in 1529, following the publication of their earlier pre-Lutheran translation of the prophets. The 'Worms' edition is the first complete Protestant translation of the Bible. Schwenckfeld's commentaries on the text are of great significance for sixteenth-century scholars and for the American Schwenkfelder communities. Besides these, however,

the volume includes manuscript commentary by Daniel Sudermann. In a manner typical of him, he wrote a poem of two
verses concerning the divine illumination necessary for rightly
understanding the printed word in the centre of the title page.
His commentaries on the text may be summerized in two categories: on the one hand, he compares the translation with the
Greek and Latin sources respectively; on the other, he adds
personal reflections based on Schwenckfeld's teaching. For example, beside John 3: 13, 'and no one ascends to Heaven but
he be come from Heaven, namely, the Son of Man,' we find
the following reference to Schwenckfeld in Sudermann's hand:
'C. S. Note: only the divine nature of the Son of Man has
its origin in Heaven, but also the nature of man, since Mary
became pregnant by the Holy Spirit. God is Father and she
the true Mother.' Numerous poems by him corroborate the
themes here addressed regarding the divine and human natures of Christ and the status of Mary, both of which were
important aspects of Christian teaching for him.[37]

Like most other books which came into his possession, Sudermann regarded Schwenckfeld's Bible as working material,
and made use of it for his own studies. At the same time,
however, he also clearly recognized the historical and theological value which the edition had for the disciples of his honored
teacher. This is obvious in the inscription on the cover, already
quoted, in which Sudermann expresses his concern regarding
the ownership of the Bible after his death. In case the persons designated as heirs should no longer be alive, he wrote:
'If these, however, have also died, it shall belong to those who
confess his teaching as true and not to one alone.'

Now, almost 300 years later, Sudermann's hope has been
fulfilled. In the existence of the Schwenkfelder community in
Pennsylvania the aims of the life and works of European religious poets, who were denied recognition by their native land,
further manifests itself in living form.

## Notes

1  *Neu-Eingerichtetes Gesang-Buch in sich haltend eine Sammlung (meh-
   renteils alter) schöner lehr-reicher und erbaulicher Lieder, Welche vor
   langer Zeit her bey den Bekennern und Liebhabern der Glorien und
   Wahrheit Jesu Christi bisz anjetzo in Uebung gewesen, Nach den Haupt-
   Stücken der Christlichen Lehr und Glaubens eingetheilet, und Mit einem*

*Verzeichnisz der Titel und dreyen nützlichen Registern versehen. An-*
*jetzo also zusammen getragen, und Zum Lobe Gottes und heilsamen*
*Erbauung im Christenthum, ans Licht gegeben* (Germantown, gedruckt
bey Christoph Saur, auf Kosten vereinigter Freunden, 1762). For further bibliography see Allen Anders Seipt, *Schwenkfelder Hymnology and*
*the Sources of the First Schwenkfelder Hymn-Book Printed in America*
(Philadelphia, 1909), 33.

2 A. F. H. Schneider, *Zur Literatur der schwenckfeldischen Liederdichter*
*bis Daniel Sudermann in Jahresbericht über die Königliche Realschule,*
*Vorschule und Elisabethschule* (Berlin, 1857).

3 VK 1-1 (1570-1579), folio 1-211; VK 1-2 (1580-1590), folio 212-700.

4 Among these are found MSS germ. quart. 101, 106, 108, 334 and 336.

5 Joachim H. Seyppel, 'Zu unbekannten Gedichten Daniel Sudermanns'
in *Zeitschrift für deutsche Philologie* 79 (1960), 150-55.

6 *Schöne ausserlesene Sinnreiche Figuren auch Gleichnuss Erklärungen*
*Gebettlein und hohe Lehren . . . Der III. theil* In verlegung Jacobs von
der Heyden, [n. d., n. pl.; Strassburg, 1625].

7 *The Genealogical Record of the Schwenkfelder Families. Seekers of Re-*
*ligious Liberty who fled from Silesia to Saxony and thence to Pennsyl-*
*vania in the Years 1731 to 1737*, edited by Samuel Kriebel Brecht (New
York, 1923), 886.

8 See *Genealogical Record*, 1258 For his help in ascertaining the original
and later owners of this volume I am especially thankful to the Director
of the Schwenkfelder Library, Mr. Dennis Moyer.

9 Anna Yeakel, (1748-1804); Anna Kriebel, nee Yeakel (1798-1875);
Reuben Kriebel (1820-1890). See *Genealogical Record*, 470 and 354,
as well as the introduction to this volume itself.

10 See also Seipt, 77f.

11 Andrew Berky, *Practitioner in Physick. A Biography of Abraham Wag-*
*ner. 1717-1763* (Pennsburg, 1954).

12 Seipt, 78.

13 Berky, 27.

14 See *Genealogical Record*, 1434f.

15 Berky, 18, 44 and 69f.

16 Berky, 30ff.

17 Berky, 146.

18 Berky, 150.

19 See 'Guide to Manuscript Volumes.'

20 See 'Guide to Manuscript Volumes' as well as the *Genealogical Record*,
964.

21 Berky, 121ff.

22 Seipt, 14.

23 Seipt, 78.

24 Seipt, 78.

25  Selina Gerhard Schultz, *A Course of Study in the Life and Teachings of Caspar Schwenckfeld von Ossig and the History of the Schwenckfelder Religious Movement* (4th ed.; Pennsburg, 1977), 135.

26  Schultz, 141.

27  Seipt, 97.

28  'Jesus der du gelitten den Tod
    Auch auferstanden mir zu gut
    Hilf dass ich also folge dir,
    Dich liebe auch absterbe mir.'
    (VN 33-12, 93 und VB 2-3, 81f. Saur edition, 256f.).

29  Seipt, 79f.

30  Erasmus Weichenhan, *Christliche Betrachtungen über die Evangelischen Texte so man zu lesen pfleget an den Sonntagen und hohen Festen* (Allentown, 1842).

31  Weichenhan, 294.

32  From the *Hohelied Auslegung* (Weichenhan, 656).

33  Weichenhan, 712.

34  See, for example, VB 4-5.

35  See also, XVIII, 601ff.

36  XXVI.

37  See, for example, 'Weil jederman sich rümet sehr,' 'Nun lasst uns hoch erschwingen,' 'Es fragen offt gemeine Leut,' 'Nun hört, ein Jungfrau hat gefragt.'

# Schwenkfelders and the Preservation of Tradition

Peter C. Erb and W. Kyrel Meschter

Like almost every German speaking group that migrated to North America in the eighteenth century, the Schwenkfelders weree concerned with the preservation of their religious tradition. The nature of their tradition, however, forced them to carry out that preservation in ways different from those of their fellows. Unlike the Lutheran and Reformed groups they could not depend on institutional structures because of their theological rejection of such structures, and unlike Anabaptist and Pietist groups like the Mennonites and the Church of the Brethren, they could not depend on ethnicity, recent charisma or the forms of a popular religion to sustain them. What they turned to were books.

From the beginnings of the movement the Schwenkfelders were a bookish people. Rooted in the intellectual tradition of humanism, Crautwald, Schwenckfeld, and other early leaders took special interest in the publication of materials to support their theological positions and to make available the works of earlier Christian writers. Even before their deaths attention was directed to the preservation of their works, and in the later sixteenth and early seventeenth centuries the next generation of leaders devoted many hours to preserving and publishing their works. With the devastation of the Thirty Years' War and the reduction of the Schwenkfelder movement to a lower cultural class in a few Silesian villages, publication became for the most part impractical, and the Schwenkfelders turned to an earlier practice of manually copying books and treatises which they wished to preserve for themselves or their children. The practice continued and grew during the troubled years of the Jesuit persecution, the flight to Saxony, and the emigration to Pennsylvania.

It is difficult to ascertain the reasons for the extensive copying of manuscripts by Schwenkfelders. From the beginnings of the Jesuit persecution in 1719 to their eventual arrival in Pennsylvania in 1734 and during the first unsettled years there, however, there was little time or opportunity to publish, and copying would have been simpler. Moreover, the Schwenkfelders were not numerous and the printing of any treatise would have been as a result highly costly. Nor was cost alone a factor. In a world which was jealous of the orthodoxy of every typeset page the individually produced manuscript was certainly less likely to attract attention. Finally, habit has a way of perpetuating itself, and this is particularly the case when the practice of copying the great spiritual masters of earlier generations not only aids in their preservation, but serves as a spiritual discipline, focussing the mind of the believing scribe on every transcribed word.

The largest collection of Schwenkfelder manuscripts is preserved in Schwenkfelder Library. The present Library collection includes approximately 200 bound manuscript volumes and some 1500 unbound volumes and individual quires, most of which were copied before 1800. This count does not include over 1000 Fraktur pieces or the extensive correspondence collection. Relatively few Schwenkfelder manuscripts are known outside of the collection at Schwenkfelder Library.

How much copying was done is not possible to estimate. The tendency for manuscripts to be lost over time was outweighed among the Schwenkfelders by the great respect they had always given to such volumes and the assiduous energy a number of major representatives of the movement devoted to the collection and preservation of materials at the close of the nineteenth and the beginning of the twentieth century. It is reasonable then to suppose that the Schwenkfelder Library collection provides an accurate indicator of the type of copying done by Schwenkfelders, particularly of their interests after their arrival in America, since most of the manuscripts were done on this continent.

A survey of the bound manuscripts alone, on which the following brief outline is based, proves highly informative. Of the manuscripts which are extant, fifty-two copyists can be identified. The most aggressive of these appears to have been Balthasar Hoffman. Twenty-three manuscript volumes can be reasonably ascribed to Hoffman, the majority comprising more than 300 folios. The first two are dated 1698 and 1717. In the

ten years between 1724 and the emigration to America, Hoffman finished seven more manuscripts in spite of the upheaval
caused by the persecution and flight, and from the time of his
arrival in Pennsylvania he copied an average of one piece every
two years until 1748 (ten in all). His decline in his later years
can be noted in that there are extant only two copies from the
1750s and two from the next decade, both interestingly done
in 1764. Hans Christoph Heebner was equally productive. Between 1736 and 1768 he copied twenty-one pieces.

The pattern for both these men was to some degree set by
their first leader in America, George Weiss, seven of whose
pre-emigration copies remain along side six manuscripts in his
hand which were done after 1734. Others too were productive.
The Hoffman family seems to have had a particular interest in
copying, Balthasar's son Christoph copying eight between 1745
and 1801, and Rosina Dresher Hoffman copying eight between
1750 and 1775. Christopher Kriebel copied eleven between
1747 and 1800, Balzer Schultz eight between 1762 and 1808,
Christopher Schultz ten between 1734 and 1783. Eleven of
the copyists were women: Susanna Heebner, Rosina Dresher
Hoffman, Barbara Krauss, Maria Kriebel, Susanna Kriebel,
Rosina Kriebel, Anna Schultz, Susanna Schultz, Maria Weiss,
and Maria Yeakel. In one case (MS C4-4) the piece was copied
by David Schultz 'and wife.' Copyists were most active during
their adult years but a number began to work quite early. Hans
Christopher Heebner, Christopher Hoffman, Barbara Krauss,
and Christopher Schultz were already copying as teenagers.
Bathasar Hoffman copied his first volume at eleven!

If the present collection is any indication the years between
1734 and 1750 marked the period of the greatest activity in
manuscript copying. An average of seven copies remain for
each of those years. In the 1750s the average drops to three,
in the 1760s to two, and thereafter until 1783 to one. Copying
after 1783 appears to have been sporadic.

The work leading to the production of the printed hymnal of 1762 is clear. Fifty-six hymn collections, forty music manuscripts, and a number of copies of the poems of
Sudermann are extant. Not surprisingly copies of works by
eighteenth-century Schwenkfelders are numerous. Twenty-six
volumes include compositions by Balthasar Hoffman, eight
with materials from George Weiss, six were compiled by or

are copies of work by Christopher Kriebel, and a dozen are primarily the works of Christopher Schultz. An additional twenty include miscellaneous materials related to the thought of the Schwenkfelders in the eighteenth-century. There are as well twelve prayer books from the period and eight copies of letter collections between Schwenkfelders in Europe and America. Eighteenth-century Schwenkfelders retained a close interest in the works of their ancestors who wrote between the death of Schwenckfeld in 1561 and their emigration to America. Forty manuscript volumes are copies of the sermons of Michael Hiller. The fact that there are only three by Erasmus Weichenhan may be a result of the publication of his sermons and their availability in print. Twenty-four volumes are miscellaneous collections of treatises and letters by Schwenkfelders who lived during this period, and there are an additional eight copies of the carefully selected and edited Epistolar which serves well as a anthology of Schwenkfelder thought to the eighteenth century.

Printed editions of many of the earliest Schwenkfelders did exist (There remain over 150 'Sammelband' collections of sixteenth-century printed treatises by Schwenckfeld. In addition there were available printed copies of the works of Schwenckfeld in the Epistolars which were published shortly after Schwenckfeld's death.). The number of manuscript copies of works by Schwenckfeld and Crautwald, for example, are relatively few. Only twenty volumes are copies of their works. Likewise there are only eight copies of works by Adam Reissner and only three by the early and popular preacher Johann Werner (both Reissner and Werner were available in printed editions), whereas there are also three copies of the treatise on the School of the Holy Spirit by the lesser-known Eisenmann, whose work was not in print.

Eighteenth-century American Schwenkfelders' interest in their founder and in the perpetuation of his ideas is marked in a number of ways. In the 1760s Christopher Schultz with the assistance of Balthasar Hoffman and others prepared a monograph, the *Erläuterung, A Vindication of Caspar Schwenckfeld von Ossig, An Elucidation of his Doctrine and the Vicissitudes of his Followers*. The volume was printed with the help of the great Silesian Schwenkfelder Carl Ehrenfried Heintze in 1771. In addition American Schwenkfelders expressed an early concern with translating Schwenckfeld's works into English. Three eighteenth-century translations exist. The most significant of these was made of Schwenckfeld's highly popular *Christian Warfare and the Knighthood of God* of 1533, a treatise which went through a number of editions and different printings in the sixteenth and seventeenth centuries (see *Corpus Schwenckfeldianorum* 6:674ff.) The translation is ascribed to Christopher Schultz who was also responsible for a translation of Schwenckfeld's *Advice to a Young Christian* of 1558 which Schultz translated for some Quakers in 1770.(CS 16:602) The third translation is by Christopher Yeakel and is of Schwenckfeld's 1541 letter to Werner on baptism.

In the nineteenth-century the concern with providing English translations of Schwenckfeld seems to have faded as attention was directed to the publication of the Silesian Reformer's works. In 1819 a collection of Schwenckfeld's letters of 1531 was printed in Allentown at the press of Heinrich Ebner and the following year Schwenckfeld's *Heavenly Balm* was published by the same press. Fifteen years later in 1835 Schwenckfeld's 1547 open letter on prayer appeared in its first American edition (Allentown, A. and W. Blumer), and in 1846 Blumer and Busch in Allentown printed a collection of Schwenckfeld's treatises, including *Christian Warfare*, *On Sin and Grace*, and *Was Christ a Sinner*. Schwenckfeld's *German Theology* was published at the direction of the Schwenkfelder community at Skippack in 1848 and this edition seems to have opened the way for the publication the following year of the large edition of Schwenckfeld's works under the title *Fünf Abhandlungen aus den Theologischen Schriften von Caspar Schwenckfeld...* including the *German Theology* and the *Great Confession* of 1538.

But these manuscript copying and publishing efforts pale in scope and significance before the *Corpus Schwenckfeldianorum* brought to fruition in 1961 by twentieth-century Schwenkfelders. After seventy five years of effort, consuming much of the lives of three principal editors and numerous associates, here in nineteen volumes of some 18,000 large pages were made readily available to scholars the critically edited texts of 1252 surviving Schwenckfeld documents. The renaissance of Schwenckfeld scholarship as these volumes appeared and in the twenty-five years since their completion, has splendidly fulfilled the wildest dreams of the initial editors, who envisioned nothing less than a reinterpretation of reformation history and Schwenckfeld's seminal role therein.

During the middle of the nineteenth century in Germany
August F. H. Schneider accumulated the most comprehensive
collection of Schwenckfeld documents assembled to that time.
After his death these collections were acquired by the Case
Memorial Library at Hartford Theological Seminary, where
Seminary Trustee Augustus C. Thompson, who had roomed
with Schneider while studying at the University of Berlin forty
years before, recognized the work of his old roommate and
brought the collections to the attention of Dr. Chester D. Hartranft, then professor of ecclesiastical history at the Seminary.

Asked to prepare and deliver a historical paper at the 150th
Gedächtniss Tag Service in 1884, Dr. Hartranft immersed himself in the Schneider documents and notebooks, became interested in Schwenckfeld and his theology, and came to feel
personally challenged by the unflattering portrait of the man
passed down through history. During the month before the
sesquicentennial service, he addressed a printed circular letter
to the Schwenkfelder community, making an appeal to edit and
publish the writings of Schwenckfeld as a literary monument.
'Surely to bring this before the world would be a more suitable
memorial of the greatness of our fathers, and of our gratitude
to God, than to raise a shaft; nor could we make a nobler
contribution to theological science and righteous living.'

Here was a project to insure preservation of Schwenckfeld's
thought and theology for posterity, and not surprisingly the
appeal struck a responsive chord. Just nine months later, in
May 1885 Dr. Hartranft was dispatched to search libraries and
archives in Germany, to compile a bibliography (over 900 documents), and to engage copyists to initiate preparation of the
documents for publication. A prospectus for a projected sixteen volumes at $6.00 per volume, or $96.00 for the set, was
circulated to raise funds for editorial costs. The sixteenth volume was to be a revisionist biography of Schwenckfeld, added
to set the historical record straight and to entice individual
subscribers.

In all the annals of literary history it is doubtful that any
work of this magnitude has been undertaken by so small a base
of sponsorship, prosecuted through so much difficulty and frustration, and yet brought to such distinguished fruition. This
paper can only hint at the vicissitudes which dogged the project
from beginning to end.

Dr. Hartranft was commissioned editor under an initial contract of four years to complete preparation of the documents and a fifth year to write the biography. Successive crises at the Seminary demanded his attention and service as President and the combined efforts predictably strained his physical and mental faculties, adding bouts of ill health to frustrate progress of the enterprise. Not until 1902 was Dr. Hartranft able to establish editorial offices in Wolfenbuettel, Germany, whose Ducal Library contained a large collection of relevant documents. Here editorial work continued down to and through World War I, when post war inflation forced the removal of headquarters to Pennsburg, Pa.

Dr. Hartranft was enthralled with the rigor of German scholarship and determined that his work would compare favorably with other productions then under way, notably the Weimar edition of Luther's works. When volume I finally appeared in 1907, subscribers and backers were aghast. In 730 pages it presented but seven documents. Hartranft projected beside reproduction of texts six critical analyses of each under the headings Bibliography, Translation, Language, History, Theology and Vocabulary. With over a thousand documents to go, 100 volumes and several lifetimes could hardly have completed the work!

As the magnitude of the task had gradually begun to emerge, in 1904 Mr. Elmer Ellsworth Schultz Johnson, a graduate of Hartford Seminary, where he had studied under Dr. Hartranft, had been dispatched to assist Dr. Hartranft and to restrain the already evident overly ambitious impulses of the editor. In August 1907 the editors returned to America, bringing with them advance sheets of Volume I, which were presented at the Fall General Conference. The first shipment of finished volumes arrived shortly thereafter, reviving the spirits of weary backers. An intensive review of the publishing program followed, along with solicitation of new subscriptions. When the editors returned to Germany in 1909, they were accompanied by Dr. Johnson's sister-in-law, Selina Schultz Gerhard as staff secretary, and by a firm direction to confine the work to the originally projected sixteen volumes.

With youthful vigor and firm direction injected, volumes two, three and four appeared by 1914, bringing the number of documents printed to 153 and wisely leaving most of the analytical supplements for the work of later scholars. In December, 1914 Dr. Hartranft died and Dr. Johnson was immediately charged with carrying on the work. No sooner had the new editor undertaken his task than the outbreak of World War I created daunting communication, funds transfer and passport problems, in spite of which, with the support of local authorities and friends, the Johnson family and Miss Schultz remained in Wolfenbuettel and quietly pursued their work. After the 1918 armistice complex negotiations finally permitted the editorial staff to return to America in April 1919, followed by 146 boxes weighing twelve tons of hastily packed editorial materials—the nucleus of the present Schwenkfelder Library collections.

At this point Dr. Johnson became Pastor of the Mennonite church in Bally, and shortly a professor of church history at Hartford Seminary. The major burden of editorial work devolved upon Miss Gerhard, now by marriage Selina Gerhard Schultz. Although assisted by a succession of associate editors, and importantly by Dr. Kurt Ernesti who officially represented the editors in Germany, only the patient perseverance of Mrs. Schultz in preparing manuscript and reading and correcting proofs allowed publication to proceed. With the 1934 Bicentennial celebration looming, a concerted effort largely completed editorial work, and by 1936 14 volumes had been delivered from the printers, Breitkopf and Härtel, in Leipzig, Germany, bringing the number of documents presented to 984.

Now once again the complications of a World War intervened. By 1936 unfavorable exchange rates forced suspension of printing. In 1939 a purchase of blocked marks permitted printing Volume XV, but shipment could not be arranged and the finished volumes had to be stored in the printer's warehouse. In December, 1943 allied bombing largely destroyed the warehouse and all the Corpus volumes stored there. Five copies of Volume XV had, however, been mailed to European subscribers, and one of these copies after the war fortunately found its way to America.

With the four hundredth anniversary of Schwenckfeld's death approaching in 1960, Mr. Wayne C. Meschter offered to donate funds if arrangements could be made to complete printing. Andrew S. Berky, Director of Schwenkfelder Library, personally carried the manuscript for volume XVI to Göttingen,

Germany, and arranged with Hubert and Co. to print the remaining volumes. Volume XV was reproduced by photographic process for printing. The last five volumes appeared by 1960, naming Mrs. Schultz as Editor and Andrew S. Berky as Managing Editor.

As earlier volumes appeared, scholarly interest quickened, and librarians and archivists turned up sixty-five previously uncataloged documents, necessitating expansion of the work to nineteen volumes. The last 350 pages of Volume XVIII present Schwenckfeld's annotations on the margins of his personal bible, in German and Latin script, often abbreviated, painstakingly translated and transcribed by Mrs. Schultz. Mrs. Schultz also prepared the long anticipated biography of Schwenckfeld, published independently in 1946 by the Schwenkfelder Board of Publication. To cap her years of dedicated effort, in 1961 Mrs. Schultz, 81 years of age, accompanied by her husband and escorted by Andrew Berky, journeyed to West Germany where on November 23 she was awarded an honorary Doctor's degree by the prestigious University of Tübingen.

As already indicated, it is not surprising that early Schwenkfelder immigrants, arriving in an unfamiliar geographical and cultural environment, should demonstrate a strong penchant for preserving memorabilia from their past, both artifacts and literary works. By the later nineteenth-century Schwenkfelder attics were crammed with such materials. Schwenkfelder historian Howard W. Kriebel began to collect these materials in his home. In the year following the initiation of the Corpus project General Conference formally charged church trustees with the gathering and preservation of these materials and designated Professor Kriebel as curator. For over forty years he pursued his studies of Schwenkfelder and local history as collector, genealogist, historian, writer and editor. His 1904 *The Schwenkfelders in Pennsylvania* outlines a fascinating study in colonial secular and religious culture, now urgently awaiting the hand of a qualified scholar to be reworked in the light of modern theological, sociological and colonial historical scholarship.

During early Corpus editorial work a large portion of this manuscript collection found its way first to Hartford, to Wolfenbuettel and then in 1919 back to Pennsburg along with the materials collected in Europe. When the Carnegie Library

was built on the grounds of Perkiomen School, the second floor
and a 'fireproof' vault down the center of a building largely of
wood, were designated as a home for the Schwenkfelder Historical Library collections. Artifacts deposited there by Schwenkfelder families mindful of past blessings, gradually accumulated
into the present museum collection.

In 1879 the Schwenkfelders were moved to prepare a genealogical record. In 1923, under the editorship of Dr. Samuel
K. Brecht the updated *Genealogical Record of Schwenkfelder
Families* was published, tracing the known descendants of the
original Schwenkfelder immigrants as close as possible to publication. At the prescient urging of Judge Heydrick, the new
Genealogical Record included a multitude of mini-biographies
of Schwenkfelder immigrants and their descendants, thereby
once again preserving for future generations their rich cultural
heritage and traditions. Genealogical materials became a significant element in Schwenkfelder Library.

In 1942 the Schwenkfelder Board of Publication, desiring
to make the work available to current generations unversed in
German, published Professor Elmer Schultz Gerhard's translation of Christopher Schultz's *Erläuterung,* originally printed in
1771, being a history of the Schwenkfelders in Silesia, the trials and tribulations leading to their emigration, and a scholarly
exposition and defense of Schwenckfeld's teachings.

During the 1940s, in an effort to distill the early Pennsylvania Schwenkfelder historical resources of the Library into a
form readable by laymen, the Board of Publication published
eleven issues of *Schwenckfeldiana,* dealing with biographies of
early Schwenkfelder ministers and leaders, relations with the
Moravians, excerpts from early Gedächtniss Tag sermons, Missionary activities and post World War II German refugee relief
work.

As collections expanded and research activities increased
the limited accommodations in the Carnegie Library handi-
capped orderly shelving and cataloging, and exposure to destruction by fire caused increasing concern. In the late 1940s
Mr. Wayne C. Meschter offered to fund a new fireproof building
under certain conditions. A non-profit corporation, Schwenkfelder Library, was formed by twenty-five ministers and leaders
of the several churches, under a charter constituting the incor-
porators as a self perpetuating governing body, subject to a

charter provision that two thirds of the members should at all times be descendants of the Schwenkfelder immigrants of the 1730s. A tract of land was acquired from Perkiomen School and a new library building erected. Library collections and certain endowment funds were formally deeded by the Board of Publication to the new corporation, and in September of 1951 Andrew S. Berky, the newly elected Library Director, supervised the removal of the literary collections from the Carnegie library to the shelves of the new library home. The Carnegie Library quarters were renovated to more adequately display the museum collections. In 1959 Mr. Meschter significantly increased the Library endowment fund, assuring maintenance of the building and its collections.

Andy Berky had a solid background in American history, an inquiring intellect and a facile pen. Under his direction for the first ten years of its existence the new library became a recognized center for the study of early Pennsylvania German history and culture, for local genealogical research, and for research into Schwenkfelder history and theology. Andy himself wrote a series of colonial culture related studies and arranged lectures by contemporary figures in public life. Visiting scholars began the series of published monographs which became the hallmark of the new institution.

In the summer of 1970 the Library was visited by Peter Erb, a doctoral candidate at the University of Toronto, Canada, preparing a dissertation on *The Role of Late Medieval Spirituality in the Work of Gottfried Arnold (1666-1714)*. The Library collections piqued Dr. Erb's interest and not long after Andrew Berky left the community for other pursuits in 1973, Dr. Erb assumed increasing responsibilities for the academic work of the Library, in time assuming the position of Associate Director. A popular lecturer and prolific writer, at home in the mainstream of Reformation scholarship, Dr. Erb has rendered distinguished service in the preservation and dissemination of Schwenkfelder history and tradition.

To celebrate the two hundred fiftieth anniversary of the arrival of the Schwenkfelder immigrants in America, in 1984 W. Kyrel Meschter prepared *Twentieth Century Schwenkfelders: A Narrative History* and Dr. Erb conceived and organized the Colloquium of which these papers are a record. The Colloquium demonstrated for all to see the vitality of post corpus

interest and research. While previous publishing and copying, including the Corpus project, was concerned principally
with preserving earlier texts, a review of the Schwenkfelder
Library Selected Bibliography prepared for the Colloquium,
suggests a new and perhaps more significant trend. The bibliography includes works by prominent scholars in the fields
of religious and historical studies who are not otherwise allied
with the Schwenkfelder community. Monographs, doctoral dis-
sertations, and books have appeared which would neither have
been inspired nor possible without the Schwenckfeld texts readily at hand in the Corpus. Dr. George Hunston Williams' 1962
study, *The Radical Reformation*, opened for the first time in
a major way the scope and significance of the Radical Reformation and presented Schwenckfeld's role in its historical and
theological context. Titles of other works published since 1950
include authors Paul L. Maier, Edward J. Furcha, Joachim
Seyppel and L. Allen Viehmeyer. Dr. Horst Weigelt's 1973
study published in German was translated by Peter Erb and
published by Schwenkfelder Library in 1985 as *The Schwenkfelders in Silesia*. In 1986 Dr. Emmet McLaughlin's *Caspar
Schwenckfeld, Reluctant Radical, his life to 1540*, was published by Yale University Press. It lucidly relates the story
of Schwenckfeld's life and clearly places it in the context of
the Reformation as it developed in Germany. It performs a
very necessary service by bringing the man Schwenckfeld and
his work within the grasp of present day laymen, frequently
possessing only sketchy knowledge of Reformation history, and
even less of the theological subtleties over which controversy
then raged.

The *Corpus Schwenckfeldianorum* enterprise had an incal-
culable formative and stimulative influence over the development of Schwenkfelder organizations and institutions during
the first half of the twentieth century. It sustained interest
in the heritage of the past and inspired institutional collection and preservation of this record. Without it it is fair to
doubt whether the Schwenkfelder traditions, treasured and preserved over four hundred and fifty years, would have survived
twentieth-century generations.

The 1984 Colloquium and these papers demonstrate for
all to see the vitality of post Corpus interest and research.

The wide range of studies and the expanding interest of scholars outside the narrow Schwenkfelder family, justify confidence that Schwenkfelder traditions will survive into the 21st century—supported as in years past by books.

# Eighteenth-Century Schwenkfelder Hymnology

## L. Allen Viehmeyer

Eighteenth-century Schwenkfelder hymn writing and compiling in Pennsylvania is a sorely neglected area of study. General encyclopedic works such as *The New Grove Dictionary of Music and Musicians* and *Die Musik in Geschichte und Gegenwart* do not contain articles on Schwenkfelder hymnology either in Europe or Pennsylvania. American Schwenkfelder hymnology has been briefly described by such scholars as J. H. Dubbs,[1], G. Haussmann,[2] and J. J. Stoudt,[3] but the only published scholarly treatise on the subject is the monograph written by Allen Anders Seipt.[4] Likewise, there have been brief sketches of several individual colonial Schwenkfelder hymnists and their poetry including Abraham Wagner (1715-1763)[5] and Balthasar Hoffman[6] (1687-1775), but very little has been written in depth about colonial Schwenkfelder hymnologists and their achievements. Moreover, the term hymnology implies tunes as well as texts, but no published, scholarly literature, not even Seipt's fine study, deals with the tonal aspects of American Schwenkfelder hymnology. In the following paper I shall review briefly the hymnological activities of colonial Schwenkfelders, then discuss broadly the 1762 Schwenkfelder hymnal, and, finally, concentrate on Balthasar Hoffman, whom I consider to be the leading eighteenth-century Schwenkfelder hymnologist.

## Hymnological Activities of Colonial Schwenkfelders

Perhaps the most important possession of a Silesian Schwenkfelder family was its hymnal, for hymnals at that time were more than just books for congregational singing on Sunday mornings—they were books of devotions for group and individual worship and study. Thus, the baggage brought by Schwenkfelder exiles to Pennsylvania contained many manuscript hymnals. Painstakingly copied by hand and pressed between two leather-covered boards, a rich heritage of Protestant

hymnody was transplanted to the New World by Schwenkfelder immigrants. Seven of these Schwenkfelder settlers stand
out especially as perpetuators of this legacy during the Colonial Period, and their supreme achievement was the printing of their own hymnal in 1762 (see Appendix D). Of these
seven, six reached Pennsylvania in the third migration of
1734. They were George Weiss (1687-1740), Balthasar Hoffman (1687-1775), David Seipt (1699-1765), Caspar Kriebel
(1700 or 1701-1771), Christopher Schultz (1718-1789), and
Christopher Kriebel (1724-1800). The seventh was Abraham
Wagner (1715-1763), a member of the sixth migration in 1737.
Collectively, the six men of the third migration were staunch,
conservative defenders of main stream Schwenkfeldianism. Although officially lacking the title of 'reverend,' George Weiss
and Balthasar Hoffman were generally regarded as spiritual
leaders. Christopher Kriebel and Christopher Schultz were officially known as 'reverend.' In 1733 David Seipt became a 'deacon.' Without title, yet a no less enthusiastic activist and organizer, was Caspar Kriebel, who opened his home for worship
services and actively worked for an organized Schwenkfelder
church and school. The non-conformist among the group was
Abraham Wagner, who leaned toward a more liberal, pietistic
spiritualism.

The names of these seven men are generally known because
some of their hymns were included in the 1762 hymnal, yet
very little is actually known about the hymnological pursuits
of most of these individuals. Because of Balthasar Hoffman's
propensity for historical detail (and a son with like bent), there
is abundant documentation of his hymnological pursuits as well
as those of his friend George Weiss, but very little, if anything,
is known about the hymnological activities of the other five. By
the time they reached Philadelphia in 1734 both George Weiss
and Balthasar Hoffman had been steeped in the hymnology of
their faith for nearly thirty-five years, editing and copying as
well as authoring more than 100 hymns each. There is no doc-
umentary evidence that the other five had pursued any hymnological activities before coming to Pennsylvania, although we
must admit that our knowledge of such pursuits by persons
other than Weiss and Hoffman is extremely limited.

Due to the inclusion of their creative efforts in the 1762
hymnal, these seven persons have enjoyed the spotlight, yet

many other Schwenkfelders were engaged in writing, studying, and copying hymns and hymnals. Their creative efforts
were not featured in the 1762 hymnal. To shed some light on
less known eighteenth-century Schwenkfelder hymnologists, we
can note some of the activities of these contributors. Christopher Wiegner (1712-1745) studied the German hymns of the
Bohemian Brethren and edited them so that they conformed
to Schwenkfelder spirituality.[7] David Schultz (1717-1797) prepared his own, eclectic manuscript hymnal during 1740 and
1741, in which he transcribed fifty-five hymns on eighty pages
along with annotations about the melodies and authors.[8] In addition, Schultz is said to have written two, if not three, hymns
intended to be eulogies of loved ones.[9] Hans Heebner (1718-
1804) is not only noted for his elegant copy of *Ein Christliches
Gesang=Buch* 1758, but he is also the author of at least two
hymns.[10] Christopher Hoffman (1728-1804), too, is noted for
his valuable contribution to Schwenkfelder hymnology in the
form of a hymnal he compiled in 1760, entitled (as is Heebner's
hymnal) *Ein Christliches Gesang=Buch*, in which he noted
the variant readings of the German hymns of the Bohemian
Brethren and the initials of the editor.

Indeed, we must look beyond the covers of the 1762 hymnal
if we are to become appreciative of the total contribution of
American Schwenkfelders to the history of German-American
hymnology.

## The 1762 Hymnal

In the sixteenth and seventeenth centuries Schwenkfeldian
hymns had been preserved in a variety of printed and handwritten compilations. In Silesia the Schwenkfelders used the
German hymnal of the Bohemian Brethren as late as the opening decade of the eighteenth century. But something different
was needed. The direct ancestor of the printed Schwenkfelder
hymnal of 1762 is a manuscript compilation completed by Caspar Weiss (1643-1712) and his son George. This effort was the
first hymnal compiled by a Schwenkfelder for Schwenkfelders.
In the preface to another manuscript hymnal which he was
copying in 1753, Balthasar Hoffman penned the earliest report
we have about the origin of the Weiss manuscript hymnal. He
relates how Caspar Weiss, the father of his friend George, was

urged by his friends to compile a new hymnal, and he soon
commenced collecting, editing, and arranging hymns, bringing
them together in a manuscript. Included were hymns written by adherents of the Schwenkfelder faith as well as many
produced outside of Schwenkfelder circles, yet deemed suitable
for Schwenkfelder worship. Totally new material included by
Weiss in this compilation were the hymns discovered among
the papers of the recently deceased Martin John, and, at the
request of his father, hymns composed by George Weiss on the
Gospel lessons. The title page of a 1733 revision of this hymnal
is dated 1709 and Hoffman, in the preface to the 1753 hymnal,
recalls making a copy of the Weiss hymnal in that year.

Continuing his account of George Weiss's hymnological endeavors, Hoffman further stated in his preface that George had
set about the task of reworking this manuscript collection only
after he had found some quiet and peace while living as an
exile in Berthelsdorf. This second edition of the Weiss hymnal
was compiled, then, sometime between 1726 and 1733, the date
on the title page. A companion volume was completed in the
following year, 1734.

In 1752 and 1753 Hoffman transcribed the Weiss two-
volume hymnal of 1733-34, adding many more interpretive remarks and scriptural references. In Pennsylvania these hymn
collections were ever increasingly felt to be the official hymnody
of the sect, and Balthasar Hoffman prepared new compilations
with some additional hymns, which were completed in 1758
and 1760. While some hymns were added during the revisions
of 1733/1734 and 1758/1760, most of the revising was in terms
of classifying and ordering of the contents. Meanwhile there
was a desire for a printed hymnal among the Schwenkfelders
for some time. A committee charged with the task of printing
the hymnal was established. Christopher Schultz was editor of
the project and the author of the Preface to the tome. After
three years of diligent effort, the first printed hymnal designed
for Schwenkfelder worship appeared late in 1762. Second and
third editions were published in 1813 and 1869 respectively.[11]

Seipt's tracing of the development of the 1762 hymnal, just
outlined, might lead one to the erroneous conclusion that it is
the ultimate, comprehensive Schwenkfelder hymnal. It is em-
phatically not. There are probably nearly as many American
Schwenkfelder hymns not in the hymnal as are in it. Besides

the albeit limited number of American Schwenkfelders whose hymns were not printed in the 1762 hymnal at all, not all the hymns of those writers represented are included.

Hardly a third of Balthasar Hoffman's hymns are included. In the case of Abraham Wagner thirty-one of the sixty-nine hymns—or nearly half—listed by Berky are not in the 1762 hymnal. The extent to which George Weiss' hymns are represented is impossible to determine at this time, but it is likely that really only a small percentage of his work is found in the 1762 hymnal. For example, not one of the three hymns composed by him for Memorial Day celebrations found its way into the printed hymnal.[12]

Moreover, it is unclear just to what extent the editor's pen was employed in revising the hymns which are in the 1762 hymnal. In his biography of Abraham Wagner, Andrew Berky reproduced a manuscript page of Wagner's hymn 'Herr mein Gott zeig mir' in Wagner's own handwriting.[13] Berky also reproduced a broadside of this same hymn printed by Christopher Sauer in 1742, which faithfully duplicates the manuscript.[14] In the 1762 hymnal, however, there are numerous deviations, usually slight, from the original. For example, the second line of the first stanza is modified to read 'Und lehr mich Dein Gebott und Steg' instead of 'Und lehr mich deine Bahn und Steg.' The second line of the second stanza in the 1762 hymnal reads 'Und zeige dir den Weg zuhand,' while the manuscript has 'Und leite dich mit deiner Hand.' Similar editing practices can also be observed in Balthasar Hoffman's hymns. Thus, we can observe that the 1762 hymnal is not exhaustive in its encompassment of American Schwenkfelder writers, nor are the pieces included without extensive emendations by the editor(s).

## Balthasar Hoffman:
### Biographical Resume

Balthasar Hoffman is not only the best represented American Schwenkfelder in the 1762 Hymnal, but next to George Weiss, perhaps the writer best known today.

Hoffman was born in Harpersdorf, Silesia, in 1687. Nothing is known about his childhood or his youth. In 1721, at the age of thirty-four, he commenced his role as a petitioner at the

Royal Court in Vienna, Austria, for Schwenkfelder tolerance. While he was in Vienna, his family remained in Harpersdorf. He had married Ursula Beier around 1712. They had two children, Anna and Rosina, nine and three years old respectively, when their father went to Vienna. Some predominantly spiritual correspondence between Balthasar and his wife, mother, father, and his only brother George, was copied by Anna into a small volume in 1728 when she was sixteen. Hoffman had remained in Vienna some four years—until 1725. On May 5, 1726, almost immediately upon his return to Harpersdorf, he fled with his wife and daughters to Berthelsdorf. While living in that community, their third child, a son called Christopher, was born on December 2, 1727. On April 24, 1734 (Christopher was six years old at the time), Hoffman sold his property in Berthelsdorf, Saxony, and joined other Schwenkfelders on the voyage to Pennsylvania. Hoffman and his family were among those who sailed from Rotterdam on June 19, 1734.

Hoffman established a home near the site of the present Salford Meeting House. He assisted George Weiss in ministering to the spiritual needs of the Schwenkfelders for nearly six years, and then, on Weiss's death in 1740, became the spiritual leader and defender of Schwenkfeldian doctrine and tradition in Pennsylvania. During the course of his ten year service in this capacity he relinquished leadership several times because of the dissonance caused by his strict, conservative teaching and preaching, and several times he resumed these responsibilities at the urgings of his friends and other conservative adherents of the Schwenkfelder faith. His final retirement came in 1749, when, at the age of sixty, he resigned because of poor health.

Throughout his whole life Hoffman was periodically engaged in the copying, ordering, collecting, interpreting and writing of hymns suitable for Schwenkfelder worship. His life-long occupation with all aspects of Schwenkfelder hymnology, including historical notations, merit our recognition of him as the leading Schwenkfelder hymnologist of the eighteenth century.

### Sources of Extant Hymns

A complete list of hymn texts written by Balthasar Hoffman has been compiled by searching through a variety of sources:

1. The manuscript folio dated 1726, containing the *Epistel Lieder*, (VB5-5)

2. *Tägliches Gesang Buchlein*, 1727. (VB1-3, [1753], VB3-4, [1743])

3. The manuscript volume of letters and other writings dated between 1721 and 1725, copied by Anna Hoffman, his daughter, in 1728, when she was 16 years old. (VA4-10)

4. *Christliches Nutzliches Gesangbuch*, 1756. (VC4-14)

5. *Ein Christliches Gesang=Buch*, 1758 (SWP 387)

6. The *Neu=Eingerichtetes Gesang=Buch*, printed in 1762 with author notations by Christopher Hoffman, Balthasar's son.

The *Epistel=Lieder* are found in only two manuscripts, EPL and VB5-5. The 1727 series on Hebrews is found only in the printed hymnals, the 1738 hymns are found only in the *Tägliches Gesang=Buch* and the printed hymnal. The other, for the most part earlier, hymns are found in a variety of manuscripts and printed hymns. The 1762 printed hymnal contains all the known hymns except the entire series of *Epistel-Lieder* and four other hymns (O Gott du Schöppfer aller Welt, Heiliger Ewiger Gott ohn Anfang, Gott unsers Lebens Anfang und Ernäher, O Jesu Christ du Gottes Lamm).

Appendix A contains a listing of Hoffman's hymns. A quick tabulation shows that 142 hymns by Hoffman are known.

## Dating Hoffman's Hymns

The source for the dates of Hoffman's hymns (except the *Epistel-Lieder*) is his son's, Christopher's, handwritten notations in many copies of the 1762 hymnal. The *Epistel-Lieder* are dated collectively as 1726 by virtue of their inclusion in a manuscript dated 1726. It is difficult to hypothesize between what dates the hymns were actually written. Their conception might date back as far as 1709 when George Weiss completed his *Gesänge über die Evangelia*. The title page of the manuscript copy of letters and hymns by Anna's father dates the contents between 1721 and 1725. Her brother's dating of the individual hymns is collaborated by this information. (We might note that Christopher dated only his father's hymns—no one else's.)

Scrutinizing the dates cited for the hymns, it appears that Hoffman's hymn writing activity fell into three distinct periods of his life. The first phase was during his stay in Vienna between 1721 and 1725; the second was the year 1738; and the final, third phase was 1761/1762, as the hymnal was going to press.

## The Three Phases

### The Vienna Years

The hymns of the first phase, the Vienna years (1721-1725), can be arranged chronologically in three groups: (1) a group of miscellaneous hymns, (2) the series called *Epistel Lieder*, and (3) the series on the Epistle to the Hebrews.

Balthasar Hoffman tells of the long, lonely hours of isolation spent in Vienna while serving as a petitioner to the Royal Court. He relates how he spent this time in study, particularly to prepare for the defense of the Schwenkfelder faith. This study and preparation resulted in three major, well-known works: the *Epistasia* of 1724, the *Hexatomus*, dated 1725, and the *Hodophaenum*, also 1725.

It is quite clear that by-products of these private studies were a translation of a Latin work on the lives of the Gospel writers, a variety of letters in pastoral tones, and a large number of hymns.

The earliest dated hymns form a group of miscellaneous songs, which Christopher Hoffman dated between 1722 and 1725. These hymns are contained in the manuscript volume penned by his older sister Anna in 1728, while the family was living in Berthelsdorf. These hymns are also found in copies of the *Tägliches Gesang-Buch*, *Christliches Nutzliches Gesang Buch*, the *Christliches Gesangbuch* as well as the 1762 hymnal. Several were even reprinted in the 1813 and 1869 hymnals.

The *Epistasia* is a study of the epistle lessons throughout the ecclesiastical year. A natural outgrowth of this study was the series of hymns called the *Epistel Lieder*. Although the manuscript containing this collection of hymns is dated 1726 and scholars such as Seipt and Gerhardt date these hymns in that year, it is perhaps more reasonable to assume that they had been written over a two to three year time span, especially since the study of the epistle lessons itself is dated 1724. Perhaps the creation of this lengthy folio manuscript dated 1726, which neatly collected these hymns into one volume, occurred in the late, wintry months of that year. The last Schwenkfelder petition to the Royal Court was denied on May 2, 1726, and Hoffman fled to Saxony with his wife and two daughters in the night of May 5, 1726. The relocation of his family in Berthelsdorf surely afforded Balthasar little time for contemplation, composing and copying until late in the year.

The *Hexatomus*, dated in the preface July 31, 1725, is a study of the Letter to the Hebrews. A series of hymns, six in number, dealing with the Epistle to the Hebrews are dated 1727 by Christopher Hoffman in the 1762 hymnal, the only source of these hymns. There is no known manuscript copy of any of the hymns in this series.

### The Hymns of 1738

The seven hymns of the second phase, all dated 1738 in the 1762 hymnal, appear earlier in the *Tägliches Gesang=Buch*. With one exception, these hymns are found in a single section of the 1762 hymnal called *Vom Worte GOTTES* in the second subsection. Whereas most of the hymns in the first phase can be shown to relate to studies and activities pursued by Balthasar Hoffman, these cannot. Hoffman was working on a catechism in 1737 and two catechical treatises in 1738, but these hymns do not seem directly related to these endeavors. This was the time, however, of attempts to organize the Schwenkfelders for worship. Deacons were appointed and places of worship were designated. These hymns do have the common thread of asking for God's grace to be open and receptive to the word of God. Perhaps these hymns were intended to serve as hymns of preparation to be sung as the corporate service in the households began.

### The Hymns of 1761/1762

The hymns of the third phase are of a great variety, and found in many sections of the 1762 hymnal. They are found only in the 1762 hymnal, and many are perpetuated in the 1813 and 1869 hymnals. The opening hymn, which is the opening hymn in all three printed Schwenkfelder hymns, is a text dated 1762. It seems likely that this hymn, a *Gloria in Excelsis Deo*, was written especially as the opening hymn of the new hymnal.

### The Hymnist

This discussion of Balthasar Hoffman as a hymnist is based on those hymns appearing in the 1762 hymnal, that is the final version of virtually all of his known hymns—except the *Epistel Lieder*. A comparison between the versions of hymns in the 1728 manuscript and the 1762 print reveal only small, insignificant variations.[15] The thirty-eight hymns forming the basis of this discussion are well representative of the hymnist's skill, since they span the entire range of his productive years and all the topics treated.

### Form

Hoffman's hymns range in length from 2 to 35 stanzas; from 12 to 272 lines. He seems to have preferred 4 and 6 line stanzas, for slightly more than half of these hymns consist either of 4 or 6 line stanzas. He employed the 2 and 14 line stanzas least frequently, there being just one each. In general, the metrical patterns tend to be iambic or trochaic.

Rhyme patterns vary. All 2 and 4 line stanzas consist of only couplets; 6 line stanzas reveal 5 different patterns (ABBACC, ABABCC, ABABCD, AABBCC, AABCCB); 7 line stanzas have three different patterns (AABBCCC, ABABCCD, ABABCCC); the 8 line stanza falls into two patterns (AABBC-CDD and ABABCDCD), while the 9 line stanza has two patterns (ABABDDCD and ABCABCDDD). The 14 line stanza has the pattern ABABCDCDEEEFFF. (See Appendix B)

By today's standards many of Hoffman's rhymes are impure or dialectical. In accented monosyllabic words and suffixes, the high fronted vowels and diphthongs blend together. For example, he rhymes *giebt* with *ubt* (310,4)[16] and *Leid* with *Freud* (319,21). With *Heil* he rhymes *Will* (320,30), *-theil* (320,32), *Seel* (319,30); he also rhymes *Seel* with *Höll* (319,4). Impure back vowels are less frequent; nevertheless, examples are *voll:Schul* (253,1) and *Gott:Rath* (383,6), *Sohn:thun* (309,10). Final consonants of monosyllabic words, especially labials and dentals often form impure rhymes, for example, *Haus:auf* (320,26), *Grab:schwach* (320,25) *grab:hat* (320,24), and *Gab:nach* (309,16). Consonants in final, unaccented syllables are rhymed occasionally with vowels, for example, *gespeiset:Weise* (320,22) and *bleibet:Leibe* (320,21).

In disyllabics the same sort of impure rhyme occurs, for example, *Sünden:finden* (303,4), *versöhnt:verdient* (310,3), *verkehrt:verhört* (309,8), and *Zierde:Ehre* (1,6). Occasionally long vowels are rhymed with short vowels, for example, *nennen:nehmen* (320,12). He also rhymes the old forms *han* and *lan* for *haben* and *lassen* (383,13) and *gahn:an* (458,11).

Intrinsically tied to the metrical patterns are the hymn tunes. With only one exception, tune names accompany all of Hoffman's hymns in the 1762 hymnal. Most of these tunes are listed in the reference works by Zahn and Tucher. Cursory investigation of these tune names reveals that nearly all of them come from the German hymnals for the Bohemian Brethren edited by Michael Weiss (1531) and Johann Horn (1544) as well as the hymn book of 1566.[17] Not found listed in any reference work are the tunes: 'O tieffe Demuth,' 'Tröst dich Gott,' 'Ach O Mensch,' and 'O Welt ich bin dein Müde.' These tune names, however, do appear as the first lines of hymn texts in the 1762 hymnal. The tunes for these texts are well known. The tune name 'Ach O Mensch' is a curious one because that is the opening line of a hymn by Hoffman. For the thirty-seven hymns bearing tune names, thirty-five of them bear a distinctive tune name. Only the tunes 'O Welt ich bin dein Müde' and 'Jesu Christ' are repeated once each. Usually the same tune name for a hymn appears in both the 1728 manuscript and the 1762 hymnal, but the tune cited for 'Ach O Mensch' in the 1728 manuscript is 'Niemand darf mich jetzt verdencken,' and in the 1762 hymnal 'O du Liebe meiner' is cited. 'Hertzliebster Jesu' is the tune cited in the 1728 manuscript for 'Wolt O Gott,' but 'O tieffe Demuth' is listed in the 1762 edition. I can also note that no hymn text is crowned with 'eigene Melodei.' Silesian Schwenkfelder hymnists, especially Hoffman, do not appear to have composed fresh tunes for their hymn texts, but to have relied upon familiar ones handed down from generation to generation. Virtually all of the tunes cited for Hoffman's hymns in the 1762 hymnal can be traced to the German hymnals of the Bohemian Brethren. (See Appendix A).

## Thematics

For years George Weiss was unhappy with the sequential order of the hymns in the 1709 hymnal. They were not arranged thematically, but chronologically for the ecclesiastical year. Consequently, the hymnal was copied again in 1733, and the hymns were placed in order for each Sunday and holy day with subdivisions for morning, forenoon, afternoon, and catechization, and then again in metrical order. Even this double ordering of the hymns was not totally satisfying, and in 1758/59 the hymnal was copied afresh with a new, thematical order. The editor(s) of the 1762 hymnal modified the categories and resequenced the hymns once more. Hence the 'newly-arranged' or 'newly-sequenced' hymnal. Thematically the 1762 hymnal is divided into two major parts (Theil): The first is called 'On the Divine Being' and the second is called 'On the Dispensation and Reign of God.' These two parts are further divided into groups or categories, and many of these categories are even subdivided. Of Hoffman's thirty-eight hymns, two were placed in the First Part and the remainder were scattered among fifteen other categories and subcategories.

Hoffman's hymns were distributed among seventeen different categories: On God and His Essence, On the Knowledge of Christ, On the Fall of Mankind, On the Nature and Essence of Faith, The Power and Fruits of Faith, The Path to Heaven, The Revelation and Realization of God's Counsel, Repentence, Prayer, Christian Life, Preparation for Worship, The Apostles and other Servants of the Church, Baptism, Communion, Authority, Marriage, Burial, Morning, and Evening Hymns. (See Appendix C).

As we read and reread Hoffman's hymns, however, we soon have a sense of the reoccurring themes in his songs. There seems to be only one major thematic thread woven throughout his hymns: Salvation. However, the hymns are not songs about his own salvation. His hymns are not personal confessions, 'I' centered exuberances about a mystical, personal interaction with God. They are dominated with 'we' and 'us,' revealing a deep and sincere concern for the salvation of all. The other themes appearing in his hymns are directly connected to those attitudes and actions which he felt were most vital for salvation. Among these themes are 'telling the story,' the fall of humanity and sinful nature, Christ's sacrifice for humanity, faith, humility, repentence, contrition, and self denial.

## Moods

Whereas 'salvation' is the thematic cornerstone of Hoffman's hymns, his means of expressing his theme are actually twofold. Either he prays to God or he admonishes his fellows.

The small index finger at the last stanza or two of most of the hymns in the 1762 hymnal directs the reader to a prayerful conclusion of the hymn. Several of Hoffman's hymns (253, 374, 383, 571, 572, 573, 579 581, 710, 855) are written in a prayerful mood or tone, in which he asks for divine forgiveness, consolation, mercy, blessing, and grace. He pleas for desire and strength to achieve righteousness and salvation. Hymn 383, dated 1723, is just such a prayer. It opens with the words:

O Gott! wir kommen jetzt zu Dir
mit Bitten und mit Flehen :/:
Erweck in uns Ernst und Begier
dass's recht von Hertzen gehe:
den Geist der Gnad und des Gebäts
gieb uns dass wir recht können
vor Dir bringen
unser Noth und dass stets,
wir hertzlich mögen singen.

Continuing, Hoffman prays in this hymn for God's uplifting of the oppressed and the imprisoned, his revelation of the truth and exposure of heresy. He prays for the spread of the gospel to all peoples and for the destruction of those who seek to cloud the knowledge of God. He asks for strength and determination to shed the old person and put on the new. He pleas for guidance from the Holy Spirit and expresses the desire to obey like children and to become brothers and sisters in Christ.

In direct contrast with the prayerful hymns are those in which he vigorously admonishes his fellow human beings. Hymn 310 opens with words echoed in many others (that is 303, 320, 350, 352, 353, 354, 355, 458, 588, 589, 618, and 627), 'O Christen=Mensch! mit Fleiss/ bedenck den Weg zu deinem Heil.' Hymn 350 (1727) stresses the necessity of repentence as a prerequisite for salvation. Hymn 458 (1723) lists stanza by stanza what one must do for the sake of salvation: practising self denial and virtue, fixing one's eyes on Heaven, spreading the gospel, despising all worldly things and pleasures.

## Scripture

A scriptural passage is quite often the inspiration for a hymn, and many hymnals today cite the scriptural source(s) for most of their contents.

For Schwenkfelder hymnists scripture was obviously a source of inspiration, too. On every page of the 1762 hymnal scripture references abound. Following most stanzas is a reference to the scriptural chapter and verse which is associated with the stanza, or even individual lines of the stanza.

Hoffman's hymns in the 1762 hymnal contain 432 references to chapter and verse in 47 books of the Bible. Hymn 253 is made up entirely of lines, for each of which there is a different scriptural reference. Hymn 319 has scriptural reference for nearly every line while hymns 458, 705, 709, 710, 755 each have a scriptural reference for every or nearly every stanza. Fifty percent of Hoffman's thirty-eight hymns have at least one scriptural reference in more than half of the stanzas, yet hymns 579, 581, 792, 854, 855, 856 have no scriptural references at all. Only a handful of his hymns indicate that the entire hymn is based on scripture. Hymn 578 is concerned with 1 Corinthians 1:4 and number 580 treats 1 Kings 8:16. There is also the series of six hymns on Hebrews. Each hymn is divided into two parts, and each part treats a separated chapter of Hebrews. Unlike many hymnists of the age, Hoffman did not write versions of the Psalms.

A closer investigation of these scriptural references reveals that these references, even for individual lines, are very rarely quotations. Examining the first line of hymn 253 reveals that its scriptural reference is but a partial quotation. This line reads: 'Schönster Jesu! König der Ehren'; the biblical reference reads: 'Wer ist derselbe König der Ehren? Es ist der Herr Zebaoth, Er ist der König der Ehren.' (Ps. 24,10). The next line reads: 'Wer zu Dir kommt, den wilst Du lehren.' Its reference states: 'Kommt her, Kinder, höret mir zu; ich will euch die Furcht des Herrn lehren.' (Ps. 34,12). Although there is a relationship between the hymn line and the reference, it is certainly not stated directly. The next line reads: 'Denn Du bist Geists und Weissheit voll,' whereas the scriptural reference states: 'Auf welchem wird ruhen der Geist des HErrn, der Geist der Weisheit und des Verstandes, der Geist des Raths und der Stärke, der Geist der Erkenntniss und der Furcht des HErrn. (Isaiah 11,2). Line 9 of this hymn implores: 'Las mich willig, Dir gefällig,' and the reference proclaims: 'Die nun sein Worte gerne annahmen, liessen sich taufen; und wurden hinzugethan an dem Tag bei drei tausend Seelen.' (Acts 2,41). These extremes from partial quotation to paraphrase to interpretative circumlocution are common to the scriptural references in Hoffman's hymns. Indeed, there are very few direct scriptural quotations.

To what extent are these scriptural references an intrinsic, inseparable part of the fabric and texture of the hymn? Comparing the 1728 edition with the 1762 edition reveals that hymns 374, 303, 320, 383, 458 plus 'O Jesu Christ du Gottes Lamm' and 'O Gott du Schöpffer aller Welt' are totally devoid of any scriptural references in the 1728 edition whereas there are several references in these hymns in the 1762 edition. The only hymn in both editions for which there are scriptural references is number 319, 'Treulich O Mensch,' yet close examination reveals that these references in the two editions do not necessarily coincide. In the 1728 edition, the references for the fourth stanza are: John 15:14; ben Sirach 17:30; Galatians 5:17; Genesis 3:10, 3:19; Romans 5:12; and Wisdom 1:3. In the 1762 edition Job (John) 15:14; Genesis 3:11; 3:19; and Wisdom 1:3 are noted. We can likewise note that the 1760 edition of hymn 458, 'Mensch! gedencke allezeit' has no scriptural references, yet there is a reference after every stanza (excepting the first) in the 1762 version.

Such evidence would suggest that scriptural references in these hymns are mainly the result of the editor's pen. In the preface of the 1762 hymnal Christopher Schultz informs the reader that one goal of that publication is to instruct. Indeed, anyone who read the hymn, looked up the references, and contemplated the significance of them for his or her life would be well edified.

Today it is difficult to ascertain when Hoffman's keen interest in Schwenkfelder hymnology and hymn writing was aroused. In the preface to his 1753 hymnal revision of the 1709 Weiss hymnal, Hoffman recalled copying the hymnal in 1709. This is his earliest involvement in Schwenkfelder hymnology, as far as is known. His association with the Weiss family in the production of this hymn collection may have been that inspiration which led him to write hymns. Certainly, the hymn writing activities of George Weiss, his boyhood friend and constant companion of the same age, made an impression on him. And perhaps it was at the urging of George, who often served as his mentor, that Hoffman tried his hand at hymn writing. We have noted that his hymn writing was sporadic. Eighty-five percent of his total output was written in the six year span between 1722 and 1728. Whereas the earlier hymns may have been inspired by his study of the scriptures at a time of relative

idleness in Vienna, his later hymns seem to be an endeavor to
fulfill a need. So, too, the unwaivering repetitive theme of salvation seems to reflect more a desire to proclaim the message
of the Christ than the fruit of being touched by the Holy Spirit.
Schwenkfelders today can be most proud of this modest spiritual leader and pioneer, who worked so diligently to preserve
and perpetuate the hymnological traditions of his faith.

## Notes

[1] J. H. Dubbs, 'Early German Hymnology of Pennsylvania,' *Reformed Quarterly Review* (1882), 584-610.

[2] William A. Haussmann, 'German-American Hymnology, 1683-1800,' *Americana Germanica*, 2 (1898).

[3] John Joseph Stoudt, Introduction to 'Pennsylvania German Poetry, 1685-1830,' *The Pennsylvania German Folklore Society*, 20 (1955), lxxx-lxxxv.

[4] Allen Anders Seipt, *Schwenkfelder Hymnology and The Sources of the First Schwenkfelder Hymn Book Printed in America* (Philadelphia, 1909).

[5] Andrew S. Berky, *Practitioner in Physick: A Biography of Abraham Wagner, 1717-1763* (Pennsburg, 1954), 120-51.

[6] Elmer S. Gerhard, 'Balthasar Hoffman (1687-1775) Scholar, Minister, Writer, Diplomat,' *Schwenkfeldiana* 1 (1941), 2, 35-52. Gerhard states there were 109 'Epistel=Lieder,' when there are actually just 101.

[7] Peter C. Erb, *The Spiritual Diary of Christopher Wiegner*, (Pennsburg, Pennsylvania, 1978), 156, n. 7.

[8] Andrew S. Berky (ed.), *The Journals and Papers of David Schultze* (Pennsburg, 1952), 1: 62-67.

[9] Ibid., Vol. 1, 67, states that David Schultz authored three poems, one each in 1743, 1750, and 1783. The 1743 hymn, 'Weil deine Stund ist kommen,' is reproduced on pages 112-16. In his later publication *Practitioner in Physick*, Berky (30) attributes this same hymn to Abraham Wagner, saying that the earlier attribution to Schultz was erroneous. The hymn written on the occasion of the murder of Schultz' wife Anna Rosina on June 14, 1750, is reprinted on pages 112-16. Berky does not seem to reprint the 1783 hymn.

[10] John Joseph Stoudt, 'Pennsylvania German Poetry, 1685-1830,' cites two poems he attributes to Hans Heebner: 'Was ist es dann geliebter Sohn" (163-64) and 'Geliebten Eltern seyd zufriden,' 165-68.

[11] Seipt gives a more detailed account of the development of the 1762 *Neu=Eingerichtetes Gesang=Buch*.

[12] Selina Gerhard Schultz, 'The First One Hundred Schwenkfelder Memorial Days, 1734-1834. Part I, 1734-1784,' *Schwenkfeldiana*, 2/3 (1952), 11, 13, 14.

[13] Berky, *Practitioner*, 52.

[14] Ibid., 122.

[15] The following variations occur in hymn 320, Ach, O Mensch! Erweg im Hertzen:

| Stanza | 1728 | 1762 |
|---|---|---|
| 1 | Dass nicht du … | Dass du nicht |
| 4 | kaum zu ergrü… | nicht zu er- |
| 5 | Auch wenn alles | Da denn alles |
| 6 | treu seyn soll | treu seyn solt |
| 8 | O jetzt hör | Aber hör |
| 11 | Eyland wird | Bald wird |
|  | welcher den Tod | der den Tod |
| 13 | Aber diss Fleisch hat must kommen | |
|  | Dis Fleisch aber muste kommen | |
| 17 | Aber bald die Zeit | Die Zeit aber bald |
| 20 | Er nimt darnach | Darnach nimt Er |
| 23 | Und giebt sich | Giebt sich |
| 24 | Endlich wird | Wird zuletzt |
| 27 | darnach thut | darnach wolt |
| 29 | Ohne diss giebet noch | Giebt auch noch. |

[16] The first number is the hymn number in the 1762 hymnal; the second number is the stanza.

[17] A listing of the tune names is found in Appendix A.

## Appendix A: Hymns with Melodies by Balthasar Hoffman in Chronological Order

| Date | Total | First Line/ Tune (Z=Zahn, T=Tucher) |
|---|---|---|
|  | 1 | O Jesu Christ du Gottes Lamm (VA4-10) |
|  |  | Erbarm Dich mein O Herre Gott (T345*) |
| 1722 | 2 | GNädiger HErre GOtt! 374 |
|  |  | O Herre Jesu=Christ (Z5088a) |
|  |  | O Gott du Schöpffer aller Welt (VA4-10) |
|  |  | Auf, Christen=Menschen, auf zum (T183) |
|  |  | Mir nach spricht Christus unser Held (T183) |
| 1723 | 5 | WOlt GOtt, du thätst, O Mensch! 303 |
|  |  | O tieffe Demuth |
|  |  | Hertzliebster Jesu, was hast du |
|  |  | ACh, O Mensch! Erweg im Hertzen 320 |
|  |  | O du Liebe meiner Liebe (Z6694) |
|  |  | Niemand darff mir jetzt verdencken |
|  |  | O GOtt! Wir kommen jetzt zu Dir 383 |
|  |  | Ich ruff zu Dir, Herr Jesu Christ (Z7400 T342) |
|  |  | Ach O Mensch (1st Line of Hymn by Hoffman) |
|  |  | MEnsch! gedencke allezeit 458 |

Wie der Hirsch in Mattigkeit (Z1237)

Heiliger ewiger Gott ohn Anfang (VA4-10)
Mein Hertz tichtet ein Lied (T436)

1725   1   FReulich, O MEnsch! Und fleissig 319

1726   101   Epistel-Lieder (SWP)

1727   7   O Mensch! Nimm wohl in acht 350
O Gott erbarm dich (Z4241)

ACh ihr Menschen! in dieser gnadreichen Zeit 351
Danck'n wir Gott dem (Z1435)

O Mensch! Du armer Erdenkloss 352
Allmächtiger ewig Gott (Z338 T235)

O Mensch! Wollest recht bedencken 353
Ein starcker Held ist (Z1614a)

O Mensch! Bedenck in dieser deiner letzten Zeit 354
Ach unser Vater der du bist im Himmelreich (Z8305)

MEnsch! der du gern wolt'st selig seyn 355
Tröst dich Gott

Gott unsers Lebens Anfang und Ernährer

1728   3   WEil ausgeruhet hat der Leib 792
Von Adam her so lange (Z307 T99*)

ALler Ding Schöpffer, HERR un GOtt! 854
Wer Gottes Diener werden will (Z321 T75)

JEsu! Du Erlöser der Welt 855
O Jesu Christ Gottes Sohn (Z340a T69)

1738   8   Schönster JEsu! 253
Heiligster Jesu (Z8408)

ACh GOtt! Vater Deiner lieben Kinder 571
Ach wie gross ist Gottes Güt u Wohlthat (Z1581 T17)

LAsst uns nun zum HErren wenden 572
JEsu! Der du meine Seele (Z6767)

So wir denn, uns zu erbauen 573
Ach O Mensch (1st Line of Hymn by Hoffman)

Nu lasst uns GOtte loben 578
O Welt ich bin dein Müde

O GOtt! Du bist aller Menschen Erschaffer 579
DAncket dem Herrn, denn er ist (Z12 T4)

JEsu! Der nach Creutz und Siegen 580
Jesu meine Freud und Lust (Z3783)

Fur Deine Gnad, HErr JEsu CHriste! 581
Heilig und zart ist Christi Menschheit (Z8515 T450)

1761   6   ALs JEsus auferstanden war 617

VAter unser im Himmelreich, der du (Z2561 T204*)

O Christen=Mensch! DIch übe 618
O Welt! Ich muss dich (Z2293a)

NAchdem JEsus Sein'n Lauff vollendt 626
Komt her zu mir spricht Gottes Sohn (Z2496a T187)

Merck auf, O Du frommer Christ 627
Jesus meine Zuversicht (Z3432)

Du Oberheit! bestellt von GOtt 705
Komt her zu mir spricht Gottes Sohn (Z2496a T187)

O GOtt! DU lieb ohn Ende 755
O Welt ich bin d

1762   8    Gebenedeyt sey allezeit 1
Allein Gott in der Hoh (Z4457 T239*)

GOtt wir loben deine Güt 309
Nun komm der Heiden Heiland (Z1174 T119*)

O CHristen=Mensch! Mit Fleiss bedenck 310
Du Friedens=Fürst (Z4373 T229*)

O CHristen=Mensch! Merck fleissig auf 588
Es ist das Heil uns kommen her (Z4430 T249*)

MEin lieber Christ! thu Acht drauf haben 589
Wer nur den lieben GOtt (Z2778)

JEsus CHristus, MEnsch und GOtt 628
Christus der uns selig macht (Z6283a T356)

LAsst uns nun singen allesam 709
Singt frölich und seyd wohlgemuth (Z4972 T461)

DIr GOtt! Zu Lob, Preiss und Ehren 710
Zeuch mich, zeuch mich mit den Armen (Z3747).

## Appendix B: Meter and Rhyme in the Hymns by Balthasar Hoffman in the 1762 Hymnal

*2 Lines*
11.11.                    (579)                    aa

*4 Lines*
7.7. 7.7.                 (309, 458)               aabb
8.7. 9.9.                 (353)
8.8. 8.8.                 (352, 792, 854, 855, 856)
10.10. 6.10.             (571)
10.10 14.14              (319)
11.11. 11.5.             (303)
11.11. 10.10.            (351)

*6 Lines*
8.7.7 8.7.7.             (580)                    abbacc

| | | |
|---|---|---|
| 7.8. 7.8. 7.7. | (627) | ababcc |
| 8.6 8.6 8.7. | (310) | ababcd |
| 8.7. 8.7. 8.8. | (710) | ababcc |
| 8.8. 8.8. 8.8. | (617) | aabbcc |
| 9.8. 9.8. 8.8. | (589) | ababcc |
| 7.7.6. 7.7.8. | (618, 578, 580, 755) | aabccb |
| 8.8.7. 8.8.7. | (626, 705) | aabccb |

*7 Lines*

| | | |
|---|---|---|
| 6.6. 7.7. 8.8.8. | (350) | aabbccc |
| 8.6. 8.6. 4.4.7. | (355) | ababccd |
| 8.7. 8.7. 8.8.7. | (1, 588) | ababccd |
| 12.15. 12.15. 15.15.15 | (354) | ababccc |

*8 Lines*

| | | |
|---|---|---|
| 6.6. 6.6. 6.6. 8.8. | (374) | aabbccdd |
| 7.6. 7.6. 7.6. 7.6. | (628) | ababcdcd |
| 8.7. 8.7. 8.7. 8.7. | (320, 573) | ababcdcd |
| 8.7. 8.7. 8.8. 7.7. | (572) | ababccdd |

*9 Lines*

| | | |
|---|---|---|
| 8.7. 8.7. 8.7. 4.6.7. | (383) | ababcddcd |
| 8.4.7. 8.4.7. 7.7.10. | (709) | abcabcddd |

*10 lines*

| | | |
|---|---|---|
| 9.9.8. 9.9.8. 6.10.8.8. | (253) | aabccbdeff |

*14 Lines*

| | | |
|---|---|---|
| 4.5.4.7. 4.5.4.7. | (581) | ababcdcdeeefff |
| 4.8.8 5.5.9 | | |

## Appendix C: Hymns by Balthasar Hoffman in the 1762 Hymnal

ERSTERTHEIL

Vom Göttlichen Wesen und Seiner Offenbahrung

durch CHristum im

Heiligen Geiste

I. Von GOTT und Seinem Wesen.

　1. Abtheilung: Vom Ewigen, Einigen Göttlichen Wesen, so
　　sich in Dreyheit offenbahret hat.

　Nr. 1. Gebenedeyt sey allezeit, 1762

XV. Vom Erkäntnis CHristi.

　JEsus CHristus eine Rose und Lilie nach Seinen
　zweyen Ständen.
　Nr. 253. SChönster JEsu!, 1738

ANDERTHEIL

Von der Oeconomie oder Offenbahrung GOttes.

im Wercke der Schöpffung, Regierung

Seiner Kirchen, und Führung

der Seinen, im Wercke der Gnaden.

III. Vom Fall des Menschen, Und Verderbung der gantzen
menschlichen Natur durch die Sünde: Sammt hertzlicher Klag
und seufszen darüber

Nr. 303. WOlt GOtt, du thätst, O Mensch!, 1723

V. Vom Glauben.

1. Abtheilung. Was eigentlich der Glaube sey; samt seiner
Würckung und Frucht im Menschen. Item: Einige
Bekäntnisse des Glaubens.

Von Ankunfft, Natur und Wesen des Glaubens.
Nr. 309. GOTT! wir loben deine Güt, 1762
Vom Nutzen, Würckung und Fruchtbarkeit des
Glaubens.
Nr. 310. O Christen=Mensch! Mit Fleiss bedenck,
1762.

2. Abtheilung. Von der Uibung des Glaubens in Christlicher
Lehre.

Innhalt vom Wege zum Himmelreich.
Nr. 319. FReulich, O Mensch! Und fleissig, 1725

Von Offenbahrung und Vollendung des Rathes GOttes
Nr. 320. ACh, O Mensch! Erweg im Hertzen, 1723

VI. Von wahrer Busse, oder Sinnes=Aenderung und Bekehrung zu GOTT

3. Abtheilung. Mancherley Ursachen, die zur Buss ermahnen
und reitzen sollen; genommen aus der Hebräer Epistel.

Nr. 350. O Mensch! Nimm wohl in acht, 1727

Nr. 351. ACh ihr Menschen! In dieser gnadreichen
Zeit, 1727

Nr. 352. O Mensch! Du armer Erdenkloss, 1727

Nr. 353. O Mensch! Wollest recht bedencken, 1727

Nr. 354. O Mensch! Bedenck in dieser deiner
letzten Zeit, 1727

Nr. 355. MEnsch! der du gern wolt'st selig seyn,
1727

VII. Vom Gebät

2. Abtheilung: Hält in sich mancherley Hertz=angelegene
Bitten, in allerley Anliegen

Aufmunterung zu rechtem Gebät
Nr. 374. GNädiger HErre GOtt!, 1722

Nr. 383. O GOtt! Wir kommen jetzt zu Dir, 1723

XII. Vom Christlichen Leben und Wandel.

    2. Abtheilung: Allerley Vermahnungen zu Christlichem
Leben, und Göttseligen Tugenden. 2. Bitten um ein
Christliches Leben. 3. Gedrohete Straffe über die, so
dem Evangelio ungehorsam sind.

Der Christen Schuldigkeit
Nr. 458. MEnsch! gedencke allezeit, 1723

XXI. Vom Worte GOTTES.

    2. Abtheilung: Begreifft Lieder: Worinnen um Aufschluss,
Anlegung, Seegen und Gedey desjenigen gebäten wird, so
beym GOttesdienst im Zeugnis geübet wird.

Nr. 571. ACH GOtt! Vater Deiner lieben Kinder!,
    1738

Nr. 572. LAsst uns nun zum HErren wenden, 1738

Nr. 573. So wir denn, uns zu erbauen, 1738

Nr. 578. NUn lasst uns GOtte loben, 1738

Nr. 579. O GOtt! Du bist aller Menschen
    Erschaffer, 1738

Nr. 580. JEsu! Der nach Creutz und Siegen, 1738

Nr. 581. Für Deine Gnad, HErr JEsu CHriste!, 1738

XXII. Von den Aposteln und Kirchen=Dienern. Von ihrem Beruff und
    Amte; item: Was für eine herrliche Wohlthat der Dienst sey;
    und wie man den HErren um treue Diener bitten soll.

Vom Dienst der Christlichen Kirchen, wem er
verordnet und was er in sich begreifft.

Nr. 588. O Christen=Menschen, Merck fleissig auf,
    1762

Was des Dienstes Gebrauch und Nutzen sey.
Nr. 589. MEin lieber Christ! thu Acht drauf
    haben, 1762

XXIV. Von den Einsetzungen CHristi und *erstlich*:

    Von der heiligen Tauffe.

    1. Abtheilung. Dass der HErr, Seinen Kindern zu gut,
symbolische Zeichen eingesetzt habe, in versamleter
Gemein zu gebrauchen: Damit die innerliche Wahrheit,
der geistlichen Reinigung und Speisung, herrlich
angezeigt und vorgestellet wird.

Von der Tauffe einsetzung, Grund und herkommen.
Nr. 617. ALs JEsus auferstanden war, 1761

Von der Tauffe Wahrheit, Gebrauch und
Unterscheidung
Nr. 618. O Christen=Mensch! Dich übe, 1761

*Zum Andern*

Vom Heiligen Abendmahl

1. Abtheilung. Hält in sich: Wenn? Warum? Worzu? und wehm? Es eingesetzt; dass durch unwürdige Geniessung sich das Gerichte aufgeladen wird: Und wie es die Christ=gläubigen herrlich begehen.

Von Abendmahl, dessen Einsetzung, Grund und Herkommen

Nr. 626. NAchdem JEsus Sein'n Lauff vollendt, 1761

Von der Wahrheit, Gebrauch und Unterscheidung des Abendmahls.

Nr. 627. Merck auf, O Du frommer Christ, 1761

Ein ander Bekäntnis=Lied

Nr. 628. JEsus CHristus, MEnsch und GOtt, 1762

XXIX. Von der Oberkeit Und ihrem Amte im weltlichen Regiment, samt der Pflicht der Unterthanen.

Nr. 705. Du Oberheit! bestellt von GOtt, 1761

XXX. Vom Ehestande. Und von der Kinder = Zucht.

Nr. 709. LAsst uns nun singen allesam, 1762

Nr. 710. DIr GOtt! Zu Lob, Preiss und Ehren, 1762

XXXII. Beym Begräbnis

2. Abtheilung. Bey dem Grabe.

Beym Begräbnis der Kinder

Der Tod kömt durch die Sünd, ergreifft offt kleine Kind

Nr. 755. O GOtt! Du Lieb ohn Ende, 1761

XXXV. Vom ewigen Leben. Zeugnis, wie CHristus Seine Gemein zu Seiner Gloria einführen = und ewiger Freude gewähren wird, und sie sich in GOtt ewig erfreuen und jubilieren werde.

*Morgen = Lieder*

2. Abtheilung: Zum Aufstehen bey angehendem Tage. Da um den Schutz durch die Nacht GOtte hertzlich gedanckt, und bey aufgehendem zeitlichen Lichte sich GOttes, als des wahren ewigen Lichtes, erinnert wird; und innerer Erleuchtung, Ihm hertzlich anbefohlen, und um ein Christliches Leben gebeten wird.

Nr. 792. WEil ausgeruhet hat der Leib, 1728

*Abend = Lieder*

Nr. 854. ALler Ding Schöpffer, HERR und GOtt!, 1728

Nr. 855. JEsu! Du Erlöser der Welt, 1728

Nr. 856. DIch Der du warst vor's Himmels Zier, 1728

## Appendix D: Hymns by American Schwenkfelders in the 1762 Hymnal according to Christoph Hoffman

Balthasar Hoffman (38 Hymns) 1, 253, 303, 309, 310, 319, 320, 350, 351, 352, 353, 354, 355, 374, 383, 458, 571, 572, 573, 578, 579, 580, 581, 588, 589 (489), 617, 618, 626, 627, 628, 705, 709, 710, 755, 792, 854, 855, 856

Caspar Kriebel (6 Hymns) 234, 311, 619, 623, 629, 717

Christopher Kriebel (8 Hymns) 492, 714, 715, 716, 743, 745, 746, 747

Christopher Schultz (7 Hymns) 157, 312, 360, 380, 469, 590, 744

David Seipt (1 Hymn) 673

Abraham Wagner (34 Hymns) 7, 10, 13, 96, 109, 139, 173, 191, 281, 293, 365, 457, 463, 478, 495, 711, 733, 742, 751, 754, 756, 763, 787, 789, 800, 801, 802, 821, 822, 826, 832, 833, 845, 850

George Weiss (27 Hymns) 3, 36, 37, 221, 222, 240, 246, 247, 248, 252, 321, 422, 423, 468, 473, 486, 509, 532, 592, 600, 601, 602, 603, 712, 713, 722, 777

(121 Hymns)

## Other Listings

Kriebel (1904), 196-197
  Erroneous attributions:
      Caspar Kriebel 326
      Christoph Kriebel 742
      Abraham Wagner 6, 14, 283, 847
Typescript 'Authorship of the hymns... (Schwenkfelder Library, n.d.)
  Erroneous attributions:
      Caspar Kriebel 326
      Balthasar Hoffman 489, 636
      Abraham Wagner 6, 847
Berky (1954), 165-167 (Wagner only)
  hymn 763 is not listed
  hymns 6, 41, 107, 706 are not attributed to anyone

# The Krauss
# Organ Builders

## Thomas S. Eader

The subject of this paper is the Krauss family of organ builders. There were four members of this family with whom we are particularly concerned, although some other family members helped. The four principal builders were: the brothers Andrew (1771-1841) and John (1770-1819), Andrew's son George, (1803-1880), and George's son, Edwin (1838-1929). The organs constructed over a period of more than a hundred years (perhaps as many as one per year) illustrate only a segment of the family's considerable skill in many areas.

The first of the organ builders, John and Andrew, were great-grandsons of Melchior and Anna Heydrich Krauss both of whom were born and raised in Silesia. On route to Pennsylvania Melchior died in Haarlem, but his wife and children continued on with five others, arriving in Pennsylvania on September 28, 1733. The entire group consisted of eleven immigrants, known as the second Schwenkfelder migration. The oldest of the Krauss children, Balzer, was born in Harpersdorf, Silesia in 1706 and in 1736 married Susanna Hoffman who had arrived in Pennsylvania in the third Schwenkfelder migration. Balzer acquired a 200 acre tract of land known as Kraussdale. This land passed from father to son for six generations. Balzer and Susanna's son was also named Balzer or Balthasar and was the father of the first organbuilders, John and Andrew. Their grandfather was still living in 1770 when John was born in the log house known as 'the Palace' because it was more spacious with its second floor than was the usual settler's cabin.

John and Andrew's father served in the Revolutionary War, probably as a teamster with the army wagon trains. No doubt at an early age his sons learned to be useful helpers on the farm, but after a day's toil, recreation could be had in the singing of hymns, pitched from a tuning fork brought from

Silesia. There were also books, pens, and paper in the house, and part of the youthful training was to learn how to read, write, and spell by copying books. The boys attended the Schwenkfelder school, begun in 1764, and in 1790 at age 20 John Krauss was admitted to the Hosensack Academy. In 1792 he attended school at Chestnut Hill, Philadelphia, specializing in languages (German, Latin, and English), mathematics (algebra, mensuration), surveying, astronomy, and navigation, as his notebooks in the Schwenkfelder Library Collection show. His access to Philadelphia broadened his mind. He apparently was always using his leisure for reading, evidence of a keen mind and a hunger for learning.

In 1794 John was engaged as a teacher at the Hosensack School and was reappointed in 1795. From this period there exists the fragment of a Psalmody, apparently his work, for use by a Choral Society. Its purpose was the cultivation of the singing of sacred music, hymn tunes, and German chorales, of which the Schwenkfelders had fine collections. Singing in worship was done without instrumental assistance. Later, about 1820, this singing organization was followed by a Choral Union. Among its members were one son and three daughters of John Krauss, three sons and two daughters of Andrew Krauss, one son of George Krauss, and four sons and one daughter of Jacob Gerhard whose wife was Helena Krauss, a sister of John, Andrew, and George.

During their schooling (c.1790) John and Andrew, with the help of their father Balthasar, planned and built a small organ. Their interest in organs at this time is documented by the inclusion in their papers of the dedication program on October 10, 1790 for David Tannenberg's largest organ at Zion Lutheran Church in Philadelphia.

Around 1791 the Krausses formed the Kraussdale Literary Society, the constitution of which is in the Library's collections. It is in English, and one of the articles states that 'no body shall talke German except he is in want of English expression, then he may ask for the word in German.' The Krauss boys asked the Rev. F. W. Geisenheimer, pastor of St. Paul's Lutheran Church (known then as the Six Cornered Church) Red Hill, to join their association. He did so, and they became close friends. This pastor was exceedingly fond of organ music and encouraged this interest in them. It is highly likely that through his

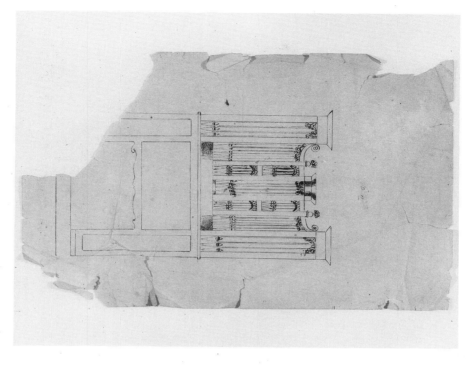

Elaborate chamber organ design. Attributed to Andrew Krauss.

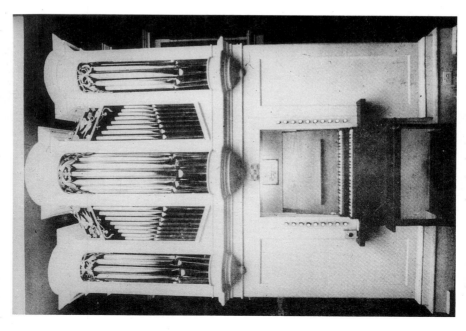

1799 organ at the Catholic Church, Bally.

influence he was able to procure for them the first order for a church organ in 1796—Long Swamp Union Lutheran and Reformed Church, Berk's County, Pa., about twenty miles from their home. About this time, because of the Schwenkfelders' opposition to the use of the organ in worship, the Krausses became members of St. Paul's Lutheran Church, Red Hill.

At the close of the eighteenth century a large portion of the Germanic settlers in Pennsylvania were familiar with church organs from their experience in their homeland. Thus, many congregations with some exceptions (Schwenkfelders, for instance, who did not admit instrumental accompaniment to singing until 1882) were anxious to obtain such instruments, thought of as both luxuries and necessities. Pennsylvania, therefore, became one of the first colonies to offer fertile ground for several organbuilders and even families who continued earlier German traditions and methods of construction.

In 1750 there had been an organ imported from Germany for the Lutheran Church at Trappe, Pa. Quite close to the Krauss home a Tannenberg organ had been installed in the Reformed Church in New Goshenhoppen (near East Greenville) in 1769. There were Tannenberg organs in the Lutheran Church at Maxatawny in 1768 (only a few miles from Palm) and others in Egypt, Easton, and Allentown. Zion Lutheran in Spring City had one in 1790 and became known far and wide as 'the organ church.' In Philadelphia other organs by Tannenberg and by Philip Feyring existed.

The Krausses heard the 1790 Tannenberg at Zion Lutheran in Philadelphia, and the 1798 Tannenberg in the Lutheran and Reformed Church, Tohickon Bucks County; John's diary records that on February 19, 1798 'I, Andrew, and Andrew Yeakle went to the church near Tohickon where we took a view of that organ.' Another entry in the diary for 1802 states, 'I and Andrew been to New Hanover to a consecration of a new organ, spent nothing.'

It must be assumed that Andrew, if not as well schooled as John (the records are not as numerable for documenting his life), was just as talented and quite knowledgeable, having been in his brother's company so much. Whatever their skill or training in organ building (and it is much to be regretted that there is so little known of this), they continued to build commercially with the first for Wentz's Church, Worcester, Montgomery County, in 1796. John's diary for November 2, 1796 states: 'I went to Worcester to set up the new organ in the Calvinist Church and did work till the 12th. Nov. 17: I went the second time to Worcester for finishing our work. The consecration of said organ was held on the 26th Sunday of the Holy Trinity by the Rev. Mister Helfenstein, and we received the sum of 54 pounds being part of 170 pounds.' By February of 1797 Andrew and John were building another organ for Longswamp Church in Berks County, and by June they had a contract for an organ at the Catholic Church in Bally at a cost of 175 pounds, due in three installments.

The resemblance to Tannenberg's organs was remarkable, and the few bits of later internal work still existing—chests, pipes, etc.—indicate the strong influence of Tannenberg. This can be explained by the fact that David Tannenberg, Jr. was in the employ of the Krauss brothers in 1798 and 1799 assisting in the work at Longswamp and Bally. Their observations during their travels, the construction of the small organ with the help of their father, and this direct connection with a master builder give us a glimpse of their determination. However, the most critical matter of all the skilled requirements necessary in the building of a tonally successful organ is the relationship between pipes not only within one stop, but between one stop and another, since the tone of an organ is a complex but concordant sounding together of many pipes. To achieve balance between bass and treble and between one stop and another has been the aim of builders for centuries. There are many different ways to accomplish this tonal personality which each organ finally possesses, but satisfactory tone cannot be achieved by consistently halving both the diameter and the length of a pipe. In other words, if a 2 foot long pipe has a chosen diamenter of 2 inches, the pipe in the same stop one octave higher must be 1 foot long, but its diameter cannot be 1 inch; it must be somewhat larger. These relationships are termed scaling, and must be carefully planned, and the pieces of wood or metal from which the pipes are made cut accordingly. The mathematical background of John Krauss was a great help in dealing with such problems.

Many contracts followed the first ones which the Krausses received. Most were for Lutheran or Reformed churches.

There were sometimes small house organs, like the one in the
Schwenkfelder Library.  Many contracts for organs built by
John and Andrew exist in the Library's collection (at least
18).  They are all in German, and often list the stops to be
contained and mention matters of payment.  In one case (for
the Reformed Church, Richmond, Berks County, 1838), the reverse page is a two diagram plan for the case, one slightly more
elaborate than the other.

All Krauss contracts in the Schwenkfelder Library are for
rural Pennsylvania churches, except one for St. Michael and
Zion Lutheran (Old Mother Churches) in Philadelphia, 1814.
At this time, the soft, lovely, unassertive tone, which the
Krauss apparently produced (I remember the tone of the Bally
organ before its recent rebuilding—soft and exquisite, not full
sounding—) would have been considered fashionable, even in
forward-looking Philadelphia, but soon a much bolder tone became the ideal.  To such changes in taste the Krausses did
not cater.  When the 1814 Krauss organ at St. Michael's in
Philadelphia was finally replaced in 1895, it was stated in an
anniversary booklet that the organ was too weak to support
congregation singing and that simple repairs could not solve
the problem.

However, many churches used these fine sounding, if not
loud, organs for many years.  The diary of John often records
the purchase of quality materials in Philadelphia for use in the
building of organs—tin and lead for pipes, spring wire, ivory,
varnish, and also piano strings and a tuning hammer in 1797
for completing a piano he sold on October 7.  Six days later he
constructed a coffin for Balzer Yeakle.

In May 1795, John married Rosina Yeakle.  They had nine
children, four of whom died in infancy.  Andrew married Susanna Schultz in 1797; they had eleven children.  In 1803
Balthasar sold part of his land to John and Andrew.  They
continued life primarily as farmers.  John supplemented the income from farming and organbuilding to pay for the house he
built in 1809 by surveying.  He kept a notebook called 'Field
Book of Calculations of Lands Surveyed, 1802-1805.'  About
1806 John became interested in wool and cotton carding and
purchased the necessary machines and built a carding house.
In addition he built and repaired these and other machines,
farmed, distilled whiskey and sold it, wrote deeds and bonds,

built more pianos, and served on juries. With all this activity, it is perhaps not surprising that he left the organ building business in 1812 to the control of his brother. He died at 49 in 1819 and is buried in the cemetery adjoining the Kraussdale Schwenkfelder Meeting House.

Andrew's sons, Joel (1801-1853) and George (1803-1880), helped in the construction of the organs and were sometimes helped by another mechanical genius, Samuel (1807-1904)— a noted clockmaker, storekeeper, foundryman, miller, and farmer. In 1823 George and Joel, barely out of their teens, wanted to organize a string band. Lacking a bass violin and the means to buy one, they went to Philadelphia, examined one recently imported, came home, and constructed one. Samuel made the brass tuning pins. Joel and George finished a melodeon in 1828. Joel also made a beaked flute of boxwood, with brass keys, ebony mouthpiece and ivory trim. George, while still a young man, made an electrical machine. Obviously, these men were as ingenious and skilled as their father and uncle.

In 1831 Andrew sent a letter to David Yost giving the costs for various sized organs: four stops, eight feet high—$200; five stops, ten feet high—$300; an organ with six stops, bellows placed without the case, front pipes in round towers, fourteen feet high—$450; eight stops—$600; ten stops, manual placed so that the organist faces the congregation—$800; twelve stops, seventeen feet high, ten feet wide—$950. The workmanship was to be good, and the front pipes to be polished like silver. Not all organs were contracted for before being built. The entry in John's diary for 1804 states that a contract was written for an 'organ already begun and for sale.' Further information on appearance can be gleaned from a diary entry which states 'We got the case up and part of it painted.'

About 1837 the Krausses built an organ, which still exists, for an unknown church. Since 1864 it has been in the Little Tulpehocken Church near Bernville. Its tone is not forceful, but rich and sweet. Its case indicates by its flat front (lacking the round towers seen in earlier organs) a slowly changing taste— it still reflects the traditional five sectional design and retains handsome carved pipe shades, presumably indicating another hand, as their design differs considerably from Krauss' carving.

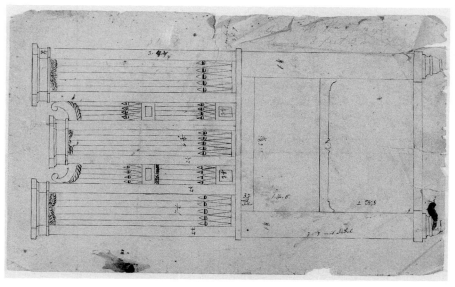

Working drawing for a less elaborate chamber organ (ca. 1830).

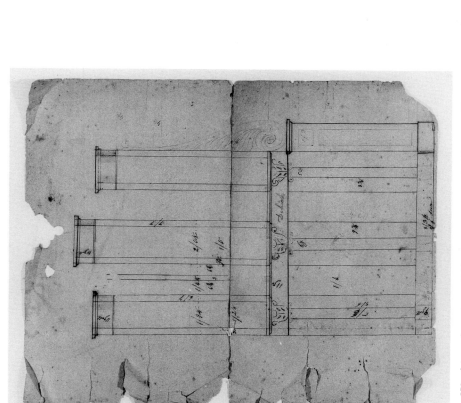

Working drawing of the organ case at Cherryville.

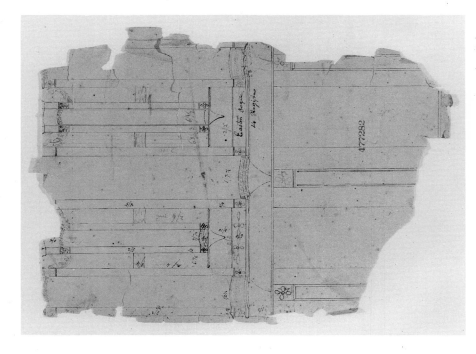

Working drawing for organ case, Easton (1832).

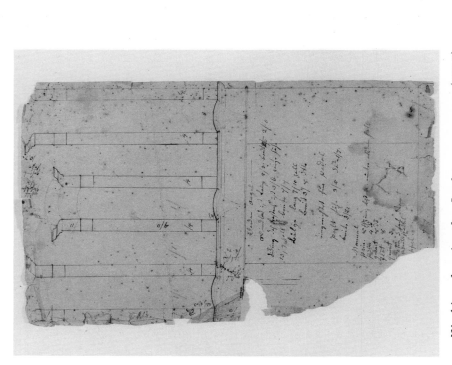

Working drawing for Jordan organ case (1813)
with stop names listed.

In 1839 the Tohickon organ built by Tannenberg in 1798 and visited then by John and Andrew was remodelled by Andrew and George. They put in a new windchest, a pedal stop, and decorative wings were added to each side of the case. The organ continued in use until 1918.

Andrew died in 1841 and was buried in the same cemetery as his brother. The year before, however, the organ building shop was moved from Kraussdale to Palm where George continued it until 1880 and Edwin until 1929.

A large organ built by George in 1852 is still used at Huff's Lutheran and Reformed Church, Huff's Church, Pa., a few miles west of Pennsburg. Its methods of construction continued the tradition of Tannenberg. Its tone is very mild. Edwin replaced the original front in the early 1880s when it was moved into an enlarged church. By this time a new system of winding was in use: the double fold reservoir. In 1850 another organbuilder, John Ziegler (an amateur who only built four chamber organs) died leaving his last instrument unfinished. George Krauss completed it. Another of the Ziegler organs was repaired by Edwin in 1913. Another chamber organ of this period by George Krauss is now in the Norriton Presbyterian Church. Its case is much like the last Ziegler organ.

Some of the earlier organs were rebuilt about this time— the 1796 organ of Long Swamp, Berks Co. in 1852 for use in the congregation's larger building. The 1799 organ at Blessed Sacrament church in Bally had a second manual and pedal pipes added in the 1860s. The organ remained in use until the 1960s and although a few old parts remain, only the case dates from 1799. The 1814 organ at St. Michael's in Philadelphia was moved in the 1870s to their new building in the Kensington section of the city, to be replaced in 1896. Huff's Church and the organ were rebuilt in the 1880s and in the 1970s the organ was restored after considerable damage was done to the pipes of the upper keyboard. That it plays so well after more than 130 years and that others were used so long is testimony to the quality of construction and the esteem in which they were held. As late as 1902 the Long Swamp Berks County organ was still in use, being rebuilt with a new front much like that in Huff's Church, as Philadelphia newspaper accounts indicate.

Surprisingly, least is known of the work of Edwin. No organ made by him is known to exist. His instrument for the

Perkiomen School was considered in the earlier years of this century to be too 'thin' in tone; a piano was preferred to accompany singing. This is another indication of changing taste, to which the Krausses did not cater, as the organs of commercial factories at this time were of great power. A drawing in Edwin's hand from about 1900 shows awareness of the style of the time. The front is flat, the pipes stenciled and there are no cornices or carving. In 1902 the Long Swamp organ of 1796 was remodeled in this style. Tastes had changed greatly, and improved transportation made factory produced organs easily obtainable. As a result, it became increasingly impossible for a hand-crafted instrument to compete. Few organs were built after 1914. The Hill Church contains a case of an organ built by Edwin in 1913.

The few remaining instruments and the records of many known to have given long service are testimony to the genius, craftsmanship, and individuality of a family whose members were not afraid to do those things their immense talents inspired.

## Technical Matters

The foregoing treatment could not cover more specific information about the technical construction of organs or known stoplists for individual Krauss organs. The information, here presented, comes from a number of organ contracts which exist, other papers in the Krauss collection, and a large number of drawings of organ cases, bellows, action components, and pipe scaling charts. These papers and drawings greatly increase our understanding of the Krauss organs.

Even so, not all we would like to know about how John and Andrew learned to build organs will likely ever be known. Their first two or three organs were apparently constructed using information they gleaned from the examination of other organs. It is quite possible they consulted David Tannenberg Jr. (son and apprentice of the famous Lititz organbuilder) as early as 1790; David Jr. was living in Easton at the time. However, by the time of the construction of the Lutheran and Reformed Church organ in 1797 and the Catholic Church organ at Goshenhoppen (now Bally) in 1798, David Tannenberg Jr. was in the employ of John and Andrew. He spent sixteen months in their employment until the summer of 1799, (he died before 1804). John copied the important work 'The Secretly Kept Art of the Scaling of Organ Pipes' written by Georg Andreas Sorge, court organist and city organist of Lobenstein, Germany in 1764 and sent to this country in two manuscript copies. (Both of Sorge's copies are in the Moravian Archives; the Krauss copy is in the Schwenkfelder Library). This manuscript gives detailed instructions on the system for planning the diameter and mouth width and height for organ pipes. Copies of the charts for this found in Sorge's work are among the Krauss drawings, made by two separate hands, different from the 1798 manuscript in John Krauss's handwriting. But without any large church organ's pipes to compare with these measurements, it cannot be determined how this material was used by the Krausses.

The contracts and the drawings which exist suggest ways in which the actual work was done. The drawings are largely unmarked and undated, but a few are identified and can be matched to contracts. The writing and style of drawing permit separation into periods—John and Andrew from the beginning to 1852, George to 1880, and Edwin to 1929. The largest number of drawings are before 1841, as are most of the contracts. Organ contracts indicated stops that the organ would contain, the size of the case with some description, and the terms—full price and period of payment. Some contract pages note payments received. Some took as long as five years to be paid in full. If the organ was already built, the contract might mention only the number of registers or stops and terms. It seems as if organs were built, not to specific spaces, but chosen to be suitable according to a set pattern of a few progressively larger schemes. The stoplists for smaller organs show a predominance of principal toned stops—often there are none but those above the 8' pitch level. In larger organs there appear varied open and stopped flute stops at 8' and 4' pitches, string stops at 8', and mixtures. No reed stops (Trumpet or Oboe) seemed to have been used until Edwin's time. Manual compass was fifty-three notes (from c - e); pedal eighteen notes (C - F) in the earlier organs. However, the 1852 organ by George Krauss existing in Huff's Church has only a thirteen note pedal range—from C - C. Later organs by Edwin contain twenty-seven note pedal compasses. Most often the pedal departments included 16' and 8' stops.

The drawings for the cases show front and side views, and sometimes the backs and other framing. They seem to fall into two categories: projected or imagined fronts and actual working drawings. The working drawings seem to be by Andrew. Several of the working drawings can be matched to contracts since the name of the church or location is noted. Some drawings have stoplists—further verification of connection to the contract. The working drawings include measurements on each important part—usually at a scale noted at 3/4 inch to the foot but are indicated also by the terms used in Sorge's work: *fuss* and *zoll*, comparable to feet and inches.[1] There are drawings of a general nature showing chest construction details, bellows' arrangements, manual and pedal keys, and a chest for an organ in a five sectional case front. Such interior work could be done by the Krausses who were more skilled in woodwork, without drawings.

The case designs show considerable variety, within a distinctive form for each period. The earlier organs were influenced by Tannenberg Sr. or by the Dieffenbachs, but a major influence came from the John Geib organ of 1806, built in New York City by an Englishman.[2] Drawings of organs in later periods show familiarity with current styles in major metropolitan American organ building centers.

A number of drawings show casework below impost level, possible only with a reversed console—a keydesk situated in front of the organ with the organist's back against the organ case. Such a design is shown in a ca. 1890 photograph of the 1813 Krauss organ at St. Michael's Lutheran Church in Philadelphia. Most case drawings do not show front pipes. Pipe shade carvings were elaborate and could also be found at the pipe foot level. Pipe mouths were of the Roman arch style. Often elaborate urn, flame, eagle, angel or ball finials surmounted the pilasters separating the sections of the flats of pipes adjoining the central towers.[3] Round towers of pipes abound, and both tower and flat compartments can be found double storied: one group of pipes above a lower. Some designs show columns below impost level which support scrollwork on the outer sides of the case which extend from impost to cornice level. Scrolls of this sort were added to the 1798 Tannenberg organ at Tohickon (rebuilt by Andrew and George in 1839), and appear in a later Victorian gothic design by George Krauss.

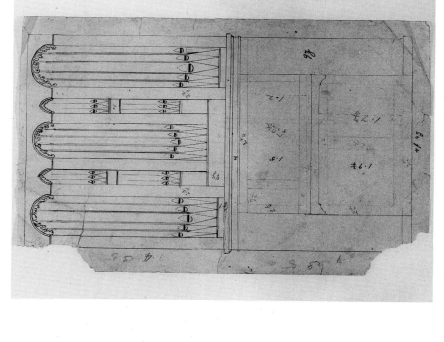

Working drawing for a chamber organ (ca. 1850). Attributed to George Krauss.

Working drawing for an organ case (ca. 1850) for use with a reversed console. Attributed to George Krauss.

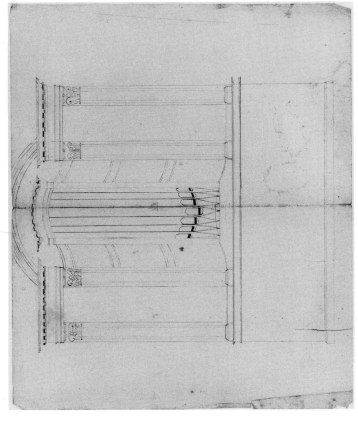

Large church organ case (ca. 1850). Attributed to George Krauss. Possibly the design of the original case at Huff's Church.

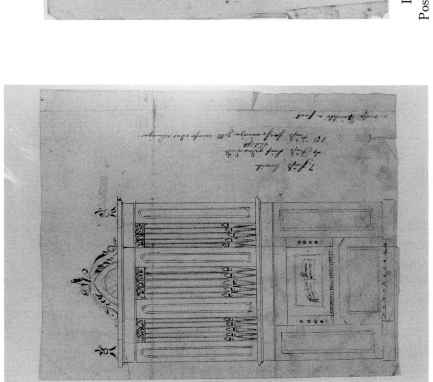

Small church organ case (ca. 1850). Attributed to George Krauss.

Bellows designs are all of the feeder and double rise ribbed reservoir type and must have been used at an early time. Earlier organs of Tannenberg and Dieffenbach used the wedge bellows, always at least in pairs (similar to forge or blacksmith bellows). These cumbersome forms had to be installed outside the organ case, often in attics above the organ gallery. When the Krausses began to use the newer arrangement is not documented.

## Notes

[1] It is a distinct possibility that all the organ cases were built by a cabinet maker in the employ of the Krausses—hence, the need for precisely measured drawings. See entries for April 6, 1797, May 24, 1802, and Sept. 22, 1806 in John's Diary in the Schwenkfelder Library. No drawings exist for the interior parts of specific organs.

[2] See Ibid., Sept. 23, 1806.

[3] See Ibid., April 22, 1805.

## Appendix

What follows is a summary list of organs built by the Krausses as known from diary notations, contract, drawings or from known or existing instruments. Stop names are not spelled the same on all documents.

### John and Andrew 1790-1812

| | | |
|---|---|---|
| ca.1790 | a house organ for their own use | diary |
| | (with the help of their father, Balthasar) | |
| 1796 | Wentz's Church | diary |
| | Worcester, Montgomery Co. | cost £170 |
| 1797 | Lutheran and Reformed Church | diary |
| | Longswamp Berks Co. | |
| | (with help from David Tannenberg, Jr.) | |
| | rebuilt 1852 by George | |
| | rebuilt 1902 by Edwin with new front | |
| 1797 | Catholic Church | diary |
| | Goshenhoppen (now Bally) | case exists |
| | (with help from David Tannenberg Jr.) | |
| | ca.1860 second manual and pedal | |
| | added by George | |
| | rebuilt by Hartmann & Beatty 1965 | |
| 1806 | Lutheran Church | contract |
| | Upper Hanover Township | cost £262.10.00 |

### Andrew 1812 - ca.1838

| | | |
|---|---|---|
| 1813 | Reformed Church | contract |

Jordan, Whitehall                                          case drawing
one manual eleven registers including                      cost $800
8 Principal              4 Principal                       Pedal
Gedact                   II-III Mixture                    (16')
                         Flot                              Coppel

1814        St. Michael's and Zion Corporation            contract
            Philadelphia                                   photograph
            Manual                                         cost $1,750
            8' Principal tin         4' Principal metal
            8' Quint A. Dina metal   4' Klein Gedact wood
            8' Flot wood             3' Quint metal
            8' Gross Gedact wood     2' Sup Octav metal
            8' Viola di Gamba wood   III Mixtur
               &metal
                                     4' Gemshorn metal
            Pedal
            16' Subbass wood         reversed console
            8' Octavbass wood
            coppel

1817        Upper Saucon Township                         contract
            manual                                         drawing
            8' Principal metal       4' Principal metal    cost $850
            8' Gedact wood           3' Quinte metal
            8' Flute wood            Cornet metal          17 1/2' high
            8' Viole d'Gambe         3 octaves tin         case 10' wide
            pedal
            16' Subbass
            8' Octavbass
            Koppel

1817        Lutheran and Reformed Church                  contract
            Colebrookdale
            Manual I
            8' Principal tin         4' Principal metal
            8' Flot                  3' Quint metal
            8' Grossgedact           Cornet
            4' Kleingedact
            8' Gamba
            Manual II                Pedal
            8' Gamba                 16' Subbass
            8' Flot                  8' Octavbass
            8' Grossgedact           Couple

1818        Church
            Peickland Township Chester Co.                contract
            manual
            8' Principal tin         4' Octav metal
            8' Gamba metal           4' (Klein?) Gedact wood

|      |                                |                     |                          |
|------|--------------------------------|---------------------|--------------------------|
|      | 8' Flot wood                   | 3' Quint metal      |                          |
|      | 8' Gedact wood                 | 2' Cornet metal     |                          |
| 1819 | Lutheran Church                |                     | contract                 |
|      | Indianfield                    |                     | cost Elfhundert Dollar   |
|      | 9 manual registers             |                     |                          |
|      | 3 pedal registers              |                     | 16' high                 |
|      | reversed console               |                     | 10' wide                 |
| 1820 | Lutheran and Reformed Church   |                     | contract                 |
|      | Hanover Township Lehigh Co.    |                     | cost $800                |
|      | manual                         |                     |                          |
|      | 8' Principal tinn              | 4' Principal metal  | 17' high                 |
|      | 8' Viol d'Gamba wood           | 3' Quinti metal     | 10' wide                 |
|      | 8' Salicional wood             | II Cornet metal     |                          |
|      | 8' Gedact wood                 | 4' Gedact wood      |                          |
|      | 8' Flot wood                   |                     |                          |
|      | pedal                          |                     |                          |
|      | 16' Subbass                    |                     |                          |
|      | 8'                             |                     |                          |
|      | Coppel                         |                     |                          |
| 1823 |                                |                     | contract                 |
|      |                                |                     | cost $400                |
| 1824 | Joseph Miller                  |                     | contract                 |
|      | Lower Milford Bucks Co.        |                     |                          |
|      | 8' Viol d'Gamba discant        |                     |                          |
|      | 8' Gedact discant              |                     |                          |
|      | 8' Bass                        |                     |                          |
|      | 4' Principal                   |                     |                          |
| 1827 | Mertz Church                   |                     | contract                 |
|      | Rockland Township Bucks Co.    |                     | cost $600                |
|      | ten registers                  |                     | $200                     |
| 1830 | Reformed Church                |                     | contract                 |
|      | Oley                           |                     | cost $1,000              |
|      | twelve registers               | balance paid        |                          |
|      |                                | 1832 Oct            |                          |
| 1833 | Stone Church                   |                     | contract                 |
|      | Allen Township                 |                     | cost $500                |
|      | Northampton Co.                |                     |                          |
| 1832 | Reformed Church Easton         |                     | contract                 |
|      | manual I                       |                     | drawing                  |
|      | 8' Principal                   | revised console     | cost $1,200              |
|      | 8' Gedact                      |                     |                          |
| 8' Salicional |                       |                     |                          |
|      | 4' Flot                        | manual II           | pedal                    |
|      | 4' Principal                   | 8' Flot             | 16' Subbass              |
|      | 3' Quinte                      | 8' Nighthorn        | 8' Octavbass             |
|      | 2' Superoctav                  | 4' Gemshorn         | Coppel                   |

|          |                                         |                  |
|----------|-----------------------------------------|------------------|
|          | II Mixtur                               |                  |
| 1837     | Sassomans Church                        | contract         |
|          | Douglass Township Montgomery Co.        | cost $800        |

manual

| 8' Principal tin    | 4'              |
|---------------------|-----------------|
| 8' Gedackt wood     | 4' Principal    |
| 8'                  | 3' Quinte       |
| 8' Viola de Gamba   | II Cornet       |

| ca. 1837 | Little Tulpehocken Church               | organ exists     |
|----------|-----------------------------------------|------------------|
|          | Bernville Berks Co.                     |                  |
| 1839     | Tohickon                                | (Organs for America) |
|          | rebuilding of 1798 Tannenberg organ     | by Armstrong     |
| no date  | Spinnersville                           | drawing          |

| partial registers | pedal        |
|-------------------|--------------|
| 8' Principal      | 16' Subbase  |
| 8' Flot           | 8' Octavbass |
| 8' Gamba          | 4' Octav     |
| 8' Gedact         | Coppel       |

| no date  | Goshenhoppen                            | drawing          |
|----------|-----------------------------------------|------------------|
| no date  | Kreidersville                           | drawing          |
| no date  | Chamber Organ                           | drawing          |
|          | Gedact Principal                        |                  |
|          | Gamba                                   |                  |
|          | Bass                                    |                  |
| no date  | Church Organ                            | drawing          |

manual

| 8' Principal | 4' Principal   |
|--------------|----------------|
| 8' Gedact    | 4' Gedact      |
| 3' Quint     | 2' Superoctav  |

There are eleven drawings for various chamber organs and about a dozen (many large) for church organs which could be either considered additional organs or unidentified drawings matching contracts. It cannot be known whether all organs built are represented by drawings or contracts. More work will certainly be required to further clarify this situation—contracts must exist in church records not presently discovered. Two small chamber organs exist, one in the Schwenkfelder Library and another of the same size and style is privately owned.

### Joel Krauss 1838

| 1838 | Reformed Church | contract         |
|------|-----------------|------------------|
|      | Reformed Berks Co. | case shown on |

| 8' Principal | 4' Principal   | rear of    |
|--------------|----------------|------------|
| 8' Gedackt   | 3' Quint       | contract   |
| 8' Flot      | 2' Superoctav  |            |

### George ca. 1838-1880

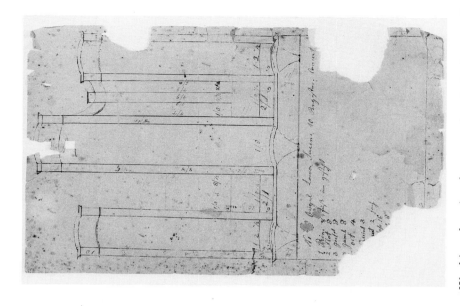

Working drawing for a number 6 sized organ for Lower Saucon.

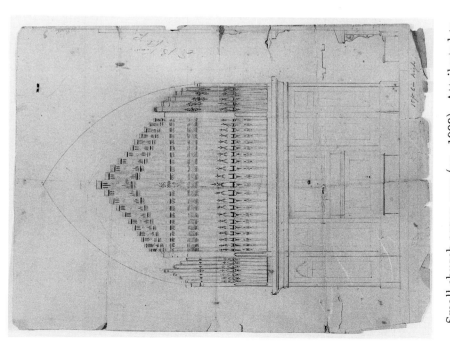

Small church organ case (ca. 1900). Attributed to Edwin Krauss.

1846        Zion Church                                    contract
            Maratawng                                      cost $725
1850        Chamber Organ                                  organ exists
            started by John Zeigler                        Landis Valley
            completed by George Krauss
ca. 1850    Chamber organ now in                           organ exists
            Norriton Presbyterian Church
1852        Lutheran and Reformed Church                   organ exists
            1883 rebuilt with new case front
            by Edwin
            manual I                manual II
            8' Principal            8' Gedackt
            8' Gedackt              8' Nighthorn
            8' Nighthorn            4' Principal
            8' Viol d'Gamba         2' Fifteenth
            4' Principal
            3' Quinte               Pedal
            2' Fifteenth            16' Open Deapasen       one rank
                                    16' Subbass             two slides
                                    Couple

1855                                                       contract
                                                           cost $600
1868        Zion Ev. Lutheran Church                       organ existed
            Long Valley, N.J.                              until late 1960s
            manual left jamb        right jamb
            8' Open Diapason        12 shared              alarm
            8' Open Flute           Stopped Basses         8' Stopped Diapason
            8' Viola share low 12 notes        8' Dulciana
            4' Principal            4' Flute (metal chimney flute)
            2' Fifteenth            Pedal
            Tremulant               16' Subbass wood
                                    8' Violencello wood
            all manual stops enclosed in       Coupler (notched
            a hitch down swell                 knob)
no date     George Krauss?                                 manuscript
            8' Principal            3' Quint
            4' Octav                2' Superoctav
            8' Gamba                4' Floet
            8' Gedact               Sesquattera
                                    Trumpet
no date     George Krauss?                                 manuscript
            8' Principal            54 notes
            4' Principal
            3' Quint                "           Pedal 18 notes
            2' Super Octav          "           16' Subbass
            4' Floet                "           Coppel

|                |                      |            |
|----------------|----------------------|------------|
|                | III Susquiattera     | 162 pipes  |
|                | 8' Gedact discant    | 36 notes   |
|                | 8' Gamba             | 41 notes   |
|                | 8' Gedact Bass       | 18 notes   |
|                | 8' Trumpet           | 41 notes   |

no date    George Krauss?                               case design

| Great manual=53 notes | Swell manual=53 notes |
|-----------------------|------------------------|
| 8' Principal          | 8' Dulciana            |
| 8' Stopt. Diapason    | 8' Nighthorn           |
| 8' Flute              | 8' Viola de Gamba      |
| 3' Quint              | Coupler to             |
| 2' Octav              | Pedal                  |
| 4' Principal          | 16' Subbass            |
| II Cornet             | 8' Octavbass           |
|                       | Coupler to Great case  |

There are eight case drawings in transitional styles, a few
in gothic styles a few with arched flats and flat cornice and
a large five sectional design which could be the plan for the
original Huff's Church front. Three undated manuscripts give
sample specifications:

| 1. Great 58 notes    | Swell 58 notes       | Pedal 25 notes        |
|----------------------|----------------------|-----------------------|
| 8' Open Diapason     | 4' Violin Diapason   | 16' Open Diapason     |
| 8' Viola di Gamba    | 8' Stpd. Diapason    | 8' Violincello        |
| 8' Melodia           | 8' Salicional        |                       |
| 8' Clarabella        | 8' Dulciana          | Couplers              |
| 4' Flute             | 4' Flute Harmonic    | Swell to Great        |
| 4' Principal         | 2' Piccolo           | Swell to Pedal        |
| 2' Fifteenth         | Tremolo              | Great to Pedal        |
| 3' Twelfth           |                      |                       |

| 2. Great 58 notes    | Swell 58 notes       | Pedal 25 notes        |
|----------------------|----------------------|-----------------------|
| 8' Open Diapason     | 8' Violin Diapason   | 16' Bourdon           |
| 8' Dulc.             | 8' Dolce             | 8' Violincello        |
| 8' Doppel Flute      | 8' Stpd. Diapason    |                       |
| 4' Gemshorn          | 4' Flute Harmanic    | Swell to Great        |
| 2' Piccolo Harmonic  | 4' Oboe or Trumpet   | Great to Pedal        |

| 3. Great 58 notes    | Swell 58 notes       | Pedal 27 notes        |
|----------------------|----------------------|-----------------------|
| 8' Open Diapason     | 8' Violin Diapason   | 16' Open Diap.        |
| 8' Dulciana          | 8' Salicional        | 8' Violincello        |
| 8' Nighthorn         | 8' Stpd. Diapason    |                       |
| 4' Octav             | 4' Flute             | Great to Pedal        |
| 4' Flute Har.        | 4' Viola             | Swell to Pedal        |
| 2' Fifteenth         | 8' Oboe              | Swell to Great        |
| 8' Trumpet           | Sur. tremolo         | bellows signal        |
|                      | pedal check          |                       |
|                      |                      | price $1,800          |

| | | |
|---|---|---|
| 1883 | Huff's Church | organ exists |
| | rebuild of 1852 George Krauss | |
| | organ with a new front to case | |
| | and low octaves of 8' Open Diapason | |
| ca. 1900 | Perkiomen School | drawing |
| 1902 | rebuild 1797 Longswamp | photograph of 1902 |
| | organ including a new case front | |
| 1913 | Hill Church | organ case only exists |
| no date | Church organ | drawing |

# Schwenkfelder Textiles

## Elizabeth R. Gamon

In its purest form, a 'sampler' is a compendium of stitches, done under supervision, by a young girl and meant to be treasured as a reference tool for the rest of her life. The earliest known sampler dates to 1502, predating by decades the founding of the Schwenkfelders. By the time of the Schwenkfelder migration to America, sampler making by young girls of good family was an established part of Germanic culture, and consequently a part of the cultural baggage of the immigrants. Research into the decorative needlework of the Schwenkfelders in America has only begun, and documentation of the needlework of Schwenkfelder women prior to the migration is a project yet to be undertaken. This paper must therefore be considered only a progress report of the research to date.

The migrating Schwenkfelders were an uncommonly well-educated group for the time. We know that many were literate, and we have records that George Weiss was hired to teach the children during the trip to America. For the first thirty years after their arrival we must assume that the immigrants were occupied with the problems of survival and establishing themselves in an undeveloped land, to the exclusion of almost all else. Until 1764 any education of the children was accomplished by parents, but in that year two schools were founded, both in private homes and both with male teachers. Other Schwenkfelder schools followed quickly—Towamencin in 1765 and the Hosensack Academy in 1790.

In the eighteenth century, one of the focal points of a woman's education was mastery of the basic sewing skills that she would need to meet the responsibilities of running a home. One accepted method of teaching these skills was by working a sampler, in the process of which the techniques of sewing, darning, and creating a design would be learned. In the years

immediately following the migration the sampler would have
been worked in the home by girls (aged 7 to 14) under the
instruction of an older, female relative. The more formal education system of the second half of the eighteenth century was
supplemented by Dame Schools, where Pennsylvania German
girls were taught reading, arithmetic, knitting, sewing, and
decorative needlework by English ladies who, in the process,
also managed to knock off a little unwanted Dutchiness. We
know of at least one Pennsylvania German girl, Elizabeth Bechtel, who attended the Dame School operated by Sara Boone in
Oley in the year 1833, and we are sure that continued research
will reveal more. Elizabeth Bechtel's sampler is a part of the
needlework collection at the Schwenkfelder Library and Museum.

The earliest documented Schwenkfelder sampler, that we
know of, is by C. Wagner, dated 1733 (Plate 1). This sampler
was worked in Germany before the migration and was carried
to America by Anna Wagner. It remains with her descendants
today. The arrangement of the sampler deviates from that
which we have come to expect in later American Schwenkfelder examples, but its iconography is almost a preview of the
symbols with which we have become so familiar—leaning corner designs (Plate 2), shields (Plate 3) in which initials, dates
or decorative motifs have been incorporated, pots of flowers,
lion rampant (Plate 4), border or divider designs (Plate 5),
alphabets (Plate 6), block and script letters (Plate 6—notice
the date of the sampler '1733' with the embroideress' initials
'CW,' people and other motifs)—clear evidence of the German heritage of Eastern Pennsylvania needlework. In spite of
this early beginning no documented Schwenkfelder decorative
needlework made between the migration and 1778 has as yet
come to light. The earliest dated piece in the Schwenkfelder
Museum collection (Plate 8, a sampler by Regina Heebner)
was worked in 1794. This sampler was pictured in *The Genealogical Record of the Schwenkfelder Families* compiled by
Samuel Brecht in 1923. Regina was the daughter of George
Heebner and Anne Schubert Heebner. She lived in Hereford
Township. There are others in private collections with slightly
earlier dates, such as the sampler worked by Christina Wagner
in 1778 (Plate 9). Christina was the daughter of Christopher
Wagner and lived on the Wagner farm in Worchester, which

became known as the Heebner farm when Christina married Abraham Heebner, having inherited the farm from her father. This sampler has remained with the Heebner descendants to the present day.

Most non-Schwenkfelder samplers (Plate 10) and the Wagner one (Plate 1) worked in Germany seem to have a constrained, pre-ordered feel to their composition when compared to the less restrained, less prescribed pieces worked in this country by Schwenkfelder and non-Schwenkfelder alike, such as the Schwenkfelder sampler worked by C. Schultz in 1801 (Plate 11).

The Show Towel (Plate 12) or door panel is a needlework form that seems to be almost exclusively of the Pennsylvania German type, in the form we are familiar with. Although earlier writers (such as Stoudt and Lichten[1]) have claimed German origin for the show towel form, lack of documented European examples and the great quantity from rural Pennsylvania seems to refute this premise. Perhaps those early scholars were confused by show towels worked in America but containing German verse, such as the show towel worked by a Kriebel in the Lansdale area (Plate 13). In function, the show towel was a highly decorated piece of needlework, designed to be hung over the more prosaic hand towel, customarily positioned near the back door and convenient to the wash basin. The show towel was often elaborately embroidered with a verse (Plate 13), names (Plate 14), and random motifs over a bottom section of drawn work and fringe (Plate 15)—Woe be unto anyone foolish enough to absentmindedly dry his or her hands on the wrong towel!

Unlike samplers, show towels were worked by young ladies in their late teens or early twenties and seldom contain the ages of their embroideress. Occasionally a man's name appears (Plate 16)—undoubtedly the name of a gentleman important to the artist. The designs worked into a show towel were often copied from the young lady's sampler, so laboriously worked at a much more tender age. It is clear that Salome Kriebel used her sampler as a pattern (Plate 17) when she worked the motifs on her show towel (Plate 18) at a later date. The needlework on a show towel often proves to be much finer than that on a sampler by the same person—indicating the continually developing skills of the embroideress. Salome was the daughter of

Melchior Kriebel and Rosina Schultz Kriebel and the grand-daughter of the Rev. Melchior and Barbara Schubert Kriebel on her paternal side and the Rev. Melchior and Salome Wagner Schultz on her maternal side.

Nowhere is the rapid acculturation of the Schwenkfelders into the English dominated society of Pennsylvania more evident than in the decorative needlework of Schwenkfelder women and girls. We can follow that acculturation, step by step, from 1733 when C. Wagner (Plate 1) worked her typically German sampler until 1857 when Phoebe Kriebel recorded with her needle her cityscape (Plate 19). We can see the random motifs of the German marking sampler of 1689, a true sampler (Plate 20) repeated on the later Schwenkfelder sampler (Plate 21) by Christine Schultz in 1799, replaced by the house, flowers, and pious verse, of what for want of a better term, we will call an English courting sampler. The latter was not really a sampler at all, but a display of needlework skills orchestrated to be posted prominently for the inspection of prospective suitors—a style absorbed by the Schwenkfelders in the early nineteenth century as witness the 1828 sampler by Rebecca Dresher (Plate 22). Rebecca was the daughter of Christopher and Anna Anders Dresher of Dreshertown in Upper Dublin Township. She married Jacob Barnett.

The Phoebe Kriebel cityscape (Plate 19) tells us even more about Schwenkfelder acculturation as it mutely attests to Phoebe's obvious familiarity with Philadelphia. With this kind of contact between nineteenth-century Schwenkfelders and their English speaking neighbors acculturation should come as no surprise.

Although the quality of decorative needlework done by Schwenkfelder girls was unusually high in both design and technique, it occasionally suffered from the same lack of needlework skills seen from time to time in the work of non-Schwenkfelder girls of comparable age. After all, not everyone could (or can) sew, or wants to! We must also keep in mind the very strong possibility that, as in everything else, only the best examples of decorative needlework have been treasured and cared for and have survived.

## Notes

†This paper is dedicated to the memory of Sara Bieler for the uncounted hours of research that she devoted to this project. Without her most of its meaning would have been lost.

[1] See John Joseph Stoudt, *Early Pennsylvania Arts and Crafts* (New York, 1964) and Frances Lichten *Folk Art of Rural Pennsylvania* (New York, 1946). Photography by Albert T. Gamon, Patricia R. Mackey, and Robert Welch.

Plate 1

Plate 2

Plate 3

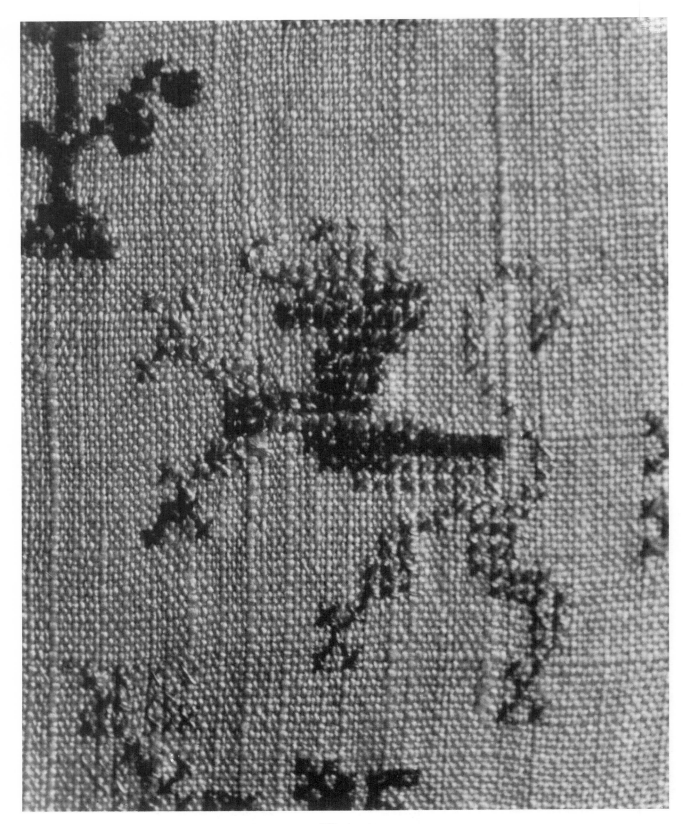

Plate 4

Plate 5

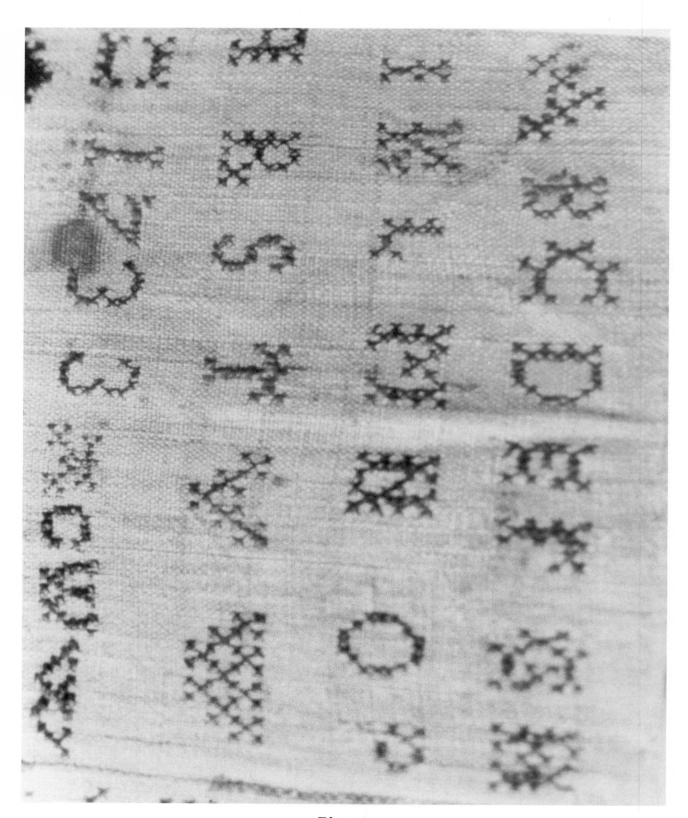

Plate 6

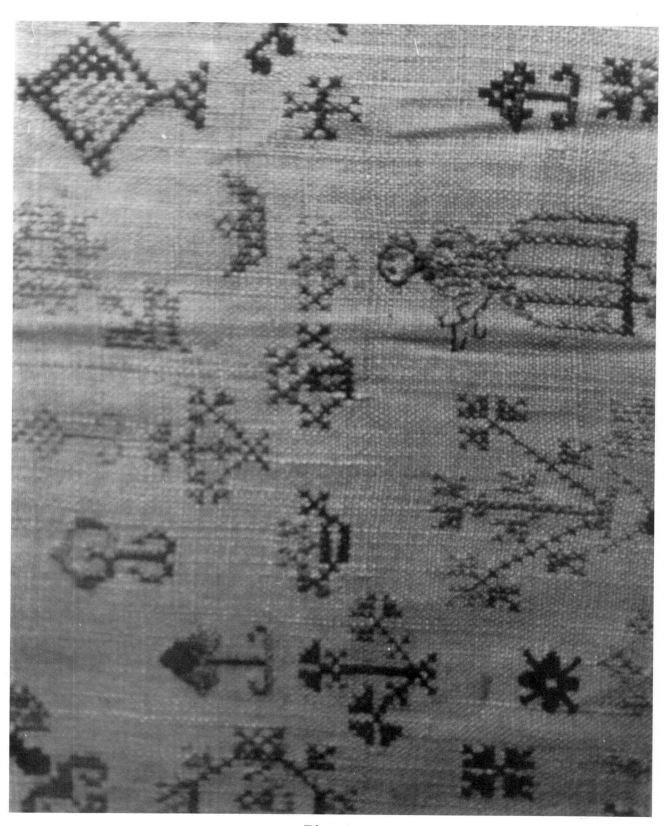

Plate 7

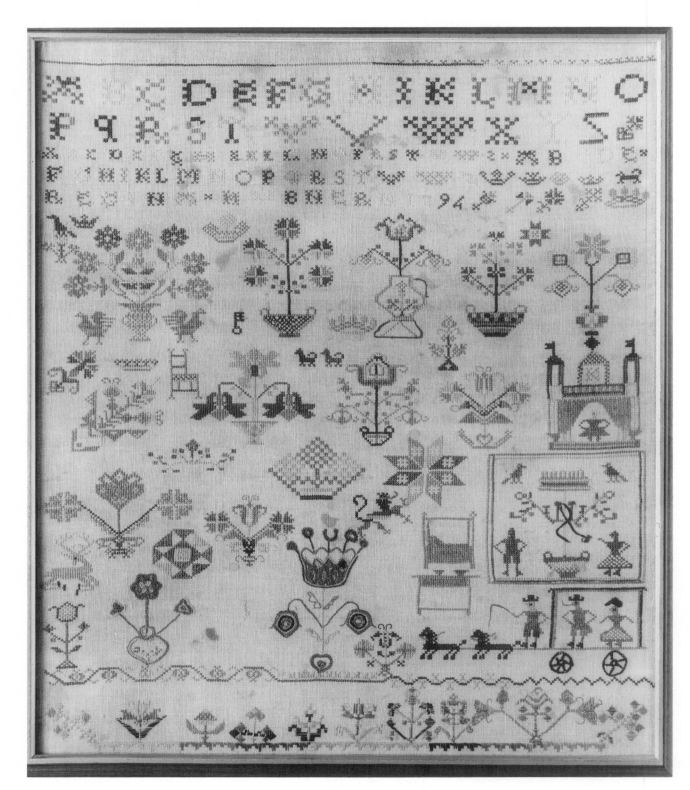

Plate 8

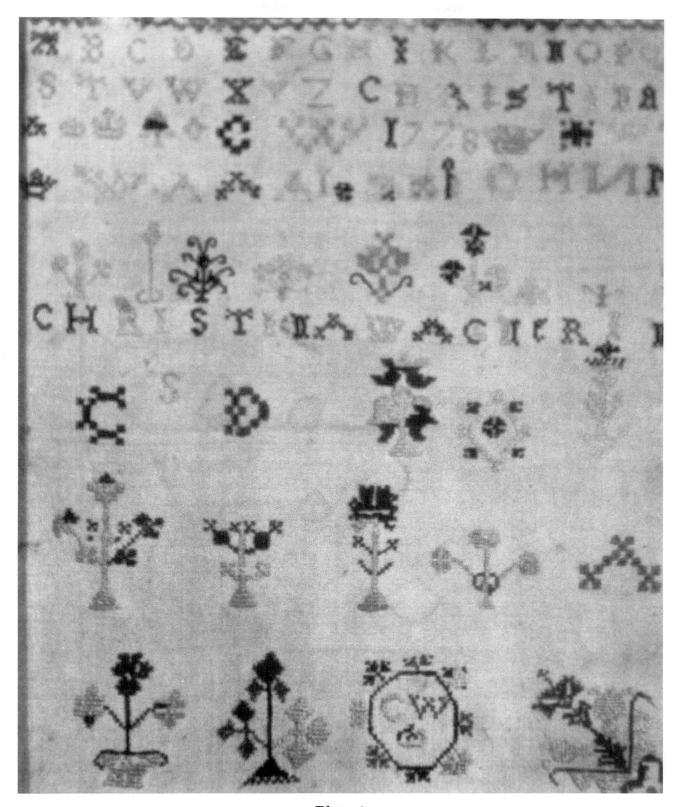

Plate 9

Plate 10

Plate 11

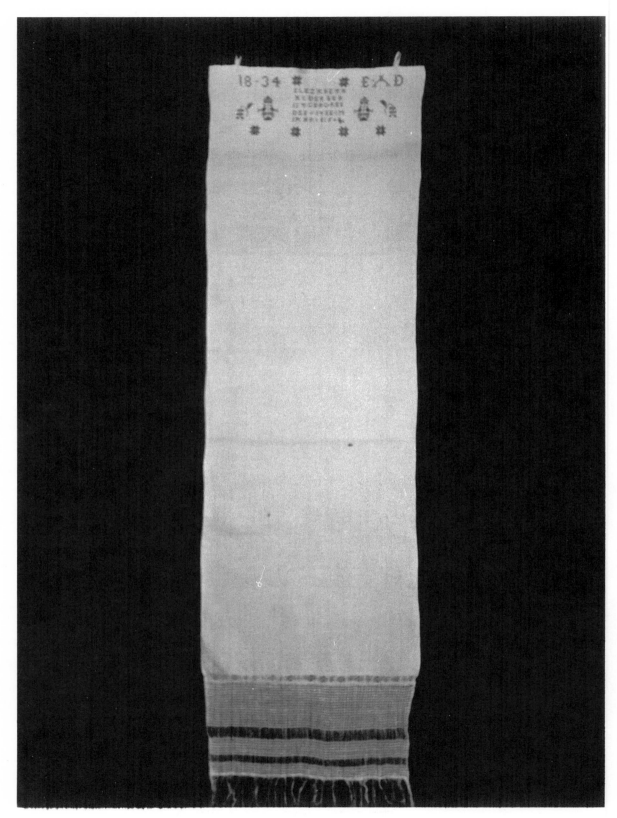

Plate 12

Plate 13

Plate 14

Plate 15

Plate 16

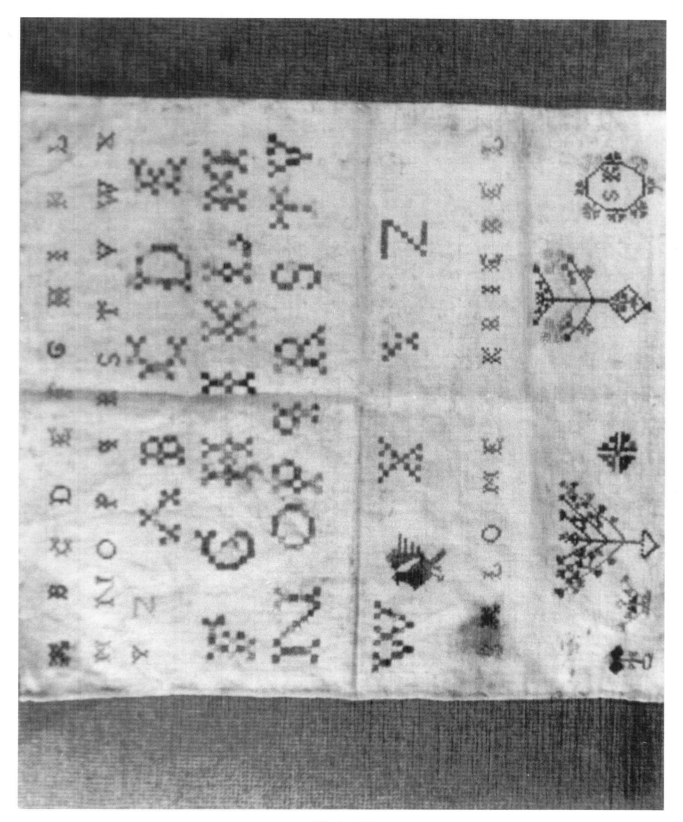

Plate **17**

Plate 18

Plate 19

Plate 20

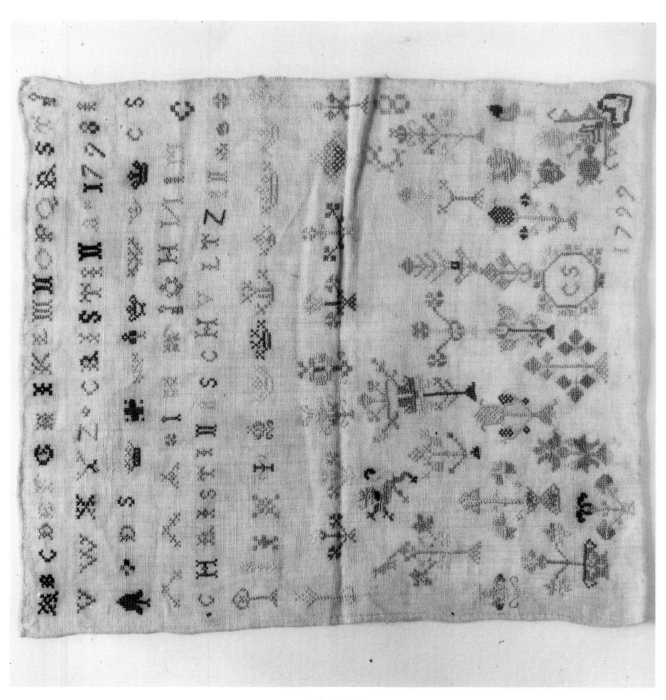

Plate 21

Plate 22

# Schwenkfelder Dairy Farming in the Early Twentieth Century

Kathleen Manolescu

Farming is an integral part of the Schwenkfelder cultural heritage. It is believed that many Schwenkfelders were farmers in Silesia. *The Genealogical Record of the Schwenkfelder Families*[1] lists the occupations of seven persons in Silesia and three of them were farmers. In Colonial Pennsylvania most Schwenkfelders were farmers or at least lived on and operated a farm. David Schultze, for example, was a busy surveyor who also ran a 180 acre farm.[2] One historian[3] has noted that the Schwenkfelders were considered good farmers during the Colonial period. Most of the members of the Palm Schwenkfelder Church were farmers until World War II. Unfortunately there is little record of Schwenkfelder or Pennsylvania German farming in the Upper Perkiomen Valley. There are still people who remember what farming was like during the first half of the twentieth century, however. These people provided the bulk of information presented here. Of special interest is the dairy operation because this is what has best survived.

## How Information was Gathered

Participant observation or watching farming activities being performed, working with farmers whenever possible, and talking with them while working was the key instrument used for gathering data for this study. It began with continuous employment and observation on a contemporary Schwenkfelder dairy farm for sixteen months. This was an invaluable introduction to what it means to be a Schwenkfelder dairy farmer. It is one thing to read about dairy farming, but quite another to farm or at least perform a range of farming activities. This experience enabled the preparation of pertinent questions for interviewing. It also served as a guide for the participant observation of the rest of the farmers studied. Seven of the persons consulted for information on early twentieth century farming still do some farming.

Formal and informal interviewing were important avenues for gathering information. A schedule of questions pertaining to a farm's physical and social resources was administered during the formal interview. Details from a specific time were requested rather than recollections from over the years. The majority of informants talked about the first year when they took over the farm. This was a momentous occasion and recollections are relatively clear about this period. For the two people who never actually ran a farm, the period referred to was that of their early teens when they learned how to farm. Ten people responded to most of the questions on both schedules. Responses focused on the 1920s for five people, on the 1930s for two, and on the 1940s for three. The formal interview also included open-ended questions about milking, feeding, breeding, and waste control for the cows and the activities performed in producing the various crops. Informal interviews were conducted over a four-year period.

Initially it was assumed that a Schwenkfelder is a person with genealogical ties to the founding population from Silesia. According to this definition, eighty percent of the persons formally interviewed would be considered Schwenkfelders. Throughout the period of study it became evident that Schwenkfelder also means membership in the Schwenkfelder Church. To some this is the primary and even sole marker. On the basis of religion only, sixty percent of the persons formally interviewed are Schwenkfelders. Non-Schwenkfelders were included in this study because of their knowledge of farming and as a means of determining if there was anything unique about Schwenkfelder dairy farmers. Because everyone interviewed was a Pennsylvania German, this presentation will refer to the group as Pennsylvania Germans. Where information pertains specifically to Schwenkfelders, it will be so noted.

Finally, written documentation was consulted to place Schwenkfelder dairy farming in an historical framework and for comparison with the state of the art. Very little information on Schwenkfelder or Pennsylvania German farming in the Upper Perkiomen Creek watershed during this period exists. There is information on the numerous inventions, discoveries,

Illustration 1. A typical Pennsylvania German farmstead in the late nineteenth century.

Illustration 2. The flock of chickens at feeding time.

and strides made in farming over the years at the state or national level or for a particular farming type, however.[4]

## Historical Background

The roots of Schwenkfelder farming in America date to the Colonial period and they parallel other Pennsylvania German farming practices in Southeast Pennsylvania. The best introduction to these practices is Lemon[5] and David Schultze's diary. This background setting will concentrate on post Civil War developments, but it is instructive to introduce comments on early Pennsylvania German farming. The traveller Schoepf, for example, found that 'everything about his farm shows order and good management in all that concerns the care of the land.'[6] The author of *American Husbandry* noted that 'few parts of America exceed the back country of Pennsylvania.'[7] This praise extended to the care of the cow. The historians Bidwell and Falconer record that better 'care of livestock was one of the many features which distinguished the farming of the thrifty Germans.'[8] They provided fine housing in winter and kept large trees in the meadow and pasture for shade in summer. The Pennsylvania German barns were uniformly praised for their size, sturdiness, practicality, and efficient layouts. Animal care was further promoted by the early construction of fences and hedgerows.

The Pennsylvania German farm was considered a legacy[9] and people strove to enhance and preserve it (Illustration 1). Farming provided the basic subsistence needs, but it was more than that. It was a way of life, a family affair. Everyone from small children and grandparents to nearby friends and relatives helped run the farm. The Pennsylvania Germans settled in compact groups with close social, religious, and economic ties.[10] People worked together and valued hard work. According to one proverb, 'Müssiggang ist aller Laster Anfang' or 'Idleness is the root of all evil'.[11] Or, as one farmer in this study noted, 'Easy tasks do not develop strong muscles or keen minds.' Murphy and Murphy observed that the Pennsylvania Germans were 'unusually thrifty, careful farmers who have spared no labor in making their land fruitful.'[12]

Colonial farming was oriented primarily to subsistence farming. This changed in the 1800s with the industrial revolution and the rise of urbanism. The tremendous population rise in cities from 1860-1910 created a large and steady demand for dairy products. The industrial revolution resulted in the development of labor-saving devices; it created a need for capital, and people left the farm to work in factories. So many changes occurred in the two decades following the Civil War that this period has been called the golden age of animal husbandry.[13] Cattle numbers increased from five to forty-five million head. A number of inventions and discoveries enabled dairying to come into its own.

The earliest changes pertinent to dairy farming affected the processing of milk. In 1861 the first creamery appeared. The creamery was a building equipped to receive and skim milk, ripen and churn cream, and work and pack butter. The practice of straining cream from milk in the springhouse in order to churn it into butter soon disappeared. Creameries benefited by the invention of a mechanical cream separator in 1879. This allowed creameries to handle more milk in less time and at a reduced cost. Refrigerated railroad cars appeared in the 1870s, facilitating the shipment of a quality product to market. A major breakthrough for dairy farming occurred in 1890 when Babcock worked out a fairly simple and effective butterfat test. Butter was the most desirable diary product at this time and the Babcock test enabled a fair payment for the amount produced. Each cow could be tested with the Babcock test so it allowed farmers an opportunity to evaluate their herds better.

The quality of milk marketed was significantly improved after discoveries made by Pasteur and Kock on the control of tuberculosis. During the nineteenth century tuberculosis was the most dreaded disease. It affected both people and cattle. People initially disliked the taste of pasteurized milk, but they came to accept it for health reasons. A machine allowing rapid pasteurization appeared in 1895 and by 1930 pasteurization was used almost everywhere. Koch isolated the tubercule bacillus and found a vaccine that identified infected animals. A program for slaughtering diseased cattle began in 1917 and by 1927 all the herds in forty-five counties in Pennsylvania were tested. Farmers received some compensation for their losses, but many were dissatisfied. A similar program during the 1930s helped control brucellosis.

Advances in animal nutrition were another factor promoting the rise of dairy farming. In 1864 a German scientist developed a table of feeding standards and a listing of the values of various feeds. In 1898 W. A. Henry published *Feeds and Feeding*, a book that was to be the standard guide to feeding into the 1960s. Revisions were made, many coming after the discovery of vitamins in 1915. The addition of vitamins to feeds made for a healthier cow. The discovery that milk has nearly every vitamin led to greater milk consumption by the public.

Two inventions had an especially dramatic impact on the farm. The first was the silo. It was introduced in the United States in 1875. Previously most farmers milked their cows only during the pasture season.[14] The silo allowed the preservation of large amounts of cheap, palatable feed during the winter and enabled dairying to become a year-round enterprise. The silo was also a labor saver. Another labor saver was the development of an effective and efficient mechanical milker in 1905. This machine reduced milking time by more than half. Its popularity rose as electricity became available.

Other important inventions were geared to the crops needed in dairy farming. Farmers already had access to a fairly full range of equipment: plow, drill, corn planter, cultivator, mower, rake, reaper, and threshing machine. In 1869 the spring-tooth harrow was invented to help prepare the seedbed. The corn picker appeared in 1911 and in 1920 the first combine came to Pennsylvania. The biggest change was the marketing of a light, general purpose tractor in 1925. This signalled the end to farming with horses and mules.

## Physical Resources

An inventory of the physical resources of farms in the Upper Perkiomen watershed during the early twentieth century is a good introduction to what people had to work with. These resources set the stage for the farming operation.

*Climate*: Southeast Pennsylvannia has a continental climate, in part because of the prevailing winds from the west. There are wide temperature fluctuations which can mean as much as a 45 degree fahrenheit temperature differential between the coldest and warmest months. The winters are mild and the summers are hot and humid. Rainfall averages 30-50 inches, spread over most of the year. Farmers can expect a 5-6 month frost free growing period.

*Areal Physical Features*: All the farms in this study are located in the upper portion of the Upper Perkiomen Creek watershed. Hosensack, Perkiomen, Molasses, West Branch Perkiomen, and Swamp Creeks are the main tributaries of the Perkiomen Creek. There are many branches of these tributaries, and springs are numerous. The topography ranges from steep ridges to broad agricultural valleys. References to the area always note the abundance of rolling hills and woodland. Population concentrations are in Hereford, Palm, East Greenville, Bally, and Congo-Niantic. The uppermost town, Hereford, is located sixty miles from Philadelphia.

*Soils*: The soils come from the Piedmont Plateau. Their geologic source materials are triassic shales and diabase, an igneous disc rock. Three major soil groups are represented: Penn-Buck, Lehigh-Brecknock, and Montalto. The average depth to bedrock for all three is 2 1/2 to 3 feet. The Penn-Buck group has good drainage, a silt loam surface soil of reddish brown color, and an average slope of five percent (2-15% extremes). Eighty percent of this group is in cropland. The Lehigh-Brecknock soils have only a fair-to-poor drainage rating, even though the surface soil is still a silt loam. The color of these soils is ashy gray and the average slope is five percent. Only forty percent of this ground is in crops while thirty percent has remained in forest. Both of these soil groups suffer draughtiness in dry seasons. The third soil group, Montalto, is steep and stony with good soil drainage, a silt loam surface soil with a brown color and an average slope of twelve percent (5-25% range). These soils are generally too stony for crops. Ninety percent has remained in forest and ten percent is kept as pasture. Overall the soils have been assessed as uniformly of fair quality.[15]

Farmers were asked to describe the ground on their farms. Three mentioned having red shale, another three described their soils as predominantly clay. Two had stony, gravelly ground and two reported some limestone soil. Two farmers had limestone kilns on their property. In the early part of the century fields were layed-out in blocks. Farmers started putting in strips on the hilly areas in the 1930s.

The acres of land owned ranged to 150. Ninety-eight acres was the average-size farm. One farmer rented all his land for the first several years and another five rented an additional thirty to eighty acres.

*Crops*: The crops sown on these acres were:

| Crop | Number Farmers | Average Number Acres |
|------|----------------|----------------------|
| Corn | 10 | 25 |
| Hay | 10 | 24 |
| Wheat | 7 | 21 |
| Oats | 4 | 10 |
| Rye | 3 | ? |
| Potatoes | 3 | 3 |
| Barley | 1 | 3 |
| Soybeans | 1 | ? |
| Sudan Grass | 1 | 10 |
| Pasture | 7 | 15 |
| Woodland | 8 | 24 |

All farmers also reported having a large garden and at least some apple trees or a small orchard.

*Animals*: All farms had cattle, pigs. chickens, and only the farmer who started at the end of the study period did not have work horses. The average farm animal population was:

| Animal | Number Farmers | Average Number Kept |
|--------|----------------|---------------------|
| Cow | 10 | 17 |
| Heifer | 5 | ? |
| Steer | 4 | 1-30 |
| Bull | 6 | 1 |
| Pig | 10 | 14 |
| Chicken | 10 | 530 |
| Work Horse | 9 | 4 |
| Mule | 2 | 3 |

Farms might have a few registered cows, but only two herds had all registered cattle. One farmer raised steers for sale while the rest raised only enough for family consumption. Half the group started raising their own replacement heifers during their period. including the two with registered herds, while the rest purchased animals as needed. Bulls were kept for breeding purposes only. Three farmers raised pigs for sale and the other seven kept them for home use only. Chickens were a popular source of added income throughout this period (Illustration 2). Work horses and mules, of course, were essential until tractors took over.

*Equipment*: Equipment inventories varied significantly from early to mid-century. A typical 1920s inventory included: a one share hand plow, harrow, and land roller to prepare the soil; a one or two row corn planter and grain drill for seeding; a mower, tedder, and rake for harvesting hay; a binder, thresher, and corn sheller for harvesting grains; a one row cultivator for weeding corn; and a manure spreader. Only two farms reported having a tractor in the 1920s. By the end of the first half of the century all farms had tractors, tractor-drawn equipment, and they probably had a disk, hay loader, and corn picker, as well.

*Buildings*: Farm buildings included a place to house the cows and horses (barn), pigs (pig stable), chickens (chicken houses or coop), and places to store milk (milkhouse), silage (silo), and equipment (sheds—Illustration 3). The barns in the area are typical Swiss or bank barns with two levels. The top level was for storing feed and threshing, and animals were kept on the first level (Figure 1[16]) illustrates a typical ground floor plan before stalls were put in. The barns had an overshoot or cantilevered forebay, with a barnyard in front on the stable area. Barns varied in size and farmers most often described them in terms of stall numbers. Stall numbers ranged from sixteen to forty-four, with twenty-six the average number. The first silos were square or rectangular horizontal models. Upright wooden ones were put in as early as 1908. No farm had more than two silos.

*Finances*: Everyone reported borrowing to buy the farm. Only three farmers ever got out-of-debt and it took them about thirteen years to do so. All three started farming before 1935. The rest reported being constantly in debt as they expanded and made improvements. Equipment took a big portion of the monies spent. Even though farmers were in debt, only one remembers struggling.

## Social Resources

While the physical resources set the stage, the social resources do the performing. Farming was not done by just one person. It was a family affair. Information about the family that might be pertinent to farming is of special interest here.

*Husband*: The husband was the head of the farm family and he made the majority of daily decisions about running the farm. All but one of the husbands was born at home on the family farm. One was born in the 1890s, three in the 1900s, and the remaining six in the 1910s. The educational achievements of the group are considerable. Thirty percent studied or received

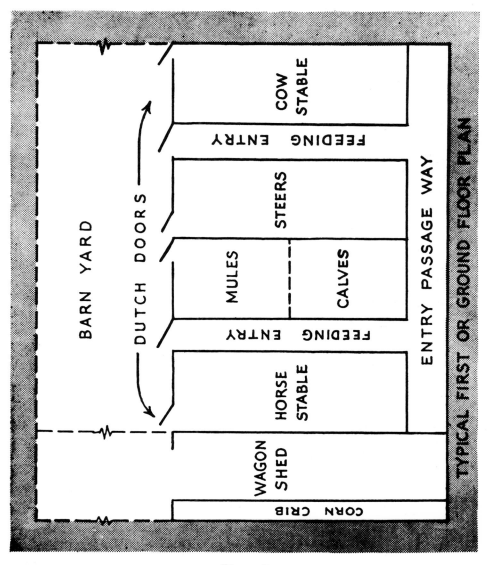

Ground floor plan for housing the animals of the farm.

Figure 1

training beyond high school and one obtained a B. Sc. degree in dairy science. The average number of school years completed for the group was eleven.

These men wanted to farm but it did not come easily for some of them. For half of them their families did not expect them to farm. One man's parents discouraged him from farming. Farming was considered hard work and they wanted something better for him. Four men worked away from the farm before they found an available farm or had enough money saved. One man taught school, another was a tester for the Dairy Herd Improvement Association, and two men did office and factory work. They did not like working away from the farm and were glad when a farming opportunity opened up. Factory work was viewed as the main alternative to farming and was considered slow and boring—'every day's the same.'

Why did people stay on the farm? Only three husbands said, 'Because it's all I ever knew' or 'Because my father farmed.' The rest chose to stay because they liked farming. They specifically mentioned the variety of work, being able to work outdoors, and planting crops. People were asked what goals they set for themselves when starting out. The replies were modest: they hoped to live one day at a time, to pay their bills, and one day to own the farm completely.

*Wife*: While the husband made most of the daily decisions about running the farm, the wife made most of the everyday decisions about the house and the children. Wives also had major responsibilities in the barn, chicken coop, and garden. All women helped with the milking, fed chickens and gathered eggs, and took care of planting, weeding, harvesting, and canning the garden produce. During canning season the work was so consuming some women took on a nanny to watch the children. Half the wives helped with fieldwork when labor was short. Husbands noted how their wives had helped plow, disk, make hay, and pick corn. And when a group of people came to the farm to help with the fieldwork, the wife had additional work preparing and serving meals. The wife was truly a partner in farming. One husband flatly stated that one could not farm in the early 1900s without a wife. People think back and nod their heads, saying 'Yes, my mother worked hard.'

Most of the farm wives of the sample were from the area. Two were not raised on a farm but they learned their new way of life quickly enough. The average number of years spent in school was ten. Only one woman had any education beyond high school. Families did not see as great a need to educate girls as boys. No women reported working away from the farm before or after getting married.

*Children*: Children were an important and valued part of the farm family. After all, one of them would take over the farm one day. The average number of children per family for the sample is four. Children played and they also helped out with chores when they were able. Each child usually had chores that were his other responsibility. Common ones were: filling the wood box, peeling potatoes, feeding chickens, gathering eggs, and bringing the cows in from pasture. Children were part of the farming activities, even if they could not help out. One husband remembered his wife putting the babies on the windowsill when she had to milk!

*Friends and Relatives*: Family extended beyond the confines of the farm. For all but one farm family most or all its close relatives also lived in the community or immediate area. There was more interaction with families then. People would go visiting once a week or once a month. After church on Sunday was a popular time for visiting relatives and friends. People also remember getting together for work projects. Wives used to mend together once a week or congregate at someone's house to make cookies or chow chow. Neighbors, friends, and relatives were also willing to help out with the fieldwork. This began to change in the 1930s when the Federal Government started implementing welfare programs and the number of people available to lend a hand dwindled.

*Family History*: The history of families farming in the area here under discussion is quite remarkable. For half the sample the family farm dates to the mid-1700s or shortly after the Schwenkfelders arrived in this area. This is a source of great pride. Three families trace their farm back about one hundred years. The remaining two families had a history of their family farming in the area, but were the first generation on the present farm.

The transfer of a farm from one generation to another was a very important undertaking. Families preferred to have one of the sons take over. If there were more than one who wanted the farm, the oldest was given the first opportunity. Generally

Illustration 3. Auxiliary buildings for housing chickens, pigs, and implements flank a nineteenth-century Swiss bank barn with over-shoot and its barnyard.

Illustration 4. A farm herd of Holsteins in the barnyard.

it seems only one wanted the farm or only one would take it. The decision was most difficult when the family was large and the parents were concerned about their childrens' welfare and about every child having an equal share. Often a third party would be called in for an estimate. In one case the farm equipment and animals were auctioned off.

*Organizational Memberships*: Beyond neighbors and relatives farm families had strong ties with the church. All attended services regularly, at east once a week. Six were members of the Schwenkfelder Church, three were Lutherans, and one belonged to an Evangelical Congregational Church. People took their church membership seriously. Besides attending services, they were active in Sunday School, church council, choir, Christian Endeavor, and they served as deacons, trustee, librarian, secretary and cemetery board.

Organizational memberships other than the church were few. There were few farm groups functioning at this time and farmers reported that those in existence were not very popular. One farmer was on the extension board and milk producer's board in the 1940s. One was on the school board, one on the township board of supervisors, and one in the Kiwanis.

*Marketing Arrangements*: In the 1920s and early 1930s farmers sold their milk to creameries. Seventy percent of the sample remember taking milk cans to the railroad station for shipment to Philadelphia. Later, local dairies bought the milk.

*Labor*: Much manual labor was done on farms during the first half of the twentieth century; as a result, much help was required. Sixty percent of the sample remembered having hired help when starting out. On one farm the farmer's father could help in the summers so he only needed hired help the rest of the year. Hired men often lived on the farm and ate meals with the family. One farmer said he hated to let his hired man go when he no longer needed him because he had become like one of the family. A common reason for letting the hired man go was that the children were old enough to help out more.

Another way of overcoming labor needs was to work in groups. At harvest time it was common for relatives and neighbors to go from one farm to the next, gathering in the yield as quickly as possible. People would also share equipment to help each other out. One farmer shared equipment with two brothers and they worked together, doing one farm at a time.

## The Farming

*The cows*: Farmers began to concentrate on dairy farming in the 1920s. One sign of this was the change in breed. Previously farmers kept mainly grade or mixed breed cows and they were more of a beef type. Butterfat testing showed the value of a good dairy cow and farmers began importing purebreds to the area. Three farmers brought cows and bulls home from New York and Wisconsin. In the late nineteenth century Jersey and Guernsey had been the most common breeds. In the twentieth century Holstein became the preferred breed because of its higher production capacity (Illustration 4). Some farmers still kept a Jersey or Guernsey in the herd for their higher butterfat.

*Milking*: Milking was by hand until the 1920s or later. Hand milking was not particularly bothersome and some people liked it. It did require more people to do the job, however. People reported that it took two persons approximately one-and-a-half hours to milk fifteen cows by hand. This amounted to about twelve minutes per cow. Machine milking cut this time by more than half. When buckets or cans were left uncovered, milk was strained before consumption (Illustration 5).

*Feeding*: Feeding programs underwent a big change as farmers focused on milk production. According to one farmer, his father fed corn fodder, wheat chaff, water, and meadow hay to the herd during the first decade of the 1900s. While some farmers continued to feed the mix of corn fodder, wheat chaff, and water until they got a corn picker, this was only a small part of the rations. With the addition of silos, corn silage became a standard feed. A special dairy mix was also developed. This consisted of ground ear corn, oats, wheat, and some source of protein, such as brewers' grain, a linseed or cottonseed oil meal, or soybeans. And farmers now fed clover and timothy hay because it 'made more milk' than meadow hay. Except for the protein supplement all the feeds were still homegrown.

The herd was fed at least twice a day. First thing in the morning it received the dairy mix (sometimes mixed with corn fodder, wheat chaff, and water). Milking commenced and then silage was fed. Silage and the dairy mix were not carefully measured but they were generally fed according to production. Later, the herd got hay or was put out on pasture. Farmers

Illustration 5. The farm wife, her daughters, and the hired girl strain the milk.

Illustration 6. The hired boy and girl bind and stack sheaves in the field.

often fed hay again at noon if the herd was housed in the barn. One farmer also fed the dairy mix again at mid-day.

*Breeding*: Breeding was accomplished with a bull prior to the 1940s. The first artificial breeding cooperative was organized in 1942 and it was not long before farmers began using it. The advantages were considerable. Superior sires were available, enhancing the prospects of obtaining superior offspring. Also, many farmers did not relish keeping a bull around. There were numerous stories regarding the eccentricities of bulls and the dangers in keeping them. Farmers were always wary of them. Bulls were raised or purchased.

*Waste Control*: Barn clean-up and manure disposal practices differed considerably from those of the late twentieth century. One early method was the use of a horse pulling a hook with three or four prongs. The prongs would catch the manure and it would be slid outside and piled in the barnyard. This was usually done every other day before gutters were put in. Later, wastes were removed daily with the aid of a wheel barrow.

In the spring and fall the manure was taken to the fields before plowing started. Sometimes it would also be used to topdress wheat in the spring or to fertilize the pasture area. Farmers remember moving manure on a horse-drawn sled and then spreading it by hand. This is how one farmer learned to drive horses at the age of eleven or twelve. Spreading manure by hand was considered a stinky, messy job that resulted in sore hands. On one farm four horses were used to pull the sled, two people loaded it up, and one unloaded. It usually took about one week to finish this job in the spring.

An early improvement to barn clean-up was the invention of a litter carrier. One farmer remembers putting stalls and a litter carrier in the barn in 1922. Some litter carriers worked with chains and a pulley system. The container was lowered to be filled, raised, pulled along tracks to the manure spreader, and then turned over. It was an improvement, but the big change came with gutter cleaners. Most farmers did not have gutter cleaners until after 1950. And it was around 1950 that farmers switched from a seasonal to a daily spreading of manure on the fields.

*The Crops*: The crops grown during the first half of the twentieth century had become established by early in the nineteenth century. Corn and the small grains (wheat, oats, barley) had long been part of the cropping program in the area. Timothy and clover were introduced around the turn of the nineteenth century and quickly gained favor. These grasses nicely balanced the grains in the rotation and they provided cheap, nutritious feed for the stock. The traditional crop rotation scheme required that a cultivated crop (for example, corn) be followed by a spring grain (oats), which would in turn be followed by a winter grain (wheat), and by one or more years of grass.

*Annual Round*: The following list summarizes the major field activities performed throughout the year. Timing depended first on the weather; as a result, these are not fixed times. Spring set everything in motion and farmers liked to start 'as soon as it warmed up!'

*January*
    Barn work, every day, every month
    Split wood
*February*
    Split wood
    Haul manure, if weather fine
*March*
    Split wood
    Seed clover
*April*
    Prepare soil for planting
    Seed oats
    Start garden
    Repair and whitewash fences
*May*
    Prepare soil for planting
    Seed corn
*June*
    Cultivate corn—two times
    Make hay
    Clean fence strips
    Harvest barley
    Beginning of canning season
*July*
    Harvest wheat, oats
    Cultivate and hill corn
*August*
    Second cutting hay
    Spread manure
*September*

Fill silo—Labour Day
Prepare soil for planting
Seed barley
Seed rye—mid month
Seed wheat—end of the month

*October*
Dig potatoes
Husk corn

*November*
Husk corn

*December*
Chop wood

*Crop Rotation*: Crop rotation principles remained basically the same, but two changes in practice were made. One change was to seed corn in the same field for two consecutive years instead of just one year. The first year most farmers would husk the corn. The second year the corn would go into the silo so the field could be prepared for a wheat seeding in late September. For the farmers who still seeded oats, some fields would be in corn for one year only, followed by oats the next spring. With increased acreage in corn, fewer acres were devoted to small grains. Everyone still raised wheat, but fewer and fewer continued to plant oats or barley. The hay crops held their own or increased in acreage. The figure below indicates the timing of the typical rotation practised.

| Spring | Fall | Spring | Fall | Spring | Fall | Spring |
|--------|------|--------|------|--------|------|--------|
| Husking | | Silo | | | | |
| Corn | | Corn | Wheat | Clover | | Grass |
| | | Oats | Wheat | Clover | | Corn |
| | | | Timothy | Timothy | | |

*Grains*: Early during the period corn became the principal grain sown. It is an easy crop to grow and a good source of feed. The plant is suited to a wide range of soil types and it thrives in the hot, humid summers of Southeast Pennsylvania. The seedlings become established and grow quickly, shading out many weeds. The plants are relatively resistant to pests. It is also a comparatively easy crop to harvest. As a feed it is the source 'par excellence' of energy. Both the grain and the entire plant are consumed and preferred by the cow. Production figures were good, but they significantly increased with the development of hybrid varieties. Hybrid seed was first introduced in Illinois in 1916. It resulted in a plant of increased vigor, stiffer stalks, and higher yields. By 1940 half the corn planted in Southeast Pennsylvania was hybrid.

The soil was prepared for planting corn by ploughing and harrowing. This was a physically demanding job done mainly by the men. Lime was usually added in the spring, just before or after ploughing. Planting began once the weather warmed sufficiently, usually in early May. One farmer mentioned that it was too cold if the dogwood had not started to bloom. The ground was not to be too wet when the corn was planted. 'It is better to plant the corn in dust and the oats in mud!' In the 1920s most farmers used a one- or two-row corn planter but one farmer hand-seeded in hills eight to ten inches apart. One farmer remembered seeding beans among the corn by hand during the 1900s, and two others recall planting field pumpkins with the corn. These pumpkins were split and fed to the cows. People mentioned using hybrid varieties as early as the 1920s. Manure was early supplemented with chemical fertilizer, which first appeared around the turn of the century.

Weed control was accomplished by cultivation. The cultivator had tines and resembled today's chisel plow. Cultivating was usually done three times to control weeds and aerate the plant's roots. The first time usually commenced once the first hay cutting was in or when the plant was three to four inches high. If the ground was hard and crusty, a spike-toothed harrow might be used. Someone, usually a child, followed the cultivator the first time over the field to uncover plants as needed and to pull grass. It was a tedious, time-consuming task the first time over the field because the plants were so fragile. For the second cultivation the plants were seven to eight inches high and much sturdier. The third time over the field, usually around July 4, different shears were used. These shears pushed the ground up around the plant for support. Some farmers also seeded ryegrass as a cover crop during this last cultivation. Cultivating was not considered a very entertaining job. As one farmer put it, 'It's a job to get sleepy.'

No one practiced chemical insect control for corn or any other crop during this period. Farmers said that there were fewer insects then. Moreover, fields were not seeded in corn for more than two years so the crop rotation program was an efficient means of controlling what insects there were.

The corn harvest began around Labor Day when stalks were cut to be put in the silo. The stalks were cut by hand and placed in small groups to be collected by a wagon. One person would load the wagon, another would unload, and a third would put the corn on the belt or feeder. An elevator was used to fill the silo before blowers were developed. Before tractors an engine such as the Springfield engine with fly wheels was used to power the elevator. Often someone would be inside the silo to insure a tight packing, especially around the outside.

Corn was not ready for husking until the kernels were dry. If the kernels were not dry enough, they would mold and spoil during storage. Again the stalks were cut by hand. Two rows were done at a time. The ears were put in a pile for storage in the corn crib and stalks were tied together in a bundle and left in the field to dry further. The stalks or corn fodder were then stored in the barn for feed. Loading corn fodder was not considered a very pleasant job. The plants were dry and sharp and clumsy to handle.

Wheat and oats were the other important grains. Wheat had been the major crop during the Colonial period but acres dwindled as western states produced it more cheaply and as yields were reduced due to infestation by the Hessian fly. In the first half of the twentieth century wheat was sown as a cash crop, for use in the dairy mix and for straw. It also fit nicely in the rotation as a nurse crop for seeding grass. Oats were raised for the dairy mix and straw, and it was a popular horse feed.

Wheat was seeded in late September and oats were sown as early as possible in the spring, preferably by mid-April. Soil preparation was the same as for corn. Chemical fertilizers were often used and wheat was sometimes fertilized with manure in the spring. Harvest times were around early July for wheat and late July for oats. The plants were cut first with a cradle and later with a machine called a binder. After cutting the sheaves would be tied together or shocked by hand (Illustration 6). Usually about ten sheaves were placed together, with two on the top for a cover. The shocks remained in the field for a week or so and were then moved to the barn for threshing. The earliest threshing was on the threshing floor in the barn with a flail. Farmers had seen this done as children, but everyone reported using a threshing machine.

Rye and barley were traditionally raised in the area, but only one farmer reported regularly sowing barley and no one sowed rye as a grain. Barley was handled the same as wheat, sown in September and harvested in July. Its straw was used for bedding and the grain was added to the dairy mix.

*Hay Crops*: Hay crops were grown to balance the grains nutritionally and environmentally. Nutritionally, hay crops are high in vitamins, minerals, and fiber, and potentially high in protein. Environmentally, hay crops are soil savers. They provide a constant cover and prevent soil erosion or gullies from forming during seasons of heavy rain. Hay crops also balance the crop rotation scheme. Corn takes nitrogen out of the soil, for example, while legumes such as clover put it back in. And finally, hay crops will grow practically anywhere while the grains can be more problematic. The main hay crops during the first half of the twentieth century were timothy, clover, and meadow grass. Some orchardgrass and alfalfa were also sown. Alfalfa did not become the chief hay crop until later when varieties more adaptable to the area were developed.

Timothy and clover were often found together in a field. Timothy, a perennial bunchgrass, does well practically anywhere. It was especially desirable for feed when work horses were needed. Red clover, a legume, is a short-lived perennial. It is higher in protein content than timothy but it only lasts one or two seasons at the most. Timothy was usually seeded with wheat in the fall in a grain drill or hand seeded with clover in a wheat field in the spring. Other than the fertilizer applied specifically for the wheat, no fertilizer was used for timothy or clover. Seeding two or three crops in the same field was effective in keeping most of the weeds back so the seedlings could get a head start.

Meadow grass was mostly a Kentucky bluegrass. To these Pennsylvania Germans the meadow is a low area where surface water is present, and the term 'meadow grass' means 'volumes of grass.' Half the sample reported irrigating the meadow when they were young. Some had a dam and everyone used ditches to transport the water throughout the meadow. With irrigation two cuttings were made. Two farmers sold their meadow hay, and another said his father fed the meadow hay so he could sell his better hay. Another farmer agreed that people were then more concerned over the quantity of hay produced than

Illustration 7. A woman uses the mechanical hay tedder to turn the hay to dry before it is raked and brought in from the field.

Illustration 8. Loading the haywagon using one of the first mechanical loaders.

the quality of hay fed. Besides meadow grass, the meadow contained an alum, *Calamus acorus* or 'Kalmus' in Pennsylvania German, which had many uses when immature. It was eaten as treatment for asthma and upset stomachs and fed to horses when heaving.

Harvesting the hay crops was a time when families and neighbors would work together. It was an especially exciting time for children. Farmers used to start cutting hay around the longest day of the year, June 21. One farmer liked to wait for a north or west wind to cut hay. He felt that a wind from the west after a rain meant good weather. Good weather for making hay requires sunshine. a breeze, low humidity, and no rain in the immediate future! The crop was cut first by hand with a scythe. Later, it was mowed, tedded (especially if it got rained on—see Illustration 7), raked, and then loaded on a wagon for transportation to the barn. A typical routine for making meadow hay was to cut it in the morning, and rake it in piles in the afternoon. The next morning it would be spread apart, and if conditions were right, it could be loaded up that afternoon (Illustration 8). Hay making was a time-consuming job but one done with care. One farmer asserted that one never saw any hay left on the ground.

Most of the hay crops were stored loose or consumed in the field. Farmers reported that they usually made only one cutting of mixed timothy and clover hay. After the first cutting farmers put up fences and pastured the cows on their hay fields. One farmer fenced in his whole farm for grazing.

## Looking Back

Before concluding the interviews each farmer was encouraged to look back over his years on the farm. Each farmer was specifically asked to note the changes he made while farming. There was a reduction or elimination of all animals kept except those in the dairy herd. Horses were removed from the barn and then eventually from the farm. However, some farmers did keep horses for a few tasks until as late as 1950. These tasks included cultivating, harrowing, and doing the ends of fields. Changes pertaining to the dairy herd included: raising more heifers, using artificial insemination for breeding more often than a bull, feeding more ensiled feed and better quality feed, spreading manure daily instead of once or twice a year, and improved health care. The physical improvements accompanying these changes were the addition of more silos, new milk houses, and many changes in the barn, such as rearranging the layout, putting in or adding stanchions, and purchasing milk machines.

Changes pertaining to the crops dealt with a shift in emphasis and a host of new equipment. Farmers began seeding more acres in corn and reducing the number of acres in small grains. Yields improved with the appearance of improved varieties and chemical fertilizers. There were improvements in existing equipment, and farmers particularly cited the tractor, hay baler, and corn picker as machines that greatly lightened the workload. Farm work was much easier physically at the end of the period than at the beginning.

In assessing changes overall, farmers felt there were more improvements in their time than in any other. When they considered today's farming equipment, they smiled and shook their heads. Alongside the wonder, there are reservations. Today's farming people see more tension and stress. Both are related to heavy financial investments and to working with so much sophisticated equipment. Farmers pointed out that one must concentrate and be ever alert when working with big machines. And the equipment must constantly be serviced and repaired. With this consideration in mind some farmers find there is less 'free time' available today. The high financial inputs have also resulted in a change in attitude. Retired farmers see farming today as more like a business than formerly. It is still a family affair and still a way of life, but they feel it must also be thought of as a business.

## Schwenkfelder Dairy Farmers

The farmers in this study have been called Pennsylvania German because a few did not consider themselves Schwenkfelders. Everyone had deep roots in the area, most had close family relatives here, and everyone spoke Pennsylvania German with family and friends. The Schwenkfelders were recognized as a unique group by everyone, but did this uniqueness carry over into farming? Every person interviewed was asked how Schwenkfelder dairy farmers might have differed from their neighbors. Only two persons noted any difference. One observed that Schwenkfelders did not do fieldwork on Sundays while others did. Another felt the Schwenkfelder emphasis on education made them stand out. For this sample, the Schwenkfelders were not more educated than the non-Schwenkfelders. The group as a whole, however, received more higher education than did a similar group of contemporary farmers. In comparing the resources and practices of Schwenkfelders with non-Schwenkfelders, no differences emerged. The study group was relatively uniform wherever data was available.

## Notes

[1] Samuel Brecht (ed.), *The Genealogical Record of the Schwenkfelder Families* (Chicago, 1923).

[2] Andrew S. Berky (ed.), *The Journals and Papers of David Schultze* (Pennsburg, 1952-1953).

[3] Leo Bressler, 'Agriculture among the Germans in Pennsylvania during the eighteenth century,' *Pennsylvania History*, 22: 131.

[4] For an introduction to dairying see John Schlebecker, *A History of American Dairying* (Chicago, 1967) and Ralph Selitzer, *The Dairy Industry in America* (new York, 1976). An excellent introduction to farming in Pennsylvania can be found in Stevenson Fletcher, *Pennsylvania Agriculture and Country Life* (Harrisburg, 1955). Walter Kollmorgen *Culture of a Contem,porary Community: The Old Order Amish of Lancaster County. Pennsylvania* (Washington, 1942) is a unique example of a Pennsylvania farming study during this period at a more local level, in this case the Old Order Amish.

[5] See J. T. Lemon. *The Best Poor Man's Country* (New York, 1972) and Berky.

[6] J. Schoepf, *Travels in the Confederation* (Philadelphia, 1911), 103.

[7] *American Husbandry* (London, 1775), 154.

[8] Percy Bidwell and John Falconer. *History of Agriculture in the Northern United States, 1620-1860* (New York, 1941), 107.

[9] See Bressler.

[10] Walter Kollmorgen, 'The Pennsylvania German Farmer,' in Ralph Wood (ed.), *The Pennsylvania Germans* (Princeton, 1942).

[11] Ibid., 51.

[12] Raymond and Marion Murphy, *Pennsylvania* (Harrisburg, 1937), 211.

[13] Norman Gras, *A History of Agriculture* (New York, 1925).

[14] See Fletcher.

[15] Murphy and Murphy, 205.

[16] John Shoemaker, *The Pennsylvania Barn* (Kutztown, 1959), 82. The illustration is reproduced with permission of the Pennsylvania German Archives.

[17] See my Ph. D. dissertation *An Approach to the Ethnography of Farming as a Culturally Structured Technological System* (University of Pennsylvania, 1986).

# Directory
# of Authors

Horst Weigelt is Professor at the Institute for Protestant Theology at the University of Bamberg, West Germany.

Lee C. Hopple is Professor of Geography at Bloomsburg University of Pennsylvania.

Rodger C. Henderson is Assistant Professor of History at Pennsylvania State University.

*William T. Parsons is Professor of History and Director of Pennsylvania German Studies at Ursinus College.

Alan G. Keyser is a specialist in Pennsylvania Folk Culture.

John B. Frantz is Assistant Professor of American History at Pennsylvania State University and Past President of the Pennsylvania Historical Association.

Don Yoder is Professor of Folklife Studies and Adjunct Professor of Religious Studies at the University of Pennsylvania.

John L. Ruth is Associate Minister at Salford Mennonite Church, Harleysville, Pa.

*Monica Pieper is an instructor in religious education and German literature at the Integrierte Gesamthochschule Ernst Bloch, Ludwigshafen, West Germany.

*Peter C. Erb is Associate Director of Schwenkfelder Library and Professor of Religion and Culture at Wilfrid Laurier University, Waterloo, Ontario, Canada.

*W. Kyrel Meschter is Vice-President of Schwenkfelder Library.

L. Allen Viehmeyer is Chairperson of the Department of Foreign Languages and Literatures at Ohio State University at Youngstown.

Thomas S. Eader is an organ restorer and has a special interest in early American organs.

Elizabeth R. Gamon is a textile restorer and conservationist.

Kathleen Manolescu is an anthropologist and has a special interest in agriculture.

Dennis Moyer is Director of Schwenkfelder Library.

The outdoor colloquium presentation of Francis Blase, Jr. on Schwenkfelder farm machinery has not been included in this volume because of its availability in a fuller form in his book *Heebner and Sons: Pioneers of Farm Machinery in America, 1840-1926* (Lansdale, 1984).

*Paper not presented at Colloquium.